Harold Schechter
Jonna Gormely Semeiks

Queens College of The City University of New York

Patterns in Popular Culture

A SOURCEBOOK FOR WRITERS

HARPER & ROW, PUBLISHERS, New York

Cambridge, Hagerstown, Philadelphia, San Francisco,
London, Mexico City, São Paulo, Sydney

1817

COVER CREDITS *(Clockwise from top right):*

Front:

St. George and the Dragon by Master IAM of Zwolle. Dutch. XV Century. The Metropolitan Museum of Art, Rogers Fund, 1933.

The Fool by Pamela Coleman Smith. From the Rider-Waite Tarot deck. Reprinted by permission of U.S. Games Systems, Inc. Copyright © 1971 by U.S. Games Systems, Inc., New York, N.Y. 10016.

The Serpent-God of the Lost Swamp by Marie and John Severin. Cover illustration for "The Forbidden Swamp," *Monsters on the Prowl,* no. 16. Copyright © 1972, Marvel Comics Group, a division of Cadence Industries Corporation. All rights reserved.

Krazy Kat by George Herriman. Copyright © King Features Syndicate, Inc.

Back:

Reynard the Fox steals the Parson's capon by Wilhelm von Kaulbach. Illustration from *Reynard the Fox* by T. J. Arnold, after the German version of Goethe (London, 1860).

Peter Schlemihl sells his shadow to the Devil by George Cruikshank. Illustration from *Peter Schlemihl* by Adelbert von Chamisso (London, 1824). Prints Division, The New York Public Library, Astor, Lenox and Tilden Foundations.

Squirrely the Squirrel by Robert Crumb. Copyright © 1973 by R. Crumb. Used by permission of the artist.

Shang-chi battles Midnight by Jim Starlin. Panel art from "Midnight Brings Dark Death," *Master of Kung Fu,* no. 16. Copyright © 1972 Marvel Comics Group, a division of Cadence Industries Corporation. All rights reserved.

Sponsoring Editor: Phillip Leininger
Project Editor: Holly Detgen
Designer: Emily Harste
Production Manager: Marion A. Palen
Compositor: Kingsport Press
Printer and Binder: Halliday Lithograph Corporation

Patterns in Popular Culture:
A SOURCEBOOK FOR WRITERS

Copyright © 1980 by Harper & Row, Publishers, Inc.

All rights reserved. Printed in the United States of America. No part of this book may be used or reproduced in any manner whatsoever without written permission except in the case of brief quotations embodied in critical articles and reviews. For information address Harper & Row, Publishers, Inc., 10 East 53rd Street, New York, N.Y. 10022.

Library of Congress Cataloging in Publication Data

Main entry under title:

Patterns in popular culture.

  Includes index.
  1. College readers. 2. English language—
Rhetoric. I. Schechter, Harold. II. Semeiks,
Jonna Gormely
PE1417.P37   808'.04275   79–18451
ISBN 0–06–045761–9

FOR OUR FAMILIES

Contents

Preface   xvii

Chapter One

The Shadow   1

SIR JAMES FRAZER	"The Myth of Osiris" 5	
THE BROTHERS GRIMM	"The Singing Bone" 9	
STEVE ENGLEHART AND JIM STARLIN	from "Midnight Brings Dark Death" 12	
GARRY CLEVELAND MYERS AND MARION HULL HAMMEL	"Goofus and Gallant" 25	
URSULA K. LE GUIN	from *A Wizard of Earthsea* 29	
ROBERT CRUMB	"Whiteman" 37	
BILLY JOEL	"The Stranger" 43	
NATHANIEL HAWTHORNE	"The Birthmark" 45	

Chapter Two

The Trickster   58

PAUL RADIN	from *The Trickster* 62	
JACQUES DOREY	"How Master Renard Enticed Ysengrin to Eat the Moon and How He Was Judged by the Court of the Lion" 66	

ANONYMOUS   "The Tar Baby" (Water-Well Version)   **69**

WARNER BROS.   "Bugs Bunny"   **74**
CARTOONS

ROBERT CRUMB   "Squirrely the Squirrel"   **86**

RUDOLPH DIRKS   *The Katzenjammer Kids*   **92**

GEORGE W. PECK   "His Pa Stabbed"   **97**

BERT KALMAR AND   from the screenplay of the Marx Brothers'
HARRY RUBY   movie *Duck Soup*   **101**

MARK TWAIN   from *The Adventures of Huckleberry
                           Finn*   **108**

Chapter Three

The Temptress 115

HOMER   "Circe" (from *The Odyssey*)   **119**

THE BROTHERS GRIMM   "The Nixie of the Mill-Pond"   **126**

SANGER D. SHAFER AND   "Bandy the Rodeo Clown"   **130**
LEFTY FRIZZELL

BILLY SHERRILL   "Woman to Woman"   **132**

DON HENLEY AND   "Witchy Woman"   **134**
BERNIE LEADON

HAL FOSTER   *Prince Valiant*   **136**

H. ANTOINE D'ARCY   "The Face Upon the Floor"   **141**

BRAM STOKER   from *Dracula*   **144**

H. RIDER HAGGARD   from *She*   **148**

JOHN KEATS   "La Belle Dame sans Merci"   **154**

Chapter Four

The Mother 158

ANONYMOUS   "Hymn to Demeter"   **162**

CHARLES PERRAULT   "Cinderella"   **168**

COURTLAND N. SMITH   "The Greatest Mother in the World"   **173**

ALMADÉN VINEYARDS   "Grapes, Like Children, Need Love and
                           Affection"   **176**

JOHN LENNON AND   "Mother Nature's Son"   **179**
PAUL MC CARTNEY

ERIC KAZ   "Mother Earth"   **180**

WALTER DONALDSON   "My Mom"   **182**

JACK KIRBY   from "Sonny Sumo"   184
IAN FLEMING   from *From Russia with Love*   195
WILLA CATHER   from *My Ántonia*   201

Chapter Five

The Wise Old Man   210

SOPHOCLES   "Teiresias the Seer" (from *Oedipus Rex*)   215
ANONYMOUS   "The Hare Herd"   223
C. C. BECK AND   "In the Beginning"   228
DENNY O'NEIL
SHEL SILVERSTEIN   "The Winner"   236
WILLIAM PETER BLATTY   from *The Exorcist*   238
CARLOS CASTANEDA   from *The Teachings of Don Juan: A Yaqui Way of Knowledge*   247
GEORGE LUCAS   from *Star Wars*   253
BENJAMIN FRANKLIN   from *Father Abraham's Speech*   258

Chapter Six

The Helpful Animal and the Holy Fool   265

EDITH HAMILTON   "Pegasus and Bellerophon"   270
THE BROTHERS GRIMM   "The Queen Bee"   273
BOB HANEY, GIL KANE,   "The Secret of the Golden Crocodile"   276
AND BERNARD SACHS
FRAN STRIKER   from *The Lone Ranger*   287
GEORGE HERRIMAN   *Krazy Kat*   296
L. FRANK BAUM   from *The Wonderful Wizard of Oz*   300
JOHN LENNON AND   "The Fool on the Hill"   306
PAUL MC CARTNEY
ISAAC BASHEVIS SINGER   "Gimpel the Fool"   308

Chapter Seven

The Quest   320

ANONYMOUS   from *The Epic of Gilgamesh*   325
THE BROTHERS GRIMM   "The Water of Life"   333

J. R. ROBERTSON   "The Weight"   337

BOB DYLAN   "A Hard Rain's A-Gonna Fall"   339

ROY THOMAS AND MARIE   "The Forbidden Swamp"   343
AND JOHN SEVERIN

J. R. R. TOLKIEN   from *The Fellowship of the Ring*   354

DASHIELL HAMMETT   from *The Maltese Falcon*   365

HERMAN MELVILLE   from *Moby-Dick*   372

Chapter Eight

Rebirth   380

OVID   "The Story of Apollo and Hyacinthus"   384

THE BROTHERS GRIMM   "The Juniper Tree"   388

JAMES DEAN AND   "I've Been Born Again"   395
DON DAVIS

JOHN DENVER AND   "Rocky Mountain High"   397
MIKE TAYLOR

WILL EISNER   "Life Below"   400

ALPHA KERI BATH OIL   "The Age-Old Secret of Younger Looking
                               Skin"   409

ARTHUR C. CLARKE   from *2001: A Space Odyssey*   412

HENRY JAMES   from *The American*   421

Appendix

Critical Essays   431

BRUNO BETTELHEIM   from *The Uses of Enchantment*   433

ROBERT JEWETT AND   from *The American Monomyth*   437
JOHN SHELTON
LAWRENCE

URSULA K. LE GUIN   "Myth and Archetype in Science
                               Fiction"   442

ALAN MC GLASHAN   "Daily Paper Pantheon"   448

ROGER B. ROLLIN   from "Beowulf to Batman"   454

Index   467

Contents by Genre

MYTHS

SIR JAMES FRAZER   "The Myth of Osiris"   5

PAUL RADIN   from *The Trickster*   62

HOMER   "Circe" (from *The Odyssey*)   119

ANONYMOUS   "Hymn to Demeter"   162

SOPHOCLES   "Teiresias the Seer" (from *Oedipus Rex*)   215

EDITH HAMILTON   "Pegasus and Bellerophon"   270

ANONYMOUS   from *The Epic of Gilgamesh*   325

OVID   "The Story of Apollo and Hyacinthus"   384

FAIRY TALES AND FOLKTALES

THE BROTHERS GRIMM   "The Singing Bone"   9

JACQUES DOREY   "How Master Renard Enticed Ysengrin to Eat the Moon and How He Was Judged by the Court of the Lion"   66

ANONYMOUS   "The Tar Baby" (Water-Well Version)   69

THE BROTHERS GRIMM   "The Nixie of the Mill-Pond"   126

CHARLES PERRAULT   "Cinderella"   168

ANONYMOUS   "The Hare Herd"   223

THE BROTHERS GRIMM   "The Queen Bee"   273

THE BROTHERS GRIMM   "The Water of Life"   333
THE BROTHERS GRIMM   "The Juniper Tree"   388

COMICS

Comic Books

STEVE ENGLEHART AND   from "Midnight Brings Dark Death"   12
JIM STARLIN

WARNER BROS.   "Bugs Bunny"   74
CARTOONS

JACK KIRBY   from "Sonny Sumo"   184

C. C. BECK AND   "In the Beginning"   228
DENNY O'NEIL

BOB HANEY, GIL KANE,   "The Secret of the Golden Crocodile"   276
AND BERNARD SACHS

ROY THOMAS AND MARIE   "The Forbidden Swamp"   343
AND JOHN SEVERIN

WILL EISNER   "Life Below"   400

Comic Strips

RUDOLPH DIRKS   *The Katzenjammer Kids*   92
HAL FOSTER   *Prince Valiant*   136
GEORGE HERRIMAN   *Krazy Kat*   296

Underground Comics

ROBERT CRUMB   "Whiteman"   37
ROBERT CRUMB   "Squirrely the Squirrel"   86

SONGS

Rock

BILLY JOEL   "The Stranger"   43

DON HENLEY AND   "Witchy Woman"   134
BERNIE LEADON

JOHN LENNON AND   "Mother Nature's Son"   179
PAUL MC CARTNEY

JOHN LENNON AND   "The Fool on the Hill"   306
PAUL MC CARTNEY

J. R. ROBERTSON   "The Weight"   337

Folk

ERIC KAZ   "Mother Earth"   180
BOB DYLAN   "A Hard Rain's A-Gonna Fall"   339

Country-Western

SANGER D. SHAFER AND LEFTY FRIZZELL   "Bandy the Rodeo Clown"   130

BILLY SHERRILL   "Woman to Woman"   132

SHEL SILVERSTEIN   "The Winner"   236

JOHN DENVER AND MIKE TAYLOR   "Rocky Mountain High"   397

Soul

JAMES DEAN AND DON DAVIS   "I've Been Born Again"   395

Sentimental

WALTER DONALDSON   "My Mom"   182

POPULAR LITERATURE

Fantasy

URSULA K. LE GUIN   from *A Wizard of Earthsea*   29

H. RIDER HAGGARD   from *She*   148

J. R. R. TOLKIEN   from *The Fellowship of the Ring*   354

Science Fiction

GEORGE LUCAS   from *Star Wars*   253

ARTHUR C. CLARKE   from *2001: A Space Odyssey*   412

Horror

BRAM STOKER   from *Dracula*   144

WILILIAM PETER BLATTY   from *The Exorcist*   238

Spy

IAN FLEMING   from *From Russia with Love*   195

Detective

DASHIELL HAMMETT   from *The Maltese Falcon*   365

Western

FRAN STRIKER   from *The Lone Ranger*   287

Humor

GEORGE W. PECK   "His Pa Stabbed"   97

Children's Literature

GARRY CLEVELAND   "Goofus and Gallant"   25
MYERS AND MARION
HULL HAMMEL

L. FRANK BAUM   from *The Wonderful Wizard of Oz*   300

Anthropology

CARLOS CASTANEDA   from *The Teachings of Don Juan: A Yaqui
                         Way of Knowledge*   247

Poetry

H. ANTOINE D'ARCY   "The Face Upon the Floor"   141

FILM

BERT KALMAR AND   from the screenplay of the Marx Brothers'
HARRY RUBY   movie *Duck Soup*   101

ADVERTISEMENTS

COURTLAND N. SMITH   "The Greatest Mother in the World"   173
ALMADÉN VINEYARDS   "Grapes, Like Children, Need Love and
                         Affection"   176
ALPHA KERI BATH OIL   "The Age-Old Secret of Younger Looking
                         Skin"   409

CLASSICS

NATHANIEL HAWTHORNE   "The Birthmark"   45
MARK TWAIN   from *The Adventures of Huckleberry
                         Finn*   108
JOHN KEATS   "La Belle Dame sans Merci"   154
WILLA CATHER   from *My Ántonia*   201
BENJAMIN FRANKLIN   from *Father Abraham's Speech*   258
ISAAC BASHEVIS SINGER   "Gimpel the Fool"   308
HERMAN MELVILLE   from *Moby-Dick*   372
HENRY JAMES   from *The American*   421

CRITICAL ESSAYS

BRUNO BETTELHEIM   from *The Uses of Enchantment*   433
ROBERT JEWETT AND   from *The American Monomyth*   437
JOHN SHELTON
LAWRENCE
URSULA K. LE GUIN   "Myth and Archetype in Science
                         Fiction"   442
ALAN MC GLASHAN   "Daily Paper Pantheon"   448
ROGER B. ROLLIN   from "Beowulf to Batman"   454

Preface

Patterns in Popular Culture is a reader which reproduces material not ordinarily studied in composition courses: sections of comic books, chapters from popular novels (detective, horror, fantasy, science fiction), Sunday newspaper strips, rock and country-western songs, a scene from the screenplay of a Marx Brothers' movie. For reasons explained below, this material is supplemented by more traditional selections: myths and folktales, literary classics, and critical essays. The contents of this book reflect our conviction, which grows out of our own classroom experience, that the use of popular culture in a writing course can make the teaching and learning of composition a lively and rewarding process for everyone involved.

We have found, for instance, that classroom discussions of movies, pop music, and comic books tend to be extremely animated. Generally, students are both knowledgeable and enthusiastic about this kind of material. They are certainly not intimidated by it and have solid ideas and strong opinions about it. As a result, they are able not only to talk but also to write about it with confidence, verve, and conviction.

Historically, many teachers have felt that the popular arts must not cross the threshold of the college classroom, and although this attitude has changed a great deal during the past few years, there is still a widespread feeling that little of value can be learned from such material. We have no intention of entering here into a lengthy defense of pop culture. The artistic excellence of works like Ursula K. Le Guin's *A Wizard of Earthsea* and George Herriman's *Krazy Kat* comic strips seems self-evident to us. But even pieces of popular art which have less to offer aesthetically are still worth paying attention to. Pop culture is important precisely because it *is* so popular. Its mass appeal is one good reason for studying it. It possesses enormous authority and exerts a major influence on all our lives. Demanding questions can and should be asked of the popular arts, and an excellent place to carry on such questioning is, of course, the college classroom.

We have found that a very fruitful approach to the popular arts is the one afforded by literary myth criticism. The premise is that certain fundamental patterns or "archetypes"—stories, characters, themes, situations—are repeated again and again in myths, fairy tales, and classic literature all over the world. But these same patterns also appear in popular art; indeed, it is often easier to distinguish them there than in more complex, highly elaborated texts. As Northrop Frye points out in *Anatomy of Criticism,* popular literature can be defined as "literature which affords an unobstructed view of archetypes." Such archetypes are ubiquitous because they give expression to universal human experiences. The reader of this textbook will learn to recognize these timeless patterns not only as they occur in cultural products of various kinds but also as they appear in life.

Each of the eight chapters of this textbook is devoted to a single archetypal or mythic pattern (with the exception of Chapter Six, which deals with two). Each begins with an introduction which defines and describes the archetype. A generous number of selections exemplifying the pattern then follows. The selections always begin with a myth and a folktale and conclude with a literary classic, generally a short story, poem or excerpt from a novel. The bulk of each chapter is devoted to the popular arts. A context in which to view and evaluate the latter is provided by the classics: students can see that the same universal images or patterns can be found in the most sophisticated as well as the most unassuming works of the human imagination.

Much of the material in *Patterns in Popular Culture* is brief enough to be read and used immediately in the classroom—a distinct advantage to the teacher who desires an easily contained, clearly directed discussion before he or she proceeds in the same hour to the writing exercise or assignment. The questions which follow each selection are divided into three categories: Language, Content, and Suggestions for Writing. The first category includes questions about diction, syntax, tone, figurative language, rhetorical strategy, and audience. The second category is meant to facilitate student understanding of plot, character, motivation, and theme. The many writing suggestions vary a great deal in difficulty, from simple descriptions and narrations to more ambitious probings of cultural issues or problems. Writing questions are always linked to the selections that precede them (although some have looser links and range farther than others). Students are asked to perform every kind of writing exercise: not only narration and description but also classification, comparison and contrast, process analysis, causal analysis, interpretation and evaluation, definition, and argumentation.

Each chapter of *Patterns in Popular Culture* concludes with additional writing suggestions more general in nature than those which follow individual selections; they are intended to draw on everything the student has learned about the particular pattern presented in the chapter. For these broader writing suggestions, as well as for the more specific ones, the student is encouraged, in formulating a response, to reach outside the text to familiar material—television programs, rock music, advertisements, fantasy and science fiction movies and novels, and so on—to substantiate claims made about the readings.

At the end of the main body of *Patterns in Popular Culture* is an appendix containing critical essays on the subjects of myth, fairy tales, and popular art. These will provide readers with a more thorough understanding of the patterns or archetypes they will be talking and writing about, of the cultural and psychological function of the popular arts, and of the complexities they offer. In addition, they will serve as examples of good expository prose, examples directed specifically at and illuminating the songs, stories, comic books, and so on that precede them. Finally, these essays, in combination with the other material in the text, will create a casebook on popular culture and its connections with classic literature. Hence, they can be used, if the teacher likes, as the basis not only for classroom discussion and weekly writing assignments but also for a research or term paper. Having these essays at the end of the book is a considerable advantage to the teacher who assigns a research paper: he or she has control over the student's research. The primary sources for the student's paper and some critical commentary on them are collected in one volume; the student need not go outside it. And the teacher will have at his or her fingertips a method of checking the student's research skills, incorporation of quotes, paraphrasing, and footnote procedures.

Finally, a supplement, *Popular Culture in the Classroom,* with complete analyses of selections, selected bibliography of Jungian literature and criticism, and a lengthy chapter "Using *Patterns in Popular Culture* to Organize the Composition Course," is available from the publisher.

Work on this book was made possible in part by several grants from the Research Foundation of the City University of New York. We are grateful for the foundation's support. Among the people who helped us in important ways with this project are: our generous and supportive colleague, Don McQuade; our friends Ray Browne and Pat Browne of the Center for the Study of Popular Culture, Bowling Green State University; Doris Albrecht of the Kristine Mann Library, C. G. Jung Foundation for Analytical Psychology; James B. Smith; Susan Mufson; Stan Willard; Tom Frosch; David Richter; David Everitt; and the students in "Myth and American Popular Culture," particularly Rhea Kirstein and Bruce Eder.

Harold Schechter
Jonna Gormely Semeiks

One

The Shadow

Who knows what evil lurks in the hearts of men? The Shadow knows!

—"The Shadow" radio program

In the myths, fairy tales, comic books, stories, and songs that make up each of the eight chapters of *Patterns in Popular Culture,* you'll be encountering a number of different patterns or *archetypes.* What is an archetype? Though its meaning changes slightly according to who is defining it (a literary critic would not describe it in the same words as a psychologist), essentially an archetype is an original pattern or model after which all subsequent things of the same type are fashioned. Obviously there are different kinds of archetypes. Henry Ford's turn-of-the-century Model T Ford is an archetype: with its four wheels, its body or cab in which people could sit, and its revolutionary motor, it served as a *pattern* on which the automobile has been modeled, with occasional alterations, ever since.

The kind of archetypes we will be dealing with in this book are patterns which occur in ancient myths, legends, and folktales, and which are repeated continually in the imaginative products of different cultures all over the world. One such pattern or motif is the Hero Slaying the Dragon. The archetypal "characters" are the hero and the dragon; the situation in which they find themselves is an archetypal battle to the death. These two figures from medieval romance can still be found alive and struggling in literature, comic books, and movies. Sometimes they appear in slightly disguised forms. In the classic nineteenth-century novel *Moby-Dick,* by Herman Melville, we see the increasingly deranged hero, Ahab, attempting to kill the elusive giant white whale, symbol of all evil to his pursuer. In the enormously successful movie *Jaws,* the dragon ravaging the bucolic countryside becomes a killer shark feasting off a quiet oceanside community, and—since the film is set in contemporary Long Island instead of Merry Old England—the hero is not a knight with a lance but a fisherman with a harpoon. And, probably because we live in a technological age which sometimes seems uncannily threatening—our machines can appear to dominate us, even to want to destroy us—a staple of science fiction since its beginnings has been the battle between heroic human beings and strange, mechanical monsters from technologically superior planets.

But it isn't only in literature or in other cultural products such as myths, songs, and television programs that we can see evidence of archetypes, of these basic and universal patterns. We can also see them in our own lives, in the kinds of people we live with and befriend, in the various things we choose to do or are forced to undergo. Archetypes are images arising from the deepest level of the mind; they burst out spontaneously in our dreams and fantasies, and then are reshaped, refined, re-expressed, by creative people, in our fairy tales and comic strips, our serious drama and country-western music. What you will do is become one of those people: you'll learn to recognize and then write about these patterns, these ancient images, not only as they appear in art—in a Beatles song, a Marx Brothers movie, a poem by John Keats—but also as they occur in your own life.

We begin with the *Shadow* archetype, which was given its name by the Swiss psychiatrist C. G. Jung (1875–1961), who introduced the concept of the archetype into modern psychology. Very simply, the Shadow is a character who appears along with and is the exact opposite of the hero. Since he *is* so different, so alien, there is often something sinister, threatening, or dangerous about him. At times, he may be an actual villain. But whatever role he plays, he always possesses a personality (and sometimes an appearance) that is in complete contrast to that of the hero.

In myths, fairy tales, and literature, the Shadow appears in certain typical forms. One of the most common of these is the dark or hostile brother. We have countless legends and folktales depicting the conflict between a good and an evil brother; the most familiar example is the biblical story of Cain and Abel. This form of the archetype is particularly prevalent in popular art. In the movie *Duel in the Sun*, for example (released in 1947 and one of the top-grossing Westerns of all time), Joseph Cotten and Gregory Peck star as the antagonistic McCanles brothers, Jesse and Lewt. Jesse—blond, well-bred, benevolent—is a spokesman for societal values: for law, order, decency. He supports the coming of the railroad, though its tracks will cut across his father's ranch, believing that it will promote the development of Texas and bring civilization to the West. Ultimately he becomes a lawyer and moves to the city. Lewt, on the other hand, is an agent of *dis*order. Brutal, lewd, and reckless, he ends up an outlaw—blowing up trains on behalf of his father—and guns Jesse down in cold blood (only to die himself at the hands of his hell-cat mistress, Pearl Chavez).

The motif of the battling brothers (symbolizing the conflict between good and evil) is not restricted to the movies. Take a look, for example, at "Midnight Brings Dark Death," from *Master of Kung Fu* no. 16 (p. 12). In this comic book, Shang-chi, the hero of the series, is forced to fight his evil foster brother, "the man-menace called Midnight," to the death. Here, the villain is actually called "a living shadow." In fact, Midnight's combat outfit is entirely black, flat black, so that, in some of the fight scenes, Shang-chi appears to be engaged in a particularly lethal form of shadow-boxing—as if his shadow had suddenly developed a mind of its own and turned on him with murderous intent. Another comic book structured around the theme of the hostile brother is *Kobra,* which first appeared early in 1976. Its plot revolves around the rivalry of two young men, Siamese twins separated at birth, who end up pursuing conflicting careers: one becomes a student at Columbia Law School, the other (less conventional), the leader of a cult of New Delhi snake worshipers and, in the words of Lieutenant Perez of the New York Police Department Special Weapons and Tactics Force, "one of the world's deadliest criminals." The central conflict of the comic is summed up on the opening page of the premier issue: "Each man is forced to be his brother's keeper. Each wishes to be his brother's killer!"

The rival brothers are not always portrayed as physical combatants—sometimes they just stand in opposition to one another, each representing a different set of values. During the late 1960s, for example, a song called "Ballad of Two Brothers" was popular in certain parts of the country. In it, the Shadow appears in the political context of the Vietnam War. The two brothers of the title are on opposite sides of the Vietnam issue: the older brother supports America's involvement in the war and is killed while fighting in Southeast Asia. His Shadow figure is his younger brother: a long-haired "hippie" who flunks out of college because he spends so much of his time protesting the war. In "Goofus and Gallant," a regular feature of the contemporary monthly magazine *Highlights for Children,* the motif of the wicked brother is used in the service of moral instruction. The good brother, Gallant, is a little paragon, a perfect gentleman—everything a nice little boy is supposed to be. Goofus, on the other hand, is a typical Shadow figure, embodying all the antisocial tendencies that children are taught to reject.

At times, the Shadow is totally unrelated to the hero—not a sibling, but a dark stranger whose character is the complete opposite of the hero's. "Whiteman," one of R. Crumb's "underground comix," provides an example. As its subtitle informs us, it is "a story of civilization in crisis." Its protagonist, the prototypical American businessman, "is on the verge of a nervous breakdown," brought on by too much work and too many tensions in the modern urban landscape he is a part of. Walking home from work one night, he encounters a parade of black men, archetypal Shadow figures for the white man. He is both terrified by them and intrigued by the possibilities of freedom they hold out to him when they ask him to join their parade ("Yo' got music in yo' soul! Remember?"). Ed Gentry, the protagonist of James Dickey's *Deliverance,* a best-seller which was made into a successful movie starring Burt Reynolds and Jon Voight, has a similar experience. A middle-aged American businessman, like Crumb's Whiteman, Gentry takes a trip into the backwoods of Georgia. There, he encounters a Shadow figure in the shape of a mountain man whose unbridled behavior (the antithesis of Ed's own civilized restraint) both repels and attracts the hero.

But the double is perhaps the commonest form of the Shadow archetype. Classic literature affords countless examples: Dostoyevsky's "The Double," Conrad's "The Secret Sharer," James's "The Jolly Corner," Hoffmann's "The Sandman," Poe's "William Wilson," Hawthorne's "Monsieur du Miroir," Maupassant's "The Horla"— these are just a few of the works in which the double (or *doppelgänger*) appears.

Double figures are no less prevalent in popular culture. In "The Enemy Within," for example, an episode of the television series "Star Trek," a malfunctioning "transporter" machine splits Captain Kirk into two individuals, one extremely meek, the other utterly animalistic. Television fantasy figures like the Bionic Woman frequently run up against evil look-alikes, criminal counterfeits created either by technology or by plastic surgery. The double is also a standard motif in adventure comics. A good example can be found in *Conan the Barbarian,* no. 54, in which the hero duels a soulless replica of himself, a "fiend-Conan" conjured up by black magic. And a recurrent character in Superman comics is an "artificial imitation" Superman named Bizarro. In a diabolical (though predictably futile) plot to destroy comicdom's mightiest hero, the mad scientist Lex Luthor constructs a duplicator ray which he trains on his foe. The result is (in Luthor's words) "your imperfect double, Superman. I created him so that he can battle you with his super-powers." Deformed, dull-witted, destructive, this "pathetic, grotesque creature" is the superhero's Shadow—the negative reflection of the noble Man of Steel.

But the Shadow is not merely a character in fantasy and fiction. Like all archetypes, the Shadow is ubiquitous in myth, fairy tales, folklore and art because it gives expression to, *symbolizes,* a universal human experience. Every human being has a Shadow. It is that side of ourselves which is the exact opposite of what we would ideally like to be, of what we like other people to think we *are.* The Shadow is that part of the personality which we consider inferior or "evil" or feel guilty about and try to conceal from everyone—even, sometimes, from ourselves. This is the meaning of Robert Louis Stevenson's *Dr. Jekyll and Mr. Hyde*—one of the most famous Shadow stories ever written. The vicious Mr. Hyde, as his name suggests, represents the *hidden* personality (just as the noble and brilliant Dr. Jekyll stands for the perfect self most people try to present to the world). Whenever "something comes over us," whenever we burst out angrily and then apologize by saying "I wasn't myself," whenever we "accidentally" let slip a nasty remark which we hadn't intended to make—those are instances of our Shadows' coming to the surface.

How does one deal with the Shadow? Many people deal with it very simply—by denying that it exists, that they possess any truly unpleasant qualities. But they are fooling themselves: all of us have dark, ignoble sides. Dr. Jekyll is aware of this fact, but he is so appalled by it, so horrified by his own wicked thoughts and desires, that he tries as hard as he can to separate himself from them. He says, in effect, "This other self is not the real me." But what such a response to the Shadow amounts to is an inability to live with oneself—a psychological state of affairs that is bound to cause trouble (as it does for Dr. Jekyll, who is ultimately destroyed by his refusal to accept his other side). The healthy approach is also the hardest; in fact, it takes a real hero, like Ged, the young wizard in Le Guin's "The Open Sea." As Ged realizes, the only way to maturity is to stop running away from those things in ourselves that we are afraid to confront—to turn and finally face them, saying, in effect, what Prospero says of the brutish Caliban at the close of Shakespeare's *The Tempest:*

> . . . this thing of darkness I
> Acknowledge mine.

SIR JAMES FRAZER

"The Myth of Osiris"

An anthropological classic, Sir James Frazer's *The Golden Bough* (from which this selection is taken) is a monumental study of primitive myth, ritual, and magic. Published in twelve volumes between 1907 and 1915, it quickly became one of the most important books of the twentieth century, exerting an enormous influence on the work of such writers as T. S. Eliot, William Butler Yeats, D. H. Lawrence, and James Joyce. Frazer's study focuses on the figure of the vegetation spirit—a ubiquitous type in ancient mythology—exemplified by deities such as Attis, Adonis, Dionysus, and the Egyptian corn-god Osiris.

As Oliver Evans and Harry Finestone point out in their book *The World of the Short Story: Archetypes in Action,* archetypes often appear in combination, and in the myth of Osiris, we find two important patterns: Death and Rebirth (see Chapter Eight) and the Shadow, here embodied in the figure of Osiris' hostile brother, Set.

Osiris was the offspring of an intrigue between the earth-god Seb (Keb or Geb, as the name is sometimes transliterated) and the sky-goddess Nut. The Greeks identified his parents with their own deities Cronus and Rhea. When the sun-god Ra perceived that his wife Nut had been unfaithful to him, he declared with a curse that she should be delivered of the child in no month and no year. But the goddess had another lover, the god Thoth or Hermes, as the Greeks called him, and he playing at draughts with the moon won from her a seventy-second part of every day, and having compounded five whole days out of these parts he added them to the Egyptian year of three hundred and sixty days. This was the mythical origin of the five supplementary days which the Egyptians annually inserted at the end of every year in order to establish a harmony between lunar and solar time. On these five days, regarded as outside the year of twelve months, the curse of the sun-god did not rest, and accordingly Osiris was born on the first of them. At his nativity a voice rang out proclaiming that the Lord of All had come into the world. Some say that a certain Pamyles heard a voice from the temple at Thebes bidding him announce with a shout that a great king, the beneficent Osiris, was born. But Osiris was not the only child of his mother. On the second of the supplementary days she gave birth to the elder Horus, on the third to the god Set, whom the Greeks called Typhon, on the fourth to the goddess Isis, and on the fifth to the goddess Nephthys. Afterwards Set married his sister Nephthys, and Osiris married his sister Isis.

Reigning as a king on earth, Osiris reclaimed the Egyptians from savagery, gave them laws, and taught them to worship the gods. Before his time the Egyptians had been cannibals. But Isis, the sister and wife of Osiris, discovered wheat and barley growing wild, and Osiris introduced the cultivation of these grains

Reprinted with permission of Macmillan Publishing Co., Inc. from *The Golden Bough* by Sir James George Frazer. Copyright 1922 by Macmillan Publishing Co., Inc., renewed 1950 by Barclays Bank Ltd. Also by permission of A. P. Watt & Son Ltd., London, England.

amongst his people, who forthwith abandoned cannibalism and took kindly to a corn diet. Moreover, Osiris is said to have been the first to gather fruit from trees, to train the vine to poles, and to tread the grapes. Eager to communicate these beneficent discoveries to all mankind, he committed the whole government of Egypt to his wife Isis, and travelled over the world, diffusing the blessings of civilisation and agriculture wherever he went. In countries where a harsh climate or niggardly soil forbade the cultivation of the vine, he taught the inhabitants to console themselves for the want of wine by brewing beer from barley. Loaded with the wealth that had been showered upon him by grateful nations, he returned to Egypt, and on account of the benefits he had conferred on mankind he was unanimously hailed and worshipped as a deity. But his brother Set (whom the Greeks called Typhon) with seventy-two others plotted against him. Having taken the measure of his good brother's body by stealth, the bad brother Typhon fashioned and highly decorated a coffer of the same size, and once when they were all drinking and making merry he brought in the coffer and jestingly promised to give it to the one whom it should fit exactly. Well, they all tried one after the other, but it fitted none of them. Last of all Osiris stepped into it and lay down. On that the conspirators ran and slammed the lid down on him, nailed it fast, soldered it with molten lead, and flung the coffer into the Nile. This happened on the seventeenth day of the month Athyr, when the sun is in the sign of the Scorpion, and in the eight-and-twentieth year of the reign or the life of Osiris. When Isis heard of it she sheared off a lock of her hair, put on a mourning attire, and wandered disconsolately up and down, seeking the body.

By the advice of the god of wisdom she took refuge in the papyrus swamps of the Delta. Seven scorpions accompanied her in her flight. One evening when she was weary she came to the house of a woman, who, alarmed at the sight of the scorpions, shut the door in her face. Then one of the scorpions crept under the door and stung the child of the woman that he died. But when Isis heard the mother's lamentation, her heart was touched, and she laid her hands on the child and uttered her powerful spells; so the poison was driven out of the child and he lived. Afterwards Isis herself gave birth to a son in the swamps. She had conceived him while she fluttered in the form of a hawk over the corpse of her dead husband. The infant was the younger Horus, who in his youth bore the name of Harpocrates, that is, the child Horus. Him Buto, the goddess of the north, hid from the wrath of his wicked uncle Set. Yet she could not guard him from all mishap; for one day when Isis came to her little son's hiding-place she found him stretched lifeless and rigid on the ground: a scorpion had stung him. Then Isis prayed to the sun-god Ra for help. The god hearkened to her and staid his bark in the sky, and sent down Thoth to teach her the spell by which she might restore her son to life. She uttered the words of power, and straightway the poison flowed from the body of Horus, air passed into him, and he lived. Then Thoth ascended up into the sky and took his place once more in the bark of the sun, and the bright pomp passed onward jubilant.

Meantime the coffer containing the body of Osiris had floated down the river and away out to sea, till at last it drifted ashore at Byblus, on the coast of Syria. Here a fine *erica*-tree shot up suddenly and enclosed the chest in its trunk. The king of the country, admiring the growth of the tree, had it cut down and made into a pillar of his house; but he did not know that the coffer with the dead Osiris was in it. Word of this came to Isis and she journeyed to Byblus, and sat down by the well, in humble guise, her face wet with tears. To none would she speak till the king's handmaidens came, and them she greeted kindly, and braided their hair, and breathed on them from her own divine body a wondrous perfume. But when the queen beheld the braids of her handmaidens' hair and smelt the sweet smell that emanated from them, she sent for the stranger woman and took her into her house and made her the nurse of her child. But Isis gave the babe her finger instead of her breast to suck, and at night she began to burn all that was mortal of him away, while she herself in the likeness of a swallow fluttered round the pillar that contained her dead brother, twittering mournfully. But the queen spied what she was doing and shrieked out when she saw her child in flames, and thereby she hindered him from becoming immortal. Then the goddess revealed herself and begged for the pillar of the roof, and they gave it her, and she cut the coffer out of it, and fell upon it and embraced it and lamented so loud that the younger of the king's children died of fright on the spot. But the trunk of the tree she wrapped in fine linen, and poured ointment on it, and gave it to the king and queen, and the wood stands in a temple of Isis and is worshipped by the people of Byblus to this day. And Isis put the coffer in a boat and took the eldest of the king's children with her and sailed away. As soon as they were alone, she opened the chest, and laying her face on the face of her brother she kissed him and wept. But the child came behind her softly and saw what she was about, and she turned and looked at him in anger, and the child could not bear her look and died; but some say that it was not so, but that he fell into the sea and was drowned. It is he whom the Egyptians sing of at their banquets under the name of Maneros.

But Isis put the coffer by and went to see her son Horus at the city of Buto, and Typhon found the coffer as he was hunting a boar one night by the light of a full moon. And he knew the body, and rent it into fourteen pieces, and scattered them abroad. But Isis sailed up and down the marshes in a shallop made of papyrus, looking for the pieces; and that is why when people sail in shallops made of papyrus, the crocodiles do not hurt them, for they fear or respect the goddess. And that is the reason, too, why there are many graves of Osiris in Egypt, for she buried each limb as she found it. But others will have it that she buried an image of him in every city, pretending it was his body, in order that Osiris might be worshipped in many places, and that if Typhon searched for the real grave he might not be able to find it. However, the genital member of Osiris had been eaten by the fishes, so Isis made an image of it instead, and the image is used by the Egyptians at their festivals to this day. "Isis," writes the historian Diodorus Siculus, "recovered all the parts of the body except the genitals; and because she wished that her husband's grave should be unknown and honoured by all who dwell in the land of Egypt, she resorted to the following device. She moulded human images out of wax and spices, corresponding to the stature of Osiris, round each one of the parts of his body. Then she called in the priests according to their families and took an oath of them all that they would reveal to no man the trust she was about to repose in them. So to each of them privately she said that to them alone she entrusted the burial of the body, and reminding them of the benefits they had received she exhorted them to bury the body in their own land and to honour Osiris as a god. She also besought them to dedicate one of the animals of their country, whichever they chose, and to honour it in life as they had formerly honoured Osiris, and when it died to grant it obsequies like his. And because she would encourage the priests in their own interest to bestow the aforesaid honours, she gave them a third part of the land to be used by them in the service and worship of the gods. Accordingly it is said that the priests, mindful of the benefits of Osiris, desirous of gratifying the queen, and moved by the prospect of gain, carried out all the injunctions of Isis. Wherefore to this day each of the priests imagines that Osiris is buried in his country, and they honour the beasts that were consecrated in the beginning, and when the animals die the priests renew at their burial the mourning for Osiris. But the sacred bulls, the one called Apis and the other Mnevis, were dedicated to Osiris, and it was ordained that they should be worshipped as gods in common by all the Egyptians, since these animals above all others had helped the discoverers of corn in sowing the seed and procuring the universal benefits of agriculture."

QUESTIONS

Language

1. Look up the following words in a dictionary: *draughts* (p. 5); *transliterate* (p. 5); *beneficent* (p. 5); *diffuse* (p. 6); *coffer* (p. 6); *niggardly* (p. 6); *papyrus* (p. 6); *shallop* (p. 7); *exhort* (p. 7); *emanate* (p. 7); *obsequies* (p. 8).
2. How would you characterize Frazer's attitude toward his subject? What is his general tone? Does he seem to make any judgments about the myth as he tells it?
3. Frazer doesn't tell the story of Osiris in a strictly linear or straightforward fashion; he embellishes it here and there with "excursions" or disgressions. Find some of them and try to decide why each is included. What do they add?
4. Discuss in class the difference between formal and informal language and between concrete and abstract words. (You will probably want to consult a dictionary or handbook to literature.) How would you characterize Frazer's prose—is it formal or informal? Is his diction largely abstract or concrete?
5. *Parallelism*, as Thrall and Hibbard define it in their *Handbook to Literature*, is "a structural arrangement of parts of a sentence, sentences, paragraphs, and larger units of composition by which one element of equal importance with another is equally developed and similarly phrased. The principle of *parallelism* simply dictates that coordinate ideas should have coordinate presentation." Show how the following sentence demonstrates parallelism: "Moreover, Osiris is said to have been the first to gather fruit from trees, to train the vine to poles, and to tread the grapes." Find other sentences like this. What effect does parallelism have on the reader?

Content

1. Talk about the gods and goddesses you encounter in this myth. What are they like and what kinds of things do they do? Does their behavior surprise you at all?
2. Why is the reader given no reasons for the enmity Set—whom Frazer elsewhere calls "the Egyptian devil"—feels toward his brother Osiris? How can we account for his hatred?
3. What is the source of animal worship in Egypt?

Suggestions for Writing

1. Write an essay which begins with the unfaithfulness—the "intrigue"—of the goddess Nut (the *cause*) and then gives in detail the main things that happened as a result of it

(the *effect*). You may want to organize your essay around good effects and bad effects, or around the effects felt only by the family and those that benefited civilization as a whole.

2. In an essay, compare and contrast the brothers Osiris and Set. Talk about the activities of both.

3. With your classmates, create a definition of sibling rivalry. Then write a personal experience essay about any feelings of sibling rivalry you have had toward a brother or sister, or any they have had toward you. (Such feelings are very common.) In the case of your family, how long did the rivalry last? What form did it take; how was it expressed? Did your parents try to discourage it, or did they unwittingly encourage it? What things did you learn from the experience?

THE BROTHERS GRIMM

"The Singing Bone"

The Grimm brothers—Jacob (1785–1863) and Wilhelm (1786–1859)—spent thirteen years collecting material for their most famous book, *Kinder- und Hausmärchen (Nursery and Household Tales)*, popularly known as *Grimm's Fairy Tales*. Published in three volumes between 1812 and 1814, it reproduced, with slight modifications, the stories they had heard from the common folk of the German countryside. As Joseph Campbell writes in his "Folkloristic Commentary" to *The Complete Grimm's Fairy Tales,* "the special distinction of the work of Jacob and Wilhelm Grimm was its scholarly regard for sources. Earlier collectors had felt free to manipulate folk materials; the Grimms were concerned to let the speech of the people break directly into print. . . . No one before the Grimms had really acquiesced to the irregularities, the boorishness, the simplicity of the folk talk." Thus, the *Hausmärchen* is not only one of the world's most popular books, but a pioneering work of folklore scholarship.

"The Singing Bone"—though little known in comparison to such favorites as "Cinderella," "Rapunzel," "Little Red Riding Hood," "Hansel and Gretel," and "Snow White"—is a fascinating story and surprisingly rich (considering its length) in archetypal imagery. In addition to the figure of the envious older brother—strikingly similar here to the bibical character Cain, probably the best-known hostile brother in Western mythology—there are, as in "The Myth of Osiris," a number of elements relating to the theme of Death and Rebirth: the wasteland; the wild boar (which in Greek mythology was the beast that slew the vegetation god Adonis); the association of the murderous brother with the west, the place where the sun sets and thus a primordial symbol of death, and of the good brother with the east, the place where the sun rises and thus a symbol of resurrection; and the corpse that comes back to life to accuse its killer.

From *The Complete Grimm's Fairy Tales,* by Jakob Ludwig and Wilhelm Karl Grimm, translated by Margaret Hunt and James Stern. Copyright 1944 by Pantheon Books and renewed 1972 by Random House, Inc. Reprinted by permission of Pantheon Books, a Division of Random House, Inc.

In a certain country there was once great lamentation over a wild boar that laid waste the farmers' fields, killed the cattle, and ripped up people's bodies with his tusks. The King promised a large reward to anyone who would free the land from this plague; but the beast was so big and strong that no one dared to go near the forest in which it lived. At last the King gave notice that whosoever should capture or kill the wild boar should have his only daughter to wife.

Now there lived in the country two brothers, sons of a poor man, who declared themselves willing to undertake the hazardous enterprise; the elder, who was crafty and shrewd, out of pride; the younger, who was innocent and simple, from a kind heart. The King said: "In order that you may be the more sure of finding the beast, you must go into the forest from opposite sides." So the elder went in on the west side, and the younger on the east.

When the younger had gone a short way, a little man stepped up to him. He held in his hand a black spear and said: "I give you this spear because your heart is pure and good; with this you can boldly attack the wild boar, and it will do you no harm."

He thanked the little man, shouldered the spear, and went on fearlessly.

Before long he saw the beast, which rushed at him; but he held the spear towards it, and in its blind fury it ran so swiftly against it that its heart was cloven in twain. Then he took the monster on his back and went homewards with it to the King.

As he came out at the other side of the wood, there stood at the entrance a house where people were making merry with wine and dancing. His elder brother had gone in here, and, thinking that after all the boar would not run away from him, was going to drink until he felt brave. But when he saw his young brother coming out of the wood laden with his booty, his envious, evil heart gave him no peace. He called out to him: "Come in, dear brother, rest and refresh yourself with a cup of wine."

The youth, who suspected no evil, went in and told him about the good little man who had given him the spear wherewith he had slain the boar.

The elder brother kept him there until the evening, and then they went away together, and when in the darkness they came to a bridge over a brook, the elder brother let the other go first; and when he was half-way across he gave him such a blow from behind that he fell down dead. He buried him beneath the bridge, took the boar, and carried it to the King, pretending that he had killed it; whereupon he obtained the King's daughter in marriage. And when his younger brother did not come back he said: "The boar must have ripped up his body," and every one believed it.

But as nothing remains hidden from God, so this black deed also was to come to light.

Years afterwards a shepherd was driving his herd across the bridge, and saw lying in the sand beneath, a snow-white little bone. He thought that it would make a good mouth-piece, so he clambered down, picked it up, and cut out of it a mouth-piece for his horn. But when he blew through it for the first time, to his great astonishment, the bone began of its own accord to sing:

"Ah, friend, thou blowest upon my bone!
Long have I lain beside the water;
My brother slew me for the boar,
And took for his wife the King's young daughter."

"What a wonderful horn!" said the shepherd; "it sings by itself; I must take it to my lord the King." And when he came with it to the King the horn again began to sing its little song. The King understood it all, and caused the ground below the bridge to be dug up, and then the whole skeleton of the murdered man came to light. The wicked brother could not deny the deed, and was sewn up in a sack and drowned. But the bones of the murdered man were laid to rest in a beautiful tomb in the churchyard.

QUESTIONS

Language

1. The Grimm stories usually start with carefully chosen words that let us know we are reading a fairy tale. What words at the beginning of "The Singing Bone" tell you you're reading a fairy tale?
2. Fairy tales were originally oral forms of communication—rather than being read, they were spoken or recited. Find "proof" in the vocabulary, syntax (the way in which words are put together to form a sentence), and structure of "The Singing Bone" that demonstrates this was an oral tale. Remember that fairy tales had to be constructed in such a way that they could be remembered and passed on for generations by people who were uneducated and usually illiterate.

Content

1. In his struggle against the boar and later against his elder brother, the hero can count on certain kinds of assistance the other character cannot count on. Why should this be so and what are these things? What does the other brother depend on for his success?
2. In "The Singing Bone," as in several other fairy tales in this book, it is the *youngest* sibling who is good and the victim of evil older brothers or sisters. Why do you think this is so?

Suggestions for Writing

1. Analyze in an essay why a child would like this fairy tale (or any other in the book you care to use for your discussion). Be as specific as you can.
2. The German poet Schiller once wrote: "Deeper meaning resides in the fairy tales told to me in my childhood than in the truth that is taught by life." Do you think fairy tales can teach us more, or "deeper," things about life than life itself can? What sorts of things does "The Singing Bone," for example, tell us? Would life teach us the same things? Discuss these questions with your classmates; then write an essay in which you argue for or against the opinion expressed by Schiller.
3. This fairy tale reflects the popular belief that "murder will out." As all of us know, however, people "get away with murder," both literally and figuratively, all the time. Based on your personal experience or observation of others, write an essay in which you describe someone you know or perhaps a public figure (a politician, for example) who has "gotten away with murder," that is, done something terrible and not been caught or punished for it. You should, of course, mention what he or she did.

STEVE ENGLEHART AND JIM STARLIN

from "Midnight Brings Dark Death"

The martial arts craze began in this country with David Carradine's television series "Kung Fu" and the importation of such Chinese action films as *Five Fingers of Death* and *Bloody Fists*. Extravagantly violent—"the master of karate/kung fu is back to break you up, smash you down, and kick you apart," reads the ad for *The Chinese Connection*—these cheaply made "chop sockies" (as *Variety* dubbed them) earned an enormous amount of money and produced a genuine box-office idol: Bruce Lee, a charismatic Chinese-American actor and kung fu expert, who died under mysterious circumstances at the age of thirty-two, on the very brink of superstardom. Lee completed four martial arts movies before his death: *Fists of Fury, The Chinese Connection, The Way of the Dragon,* and (what is generally considered his finest) *Enter the Dragon*.

Comics were quick to cash in on the craze with magazines like *Iron Fist, Yang,* and *Richard Dragon—Kung Fu Fighter*. The best of the bunch, and a popular title still, is Marvel Comics' *Master of Kung Fu*. Shang-chi, the hero of the series, is the son of the Oriental archfiend Fu Manchu. Deceived by his father into believing that an Englishman named Dr. Petrie is "the most evil man alive," Shang-chi has assassinated Petrie. As a result, the young hero is now being sought by the police. At the same time, he has become the sworn enemy of Fu Manchu, having learned that the true villain is his own father. In the story which follows (from *Master of Kung Fu,* no. 16, written by Steve Englehart and drawn by Jim Starlin) the treacherous Mandarin, who has vowed to use all the evil means at his disposal to destroy his gallant son, forces Shang-chi into a deadly duel with his foster brother, "the man-menace called Midnight."

Reprinted with permission of Marvel Comics from *Master of Kung Fu,* no. 16. Copyright © 1974 by Marvel Comics Group. All rights reserved.

"THE SOUTHERN SECTION OF MANHATTAN ISLAND.

"THOUGH NEW YORK IS A CITY WITHOUT *REPOSE*, THIS AREA SEEMS ENTIRELY *EMPTIED* AFTER DARK.

"IT LOOMS WITH GREAT GRAY *WAREHOUSES*, AND *TWISTS* WITH SUDDEN *ALLEYWAYS* THAT MELT AWAY THE MIDDLE OF *BLOCKS*.

"IN ANY *DIRECTION*, I HEAR ONLY MY *HEART*.

"BUT NOW, A *SHADOW*--

"--HURLED INTO *ENORMITY* AGAINST A ROTTED BUILDING'S WALL BY SOME LOW-LYING *LAMP* AROUND THE CORNER.

"I SLIP *FORWARD*, THE COOL *WIND* MAKING MORE SOUND THAN MY *PASSAGE* --BUT NO ONE IS *THERE*.

"NOW *ANOTHER* SHADOW, FARTHER UP AN *ALLEY*.

"ALL OF MY TRAINED SENSES FUNCTIONING *FULLY*, I GLIDE INTO THE *WAITING DARK*, SEARCHING...

SNAP

"*BEHIND* ME!

"HE STEPS OUT *SOLIDLY*, A LIVING SHADOW IN A *REALM OF SHADOWS*.

"FAR AWAY, ACROSS *WATER*, A CLOCK TOLLS *MIDNIGHT*.

I SEE, MY BROTHER, THAT YOU HAVE COME TO *DIE*.

NO, M'NAI. I HAVE COME TO *LIVE*.

"NO FURTHER WORDS ARE NECESSARY.

TOK!

"NEITHER OF US HARBORS ANY ILLUSIONS AS TO WHY WE ARE HERE. FRIENDSHIP BETWEEN TWO MASTERS OF THE MARTIAL ARTS HAS NOTHING TO DO WITH COMBAT.

"BUT IN THINKING OF SUCH THINGS NOW, I DO DWELL UPON OUR FRIENDSHIP INSTEAD OF OUR FIGHT... TO MY COST.

"HE BREATHES LIGHTLY, SURPRISE THAT HIS FOOT DID NOT FIND ME IN THE CLOAK IS EVIDENT IN HIS STANCE.

YOU RECOVER QUICKLY, SHANG-CHI. I AM NOT DISAPPOINTED.

"HE SPEAKS! THE MENTAL PRESSURE OF OUR DUEL AFFECTS HIM AFTER ALL.

"I AM DISAPPOINTED. THIS WILL IMPROVE MY CHANCE OF SURVIVAL -- BUT I EXPECTED BETTER FROM M'NAI.

ARE YOU YET A MASTER OF WEAPONRY?

"HE KNOWS I COME PREPARED. MY NUNCHAKU WHIZZ FREE EVEN AS THE ALLEY WALLS RETURN THE SOUND OF HIS VOICE.

"HE STRIKES WELL. I RECOIL WELL. HE MISSES.

"I STEP AROUND THE BLADE AS HE RECOVERS HIMSELF, SMASHING HIM FOUR TIMES RUNNING WITH THE ON-SWEEPING MOTION OF MY ARM.

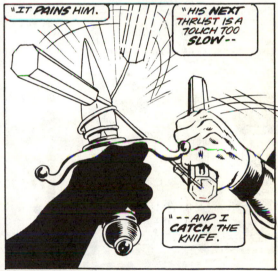

"IT PAINS HIM.

"HIS NEXT THRUST IS A TOUCH TOO SLOW--

"--AND I CATCH THE KNIFE.

"A TWIST TO PULL IT FROM HIS HAND, AND NOW --

WEAPONS WERE A MERCY OF A SORT, SHANG-CHI. IN UNARMED COMBAT, I SHALL BE YOUR SUPERIOR--

--FOR YOUR PATH IS NEW TO YOU, AND MINE IS AS OLD AS MY MEMORIES!

NEW YORK'S **FINEST** DON'T GO FOR BEATIN' UP **COPS**, PALLY, AN' WE'RE NOT AS **INEPT** AS YOU **THINK**!

NOW REACH--

TRACKIN' YOU DOWN WAS NO HARDER THAN CHECKIN' YER **DESCRIPTION**, MR. **SHANG-CHI**, MURDERER!

I SHALL FIND YOU **LATER**, MY BROTHER.

HEY!

WELL, I'LL BE--! THE KID'S GOT **GUTS**, AT ANY **RATE**!

BUT, BOY, AM I GONNA GET THE **HORSELAUGH** BACK AT THE **STATION**!

OKAY, BOSTON BLACKIE--AT LEAST I COLLARED **YOU**, SO LET'S--

HOLY CROW!

HE'S GONE, TOO!

"THE SKY IS STREAKED WITH THE PROMISE OF **DAWN** NOW. I STAND HIGH AND SILENT, **SEARCHING.**

"AS THE **FALCON** SEEKS HIS PREY **BELOW** HIM, I USE MY **VANTAGE POINT** TO SCAN THE STREETS BENEATH. ALSO I USE IT FOR **PROTECTION**, FOR M'NAI'S SKILL IN BLENDING WITH **SHADOWS** HAS MADE HIM COMPLETELY **SILENT**, EVEN TO **MY** EARS.

WOK!

DEAL ONLY WITH THE **PRESENT**, M'NAI! THE FUTURE LIES **ALWAYS** BEYOND ONE'S GRASP!

I AM THE **ONLY** MAN WHO CAN APPROACH YOU UNHEARD, SHANG-CHI--A FACT THAT DETERMINES MY **VICTORY**--

--AND YOUR **DEATH**!

"I HANG BY MY **FINGER-TIPS**, BUT THEY ARE STRONG AS **STEEL** -- STRONG ENOUGH TO **ANCHOR** ME AS I TWIST MY BODY TO THE **OFFENSE**.

WUMP!

"TECHNIQUES FOR **UNARMED COMBAT** AGAINST AN OPPONENT WITH A **BO*** FLASH THROUGH MY **BRAIN**, MY **HANDS** AND **FEET** --

"-- YET **NONE** ARE SO DESIRABLE AS **AVOIDANCE** OF SUCH COMBAT.

* STAFF. --R.T.

"HOWEVER, AS I **CARRY** MYSELF HAND-OVER-HAND ACROSS THE FIFTY-FOOT ABYSS, M'NAI LEAPS OUT TO **WALK THE WIRE** ON HIS TOES, USING THE STAFF FOR **BALANCE**!

"I HAVE MADE **ANOTHER** ERROR.

"ONLY MY **SPEED** AND A LAST-SECOND DROP TO A **LEDGE** BELOW --

"-- ALLOW ME TO **ESCAPE** THE BLACK-CLAD FEET THAT SEEK TO **CRUSH** MY FINGERS AND CAUSE ME TO **FALL**.

"AND NOW EVEN THIS HAVEN IS DENIED ME!

"KNIFE-EDGED **STARS** SLICE PAST! M'NAI WILL NOT MISS FOR **LONG**!

"I DROP **THREE STORIES** TO THE STREET.

THUDD!

"AN *ANSWERING* THUD ANNOUNCES *MIDNIGHT'S* ARRIVAL.

SURRENDER, SHANG-CHI! DO NOT PROLONG THIS *FURTHER!*

"A *CONSTRUCTION* SITE! THERE MUST BE--

"--PIPES!

NOW, MIDNIGHT--NOW WE SHALL FACE EACH OTHER *EVENLY* MATCHED!

YOU--NO LONGER CALL ME BY MY *GIVEN NAME!* YOU CALL ME BY MY *NOM DE GUERRE,* MY *BROTHER!*

GIVEN NAMES ARE FOR *FRIENDS,* MIDNIGHT.

YOU HAVE *FORFEITED* OUR FRIENDSHIP!

A PATH *CAN* CONNECT TWO OPPOSITE POINTS, BUT A MAN CANNOT TRAVEL TOWARD *BOTH* AT THE *SAME TIME!*

IF YOUR LOVE FOR MY *FATHER* OUT-WEIGHS YOUR LOVE FOR *ME,* I CAN ONLY *RECOGNIZE* IT, AND ACT *ACCORDINGLY!*

TONG!

FFTTT!

CHAK!

KLUD

BRUN!

"RAGE HAS DRIVEN HIM TO MORE BRAVADO THAN SCIENCE IN HIS BLOWS, AND THOUGH THAT USUALLY BRINGS DISASTER--

"--I FIND IT IS I WHO MUST FLEE AGAIN!

CLIMBING THE CRANE WILL NOT SAVE YOU! I WILL NOT DESERT MY PATH! I WILL FOLLOW IT FOREVER!

THEN FOLLOW!

I CRAVE NOT ESCAPE -- ONLY TIME!

"INSTANTLY, HE SWINGS ONTO THE SCAFFOLDING, SKITTERING UPWARD LIKE A GREAT BLACK SPIDER--

"--CLINGING GREEDILY TO A STEEL-STRAND WEB!

"AND I AM THE FLY.

"THIS IMAGE STICKS IN MY THOUGHTS LIKE FLY-PAPER -- AND SUDDENLY, A NEW UNDERSTANDING OF MYSELF OPENS BEFORE ME!

"I ACCEPTED THE INEVITABILITY OF OUR BATTLE --ACCEPTED THE BATTLE ITSELF--

"I UNDERSTAND NOW-- THAT I MUST NO LONGER HOLD BACK!

TUNK!

DOES FRIENDSHIP CLOUD YOUR MIND AGAIN, SHANG-CHI?

OR DO YOU HALT BECAUSE YOU UNDERSTAND THAT YOU CANNOT BEST ME?

HATE DRIVES MY ATTACK, MY BROTHER-- HATE THAT TWISTS THE ALREADY-TWISTED FACE UNDER THE MASK INTO A SIGHT THAT COULD KILL YOU IN ITSELF!

YOU SPOKE OF LOVE BEFORE-- FOR YOU AND YOUR FATHER--

--BUT LOVE IS NOT MINE TO HAVE-- LET ALONE TO GIVE!

WOW!

YOU EASED MY DAYS AS A YOUTH, YET I DO NOT NEED YOU FOR THE REMAINDER OF MY DAYS!

I NEED NO ONE!

I AM ALONE!

PAK!

I UNDERSTAND IT NOW! I AM NO MAN LIKE OTHER MEN! I CANNOT BE THAT! I AM A WEAPON!

"HIS KICKS HAVE BLOODIED MY FACE, YET NOW HIS VOICE CRESCENDOS IN BLIND PASSION--

"--AND NOW I SWING AWAY!

"HIS WEIGHT ALL RIDES IN HIS FOOT-- AND HIS FOOT ENCOUNTERS NOTHING BUT AIR!

"OFF-BALANCE, HE CANNOT CONTROL HIS FALL AS BEFORE! I SHALL HAVE HIM!

AIIEE!

"THE HOOK! HIS CAPE CAUGHT ON THE HOOK!"

"THE SOUND OF HIS NECK SNAPPING WAS LIKE THE CRACK OF DOOM!"

"I CLIMB NUMBLY FROM MY PERCH. STRANGELY -- OR PERHAPS NOT SO STRANGELY -- A THOUGHT SLIPS UNCALLED FROM THE PAST.

"I ALWAYS WANTED TO SEE HIS FACE, TO SEE WHAT DROVE HIM.

"NOW IS MY CHANCE, I KNOW. I HAVE ONLY TO CLIMB AGAIN, AND PULL HIM TO ME --

" -- BUT EVEN WITHOUT THE SEEING, I NOW KNOW THE SCARS THAT PLAGUED HIM.

"FARE- WELL, M'NAI... MY BROTHER."

By NATURE, men are nearly ALIKE; by PRACTICE, they get to be WIDE APART.

NEXT: THE RETURN OF SIR DENIS NAYLAND SMITH AND THE LAIR OF THE LOST!

QUESTIONS

Language

1. How would you characterize Shang-chi's diction? Is it different from the way his foster brother M'nai speaks? From the way the policeman talks? What is Englehart trying to suggest with Shang-chi and M'nai's speech?
2. Shang-chi says on page 14, "Friendship between two masters of the martial arts has nothing to do with conflict." What does he mean? Can you think of a better way of saying this?
3. A *metaphor,* according to Thrall and Hibbard in *A Handbook to Literature,* is "an implied analogy which imaginatively identifies one object with another and ascribes to the first one or more of the qualities of the second or invests the first with emotional or imaginative qualities associated with the second." There are a number of metaphors in this selection; see how many you can find. What do they add to the story?

Content

1. M'nai's face is horribly scarred; thus he wears a mask. But can you think of any other reason the author masked him? What does Shang-chi mean at the end when he says of M'nai, "But even without the seeing, I now know the scars that plagued him"?
2. What kind of hero is Shang-chi? Describe him and his actions as completely as you can. What is M'nai like?
3. At one point in the story, Shang-chi refuses to call his foster brother "M'nai." Why? And why, at the end, does the hero again call him "M'nai"?
4. Is it absolutely clear that, of the two brothers, it is M'nai who is more filled with hatred, M'nai who cares less about his rival and is more determined to destroy him? Explain.
5. What must Shang-chi acknowledge before he can vanquish his enemy Midnight?
6. What does M'nai mean when he says to Shang-chi that he, M'nai, will be the victor because "your path is new to you, and mine is as old as my memories"?

Suggestions for Writing

1. Write an essay comparing and contrasting the two brothers M'nai and Shang-chi.
2. At the end of this story, the narrator comments, "By nature, men are nearly alike; by practice, they get to be wide apart." Write an essay evaluating this "moral" as an adequate explanation of what has happened in the story.

GARRY CLEVELAND MYERS AND
MARION HULL HAMMEL

"Goofus and Gallant"

Highlights for Children, like most juvenile magazines, is designed both to delight and instruct. Published monthly, it is filled with games, puzzles, handicraft hints, and stories with a moral tag. A regular feature is "Goofus and Gallant," which uses the motif of the good and bad twins to promote proper conduct in children.

As we point out in our introduction to this chapter, the Shadow is that part of our personalities which we often regard as shameful or immoral—generally, our sexual and aggressive drives and desires. But the Shadow is not completely evil, for these same instinctual drives are the source of much of our creative energy. In literature, myths, and popular art, therefore, Shadow figures are often characterized by their high animal spirits and possess a vitality that the "good guys" lack. In the western movie *Duel in the Sun,* for example, Gregory Peck, though utterly villainous, is a far more attractive character than the citified, almost sissified hero, Joseph Cotten. Similarly, though Goofus is clearly meant to be obnoxious, even destructive—a bundle of unbridled aggression—he sometimes seems more appealing than the do-gooder Gallant. Concerned, apparently, that readers might miss the point and emulate the wrong brother, the writer, Garry Cleveland Myers, includes a little explanatory note at the bottom of each page: "Gallant shows correct behavior."

Copyright © 1972 and 1973, Highlights for Children, Inc., Columbus, Ohio.

Goofus and Gallant

By Garry Cleveland Myers

Pictures by Marion Hull Hammel

Goofus leaves dirt from his hands on the towel.

Gallant washes his hands well before using the towel.

Goofus places his used knife· and spoon on the tablecloth.

Gallant places his knife and spoon on his plate.

Goofus never washes the bathtub after taking a bath.

Gallant always cleans the bathtub neatly after bathing.

★ Gallant sets a good example.

Goofus and Gallant

By Garry Cleveland Myers

Pictures by Marion Hull Hammel

Goofus reads many comic books at the drugstore.

Gallant doesn't handle things he doesn't want to buy.

At the food store Goofus runs all over the place.

Gallant stays with his mother and helps her.

Goofus goes with a pal to look at things in the store, not to buy them.

Gallant goes into the store with an older person to buy things there.

★ Gallant shows correct behavior.

Goofus and Gallant

By Garry Cleveland Myers

Pictures by Marion Hull Hammel

Goofus argues when he is asked to do something.

Gallant gets right at a job when he is asked.

When Mother calls Goofus from another room he doesn't answer.

Gallant says, "Coming, Mother," when he is called.

Goofus is rude to the woman who helps.

"It's nice you help keep the house tidy."

QUESTIONS

Language

1. How would you characterize the language in these "lessons"? What effect does it have on you?

Content

1. Why are two boys featured in this series rather than two girls or a girl and a boy?
2. Using "Goofus and Gallant" as a model, imagine a series that offers praise and admonition to two little girls, concentrating on the lessons you think are *most* important for girls to learn; write the lessons down on a piece of paper. Then discuss with your classmates how much your series differs from theirs as well as from Myers' original. Do any of the series indicate that many people believe small boys and girls should be taught different lessons and be prepared for different futures?

Suggestions for Writing

1. Does "Goofus and Gallant" seem old-fashioned to you? Why or why not? In you essay, support your opinion by referring to the things the two boys do and don't do, the lessons the reader is being taught, the way the boys are drawn, and the *tone* of the writer.
2. Write psychological profiles depicting Goofus and Gallant as adults. Compare and contrast the two.
3. "Goofus and Gallant" is trying to instill certain kinds of behavior in children. What are they? In your essay, try to get at some of the underlying assumptions beneath these prescriptions for behavior. For example, what role do property and material possessions play here?

URSULA K. LE GUIN

from *A Wizard of Earthsea*

A marvelous storyteller with an elegant, poetic style, Ursula K. Le Guin is, in the words of critic Leslie Fiedler, "one of the best writers of science fiction in the United States at the moment, which is to say one of the best writers of fiction." She has published poetry, short stories, critical essays (see Appendix), and several superb science fiction novels, including *Rocannon's World, Planet of Exile, City of Illusions, The Lathe of Heaven, The Left Hand of Darkness, The Dispossessed.* The last two were both winners of the coveted Hugo and Nebula Awards for best science fiction novel of the year.

"The Open Sea" is the concluding chapter of Le Guin's fantasy novel *A Wizard of Earthsea,* volume one of *The Earthsea Trilogy* (followed by *The Tombs of Atuan* and *The Farthest Shore*). In it, young Ged, an apprentice wizard, abuses his training by toying with powers he has not yet learned to control. As a result, he unleashes

Reprinted with permission of Parnassus Press from *A Wizard of Earthsea* by Ursula K. Le Guin. Copyright 1968 by Ursula K. Le Guin.

a fearful shadow which pursues him across the far reaches of Earthsea until, in this climactic episode, Ged turns and sails out to face his foe.

THE OPEN SEA

The haven now was sunk from sight and *Lookfar's* painted eyes, wave-drenched, looked ahead on seas ever wider and more desolate. In two days and nights the companions made the crossing from Iffish to Soders Island, a hundred miles of foul weather and contrary winds. They stayed in port there only briefly, long enough to refill a waterskin, and to buy a tar-smeared sailcloth to protect some of their gear in the undecked boat from seawater and rain. They had not provided this earlier, because ordinarily a wizard looks after such small conveniences by way of spells, the very least and commonest kind of spells, and indeed it takes little more magic to freshen seawater and so save the bother of carrying fresh water. But Ged seemed most unwilling to use his craft, or to let Vetch use his. He said only, "It's better not," and his friend did not ask or argue. For as the wind first filled their sail, both had felt a heavy foreboding, cold as that winter wind. Haven, harbor, peace, safety, all that was behind. They had turned away. They went now a way in which all events were perilous, and no acts were meaningless. On the course on which they were embarked, the saying of the least spell might change chance and move the balance of power and of doom: for they went now toward the very center of that balance, toward the place where light and darkness meet. Those who travel thus say no word carelessly.

• • •

In these days and nights of sailing Ged never spoke of the shadow, nor directly of his quest; and the nearest Vetch came to asking any question was (as they followed the same course farther and farther out and away from the known lands of Earthsea)—"Are you sure?—" To this Ged answered only, "Is the iron sure where the magnet lies?" Vetch nodded and they went on, no more being said by either. But from time to time they talked of the crafts and devices that mages of old days had used to find out the hidden name of baneful powers and beings: how Nereger of Paln had learned the Black Mage's name from overhearing the conversation of dragons, and how Morred had seen his enemy's name written by falling raindrops in the dust of the battlefield of the Plains of Enlad. They spoke of finding-spells, and invocations, and those Answerable Questions which only the Master Patterner of Roke can ask. But often Ged would end by murmuring words which Ogion had said to him on the shoulder of Gont Mountain in an autumn long ago: "To hear, one must be silent. . . ." And he would fall silent, and ponder, hour by hour, always watching the sea ahead of the boat's way. Sometimes it seemed to Vetch that his friend saw, across the waves and miles and grey days yet to come, the thing they followed and the dark end of their voyage.

They passed between Kornay and Gosk in foul weather, seeing neither isle in the fog and rain, and knowing they had passed them only on the next day when they saw ahead of them an isle of pinnacled cliffs above which sea-gulls wheeled in huge flocks whose mewing clamor could be heard from far over the sea. Vetch said, "That will be Astowell, from the look of it. Lastland. East and south of it the charts are empty."

"Yet they who live there may know of farther lands," Ged answered.

"Why do you say so?" Vetch asked, for Ged had spoken uneasily; and his answer to this again was halting and strange. "Not there," he said, gazing at Astowell ahead, and past it, or through it—"Not there. Not on the sea. Not on the sea but on dry land: what land? Before the springs of the open sea, beyond the sources, behind the gates of daylight—"

Then he fell silent, and when he spoke again it was in an ordinary voice, as if he had been freed from a spell or a vision, and had no clear memory of it.

The port of Astowell, a creek-mouth between rocky heights, was on the northern shore of the isle, and all the huts of the town faced north and west; it was as if the island turned its face, though from so far away, always towards Earthsea, towards mankind.

Excitement and dismay attended the arrival of strangers, in a season when no boat had ever braved the seas round Astowell. The women all stayed in the wattle huts, peering out the door, hiding their children behind their skirts, drawing back fearfully into the darkness of the huts as the strangers came up from the beach. The men, lean fellows ill-clothed against the cold, gathered in a solemn circle about Vetch and Ged, and each one held a stone hand-axe or a knife of shell. But once their fear was past they made the strangers very welcome, and there was no end to their questions. Seldom did any ship come to them even from Soders or Rolameny, they having nothing to trade for bronze or fine wares; they had not even any wood. Their boats were coracles woven of reed, and it was a brave sailor who would go as far as Gosk or Kornay in such a craft. They dwelt all alone here at the edge of all the maps. They had no witch or sorcerer, and seemed not to recognise the young wizards' staffs for what they were, admiring them only for the precious stuff they were made of, wood. Their chief or Isle-Man was very old, and he alone of his people had ever before seen a man born in the Archipelago. Ged, therefore, was a marvel to them; the men brought their little sons to look at the Archipelagan, so they might remember him when they were old. They had never heard of Gont, only of Havnor and Éa, and took him for a Lord of Havnor. He did his best to answer their questions about the white city he had never seen. But he was restless as the evening wore on, and at last he asked the men of the village, as they sat crowded round the firepit in the lodgehouse in the reeking warmth of the goat-dung and broom-faggots that were all their fuel, "What lies eastward of your land?"

They were silent, some grinning others grim.

The old Isle-Man answered, "The sea."

"There is no land beyond?"

"This is Lastland. There is no land beyond. There is nothing but water till world's edge."

"These are wise men, father," said a younger man, "seafarers, voyagers. Maybe they know of a land we do not know of."

"There is no land east of this land," said the old man, and he looked long at Ged, and spoke no more to him.

The companions slept that night in the smoky warmth of the lodge. Before daylight Ged roused his friend, whispering, "Estarriol, wake. We cannot stay, we must go."

"Why so soon?" Vetch asked, full of sleep.

"Not soon—late. I have followed too slow. It has found the way to escape me, and so doom me. It must not escape me, for I must follow it however far it goes. If I lose it I am lost."

"Where do we follow it?"

"Eastward. Come. I filled the waterskins."

So they left the lodge before any in the village was awake, except a baby that cried a little in the darkness of some hut, and fell still again. By the vague starlight they found the way down to the creek-mouth, and untied *Lookfar* from the rock cairn where she had been made fast, and pushed her out into the black water. So they set out eastward from Astowell into the Open Sea, on the first day of the Fallows, before sunrise.

That day they had clear skies. The world's wind was cold and gusty from the northeast, but Ged had raised the magewind: the first act of magery he had done since he left the Isle of the Hands. They sailed very fast due eastward. The boat shuddered with the great, smoking, sunlit waves that hit her as she ran, but she went gallantly as her builder had promised, answering the magewind as true as any spell-enwoven ship of Roke.

Ged spoke not at all that morning, except to renew the power of the wind-spell or to keep a charmed strength in the sail, and Vetch finished his sleep, though uneasily, in the stern of the boat. At noon they ate. Ged doled their food out sparingly, and the portent of this was plain, but both of them chewed their bit of salt fish and wheaten cake, and neither said anything.

All afternoon they cleaved eastward never turning nor slackening pace. Once Ged broke his silence, saying, "Do you hold with those who think the world is all landless sea beyond the Outer Reaches, or with those who imagine other Archipelagoes or vast undiscovered lands on the other face of the world?"

"At this time," said Vetch, "I hold with those who think the world has but one face, and he who sails too far will fall off the edge of it."

Ged did not smile; there was no mirth left in him. "Who knows what a man might meet, out there? Not we, who keep always to our coasts and shores."

"Some have sought to know, and have not returned. And no ship has ever come to us from lands we do not know."

Ged made no reply.

All that day, all that night they went driven by the powerful wind of magery over the great swells of ocean, eastward. Ged kept watch from dusk till dawn, for in darkness the force that drew or drove him grew stronger yet. Always he watched ahead, though his eyes in the moonless night could see no more than the painted eyes aside the boat's blind prow. By daybreak his dark face was grey with weariness, and he was so cramped with cold that he could hardly stretch out to rest. He said whispering, "Hold the magewind from the west, Estarriol," and then he slept.

There was no sunrise, and presently rain came beating across the bow from the northeast. It was no storm, only the long, cold winds and rains of winter. Soon all things in the open boat were wet through, despite the sailcloth cover they had bought; and Vetch felt as if he too were soaked clear to the bone; and Ged shivered in his sleep. In pity for his friend, and perhaps for himself, Vetch tried to turn aside for a little that rude ceaseless wind that bore the rain. But though, following Ged's will, he could keep the magewind strong and steady, his weatherworking had small power here so far from land, and the wind of the Open Sea did not listen to his voice.

And at this a certain fear came into Vetch, as he began to wonder how much wizardly power would be left to him and Ged, if they went on and on away from the lands where men were meant to live.

Ged watched again that night, and all night held the boat eastward. When day came the world's wind slackened somewhat, and the sun shone fitfully; but the great swells ran so high that *Lookfar* must tilt and climb up them as if they were hills, and hang at the hillcrest and plunge suddenly, and climb up the next again, and the next, and the next, unending.

In the evening of that day Vetch spoke out of long silence. "My friend," he said, "you spoke once as if sure we would come to land at last. I would not question your vision but for this, that it might be a trick, a deception made by that which you follow, to lure you on farther than a man can go over ocean. For our power may change and weaken on strange seas. And a shadow does not tire, or starve, or drown."

They sat side by side on the thwart, yet Ged looked at him now as if from a distance, across a wide abyss. His eyes were troubled, and he was slow to answer.

At last he said, "Estarriol, we are coming near."

Hearing his words, his friend knew them to be true. He was afraid, then. But he put his hand on Ged's shoulder and said only, "Well, then, good, that is good."

Again that night Ged watched, for he could not sleep in the dark. Nor would he sleep when the third day came. Still they ran with that ceaseless, light, terrible swiftness over the sea, and Vetch wondered at Ged's power that could hold so strong a magewind hour after hour, here on the Open Sea where Vetch felt his own power all weakened and astray. And they went on, until it seemed to Vetch that what Ged had spoken would come true, and they were going beyond the sources of the sea and eastward behind the gates of daylight. Ged stayed forward in the boat, looking ahead as always. But he was not watching the ocean now, or not the ocean that Vetch saw, a waste of heaving water to the rim of the sky. In Ged's eyes there was a dark vision that overlapped and veiled the grey sea and the grey sky, and the darkness grew, and the veil thickened. None of this was visible to Vetch, except when he looked at his friend's face; then he too saw the darkness for a moment. They went on, and on. And it was as if, though one wind drove them in one boat, Vetch went east over the world's sea, while Ged went alone into a realm where there was no east or west, no rising or setting of the sun, or of the stars.

Ged stood up suddenly in the prow, and spoke aloud. The magewind dropped. *Lookfar* lost headway, and rose and fell on the vast surges like a chip of wood. Though the world's wind blew strong as ever straight from the north now, the brown sail hung slack, unstirred. And so the boat hung on the waves, swung by their great slow swinging, but going no direction.

Ged said, "Take down the sail," and Vetch did so quickly, while Ged unlashed the oars and set them in the locks and bent his back to rowing.

Vetch, seeing only the waves heaving up and down clear to the end of sight, could not understand why they went now by oars; but he waited, and presently he was aware that the world's wind was growing faint and the swells diminishing. The climb and plunge of the boat grew less and less, till at last she seemed to go forward under Ged's strong oarstrokes over water that lay almost still, as in a land-locked bay. And though Vetch could not see what Ged saw, when between his strokes he looked ever and again over his shoulder at what lay before the boat's way—though Vetch could not see the dark slopes beneath unmoving stars, yet he began to see with his wizard's eye a darkness that welled up in the hollows of the waves all around the boat, and he saw the billows grow low and sluggish as they were choked with sand.

If this were an enchantment of illusion, it was powerful beyond belief; to make the Open Sea seem land. Trying to collect his wits and courage, Vetch spoke the Revelation-spell, watching between each slow-syllabled word for change or tremor of illusion in this strange drying and shallowing of the abyss of ocean. But there was none. Perhaps the spell, though it should affect only his own vision and not the magic at work about them, had no power here. Or perhaps there was no illusion, and they had come to world's end.

Unheeding, Ged rowed always slower, looking over his shoulder, choosing a way among channels or shoals and shallows that he alone could see. The boat shuddered as her keel dragged. Under that keel lay the vast deeps of the sea, yet they were aground. Ged drew the oars up rattling in their locks, and that noise was terrible, for there was no other sound. All sounds of water, wind, wood, sail, were gone, lost in a huge profound silence that might have been unbroken for ever. The boat lay motionless. No breath of wind moved. The sea had turned to sand, shadowy, unstirred. Nothing moved in the dark sky or on that dry unreal ground that went on and on into gathering darkness all around the boat as far as eye could see.

Ged stood up, and took his staff, and lightly stepped over the side of the boat. Vetch thought to see him fall and sink down in the sea, the sea that surely was there behind this dry, dim veil that hid away water, sky, and light. But there was no sea any more. Ged walked away from the boat. The dark sand showed his footprints where he went, and whispered a little under his step.

His staff began to shine, not with the werelight but with a clear white glow, that soon grew so bright that it reddened his fingers where they held the radiant wood.

He strode forward, away from the boat, but in no direction. There were no directions here, no north or south or east or west, only towards and away.

To Vetch, watching, the light he bore seemed like a great slow star that moved through the darkness. And the darkness about it thickened, blackened, drew together. This also Ged saw, watching always ahead through the light. And after a while he saw at the faint outermost edge of the light a shadow that came towards him over the sand.

At first it was shapeless, but as it drew nearer it took on the look of a man. An old man it seemed, grey and grim, coming towards Ged; but even as Ged saw his father the smith in that figure, he saw that it was not an old man but a young one. It was Jasper: Jasper's insolent handsome young face, and silver-clasped grey cloak, and stiff stride. Hateful was the look he fixed on Ged across the dark intervening air. Ged did not stop, but slowed his pace, and as he went forward he raised his staff up a little higher. It brightened, and in its light the look of Jasper fell from the figure that approached, and it became Pechvarry. But Pechvarry's face was all bloated and pallid like the face of a drowned man, and he reached out his hand strangely as if beckoning. Still Ged did not stop, but went forward, though there were only a few yards left between them now.

Then the thing that faced him changed utterly, spreading out to either side as if it opened enormous thin wings, and it writhed, and swelled, and shrank again. Ged saw in it for an instant Skiorh's white face, and then a pair of clouded, staring eyes, and then suddenly a fearful face he did not know, man or monster, with writhing lips and eyes that were like pits going back into black emptiness.

At that Ged lifted up the staff high, and the radiance of it brightened intolerably, burning with so white and great a light that it compelled and harrowed even that ancient darkness. In that light all form of man sloughed off the thing that came towards Ged. It drew together and shrank and blackened, crawling on four short taloned legs upon the sand. But still it came forward, lifting up to him a blind unformed snout without lips or ears or eyes. As they came right together it became utterly black in the white mage-radiance that burned about it, and it heaved itself upright. In silence, man and shadow met face to face, and stopped.

Aloud and clearly, breaking that old silence, Ged spoke the shadow's name and in the same moment the shadow spoke without lips or tongue, saying the same word: "Ged." And the two voices were one voice.

Ged reached out his hands, dropping his staff, and took hold of his shadow, of the black self that reached out to him. Light and darkness met, and joined, and were one.

But to Vetch, watching in terror through the dark twilight from far off over the sand, it seemed that Ged was overcome, for he saw the clear radiance fail and grow dim. Rage and despair filled him, and he sprang out on the sand to help his friend or die with him, and ran towards that small fading glimmer of light in the empty dusk of the dry land. But as he ran the sand sank under his feet, and he struggled in it as in quicksand, as through a heavy flow of water: until with a roar of noise and a glory of daylight, and the bitter cold of winter, and the bitter taste of salt, the world was restored to him and he floundered in the sudden, true, and living sea.

Nearby the boat rocked on the grey waves, empty. Vetch could see nothing else on the water; the battering wave-tops filled his eyes and blinded him. No strong swimmer, he struggled as best he could to the boat, and pulled himself up into her. Coughing and trying to wipe away the water that streamed from his hair, he looked about desperately, not knowing now which way to look. And at last he made out something dark among the waves, a long way off across what had been sand and now was wild water. Then he leapt to the oars and rowed mightily to his friend, and catching Ged's arms helped and hauled him up over the side.

Ged was dazed and his eyes stared as if they saw nothing, but there was no hurt to be seen on him. His staff, black yew wood, all radiance quenched, was grasped in his right hand, and he would not let go of it. He said no word. Spent and soaked and shaking he lay huddled up against the mast, never looking at Vetch who raised the sail and turned the boat to catch the north-east wind. He saw nothing of the world until, straight ahead of their course, in the sky that darkened where the sun had set, between long clouds in a bay of clear blue light, the new moon shone: a ring of ivory, a rim of horn, reflected sunlight shining across the ocean of the dark.

Ged lifted his face and gazed at that remote bright crescent in the west.

He gazed for a long time, and then he stood up erect, holding his staff in his two hands as a warrior holds his long sword. He looked about at the sky, the sea, the brown swelling sail above him, his friend's face.

"Estarriol," he said, "look, it is done. It is over." He laughed. "The wound is healed," he said, "I am whole, I am free." Then he bent over and hid his face in his arms, weeping like a boy.

Until that moment Vetch had watched him with an anxious dread, for he was not sure what had happened there in the dark land. He did not know if this was Ged in the boat with him, and his hand had been for hours ready to the anchor, to stave in the boat's planking and sink her there in midsea, rather than carry back to the harbors of Earthsea the evil thing that he feared might have taken Ged's look and form. Now when he saw his friend and heard him speak, his doubt vanished. And he began to see the truth, that Ged had neither lost nor won but, naming the shadow of his death with his own name, had made himself whole: a man: who, knowing his whole true self, cannot be used or possessed by any power other than himself, and whose life therefore is lived for life's sake and never in the service of ruin, or pain, or hatred, or the dark. In the *Creation of Éa,* which is the oldest song, it is said, "Only in silence the word, only in dark the light, only in dying life: bright the hawk's flight on the empty sky." That song Vetch sang aloud now as he held the boat westward, going before the cold wind of the winter night that blew at their backs from the vastness of the Open Sea.

QUESTIONS

Language

1. What effect does the first part of this story have on you? How would you describe its tone or mood? Find specific words, phrases, or metaphors that contribute to the effect which the author intends and which you feel.
2. Why does Le Guin include so many names of places in her story? What would be the effect if she took them all out?
3. How would you characterize the diction of Ged and Vetch? Suppose they spoke in contemporary, conversational English, unadorned by metaphor or figure of speech. How would that change the story?
4. Is the language in this story basically abstract or concrete? Point to specific examples.

Content

1. Try to find all the examples you can of storytelling and mythmaking in "The Open Sea." Why do these legends and tales play such a prominent part in it?
2. How does the writer build suspense in this episode?
3. What kind of reception do Ged and Vetch receive on Astowell (Lastland)? How are the inhabitants the two encounter there different from themselves?
4. Why does the shadow keep changing shape as it moves toward Ged?
5. What are the results of Ged's encounter with the shadow?

Suggestions for Writing

1. Write an essay examining the various means by which Le Guin has created a strange, enchanted world—a fantasy world. Refer to specific details of setting, language, manners, behavior, characterization, plot.

2. Create your own fantasy world—a place where the impossible is commonplace. Take the reader on a tour through this imaginary land. Show its scenery, inhabitants, creatures, and so on. You may want simply to describe it, or you may want to write a short narrative, or story, set in it. Read your essay or story to your classmates. Whose do you like best? Why?

ROBERT CRUMB

"Whiteman"

The creator of such characters as Fritz the Cat and Mr. Natural—and the man who made "Keep on Truckin' " one of the hip slogans of the sixties—Robert Crumb (b. 1943) is undoubtedly the best known of the underground cartoonists. He is also the most highly regarded, both by comic fans and critics. His drawings have been displayed in museums and analyzed in scholarly journals. Assessing his achievement, most critics refer to Crumb's astute social commentary. In his essay "The New Comics and American Culture," for example (*Tri-Quarterly*, Winter/Spring 1972), Paul Buhle writes that "Robert Crumb most thoroughly of all the [underground] artists comprehends, portrays, and embodies the dilemmas of the middle class." And Thomas Maremaa, writing in the *New York Times Magazine* ("Who is this Crumb?" October 1, 1972), argues that "what Jules Feiffer was to the neurotic fifties, Crumb has been to the cultural radicalism of the late sixties."

While critics like Buhle and Maremaa are undoubtedly right, they tend to overlook an important aspect of Crumb's work. For though Crumb may be, as Buhle claims, "a supreme realist," he is realistic only part of the time. In *Zap, Despair, Motor City, Uneeda Comix* and others, he does indeed provide "a powerful cultural critique of American life." But a story like "Whiteman" (from *Zap,* no. 1) reveals something else: that Crumb's imagination is strikingly mythological. Crumb's "head comix," that is to say, derive their special appeal, not only from the social satire they contain, but from the richness of their mythic imagery, from their archetypal symbolism. "Whiteman" also provides insight into the psychological sources of racism, for it illustrates the way in which people who are different from us can become a kind of screen onto which we project precisely those things we most fear in ourselves.

Reprinted with permission of R. Crumb from *Zap Comix,* no. 1. Copyright 1967 by R. Crumb.

QUESTIONS

Language

1. What is the author's attitude toward his main character, Whiteman? Look at Crumb's comments as narrator. What do they reveal? What is Crumb's tone?

Content

1. How would you characterize Crumb's attitude toward American society?
2. Describe Whiteman's public and private faces. What kind of condition is he in?
3. Why does Crumb depict the black paraders as he does? Is he trying to say something about white prejudice?
4. What attitudes does Whiteman have toward the community of which he is a part? Do they seem contradictory to you?

Suggestions for Writing

1. Whiteman tries to deny his violent impulses as well as his sexual desires—thus, paradoxically, he is always thinking about them. Do you think Americans are overly preoccupied with sex and violence? After a discussion with your classmates, write an essay in which you support your opinion with examples drawn from movies, books, television, music, advertising, and journalism.
2. With your classmates, decide what Robert Crumb's comic has to say about the strains men have traditionally faced in America as they strive to be, at all times and in all circumstances, "real men." What is a "real man," or a "he-man"? Are the pressures on men changing as our image of manliness changes? After your discussion, write an essay in which you first define what a "real man" or "he-man" has traditionally been; then discuss the difficulties men have had conforming to this image; and finally, indicate what changes you see today, if any, in that image.
3. Note how the unnamed American city in "Whiteman" is portrayed. It is noisy, crowded and lawless, altogether a place threatening to life and mental health—a view of big city conditions showing up increasingly on the pages of newspapers, in books and movies, and on television. What is your opinion? Are big cities simply getting a "bad press" or are they places one would not even want to visit, much less live in? In your essay, support your opinion with your own experiences, your reading, and so on.
4. Write an essay in which you explore the *causes* of what happens to Whiteman. What are the circumstances of Whiteman's life that lead up to his confrontation with the black paraders? In what way is that meeting the inevitable result of certain forces in Whiteman's life and personality?

BILLY JOEL

"The Stranger"

After early training in classical piano, Billy Joel began his career at age fifteen, playing in various bar bands on Long Island. He recorded his first solo album, *Cold Spring Harbor,* in 1971 and, shortly after its release, moved to Los Angeles, where he played piano in a bar called The Executive Lounge for six months. His experiences during this time formed the basis for his autobiographical song "Piano Man," which became his first hit single and the title song of his second album. Since his rise to pop music prominence, he has toured widely and recorded several more albums, including *Streetlite Serenade* (1974), *Turnstiles* (1976), *The Stranger* (1977), and *52nd Street* (1978).

Billy Joel's songs on *The Stranger* are melodically varied, ranging from upbeat "rockers" to gentle ballads; lyrically, his pieces tend to portray the world of the city and the lives of its middle- and working-class men and women. The album's title cut, reprinted below, is a song which displays a high degree of psychological sophistication. It describes the Shadow side of the human personality—that part of ourselves which we all "hide away forever"—and wisely reminds us that the healthiest way of dealing with the stranger is to recognize and accept his existence.

"The Stranger"

Well we all have a face
That we hide away forever
And we take them out and
Show ourselves
When everyone has gone
Some are satin some are steel
Some are silk and some are leather
They're the faces of the stranger
But we love to try them on
Well we all fall in love
But we disregard the danger
Though we share so many secrets
There are some we never tell
Why were you so surprised
That you never saw the stranger
Did you ever let your lover see
The stranger in yourself?
Don't be afraid to try again
Everyone goes south
Every now and then
You've done it, why can't
Someone else?

Reprinted with permission of Home Run. Copyright 1977.

You should know by now
You've been there yourself
Once I used to believe
I was such a great romancer
Then I came home to a woman
That I could not recognize
When I pressed her for a reason
She refused to even answer
It was then I felt the stranger
Kick me right between the eyes
Well we all fall in love
But we disregard the danger
Though we share so many secrets
There are some we never tell
Why were you so surprised
That you never saw the stranger
Did you ever let your lover see
The stranger in yourself?
Don't be afraid to try again
Everyone goes south
Every now and then
You've done it, why can't
Someone else?
You should know by now
You've been there yourself
You may never understand
How the stranger is inspired
But he isn't always evil
And he isn't always wrong
Though you drown in good intentions
You will never quench the fire
You'll give in to your desire
When the stranger comes along.

QUESTIONS

Language

1. The printed lyrics of this song can be initially difficult to make any sense of because they are not divided into stanzas and have virtually no punctuation. Punctuate "The Stranger" and divide it into stanzas, justifying your divisions.
2. Billy Joel's song is highly metaphorical. For example, the stranger is itself a metaphor: it *stands for* or represents something in each of us. "Going south" is another metaphor. What do these things mean? Find any other metaphors you can and say what Joel means by them.

Content

1. Who is the speaker of this song? To whom is he speaking? What kind of relationship do the speaker and the listener seem to have?

2. What things do we know—or what things are suggested—about the personal histories and lives of the speaker and the listener?
3. Do the speaker and the person to whom he is speaking have different attitudes toward the stranger? Does the speaker claim to know what all of us feel about the stranger? Explain. Referring to ''the faces of the stranger,'' the speaker says we ''love to try them on.'' Do you agree?
4. Why does the speaker say his friend shouldn't have been surprised by events?
5. What is the ''danger'' referred to in the refrain of this song? And what do the last four lines mean?

Suggestions for Writing

1. The speaker of this song offers advice and insight to a confused, unhappy friend. Pretend you are this speaker and rephrase, in your own words, what he says to his friend. Where Joel uses metaphors and indirect language, you should be as literal as possible. Then discuss with your classmates the essays you've written. Compare and contrast them to the song. Do you find the essays easier to understand? Does the song lose anything when it is rephrased in prose?
2. Describe an incident in which someone you thought you knew very well—a close friend, lover, or relative—suddenly revealed a side to his or her personality that you had never seen before. Be sure to include your emotional reaction in addition to the facts of the incident. Did your discovery of ''the stranger'' in this person change your relationship?

NATHANIEL HAWTHORNE

''The Birthmark''

Born and raised in Salem, Massachusetts, Nathaniel Hawthorne (1804–1864) was a member of a prominent Puritan family, one of whose members—Hawthorne's great-grandfather, John Hathorne—had been a judge at the Salem witchcraft trials. After four years at Bowdoin college, Hawthorne returned home to Salem and entered his ''lonely chamber period'': twelve years of seclusion devoted to learning his craft. *Twice-Told Tales,* published in 1837, was a collection of his earliest stories—dark allegories pervaded by a ''Puritanic gloom'' (to use one of his friend Herman Melville's phrases) and preoccupied with the themes of sin, secret guilt, spiritual isolation and intellectual pride. Another collection of short stories, *Mosses from an Old Manse,* appeared in 1846, followed four years later by his masterpiece, *The Scarlet Letter.*

''The Birthmark,'' which first appeared in *Mosses,* is one of Hawthorne's greatest and most typical tales. It is the richly symbolic story of Aylmer, the ''higher intellect,'' who, in choosing the life of the mind over that of the heart, eventually comes to regard human beings as nothing more than objects to be manipulated for the sake of scientific investigation; of Georgiana, his devoted wife, ''flawed'' (in Aylmer's eyes) by the mark of her mortality, her imperfect human nature; and of the hulking brute Aminadab, Aylmer's crude, earthly counterpart.

In the latter part of the last century, there lived a man of science, an eminent proficient in every branch of natural philosophy, who not long before our story opens had made experience of a spiritual affinity more attractive than any chemical one. He had left his laboratory to the care of an assistant, cleared his fine countenance from the furnace smoke, washed the stain of acids from his fingers, and persuaded a beautiful woman to become his wife. In those days when the comparatively recent discovery of electricity and other kindred mysteries of Nature seemed to open paths into the region of miracle, it was not unusual for the love of science to rival the love of woman in its depth and absorbing energy. The higher intellect, the imagination, the spirit, and even the heart might all find their congenial aliment in pursuits which, as some of their ardent votaries believed, would ascend from one step of powerful intelligence to another, until the philosopher should lay his hand on the secret of creative force and perhaps make new worlds for himself. We know not whether Aylmer possessed this degree of faith in man's ultimate control over Nature. He had devoted himself, however, too unreservedly to scientific studies ever to be weaned from them by any second passion. His love for his young wife might prove the stronger of the two; but it could only be by intertwining itself with his love of science, and uniting the strength of the latter to his own.

Such a union accordingly took place, and was attended with truly remarkable consequences and a deeply impressive moral. One day, very soon after their marriage, Aylmer sat gazing at his wife with a trouble in his countenance that grew stronger until he spoke.

"Georgiana," said he, "has it never occurred to you that the mark upon your cheek might be removed?"

"No, indeed," said she, smiling; but perceiving the seriousness of his manner, she blushed deeply. "To tell you the truth, it has been so often called a charm that I was simple enough to imagine it might be so."

"Ah, upon another face perhaps it might," replied her husband, "but never on yours. No, dearest Georgiana, you came so nearly perfect from the hand of Nature that this slightest possible defect, which we hesitate whether to term a defect or a beauty, shocks me, as being the visible mark of earthly imperfection."

"Shocks you, my husband!" cried Georgiana, deeply hurt; at first reddening with momentary anger, but then bursting into tears. "Then why did you take me from my mother's side? You cannot love what shocks you!"

To explain this conversation, it must be mentioned that in the center of Georgiana's left cheek there was a singular mark, deeply interwoven, as it were, with the texture and substance of her face. In the usual state of her complexion— a healthy though delicate bloom—the mark wore a tint of deeper crimson, which imperfectly defined its shape amid the surrounding rosiness. When she blushed, it gradually became more indistinct, and finally vanished amid the triumphant rush of blood that bathed the whole cheek with its brilliant glow. But if any shifting motion caused her to turn pale, there was the mark again, a crimson stain upon the snow, in what Aylmer sometimes deemed an almost fearful distinctness. Its shape bore not a little similarity to the human hand, though of the smallest pygmy size. Georgiana's lovers were wont to say that some fairy at her birth hour had laid her tiny hand upon the infant's cheek, and left this impress there in token of the magic endowments that were to give her such sway over all hearts. Many a desperate swain would have risked life for the privilege of pressing his lips to the mysterious hand. It must not be concealed, however, that the impression wrought by this fairy sign manual varied exceedingly, according to the difference of temperament in the beholders. Some fastidious persons—but they were exclusively of her own sex—affirmed that the bloody hand, as they chose to call it, quite destroyed the effect of Georgiana's beauty, and rendered her countenance even hideous. But it would be as reasonable to say that one of those small blue stains which sometimes occur in the purest statuary marble would convert the Eve of Powers to a monster. Masculine observers, if the birthmark did not heighten their admiration, contented themselves with wishing it away, that the world might possess one living specimen of ideal loveliness without the semblance of a flaw. After his marriage—for he thought little or nothing of the matter before—Aylmer discovered that this was the case with himself.

Had she been less beautiful—if Envy's self could have found aught else to sneer at—he might have felt his affection heightened by the prettiness of this mimic hand, now vaguely portrayed, now lost, now stealing forth again and glimmering to and fro with every pulse of emotion that throbbed within her heart; but seeing her otherwise so perfect, he found this one defect grow more and more intolerable with every moment of their united lives. It was the fatal flaw of humanity which Nature, in one shape or another, stamps ineffaceably on all her productions, either to imply that they are temporary and finite, or that their perfection must be wrought by toil and pain. The crimson hand expressed the ineludible grip in which mortality clutches the highest and purest of earthly mold, degrading them into kindred with the lowest, and even with the very brutes, like whom their visible frames return to dust. In this manner, selecting it as the symbol of his wife's liability to sin, sorrow, decay, and death, Aylmer's somber imagination was not long in rendering the birthmark a frightful object, causing him more trouble and horror than ever Georgiana's beauty, whether of soul or sense, had given him delight.

At all the seasons which should have been their happiest, he invariably and without intending it, nay, in spite of a purpose to the contrary, reverted to this one disastrous topic. Trifling as it at first appeared, it so connected itself with innumerable trains of thought and modes of feeling that it became the central point of all. With the morning twilight, Aylmer opened his eyes upon his wife's face and recognized the symbol of imperfection; and when they sat together at the evening hearth, his eyes wandered stealthily to her cheek, and beheld, flickering with the blaze of the wood fire, the spectral hand that wrote mortality where he would fain have worshiped. Georgiana soon learned to shudder at his gaze. It needed but a glance with the peculiar expression that his face often wore to change the roses of her cheek into a deathlike paleness, amid which the crimson hand was brought strongly out, like a bas-relief of ruby on the whitest marble.

Late one night, when the lights were growing dim, so as hardly to betray the stain on the poor wife's cheek, she herself, for the first time, voluntarily took up the subject.

"Do you remember, my dear Aylmer," said she, with a feeble attempt at a smile, "have you any recollection of a dream last night about this odious hand?"

"None! none whatever!" replied Aylmer, starting; but then he added, in a dry, cold tone, affected for the sake of concealing the real depth of his emotion,

"I might well dream of it; for before I fell asleep it had taken a pretty firm hold of my fancy."

"And you did dream of it?" continued Georgiana, hastily; for she dreaded lest a gush of tears should interrupt what she had to say. "A terrible dream! I wonder that you can forget it. Is it possible to forget this one expression?—'It is in her heart now; we must have it out!' Reflect, my husband; for by all means I would have you recall that dream."

The mind is in a sad state when Sleep, the all-involving, cannot confine her specters within the dim region of her sway, but suffers them to break forth, affrighting this actual life with secrets that perchance belong to a deeper one. Aylmer now remembered his dream. He had fancied himself with his servant Aminadab, attempting an operation for the removal of the birthmark; but the deeper went the knife, the deeper sank the hand, until at length its tiny grasp appeared to have caught hold of Georgiana's heart; whence, however, her husband was inexorably resolved to cut or wrench it away.

When the dream had shaped itself perfectly in his memory, Aylmer sat in his wife's presence with a guilty feeling. Truth often finds its way to the mind close muffled in robes of sleep, and then speaks with uncompromising directness of matters in regard to which we practice an unconscious self-deception during our waking moments. Until now he had not been aware of the tyrannizing influence acquired by one idea over his mind, and of the lengths which he might find in his heart to go for the sake of giving himself peace.

"Aylmer," resumed Georgiana, solemnly, "I know not what may be the cost to both of us to rid me of this fatal birthmark. Perhaps its removal may cause cureless deformity; or it may be the stain goes as deep as life itself. Again, do we know that there is a possibility, on any terms, of unclasping the firm grip of this little hand which was laid upon me before I came into the world?"

"Dearest Georgiana, I have spent much thought upon the subject," hastily interrupted Aylmer. "I am convinced of the perfect practicability of its removal."

"If there be the remotest possibility of it," continued Georgiana, "let the attempt be made at whatever risk. Danger is nothing to me; for life, while this hateful mark makes me the object of your horror and disgust—life is a burden which I would fling down with joy. Either remove this dreadful hand, or take my wretched life! You have deep science. All the world bears witness of it. You have achieved great wonders. Cannot you remove this little, little mark, which I cover with the tips of two small fingers? Is this beyond your power, for the sake of your own peace, and to save your poor wife from madness?"

"Noblest, dearest, tenderest wife," cried Aylmer, rapturously, "doubt not my power. I have already given this matter the deepest thought—thought which might almost have enlightened me to create a being less perfect than yourself. Georgiana, you have led me deeper than ever into the heart of science. I feel myself fully competent to render this dear cheek as faultless as its fellow; and then, most beloved, what will be my triumph when I shall have corrected what Nature left imperfect in her fairest work! Even Pygmalion, when his sculptured woman assumed life, felt not greater ecstasy than mine will be."

"It is resolved, then," said Georgiana, faintly smiling. "And, Aylmer, spare me not, though you should find the birthmark take refuge in my heart at last."

Her husband tenderly kissed her cheek—her right cheek, not that which bore the impress of the crimson hand.

The next day, Aylmer apprised his wife of a plan that he had formed whereby he might have opportunity for the intense thought and constant watchfulness which the proposed operation would require; while Georgiana, likewise, would enjoy the perfect repose essential to its success. They were to seclude themselves in the extensive apartments occupied by Aylmer as a laboratory, and where, during his toilsome youth, he had made discoveries in the elemental powers of Nature that had roused the admiration of all the learned societies in Europe. Seated calmly in this laboratory, the pale philosopher had investigated the secrets of the highest cloud region and of the profoundest mines; he had satisfied himself of the causes that kindled and kept alive the fires of the volcano; and had explained the mystery of fountains, and how it is that they gush forth, some so bright and pure, and others with such rich medicinal virtues, from the dark bosom of the earth. Here, too, at an earlier period, he had studied the wonders of the human frame, and attempted to fathom the very process by which Nature assimilates all her precious influences from earth and air, and from the spiritual world, to create and foster man, her masterpiece. The latter pursuit, however, Aylmer had long laid aside in unwilling recognition of the truth—against which all seekers sooner or later stumble—that our great creative Mother, while she amuses us with apparently working in the broadest sunshine, is yet severely careful to keep her own secrets, and, in spite of her pretended openness, shows us nothing but results. She permits us, indeed, to mar, but seldom to mend, and, like a jealous patentee, on no account to make. Now, however, Aylmer resumed these half-forgotten investigations; not, of course, with such hopes or wishes as first suggested them; but because they involved much physiological truth and lay in the path of his proposed scheme for the treatment of Georgiana.

As he led her over the threshold of the laboratory, Georgiana was cold and tremulous. Aylmer looked cheerfully into her face, with intent to reassure her, but was so startled with the intense glow of the birthmark upon the whiteness of her cheek that he could not restrain a strong, convulsive shudder. His wife fainted.

"Aminadab! Aminadab!" shouted Aylmer, stamping violently on the floor.

Forthwith there issued from an inner apartment a man of low stature, but bulky frame, with shaggy hair hanging about his visage, which was grimed with the vapors of the furnace. This personage had been Aylmer's underworker during his whole scientific career, and was admirably fitted for that office by his great mechanical readiness, and the skill with which, while incapable of comprehending a single principle, he executed all the details of his master's experiments. With his vast strength, his shaggy hair, his smoky aspect, and the indescribable earthiness that incrusted him, he seemed to represent man's physical nature; while Aylmer's slender figure, and pale, intellectual face, were no less apt a type of the spiritual element.

"Throw open the door of the boudoir, Aminadab," said Aylmer, "and burn a pastille."

"Yes, master," answered Aminadab, looking intently at the lifeless form of Georgiana; and then he muttered to himself, "If she were my wife, I'd never part with that birthmark."

When Georgiana recovered consciousness, she found herself breathing an atmosphere of penetrating fragrance, the gentle potency of which had recalled her from her deathlike faintness. The scene around her looked like enchantment.

Aylmer had converted those smoky, dingy, somber rooms, where he had spent his brightest years in recondite pursuits, into a series of beautiful apartments not unfit to be the secluded abode of a lovely woman. The walls were hung with gorgeous curtains, which imparted the combination of grandeur and grace that no other species of adornment can achieve; and as they fell from the ceiling to the floor, their rich and ponderous folds, concealing all angles and straight lines, appeared to shut in the scene from infinite space. For aught Georgiana knew, it might be a pavilion among the clouds. And Aylmer, excluding the sunshine, which would have interfered with his chemical processes, had supplied its place with perfumed lamps, emitting flames of various hue, but all uniting in a soft, empurpled radiance. He now knelt by his wife's side, watching her earnestly, but without alarm; for he was confident in his science, and felt that he could draw a magic circle round her within which no evil might intrude.

"Where am I? Ah, I remember," said Georgiana, faintly; and she placed her hand over her cheek to hide the terrible mark from her husband's eyes.

"Fear not, dearest!" exclaimed he. "Do not shrink from me! Believe me, Georgiana, I even rejoice in this single imperfection, since it will be such a rapture to remove it."

"Oh, spare me!" sadly replied his wife. "Pray do not look at it again. I never can forget that convulsive shudder."

In order to soothe Georgiana, and, as it were, to release her mind from the burden of actual things, Aylmer now put in practice some of the light and playful secrets which science had taught him among its profounder lore. Airy figures, absolutely bodiless ideas, and forms of unsubstantial beauty came and danced before her, imprinting their momentary footsteps on beams of light. Though she had some indistinct idea of the method of these optical phenomena, still the illusion was almost perfect enough to warrant the belief that her husband possessed sway over the spiritual world. Then again, when she felt a wish to look forth from her seclusion, immediately, as if her thoughts were answered, the procession of external existence flitted across a screen. The scenery and the figures of actual life were perfectly represented, but with that bewitching yet indescribable difference which always makes a picture, an image, or a shadow so much more attractive than the original. When wearied of this, Aylmer bade her cast her eyes upon a vessel containing a quantity of earth. She did so, with little interest at first; but was soon startled to perceive the germ of a plant shooting upward from the soil. Then came the slender stalk; the leaves gradually unfolded themselves; and amid them was a perfect and lovely flower.

"It is magical!" cried Georgiana. "I dare not touch it."

"Nay, pluck it," answered Aylmer, "pluck it, and inhale its brief perfume while you may. The flower will wither in a few moments and leave nothing save its brown seed vessels; but thence may be perpetuated a race as ephemeral as itself."

But Georgiana had no sooner touched the flower than the whole plant suffered a blight, its leaves turning coal black as if by the agency of fire.

"There was too powerful a stimulus," said Aylmer, thoughtfully.

To make up for this abortive experiment, he proposed to take her portrait by a scientific process of his own invention. It was to be effected by rays of light striking upon a polished plate of metal. Georgiana assented; but, on looking at the results, was affrighted to find the features of the portrait blurred and indefinable; while the minute figure of a hand appeared where the cheek should have been. Aylmer snatched the metallic plate and threw it into a jar of corrosive acid.

Soon, however, he forgot these mortifying failures. In the intervals of study and chemical experiment, he came to her flushed and exhausted, but seemed invigorated by her presence, and spoke in glowing language of the resources of his art. He gave a history of the long dynasty of the alchemists, who spent so many ages in quest of the universal solvent by which the golden principle might be elicited from all things vile and base. Aylmer appeared to believe that, by the plainest scientific logic, it was altogether within the limits of possibility to discover this long-sought medium; "but," he added, "a philosopher who should go deep enough to acquire the power would attain too lofty a wisdom to stoop to the exercise of it." Not less singular were his opinions in regard to the elixir vitae. He more than intimated that it was at his option to concoct a liquid that should prolong life for years, perhaps interminably; but that it would produce a discord in Nature which all the world, and chiefly the quaffer of the immortal nostrum, would find cause to curse.

"Aylmer, are you in earnest?" asked Georgiana, looking at him with amazement and fear. "It is terrible to possess such power, or even to dream of possessing it."

"Oh, do not tremble, my love," said her husband. "I would not wrong either you or myself by working such inharmonious effects upon our lives; but I would have you consider how trifling, in comparison, is the skill requisite to remove this little hand."

At the mention of the birthmark, Georgiana, as usual, shrank as if a red-hot iron had touched her cheek.

Again Aylmer applied himself to his labors. She could hear his voice in the distant furnace room, giving directions to Aminadab, whose harsh, uncouth, misshapen tones were audible in response, more like the grunt or growl of a brute than human speech. After hours of absence, Aylmer reappeared and proposed that she should now examine his cabinet of chemical products and natural treasures of the earth. Among the former he showed her a small vial, in which, he remarked, was contained a gentle yet most powerful fragrance, capable of impregnating all the breezes that blow across a kingdom. They were of inestimable value, the contents of that little vial; and, as he said so, he threw some of the perfume into the air and filled the room with piercing and invigorating delight.

"And what is this?" asked Georgiana, pointing to a small crystal globe containing a gold-colored liquid. "It is so beautiful to the eye that I could imagine it the elixir of life."

"In one sense it is," replied Aylmer, "or, rather, the elixir of immortality. It is the most precious poison that ever was concocted in this world. By its aid, I could apportion the lifetime of any mortal at whom you might point your finger. The strength of the dose would determine whether he were to linger out years, or drop dead in the midst of a breath. No king on his guarded throne could keep his life if I, in my private station, should deem that the welfare of millions justified me in depriving him of it."

"Why do you keep such a terrific drug?" inquired Georgiana in horror.

"Do not mistrust me, dearest," said her husband, smiling. "Its virtuous potency is yet greater than its harmful one. But see! here is a powerful cosmetic.

With a few drops of this in a vase of water, freckles may be washed away as easily as the hands are cleansed. A stronger infusion would take the blood out of the cheek, and leave the rosiest beauty a pale ghost."

"Is it with this lotion that you intend to bathe my cheek?" asked Georgiana, anxiously.

"Oh, no," hastily replied her husband, "this is merely superficial. Your case demands a remedy that shall go deeper."

In his interviews with Georgiana, Aylmer generally made minute inquiries as to her sensations and whether the confinement of the rooms and the temperature of the atmosphere agreed with her. These questions had such a particular drift that Georgiana began to conjecture that she was already subjected to certain physical influences, either breathed in with the fragrant air or taken with her food. She fancied likewise, but it might be altogether fancy, that there was a stirring up of her system—a strange, indefinite sensation creeping through her veins, and tingling, half painfully, half pleasurably, at her heart. Still, whenever she dared to look into the mirror, there she beheld herself pale as a white rose and with the crimson birthmark stamped upon her cheek. Not even Aylmer now hated it so much as she.

To dispel the tedium of the hours which her husband found it necessary to devote to the processes of combination and analysis, Georgiana turned over the volumes of his scientific library. In many dark old tomes she met with chapters full of romance and poetry. They were the works of the philosophers of the Middle Ages, such as Albertus Magnus, Cornelius Agrippa, Paracelsus, and the famous friar who created the prophetic Brazen Head. All these antique naturalists stood in advance of their centuries, yet were imbued with some of their credulity, and therefore were believed, and perhaps imagined themselves to have acquired from the investigation of Nature a power above Nature, and from physics a sway over the spiritual world. Hardly less curious and imaginative were the early volumes of the Transactions of the Royal Society, in which the members, knowing little of the limits of natural possibility, were continually recording wonders or proposing methods whereby wonders might be wrought.

But to Georgiana, the most engrossing volume was a large folio from her husband's own hand, in which he had recorded every experiment of his scientific career, its original aim, the methods adopted for its development, and its final success or failure, with the circumstances to which either event was attributable. The book, in truth, was both the history and emblem of his ardent, ambitious, imaginative, yet practical and laborious life. He handled physical details as if there were nothing beyond them; yet spiritualized them all, and redeemed himself from materialism by his strong and eager aspiration towards the infinite. In his grasp, the veriest clod of earth assumed a soul. Georgiana, as she read, reverenced Aylmer and loved him more profoundly than ever, but with a less entire dependence on his judgment than heretofore. Much as he had accomplished, she could not but observe that his most splendid successes were almost invariably failures, if compared with the ideal at which he aimed. His brightest diamonds were the merest pebbles, and felt to be so by himself, in comparison with the inestimable gems which lay hidden beyond his reach. The volume, rich with achievements that had won renown for its author, was yet as melancholy a record as ever mortal hand had penned. It was the sad confession and continual exemplification of the shortcomings of the composite man, the spirit burdened with clay and working in matter, and of the despair that assails the higher nature at finding itself so miserably thwarted by the earthly part. Perhaps every man of genius in whatever sphere might recognize the image of his own experience in Aylmer's journal.

So deeply did these reflections affect Georgiana that she laid her face upon the open volume and burst into tears. In this situation she was found by her husband.

"It is dangerous to read in a sorcerer's books," said he with a smile, though his countenance was uneasy and displeased. "Georgiana, there are pages in that volume which I can scarcely glance over and keep my senses. Take heed lest it prove as detrimental to you."

"It has made me worship you more than ever," said she.

"Ah, wait for this one success," rejoined he, "then worship me if you will. I shall deem myself hardly unworthy of it. But come, I have sought you for the luxury of your voice. Sing to me, dearest."

So she poured out the liquid music of her voice to quench the thirst of his spirit. He then took his leave with a boyish exuberance of gaiety, assuring her that her seclusion would endure but a little longer, and that the result was already certain. Scarcely had he departed when Georgiana felt irresistibly impelled to follow him. She had forgotten to inform Aylmer of a symptom which for two or three hours past had begun to excite her attention. It was a sensation in the fatal birthmark, not painful, but which induced a restlessness throughout her system. Hastening after her husband, she intruded for the first time into the laboratory.

The first thing that struck her eye was the furnace, that hot and feverish worker, with the intense glow of its fire, which by the quantities of soot clustered above it seemed to have been burning for ages. There was a distilling apparatus in full operation. Around the room were retorts, tubes, cylinders, crucibles, and other apparatus of chemical research. An electrical machine stood ready for immediate use. The atmosphere felt oppressively close, and was tainted with gaseous odors which had been tormented forth by the processes of science. The severe and homely simplicity of the apartment, with its naked walls and brick pavement, looked strange, accustomed as Georgiana had become to the fantastic elegance of her boudoir. But what chiefly, indeed almost solely, drew her attention was the aspect of Aylmer himself.

He was pale as death, anxious and absorbed, and hung over the furnace as if it depended upon his utmost watchfulness whether the liquid which it was distilling should be the draught of immortal happiness or misery. How different from the sanguine and joyous mien that he had assumed for Georgiana's encouragement!

"Carefully now, Aminadab; carefully, thou human machine; carefully, thou man of clay!" muttered Aylmer, more to himself than his assistant. "Now, if there be a thought too much or too little, it is all over."

"Ho! ho!" mumbled Aminadab. "Look, master! look!"

Aylmer raised his eyes hastily, and at first reddened, then grew paler than ever, on beholding Georgiana. He rushed towards her and seized her arm with a grip that left the print of his fingers upon it.

"Why do you come hither? Have you no trust in your husband?" cried he, impetuously. "Would you throw the blight of that fatal birthmark over my labors? It is not well done. Go, prying woman, go!"

"Nay, Aylmer," said Georgiana with the firmness of which she possessed no stinted endowment. "It is not you that have a right to complain. You mistrust your wife; you have concealed the anxiety with which you watch the development of this experiment. Think not so unworthily of me, my husband. Tell me all the risk we run, and fear not that I shall shrink; for my share in it is far less than your own."

"No, no, Georgiana!" said Aylmer, impatiently. "It must not be."

"I submit," replied she, calmly. "And, Aylmer, I shall quaff whatever draught you bring me; but it will be on the same principle that would induce me to take a dose of poison if offered by your hand."

"My noble wife," said Aylmer, deeply moved, "I knew not the height and depth of your nature until now. Nothing shall be concealed. Know, then, that this crimson hand, superficial as it seems, has clutched its grasp into your being with a strength of which I had no previous conception. I have already administered agents powerful enough to do aught except to change your entire physical system. Only one thing remains to be tried. If that fails us, we are ruined."

"Why did you hesitate to tell me this?" asked she.

"Because, Georgiana," said Aylmer, in a low voice, "there is danger."

"Danger? There is but one danger—that this horrible stigma shall be left upon my cheek!" cried Georgiana. "Remove it, remove it, whatever be the cost, or we shall both go mad!"

"Heaven knows your words are too true," said Aylmer, sadly. "And now, dearest, return to your boudoir. In a little while, all will be tested."

He conducted her back and took leave of her with a solemn tenderness which spoke far more than his words how much was now at stake. After his departure, Georgiana became rapt in musings. She considered the character of Aylmer, and did it completer justice than at any previous moment. Her heart exulted, while it trembled, at his honorable love—so pure and lofty that it would accept nothing less than perfection nor miserably make itself contented with an earthlier nature than he had dreamed of. She felt how much more precious was such a sentiment than that meaner kind which would have borne with the imperfection for her sake, and have been guilty of treason to holy love by degrading its perfect idea to the level of the actual; and with her whole spirit, she prayed that, for a single moment, she might satisfy his highest and deepest conception. Longer than one moment she well knew it could not be; for his spirit was ever on the march, ever ascending, and each instant required something that was beyond the scope of the instant before.

The sound of her husband's footsteps aroused her. He bore a crystal goblet containing a liquor colorless as water, but bright enough to be the draught of immortality. Aylmer was pale; but it seemed rather the consequence of a highly wrought state of mind and tension of spirit than of fear or doubt.

"The concoction of the draught has been perfect," said he, in answer to Georgiana's look. "Unless all my science have deceived me, it cannot fail."

"Save on your account, my dearest Aylmer," observed his wife, "I might wish to put off this birthmark of mortality by relinquishing mortality itself in preference to any other mode. Life is but a sad possession to those who have attained precisely the degree of moral advancement at which I stand. Were I weaker and blinder, it might be happiness. Were I stronger, it might be endured hopefully. But, being what I find myself, methinks I am of all mortals the most fit to die."

"You are fit for heaven without tasting death!" replied her husband. "But why do we speak of dying? The draught cannot fail. Behold its effect upon this plant."

On the window seat there stood a geranium diseased with yellow blotches, which had overspread all its leaves. Aylmer poured a small quantity of the liquid upon the soil in which it grew. In a little time, when the roots of the plant had taken up the moisture, the unsightly blotches began to be extinguished in a living verdure.

"There needed no proof," said Georgiana, quietly. "Give me the goblet. I joyfully stake all upon your word."

"Drink, then, thou lofty creature!" exclaimed Aylmer, with fervid admiration. "There is no taint of imperfection on thy spirit. Thy sensible frame, too, shall soon be all perfect."

She quaffed the liquid and returned the goblet to his hand.

"It is grateful," said she, with a placid smile. "Methinks it is like water from a heavenly fountain; for it contains I know not what of unobtrusive fragrance and deliciousness. It allays a feverish thirst that had parched me for many days. Now, dearest, let me sleep. My earthly senses are closing over my spirit like the leaves around the heart of a rose at sunset."

She spoke the last words with a gentle reluctance, as if it required almost more energy than she could command to pronounce the faint and lingering syllables. Scarcely had they loitered through her lips ere she was lost in slumber. Aylmer sat by her side, watching her aspect with the emotions proper to a man the whole value of whose existence was involved in the process now to be tested. Mingled with this mood, however, was the philosophic investigation characteristic of the man of science. Not the minutest symptom escaped him. A heightened flush of the cheek, a slight irregularity of breath, a quiver of the eyelid, a hardly perceptible tremor through the frame—such were the details which, as the moments passed, he wrote down in his folio volume. Intense thought had set its stamp upon every previous page of that volume, but the thoughts of years were all concentrated upon the last.

While thus employed, he failed not to gaze often at the fatal hand, and not without a shudder. Yet once, by a strange and unaccountable impulse, he pressed it with his lips. His spirit recoiled, however, in the very act; and Georgiana, out of the midst of her deep sleep, moved uneasily and murmured as if in remonstrance. Again Aylmer resumed his watch. Nor was it without avail. The crimson hand, which at first had been strongly visible upon the marble paleness of Georgiana's cheek, now grew more faintly outlined. She remained not less pale than ever; but the birthmark, with every breath that came and went, lost somewhat of its former distinctness. Its presence had been awful; its departure was more awful still. Watch the stain of the rainbow fading out of the sky, and you will know how that mysterious symbol passed away.

"By Heaven! it is well-nigh gone!" said Aylmer to himself, in almost irrepressible ecstasy. "I can scarcely trace it now. Success! success! And now it is like the faintest rose color. The lightest flush of blood across her cheek would overcome it. But she is so pale!"

He drew aside the window curtain and suffered the light of natural day to fall into the room and rest upon her cheek. At the same time, he heard a gross, hoarse chuckle, which he had long known as his servant Aminadab's expression of delight.

"Ah, clod! Ah, earthly mass!" cried Aylmer, laughing in a sort of frenzy, "you have served me well! Matter and spirit—earth and heaven—have both done their part in this! Laugh, thing of the senses! You have earned the right to laugh."

These exclamations broke Georgiana's sleep. She slowly unclosed her eyes and gazed into the mirror which her husband had arranged for that purpose. A faint smile flitted over her lips when she recognized how barely perceptible was now that crimson hand which had once blazed forth with such disastrous brilliancy as to scare away all their happiness. But then her eyes sought Aylmer's face with a trouble and anxiety that he could by no means account for.

"My poor Aylmer!" murmured she.

"Poor? Nay, richest, happiest, most favored!" exclaimed he. "My peerless bride, it is successful! You are perfect!"

"My poor Aylmer," she repeated, with a more than human tenderness, "you have aimed loftily; you have done nobly. Do not repent that with so high and pure a feeling, you have rejected the best the earth could offer. Aylmer, dearest Aylmer, I am dying!"

Alas! it was too true! The fatal hand had grappled with the mystery of life, and was the bond by which an angelic spirit kept itself in union with a mortal frame. As the last crimson tint of the birthmark—that sole token of human imperfection—faded from her cheek, the parting breath of the now perfect woman passed into the atmosphere, and her soul, lingering a moment near her husband, took its heavenward flight. Then a hoarse, chuckling laugh was heard again! Thus ever does the gross fatality of earth exult in its invariable triumph over the immortal essence which, in this dim sphere of half development, demands the completeness of a higher state. Yet, had Aylmer reached a profounder wisdom, he need not thus have flung away the happiness which would have woven his mortal life of the selfsame texture with the celestial. The momentary circumstance was too strong for him; he failed to look beyond the shadowy scope of time, and, living once for all in eternity, to find the perfect future in the present.

QUESTIONS

Language

1. In *American Renaissance*, the critic F. O. Matthiessen quotes a remark by the poet Walter Savage Landor: "My friend wrote excellent English, a language now obsolete." Matthiessen applies this remark to Hawthorne. Discuss this idea, with specific references to the language of "The Birthmark."
2. What techniques does Aylmer use to persuade his wife to let him "experiment" on her? Discuss both his actions and his words.

Content

1. Define a symbol, consulting a good dictionary or handbook to literature. Talk about Hawthorne's use of symbols in this story. How many can you find? What do they mean?
2. Identify Aylmer's Shadow in this story. What is his Shadow figure like? In what way is he the precise opposite of Aylmer?

3. How does Georgiana feel about her birthmark? Does her attitude change as the story progresses? How and why?

4. How does Aminadab feel about the birthmark? Does his attitude seem significant to you?

5. Why does Aylmer isolate his wife in a chamber—which, "for aught Georgiana knew," might have been a "pavilion among the clouds"—and exclude from it all sunlight? What symbolic value do these facts have?

6. *Foreshadowing* is a technique a writer uses to indicate, before the end of a story, what the probable resolution of that story will be. Clues are dropped, in the form of phrases, symbols, or analogical events, that help the reader sense what is going to happen in the story. Find examples of foreshadowing in "The Birthmark" and talk about how each works.

7. Why is Aminadab laughing at the end of Hawthorne's story?

Suggestions for Writing

1. Why is it significant that the birthmark Aylmer is trying to eliminate belongs to a woman? What kind of psychological truth, in terms of the traditional relationship between the sexes, does this story have? What value have female beauty and submissiveness had for men? Discuss these questions in class; then write an essay about what can be learned from the Hawthorne story. You might begin by *summarizing* the story briefly.

2. Aylmer, through his experiments and research, is trying to gain mastery over physical life, to eliminate Nature's imperfections, to correct its "mistakes." Write an essay which compares and contrasts Aylmer to modern scientists. Do scientists today still strive to do these things? Can you think of any specific examples? Do some scientists end up destroying what they sought to "improve"?

3. The figure of the mad/evil research doctor or scientist appears frequently in American popular as well as classic culture. With your classmates, draw up a list of these figures you have encountered in films, fiction, drama, and television. Then *classify* them according to what they have in common. Finally, *analyze* what they seem to indicate about American attitudes toward the research doctor/scientist.

ADDITIONAL WRITING SUGGESTIONS FOR CHAPTER ONE

1. Describe a friend or enemy—someone to whom you are strongly attached or by whom you are deeply repelled. What is there about this person that makes you feel the way you do? Can you see any parts of your own personality reflected in him or her?

2. Describe some situation in which you felt like an outsider, an outcast, an alien. What happened? What were your emotions?

3. Write an essay describing *your* Shadow: that side of yourself you are ashamed of, afraid of, made uneasy by; that side you try to keep hidden from others, perhaps even from yourself.

4. Discuss in class, and then write an essay about, the Shadow side of America. Naturally you will have to think in generalities to do this, though you should anchor your generalities to specific illustrations or pieces of evidence as much as you can. If America has a conscious identity, a deliberately defined character, a public face that it shows to the world, what then is its underside, its private face, that part of itself it tries to repress and refuses to acknowledge? What things does America stand for? Are there realities that contradict those things?

The Trickster

"I am afraid you are a terror," said the grocery man, as he looked at the innocent face of the boy. "You are always making your parents some trouble, and it is a wonder to me that they don't send you to some reform school. What deviltry were you up to last night . . . ?"

"No deviltry, just a little fun."

—George W. Peck, *Peck's Bad Boy and His Pa*

The *Trickster* is one of humanity's oldest and most widespread mythic figures. It is "found in clearly recognizable form among the simplest aboriginal tribes and the most complex," writes the anthropologist Paul Radin in his pioneering study, *The Trickster;* it can be found in the mythology of ancient Greece, Japan, China, and the Middle East. Many characteristics of the Trickster, Radin notes, "were perpetuated in the figure of the medieval jester, and have survived right up to the present day in the Punch-and-Judy plays and in the clown." The Trickster is also alive and kicking in newspaper comic strips and in "sitcoms" on television.

Before we try to account for the special appeal of the Trickster, we must ask, who is he? Like all such symbols, the Trickster archetype takes on different forms, depending on the particular culture in which it is found. In Norse mythology, for example, the Trickster appears as the god Loki, "full of wile," whose evil pranks ultimately lead to the destruction of the world. Among the Indian tribes of North America, on the other hand, the Trickster assumes a variety of animal shapes: Coyote, Raven, Blue Jay, and Hare. And in our own time and place, the Trickster may be an all-American mischief-maker like Dennis the Menace. But whatever their particular shapes, all Trickster figures possess the same essential traits. These are vividly illustrated in an anecdote quoted by the mythologist Joseph Campbell in his book *Hero with a Thousand Faces*. The tale, from Yorubaland in West Africa, concerns a Trickster divinity named Edshu:

One day, this odd god came walking along a path between two fields. "He beheld in either field a farmer at work and proposed to play the two a turn. He donned a hat that was on the one side red but on the other white . . . ; so that when the two friendly farmers had gone home to their village and the one had said to the other, 'Did you see that old fellow go by today in the white hat?' the other replied, 'Why, the hat was red.' To which the first retorted, 'It was not; it was white.' 'But it was red,' insisted the friend, 'I saw it with my own two eyes.' 'Well, you must be blind,' declared the first. 'You must be drunk,' rejoined the other. And so the argument developed and the two came to blows. When they began to knife each other, they were brought by neighbors before the headman for judgment. Edshu was among the crowd at the trial, and when the headman sat at a loss to know where justice lay, the old trickster revealed himself, made known his prank, and showed the hat. 'The two could not help but quarrel,' he said. 'I wanted it that way. Spreading strife is my greatest joy.' "

As this African folktale shows, the Trickster is a born troublemaker, a being who is happiest when creating chaos, disturbing the peace. Just as nature abhors a vacuum, so the Trickster cannot abide tranquility. He is a compulsive prankster, a lover of anarchy and discord, who, in the words of C. G. Jung, "does the most atrocious things" for the sheer joy of doing them. Take a look, for instance, at R. Crumb's "Squirrely the Squirrel" (p. 86), a comic with interesting similarities to the story of Edshu. Hoping to have a little "fun," Squirrely visits his old adversary Farnsworth the Fox, and finds him peacefully tending a garden ("I'm tired of chasing rabbits and squirrels," Farny declares. "So I've become a vegetarian"). Squirrely cannot endure this untroubled state of affairs, any more than Edshu could, and isn't satisfied until he has taunted Farny into chasing him. Then, with a cruelty that is characteristic of many Trickster figures, he hurls a bottleful of blinding insect killer into Farny's eyes. "Ta, ha, ha," laughs Squirrely, as Farny screeches in pain. "I love to agitate him!" Even crueler is Wadjunkaga, the brutish Trickster of the Winnebago Indians, who is known, as Jung observes, for "his pointless orgies of destruction." In a story we reprint in this chapter, for example, Wadjunkaga tricks two raccoon-women into leaving their babies with him, promising to take care of the children while their mothers go off to search for some fruit. The moment the two women are out of sight, however, Wadjunkaga kills the children.

Now, the Trickster's appeal lies partly in his humor; he is most often meant to make us laugh in his role of jester, practical joker, or clown. But as the story of Wadjunkaga illustrates, he has a darker aspect which is savage, even satanic. Indeed, the merry prankster of comedy may easily become, in more serious literature, the devil himself; there is a fine line separating the two.

We can see just how fine this line is by looking at Elizabethan drama. The very first English comedy, for example, Nicholas Udall's *Ralph Roister Doister* (1552), features a mischievous figure named Matthew Merygreeke, who spends all his time playing prank after sadistic prank on the pompous hero, Ralph. True Trickster that he is, Matthew admits at one point that he puts his "sporte" (which consists of humiliating Ralph by making him the butt of endless practical jokes) before everything else in life, even eating. But when the same kind of character—the single-minded manipulator and humiliator of other people—is transposed to tragedy, he becomes monstrous: Matthew Merygreeke turns into Iago, the villain of Shakespeare's *Othello*. For years, critics have puzzled over Iago's motivation:

what makes him lie to and deceive the noble Othello; why is he so eager to orchestrate the destruction of this heroic man? The answer is found in the African story of Edshu. Like all Trickster figures, Iago causes havoc because it is part of his nature—because it *is* his nature—to do so. As Edshu explains, "Spreading strife is my greatest joy!" This satanic side of the Trickster can still be seen in comic book villains like the Green Goblin, a demonic creature dressed in a bizarre Halloween costume and armed with a bagful of lethal tricks (from *Spider-Man* comics); the Prankster, one of Superman's old enemies, who commits crimes by means of elaborate practical jokes; and the Joker, the harlequin-faced archfiend of *Batman.*

Unlike such early figures as Wadjunkaga and Edshu, however, most of the Tricksters that appear in modern popular culture are more cuddly than cruel—cute little mischief-makers in the form of "funny animals" like Heckle and Jeckle, Woody Woodpecker, and Ignatz the Mouse (from George Herriman's classic *Krazy Kat*). Perhaps the most popular cartoon Trickster is the wisecracking Bugs Bunny, who can still be seen on television every Saturday morning, making life miserable for his favorite "fall guy," Elmer Fudd.

Two more forms which the Trickster archetype typically assumes in our culture are the bad boy and the con artist. Far from arousing our indignation at their immoral behavior and even their crimes, these characters frequently delight us. The bad boy was an especially popular figure in late nineteenth- and early twentieth-century American literature, appearing in such best-selling books as Mark Twain's *The Adventures of Tom Sawyer* (1876) and *The Adventures of Huckleberry Finn* (1884), George W. Peck's *Peck's Bad Boy and His Pa* (1883), Thomas Bailey Aldrich's *The Story of a Bad Boy* (1870), and Booth Tarkington's three Penrod novels (1914–1916). The bad boy has also been a favorite character in comic strips. Hans and Fritz (the Katzenjammer Kids) and Dennis the Menace are probably the best-known examples.

The con artist has an even longer history in the literature, legends, and popular art of our nation. A favorite character in eighteenth-century folklore was the slick Yankee peddler, who traveled around the countryside taking advantage of gullible farmers, selling them things they didn't need, charging them ridiculously high prices for useless items. The fast-talking, itinerant medicine man, hawking his bottles of snake oil and often only one step ahead of the law, is a familiar figure to most of us. In our nineteenth-century literature, con artists play central roles in such classic novels as *The Adventures of Huckleberry Finn* (where the title character meets up with a pair of "low-down humbugs and frauds" called the Duke and Dauphin) and Herman Melville's *The Confidence Man.* Recent examples of the con man in our popular culture include television's Sergeant Bilko and Hogan's Heroes.

In order to make trouble, of course, the Trickster needs a victim. More often than not, the "sucker" is some stuffy authority figure—another reason for the Trickster's appeal to the rest of us. Hennery, Peck's Bad Boy, spends all his time visiting endless humiliations on his pompous Pa. The Marx Brothers—Groucho, Chico, and Harpo—are happiest when they are poking needles through some inflated windbag like Ambassador Trentino (in the movie *Duck Soup*) or making a haughty "society dame" look stupid. Sergeant Bilko's perennial mark is the powerful army brass, embodied in the figure of his straitlaced superior officer, Colonel J. T. Hall, while Hogan's Heroes are continually outfoxing the blowhard Commandant Klink and his strutting, buffoonish sidekick, Sergeant Schulz. Another interesting example from the world of television is Froggy the Gremlin, a mischievous little puppet who was featured on a now-defunct children's show called "Andy's Gang." Froggy was the nemesis of a pudgy professor who appeared every week to impart some important bit of wisdom to the audience—the proper method of preparing spaghetti, for example. The professor would be in the midst of his lesson when suddenly, at his shoulder, Froggy would materialize in a puff of smoke. "Then you take the spaghetti," the professor would explain, holding a bowlful of the stuff in his hands. "And pour it over your head," Froggy would croak in his ear. "Yes, and pour it over your head, like so," the suggestible scholar would say, dumping the noodles all over his own head. Here we see a central motif of many Trickster stories: the puppet who pulls the strings. The Trickster is the archenemy of dignity and discipline, and though he often seems small and insignificant—he may be a servant, a child, a pet, or a puppet—he manages to turn things topsy-turvy, and ends up in control.

When we were children, we liked to see the bully of our block get his comeuppance, and as adults, we like to feel we have some chance against powerful and unjust people and institutions. Hence the appeal of another common Trickster theme, closely related to that of the puppet who pulls the strings: the theme of the weak and lowly creature who overcomes a powerful foe by means of wit and cunning. The small hero who defeats a giant or ogre by pretending to possess superhuman strength is a very common figure in European folktales, according to Richard Dorson in his book *American Folklore*. As an example, he quotes a tale, set in ancient Greece, of a young man who joins a gang of giants.

> When night fell he placed his overcoat over a pile of stones, to simulate a man sleeping, and hid in the hills. The giants attempted to kill the little fellow by pounding his bed with an ax. But in the morning the youth, whom they had presumably chopped in a thousand pieces, reappeared, complaining that the bedbugs had been scratching him all night long. Impressed and overawed, the giants named him captain and thenceforth carried out his orders.

Not every Trickster is as successful as the young man in this anecdote, however, and some stories show the Trickster getting caught and punished, or himself falling victim to a prank ("the Trickster tricked"). After subjecting his father to countless physical and psychological tortures, Peck's Bad Boy finally has the tables turned on him when his Pa persuades the boy (who is eager to have whiskers) that the best way for him to make his moustache grow quickly is to rub tar on his upper lip each night and scrub it off each morning with a scouring-brick. The Winnebago Trickster Wadjunkaga is occasionally outsmarted by other, more cunning creatures such as the mink and the chipmunk and even, at times, undone by his own unpredictable body. One well-known story of Wadjunkaga tells of the day his two arms began battling each other over a slain buffalo which the Trickster had been skinning—a fight which only ended after the knife-wielding right hand had severely wounded the left.

We have suggested some of the reasons the Trickster has already appealed to human beings and has shown up so often in all cultures. The question we must now ask is, where do we find it in our lives? Most obviously, we see it in those people who, in their own behavior, act like Tricksters (for there *are* people who unconsciously identify with and live out archetypes)—the inveterate practical joker, for instance, who can't shake hands without having an electric "joy buzzer" concealed in his palm, and who considers a squirting lapel flower to be the highest form of humor. But the Trickster also represents something found in every one of us. It stands for that mischievous and uncontrollable part of ourselves which trips us up at the worst possible times (making us say something absolutely stupid, for example, at the very moment we are trying to impress someone with our intelligence), or which stirs up trouble when our lives are running smoothly, making us dissatisfied when we should feel most content. Edgar Allan Poe called this diabolical element in the human personality the "Imp of the Perverse," and described it (in the story of the same name) as a primitive impulse which causes us to do the wrong thing precisely "because we feel that we should *not.*"

There is, however, a more positive aspect to this Trickster impulse. Most archetypes have two sides to them; even the Shadow, as we have seen, can play a helpful part in our lives by leading us to self-realization. While the Trickster is usually represented as a disruptive, even a destructive being, he is also often portrayed as a creator—a benefactor as well as a buffoon (in the words of Paul Radin). In the myths of certain American Indians, for example, it is the Trickster (in the form of Coyote, Raven, or Hare, depending on the particular tribe) who steals fire from the Fire People and passes it along to humanity. Psychologically speaking, the Trickster archetype in its more positive forms stands for that part of ourselves which retains a healthy disrespect for the authoritarian, the regimented, the pretentious. It is that part of ourselves which, despite the best efforts of society to tame it, remains filled with a kind of animal vitality and childlike spontaneity. Of course, these are not qualities which the disciplinarian holds very dear; but insofar as they impel us to struggle against those forces that would stifle or subdue us (extreme social conformity, for example), they are qualities which, in the words of Joseph Campbell, are "not to be despised."

PAUL RADIN

from *The Trickster*

Though Trickster myths are found among nearly all the Indian tribes of North America, the most complete collection of these stories available to us is the so-called Trickster Cycle of the Winnebago Indians, a Siouan-speaking tribe living in central Wisconsin and eastern Nebraska. This cycle—a series of forty-nine loosely interrelated episodes concerning the figure known as Wadjunkaga (The Tricky One)—was recorded in 1912 by the well-known anthropologist Paul Radin

Reprinted with permission of The Philosophical Library and Routledge & Kegan Paul Ltd. from *The Trickster: A Study in American Indian Mythology* by Paul Radin. Copyright 1956.

(1883–1959), who obtained it from an Indian informant and raconteur named Sam Blowsnake.

The Trickster is an amorphous and often contradictory character. Though he is sometimes known by animal names—Raven, Spider, Coyote, Hare—and though he can, in fact, easily transform himself into almost any shape, he is, at the start of the Winnebago Cycle, a creature of indeterminate form, his most striking physical characteristics being enormously long intestines, which he wears wrapped around his body, and an equally long penis. The Trickster figure of the Blackfoot and Crow Indians is known as Old Man, though in this context the word *old* implies not that the Trickster is a graybeard, but that he is ageless, that he has existed from the beginning of time. Similarly, his animal names are meant to be more metaphoric than literal, a reference to his animalistic nature. In the words of Radin, Trickster is a hero "who is always wandering, who is always hungry, who is not guided by moral conceptions of good or evil, who is either playing tricks on people or having them played on him, and who is highly sexed." He is, in short, a creature impelled by unbridled instinct. As the Winnebago Cycle progresses, however, Trickster becomes increasingly socialized and even humanized until, by the end of the stories, he has evolved into "a figure foreshadowing the shape of man." In addition—and this is the central paradox of these stories—Trickster is not only destructive but creative as well, a "benefactor *and* buffoon," who is responsible (though at times inadvertently) for bringing food, fire and even, in certain versions of these myths, the world into existence.

The following episodes, sections 27–29 in the cycle, show Wadjunkaga at his cruelest.

As he was engaged in this cleansing he happened to look in the water and much to his surprise he saw many plums there. He surveyed them very carefully and then he dived down into the water to get some. But only small stones did he bring back in his hands. Again he dived into the water. But this time he knocked himself unconscious against a rock at the bottom. After a while he floated up and gradually came to. He was lying on the water, flat on his back, when he came to and, as he opened his eyes, there on the top of the bank he saw many plums. What he had seen in the water was only the reflection. Then he realized what he had done. "Oh, my, what a stupid fellow I must be! I should have recognized this. Here I have caused myself a great deal of pain."

Then he went on to the shore and ate as many plums as possible, and putting a belt around his racoon-skin blanket he filled it likewise with plums and proceeded downstream.

Much to his surprise as he travelled along he came upon an oval lodge. He peeped in and saw two women with many children. He took one of the plums and threw it through the top of the lodge. It made a great noise. The women grabbed it. This he repeated and soon one of the women came out and saw, unexpectedly, a man standing there. "Aha, it is my older brother who is doing this." She and her companion asked him to come in, and as he entered the lodge he gave a plum apiece to each of the women. Then they asked him, "Where did you pick these, older brother?" "There are many of these at a particular place, sisters, and if you wish to pick them I will tell you where to go." "We would like very much to have some, brother," they said. "However, we cannot leave our children alone for they are very disobedient." "Sisters, if you wish to go, I will take care of the children for you," he said. "You are very good, older brother," they said. "You cannot possibly miss the place," he added, "for there are so many plums there. You cannot really pick them all for they are too plentiful. If, toward evening, as the sun sets, you see the sky red, you will know that the plums are causing it. Do not turn back for you will surely find it."

They started out and as soon as they were out of sight, he killed the children, singed them, and then boiled them. They were racoons. "Well, now, for once I am going to have a good meal," he said. There he ate a good deal; he ate a good deal of singed racoon meat. When he was finished, he cut off the head of one of the children, put a stick through its neck and placed it at the door as though the child were peeping out and laughing. After that he went to a hill that was not far off.

• • •

Soon the women came along. He saw them in the distance. When they saw him he went inside of the hill. As they got nearer home, they were getting quite angry for they had not been able to find any plums. As they approached their lodge, much to their annoyance, one of the children was peeping out of the door. It was smiling at them. "What kind of a joke is this? We were not able to get any plums." "I am angry," said one of the women. So she slapped the child on the cheek and the head toppled over. There, much to her horror, she noticed that it was only the child's head. Then both of the women cried out, "Oh, my children! He has killed them! It must have been Trickster! He must have been the one who went into the hill!" They wept very much.

Soon Trickster came over to them again. He had changed himself into another person and his face was blackened. When he got to them he said, "Sisters, what are you crying about?" And they answered, "Trickster has killed both of our children and has eaten them." "Oh, my, I wish I could get hold of him for you! When they tell me such things about him, I always long to get hold of him! In what direction did he go? Do you know?" They said, "Some time ago a person went into the hill, that must have been he." "He is going to get it now! Which way do you mean? Come and show it to me." So they went and there they saw a hole, a very large one, where the dirt had been freshly disturbed. "Now he is going to get it! He is certainly the one that did it," said the man. Then he went in the hole and after he was in a while he made quite a commotion as if he were striking something. Then they heard something like a groan inside the hill. Soon he came out all bloody. His nose was all covered with blood and bruised. He had, of course, bruised his own nose and then come out. "My, what a large fellow he was! I suppose that is why they talk about him so much! He fought with great fierceness against me. But I killed him. I am sure you heard us inside. He is inside there. You ought to go and get him. He is dead so that you need not be in the least afraid of him." Thus spoke Trickster to the women.

Then the women went in. After a few minutes, however, they turned back. "He is inside, a little farther up. Don't be afraid of him." So they went farther in and as soon as they were well in, he put some hay inside and set fire to it. Then he ran to the other side of the hill [where there was an exit hole], put some hay in and set fire to it. When the hay was entirely burnt up he went inside and took the racoons out. They had been thoroughly singed. "Now is the time that I will eat some fat," he said.

QUESTIONS

Language

1. How would you characterize each of the conversations Trickster has with the women in this myth? Does the *way* that he speaks to them have something to do with his ability to trick them twice?
2. Instead of telling the women exactly where the plums are, Trickster fools them with a rather poetic figure of speech—that is, language which is not used in its literal sense. What is this figure of speech and why is it so effective?

Content

1. What kind of person does Trickster seem to be when we first meet him? What do the women think of him?
2. Why do the women leave their children with Trickster? What qualities of theirs contribute to Trickster's success? Must they bear some responsibility for what happens?
3. Describe Trickster's real nature as completely as you can. What do you think of him? How do you respond to him?
4. Look up the word *transformation* in a good dictionary; then talk about the various transformations that take place in this tale.

Suggestions for Writing

1. Think about and discuss in class any vivid dreams you have had, particularly nightmares. Write an essay about the qualities in this Trickster myth that make it seem like a dream.
2. Using your classroom discussions, the essay you have just written, plus any other myths in this book as sources of insight and information, write more generally about the relationship of myths and dreams. What are the similarities? The differences?
3. Take a look at the Bugs Bunny comic (p. 74). Write an essay comparing the world which Bugs and his friends inhabit with the world inhabited by Trickster in this myth. If the setting of the comic, a comfortable, typical, safe, suburban neighborhood of the 1950's, tells us something about the kind of world modern Americans live in, what does the Winnebago myth tell us about the world the first Americans, the Indians, lived in?

JACQUES DOREY

"How Master Renard Enticed Ysengrin to Eat the Moon and How He Was Judged by the Court of the Lion"

Just as the owl is associated with wisdom, the lion with courage, and the lamb with meekness, the fox has always symbolized slyness and craft. As a result, foxes have often been portrayed as Tricksters in folklore and literature (though in some works—"The Tar Baby" and "Squirrely the Squirrel," for example—the fox himself is outsmarted by smaller, even cleverer creatures). The use of the fox as Trickster can be found at least as far back as the sixth century B.C., in the animal fables of Aesop.

During the middle ages, a group of fables known as beast epics became highly popular in France, Germany, and the Low Countries. The hero of these stories was the master Trickster Renard (or Reynard) the Fox. Sometime between the twelfth and fourteenth centuries, *Le Roman de Reynard*, a collection of fables concerning this cunning animal, was produced in France. A High German version of the Renard stories, called *Reinecke Fuchs,* was popular throughout the medieval period. In 1481, William Caxton, the first English printer, published his *Historie of Reynart the Foxe,* a translation of a Flemish version of the fables. Modern English renditions of these stories include T. J. Arnold's translation (1860) of Goethe's *Reinecke Fuchs* (a paraphrase of the famous medieval collection), William Rose's *Epic of the Beasts* (1924), and Jacques Dorey's *Three and the Moon: Legendary Stories of Old Brittany, Normandy, and Provence* (1929), from which the present selection has been taken.

Though the stories were originally satirical in intent, expressing the peasant's contempt for the upper classes, their appeal does not depend on their political meaning. Renard's quick-witted deceptions of his archfoe Ysengrin the Wolf, and the quick-tongued argument he makes in his own defense when called before King Noble the Lion, make these tales as enjoyable today as they were when they were first written.

The earth, heavy with the heat of summer, breathed out into the night. The sad, monotonous croaking of frogs rose over dank marshes and the cloudy moon was set in the shell of the sky. Close to dark villages, huddled under the weight of sleep, Renard was softly prowling, his red tongue lolling over his chest, as he hunted the partridge or dozed in the shade. All day his throat had been parched. He saw near to a farm the shadow of a well, with its two buckets swaying in

From *Three and the Moon: Legendary Stories of Old Brittany, Normandy, and Provence* by Jacques Dorey. Copyright 1929 by Alfred A. Knopf, Inc. Reprinted by permission of Alfred A. Knopf, Inc., a Division of Random House, Inc.

the breeze. Every one was asleep; nowhere was there a trace of a dog nor the shadow of a man. The strident song of grasshoppers rang out from the meadows.

Renard jumped on to the edge of the well, and he felt the welcome freshness of the water below. His parched throat now burning still more from impatience, he threw prudence to the wind. He jumped into an empty bucket; the chain unravelled and creaked on the pulley. In a whirling rapid descent, he went to the bottom of the well. Greedily he lapped the silent waters and an exquisite freshness stole over his body.

His thirst quenched, he lost his weariness and, terrified, he suddenly thought of his return. The second bucket high up on the pulley blocked his way, and only by a heavy weight in it could he be raised to the well-brim.

"How can I find a beast silly enough to take my place?" wondered Renard, dejectedly.

Destiny's reply was swifter than the flight of swallows. Renard raised his muzzle and saw Ysengrin's head and sharp pointed ears over the edge of the well. He was calmly admiring his reflection in the water and grunting with pleasure.

"Seek a fool, and Ysengrin is sure to be there," chuckled Renard to himself and smacked his wet chops.

"Hi, there, my old friend Ysengrin," he shouted to the wolf, "have you not heard Dame Hermeline shouting to all the echoes for the last two hours?"

At the sound of this sepulchral voice from the depths of the well, Ysengrin sprang back terrified, then timidly he ventured to push his muzzle over the edge of the well.

"Can it be you, Master Cheat and Rogue, who calls to me, from hell?" he asked.

"Say rather from paradise, and what a delicious paradise, too," replied sly Renard. "Do you not see by my side this marvellous cheese with which I delight my eye and regale my gullet?" And he pointed his paw at the moon's white reflection in the well.

"If your cheese is as tasty as the fish from the pond, then I do not envy you your meal," replied Ysengrin with distrust.

"Who has invited you, silly ninny?" retorted Renard, feigning impatience. "You can fast, my friend, what do I care? I would sooner pluck out my silky moustache than try to convince you. Only, on thy way home, tell Dame Hermeline, my spouse, to come to me. Tell her this cheese is cream and velvet and I am sorry to have eaten a whole quarter without her."

The moon was in the third phase of her slow waxing and her face seemed to have been cut by a sharp knife.

Ysengrin, enticed, believed Renard's words and his mistrust gave way to greed.

"I will gladly fetch your wife and even your three sons," said Ysengrin, "but before that will you not offer me a bite of this cheese?"

Renard seemed to waver for a second.

"You hardly deserve it, but I have a kind heart and do not nurse grudges. Jump into the bucket that hangs on the pulley and come and share my banquet."

Ysengrin jumped joyfully into the bucket and, knocking against the sides of the well, he reached the bottom. Lifted up by Ysengrin's weight, Master Renard said to him, amiably:

"I have had my fill of this cheese. It is really rather tasteless. Help yourself, old friend, but do not eat too much of it or else your skin at dawn may deck the door of some peasant."

He climbed over the edge of the well and ran off into the night.

Ysengrin, deep down in the well, called plaintively for help.

He howled so much and so well that peasants armed with forks came out from the farmsteads and hurled stones at him at the bottom of the well. At dawn, Brichemer, the stag, brayed over the whole forest the news of Ysengrin's death and the Lion gathered his subjects together for the solemn burial of the wolf and the judgment of Renard. It was a wonderful gathering for there was no beast, feathered or furred, bold enough to ignore the King's call. All left their hunt or travels and came out of thickets, shrubs, lairs, and caves, and down from the branches. Ysengrin's body was buried in a grave dug by Beaucent, the boar, and a marble slab gave his name and martyrdom to posterity. Tardiff, the snail, Brichemer, the stag, and Tilbert, the cat, sang the burial service. The mourners were headed by Dame Hersent, the widow of the wolf. The lion presided under an oak tree.

Roonel, the dog, guarded Renard, whose feet were bound together. Bruin, the bear, a procurator's cap on his head, insisted on death to the prisoner in the name of the law of the forest, but Grimbert, the badger, Renard's cousin, cleverly pleaded for him and the Lion hesitated when the accused spoke thus:

"O most powerful of all sovereigns, and all ye proud barons, know ye that my heart is free from sin. Ysengrin died through his own folly. The law of the forest only punishes him who by violence delivers his friend into the hands of man. How, how could I have forced the wolf to come down into the well when I, myself, was sitting inside it in a bucket? If he came down it was of his own free will and because he was drawn by foolish greed. When I compared the moon to a cheese it was just poetry that inspired me. Ysengrin, the dense blockhead, did not understand my metaphor. Weary of life for some time now, I have long planned to go to Rome to see the Pope and then to retire as a humble hermit into the desert. Do not frustrate my pious projects by an unjust death."

Sire Noble, weary of all this talk, pardoned him.

Wrapped in a scarf and armed with a pilgrim's staff, Renard drew up his last will and testament on a parchment of donkey's skin.

To Hermeline, his spouse, he left his memories.

To his children, his wiles.

To the forest wind, his scent.

To the night, his sight.

This done, he set out on the road to Rome, his head covered with ashes.

History does not relate that he ever arrived.

QUESTIONS

Language

1. Compare the beginning of this tale to those of any of the fairy tales in this book. Describe the differences you find. Do the writers seem to be striving for different effects?
2. Suppose the story of Renard the Fox had begun: "One hot summer night, Renard was prowling around. He was very thirsty. Suddenly he saw a well on a farm, and fortunately

no one was around to see him, for he intended to take some water.'' What would have been lost in this version?

3. Are there any similarities between the way Renard speaks to Ysengrin and the way Trickster in the Winnebago Cycle (p. 62) speaks to the women? What are they?

Content

1. How does Renard manage to trick Ysengrin the Wolf down into the well? What qualities of Ysengrin's make him an easy victim?
2. Who else besides Ysengrin does sly Renard trick? How?
3. Is the Lion a good ruler? Why or why not?
4. The *American Heritage Dictionary* defines a fable as ''a concise narrative making an edifying or cautionary point and often employing as characters animals that speak and act like human beings.'' Such a narrative, in other words, warns or admonishes or paints a *moral.* Would you call this tale a fable? If so, what is the moral?
5. How do you interpret the last line of this selection?

Suggestions for Writing

1. Write a fable of your own. Decide what moral you want to offer to your reader and then construct a narrative, a story, featuring talking animals, which leads up to and illustrates that moral. Morals can be found anywhere. You can invent one yourself or you can use any conventional proverb—for example, ''A rolling stone gathers no moss'' or ''Don't count your chickens before they're hatched.'' Or, consult the collection of proverbs in Benjamin Franklin's *Father Abraham's Speech* (p. 258) for additional ideas.
2. Ysengrin is stoned to death by the peasants because of his own greed (and, of course, Renard's treachery). Write an essay in which you discuss the possible consequences of greed. Begin with a fable about animals that you yourself write. If you like, *reward* your animal for greed.
3. Write an essay exploring the question of how fast and skillful talking can get one out of a tight situation. Use the fable about Renard and Ysengrin plus anything from your own history as examples.

ANONYMOUS

"The Tar Baby" (Water-Well Version)

The slaves who were brought to America carried with them a wealth of African folklore, much of which was gradually adapted to New World settings and situations. By the nineteenth century, a South African Hare Trickster had evolved into the popular folk hero, Brer Rabbit. (The Creek Indians of the southeastern United States also had a Trickster god called Hare, some of whose exploits seem to have been incorporated into the legends of Brer Rabbit.) The adventures of Brer Rabbit were popularized during the late 1800s by the southern writer Joel Chandler

Reprinted with permission of the American Folklore Society from *Negro Tales from West Virginia* by John Harrington Cox. Copyright 1934.

Harris (1848–1908). Harris, who had learned these folktales as a boy from the slaves on his employer's plantation, published them in the highly successful series of Uncle Remus books, named after their central character and narrator, a kindly and wise old slave whose shrewd, humorous fables were recited for the benefit of his tireless audience of one, his master's little boy.

The best-known of the Brer Rabbit tales is "The Wonderful Tar Baby Story," which first appeared in the 1880 collection *Uncle Remus, His Songs and His Sayings.* In this story, Brer Fox captures Brer Rabbit by setting up a figure fashioned of tar in the middle of the road. Coming upon the Tar Baby, Brer Rabbit greets it in a friendly way, but when the little figure fails to respond, the incensed animal punches it, kicks it, and butts it with his head, thereby becoming hopelessly ensnared. He escapes, however, by using reverse psychology on Brer Fox, claiming to prefer any form of punishment—being hanged, burned, or skinned alive—to being thrown into the brier patch on the side of the road. Naturally the gullible fox immediately tosses his hated enemy into the brier patch. A few moments later, Brer Rabbit hops out, cleaning his fur with a wood chip and singing, "Bred and born in a brier patch, Brer Fox—bred and born in a brier patch!"

The Uncle Remus stories are written in a dialect which is difficult for the modern reader, though it is apparently very accurate. (Mark Twain, who wrote the same kind of dialect in *The Adventures of Huckleberry Finn,* acknowledged Harris as the master.) The following version of the "Tar Baby Story" is a variant form from West Virginia. Though it differs in certain respects from Chandler's version (among other differences, the hero is referred to as Mr. Rabbit and the setting seems to be a combination of Africa and the United States), it contains the same tar baby trick as the Uncle Remus tale and a similar denouement. (The tar baby trick, incidentally, is a form of a common folklore motif known as the "stick-fast trap.")

Once upon a time there was a water famine, and the runs went dry and the creeks went dry and the rivers went dry, and there wasn't any water to be found anywhere, so all the animals in the forest met together to see what could be done about it. The lion and the bear and the wolf and the fox and the giraffe and the monkey and elephant, and even the rabbit,—everybody who lived in the forest was there, and they all tried to think of some plan by which they could get water. At last they decided to dig a well, and everybody said he would help,—all except the rabbit, who always was a lazy little bugger, and he said he wouldn't dig. So the animals all said, "Very well, Mr. Rabbit, if you won't help dig this well, you shan't have one drop of water to drink." But the rabbit just laughed and said, as smart as you please, "Never mind, you dig the well and I'll get a drink all right."

Now the animals all worked very hard, all except the rabbit, and soon they had the well so deep that they struck water and they all got a drink and went away to their homes in the forest. But the very next morning what should they find but the rabbit's footprints in the mud at the mouth of the well, and they knew he had come in the night and stolen some water. So they all began to think how they could keep that lazy little rabbit from getting a drink, and they all talked and talked and talked, and after a while they decided that someone must watch the well, but no one seemed to want to stay up to do it. Finally, the bear said, "I'll watch the well the first night. You just go to bed, and I'll show old Mr. Rabbit that he won't get any water while I'm around."

So all the animals went away and left him, and the bear sat down by the well. By and by the rabbit came out of the thicket on the hillside and there he saw the old bear guarding the well. At first he didn't know what to do. Then he sat down and began to sing:

"Cha ra ra, will you, will you, can you?
Cha ra ra, will you, will you, can you?"

Presently the old bear lifted up his head and looked around. "Where's all that pretty music coming from?" he said. The rabbit kept on singing:

"Cha ra ra, will you, will you, can you?
Cha ra ra, will you, will you, can you?"

This time the bear got up on his hind feet. The rabbit kept on singing:

"Cha ra ra, will you, will you, can you?
Cha ra ra, will you, will you, can you?"

Then the bear began to dance, and after a while he danced so far away that the rabbit wasn't afraid of him any longer, and so he climbed down into the well and got a drink and ran away into the thicket.

Now when the animals came the next morning and found the rabbit's footprints in the mud, they made all kinds of fun of old Mr. Bear. They said, "Mr. Bear, you are a fine person to watch a well. Why, even Mr. Rabbit can outwit you." But the bear said, "The rabbit had nothing to do with it. I was sitting here wide-awake, when suddenly the most beautiful music came right down out of the sky. At least I think it came down out of the sky, for when I went to look for it, I could not find it, and it must have been while I was gone that Mr. Rabbit stole the water." "Anyway," said the other animals, "we can't trust you any more. Mr. Monkey, you had better watch the well tonight, and mind you, you'd better be pretty careful or old Mr. Rabbit will fool you." "I'd like to see him do it," said the monkey. "Just let him try." So the animals set the monkey to watch the well.

Presently it grew dark, and all the stars came out; and then the rabbit slipped out of the thicket and peeped over in the direction of the well. There he saw the monkey. Then he sat down on the hillside and began to sing:

"Cha ra ra, will you, will you, can you?
Cha ra ra, will you, will you, can you?"

Then the monkey peered down into the well. "It isn't the water," said he. The rabbit kept on singing:

"Cha ra ra, will you, will you, can you?
Cha ra ra, will you, will you, can you?"

This time the monkey looked into the sky. "It isn't the stars," said he. The rabbit kept on singing.

This time the monkey looked toward the forest. "It must be the leaves." said he. "Anyway, it's too good music to let go to waste." So he began to dance, and after a while he danced so far away that the rabbit wasn't afraid, so he climbed down into the well and got a drink and ran off into the thicket.

Well, the next morning, when all the animals came down and found the footprints again, you should have heard them talk to that monkey. They said, "Mr. Monkey, you are no better than Mr. Bear; neither of you is of any account. You can't catch a rabbit." And the monkey said, "It wasn't old Mr. Rabbit's fault at all that I left the well. He had nothing to do with it. All at once the most beautiful music that you ever heard came out of the woods, and I went to see who was making it." But the animals only laughed at him. Then they tried to get someone else to watch the well that night. No one would do it. So they thought and thought and thought about what to do next. Finally the fox spoke up. "I'll tell you what let's do," said he. "Let's make a tar man and set him to watch the well." "Let's do," said all the other animals together. So they worked the whole day long building a tar man and set him to watch the well.

That night the rabbit crept out of the thicket, and there he saw the tar man. So he sat down on the hillside and began to sing:

"Cha ra ra, will you, will you, can you?
Cha ra ra, will you, will you, can you?"

But the man never heard. The rabbit kept on singing:

"Cha ra ra, will you, will you, can you?
Cha ra ra, will you, will you, can you?"

But the tar man never heard a word. The rabbit came a little closer:

"Cha ra ra, will you, will you, can you?
Cha ra ra, will you, will you, can you?"

The tar man never spoke. The rabbit came a little closer yet:

"Cha ra ra, will you, will you, can you?
Cha ra ra, will you, will you, can you?"

The tar man never spoke a word.

The rabbit came up close to the tar man. "Look here," he said, "you get out of my way and let me down into that well." The tar man never moved. "If you don't get out of my way, I'll hit you with my fist," said the rabbit. The tar man never moved a finger. Then the rabbit raised his fist and struck the tar man as hard as he could, and his right fist stuck tight in the tar. "Now you let go of my fist or I'll hit you with my other fist," said the rabbit. The tar man never budged. Then the rabbit struck him with his left fist, and his left fist stuck tight in the tar. "Now you let go of my fists or I'll kick you with my foot," said the rabbit. The tar man never budged an inch. Then the rabbit kicked him with his right foot, and his right foot stuck tight in the tar. "Now you let go of my foot or I'll kick you with my other foot," said the rabbit. The tar man never stirred. Then the rabbit kicked him with his left foot, and his left foot stuck tight in the tar. "Now you let me go or I'll butt you with my head," said the rabbit. And he butted him with his head, and there he was; and there the other animals found him the next morning.

Well, you should have heard those animals laugh. "Oh, ho, Mr. Rabbit," they said. "Now we'll see whether you steal any more of our water or not.

We're going to lay you across a log and cut your head off." "Oh, please do," said the rabbit. "I've always wanted to have my head cut off. I'd rather die that way than any other way I know." "Then we won't do it," said the other animals. "We are not going to kill you any way you like. We are going to shoot you." "That's better," said the rabbit. "If I had just stopped to think, I'd have asked you to do that in the first place. Please shoot me." "No, we'll not shoot you," said the other animals; and then they had to think and think for a long time.

"I'll tell you what we'll do," said the bear. "We'll put you into a cupboard and let you eat and eat and eat until you are as fat as butter, and then we'll throw you up into the air and let you come down and burst." "Oh, please don't!" said the rabbit. "I never wanted to die that way. Just do anything else, but please don't burst me." "Then that's exactly what we'll do," said all the other animals together.

So they put the rabbit into the cupboard and they fed him pie and cake and sugar, everything that was good; and by and by he got just as fat as butter. And then they took him out on the hillside and the lion took a paw, and the fox took a paw, and the bear took a paw, and the monkey took a paw; and then they swung him back and forth, and back and forth, saying: "One for the money, two for the show, three to make ready, and four to go." And up they tossed him into the air, and he came down and lit on his feet and said:

"Yip, my name's Molly Cotton-tail;
Catch me if you can."

And off he ran into the thicket.

QUESTIONS

Language

1. What is the predominant tone or mood of this folk story? That is, would you say it is a serious or a light-hearted story? Were you surprised when all the forest animals decided to kill Mr. Rabbit? Did you somehow *know* they would not succeed? If so, how?
2. There is a great deal of repetition in this story, repetition of incident as well as of words, phrases, and sentences. Can you find examples of repeated language? Why do you suppose there is so much of it? What purpose does it serve?
3. Compare the first paragraph of this folk story with the first of the fable "How Master Renard Enticed Ysengrin to Eat the Moon" (p. 66). Which seems simpler to you? Which would be easier to remember and repeat? Which is more formal? Which shows more evidence of deliberate artistic shaping? Find words and phrases to support your opinions.

Content

1. Why won't Mr. Rabbit help dig the well? Can you think of any other reasons besides the one the narrator gives you?
2. How is Mr. Rabbit different from the other animals in the forest? What advantages does he have over them? Is he completely infallible, incapable of mistakes?
3. How does Mr. Rabbit manage to defeat his captors? Does he understand them better than they understand him?

Suggestions for Writing

1. Write an essay in which you try to account for the appeal of stories about animals, particularly one in which a small, weak animal triumphs over a group of larger, stronger ones.

2. The animal characters in the story have conflicting attitudes toward work. Write an essay in which you explore what those differences are and which view seems to be supported by the end of the story.

WARNER BROS. CARTOONS

"Bugs Bunny"

A twentieth-century descendant of Brer Rabbit, Bugs Bunny made his earliest appearance in a 1930s Porky Pig cartoon called "Porky's Hare Hunt," directed by Ben Hardaway (whose nickname was Bugs) and Cal Dalton, although at this time the rabbit was unnamed and bore little resemblance to the present-day version. He was later christened Bugs after Hardaway. His physical appearance continued to be altered in successive releases—"Hare-um Scare-um," "Presto Change-o," "Elmer's Candid Camera"—until, by the 1939 "A Wild Hare," he had attained his definitive form. It was in this film, too, that the rabbit first spoke his famous line, "What's up, Doc?"

For the past forty years, Bugs, along with his faithful patsy, Elmer Fudd, has been featured, not only in theatrical cartoons and comic books, but in newspaper strips, television shows, records, and books. In the early seventies a feature-length anthology film of his greatest cartoons, entitled *Bugs Bunny, Superstar,* was a box-office hit, proving the enduring popularity of this wise-cracking, carrot-chomping Trickster.

The following Bugs Bunny story originally appeared in the February, 1953, issue of the comic book *Looney Tunes & Merry Melodies.*

Reprinted with permission of Licensing Corporation of America from *Looney Tunes & Merry Melodies,* February 1953. Copyright 1953.

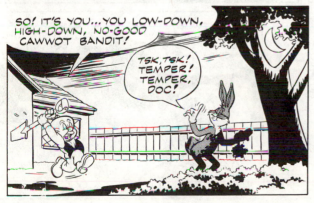

THANKS, WABBIT! I NEVER THOUGHT I'D EVER SEE YOU PWOMOTING AN ACTUAL NON-PWOFIT PLAN!

?

NON-PROFIT, HE SAYS! SILLY BOY!

I C-COULDN'T HELP OVERHEARING, BUGS! ER...HOW DO YOU PLAN TO M-MAKE ANY MONEY OUT OF THIS NEW BUSINESS?

OH, I'LL MANAGE, PORKY!

I KNOW YOU'RE NOT DOING IT F-FOR YOUR HEALTH... .

EH... PARDON ME, PAL!

I ALSO WANT TO DROP IN ON *YOSEMITE SAM* FOR A SECOND!

LET'S SEE NOW... I NEVER CAN REMEMBER WHICH IS HIS HOUSE...THEY BOTH LOOK ALIKE!

OOPS! NOW I KNOW!

THAT'S YOSEMITE'S! HE'S ALWAYS RAISING THE ROOF ABOUT SOMETHING!

L &M #136 - 532(9)

QUESTIONS

Language

1. Each of the characters in this story has a distinctive way of speaking. Describe the speech patterns of each. What do these patterns reveal about the characters' personalities?

2. Find examples of Bugs Bunny's verbal playfulness.

Content

1. Elmer Fudd is Bugs Bunny's usual victim. What is he like? Why is he such an ideal victim for a Trickster figure?

2. What do Yosemite Sam and Elmer Fudd have in common? What values and traits do they share?

3. How is Bugs Bunny's trick exposed in this story? Compare and contrast what happens to *him* with what happens to Mr. Rabbit in "The Tar Baby" (p. 69).

4. What role does Porky Pig play? Porky is, or course, the only other animal character in this story. How is he different from Bugs?

5. Why do you suppose the creators of this comic strip chose to set their story in suburbia?

Suggestions for Writing

1. Bugs Bunny has been popular in America for a very long time; he had appeared in a number of films before he first asked the befuddled Elmer Fudd, "What's up, Doc?" Write an essay in which you offer three or four reasons for the success of this comic character.

2. Two of the Tricksters in this chapter have been rabbits: Bugs Bunny and Mr. Rabbit of "The Tar Baby." They share certain characteristics and pursue essentially the same ends. Write an essay comparing and contrasting the two rabbits. Remember not to ignore any *differences* you find.

3. Using this story and "The Tar Baby" in addition to your personal experience as specific examples or illustrations, write an essay about the dangers of being overconfident or underestimating your opponents.

ROBERT CRUMB

"Squirrely the Squirrel"

Though the anthropomorphic animals that populate the underground "comix" of R. Crumb (see headnote for "Whiteman," p. 37) resemble the cute, furry creatures of the "funny animal" cartoons, they tend to possess repellent, if not actually criminal, personalities. Squirrely the Squirrel—"the nuttiest li'l guy that ever walked across a piece o' paper"—is no exception. Like much of Crumb's art, this comic strip is a sharp reflection of American culture in the sixties, a time which saw a terrifying escalation of violence in the mass arts and in real life. "Squirrely the Squirrel," which originally appeared in *Black and White Comics,* might be seen as a comic strip equivalent of a movie like *The Wild Bunch,* as if a "Tom and Jerry" cartoon had been filmed by Sam Peckinpah. By taking a situation common to the "funny animal" cartoons—in which cats and mice, foxes and crows, coyotes and roadrunners routinely shoot, stab, and throw bombs at each other—and treating it in this blatantly sadistic fashion, Crumb creates, not only a pointed commentary on contemporary American life but also a character with the same cruel, amoral personality as archaic Trickster gods like Edshu and Wadjunkaga.

Reprinted with permission of R. Crumb from *Black and White Comics*. Copyright 1973 by R. Crumb.

QUESTIONS

Language

1. How would you characterize the way Squirrely speaks? Do you know any people who talk the way he does? Do you think the artist, R. Crumb, captures the real sounds of American speech?
2. How does Farnsworth speak? Look at his dialogue with Squirrely. Do they both sound the same? If not, what are the differences?
3. What do you think of Squirrely's casual comment "I love to agitate him" after he has blinded Farnsworth with the insect killer? Does his language fit his act?

Content

1. What kind of sense of humor does Squirrely have? How do you respond to it?
2. Most of us have preconceived notions of how animals in cartoons and comics should look and act. How do you think a fox should be portrayed? A squirrel? How do R. Crumb's animals differ from your conceptions?
3. Most of the Tricksters we have encountered or will encounter in this chapter must talk their way out of difficult situations. (They don't, of course, always succeed.) But how does Squirrely escape Farnsworth's clutches?
4. Why do you suppose Crumb draws Farnsworth with no tail?
5. Which animal characters seem more human to you: those in the Bugs Bunny comic (p. 74) or in the R. Crumb comic? Why?

Suggestions for Writing

1. Write an essay comparing and contrasting the Trickster of the Winnebago myth (p. 62) with Squirrely. What characteristics do they share? Are there any differences between the two?
2. The Bugs Bunny comic in this chapter was written in 1953; "Squirrely the Squirrel," in 1973. Though a Trickster appears in each, there are some major differences between these comics, especially in the action that takes place. Write an essay on the differences you find. You might want to share your opinions with your classmates, and then consider whether the changes you see in the comics reflect changes in *us,* the audience for the comics.
3. As we mention in our headnote to "Whiteman" in the first chapter, R. Crumb's comics are characterized by their social satire. Write an essay analyzing what "Squirrely the Squirrel" says about our system of justice.

RUDOLPH DIRKS

The Katzenjammer Kids

The oldest comic strip still in existence, *The Katzenjammer Kids* originated in the late nineteenth century, when "bad boy" stories were at the peak of their popularity in this country. Created by Rudolph Dirks (1877–1968)—who derived the idea from a well-known children's picture book, *Max und Moritz,* by the German artist/writer Wilhelm Busch—the strip first appeared in the December 12, 1897, issue of *The American Humorist,* the Sunday supplement to William Randolph Hearst's newspaper, the New York *Journal.*

Hans and Fritz, the two "Katzies," as they are sometimes called, are compact bundles of sheer destructive energy, who make life endlessly miserable for the other members of their rather peculiar household: die Mama (their mother), der Captain (an old sailor who lives with them and serves as a surrogate father), and the Inspector (a truant officer who apparently came after the Kids one day and inexplicably stayed around to become one of their favorite victims).

When, in 1912, Dirks left the *Journal* for the New York *World* and tried to take the strip with him, he was sued by Hearst. The legal decision which resulted allowed Dirks to use his characters but required that he change the name of the strip. (He did: first to *Hans and Fritz,* then to *The Captain and the Kids*). Hearst won the rights to the original title. In 1914, *The Katzenjammer Kids* reappeared in the *Journal,* drawn by an artist named Harold Knerr, who produced the strip until his death in 1949, when it passed into other hands.

The following strips by the Katzies' original creator, Rudolph Dirks, appeared in the New York *Journal* between 1906 and 1907.

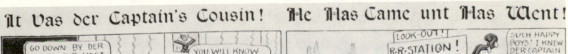

No. The Katzenjammer Kids Couldn't Stand the Strain!

QUESTIONS

Language

1. How, besides having the characters speak in a crude German-American dialect, does the creator of this comic strip, Rudolf Dirks, suggest that they belong to an ethnic group? Do you notice anything peculiar in the actual *syntax* of some of the speeches—that is, in the way the words are arranged, in the actual order they have within a sentence?
2. Dialect humor—humor which pokes fun at, among other things, the way people of different races, nationalities, or regions speak—has long been a very popular form of humor in America (and in other countries, of course). Why do you think this is so? Who is most likely to appreciate this sort of humor? Who least likely? If you were trying to achieve this kind of comic effect, would it be better to approximate only crudely a people's accent, or should you make it as subtle as it often is in real life? Why?

Content

1. Why do the Katzenjammer Kids, Hans and Fritz, act the way they do? Why aren't they able to "stand the strain" of behaving themselves?
2. Look at panel two of "It Vas der Captain's Cousin!" What is funny about it?
3. What is the Captain's initial reaction to his cousin's predicament? At what point does he become enlightened?

Suggestions for Writing

1. Look at the ending to R. Crumb's "Squirrely the Squirrel" (p. 86) and compare it to that of the second *The Katzenjammer Kids* comic. Which ending appeals to you most? Which ending is the more unexpected? Order is restored by both conclusions, but do you, as a reader, expect a certain *kind* of order at the end of a comic? If so, what kind? Discuss these questions with your classmates; then write an essay comparing the two conclusions and commenting on their effect on you.
2. Do Hans and Fritz seem typical of young boys to you? Write an essay arguing either that they are typical or that they are not. Don't let surface details—the rural setting, for example—influence your argument.
3. What kind of people do you think Hans and Fritz Katzenjammer will grow up to be? Write a story featuring the two of them as young men of about twenty-one.

GEORGE W. PECK

"His Pa Stabbed"

The prime example of the "bad boy" type in American popular art is Peck's Bad Boy, an incorrigible young prankster who appeared in a long, highly successful series of newspaper pieces (later collected into several books, the best-known of which is the 1883 volume *Peck's Bad Boy and His Pa*) written by the Wisconsin humorist George Wilbur Peck (1840–1916). Peck achieved his earliest success writing comic articles on political matters in Irish dialect—articles later collected in the book *Adventures of One Terence McGrant* (1873). After working on several newspapers, he started his own, the Milwaukee *Sun*, in 1874. It was in the *Sun* that the adventures of the bad boy were first published. Peck's great popularity as a journalist enabled him to run successfully for political office: he served for a year as mayor of Milwaukee (1890–1891) and for two terms as governor of Wisconsin (1891–1895).

High-spirited and often ingenious, the individual bad boy stories are still entertaining, though it is difficult to read through an entire book of them without becoming a bit bored, since they all follow the same formula. In each, the bad boy plays a practical joke on the grocery man, all the while bragging to the grocer of some recent piece of "deviltry"—invariably a sadistic prank the boy has contrived to humiliate his pompous "old man." While the bad boy's tricks often cross the boundary which separates the mischievous from the cruel, Peck's attitude toward his hero's behavior was not merely indulgent but admiring. Clearly Peck, along with his audience, regarded the bad boy's "gumption" and cunning as valuable qualities for a young man to possess in the competitive, increasingly commercial world of turn-of-the-century America.

THE GROCERY MAN SETS A TRAP IN VAIN—A BOOM

IN LINIMENT—HIS PA GOES TO THE LANGTRY

SHOW—THE BAD BOY TURNS BURGLAR—

THE OLD MAN STABBED—HIS AC-

COUNT OF THE FRAY—A GOOD

SINGLE HANDED LIAR.

"I hear you had burglars over to your house last night," said the grocery man to the bad boy, as he came in and sat on the counter right over a little gimlet hole, where the grocery man had fixed a darning needle so that by pulling a string the needle would fly up through the hole and run into the boy about an inch. The grocery man had been laying for the boy about two days, and now that he had got him right over the hole the first time, it made him laugh to think how he would make him jump and yell, and as he edged off and got hold of the string the boy looked unconscious of impending danger. The grocery man pulled, and the boy sat still. He pulled again, and again, and finally the boy said:

"Yes, it is reported that we had burglars over there. O, you needn't pull that string any more. I heard you was setting a trap for me, and I put a piece of board inside my pants, and thought I would let you exercise yourself. Go ahead if it amuses you. It don't hurt me."

The grocery man looked sad, and then smiled a sickly sort of a smile, at the failure of his plan to puncture the boy, and then he said, "Well, how was it? The policeman didn't seem to know much about the particulars. He said there was so much deviltry going on at your house that nobody could tell when anything was serious, and he was inclined to think it was a put up job."

"Now let's have an understanding," says the boy. "Whatever I say, you are not to give me away. It's a go, is it? I have always been afraid of you, because you have a sort of decayed egg look about you. You are like a peck of potatoes with the big ones on top, a sort of a strawberry box, with the bottom raised up, so I have thought you would go back on a fellow. But if you won't give this away, here goes. You see, I heard Ma tell Pa to bring up another bottle of liniment last night. When Ma corks herself, or has a pain anywhere, she just uses liniment for all that is out, and a pint bottle don't last more than a week. Well, I told my chum, and we laid for Pa. This liniment Ma uses is offul hot, and almost blisters. Pa went to the Langtry show, and did not get home till eleven o'clock, and me and my chum decided to teach Pa a lesson. I don't think it is right for a man to go to the theaters and not take his wife or his little boy.

"So we concluded to burgle Pa. We agreed to lay on the stairs, and when he came up my chum was to hit him on the head with a dried bladder, and I was to stab him on his breast pocket with a stick, and break the liniment bottle, and make him think he was killed.

"It couldn't have worked better if we had rehearsed it. We had talked about burglars at supper time, and got Pa nervous, so when he came up stairs and was hit on the head with the bladder, the first thing he said was 'Burglars, by mighty,' and he started to go back, and I hit him on the breast pocket, where the bottle was, and then we rushed by him, down stairs, and I said in a stage whisper, 'I guess he's a dead man,' and we went down cellar and up the back stairs to my room and undressed. Pa hollered to Ma that he was murdered, and Ma called me, and I came down in my night-shirt, and the hired girl she came down, and Pa was on the lounge, and he said his life-blood was fast ebbing away. He held his hand on the wound, and said he could feel the warm blood trickling clear down to his boots. I told Pa to stuff some tar into the wound, such as he told me to put on my lip to make my mustache grow, and Pa said, 'My boy, this is no time for trifling. Your Pa is on his last legs. When I came up stairs I met six burglars, and I attacked them, and forced four of them down, and was going to hold them and send for the police, when two more, that I did not know about, jumped on me, and I was getting the best of them when one of them struck me over the head with a crowbar, and the other stabbed me to the heart with a butcher knife. I have received my death wound, my boy, and my hot southern blood, that I offered up so freely for my country in her time of need, is passing from my body, and soon your Pa will be only a piece of poor clay. Get some ice and put on my stomach, and all the way down, for I am burning up.' I went to the water pitcher and got a chunk of ice and put inside Pa's shirt, and while Ma was tearing up an old skirt to stop the flow of blood, I asked Pa if he felt better, and if he could describe the villains who had murdered him. Pa gasped and moved his legs to get them cool from the clotted blood, he said, and he went on, 'One of them was about six foot high, and had a sandy mustache. It got him down and hit him on the nose, and if the police find him, his nose will be broke. The second one was thick set, and weighed about two hundred. I had him down, and my boot was on his neck, and I was knocking two more down when I was hit. The thick set one will have the mark of boot heels on his throat. Tell the police when I'm gone, about the boot heel marks.'

"By this time Ma had got the skirt tore up, and she stuffed it under Pa's shirt, right where he said he was hit, and Pa was telling us what to do to settle his estate, when Ma began to smell the liniment, and she found the broken bottle in his pocket, and searched Pa for the place where he was stabbed, and then she began to laugh, and Pa got mad and said he didn't see as a death-bed scene was such an almighty funny affair; and then she told him he was not hurt, but that he had fallen on the stairs and broke his bottle, and that there was no blood on him, and he said, 'Do you mean to tell me my body and legs are not bathed in human gore?' and then Pa got up and found it was only the liniment. He got mad and asked Ma why she didn't fly around and get something to take that liniment off his legs, as it was eating them right through to the bone; and then he saw my chum put his head in the door, with one gallus hanging down, and Pa looked at me, and then he said, 'Lookahere, if I find out it was you boys that put up this job on me, I'll make it so hot for you that you will think liniment is ice cream in comparison.' I told Pa it didn't look reasonable that me and my chum could be six burglars, six feet high, with our noses broke, and boot-heel marks on our neck, and Pa, he said for us to go to bed alfired quick, and give him a chance to rinse off that liniment, and we retired. Say, how does my Pa strike you as a good, single-handed liar?" and the boy went up to the counter, while the grocery man went after a scuttle of coal.

In the meantime, one of the grocery man's best customers—a deacon in the church—had come in and sat down on the counter, over the darning needle, and as the grocery man came in with the coal, the boy pulled the string, and went out door and tipped over a basket of rutabagas, while the deacon got down off the counter with his hand clasped, and anger in every feature, and told the grocery man he could whip him in two minutes. The grocery man asked what was the matter, and the deacon hunted up the source from whence the darning needle came through the counter, and as the boy went across the street, the deacon and the grocery man were rolling on the floor, the grocery man trying to hold the deacon's fists while he explained about the darning needle, and that it was intended for the boy. How it came out the boy did not wait to see.

QUESTIONS

Language

1. Can you find any examples of incorrect grammar in this selection? Why would the author deliberately use bad grammar?

2. Look up the word *metaphor* in a dictionary. The bad boy uses several metaphors to describe the grocer on p. 98. What are they? Do they help to reveal the grocer's character to you? Do you find them fresh and vivid? Would the grocer have any trouble understanding what the boy means?

3. Look at the father's speeches about the attack. What kind of person do you think he is? Does he speak differently from his son?

Content

1. What sort of people does the bad boy play tricks on? Why does he choose these people for his targets?

2. What are the various tricks the bad boy performs? Can he himself be tricked, as can other Tricksters we have seen in this chapter?

3. How mature does the grocer seem to you? What kind of relationship does he have with the bad boy?

4. Why does the father lie about the attack by the "burglars"? Why does he get angry at his wife? Does this seem a realistic reaction to you? Why?

5. How does the bad boy cleverly avoid being punished by his father?

Suggestions for Writing

1. Retell this story from the father's point of view, beginning with the dinner conversation about burglars. Try for an even balance between narration, such as you see in the first paragraph of this selection, and dialogue. Compare your version with you classmates' versions. How are they different?
2. Write an essay in which you defend or condemn the bad boy for his actions. Give *reasons* for your position.
3. The *Peck's Bad Boy* stories were extremely popular in late nineteenth-century America. Do you think a series of the same sort featuring a *girl* would have been as popular or successful? Why or why not? Discuss this question in class and then write an essay arguing one side or the other, using some of the insights produced by the class discussion to round out your argument.

BERT KALMAR AND HARRY RUBY

from the screenplay of the Marx Brothers' movie *Duck Soup*

Born and raised in a slum district of New York City, the five Marx Brothers—Groucho, Chico, Harpo, Zeppo, and Gummo (the nicknames, respectively, of Julius, Leonard, Adolph, Herbert, and Milton)—were encouraged to enter show business at an early age by their mother, Minnie, sister of the vaudeville star Al Shean. Originally a musical act, they switched to comedy around 1914, with the introduction of a skit called "Fun in Hi Skule" into their act. After years of touring the midwestern vaudeville circuit, the group (minus Gummo, who had enlisted in the army) finally made it to Broadway in 1924, in a review called *I'll Say She Is,* which became their first theatrical hit. It was followed by two more successful shows, both of which were later filmed: *The Cocoanuts* (1929) and *Animal Crackers* (1930). After the completion of *Animal Crackers,* the Marx Brothers moved out to Hollywood where, for the next six years, they made a series of classic screen comedies: *Monkey Business* (1931), *Horse Feathers* (1932), *Duck Soup* (1933), *A Night at the Opera* (1935, generally considered their greatest film), and *A Day at the Races* (1937). Between 1938 and 1949, they made six more movies, which, though brilliantly funny at times, were not, in general, as successful as the earlier films.

The comic personalities of Groucho, Chico, and Harpo (Zeppo, a rather wooden and colorless straight man, dropped out of the act in 1933) were fixed at an early stage and never changed, though the names of the characters they played were different in every movie. Groucho, the sharp-tongued "mangy lover," is in-

From *Duck Soup* by Bert Kalmar and Harry Ruby. Reprinted with permission of Lorimer Publishing Ltd. from *The Four Marx Brothers in Monkey Business and Duck Soup.* Copyright 1972 by Lorimer Publishing Ltd. Published by Simon and Schuster.

stantly identifiable by his black, swallow-tailed coat, thick, greasepaint eyebrows and moustache, leering grin, loping walk, and ever-present cigar. Chico, with his blatantly phony Italian accent, generally plays good-natured, hopelessly stupid con men, while Harpo, a master mime, is a mute, childlike agent of chaos, dressed in an oversized trenchcoat whose pockets and sleeves contain everything from a taxi horn to silverware service for ten to a flaming blowtorch. Their style of comedy can perhaps best be described as anarchic, and like most of their movies, *Duck Soup* is essentially plotless. In it Groucho plays Rufus T. Firefly, president of the mythical country of Freedonia, while Harpo and Chico (here named Pinky and Chicolini) are spies for Ambassador Trentino, leader of the rival nation, Sylvania. In the following scene, Harpo and Chico report their latest undercover activities to their boss.

> *Fade in to a flag waving from a mast. Music. The word SYLVANIA appears over it, then we wipe to a shot of Sylvania itself. It is another Ruritanian town, of more southern aspect than Freedonia.*
> *The music ends as a diagonal wipe transports us to* TRENTINO's *office.* TRENTINO *is seated at his desk in close-up, holding a newspaper.*

AGITATOR *off* : I have failed, Ambassador.

TRENTINO : I know it, I know it, you idiot!

> *Close-up of the* AGITATOR, *leaning over* TRENTINO's *desk with a cringing expression.*

AGITATOR : I'm sorry.

TRENTINO *off* : You have muddled everything.

> *We now see him at his desk in the foreground, with the* AGITATOR *beyond him.*

TRENTINO : If you'd started the revolution as I planned, during the turmoil I could have stepped in and placed Freedonia under the Sylvanian flag—our flag.

> *Close-up of the* AGITATOR, *leaning over the desk.*

AGITATOR : But Firefly blocked us. Your Excellency . . .

> *Resume on* TRENTINO *from his point of view.*

AGITATOR *off* : . . . you have no idea how popular he is in Freedonia.

TRENTINO : Oh, yes, I've known of that too. That's why I have two spies shadowing him. I want to find out something about him—something to disgrace him, to discredit him with the people.

> *He turns as the door opens off-screen and we cut to* TRENTINO's SECRETARY, *who has come in through the door.*

SECRETARY : Ambassador, Chicolini and Pinky are here.

> *Resume on* TRENTINO *at his desk, with the* AGITATOR *in back view.*

TRENTINO : Ah, those are my two spies. Show them in. *To the* AGITATOR : Wait outside.

> *The* AGITATOR *hurries off in the background and we cut back to the* SECRETARY *as she opens the door, revealing* PINKY *in disguise.*

We see CHICOLINI *and* PINKY *standing in the doorway, both wearing bearded masks and hats. The eyes on* PINKY's *mask whirl round.* CHICOLINI *removes his mask and grins, then spins* PINKY *round to reveal his face on the other side.*

CHICOLINI : We fool you good, heh?

Shot of TRENTINO.

TRENTINO *genially* : Gentlemen! *He starts forward.*

Resume on the door, which the SECRETARY *is holding open.* TRENTINO *advances towards* CHICOLINI *and* PINKY *with open arms, but they suddenly dive past him to the desk as a bell rings.*
At the desk, PINKY *answers first one phone, then the other, but the bell goes on ringing.*

TRENTINO : Gentlemen, what is this?

A closer shot excludes him as CHICOLINI *replies :*

CHICOLINI : Sssh! This is spy stuff!

PINKY *listens to both phones at once but the bell still goes on ringing. Finally he gives a grin and pulls a large alarm clock out of his pocket.* CHICOLINI *laughs.*

SECRETARY *off* : A telegram for you sir.

As she finishes, we see her and TRENTINO.

TRENTINO : Oh!

CHICOLINI *and* PINKY *rush round beside him.* PINKY *grabs the telegram, looks at it, then screws it up and throws it on the floor in a rage.*

CHICOLINI : He gets mad because he can't read.

The SECRETARY *exits and* PINKY *leers after her.*

TRENTINO : Oh, I see. Well, gentlemen, we have serious matters to discuss.

Camera pans with them to the desk, then cuts to show them from a high angle.

TRENTINO : So please be seated.

CHICOLINI *and* PINKY *slide under* TRENTINO *as he sits down.* PINKY *whistles while* CHICOLINI *sings:*

CHICOLINI : Rock-a-bye . . .

In a medium shot of the group, PINKY *continues to whistle and puts his feet up on the desk while the other two get up again.*

TRENTINO : Gentlemen! Gentlemen! Now, about that information I asked you to get.

CHICOLINI *reaches in his pocket.*

CHICOLINI : Wait, wait, wait, wait. Here, have a cigar.

We see his hands as he holds out the charred butt of a cigar. TRENTINO'S *hand takes it from him.*
Seen from below TRENTINO *looks at the butt with distaste.*

CHICOLINI *off* : That's a good quarter cigar.

Back to the group.

CHICOLINI : I smoked the other three-quarters myself.
TRENTINO : Yes. Well, no thank you. I have one of my own.

He throws down the butt and produces a cigar from a box on the desk.
PINKY *leaps up and grabs it in his mouth.*

TRENTINO : Here, try one of these.

Shot of PINKY *and* CHICOLINI. PINKY *tries to light the cigar with the telephone receiver.*

CHICOLINI : Aw, 'at'sa no good.

He takes out a lighter but finds that it does not work.
Resume on all three of them as PINKY *pulls a blowlamp out of his pocket. It ignites with a roar, and he lights his own cigar, then* TRENTINO'S.

CHICOLINI : 'At'sa good, all right. 'At'sa fine. 'At'sa good.

PINKY *blows out the flame.*
In another shot of the group camera pans, excluding CHICOLINI, *while* PINKY *puts the blowlamp down on the desk behind* TRENTINO. *The Sylvanian ambassador turns to* CHICOLINI, *holding his cigar behind his back.*

TRENTINO : Now, let's concentrate. Have you been trailing Firefly?

PINKY *opens a drawer in the desk and snips the end off* TRENTINO'S *cigar with a pair of scissors; it falls into the drawer. Camera pans to include* CHICOLINI *again.*

CHICOLINI *laughing* : Have we been trailing Firefly? Why, my partner—he's got a nose just like a bloodhound.

TRENTIONO *turning to look at* PINKY: Really?

CHICOLINI : Yeah, and the rest of his face don't look so good either.

The three of them are seen standing in a row behind the desk. TRENTINO *tries to puff on his truncated cigar, then looks suspiciously at* PINKY.

CHICOLINI : Look. We find out all about this Firefly. *He pulls out a letter.* Here, look at this.

TRENTINO *grabs it and sits down.*

TRENTINO : Ah very good, very good. Wait a minute. We must not be disturbed.

Close-up of his hand pressing a buzzer on the desk.
The trio are seen from the side as the SECRETARY *enters in the background and comes up to the desk.*

SECRETARY : Yes, sir?

TRENTINO : Oh . . . This is a very important conference, and I do not wish to be interrupted.

Shot of TRENTINO, PINKY *and the* SECRETARY.

SECRETARY : Yes sir.

She sees PINKY *leering at her and backs away nervously.* PINKY *starts to follow, but* CHICOLINI *restrains him.*

CHICOLINI *off* : Ah-ah! Ah-ha! *He snaps his fingers.*

Resume on the three of them beyond the desk. TRENTINO *gets up in exasperation.*

TRENTINO : Gentlemen, we are not getting anywhere. *He puts his cigar in the ashtray.*

Close-up of PINKY'S *hand as he balances the cigar on the end of the buzzer board.*
PINKY *hits the cigar in the air with a ruler and belts it across the room.*
We see the others as PINKY *runs to first base by the door, then back to the desk. He throws himself down on the carpet and* CHICOLINI *stands over him.*

CHICOLINI : You're out!

He goes back to the other side of TRENTINO. PINKY *tries to press the buzzer, but* TRENTINO *raises a finger.*

TRENTINO *to* PINKY : Ah-ah-ah! *To both of them* : Now, gentlemen, please! Will you tell me what you found out about Firefly?

Shot of him and CHICOLINI.

CHICOLINI : Well, you remember you gave us a picture of a man and said follow him?

TRENTINO : Oh, yes.

CHICOLINI: Well, we get on the job right away . . . *He gestures dramatically* . . . and in one hour . . . even in less than one hour . . .

TRENTINO *excitedly* : Yes?

CHICOLINI : . . . we lose-a da picsh . . . TRENTINO *sighs* . . . Dat'sa pretty quick work, huh?

TRENTINO : But I asked you to dig up something I can use against Firefly. Did you bring me his record?

Resume on the three. PINKY *gets out a gramophone record from under his coat and hands it to* TRENTINO. *The ambassador gets up, at his wits' end.*

TRENTINO : No, no!

He throws the record over his shoulder. PINKY *pulls out a gun. We see the record flying through the air. A shot rings out and it disintegrates.*
Back to the group as CHICOLINI *rings a handbell which he has found on the desk and hands* PINKY *a cigar from the box.*

CHICOLINI : And da boy get a cigar.

He slams the lid on TRENTINO'S *fingers.*

TRENTINO : Oww! *He shakes his fingers;* PINKY *commiserates.* Now, Chicolini . . .

Shot of CHICOLINI *and* TRENTINO. TRENTINO *sits down.*

TRENTINO *wagging a finger* : . . . I want a full detailed report of your investigation.

PINKY *is partly visible to the right.*

CHICOLINI : All right, I tell you. Monday we watch Firefly's house, but he no come out. He wasn't home. Tuesday we go to the ball game, but he fool us. He no show up. Wednesday he go to the ball game, and we fool him. We no show up. Thursday was a double header. Nobody show up. Friday it rained all day. There was no ball game so we stayed home and we listened to it over the radio.

TRENTINO *exasperated* : Then you didn't shadow Firefly?
CHICOLINI : Oh, sure we shadow Firefly. We shadow him all day.
TRENTINO : But what day was that?
CHICOLINI : Shadderday.

Cut to include PINKY. TRENTINO *clutches his head in his hands.*

CHICOLINI *laughing* : 'At'sa some joke, eh, Boss?

PINKY *snips at* TRENTINO'S *hair, which is standing up between his fingers. Resume on* TRENTINO *and* CHICOLINI.

TRENTINO : Now, will you tell me what happened on Saturday?
CHICOLINI : I'm glad you asked me. We follow this man down to a roadhouse and at this roadhouse he meet a married lady.
TRENTINO : A married lady?
CHICOLINI : Yeah. I think it was his wife.
TRENTINO : Firefly has no wife.
CHICOLINI : No?
TRENTINO : No.
CHICOLINI : Den you know what I think, Boss?
TRENTINO : What?
CHICOLINI : I think we follow da wrong man.

We see the three of them again, facing camera. TRENTINO *gets up.*

TRENTINO : Oh, gentlemen, I am disappointed. *They hang their heads.* I entrusted you with a mission of great importance . . . *They look up eagerly* . . . and you failed. *They hang their heads again.* However . . . *They look up again* . . . I am going to give you one more chance.

A closer shot of the three of them, from the side. TRENTINO *bends over, looking in a drawer, and* PINKY *cuts off his coat tails.*

TRENTINO : I have credentials here that will get you into any place in Freedonia. If I can only . . . Ah, here we are.

He straightens up and hands CHICOLINI *a document. Shot of* TRENTINO *and* PINKY.

TRENTINO : Now, are you sure that you can trap Firefly?

> PINKY *nods and pulls out a mousetrap.*
> *We see* PINKY's *hands with the mousetrap. It snaps shut.*
> *Back to* TRENTINO *and* PINKY. TRENTINO *sighs in despair.*
> *We see the three of them from the side again.* TRENTINO *turns towards* CHICOLINI
> *in the background, while* PINKY *picks up a paste pot.*

TRENTINO : Remember, this time . . .

> PINKY's *hand dips the brush in the paste.*

TRENTINO *off* : . . . . I expect results.

> *Resume on the group as* TRENTINO *bends over, shaking hands with* CHICOLINI.

TRENTINO : Goodbye, and good luck.

> PINKY *smears paste on the seat of* TRENTINO's *trousers.*

CHICOLINI : Okay, Cap. Come on, Pinky.

> *He goes off, while* PINKY *waves to* TRENTINO. *Another shot looking towards
> the door.* TRENTINO *sits on the desk with his hand outstretched.*

TRENTINO : Goodbye.

> PINKY *shakes his hand and exits, leaving* TRENTINO's *fingers caught in the
> mousetrap.* TRENTINO *gets up with an agonised expression—and the newspaper
> stuck to his backside. He groans and tries to remove his fingers from the
> trap. Fade out.*

QUESTIONS

Language

1. Most of the humor in this excerpt from the screenplay involves physical action of some kind. But in addition to numerous sight gags, there is considerable verbal humor as well. What are some examples of the latter?
2. Ambassador Trentino speaks very differently from Chicolini (and you will note Pinky never speaks at all). How would you characterize the difference?
3. What is the function of the dialogue between the Agitator and Trentino at the beginning of this scene?

Content

1. Which of the two, Chicolini or Pinky, is a better example of the Trickster? Why?
2. What kind of relationship do the two "spies" have? How does Chicolini react to Pinky's jokes?
3. What are the tricks Pinky plays? Which ones do you think are funniest? Are there some you feel must be seen—not read about—to be funny? If so, which?
4. Comparatively little space is devoted in this scene to a report of the shadowing the spies are supposed to have done. Why?

Suggestions for Writing

1. Nearly everyone has seen movies or television programs about spies—if not espionage agents, then police spies or private detectives who shadow suspicious people. As a

result, we have certain ideas about how that spying should be conducted, about its dangers and so on. Keeping these conventional ideas or expectations in mind, write an essay about why Chicolini's long-awaited report to Trentino about his and his partner's activities is so funny. This is a comparison and contrast essay: you will be *comparing* the typical spy's attitude, technique, and success with Chicolini and Pinky's.

2. *Duck Soup* was released in late 1933, eight years before the attack on Pearl Harbor that initiated America's entrance into World War II. Discuss with your classmates whether this Marx Brothers' movie could have been made during the Second World War; if so, would it have been successful? Would America have laughed at and enjoyed it? Why or why not? After your discussion, write an essay on this topic.

3. Look up the word *slapstick* in good dictionary. Then write an essay defining the word, using incidents from *Duck Soup* to illustrate your definition. Make it *interesting*.

MARK TWAIN

from *The Adventures of Huckleberry Finn*

"The Lincoln of our literature," as his friend William Dean Howells described him, Mark Twain—pseudonym of Samuel Langhorne Clemens (1835–1910)—began his literary career writing humorous articles for the Virginia City *Territorial Enterprise.* His story "The Celebrated Jumping Frog of Calaveras County" brought him immediate nationwide recognition upon its appearance in 1865. Published first in the New York *Saturday Press,* it was soon reprinted in newspapers across the country and became the title story of Twain's first book. Two travel books followed: *The Innocents Abroad* (1869) and *Roughing It* (1872), humorous accounts of the author's experiences during, respectively, a pilgrimage to the Holy Land and a trip to the Far West. His best-known works are *The Prince and the Pauper* (1882), *A Connecticut Yankee in King Arthur's Court* (1889), *The Adventures of Tom Sawyer* (1876), and its sequel *The Adventures of Huckleberry Finn* (1884), the last two of which are based on Twain's memories of his boyhood in the small town of Hannibal, Missouri. Twain's later life was marked by a string of tragedies, including a plunge into bankruptcy and the death of his wife and two beloved daughters. As a result, his final writings are pervaded by pessimism and gloom.

The Adventures of Huckleberry Finn is Twain's masterpiece, "the epic of American democracy" (in the words of critic Darrel Abel), and a brilliant re-creation of frontier life on the Mississippi River. Narrated by the "ignorant village boy," Huck, the novel tells of his experiences while floating on a raft down the Mississippi, accompanied by the runaway slave, Jim. Among the many characters Huck and Jim encounter on their journey are a pair of outrageous con men who call themselves the Duke and the Dauphin.

Towards night it begun to darken up and look like rain; the heat lightning was squirting around low down in the sky, and the leaves was beginning to shiver—

it was going to be pretty ugly, it was easy to see that. So the duke and the king went to overhauling our wigwam, to see what the beds was like. My bed was a straw tick—better than Jim's, which was a corn shuck tick; there's always cobs around about in a shuck tick, and they poke into you and hurt; and when you roll over the dry shucks sound like you was rolling over in a pile of dead leaves; it makes such a rustling that you wake up. Well, the duke allowed he would take my bed; but the king allowed he wouldn't. He says:

"I should 'a' reckoned the difference in rank would a sejested to you that a cornshuck bed warn't just fitten for me to sleep on. Your Grace 'll take the shuck bed yourself."

Jim and me was in a sweat again for a minute, being afraid there was going to be some trouble amongst them; so we was pretty glad when the duke says:

" 'Tis my fate to be always ground into the mire under the iron heel of oppression. Misfortune has broken my once haughty spirit; I yield, I submit; 'tis my fate. I am alone in the world—let me suffer; I can bear it."

We got away as soon as it was good and dark. The king told us to stand well out towards the middle of the river, and not show a light till we got a long ways below the town. We come in sight of the little bunch of lights by and by—that was the town, you know—and slid by, about a half a mile out, all right. When we was three-quarters of a mile below we hoisted up our signal lantern; and about ten o'clock it come on to rain and blow and thunder and lighten like everything; so the king told us to both stay on watch till the weather got better; then him and the duke crawled into the wigwam and turned in for the night. It was my watch below till twelve, but I wouldn't 'a' turned in anyway if I'd had a bed, because a body don't see such a storm as that every day in the week, not by a long sight. My souls, how the wind did scream along! And every second or two there'd come a glare that lit up the whitecaps for a half a mile around, and you'd see the islands looking dusty through the rain, and the trees thrashing around in the wind; then comes a *h-whack*—bum! bum! bumble-umble-umbum-bum-bum-bum—and the thunder would go rumbling and grumbling away, and quit—and then *rip* comes another flash and another sockdolager. The waves most washed me off the raft sometimes, but I hadn't any clothes on, and didn't mind. We didn't have no trouble about snags; the lightning was glaring and flittering around so constant that we could see them plenty soon enough to throw her head this way or that and miss them.

I had the middle watch, you know, but I was pretty sleepy by that time, so Jim he said he would stand the first half of it for me; he was always mighty good that way, Jim was. I crawled into the wigwam, but the king and the duke had their legs sprawled around so there warn't no show for me; so I laid outside—I didn't mind the rain, because it was warm, and the waves warn't running so high now. About two they come up again, though, and Jim was going to call me; but he changed his mind, because he reckoned they warn't high enough yet to do any harm; but he was mistaken about that, for pretty soon all of a sudden along comes a regular ripper and washed me overboard. It most killed Jim a-laughing. He was the easiest nigger to laugh that ever was, anyway.

I took the watch, and Jim he laid down and snored away; and by and by the storm let up for good and all; and the first cabin light that showed I rousted him out, and we slid the raft into hiding quarters for the day.

The king got out an old ratty deck of cards after breakfast, and him and the duke played seven-up awhile, five cents a game. Then they got tired of it, and allowed they would "lay out a campaign," as they called it. The duke went down into his carpetbag, and fetched up a lot of little printed bills and read them out loud. One bill said, "The celebrated Dr. Armand de Montalban, of Paris," would "lecture on the Science of Phrenology" at such and such a place, on the blank day of blank, at ten cents admission, and "furnish charts of character at twenty-five cents apiece." The duke said that was *him*. In another bill he was the "world-renowned Shakespearian tragedian, Garrick the Younger, of Drury Lane, London." In other bills he had a lot of other names and done other wonderful things, like finding water and gold with a "divining-rod," "dissipating witch spells," and so on. By and by he says:

"But the histrionic muse is the darling. Have you ever trod the boards, Royalty?"

"No," says the king.

"You shall, then, before you're three days older, Fallen Grandeur," says the duke. "The first good town we come to we'll hire a hall to do the swordfight in 'Richard III,' and the balcony scene in 'Romeo and Juliet.' How does that strike you?"

"I'm in, up to the hub, for anything that will pay, Bilgewater; but, you see, I don't know nothing about play-actin', and hain't ever seen much of it. I was too small when pap used to have 'em at the palace. Do you reckon you can learn me?"

"Easy!"

"All right. I'm jist a-freezin' for something fresh, anyway. Le's commence right away."

So the duke told him all about who Romeo was and who Juliet was, and said he was used to being Romeo, so the king could be Juliet.

"But if Juliet's such a young gal, duke, my peeled head and my white whiskers is goin' to look oncommon odd on her, maybe."

"No, don't you worry; these county jakes won't ever think of that. Besides, you know, you'll be in costume, and that makes all the difference in the world; Juliet's in a balcony, enjoying the moonlight before she goes to bed, and she's got on her nightgown and her ruffled nightcap. Here are the costumes for the parts."

He got out two or three curtain-calico suits, which he said was meedyevil armor for Richard III and t'other chap, and a long white cotton nightshirt and a ruffled nightcap to match. The king was satisfied; so the duke got out his book and read the parts over in the most splendid spread-eagle way, prancing around and acting at the same time, to show how it had got to be done; then he give the book to the king and told him to get his part by heart.

There was a little one-horse town about three mile down the bend, and after dinner the duke said he had ciphered out his idea about how to run in daylight without it being dangersome for Jim; so he allowed he would go down to the town and fix that thing. The king allowed he would go, too, and see if he couldn't strike something. We was out of coffee, so Jim said I better go along with them in the canoe and get some.

When we got there warn't nobody stirring; streets empty, and perfectly dead and still, like Sunday. We found a sick nigger sunning himself in a back yard, and he said everybody that warn't too young or too sick or too old was gone to camp meeting, about two mile back in the woods. The king got the directions, and allowed he'd go and work that camp meeting for all it was worth, and I might go, too.

The duke said what he was after was a printing office. We found it; a little bit of a concern, up over a carpenter shop—carpenters and printers all gone to the meeting, and no doors locked. It was a dirty, littered-up place, and had ink marks, and handbills with pictures of horses and runaway niggers on them, all over the walls. The duke shed his coat and said he was all right now. So me and the king lit out for the camp meeting.

We got there in about a half an hour fairly dripping, for it was a most awful hot day. There was as much as a thousand people there from twenty mile around. The woods was full of teams and wagons, hitched everywheres, feeding out of the wagon troughs and stomping to keep off the flies. There was sheds made out of poles and roofed over with branches, where they had lemonade and gingerbread to sell, and piles of watermelons and green corn and such-like truck.

The preaching was going on under the same kinds of sheds, only they was bigger and held crowds of people. The benches was made out of outside slabs of logs, with holes bored in the round side to drive sticks into for legs. They didn't have no backs. The preachers had high platforms to stand on at one end of the sheds. The women had on sunbonnets; and some had linsey-woolsey frocks, some gingham ones, and a few of the young ones had on calico. Some of the young men was barefooted, and some of the children didn't have on any clothes but just a tow-linen shirt. Some of the old women was knitting, and some of the young folks was courting on the sly.

The first shed we come to the preacher was lining out a hymn. He lined out two lines, everybody sung it, and it was kind of grand to hear it, there was so many of them and they done it in such a rousing way; then he lined out two more for them to sing—and so on. The people woke up more and more, and sung louder and louder; and towards the end some begun to groan, and some begun to shout. Then the preacher begun to preach, and begun in earnest, too; and went weaving first to one side of the platform and then the other, and then a-leaning down over the front of it, and his arms and his body going all the time, and shouting his words out with all his might; and every now and then he would hold up his Bible and spread it open, and kind of pass it around this way and that, shouting, "It's the brazen serpent in the wilderness! Look upon it and live!" And people would shout out, "Glory!—A-a-men!" And so he went on, and the people groaning and crying and saying amen:

"Oh, come to the mourners' bench! come, black with sin! (*amen!*) come, sick and sore! (*amen!*) come, lame and halt and blind! (*amen!*) come, pore and needy, sunk in shame! (*a-a-men!*) come, all that's worn and soiled and suffering!—come with a broken spirit! come with a contrite heart! come in your rags and sin and dirt! the waters that cleanse is free, the door of heaven stands open—oh, enter in and be at rest!" (*a-a-men! glory, glory hallelujah!*)

And so on. You couldn't make out what the preacher said any more, on account of the shouting and crying. Folks got up everywheres in the crowd, and worked their way just by main strength to the mourners' bench, with the tears running down their faces; and when all the mourners had got up there to the front benches in a crowd, they sung and shouted and flung themselves down on the straw, just crazy and wild.

Well, the first I knowed the king got a-going, and you could hear him over everybody; and next he went a-charging up onto the platform, and the preacher he begged him to speak to the people, and he done it. He told them he was a pirate—been a pirate for thirty years out in the Indian Ocean—and his crew was thinned out considerable last spring in a fight, and he was home now to take out some fresh men, and thanks to goodness he'd been robbed last night and put ashore off of a steamboat without a cent, and he was glad of it; it was the blessedest thing that ever happened to him, because he was a changed man now, and happy for the first time in his life; and, poor as he was, he was going to start right off and work his way back to the Indian Ocean, and put in the rest of his life trying to turn the pirates into the true path; for he could do it better than anybody else, being acquainted with all pirate crews in that ocean; and though it would take him a long time to get there without money, he would get there anyway, and every time he convinced a pirate he would say to him, "Don't you thank me, don't you give me no credit; it all belongs to them dear people in Pokeville camp meeting, natural brothers and benefactors of the race, and that dear preacher there, the truest friend a pirate ever had!"

And then he busted into tears, and so did everybody. Then somebody sings out, "Take up a collection for him, take up a collection!" Well, a half a dozen made a jump to do it, but somebody sings out, "Let *him* pass the hat around!" Then everybody said it, the preacher too.

So the king went all through the crowd with his hat, swabbing his eyes, and blessing the people and praising them and thanking them for being so good to the poor pirates away off there; and every little while the prettiest kind of girls, with the tears running down their cheeks, would up and ask him would he let them kiss him for to remember him by; and he always done it; and some of them he hugged and kissed as many as five or six times—and he was invited to stay a week; and everybody wanted him to live in their houses, and said they'd think it was an honor; but he said as this was the last day of the camp meeting he couldn't do no good, and besides he was in a sweat to get to the Indian Ocean right off and go to work on the pirates.

When we got back to the raft and he come to count up he found he had collected eighty-seven dollars and seventy-five cents. And then he had fetched away a three-gallon jug of whisky, too, that he found under a wagon when he was starting home through the woods. The king said, take it all around, it laid over any day he'd ever put in in the missionarying line. He said it warn't no use talking, heathens don't amount to shucks alongside of pirates to work a camp meeting with.

The duke was thinking *he'd* been doing pretty well till the king come to show up, but after that he didn't think so so much. He had set up and printed off two little jobs for farmers in that printing-office—horse bills—and took the money, four dollars. And he had got in ten dollars' worth of advertisements for the paper, which he said he would put in for four dollars if they would pay in advance—so they done it. The price of the paper was two dollars a year, but he took in three subscriptions for half a dollar apiece on condition of them paying him in advance; they were going to pay in cordwood and onions as usual, but he said he had just bought the concern and knocked down the price as low as he could afford it, and was going to run it for cash. He set up a little piece of poetry, which he made, himself, out of his own head—three verses—kind of sweet and saddish—the name of it was, "Yes, crush, cold world, this breaking heart"—and he left that all set up and ready to print in the paper, and didn't charge nothing for it. Well, he took in nine dollars and a half, and said he'd done a pretty square day's work for it.

QUESTIONS

Language

1. What do the following words and phrases mean? *divining rod* (p. 110); *trod the boards* (p. 110); *up to the hub* (p. 110); *jakes* (p. 110); *spread-eagle way* (p. 110); *one-horse town* (p. 110); *truck* (p. 111); *lining out a hymn* (p. 111); *by main strength* (p. 111).
2. Find examples of Huck Finn's ungrammatical English. Why would Mark Twain have him speak this way?
3. Though Huck and Jim, when they first meet the king and the duke, believe they are in the presence of royalty, they very quickly see through their new acquaintances. What besides the duke and the king's unscrupulous, undignified conduct—their dishonest tricks—would tip any sensible person off to their real identity?
4. Look at the description of the contents of the duke's carpetbag in the second paragraph on page 110 and of the appearance of the people at the camp meeting and the food offered for sale there (p. 111). Twain *could* have simplified here, *could* have cut out much of this description. But what does such detail add; what does it do for the whole?

Content

1. What is the king's trick? The duke's? What is Huck Finn's reaction to their activities? Is Huck a good reporter of events? Why?
2. Describe the camp meeting and the people who are at it as completely as you can. Why is a religious meeting a good place for an unprincipled person to make a lot of money?
3. What qualities do you think the king and the duke would need to cheat people so easily? What qualities would their victims have to have?

Suggestion for Writing

1. *The Adventures of Huckleberry Finn* is told entirely by Huck, a young adolescent runaway; everything is seen through his eyes. Using this short selection from the book, construct a portrait of the narrator. Look at the way Huck speaks, the things he does, the things he notices.
2. *Huckleberry Finn* is set in the early nineteenth century; the action takes place in the rural South, on the Mississippi River and in the small towns and villages that line its banks. Write an essay summarizing the picture Twain gives you of the American South in the early 1800s: its people, their activities, the scenery.
3. Discuss in class your reaction to the tricks the duke and the king play on the naive riverbank people at the camp meeting and in the printer's office. Are you upset that (for the time being, anyway) the two Tricksters get away with their deception? Are you glad? Write an essay giving the reasons for your reaction.
4. Renard the Fox (see p. 66) fools the Lion's court; the king in *Huckleberry Finn* fools the camp meeting in a similar way. Write an essay comparing the methods these two Tricksters use. How do they use, for example, religious sentiment to their own advantage?

5. At the beginning of this excerpt, Huck stays up late to watch a storm ''because a body don't see such a storm as that every day in the week, not by a long sight.'' Describe in an essay the worst storm you have ever witnessed or been out in. Make your description as vivid and concrete as you can. Include your reactions to the storm.

6. The king fools the people at the camp meeting by telling them an outrageous lie. Write an essay about lying. Are you a ''good'' liar? Do you find it impossible to lie? Why? Have you ever told a lie and gotten away with it? Or was your lie eventually discovered? How do you feel about other people who lie?

ADDITIONAL WRITING SUGGESTIONS FOR CHAPTER TWO

1. Bugs Bunny (see p. 74) became a popular cartoon character with the average American in the middle 1930s, just as the country was beginning to recover from the disastrous conditions of the Great Depression. Stories like ''The Tar Baby'' (p. 69) featuring a rabbit Trickster were extremely popular among oppressed black slaves in the pre-Civil War South. Write an essay in which you try to account for the popularity of Tricksters during these two different historical periods. In other words, try to answer the question of why Bugs would have appealed to the ordinary American worker, and the rabbit Trickster to the black slave. Look at the two selections in this chapter carefully in order to help formulate your answer.

2. Think of all your friends, acquaintances, classmates, and relatives. Do you know anyone who is a Trickster? Write a description of him or her—include some of that person's ''best'' tricks—and then try to analyze the reasons for his or her behavior.

3. Write an essay about authority and freedom (first consulting a good dictionary for a definition of both words) and the Trickster's relationship to both.

4. The Tricksters assembled in this chapter are a varied lot: some are cruel, even vicious in nature, while others are merely playful—rather than shock or repel us, they make us laugh. Write an essay in which you range all of the Tricksters you've encountered along a scale, from most innocuous or harmless to most cruel. You will be comparing and contrasting nine different figures (you can count the Katzenjammer Kids as one figure). In making your decisions, keep the *tone* of the authors—the attitudes they seem to have toward their stories—in mind. It is possible, for example, that two Tricksters can do equally cruel things, and yet, because of the way the authors have treated their material, one won't seem as bad as the other.

5. Write your own Trickster narrative or story, using either an animal—or a bird or insect, for that matter—or a human being as your central character. Be sure to show him, her, or it performing enough tricks to be easily described by someone else; that is, give your Trickster a definite personality. Be as fanciful and elaborate as you please. Then read your narratives in class and discuss each other's Tricksters. In terms of their personalities and the kinds of actions they perform, how different are they? Talk about why you made yours the way you did.

6. Think of children's cartoons. Many of them feature a Trickster. Write an essay speculating on why this archetypal figure would appeal especially to children.

7. Is there a bit of the Trickster in you? Has it ever been expressed? When? Describe what happened and what the consequences, if any, were.

Three

The Temptress

"It's funny, but you remember a bad gal longer than a good one!—The only women who get their names in history books are th' ones who ruined empires, or poisoned a bunch o' guys!"

—from the comic strip *Terry and the Pirates* by Milton Caniff

The two archetypes we have looked at so far are not limited to either sex. Shadow figures can be female as well as male; *every* human being, after all, has a hidden "shadow side" to his or her personality. In Brian de Palma's horror movie *Sisters,* for example, the good and evil siblings are women—Siamese twin sisters, one a sweet young girl, the other a homicidal maniac. There are also female Tricksters. A good example is the comic strip character Little Iodine, who, in the tradition of Peck's Bad Boy and the Katzenjammer Kids, devotes all of her demonic energies to tormenting her poor father, Henry Tremblechin.

It is, however, an unfortunate fact that, for social and political reasons far too complicated to discuss here, Western culture has always been dominated by men. As a result, many of the myths and literary works produced in our society are filled with specifically male fantasies—masculine daydreams (or nightmares) turned into art. And one of the most powerful and prevalent male fantasies is that of the lovely but lethal woman who bewitches men with her beauty, then lures them to destruction. This is the archetypal figure of the Temptress or Fatal Woman (*femme fatale*).

Where does this fantasy come from? Partly, at least, it seems to grow out of a very primitive and irrational fear which man has of woman's sexual influence over him—of that power which, precisely because it is so irresistible, threatens to over-whelm him, robbing him of his will and vitality. Often, for example, the Temptress is shown to be a supernatural female whose ravenous sexual appetite literally drains men dry. The folktales, myths, and superstitions of the world are filled with these sinister creatures. There is the ancient Hebrew demoness Lilith, for instance—the "night hag" who, according to legend, was Adam's first wife. Lawless and lewd, she flew into the sky and became a living nightmare, a monster who murdered sleeping babies and seduced solitary men in their beds, filling their minds with sexual dreams and sucking their blood. There is the succubus of medieval tradition, the female demon who lies with mortal men and drains their "vital fluids" in the dark. And more recently, there is the vampire-woman, with her raven black hair, deathly pale complexion, and (to borrow a line from Swinburne's poem "Dolores") "cruel red mouth like a venomous flower"—a figure familiar to us from scores of Dracula movies and horror comics like *Creepy* and *Vampirella*.

Creatures such as these combine both terror and temptation, danger and desirability; indeed, it is precisely their intense eroticism which makes them so scary to the male, who imagines that he will be absorbed and perhaps even annihilated by the woman's sexuality—drawn like a moth to a flame and then consumed by the heat. This mixture of fear and erotic attraction is powerfully captured by Bram Stoker in his classic nineteenth-century novel, *Dracula.* In the following scene, Arthur Holmwood, who has traveled to a midnight graveyard in the company of his friends John Seward (the narrator) and Professor Van Helsing, must resist the enticements of his horribly altered fiancée, Lucy Westenra, an innocent girl transformed by Count Dracula into a demon who leaves her coffin each night to feed on the blood of young children:

> When Lucy—I call the thing that was before us Lucy because it bore her shape—saw us she drew back with an angry snarl, such as a cat gives when taken unawares; then her eyes ranged over us. Lucy's eyes in form and colour; but Lucy's eyes unclean and full of hell-fire, instead of the pure, gentle orbs we knew. . . . As she looked, her eyes blazed with unholy light, and the face became wreathed with a voluptuous smile. Oh, God, how it made me shudder to see it! With a careless motion, she flung to the ground, callous as a devil, the child that up to now she had clutched strenuously to her breast, growling over it as a dog growls over a bone. The child gave a sharp cry, and lay there moaning. There was a cold-bloodedness in the act which wrung a groan from Arthur; when she advanced to him with outstretched arms and a wanton smile he fell back and hid his face in his hands.
>
> She still advanced, however, and with a languorous, voluptuous grace, said:—
>
> "Come to me, Arthur. Leave these others and come to me. My arms are hungry for you. Come, and we can rest together. Come, my husband, come!"
>
> There was something diabolically sweet in her tones—something of the tingling of glass when struck—which rang through the brains even of us who heard the words addressed to another. As for Arthur, he seemed under a spell; moving his hands from his face, he opened wide his arms. She was leaping for them, when Van Helsing sprang forward and held between them his little golden crucifix. She recoiled from it, and, with a suddenly distorted face, full of rage, dashed past him as if to enter the tomb.

The vampire or succubus—the blood-drinker, the man-eater, the sexual cannibal who, like the female praying mantis, consumes the body of the male in the very act of mating with him—is only one form of the Temptress archetype. Often, the Fatal Woman is portrayed as vampiric, not in a physical, but in a spiritual or psychic sense: a woman who drains men of their souls, turning them into slaves, clowns, or mindless beasts. Such women abound in the most ancient stories known to us, as well as in today's most popular movies, best-sellers, and songs. The Bible tells, for example, of the Philistine Temptress Delilah, who robbed Samson of his manhood by shearing off his hair (an act which, according to psychoanalysis, symbolizes castration). There is the fabled Egyptian queen Cleopatra, who brought ruin to the mighty Mark Antony, transforming that noble Roman soldier "into a strumpet's fool" (to quote a phrase from Shakespeare's play *Antony and Cleopatra*). And a famous character from ancient Greek mythology is the beautiful enchantress Circe, whose sorcery turned men into swine.

In modern times, we find these Fatal Women in every area of popular culture. A well-known work in nineteenth-century America, for instance—often reprinted in early anthologies of "best-loved" verse—was Hugh D'Arcy's sentimental "The Face Upon the Floor," a poem about a promising young artist whose life is destroyed by a fickle beauty. The Temptress is also a popular type in the movies. In the 1920s, Hollywood even coined a name for the sexually alluring but sinister female (exemplified by the silent film actress Theda Bara), calling this kind of woman, fittingly enough, a "vamp." Perhaps the most famous *femme fatale* in cinematic history is the character Lola, played by Marlene Dietrich, in *The Blue Angel*. This classic film tells the story of the proper, even priggish, Immanuel Rath, a professor of English at a boys' high school in Germany, who falls under the spell of the sultry cabaret singer Lola Lola, marries her, and becomes, in effect, her slave. We watch in "pity and fear" the utter degradation of this dignified, middle-aged man: his transformation from a respectable teacher into Lola's doting servant and finally, after she forces him to join the show and help bring in some money, into a pathetic buffoon, a grotesque clown in a horrible, humiliating vaudeville routine. It is significant that, at the end of the film—which takes place over the course of several years and shows the steady decline of Rath from a robust man into a gaunt and grubby ruin—Lola looks as young and voluptuous as she does at the beginning. One of the traits of the Temptress is that she never seems to age. Her beauty is eternal, though it can only be maintained at the expense of her men. The Fatal Woman keeps her vitality by draining the life, whether physical or spiritual, from her lovers.

This fantasy of woman as Temptress is very deeply rooted in the antifeminine bias of Western culture. The Bible itself tells us that the very first woman was a Temptress: Eve, who brought sin and death into the world when she persuaded her mate Adam to taste the forbidden fruit. And who isn't familiar with the ancient Greek legend of Pandora, who let "infinite calamities" loose among men by opening the lid of a box filled with evil spirits? All of us, people of *both* sexes, are conditioned from childhood to see women as dangerous creatures. We are constantly coming across Fatal Women in the classic literature we read in school, from Homer's *Odyssey*, which contains the story of Circe; to Hawthorne's "Rappaccini's Daughter," a tale about a beautiful girl raised in a garden of deadly flowers whose poison has so filled her system that she can kill a man with a kiss; to a modern story like Hemingway's "The Short Happy Life of Francis Macomber," in which the title character's wife "accidentally" blows off his head with a shotgun. Outside of school, the mass media are always bombarding us with images of the *femme fatale,* a fantasy they exploit (along with so many others) for commercial reasons. Our male-dominated society actually sets this fantasy up as a model for women to imitate. Women are encouraged to look and behave like Temptresses, to play a role created for them by man's dark erotic dreams. Cosmetic ads promise to give women the "Cleopatra look": "the sultry, sweet-lipped, sloe-eyed look that shook the pyramids, shocked the world!" (Revlon's "Sphinx Pink" lipstick and nail polish). And widely read *Cosmopolitan* magazine offers to show its readers "How to be a Bitch . . . and Make Men Like it!"

Over the past ten years or so, the feminist movement has worked hard to change our perception of women by teaching the members of both sexes to stop seeing each other (and themselves) in stereotyped sexual roles. But the myth of the Temptress, which seems to be as old as humanity itself, will not disappear overnight. Indeed it sometimes appears, paradoxically enough, as if one effect of the feminist movement has been to make the fantasy image of the deadly female more widespread. Perhaps because many men feel threatened by "women's lib," contemporary works of popular culture (which are still largely produced by males) seem particularly preoccupied with the figure of the Fatal Woman. Rock musicians sing about her all the time: she is Ringo Starr's "Devil Woman," Blood, Sweat, and Tears' "Lucretia MacEvil," The Doors' "Twentieth Century Fox," the Eagles' "Witchy Woman," LaBelle's "Lady Marmalade," the Beatles' "Sexy Sadie," The Who's "The Acid Queen," and Bob Dylan's "Sad-Eyed Lady of the Lowlands." She is also a favorite subject of country-western musicians. In "Bandy the Rodeo Clown," for example, the singer (Moe Bandy) tells the sad (and familiar) story of a rugged rodeo star, "a bull hookin' son-of-a-gun," who "was ridin' high 'til a pretty girl rode him to the ground." Once a first-class bronc-buster who "was closin' in on number one," he is now a pathetic figure, a drunken rodeo clown who keeps the crowds entertained between the "ropin' and ridin' " events. The song is a kind of country music version of the film *The Blue Angel*. This theme of the beautiful woman who turns men into clowns is common in popular music. Another well-known example is the Everly Brothers' rock 'n' roll hit of the fifties, "Cathy's Clown."

On television, the *femme fatale* seems to appear most frequently on the "soaps." "All My Children," "Guiding Light," "As the World Turns," and "Edge of Night" are all loaded with catty females, seductresses, home-wreckers, adulteresses, and, most fearsome of all, aggressive "career women." The same kind of character—the driven, power-hungry female who will stop at nothing to further her career—can be seen in the hit movie *Network,* in the role played by Faye Dunaway: a television executive who casually wrecks William Holden's long-standing marriage in her single-minded quest for corporate success. Another good example of a modern movie Temptress is Mrs. Robinson, the cold-hearted, middle-aged beauty (played by Anne Bancroft) who seduces young Benjamin Braddock (Dustin Hoffman) in the film *The Graduate*.

Finally, there are the comics, a form of pop culture that not only features a great many Temptress figures, but also (and in this respect, we believe, the comics are unique among the popular arts) makes them into heroines—dangerous women whose destructive powers are directed only at criminals. Recent examples of such comic book superwomen include Vampirella, the blood-sucking beauty from the planet Drakulon; Red Sonja, "the she-devil with a sword"; and Spider-Woman ("To know her is to fear her!" warns the cover of her magazine). More traditional femmes fatales—which is to say, more evil ones—can be found all the time in the Conan the Barbarian series of comic books. Indeed, it is a rare issue of Conan that does not contain at least one sorceress, wolf-woman, hell-cat, or queen of the underworld. One of the most sinister "she-creatures" of all appears in a story called "The Flame Winds of Lost Khitai" (Conan no. 32), in which the hero is nearly dragged to a watery grave by a blonde "sloe-eyed wench" of hypnotic beauty who lures him into a bottomless pool and then changes into a half-human monster with octopus tentacles. This deadly female has many mythological cousins: the sirens, the Lorelei, the Rusalka, the nixies—lovely water-spirits whose songs lure men to their deaths. In his essay "Archetypes of the Collective Unconscious," C. G. Jung quotes a short passage of poetry which perfectly sums up the nature of the meeting with this kind of Fatal Woman—her irresistible allure, her victim's own willingness to place himself in her power, and the inevitable outcome of the confrontation with such a creature:

> Half she drew him down,
> Half sank he down
> And nevermore was seen.

HOMER

"Circe" (from *The Odyssey*)

Though some modern scholars doubt that *The Iliad* and *The Odyssey,* the great epic poems of ancient Greece, were created by the same person, or even during the same period, tradition assigns the composition of both to Homer, an "oral poet" (that is, one who communicated his works orally, in song, rather than in writing) who lived in the region of Ionia sometime during the eighth century B.C. The oldest known sources of Greek mythology, as well as the greatest stories of heroic adventure ever told, the two epics have had an incalculable impact on Western culture since the classical age of Greece.

The Iliad is the history of the final days of the Trojan War. Odysseus, the King of Ithaca and a clever and courageous warrior, figures prominently in the story (indeed, it is he who devises the plan for the Trojan Horse and commands the party of Greek soldiers concealed inside it). *The Odyssey* tells of the fantastic and largely terrifying adventures which befall him and his crew on the long voyage home, following the destruction of Troy. Along the way, they are captured by a tribe of cannibal giants, caught between a titanic whirlpool and a six-headed monster, and—in the episode reprinted below (from Book Ten of *The Odyssey*)—bewitched by the enchantress Circe, who has the power to transform men into swine.

Reprinted with permission of Thomas Nelson, Inc. from *The Odyssey,* translated by H. D. Rouse. Copyright 1937 by H. D. Rouse.

"From that place we sailed on, glad enough to have come off with our lives, but sad to lose our companions. Next we reached the island of Aiaia. There Circê lived, a terrible goddess with lovely hair, who spoke in the language of men, own sister to murderous Aietas; their father was Helios, who gives light to mankind, and their mother was Persê, a daughter of Oceanos.[1] We brought our ship to the shore in silence, and some providence guided us into a harbour where ships could lie. There we spent two days and two nights on shore, eating out our hearts with weariness and woe.

"On the third day, as soon as dawn showed the first streaks of light, I took spear and sword and climbed to a high place, where I had a look round to see if there was any one about or any voice to be heard. Standing on the top of a rock, I saw smoke rising into the air from the house where Circê lived in the middle of thick bushes and trees.

"When I saw the smoke glowing, I considered whether I should go and inquire. The best plan seemed to be that I should return first to our ship on the shore and give the men something to eat, and then send out to inquire. Just as I came near to the ship, some god must have pitied me there so lonely, and sent me a stag with towering antlers right on my path: he was going down to the river from his woodland range to drink, for the sun's heat was heavy on him. As he came out, I struck him on the spine in the middle of the back, and the spear ran right through: down he fell in the dust with a moan, and died. I set my foot on him and drew out the spear from the wound. Then I laid the body flat on the ground, and pulled a quantity of twigs and withies, which I plaited across and twisted into a strong rope of a fathom's length: with this rope I tied together the legs of the great creature, and strung him over my neck, and so carried him down to the ship, leaning upon my spear; I could not have carried him on the shoulder with one hand, for he was a huge beast.

"I threw him down in front of the ship, and cheered up my friends with encouraging words as I turned from one to another. 'We are not going to die yet, my friends, for all our troubles: we shall not see the house of Hadês[2] before our day comes. While there's food and drink in the ship, don't let us forget to eat! we need not die of starvation, at all events!'

"They were all sitting about with their faces muffled up in their cloaks; but at my words they threw off the cloaks, and got up quickly to stare at the stag lying on the beach; for he was a huge beast. When they had feasted their eyes on the welcome sight, they began to think of another kind of feast; so they swilled their hands in due form, and got him ready. All day long until sunset we sat enjoying ourselves with our meat and wine; and when the sun went down and the darkness came, we lay down to sleep on the seashore.

"As soon as morning dawned, I called my companions together and addressed them:

" 'My friends, we do not know east from west, we don't know where the sun rises to give light to all mankind, and where he goes down under the earth.

---

[1] Helios (or Helius) was the Greek sun god who drove across the sky each day in a golden chariot drawn by four winged horses. His wife Perse (or Perseïs) was a daughter of Oceanus and Tethys, two of the Titans (the "Elder Gods"). She was regarded as a patron of youth. Oceanus was the god of the great river which was believed to surround the earth. He was worshiped as the source of all rivers, seas, and "waters which gushed from the earth."
[2] The god of the Underworld.

Well, then, what are we to do? We must try to think of something at once, and for my part, I can't think of anything. I have just been up on the cliffs to look around. We are on some island in the middle of the sea, with no land in sight. The island is flat, and I saw smoke rising in the air above a coppice of bushes and trees.'

"When I said this, their hearts were crushed with foreboding: for they remembered the doings of Laistrygonian Antiphatês, and the violence of that audacious cannibal the goggle-eye Cyclops.[3] The tears ran down their cheeks, and much good it did to weep!

"However, I divided them into two parts of equal number, and chose a captain for each: one I took myself, the other I gave to an excellent man, Eurylochos. Quickly then we shook lots in a helmet, and out leapt the lot of Eurylochos. Off he went, with his two-and-twenty men, groaning and grumbling, and we were left groaning and grumbling behind.

"They found in a dell the house of Circê, well built with shaped stones, and set in a clearing. All round it were wolves and lions of the mountains, really men whom she had bewitched by giving them poisonous drugs. They did not attack the men, but ramped up fawning on them and wagging their long tails, just like a lot of dogs playing about their master when he comes out after dinner, because they know he has always something nice for them in his pocket. So these wolves and lions with their sharp claws played about and pawed my men, who were frightened out of their wits by the terrible creatures.

"They stopt at the outer doors of the courtyard, and heard the beautiful goddess within singing in a lovely voice, as she worked at the web on her loom, a large web of incorruptible stuff, a glorious thing of delicate gossamer fabric, such as goddesses make. The silence was broken by Politês, who was nearest and dearest to me of all my companions, and the most trusty. He said:

" 'Friends, I hear a voice in the house, some woman singing prettily at the loom, and the whole place echoes with it. Goddess or woman, let's go in and speak to her.'

"Then they called her loudly. She came out at once, and opened the shining doors, and asked them to come in; they all followed her, in their innocence, only Eurylochos remained behind, for he suspected a trap. She gave them all comfortable seats, and made them a posset, cheese and meal and pale honey mixt with Pramneian wine; but she put dangerous drugs in the mess, to make them wholly forget their native land. When they had swallowed it, she gave them a tap of her wand at once and herded them into pens; for they now had pigs' heads and grunts and bristles, pigs all over except that their minds were the same as before. There they were then, miserably shut up in the pigsty. Circê threw them a lot of beechnuts and acorns and cornel-beans to eat, such as the earth-bedded swine are used to.

---

[3] The Laistrygonians were cannibal giants who lived in the city of Telepylus. Arriving in the harbor of the city, Odysseus sent out a three-man scouting party. The Greeks were brought before King Antiphates, who immediately ate one of them. The other two fled back to the boats. Though Odysseus escaped, the rest of his fleet was destroyed by the giants, who crushed the ships with huge stones, speared the swimmers, and devoured them.

    The Cyclopes were a race of cannibal giants, each with a single eye in the center of his brow. Odysseus and his men were captured by a Cyclops named Polyphemus, who proceeded to devour the Greeks one by one, until Odysseus managed to blind the monster and, through trickery, contrive an escape.

"But Eurylochos came back to the ship, to tell the tale of his companions and their unkind fate. At first he could not utter a word, he was so dumbfounded with this misfortune; his eyes were full of tears, his mind foreboded trouble. At last when we were fairly flummoxed with asking questions, he found his tongue and told us how all his companions had come to grief.

" 'We went out into the wood, as you told us, most renowned chief; found a well-built house in a dell, and there some one was singing loudly as she worked the loom, goddess or woman: they called to her. She came out at once and opened the doors and asked them in: they all followed in the simplicity of their hearts, but I stayed behind because I suspected a trap. They all disappeared at once, not a soul was to be seen, and I stayed there a long time to spy.'

"When he said this, at once I slung my sword over my shoulders, the large one, bronze with silver knobs, and the bow with it, and told him to go back with me and show me the way. But he threw his arms about my knees and begged and prayed without disguise—'Don't take me there, my prince; I don't want to go. Let me stay here. I am sure you will never come back again, nor will any one who goes with you. Let us get away with those who are here while we can: we have still a chance to escape the day of destruction!'

"But I answered, 'Very well, Eurylochos, you may stay here in this place, eat and drink beside the ship. But as for me, go I must, and go I will.'

"So I made my way up from the sea-side. But just as I was on the point of entering the sacred dell and finding the house of that mistress of many spells, who should meet me but Hermês[4] with his golden rod: he looked like a young man with the first down on his lip, in the most charming time of youth. He grasped my hand, and said:

" 'Whither away again, you poor fellow, alone on the hills, in a country you do not know? Your companions are shut up yonder in Circê's, like so many pigs cosy in their pigsties. Are you going to set them free? Why, I warn you that you will never come back, you will stay here with the others.—All right, I will help you and keep you safe. Here, take this charm, and then you may enter the house of Circê: this will keep destruction from your head.

" 'I will reveal to you all the malign arts of Circê. She will make you a posset, and put drugs in the mess. But she will not be able to bewitch you for all that; for the good charm which I will give you will foil her. I will tell you exactly what to do.

" 'As soon as Circê gives you a tap with her long rod, draw your sword at once and rush upon her as if you meant to kill her. She will be terrified, and will invite you to lie with her. Do not refuse, for you want her to free your companions and to entertain you; but tell her to swear the most solemn oath of the blessed gods that she will never attempt any other evil against you, or else when you are stript she may unman you and make you a weakling.'

"With these words Argeiphontês handed me the charm which he had pulled out of the soil, and explained its nature. The root was black, but the flower was milk-white. The gods call it moly: it is hard for mortals to find it, but the gods can do all things.

---

[4] The messenger of the gods and guide of travelers. On his head, he wears a winged hat; on his feet, winged sandals; in his hand, he carries a magic staff called the *caduceus*. He is also sometimes called Argeïphontes.

"Then Hermês departed through the woody island to high Olympos,[5] but I went on to Circê's house, and I mused deeply as I went. I stood at the doors; as I stood I called loudly, and the beautiful goddess heard. Quickly she came out and opened the doors, and I followed her much troubled.

"She led me to a fine carven chair covered with silver knobs, with a footstool for my feet. Then she mixt me a posset, and dropt in her drugs with her heart full of wicked hopes. I swallowed it, but it did not bewitch me; then she gave me a tap with her wand, and said:

" 'Now then, to the sty with you, and join your companions!'

"I drew my sharp sword and leapt at Circê as though to kill her. She let out a loud shriek, and ran up and embraced my knees, and blurted out in dismay:

" 'Who are you, where do you come from in the wide world? Where is your city, who are your parents? I am amazed that you have swallowed my drugs and you are not bewitched. Indeed, there never was another man who could stand these drugs once he had let them pass his teeth! But you must have a mind that cannot be bewitched. Surely you are Odysseus, the man who is never at a loss! Argeiphontês Goldenrod used to say that you would come on your way from Troy in a ship. Come now, put up your sword in the sheath, let us lie down on my bed and trust each other in love!'

"I answered her, 'Ah, Circê, how could you bid me be gentle to you, when you have turned my companions into pigs in this house? And now that you have me here, with deceitfulness in your heart you bid me to go to your bed in your chamber, that when I am stript you may unman me and make me a weakling. I will not enter your bed unless you can bring yourself to swear a solemn oath that you will never attempt any evil thing against me.'

"She swore the oath at once; and when she had sworn the oath fully and fairly, I entered the bed of Circê.

"Meanwhile, the four maids who served her had been doing their work in the house. These were daughters of springs and trees and sacred rivers that run down into the sea. One of them spread fine coverings upon the seats, a linen sheet beneath and a purple cloth upon it. The second drew tables of silver in front of the seats, and laid on them golden baskets. The third mixt wine in a silver mixer, delicious honey-hearted wine, and set out cups of gold. The fourth brought water and kindled a great fire under a copper. The water grew warm; and when it boiled in the glittering cauldron, she led me to the bath, and bathed me with water out of the cauldron, when she had tempered it to a pleasant warmth, pouring it over my head and shoulders to soothe the heart-breaking weariness from my limbs. And when she had bathed me and rubbed me with olive oil, she gave me a tunic and a wrap to wear.

"Then she led me to the fine carven seat, and set a foot-stool under my feet, and invited me to fall to. But this displeased me; I sat still half-dazed, and my heart was full of foreboding.

"When Circê noticed that I sat still and did not touch the vittles, when she saw how deeply I was troubled, she came near and spoke her mind plainly:

" 'Why do you sit there like a dumb man, Odysseus, and eat your heart out instead of eating your dinner? I suppose you expect some other treachery! You need not be afraid; I have sworn you a solemn oath.'

---

[5] A mountain range in Thessaly, believed by the ancient Greeks to be the home of the gods.

"I answered, 'Ah, Circê! What man with any decent feeling could have the heart to taste food and drink, until he should see his friends free and standing before his eyes? If you really mean this invitation to eat and drink, set them free, that I may see my friends before my eyes!'

"Then Circê took her wand in hand, and walked through the hall, and opened the doors of the sty, and drove them out, looking like a lot of nine-year hogs. As they stood there, she went among them and rubbed a new drug upon each; then the bristles all dropt off which the pernicious drug had grown upon their skin. They became men once more, younger than they were before, and handsomer and taller.

"They knew me, and each grasped my hand; they sobbed aloud for joy till the hall rang again with the noise, and even the goddess was touched. She came close to me, and said:

"'Prince Laërtiadês,[6] Odysseus never at fault! Go down to the seashore where your ship lies. First of all draw up the ship on the beach, and stow all your goods and tackle in a cave; then come back yourself and bring the rest of your companions with you.'

"So I went; and when I reached the shore, I found my companions sitting beside the ship in deep distress. But as soon as they saw me, they were like so many calves in a barnyard, skipping about a drove of cows as they come back to the midden after a good feed of grass; they cannot keep in their pens, but frolic round their dams lowing in a deafening chorus. So the men crowded round me, with tears running down over their cheeks; they felt as glad as if they had come back to their native land, to rugged Ithaca, their home where they were born and bred; and they cried out from their hearts:

"'You are back again, my prince! How glad we are, as glad as if we had come safe home to Ithaca! Now do tell us what has become of our companions!'

"I answered gently, 'First of all we will draw up the ship on shore, and store the tackle and all our belongings in some cave. Then bestir yourselves and come with me, all of you, and you shall see your companions in the sacred house of Circê, eating and drinking. They have enough and to spare.'

"At once they set about the work. And now what should I see but Eurylochos alone trying to stop them! He made no secret of his thoughts:

"'Oh, you poor fools!' he cried out, 'where are we going? Do you want to run your heads into trouble? Go to Circê's house, and let her turn you all into lions or wolves to keep watch for her whether we like it or not? Just Cyclops over again, when our fellows went into his yard, and this same bold Odysseus with them! It was only his rashness that brought them to destruction!'

"When I heard this, I thought for a moment that I would draw my sword and cut off his head, and let it roll on the ground, for all he was my near relation. But the others held me back and did their best to soften me:

"'Let us leave the man here, prince, if you please, let him stay by the ship and look after the ship. Lead the way! We are going with you to Circê's house!'

"Then away they went up from the shore. Indeed, Eurylochos would not be left behind; he came too, for he had a terror of my rough tongue.

"Then Circê gave a bath in her house to my companions, and had them

---

[6] A formal mode of address, signifying that Odysseus is the son of King Laërtes.

rubbed with olive oil, and gave them tunics and woollen wraps. We found all the others feasting merrily in the hall. When they saw one another face to face, and knew one another, their feelings were too much for them; they made such a noise that the roof rang again. And the radiant goddess came up to me, and said:

" 'No more lamentations now, Odysseus! I know myself how many hardships you have suffered on the seas, and how many cruel enemies have attacked you on land. Now then, eat your food and drink your wine until you become as gay as when you first left your rugged home in Ithaca. Just now you are withered and down-hearted, you can't forget your dismal wanderings. Your feelings are not in tune with good cheer, for assuredly you have suffered much.'

"We took her advice; and there we remained for a whole year, with plenty to eat and good wine to drink. . . ."

QUESTIONS

Language

1. Look up the word *simile* in a good dictionary. Find two similes in this selection. Discuss whether they successfully convey the emotions they are meant to suggest. Try making up your own similes to convey the same emotions.
2. Odysseus is telling the story of his encounter with Circe to a large audience some time after it happened. What kind of a storyteller is he? Is his story elaborate or simple? Does he use plain language? Does he give you a complete picture of what happened?
3. Look at the confrontation between Eurylochos and Odysseus on p. 124. Does Odysseus' reaction surprise you? What is his tone when he describes his reaction? Do these things affect your opinion of him?

Content

1. Why must Odysseus' men approach Circe's house? Why are they so apprehensive about doing so? What happens when they arrive at her residence? Given the men's fear, why do you suppose they enter the house so eagerly and carelessly? Does Odysseus enter in a different spirit? Does this seem to you significant?
2. What is Circe like? What is her house like? What reasons are we given for her behavior?
3. What kind of relationship do Odysseus' men have with each other? Does it surprise you that this band of warriors shows emotion so easily?
4. Could Odysseus have defeated the goddess Circe on his own, exceptional mortal that he is? The charm that Hermes gives him, the moly, is a kind of lily; and the lily has long symbolized purity, especially sexual purity. Does the choice of the lily as a charm, then, seem significant to you?
5. When Circe enchants men, what do they lose besides their human shape?

Suggestions for Writing

1. Odysseus is one of the earliest and greatest heroes and leaders of men in Western literature. Most of us have certain ideas about how a hero and leader should act, what he should be like. Write a paper describing Odysseus' character and actions, and evaluating how well he fits *your* version of the hero and leader.
2. Write an essay which examines how women are portrayed in Homer's story. What *feelings* about women seem to be expressed by this narrative?

3. With your classmates, look at Circe's treatment of the men who stumble into her path and her much different confrontation with Odysseus. Why do Odysseus' men lose? How does Odysseus vanquish Circe? Before they even exchange a word with the goddess, do Odysseus and his men have different attitudes toward her? What sorts of things are being said about the relationship between men and women, about the "battle between the sexes"? Write an essay in which you first state what Homer seems to be saying about a woman's attitude toward a man and about how a man should "handle" this woman; then say whether you agree or disagree with the poet.

THE BROTHERS GRIMM

"The Nixie of the Mill-Pond"

Like her supernatural sisters—the sirens, Rusalka, and Lorelei—the nixie in the following Grimms' fairy tale (see the headnote for "The Singing Bone," p. 9) is an alluring but dangerous water-spirit who will promise a man bliss only to exact a terrible payment. As the unfortunate miller in the story discovers, the nixie's gift is not as generous as it seems, for her open-handed gesture soon becomes a death grip which closes on the miller's only son, drawing the young man down into the waters of her dark, enchanted pool.

There was once upon a time a miller who lived with his wife in great contentment. They had money and land, and their prosperity increased year by year more and more. But ill luck comes like a thief in the night: as their wealth had increased so did it again decrease, year by year, and at last the miller could hardly call the mill in which he lived, his own. He was in great distress, and when he lay down after his day's work, found no rest, but tossed about in his bed, sorely troubled. One morning he rose before daybreak and went out into the open air, thinking that perhaps there his heart might become lighter. As he was stepping over the mill-dam the first sunbeam was just breaking forth, and he heard a rippling sound in the pond. He turned round and perceived a beautiful woman, rising slowly out of the water. Her long hair, which she was holding off her shoulders with her soft hands, fell down on both sides, and covered her white body. He soon saw that she was the nixie of the mill-pond, and in his fright did not know whether he should run away or stay where he was. But the nixie made her sweet voice heard, called him by his name, and asked him why he was so sad. The miller was at first struck dumb, but when he heard her speak so kindly, he took heart, and told her how he had formerly lived in wealth and happiness, but that now he was so poor that he did not know what to do. "Be easy," answered the nixie, "I will make you richer and happier than you have ever been before, only you must promise to give me the young thing which has just been born in your house." "What else can that be," thought the miller, "but a puppy or a kitten?" and he promised her what she desired. The nixie

From *The Complete Grimm's Fairy Tales,* by Jakob Ludwig and Wilhelm Karl Grimm, translated by Margaret Hunt and James Stern. Copyright 1944 by Pantheon Books and renewed 1972 by Random House, Inc. Reprinted by permission of Pantheon Books, a Division of Random House, Inc.

descended into the water again, and he hurried back to his mill, consoled and in good spirits. He had not yet reached it, when the maid-servant came out of the house, and cried to him to rejoice, for his wife had given birth to a little boy. The miller stood as if struck by lightning; he saw very well that the cunning nixie had been aware of it, and had cheated him. Hanging his head, he went up to his wife's bedside and when she said: "Why do you not rejoice over the fine boy?" he told her what had befallen him, and what kind of a promise he had given to the nixie. "Of what use to me are riches and prosperity?" he added, "if I am to lose my child; but what can I do?" Even the relatives, who had come thither to wish them joy, did not know what to say. In the meantime prosperity again returned to the miller's house. All that he undertook succeeded. It was as if presses and coffers filled themselves of their own accord, and as if money multiplied nightly in the cupboards. It was not long before his wealth was greater than it had ever been before. But he could not rejoice over it untroubled, for the bargain which he had made with the nixie tormented his soul. Whenever he passed the mill-pond, he feared she might ascend and remind him of his debt. He never let the boy himself go near the water. "Beware," he said to him, "if you do but touch the water, a hand will rise, seize you, and draw you down." But as year after year went by and the nixie did not show herself again, the miller began to feel at ease. The boy grew up to be a youth and was apprenticed to a huntsman. When he had learnt everything, and had become an excellent huntsman, the lord of the village took him into his service. In the village lived a beautiful and true-hearted maiden, who pleased the huntsman, and when his master perceived that, he gave him a little house, the two were married, lived peacefully and happily, and loved each other with all their hearts.

One day the huntsman was chasing a roe; and when the animal turned aside from the forest into the open country, he pursued it and at last shot it. He did not notice that he was now in the neighborhood of the dangerous mill-pond, and went, after he had disembowelled the roe, to the water, in order to wash his blood-stained hands. Scarcely, however, had he dipped them in than the nixie ascended, smilingly wound her dripping arms around him, and drew him quickly down under the waves, which closed over him. When it was evening, and the huntsman did not return home, his wife became alarmed. She went out to seek him, and as he had often told her that he had to be on his guard against the snares of the nixie, and dared not venture into the neighborhood of the mill-pond, she already suspected what had happened. She hastened to the water, and when she found his hunting-pouch lying on the shore, she could no longer have any doubt of the misfortune. Lamenting her sorrow, and wringing her hands, she called on her beloved by name, but in vain. She hurried across to the other side of the pond, and called him anew; she reviled the nixie with harsh words, but no answer greeted her. The surface of the water remained calm, only the crescent moon stared steadily back at her. The poor woman did not leave the pond. With hasty steps, she paced round and round it, without resting a moment, sometimes in silence, sometimes uttering a loud cry, sometimes softly sobbing. At last her strength came to an end, she sank down to the ground and fell into a heavy sleep. Presently a dream took possession of her.

She was anxiously climbing upwards between great masses of rock; thorns and briars caught her feet, the rain beat in her face, and the wind tossed her long hair about. When she had reached the summit, quite a different sight presented itself to her; the sky was blue, the air soft, the ground sloped gently downwards, and on a green meadow, gay with flowers of every color, stood a pretty cottage. She went up to it and opened the door; there sat an old woman with white hair, who beckoned to her kindly. At that very moment, the poor woman awoke, day had already dawned, and she at once resolved to act in accordance with her dream. She laboriously climbed the mountain; everything was exactly as she had seen it in the night. The old woman received her kindly, and pointed out a chair on which she might sit. "You must have met with a misfortune," she said, "since you have sought out my lonely cottage." With tears, the woman related what had befallen her. "Be comforted," said the old woman, "I will help you. Here is a golden comb for you. Tarry till the full moon has risen, then go to the mill-pond, seat yourself on the shore, and comb your long black hair with this comb. When you have done, lay it down on the bank, and you will see what will happen." The woman returned home, but the time till the full moon came, passed slowly. When at last the shining disc appeared in the heavens, she went out to the mill-pond, sat down and combed her long black hair with the golden comb, and when she had finished, she laid it down at the water's edge. It was not long before there was a movement in the depths, a wave rose, rolled to the shore, and bore the comb away with it. In not more than the time necessary for the comb to sink to the bottom, the surface of the water parted, and the head of the huntsman arose. He did not speak, but looked at his wife with sorrowful glances. At the same instant, a second wave came rushing up, and covered the man's head. All had vanished, the mill-pond lay peaceful as before, and nothing but the face of the full moon shone on it.

Full of sorrow, the woman went back, but again the dream showed her the cottage of the old woman. Next morning she again set out and complained of her woes to the wise woman. The old woman gave her a golden flute, and said: "Tarry till the full moon comes again, then take this flute; play a beautiful air on it, and when you have finished, lay it on the sand; then you will see what will happen." The wife did as the old woman told her. No sooner was the flute lying on the sand than there was a stirring in the depths, and a wave rushed up and bore the flute away with it. Immediately afterwards the water parted, and not only the head of the man, but half of his body also arose. He stretched out his arms longingly towards her, but a second wave came up, covered him, and drew him down again. "Alas, what does it help me," said the unhappy woman, "that I should see my beloved, only to lose him again?" Despair filled her heart anew, but the dream led her a third time to the house of the old woman. She set out, and the wise woman gave her a golden spinning-wheel, consoled her and said: "All is not yet fulfilled, tarry until the time of the full moon, then take the spinning-wheel, seat yourself on the shore, and spin the spool full, and when you have done that, place the spinning-wheel near the water, and you will see what will happen." The woman obeyed all she said exactly; as soon as the full moon showed itself, she carried the golden spinning-wheel to the shore, and span industriously until the flax came to an end, and the spool was quite filled with the threads. No sooner was the wheel standing on the shore than there was a more violent movement than before in the depths of the pond, and a mighty wave rushed up, and bore the wheel away with it. Immediately the head and the whole body of the man rose into the air, in a water-spout. He quickly sprang to the shore, caught his wife by the hand and fled. But they had scarcely gone a very little distance, when the whole pond rose with a frightful roar, and streamed out over the open country. The fugitives already saw death before their eyes, when the woman in her terror implored the help of the old woman, and in an instant they were transformed, she into a toad, he into a frog. The flood which had overtaken them could not destroy them, but it tore them apart and carried them far away.

When the water had dispersed and they both touched dry land again, they regained their human form, but neither knew where the other was; they found themselves among strange people, who did not know their native land. High mountains and deep valleys lay between them. In order to keep themselves alive, they were both obliged to tend sheep. For many long years they drove their flocks through field and forest and were full of sorrow and longing.

When spring had once more broken forth on the earth, they both went out one day with their flocks, and as chance would have it they drew near each other. They met in a valley, but did not recognize each other; yet they rejoiced that they were no longer so lonely. Henceforth they each day drove their flocks to the same place; they did not speak much, but they felt comforted. One evening when the full moon was shining in the sky, and the sheep were already at rest, the shepherd pulled the flute out of his pocket, and played on it a beautiful but sorrowful air. When he had finished he saw that the shepherdess was weeping bitterly. "Why are you weeping?" he asked. "Alas," answered she, "thus shone the full moon when I played this air on the flute for the last time, and the head of my beloved rose out of the water." He looked at her, and it seemed as if a veil fell from his eyes, and he recognized his dear wife, and when she looked at him, and the moon shone in his face she knew him also. They embraced and kissed each other, and no one need ask if they were happy.

QUESTIONS

Language

1. Look at the paragraph divisions in this fairy tale; as is often the case with this kind of story, the paragraphs are unusually long. With your class, discuss how each long paragraph might be separated into two or more smaller paragraphs. Indicate in each case which sentence would begin a new paragraph, and justify your choice of division points. Afterwards, generalize about what you've just done: formulate general rules for paragraph division.

Content

1. What makes the miller trust the nixie? Do you think he is foolish to bargain with her when he's not absolutely sure what she wants? Is he guilty of underestimating her?
2. Does it seem strange to you that the miller would not know his wife is pregnant? Is it unfair that the son must pay for his father's prosperity?
3. The young man has been warned repeatedly that he must not approach the mill-pond, yet one day he carelessly does so. Do you think he could have successfully avoided it forever?
4. Look at the last two paragraphs of this fairy tale. Do they seem to belong to the rest of it? Write your own alternative ending for the story.
5. The wife offers the nixie a golden comb, flute, and spinning wheel. What do you think the significance of these three gifts is?
6. Why do you think the husband and wife don't know each other when they finally meet again?

Suggestions for Writing

1. The nixie, like all such Temptresses, represents certain negative characteristics which male fantasy often attributes to women. What are these negative characteristics? That is to say, what is the nixie like? How is she different from the wife, the other beautiful young woman in this tale? Do you think the wife is idealized? Write an essay comparing and contrasting the two female figures and the qualities they possess.

2. Write a story which tells what happens to the young man from the time he is pulled down under the water by the nixie until the time he is released by his wife's third gift. Imagine the underwater world as completely as possible; include many concrete details; and record the young man's feelings about what is happening to him. Try to capture the *tone* of the Grimm fairy tale, and use its same level of vocabulary.

3. One way to look at this tale is to see it as a symbolic means of showing what happens when a young husband leaves the security of his home and, rather without thinking, becomes involved with another woman. Write a paper exploring the fairy tale in these terms. (You might want to ask yourself who the old woman the young wife seeks out is.) What might the *function* of the fairy tale then be? Why would people tell it to each other and read it for centuries?

SANGER D. SHAFER AND LEFTY FRIZZELL

"Bandy the Rodeo Clown"

(as recorded by Moe Bandy)

A common masculine fear connected with the fantasy of the Temptress is that of being drained of power by such a woman, of being emasculated, reduced to something less than a man—to her servant, pet, or fool. A country-western song which gives expression to this fear, "Bandy the Rodeo Clown" tells the story of a robust, virile man, a champion "bronco buster," who falls victim to a beautiful but faithless woman and degenerates into a pitiful buffoon. The song was a big success for Moe Bandy, a one-time rodeo rider himself, who has recorded several hit singles since 1973, including "I Just Started Hatin' Cheatin' Songs Today," "It Was Always So Easy to Find an Unhappy Woman," "She Took More than Her Share," and "Hank Williams, You Wrote My Life."

"Bandy the Rodeo Clown"

Who was once a bull hookin' son-of-a-gun
Now, who keeps a pint hid out behind chute number one
Who was ridin' high 'til a pretty girl rode him to the ground
    Any kid knows where to find me
    I'm Bandy, the rodeo clown.

"Bandy the Rodeo Clown" by Sanger D. Shafer and Lefty Frizzell. © Copyright 1975 by Acuff-Rose Publications, Inc. Used by permission of the publisher. All rights reserved.

I could ride 'em all
The bulls and the broncs know I was boss
But the ride that woman took me on
Broke a whole lot more than this ole cowboy's bones
While the tears on my make-up melt my painted smile into a frown
   The crowd thinks I'm a dandy
     I'm Bandy the rodeo clown.

In the ridin' and ropin' I was closin' in on number one
Now in dreams at night I ride on that silver saddle I never won
Since she left me the whiskey takes me to the rodeo grounds
   Where the cowboys think I'm handy
     I'm Bandy the rodeo clown.

QUESTIONS

Language

1. Not until the end of the first stanza or verse of this song do we learn who the speaker is. Why do the lyricists begin their song in the way they do? Would the impact of the stanza be changed much if each of the first three lines began with "I" instead of the relative pronoun "who"?
2. The speaker or singer uses several rodeo metaphors to characterize the woman who betrayed him. What are they? Would a cowboy express himself this way? Why or why not?
3. How would you describe the *tone* of the speaker's voice? That is, what sorts of things does he seem to be feeling as he sings his story?

Content

1. What was the speaker like before the Temptress entered his life? And after? How does he evaluate himself?
2. The speaker tells us how the crowd—the rodeo audience—and the cowboys respond to him. How do you think he feels about their view of him?
3. Do you think other people know about Bandy's trouble? What means does he use to cover it up?

Suggestions for Writing

1. Have you ever had a close relationship with another person come to an end because that person didn't want to be involved with you any longer? How did you react? Did your reactions change as the days went by; did your *view* of the relationship and its end change also? Write an essay on this topic, paying particular attention to the effects the sudden end of the relationship had on you. Alternatively, write an essay about your decision to terminate a relationship with another person, the events and feelings leading up to your decision, and the effect on you afterwards.
2. Beneath the surface of this song lies an ancient male fear: that excessive romantic involvement with a woman prevents men from achieving their goals, whatever they are—athletic, intellectual, practical, etc. Discuss in class whether you think this fear is justified; then write an essay arguing that it is or isn't, supporting your opinion with personal experiences or observations.

BILLY SHERRILL

"Woman to Woman"

(as recorded by Tammy Wynette)

One of the "queens of country music," Tammy Wynette (the professional name of Wynette Pugh) was born in Tupelo, Mississippi, in 1942, though she grew up in Birmingham, Alabama, where her mother had moved after the death of the young girl's father. Even as a child, Wynette aspired to a career as a singer, but after marrying at the age of seventeen, she settled down instead to a life as a housewife and part-time beautician. During her third pregnancy, however, her marriage broke up, and when the baby subsequently developed spinal meningitis, she decided to supplement her beautician's wages by becoming a professional singer. After a stint during the mid-sixties on a local Birmingham television program, "The Country Boy Eddie Show," Wynette traveled to Nashville and auditioned with several record companies. Signing with Epic Records, she cut a string of enormously successful singles—"Apartment No. 9" "Your Good Girl's Gonna Go Bad," "I Don't Want to Play House," "D-I-V-O-R-C-E," "Stand by Your Man," and others—all made with record producer Billy Sherrill, who also wrote some of her hits, including the one reprinted here. In 1968, she married country star George Jones, who became her partner in a popular singing team, which lasted until their highly publicized divorce in 1975.

"Woman to Woman" is typical of Tammy Wynette's songs (and indeed of contemporary country-western music in general), which often deal with the problem of marital infidelity—or "cheatin'"—and the inability of men to resist the charms of housebreaking Temptresses.

"Woman to Woman"

If you think you got your man in the
   palm of your hand, you better listen,
And if you think you got it made and his
   love will never fade, you better listen.

She's out there, too, and she's a whole lot
   better lookin' than me and you,
And she can do things to a man you
   never dreamed a woman can do.

If you think you keep your man with a
   golden wedding band, you better listen,
And if you're sittin' there at home thinking'
   how good you turn him on, you better listen.

Reprinted with permission of Algee Music. Copyright © 1974.

She's sweet when she talks and she bounces
   all over when she walks,
And she's forgot more about a man than your
   Sweet mama ever told you.

I'm talkin' woman to woman,
Heart to heart,
I'm singin' straight to you.
Just woman to woman,
Right from my heart.
And you can take it or leave it,
Ah, but it's true.
Woman to woman,
Me to you.

QUESTIONS

Language

1. What is the tone of this song? What kind of mood does the speaker (the woman who is talking) seem to be in? What emotional response is the song supposed to produce in the woman being spoken to? How do *you* respond?
2. In this song we learn about the Temptress through the eyes of another woman. We are told some specific things directly; in addition other characteristics of the Temptress are merely hinted at. What do we know about her? Which line or phrase best conveys her dangerous nature?
3. Find the words that rhyme in the lines of this song. Why doesn't every line contain a rhyme? Why do popular song writers use rhymes at all?

Content

1. Try to describe what the speaker of this song looks like, acts like, and so on. Then picture and describe the woman she is speaking about. How are they different? What might be the personal history of each woman?
2. What kind of relationship does the speaker seem to have with the woman she is talking to? Do you think they are close? Would you say they're about the same age?
3. This song is essentially a warning. What are the things the speaker warns the listening woman about? That is, is it a warning about more than the Temptress?
4. How are women viewed by the speaker of this song? Do you think her ideas are silly? Why or why not?
5. Though recorded by a woman, this song was written by a man. Does this fact make the song more or less threatening to women? Why?

Suggestions for Writing

1. Discuss in class your reaction to this song. Is the female students' emotional reaction to it different from that of the male students? If so, why? Is the Temptress figure in this song viewed differently by each sex? After your discussion, write an essay comparing and contrasting the two reactions.
2. That a certain view of women is expressed by this song is clear; less clear, perhaps, is the fact that a particular view of *men* is expressed. Write an essay analyzing what the man pictured by ''Woman to Woman'' is like.

3. Have you ever had to call a friend and criticize or give him or her some unpleasant news? What happened? Was it hard for you to do? How did the friend react? Did your friendship survive the incident? Write a personal experience paper which presents the events that led up to the call (the *causes* for the action you took) and the *effects* of it.

DON HENLEY AND BERNIE LEADON

"Witchy Woman"

(as recorded by the Eagles)

With singles and albums that consistently "go platinum" (music industry jargon, meaning that a record has sold a million or more copies), the Eagles are one of the most popular of contemporary rock acts. Originally the back-up band for country star Linda Ronstadt, the four-member group—consisting of Glenn Frey and Don Henley (who write most of the lyrics), Randy Meisner, and Bernie Leadon—made its first album, *Eagles,* in 1972. Two more bestselling LPs followed: *Desperado* (a "concept" album which uses the metaphor of the Western outlaw to explore the rock musician's way of life) and *On the Border,* a record made with the assistance of slide-guitarist Don Felder, who subsequently joined the group. In 1976, following the release of a fourth album, *One of These Nights,* Leadon quit the band and was replaced by Joe Walsh, whose first album with the Eagles was *Hotel California.* Like its predecessors, this LP is characterized by country-flavored music, slick harmonies, and lyrics which—either directly or in allegorical form—portray the seductions and dangers of fast-paced West Coast life-styles.

"Witchy Woman," from the 1972 debut album, *Eagles,* was an early hit single for the group.

"Witchy Woman"

Raven hair and ruby lips,
Sparks fly from her fingertips,
Echoed voices in the night,
She's a restless spirit on an endless flight.

Woo-hoo witchy woman
See how high she flies.
Woo-hoo witchy woman,
She got the moon in her eyes.

She held me spellbound in the night,
Dancing shadows and firelight,
Crazy laughter in another room,
And she drove herself to madness with a silver spoon.

© 1973 WB Music Corp. & Kicking Bear Music. All rights reserved. Used by permission.

I know you love her,
But let me tell you brother,
She's been sleepin' in the devil's bed.
There's some rumors goin' round,
Someone's underground,
She can rock you in the night until your skin turn red.

Woo-hoo witchy woman,
See how high she flies.
Woo-hoo witchy woman,
She got the moon in her eyes.

QUESTIONS

Language

1. Which lines or phrases best convey the *strangeness* of the woman in the Eagles' song? Why would the singer or speaker describe her in such bizarre terms?
2. The Temptress is called a "witch," which becomes the central metaphor of the song. Find the various phrases and lines that help develop or expand this metaphor, that reemphasize the woman's "witchiness."
3. Rock musicians, like all popular music composers, try to capture the feel of ordinary speech in their lyrics. Find words or phrases in "Witchy Woman" that prove this.

Content

1. What do you think the line "She drove herself to madness with a silver spoon" means? What is the silver spoon? And do you think the speaker means that the woman has destroyed herself as well as her victims?
2. What does the line "Someone's underground" suggest?
3. What is the appeal of the "witchy woman"? Why is it necessary for the speaker to warn others against her? Do her victims participate willingly in what she does to them? How does she get the power she has over them?
4. Discuss whether you think the song would have the same impact if the woman in it had blond hair and blue eyes. Why or why not?

Suggestions for Writing

1. Can you picture the woman of the song during the day? If so, what would she be like? Act like? What would her daily life be like? If you *can't* picture her during the day, why not? Do the words of the song prevent you from doing it? How? Discuss this issue in class; then write an essay maintaining either that you can picture her or that you can't, elaborating on your position.
2. Both "Woman to Woman" (p. 132) and this song (which might be called "Man to Man") are *warnings* about a particular kind of woman, and the men who fall prey to her. Compare and contrast how the two songs portray that woman, her male victims, the relationship between the Temptress and her prey, and how the songs apportion blame—how much they blame the woman and how much they blame her "victims." Remember that both songs are written by men.

HAL FOSTER

Prince Valiant

As a young man growing up in Canada, Harold ("Hal") Foster (b. 1892) led an adventurous life which included periods spent as a fur trapper, prize fighter, and—later on, along with his wife—gold prospector and wilderness guide. Having displayed a talent for drawing at an early age, he also supported himself intermittently by working as a staff artist for a mail-order house and as a free-lance illustrator. In 1921, having earned and then lost a fortune as a miner, he decided to study art seriously and traveled by bicycle from Manitoba to Chicago, where he attended the Arts Institute, the National Academy of Design, and the Chicago Academy of Fine Arts. He worked for several years as an advertising artist and magazine illustrator and then, in 1929, accepted a job drawing the first newspaper comic strip version of Edgar Rice Burroughs' *Tarzan of the Apes.* After the completion of the ten-week serialization (consisting of sixty daily strips), he went back to his advertising work, but returned to the *Tarzan* strip in 1931 as the illustrator of the Sunday color pages, which he drew for the next six years.

As early as 1934, Foster had wanted to do his own adventure strip, a saga set in medieval times and based on the legends of King Arthur and his knights. His chance finally came in 1937; in February of that year the first episode of *Prince Valiant* appeared in the pages of the New York *Journal.* Foster's famous strip is remarkable for the virtuosity of the draftsmanship, the complexity of the plot and characterizations, and the richness and authenticity of the background details. These qualities—plus Foster's technique of printing his text along the top or bottom edges of each panel, thereby eliminating word "balloons" from the drawings—make *Prince Valiant* seem more like an illustrated novel than a conventional comic strip.

The story centers on Valiant, the son of the exiled King of Thule. After a rough and adventurous boyhood in the British marshes, Val journeys to Camelot, where he first becomes squire to Sir Gawain and later, after winning the admiration of King Arthur, a full-fledged Knight of the Round Table. Returning to his home, he helps his father regain his throne, then sets out on a life of adventure, as a wandering "knight errant." In subsequent years, he marries Princess Aleta, "Queen of the Misty Isles," settles down and has four children, including a son named Arn who gradually takes over as the strip's central character.

Foster gave up drawing the strip in 1971, though he continued to write it. The following pages originally appeared in April, 1939.

© King Features Syndicate, Inc. 1939

Prince Valiant

Registered U. S. Patent Office

IN THE DAYS OF
KING ARTHUR
BY
HAROLD R. FOSTER

SYNOPSIS—VAL TAKES REFUGE FROM A STORM IN WHAT HE BELIEVES IS AN EMPTY CAVE. HEARING A SLIGHT COUGH HE TURNS, STARTLED, TO FIND A STRANGE WOMAN STANDING BEHIND HIM.

"PARDON, LADY, DO I TRESPASS?"

"NO, LAD, FOR SOONER OR LATER ALL THINGS MUST COME AT LAST TO THIS FORLORN PLACE," ANSWERED THE WITCH-WOMAN. "SHALL WE DINE?"

"I DO NOT UNDERSTAND THE MEANING OF YOUR WORDS, BUT YOUR WINE IS POTENT, ALREADY MY HEAD SWIMS."

"THIS CAVE IS THE TROPHY-ROOM OF TIME, WHICH NO ONE DARE ENTER."

"I'LL DARE ANY ADVENTURE!" AND DRAWING THE 'SINGING SWORD', VAL ENTERS THE SILENT GLOOM.

A BLUE AND SINISTER GLOW ILLUMINATES THIS MISCHANCY PLACE. IN A FAR CORNER THE BENT FIGURE OF AN AGED MAN CAN BE DIMLY SEEN.

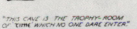

"WHO ARE YOU?" FALTERS THE SCARED YOUTH. "I AM THE ULTIMATE CONQUEROR OF ALL THINGS AND MY TROPHIES ARE THE ALTARS OF FORGOTTEN GODS, THE THRONES OF KINGS, SPLENDID CITIES AND FORTRESSES UNCONQUERABLE."

"NONE MAY WITHSTAND TIME.... I VANQUISH THEM ALL IN THE END.... WOULD YOU CARE TO WRESTLE WITH ME?"

NEXT WEEK: THE CONTEST

Prince Valiant

Registered U. S. Patent Office.

IN THE DAYS OF
KING ARTHUR
BY
HAROLD R FOSTER

SYNOPSIS: IN THE SHELTER OF A GREAT CAVE VAL MEETS A WITCH-WOMAN WHO GIVES HIM A POTENT DRINK AND A GRIM WARNING, WHICH HE IGNORES AND ENTERS THE ABODE OF "TIME."

"YOU DON'T BELIEVE THAT 'TIME' IS UNCONQUERABLE...THEN SHALL WE WRESTLE?"

THE STALWART YOUTH PICKS UP THE SENILE OLD MAN TO FLING HIM AMONG HIS DUSTY TROPHIES.

BUT THE ANCIENT CREATURE CLINGS TENA-CIOUSLY WITH WEAK, FRAIL HANDS, AS VAL STRIVES TO FREE HIMSELF.

HOW LONG THEY STRUGGLED IN THAT WEIRD, DIM PLACE VAL COULD NEVER AFTERWARDS TELL, BUT HE GROWS WEARY... WEARY....

WITH A CACKLING LAUGH "TIME" HURLS HIS SKINNY ADVERSARY AMONG THE WORLD'S DISCARDED TOYS.

AS VAL STUMBLES OUT OF THAT FANTASTIC CAVERN HE HEARS A THIN, CRACKED VOICE GLOATING, "ALL CONTEND WITH 'TIME' AND ALL ARE VANQUISHED."

SAVE THIS STAMP

MORGAN LE FEY

AT THE CAVE'S MOUTH THE WITCH-WOMAN CALMLY WAITS THE RETURN OF ALL THAT REMAINS OF A PROUD PRINCE.

"YOU MUST BE TIRED, GRANDFATHER, SIT DOWN AND REFRESH YOURSELF."

116   4-30-39

VAL DRAINS THE CUP.

NEXT WEEK: THE WANDERER

Prince Valiant

IN THE DAYS OF KING ARTHUR BY HAROLD R. FOSTER

Registered U.S. Patent Office.

SYNOPSIS: THE WITCH-WOMAN GIVES VAL A POTENT DRINK AND A WARNING WHICH HE IGNORES. ENTERING THE CAVE HE WRESTLES WITH **TIME** AND IS VANQUISHED.

"DRINK AND BE REFRESHED POOR, RECKLESS FOOL." THE WEARY OLD PRINCE GRASPS THE GOBLET.

"AH! HOW STIMULATING IS THE WINE," SAYS VAL, LOWERING THE CUP.

THEN TERROR SEIZES HIM AND HE FLEES "'TIS A HORRIBLE TRICK, NO SUCH THING COULD POSSIBLY HAVE HAPPENED!"

"HOW TERRIBLE TO BE OLD AND WEAK AND HOW GOOD IT IS TO BE YOUNG AND STRONG AGAIN — I MUST REMEMBER THAT."

HE RIDES FAR AND COMES TO THE SEA OVER WHICH A GREAT STORM IS APPROACHING.

LIGHTS SHINING THROUGH THE STORM PROMISE SHELTER.

HE FINDS A TAVERN FREQUENTED BY SAILORS AND TRAVELERS FROM FAR, STRANGE LANDS.

117-5-7-39

AS THE STORM WITHOUT RAGES, WEIRD TALES ARE TOLD OF FABULOUS ISLES AND WONDROUS WALLED CITIES.

AND ALL THIS WHILE A HAGGARD WANDERER IS NEARING THE TAVERN WITH ASTOUNDING NEWS.

NEXT WEEK "ROME HAS FALLEN!"

BATTERING RAM — SAVE THIS STAMP

SIEGE TOWER — SAVE THIS STAMP

MANGONEL — SAVE THIS STAMP

CHARIOT OF WAR — SAVE THIS STAMP

QUESTIONS

Language

1. Foster says that the cave Prince Valiant enters is a "mischancy" place. Does such a word exist? What effect is Foster trying to achieve in using it?
2. Look at the conversations the various characters in this comic have with one another. How would you describe their language? Do they sound like the characters in some of the other comics in this book? Do you think the way Foster's figures speak is appropriate to the rest of the material that makes up his strip?

Content

1. Both the woman and Val *seem* to be about the same age, yet she calls him "lad." Does this tell us something important about her? Look at her speech in the second panel. What do you think her tone is here? How would you interpret the expression on her face?
2. What kind of young man is Val? What are his good qualities? His bad? Describe him as fully as you can.
3. Exactly how does the witch-woman get Val to enter more deeply into her cave?
4. The old man tells Val that his trophies include "the altars of forgotten gods, the thrones of kings, splendid cities and fortresses unconquerable." What do all these things have in common? What is he trying to tell Val?
5. Do the woman and the old man seem to share the same attitude toward Val? Do they each help to deplete and defeat him? What kind of powers does the witch-woman have?
6. Val has ridden his horse partly into the cave. Note that when he is defeated and aged, his horse becomes a pile of bones, but is resurrected as Val is magically restored to youth and vigor by the woman. Why would Foster involve the horse this way?

Suggestions for Writing

1. Val's terrible trials begin when he enters the home of a beautiful woman, decides to spend the night, and accepts the food and drink she offers. Remembering that Val is a warrior who has dedicated his life to heroic ideals and action rather than to leisure and pleasure, write an essay on the *moral* of this comic strip.
2. Hal Foster's *Prince Valiant* has been running continuously in American newspapers since 1937; his young hero's face is familiar to readers from California to New York. Yet a comic strip further removed from modern America in plot, character, costume, setting, manners, and ways of speaking can hardly be imagined. Discuss in class and then write an essay about the perennial appeal of the Foster comic. What makes it so popular? What need does it satisfy?
3. Write an essay saying how this episode from Prince Valiant is like a dream or nightmare. Refer to specific details in the pictures, to the things that happen to Val, to the lack of logic or reality in the cave Val enters.

H. ANTOINE D'ARCY

"The Face Upon the Floor"

The child of a French father and English mother, Hugh Antoine D'Arcy (1843–1925) was born in France but, at an early age, emigrated to England with his parents. At fifteen, he began working in the theater, playing juvenile roles on the stage; later, he attended Ipswich University. Moving to America in 1871, he pursued a career as an actor, manager, and popular poet. His best-known work is the sentimental ballad "The Face Upon the Floor," supposedly inspired by an incident which occurred one evening in Joe Schmidt's tavern, a popular gathering place for theater people in turn-of-the-century New York.

The piece appeared first in the New York *Dispatch* in 1887 and was an immediate hit. Copies of the poem soon reached England and "in no time," D'Arcy reports, "it was being read in three of the biggest music halls in London." But, despite the poem's success, D'Arcy never made a penny from it, partly because a rival version, entitled "The Face on the Barroom Floor," soon began making the rounds. To set the record straight, D'Arcy issued, in 1912, a slim volume of poems entitled *The Face Upon the Floor and Other Ballads*, from which the following—"the true and original story"—is taken.

"The Face Upon the Floor"

'Twas a balmy summer evening, and a goodly crowd was there,
Which well-nigh filled Joe's bar-room on the corner of the square;
And as songs and witty stories came through the open door
A vagabond crept slowly in and posed upon the floor.

"Where did it come from?" some one said. "The wind has blown it in."
"What does it want?" another cried. "Some whiskey, rum or gin."
"Here, Toby, sic him if your stomach's equal to the work—
I wouldn't touch him with a fork, he's as filthy as a Turk."

This badinage the poor wretch took with stoical good grace;
In fact he smiled, as though he thought he'd struck the proper place.
"Come, boys, I know there's burly hearts among so good a crowd,
To be in such good company would make a deacon proud.

"Give me a drink—that's what I want—I'm out of funds you know,
When I had cash to treat the gang this hand was never slow.
What? You laugh as though you thought this pocket never held a sou!
I once was fixed as well, my boys, as any one of you.

"There, thanks! that's braced me nicely. God bless you one and all!
Next time I pass this good saloon I'll make another call.
Give you a song? No, I can't do that; my singing days are past;
My voice is cracked, my throat's worn out, and my lungs are going fast.

From *The Face Upon the Floor and Other Ballads*, by Hugh Antoine D'Arcy, 1912.

"Say! give me another whiskey, and I tell you what I'll do—
I'll tell you a funny story, and a fact, I promise, too.
That I was ever a decent man not one of you would think;
But I was, some four or five years back. Say, give me another drink.

"Fill her up, Joe; I want to put some life into my frame—
Such little drinks to a bum like me are miserably tame;
Five fingers—there, that's the scheme—and corking whiskey, too!
Well, here's luck, boys! and, landlord, my best regards to you!

"You've treated me pretty kindly, and I'd like to tell you how
I came to be the dirty sot you see before you now.
As I told you, once I was a man, with muscle, frame and health,
And but for a blunder ought to have made considerable wealth.

"I was a painter—not one that daubs on bricks and wood;
But an artist, and for my age was rated pretty good.
I worked hard at my canvas, and was bidding fair to rise,
For gradually I saw the star of fame before my eyes.

"I made a picture perhaps you've seen, 'tis called 'The Chase of Fame?'
It brought me fifteen hundred pounds and added to my name.
And then I met a woman—now comes the funny part—
With eyes that petrified my brain and sunk into my heart.

"Why don't you laugh? 'Tis funny that the vagabond you see
Could ever love a woman and expect her love for me;
But 'twas so, and for a month or two her smiles were freely given,
And when her lovely lips touched mine it carried me to heaven.

"Did you ever see a woman for whom your soul you'd give,
With a form like the Milo Venus, too beautiful to live;
With eyes that would beat the Koh-i-noor,[1] and a wealth of chestnut hair?
If so, 'twas she, for there never was another half so fair.

"I was working on a portrait, one afternoon in May,
Of a fair-haired boy, a friend of mine, who lived across the way;
And Madeleine admired it, and, much to my surprise;
Said that she'd like to know the man that had such dreamy eyes.

"It didn't take long to know him, and before the month had flown
My friend had stolen my darling, and I was left alone;
And ere a year of misery had passed above my head
The jewel I had treasured so had tarnished, and was dead!

"That's why I took to drink, boys. Why, I never saw you smile!
I thought you'd be amused, and laughing all the while.
Why, what's the matter, friend? There's a tear-drop in your eye!
Come, laugh, like me; 'tis only babes and women that should cry.

---

[1] From the Persian kŏh-i-nūr, meaning "mountain of light": a 109-carat diamond discovered in India
and added to the British crown jewels in 1849.

"Say, boys! if you give me just another whiskey I'll be glad,
And I'll draw right here a picture of the face that drove me mad.
Give me that piece of chalk with which you mark the baseball score,
You shall see the lovely Madeleine upon the bar-room floor."

Another drink, and with chalk in hand the vagabond began
To sketch a face that well might buy the soul of any man;
Then as he placed another lock upon the shapely head,
With a fearful shriek he leaped and fell across the picture—dead.

QUESTIONS

Language

1. Most of this poem is a monologue delivered by the vagabond. How does D'Arcy let you know what is happening in the room as the vagabond is speaking?
2. What does the ex-painter mean in the seventh stanza by "five fingers"? And what is "corking whiskey"?
3. What words does the vagabond use to refer to himself? What do they reveal about his opinion of himself?

Content

1. How do the men in the bar greet the new arrival? Do you think they are mean or just humorous?
2. How does the ex-painter react to his tormentors? How does he get a drink out of them?
3. The ex-painter says Madeleine was the kind of woman "for whom your soul you'd give . . ." In what sense did he lose his soul for her?
4. The vagabond repeatedly calls his story "funny." Do you think he thinks it is? Do his listeners? Do you? Can you find elements of humor in it, or in the way it's told?
5. Do you like the poem's ending? What point do you think D'Arcy is trying to make by having the vagabond die in the way he does?

Suggestions for Writing

1. Picture Joe's barroom to yourself—its furnishings, its inhabitants—and then describe it in as much detail as you can. Make your description vivid and interesting.
2. Write the story of Madeleine's relationship with the painter from *her* point of view; tell the story in the first person.
3. Alternatively, write a short narrative which indicates what happened during the year after Madeleine abandoned the painter. End with her death, and *account* for her death, as D'Arcy does not.

BRAM STOKER

from *Dracula*

Dracula was the creation of Abraham ("Bram") Stoker (1847–1922), a British writer who based his famous horror story, which was published in 1897, on eastern European vampire lore as well as on legends of an actual Rumanian count called Vlad the Impaler (also known as Dracula, "Son of the Devil"). Stoker, born in Dublin, was a sickly child and an invalid throughout most of his boyhood, though by the time he entered Dublin University in 1864, he had so developed his strength that he distinguished himself as a college athlete. During his twenties, while working for the Irish Civil Service, he began writing drama reviews for the Dublin *Mail.* Enthralled by the performances of the famous English actor Henry Irving, Stoker quit his government job in 1878 to become Irving's private secretary, remaining with him for the next twenty-seven years.

Dracula is told from various points of view, through the letters, diaries, journals, and even phonograph recordings of its principal characters. As the book opens, we are introduced to young Jonathan Harker, a real-estate agent from London, who is on his way to Transylvania to arrange for the sale of an English estate to the mysterious Count Dracula. Dracula's purpose in moving to England is to find fresh blood, though Harker, of course, does not know this. By the time he discovers just who—or what—the count is, he can do nothing to prevent the diabolical plan, for he discovers at the same time that he is a helpless prisoner in the vampire's unholy castle, which is also inhabited by Dracula's ghoulish brides. The vampire sails for England, and the rest of the novel focuses on his attacks on two women— Lucy Westenra and Harker's own wife, Mina—and on the attempts of a closely knit group of companions, led by the Dutch vampire expert, Dr. Abraham Van Helsing, to find and destroy the monster.

As this scene from the novel opens, Harker has left his own rooms in the Transylvania castle and wandered into a part of it Dracula has warned him not to enter.

JONATHAN HARKER'S JOURNAL—*continued.*

15 May.— . . . I was now in a wing of the castle further to the right than the rooms I knew and a storey lower down. From the windows I could see that the suite of rooms lay along to the south of the castle, the windows of the end room looking out both west and south. On the latter side, as well as to the former, there was a great precipice. The castle was built on the corner of a great rock, so that on three sides it was quite impregnable, and great windows were placed here where sling, or bow, or culverin could not reach, and consequently light and comfort, impossible to a position which had to be guarded, were secured. To the west was a great valley, and then, rising far away, great jagged mountain fastnesses, rising peak on peak, the sheer rock studded with mountain ash and thorn, whose roots clung in cracks and crevices and crannies of the stone. This was evidently the portion of the castle occupied by the ladies in bygone days, for the furniture had more air of comfort than any I had seen. The windows were curtainless, and the yellow moonlight, flooding in through the diamond panes, enabled one to see even colours, whilst it softened the wealth of dust which lay over all and disguised in some measure the ravages of time and the moth. My lamp seemed to be of little effect in the brilliant moonlight, but I was glad to have it with me, for there was a dread loneliness in the place which chilled my heart and made my nerves tremble. Still, it was better than living alone in the rooms which I had come to hate from the presence of the Count, and after trying a little to school my nerves, I found a soft quietude come over me. Here I am, sitting at a little oak table where in old times possibly some fair lady sat to pen, with much thought and many blushes, her ill-spelt love-letter, and writing in my diary in shorthand all that has happened since I closed it last. It is nineteenth century up-to-date with a vengeance. And yet, unless my senses deceive me, the old centuries had, and have, powers of their own which mere "modernity" cannot kill.

Later: the Morning of 16 May.—God preserve my sanity, for to this I am reduced. Safety and the assurance of safety are things of the past. Whilst I live on here there is but one thing to hope for, that I may not go mad, if, indeed, I be not mad already. If I be sane, then surely it is maddening to think that of all the foul things that lurk in this hateful place the Count is the least dreadful to me; that to him alone I can look for safety, even though this be only whilst I can serve his purpose. Great God! merciful God! Let me be calm, for out of that way lies madness indeed. I begin to get new lights on certain things which have puzzled me. Up to now I never quite knew what Shakespeare meant when he made Hamlet say:—

"My tablets! quick, my tablets!
'Tis meet that I put it down," etc.,

for now, feeling as though my own brain were unhinged or as if the shock had come which must end in its undoing, I turn to my diary for repose. The habit of entering accurately must help to soothe me.

The Count's mysterious warning frightened me at the time; it frightens me more now when I think of it, for in future he has a fearful hold upon me. I shall fear to doubt what he may say!

When I had written in my diary and had fortunately replaced the book and pen in my pocket I felt sleepy. The Count's warning came into my mind, but I took a pleasure in disobeying it. The sense of sleep was upon me, and with it the obstinacy which sleep brings as outrider. The soft moonlight soothed, and the wide expanse without gave a sense of freedom which refreshed me. I determined not to return to-night to the gloom-haunted rooms, but to sleep here, where, of old, ladies had sat and sung and lived sweet lives whilst their gentle breasts were sad for their menfolk away in the midst of remorseless wars. I drew a great couch out of its place near the corner, so that as I lay, I could look at the lovely view to east and south, and unthinking of and uncaring for the dust, composed myself for sleep. I suppose I must have fallen asleep; I hope so, but I fear, for all that followed was startlingly real—so real that now sitting here in the broad, full sunlight of the morning, I cannot in the least believe that it was all sleep.

I was not alone. The room was the same, unchanged in any way since I came into it; I could see along the floor, in the brilliant moonlight, my own footsteps marked where I had disturbed the long accumulation of dust. In the moonlight opposite me were three young women, ladies by their dress and manner. I thought at the time that I must be dreaming when I saw them, for, though the moonlight was behind them, they threw no shadow on the floor. They came close to me, and looked at me for some time, and then whispered together. Two were dark, and had high aquiline noses, like the Count, and great dark, piercing eyes, that seemed to be almost red when contrasted with the pale yellow moon. The other was fair, as fair as can be, with great wavy masses of golden hair and eyes like pale sapphires. I seemed somehow to know her face, and to know it in connection with some dreamy fear, but I could not recollect at the moment how or where. All three had brilliant white teeth that shone like pearls against the ruby of their voluptuous lips. There was something about them that made me uneasy, some longing and at the same time some deadly fear. I felt in my heart a wicked, burning desire that they would kiss me with those red lips. It is not good to note this down; lest some day it should meet Mina's eyes and cause her pain; but it is the truth. They whispered together, and then they all three laughed—such a silvery, musical laugh, but as hard as though the sound never could have come through the softness of human lips. It was like the intolerable, tingling sweetness of water-glasses when played on by a cunning hand. The fair girl shook her head coquettishly, and the other two urged her on. One said:—

"Go on! You are first, and we shall follow; yours is the right to begin." The other added:—

"He is young and strong; there are kisses for us all." I lay quiet, looking out under my eyelashes in an agony of delightful anticipation. The fair girl advanced and bent over me till I could feel the movement of her breath upon me. Sweet it was in one sense, honey-sweet, and sent the same tingling through the nerves as her voice, but with a bitter underlying the sweet, a bitter offensiveness, as one smells in blood.

I was afraid to raise my eyelids, but looked out and saw perfectly under the lashes. The girl went on her knees, and bent over me, simply gloating. There was a deliberate voluptuousness which was both thrilling and repulsive, and as she arched her neck she actually licked her lips like an animal, till I could see in the moonlight the moisture shining on the scarlet lips and on the red tongue as it lapped the white sharp teeth. Lower and lower went her head as the lips went below the range of my mouth and chin and seemed about to fasten on my throat. Then she paused, and I could hear the churning sound of her tongue as it licked her teeth and lips, and could feel the hot breath on my neck. Then the skin of my throat began to tingle as one's flesh does when the hand that is to tickle it approaches nearer—nearer. I could feel the soft, shivering touch of the lips on the super-sensitive skin of my throat, and the hard dents of two sharp teeth, just touching and pausing there. I closed my eyes in a languorous ecstasy and waited—waited with beating heart.

But at that instant, another sensation swept through me as quick as lightning. I was conscious of the presence of the Count, and of his being as if lapped in a storm of fury. As my eyes opened involuntarily I saw his strong hand grasp the slender neck of the fair woman and with giant's power draw it back, the blue eyes transformed with fury, the white teeth champing with rage, and the fair cheeks blazing with passion. But the Count! Never did I imagine such wrath and fury, even to the demons of the pit. His eyes were positively blazing. The red light in them was lurid, as if the flames of hell-fire blazed behind them. His face was deathly pale, and the lines of it were hard like drawn wires; the thick eyebrows that met over the nose now seemed like a heaving bar of white-hot metal. With a fierce sweep of his arm, he hurled the woman from him, and then motioned to the others, as though he were beating them back; it was the same imperious gesture that I had seen used to the wolves. In a voice which, though low and almost in a whisper, seemed to cut through the air and then ring round the room he said:—

"How dare you touch him, any of you? How dare you cast eyes on him when I had forbidden it? Back, I tell you all! This man belongs to me! Beware how you meddle with him, or you'll have to deal with me." The fair girl, with a laugh of ribald coquetry, turned to answer him:—

"You yourself never loved; you never love!" On this the other women joined, and such a mirthless, hard, soulless laughter rang through the room that it almost made me faint to hear; it seemed like the pleasure of fiends. Then the Count turned, after looking at my face attentively, and said in a soft whisper:—

"Yes, I too can love; you yourselves can tell it from the past. Is it not so? Well, now I promise you that when I am done with him you shall kiss him at your will. Now go! go! I must awaken him, for there is work to be done."

"Are we to have nothing to-night?" said one of them, with a low laugh, as she pointed to the bag which he had thrown upon the floor, and which moved as though there were some living thing within it. For answer he nodded his head. One of the women jumped forward and opened it. If my ears did not deceive me there was a gasp and a low wail, as of a half-smothered child. The women closed round, whilst I was aghast with horror; but as I looked they disappeared, and with them the dreadful bag. There was no door near them, and they could not have passed me without my noticing. They simply seemed to fade into the rays of the moonlight and pass out through the window, for I could see outside the dim, shadowy forms for a moment before they entirely faded away.

Then the horror overcame me, and I sank down unconscious.

QUESTIONS

Language

1. Stoker carefully makes the three night visitors to Harker's room both alluring and repulsive. How does he do this? Find phrases and metaphors that attract and repel you.
2. Though the fair-haired bride of Dracula has a human form, Stoker's description makes her seem like an animal. Find words and phrases that suggest her animality. What kind of creature does she most remind you of?

Content

1. How does Stoker set the scene for what is going to happen to Harker? Do you expect the subsequent events or not?

2. What kind of emotional state is Harker in on the morning of May 16? What has put him in this state?

3. Much of *Dracula* is written in the form of diary entries. Stoker must therefore have Harker write down his experiences as soon as possible after they occur. How does he make Harker's diary-keeping seem natural or right?

4. Why does Harker decide to sleep in the room Dracula has warned him against? What kind of room does he think it is? What sort of people does he imagine have used it?

5. Why does Count Dracula represent Harker's only safety?

6. How does Harker feel about the three women who visit him during the night?

7. What do you think Harker means when he reflects, "the old centuries had, and have, powers of their own which mere 'modernity' cannot kill"? Do you agree with him?

Suggestions for Writing

1. Discuss with your classmates the lasting appeal of the Dracula story. Some of you— perhaps many of you—have probably read the novel or seen one of the television or movie versions of Stoker's *Dracula*. Why has it been retold again and again since 1897? What fears of ours does it reveal? What fantasies or dreams? You may want to extend your discussion to include the appeal of all horror stories. Then write an essay in which you account for the perennial popularity of *Dracula*.

2. Before Harker falls asleep, he fantasizes about the kind of "ladies" who have in the past used the room he is in. Later, of course, the three young "women" (note the difference in terms) invade his privacy. Compare and contrast these females. Then write an essay in which you try to answer the question of whether you think men tend to divide women into extreme categories such as Stoker has done. Use your own experience here, your friends' attitudes, and so on, to arrive at an opinion.

H. RIDER HAGGARD

from *She*

One of the most popular adventure yarns of all time, Sir Henry Rider Haggard's *She* has been continuously in print since its first appearance in 1887. Haggard was born in Norfolk, England, in 1856. Following an early governmental career in South Africa, he settled in London in 1881, and there began to study law and write in his spare time. His African adventure story *King Solomon's Mines* (1885) was so successful and earned Haggard so much money that he abandoned law entirely and devoted himself to literature. Haggard was knighted in 1912; by the time of his death thirteen years later, he had published more than forty novels.

Written in only six weeks, in a "white heat" of inspiration (as Haggard later recalled), *She* is the story of the mysterious, awesomely beautiful, and seemingly immortal Queen Ayesha, She-Who-Must-Be-Obeyed. Two thousand years before the time of the story (which begins in Victorian England), Ayesha had slain the Egyptian Kallikrates—the man she loved—in a fit of jealous fury. Throughout the intervening centuries, convinced that her lover would be reborn, Ayesha waited faithfully for his return, her youth preserved by the flaming Pillar of Life. The hero of the tale is the Englishman Leo Vincey, a direct descendant (and exact duplicate) of Kallikrates, who learns of the legend of She from the inscription on an ancient pottery shard left him by his father. Along with his guardian Holly (a brave and brilliant man, but as ugly as Leo is handsome) and their servant Job, he travels to Africa to ascertain the truth of the story and falls under the spell of She.

In the course of the journey, Leo meets the simple native girl Ustane, who falls deeply in love with him and (after the custom of her people) declares herself his wife. Banished by the jealous queen, Ustane defies the order and sneaks back during a tribal ceremony, disguised in the skin of a leopard. She is betrayed, however, by the "brand"—three white stripes—which the queen has set upon her hair as a sign of the girl's disgrace. In the following episode, She-Who-Must-Be-Obeyed takes a terrible vengeance on Ustane. Then, with the young girl's corpse lying at Leo's feet, this "modern Circe" (as Holly describes Ayesha) displays the irresistible power of her "awful beauty."

TRIUMPH

Then followed a moment of the most painful silence that I ever endured. It was broken by Ayesha, who addressed herself to Leo.

'Nay, now, my lord and guest,' she said in her softest tones, which yet had the ring of steel about them, 'look not so bashful. Surely the sight was a pretty one—the leopard and the lion!'

'Oh, bother!' said Leo in English.

'And thou, Ustane,' she went on, 'in truth I should have passed thee by, had not the light fallen on the stripes across thy hair,' and she pointed to the bright edge of the rising moon which was now appearing above the horizon. 'Well! well! the dance is done—see, the tapers have burnt down, and all things end in silence and in ashes. So thou thoughtest it a fit time for love, Ustane, my servant—and I, dreaming not that I could be disobeyed, deemed thee already far away.'

'Play not with me,' moaned the wretched woman; 'kill me, and let there be an end.'

'Nay, why? It is not well to go so swift from the hot lips of love down to the cold mouth of the grave,' and Ayesha motioned to the mutes, who instantly stepped up and caught the girl by either arm. With an oath Leo sprang upon the nearest, and hurled him to the ground, and then stood over him with his face set and his fist ready.

Again Ayesha laughed. 'It was well thrown, my guest; thou hast a strong arm for one who so late was sick. But now of thy courtesy I pray thee let that man live and do my bidding. He shall not harm the girl; the night air grows chill, and I would welcome her in mine own place. Surely she whom thou dost favour shall be favoured of me also.'

I took Leo by the arm, dragging him from the prostrate mute, and, half bewildered, he yielded and left the man. Then we set out for the cave across the plateau, whence the dancers had vanished, and where a pile of white human ashes was all that remained of the fire which had lit their dancing.

In due course we gained Ayesha's boudoir—all too soon it seemed to me, having a sad presage of what was to come lying heavy on my heart.

Ayesha seated herself upon her cushions, and, having dismissed Job and Billali, by signs she bade the mutes tend the lamps and retire—all save one girl, who was her favourite personal attendant. We three remained standing, the unfortunate Ustane a little to the left of the rest of us.

'Now, O Holly,' Ayesha began, 'how came it that thou who didst hear my words bidding this evil-doer'—and she pointed to Ustane—'to go hence—thou at whose prayer I weakly spared her life—how came it, I say, that thou hadst part in what I saw to-night? Answer, and for thine own sake, I say, speak all the truth, for I am not minded to hear lies upon this matter!'

'It was by accident, O Queen,' I answered. 'I knew nothing of it.'

'I believe thee, Holly,' she answered coldly, 'and well it is for thee that I do. Then does the whole guilt rest upon her.'

'I do not find any guilt herein,' interrupted Leo. 'She is no other man's wife, and it seems that she has married me according to the custom of this awful place, so who is harmed? Any way, madam, whatever she has done I have done, so if she is to be punished let me be punished also; and I tell thee,' he went on, working himself up into a fury, 'that if thou biddest one of those deaf and dumb villains to touch her again I will tear him to pieces!'

Ayesha listened in icy silence, and made no remark. When he had finished, however, she addressed Ustane.

'Hast thou aught to say, woman? Thou silly straw, thou feather, who didst think to float towards thy passion's petty ends, even against the great wind of my will! Tell me, for I fain would understand, why didst thou this thing?'

Then I think that I saw the most wonderful example of moral courage and intrepidity which it is possible to conceive. For this poor doomed girl, knowing what she had to expect at the hands of her terrible Queen, knowing, too, from bitter experience, how great was her adversary's power, yet stood unshaken, and out of the very depths of her despair drew the strength to defy her.

'I did it, O *She,*' she answered, drawing herself up to the full of her stately height, and throwing back the panther skin from her head, 'because my love is deeper than the grave. I did it because my life without this man whom my heart chose would be but a living death. Therefore I risked my life, and now, when I know that it is forfeit to thine anger, still am I glad that I risked it, and must pay it away in the risking, ay, because he embraced me once, and told me that he loved me yet.'

Here Ayesha half rose from her couch, and then sank down again.

'I have no magic,' went on Ustane, her rich voice ringing strong and full, 'and I am not a Queen, nor do I live for ever: but a woman's heart is heavy to sink through waters, however deep, O Queen! and a woman's eyes are quick to see—even through thy veil, O Queen!

'Listen: I know it, thou dost love this man thyself, and therefore wouldst thou destroy me who stand across thy path. Ay, I die—I die, and go into the darkness, nor know I whither I go. But this I know. There is a light shining in my breast, and by that light, as by a lamp, I see the truth, and the future that I shall not share, unroll itself before me like a scroll. When first I knew my lord,' and she pointed to Leo, 'I knew also that death would be the bridal gift he gave me—it rushed upon me of a sudden, but I turned not back, being ready to pay the price, and, behold, death is here! And now, even as I knew this, so, standing on the steps of doom, do I know that thou shalt not reap the profit of thy crime. Mine he is, and, though thy beauty shine like a sun among the stars, mine he shall remain for thee. Never here in this life shall he look thee in the eyes and call thee spouse. Thou too art doomed, I see'—and her voice rose like the cry of an inspired prophetess; 'ah, I see——'

Then there rang an answering cry of rage and terror. I turned my head. Ayesha had risen, and was standing with her outstretched hand pointing at Ustane, who had suddenly become silent. I gazed at the poor woman, and as I gazed there fell upon her face that same woful, fixed expression of terror which I had seen before when she broke into her wild chant. Her eyes grew large, her nostrils dilated, and her lips blanched.

Ayesha said nothing, she made no sound, she only drew herself up, stretched out her arm, and, her tall veiled frame quivering like an aspen leaf, appeared to look fixedly at her victim. Even as she looked Ustane put her hands to her head, uttered one piercing scream, turned round twice, and then fell backwards with a thud—prone upon the floor. Both Leo and myself rushed to her. She was stone dead—blasted into death by some mysterious electric agency or overwhelming will-force whereof the dread *She* had command.

For a moment Leo did not quite understand what had happened. But, when it came home to him, his face was awful to see. With a savage oath he rose from beside the corpse, and, turning, literally sprang at Ayesha. But she was watching, and, seeing him come, stretched out her hand again, and he went staggering back towards me, and would have fallen, had I not caught him. Afterwards he told me that he felt as though he had suddenly received a violent blow in the chest, and, what is more, utterly cowed, as if all the manhood had been taken out of him.

Then Ayesha spoke. 'Forgive me, my guest,' she said softly, addressing him, 'if I have shocked thee with my justice.'

'Forgive thee, thou fiend!' shouted poor Leo, wringing his hands in his rage and grief. 'Forgive thee, thou murderess! By Heaven, I will kill thee if I can!'

'Nay, nay,' she answered in the same soft voice, 'thou dost not understand—the time has come for thee to learn. *Thou* art my love, my Kallikrates, my Beautiful, my Strong! For two thousand years, Kallikrates, I have waited for *thee,* and now at length thou hast come back to me; and as for this woman,' pointing to the corpse, 'she stood between me and thee, therefore have I laid her in the dust, Kallikrates.'

'It is a lie!' said Leo. 'My name is not Kallikrates! I am Leo Vincey; my ancestor was Kallikrates—at least, I believe he was.'

'Ah, thou sayest it—thine ancestor was Kallikrates, and thou, even thou, art Kallikrates reborn, come back—and mine own dear lord!'

'I am not Kallikrates, and as for being thy lord, or having aught to do with thee, I had sooner be the lord of a fiend from hell, for she would be better than thou.'

'Sayest thou so—sayest thou so, Kallikrates? Nay, but thou hast not seen me for so long a time that no memory remains. Yet am I very fair, Kallikrates!'

'I hate thee, murderess, and I have no wish to see thee. What is it to me how fair thou art? I hate thee, I say.'

'Yet within a very little space shalt thou creep to my knee, and swear that thou dost love me,' answered Ayesha, with a sweet, mocking laugh. 'Come, there is no time like the present time. Here, before this dead girl who loved thee, let us put it to the proof.

'Look now on me, Kallikrates!' and with a sudden motion she shook her gauzy covering from her, and stood forth in her low kirtle and her snaky zone, in her glorious radiant beauty and her imperial grace, rising from her wrappings, as it were, like Venus from the wave, or Galatea[1] from her marble, or a beatified spirit from the tomb. She stood forth, and fixed her deep and glowing eyes upon Leo's eyes, and I saw his clenched fists unclasp, and his set and quivering features relax beneath her gaze. I saw his wonder and astonishment grow into admiration, then into longing, and the more he struggled the more I saw the power of her dread beauty fasten on him and take hold of his senses, drugging them, and drawing the heart out of him. Did I not know the process? Had not I, who was twice his age, gone through it myself? Was I not going through it afresh even then, although her sweet and passionate gaze was not for me? Yes, alas! I was. Alas! that I should have to confess that at this very moment I was rent by mad and furious jealousy. I could have flown at him, shame upon me! This woman had confounded and almost destroyed my moral sense, as indeed she must confound all who looked upon her superhuman loveliness. But—I do not know how—I mastered myself, and once more turned to see the climax of the awful tragedy.

'Oh, great Heaven!' gasped Leo, 'art thou a woman?'

'A woman in truth—in very truth—and thine own spouse, Kallikrates!' she answered, stretching out her rounded ivory arms towards him, and smiling, ah, so sweetly!

He looked and looked, and slowly I perceived that he was drawing nearer to her. Suddenly his eye fell upon the corpse of poor Ustane, and he shuddered and stood still.

'How can I?' he said hoarsely. 'Thou art a murderess; she loved me.'

Observe, he was already forgetting that he had loved her.

'It is nothing,' Ayesha murmured, and her voice sounded sweet as the night-wind passing through the trees. 'It is naught at all. If I have sinned, let my beauty answer for my sin. If I have sinned, it is for love of thee: let my sin, therefore, be put away and forgotten;' and once more she stretched out her arms and whispered *'Come.'* Then in a few seconds it was over.

I saw him struggle—I saw him even turn to fly; but her eyes drew him more strongly than iron bonds, and the magic of her beauty and concentrated will and passion entered into him and overpowered him—ay, even there, in the presence of the body of the woman who had loved him well enough to die for him. It sounds horrible and wicked indeed, but he should not be too greatly blamed, and be sure his sin has found him out. The temptress who drew him into evil was more than human, and her beauty was greater than the loveliness of the daughters of men.

I looked up again, and now her perfect form lay in his arms, and her lips were pressed against his own; and thus, with the corpse of his dead love for an altar, did Leo Vincey plight his troth to her red-handed murderess—plight it

---

[1] According to Greek mythology, the sculptor Pygmalion carved a statue of a beautiful maiden and fell so passionately in love with it that he prayed to Aphrodite, goddess of love, to send him a woman like his statue. Aphrodite, moved by Pygmalion's plea, brought his statue to life, and the sculptor and maiden—whom he named Galatea—were wed.

for ever and a day. For those who sell themselves into a like dominion, paying down the price of their own honour, and throwing their soul into the balance to sink the scale to the level of their lusts, must win deliverance hardly. As they have sown, so shall they reap and reap, even when the poppy flowers of passion have withered in their hands, and their harvest is but bitter tares, garnered in satiety.

Suddenly, with a snake-like motion, she seemed to slip from his embrace, and again she broke out into her low laugh of triumphant mockery, and said, pointing to the dead Ustane:

'Did I not tell thee that within a little space thou wouldst creep to my knee, O Kallikrates? Surely the space has been no great one!'

QUESTIONS

Language

1. Look at the way the characters speak in this excerpt from *She*. Why do Ayesha and Ustane sound the way they do? Is Leo Vincey's speech consistent? Does he sound like a nineteenth-century gentleman?
2. What does Ustane mean when she says to the queen, "A woman's heart is heavy to sink through waters, however deep . . ."?
3. What do *kirtle* (p. 152) and *tares* (p. 153) mean?
4. Find all the metaphors you can in this selection. Which are the ones you like best? Which are most powerful? Why do you think a writer uses metaphors? Take one of the most vivid metaphors in *She* and rephrase it in ordinary, literal language. Which version do you like best? Why?

Content

1. Compare Leo with the narrator, Holly. Who is the more realistic? The wiser? Who has more courage?
2. Why does Ustane, knowing the dreadful power Ayesha has, return to Leo after her banishment?
3. Why does Leo yield to Ayesha? How has he felt about her up to the point he surrenders?
4. Do you think Holly condemns Leo for his weakness? Why or why not? Find remarks in the text which support your point of view.
5. How does Ayesha justify her murder of Ustane? Does Leo accept her excuse?
6. Look at the paragraph on p. 152 beginning "I looked up again, . . ." What is going on here? Why is Holly so pessimistic about Leo's chances for freedom? What kind of freedom will he never have?

Suggestions for Writing

1. The two women struggling for possession of Leo Vincey afford a good contrast. Write an essay comparing the two women. How are they different?
2. A critic has said that although H. Rider Haggard's novels were written for adults, they were "for the most part devoured by adolescents." Do you think a novel like *She* would appeal to the contemporary adolescent? Write an essay analyzing why or why not.
3. In some respects, the position of women in *She* is novel: the country is ruled by a woman; families in it trace their descent through women—their mothers—not through their fathers; women choose and discard their husbands (who do not protest against

the custom) whenever they like and generally enjoy equality with them. But are women portrayed here radically differently from the way they are pictured in most of the literature we read? Do they behave differently? Do they have different kinds of relationships with men and with other women? Discuss this question with your classmates and then, after arriving at your own decision, write an essay presenting it.

4. What if Haggard had written a book entitled *He* instead of *She?* Rewrite the scene above, substituting a jealous king for the jealous queen, a rival male for Ustane, and a beloved woman for the character Leo.

JOHN KEATS

"La Belle Dame sans Merci"

John Keats lived only twenty-five years, but during that time created some of the most beautiful poetry in the English language. Born over his father's livery stable in 1795, Keats became interested in literature through the influence of his friend and teacher, Charles Cowden Clarke. In 1811, however, he was withdrawn from school by his legal guardians—his father having died when Keats was eight, his mother when he was fourteen—and was apprenticed to a surgeon. During the five subsequent years that he studied medicine, he paid frequent visits to Clarke, who continued to introduce his friend to the writings of important English poets and encouraged Keats' own early attempts at verse. Though he traveled to London in 1815 to pursue his medical studies, Keats was spending more and more of his time writing, and after obtaining a license to set up as an apothecary, he decided, much to the dismay of his guardians, to devote himself entirely to poetry.

Keats' early works—his first volume, *Poems,* appeared in 1817 and was followed a year later by *Endymion*—were so savagely attacked by reviewers that his friends later blamed the critics for the poet's early death. But despite these attacks and other blows far more severe (including the death of his brother by tuberculosis, the discovery of the disease in himself, and a passionate but hopeless love affair with a woman named Fanny Brawne), he never turned aside from his committment to his art. Indeed, adversity seemed to fuel Keats' genius, and in the few months following his brother's death, he produced an astonishing number of masterpieces, collected in his third volume *Lamia, Isabella, The Eve of St. Agnes and Other Poems* (1820). In September of that year, in the faint hope that a warmer climate might improve his health, he traveled to Italy with a friend, but died in Rome on February 23, 1821.

The haunting ballad, "La Belle Dame sans Merci," tells of a knight who encounters a lovely young woman and soon discovers that he has fallen under a terrible spell of "The Beautiful Lady without Pity."

"La Belle Dame sans Merci"

O what can ail thee, knight-at-arms,
  Alone and palely loitering?
The sedge has withered from the lake,
  And no birds sing.

O what can ail thee, knight-at-arms,
  So haggard and so woe-begone?
The squirrel's granary is full,
  And the harvest's done.

I see a lily on thy brow
  With anguish moist and fever dew,
And on thy cheek a fading rose
  Fast withereth too.

I met a lady in the meads,
  Full beautiful—a faery's child;
Her hair was long, her foot was light,
  And her eyes were wild.

I made a garland for her head,
  And bracelets too, and fragrant zone;
She looked at me as she did love,
  And made sweet moan.

I set her on my pacing steed,
  And nothing else saw all day long,
For sidelong would she bend, and sing
  A faery's song.

She found me roots of relish sweet,
  And honey wild, and manna dew,
And sure in language strange she said—
  "I love thee true!"

She took me to her elfin grot,
  And there she wept and sighed full sore,
And there I shut her wild, wild eyes
  With kisses four.

And there she lullèd me asleep,
  And there I dreamed—ah! woe betide!
The latest dream I ever dreamed
  On the cold hill's side.

I saw pale kings and princes too,
  Pale warriors, death-pale were they all;
They cried—"La Belle Dame sans Merci
  Hath thee in thrall!"

I saw their starved lips in the gloam,
  With horrid warning gapèd wide,
And I awoke and found me here,
  On the cold hill's side.

And this is why I sojourn here,
  Alone and palely loitering,
Though the sedge is withered from the lake
  And no birds sing.

QUESTIONS

Language

1. Keats uses words in this poem you may not be familiar with; some of them are archaic. Look up the following words in a good dictionary: *sedge, granary, meads, zone, manna, elfin, grot, gloam.*
2. Why does Keats use the word *grot* instead of *grotto*, or spell *lullèd* and *gapèd* unconventionally?
3. We are told by the stranger who encounters the knight that that unfortunate young man has a lily on his forehead. What does Keats mean by this? Is there literally a lily on his face, or a rose, for that matter? What is language like this called? Why do poets use it?

Content

1. How many speakers are there in this poem? When does the second speaker begin to talk?
2. What does the knight look like? What is he doing when the stranger first meets him?
3. Describe the events of the young man's day with La Belle Dame sans Merci. What does the Temptress look like; how does she behave? Does Keats want us to think of her as the usual young noblewoman the knight might meet at court in his native country?
4. What kind of man does the Temptress in this poem choose for her victim?
5. Why is it that the knight sees nothing else all day long but the lady he has met? And in stanza nine, why does he call his terrible dream "the latest dream I ever dreamed"?
6. What season is it in the poem? How do you know? And why does Keats bother to mention the season and details of the landscape? Suppose he had made it a warm summer day, with the birds singing and a pleasant breeze blowing: would the poem be different? Why or why not?

Suggestions for Writing

1. Compare Keats' "La Bella Dame sans Merci" to the Eagles' "Witchy Woman" (p. 134). What similarities can you find? What differences? You might begin by deciding what categories of things you *can* fruitfully compare. (An obvious category is the woman in each work.) Then, write an essay comparing and contrasting the song and the poem.
2. Notice that the knight tells us in the eighth stanza that La Belle Dame sans Merci, once inside her grotto with him, "wept and sighed full sore"; but we do not hear why, nor do we hear any more details. *Her* story remains untold, as is the case with all the Temptresses we have read about in this chapter. Discuss this with your classmates; why don't we hear the Temptress' version of things? What might her story be? Why does she do the things she does to men? Does she hate them? Envy them? Or would she tell a very different tale? Would she claim that *she* is victimized by men? Look at

specific Temptresses in this chapter as you attempt to answer these questions. Then write an essay in which you maintain either that there are good reasons for the Temptress' behavior (explain them) or that her behavior is evil and incomprehensible (justify your opinion). Refer to specific Temptresses in your argument.

ADDITIONAL WRITING SUGGESTIONS FOR CHAPTER THREE

1. All of the Temptresses we have encountered in this chapter—from Homer's Circe to Keats' La Belle Dame sans Merci—have had enormous *power* over men: the unlimited power to attract and delight but also to enslave, to unman, to degrade, to destroy, to drain of vitality, purpose, and identity. Have a discussion with your classmates about the balance of power between men and women. Who has more, men or women? What kind of power do men have? What kind do women have? Do you see changes in the way power is apportioned to each sex? After your discussion, which will undoubtedly be rather general in nature, write an essay on some aspect of it that interests you.

2. Another way of approaching the same subject is from a more personal perspective. Reflect on a serious relationship you now have or have had with a young adult of the opposite sex, or observe the relationship of your parents or other close relatives. How is power—authority, decision-making, responsibility, influence—shared? Do you see any problems with the way it is divided up? Write an essay about this subject. You might begin by describing the relationship and the division of power within it and then go on to analyze how successful the relationship is.

3. Many women critics have charged that rock music—which is even today still largely written by and performed by males—is sexist: that is, rock songs are often hostile to women and portray them in negative, demeaning and/or stereotypical ways. Using "Witchy Woman" and any other rock songs you know well, write an essay agreeing or disagreeing with these critics. Quote rock lyrics frequently to support your opinion and to illustrate individual points.

4. Look back at the men who succumb to the Temptress in this chapter: they are almost always soldiers, adventurers, heroes, leaders, cowboys. Why are these men most vulnerable, apparently, to the Temptress? With your classmates, try to decide and then write an essay about what all of these men have in common and what makes them such ideal victims. What characteristics do they share? What patterns of behavior? Might they have the same values? What in any of these things makes them perfect targets for the Temptress?

5. Are there men who play the role of Temptress to women, men who are fascinating but destructive, men who snare women only to ruin them? Discuss this in class; get both male and female perspectives. What would such a man be like? What kind of woman would he probably attract? What would happen to her? After your discussion, either write an essay describing this man and his victim and analyzing their relationship, or write a story or poem about them. Alternatively, argue in an essay that such a man—the male counterpart to the Temptress—does not exist.

Four

The Mother

When I find myself in times of trouble,
Mother Mary comes to me,
Speaking words of wisdom—
Let it be.*

—the Beatles, "Let It Be"

Though the Temptress archetype is, as we have seen, extremely widespread in imaginative works of every kind, from classical myths to comic books, poetry to popular music, it is by no means the only way in which women have been typically portrayed. Other archetypal roles which they play in fantasy and art include the ministering angel, captive princess, amazon, muse, nymph, and—one of the most powerful mythic figures of all—the Mother. From time immemorial, humanity's hunger for security in a hard, uncertain world has expressed itself symbolically, in the form of all-powerful Good Mother figures who offer shelter and solace at moments of distress.

One such figure, in religious tradition, is the Virgin Mary. Until the Reformation, she was revered nearly as much as Christ, and was viewed by all Christians— and still is by Roman Catholics—as an inexhaustible source of mercy, tenderness, love, and patience. She was forever generous to and forgiving of those who, in prayer, sought her aid. The same qualities of love and compassion that characterize the Madonna can be seen in other, more secularized, versions of the Good Mother archetype. One of the most famous advertisements ever created, for example, was an appeal, put out during World War I, for donations to the Red Cross. In it, this humanitarian organization is portrayed in personified form as "the Greatest

* "Let It Be" (John Lennon and Paul McCartney) Copyright © 1970 Northern Songs Limited. All rights for the U.S.A., Canada and Mexico controlled by Maclen Music, Inc. c/o ATV Music Corp. Used by permission, all rights reserved.

Mother in the World'': a giant protectress who, in a pose reminiscent of a pietà, cradles the body of a wounded soldier in her strong yet gentle arms. And in a much lighter vein, there is the well-known comic strip character Mary Worth, a kindly white-haired widow to whom people are always turning for comfort and advice.

But it is not merely emotional support that the Good Mother provides; the sustenance she bestows is physical as well as spiritual. The newborn baby, in its helpless and dependent state, experiences the mother as the original source of life-giving food; and even as adults, we tend to identify (on some deep level of the mind) mothering with feeding. Perhaps because of this ancient association, people have, throughout history, conceived of the earth itself, with its fruits and vegetables, its water and wild grains, as maternal: the mother who brings forth and nourishes all living things. ''In the West,'' writes Eric J. Sharpe in *Man, Myth, and Magic* (1970), ''God is generally spoken of as 'Our Father which art in heaven,' but the naive question, 'If God is Father, then who is Mother?' still deserves to be asked. Historically the answer would be: 'The earth on which we live.' '' Earth Mother goddesses—who rule over plant and animal life, who make nature and humanity fruitful—are among the oldest deities known to us. In fact, the earliest sculptures archeologists have unearthed, dating back to the Stone Age, are female fertility figures, like the famous ''Venus of Willendorf'': small, crudely carved statuettes with bulging bellies and swelling breasts, representing the maternal abundance and fecundity of nature. The Earth Mother, creator of vegetation, is a familiar figure in ancient mythology, known by different names in different parts of the world: in Babylonia as Ishtar, ''The Green One,'' ''The Mistress of the Field''; in Egypt as Isis, the ''Lady of Abundance'' who gives ''birth to the fruits of the field''; in ancient Greece, as Demeter, the ''Corn Mother.''

As the food giver, ''the great nourisher'' (so-called by Erich Neumann in his classic study *The Great Mother* [1955]), the goddess is often associated with the symbol of the full, flowing breast. Both the Mexican goddess Mayauel and the Roman Diana, for instance, are depicted, in statuary and painting, with clusters of breasts, like bunches of fruit, covering their upper torsos. (Mayauel, in fact, is known as ''the woman with the four hundred breasts,'' and Diana as ''the Many-Breasted Mother.'') Other images connected with the Earth Mother include caves, ovens, wells, trees, fruits, grains, gardens, milk, and honey (along with the creatures that produce these last two substances: cows and bees).

Though the worship of the Earth Mother goddess has long since disappeared from Western religion, she still survives in the familiar, desacralized form of ''Mother Nature''—a figure who has lately begun to assume a special significance in American society. We have always been a people enamored of technology, for whom progress is equivalent to new and more splendid machines. But many of us have started to feel that American technology, which is rapidly turning our ''fruited plains'' into landscapes of concrete and steel, has gotten out of hand. And one of the results of this widespread sense that the machines are taking over, if not actually destroying, our land has been a renewed appreciation, even glorification, of nature. This reawakened reverence for Mother Earth can be seen most clearly in our increasing concern with ecology and conservation and in the astonishing growth, in recent years, of the ''back-to-nature'' movement. Even in the hearts of our cities (indeed, perhaps most intensely there), people have begun to long for some contact with the natural world, with plant life. We want greenery, and not just machinery, near at hand. And so we fill our houses not only with the newest technological marvels, the latest in labor-saving machines, but also with houseplants—begonias, Swiss ivy, African violets—whose companionship we have started to crave.

Like so many other things in our society, this new feeling for nature has become faddish and extremely commercialized. Every item on the market pretends to be "natural" these days; the label is apparently a guarantee of success. There are natural cereals, natural cigarettes, natural shoes, even "natural" synthetic sweaters! And because we have become so concerned that the products we buy be "natural," Madison Avenue has been quick to exploit the image of Mother Nature in its ads. To some extent, of course, this has always been true; because of its elementary associations with loving care and nourishment, the symbol of the Good Mother has for years been used to sell food. Betty Crocker, Sarah Lee, Aunt Jemima, Mrs. Paul, and Borden's Elsie the Cow (who bears an interesting similarity to the ancient Egyptian cow-goddess Hathor, who, to quote Erich Neumann again, "waters the earth with her rain-milk") are characters who have been with us so long that they have achieved a near mythical status in our society. We perceive them as larger-than-life Mother figures, bestowers of the earth's endless bounty.

But these days, given our current hunger for "health foods" and our preoccupation with the natural, Good Mother images are appearing in advertisements more frequently than ever before. They promote such products as maple syrup (Mrs. Butterworth), frozen pizza (Mama Celeste), and pumpkin custard pie (Mrs. Smith)—all with the natural "flavor of home." After consumers have given themselves indigestion from eating all these homestyle treats, there is even a Good Mother figure handy to offer relief: Mother Tums, who supplies the dual comforts of sympathy ("Tell me where it hurts") and antacid tablets. Several years ago, Madison Avenue actually created a successful television commercial which used Mother Nature to peddle artificial butter! (Chiffon Margarine's "It's Not Nice to Fool Mother Nature.") Advertisements like these are appealing and successful because, in our reaction against the onslaughts of technology, we seem to have swung to the other extreme and have made the words "natural" and "beneficial" synonymous.

To equate nature with goodness, however, is to ignore a significant point. It is all very well for John Denver to celebrate, in his songs, the glories of the Rocky Mountains. His music, though, ignores an important fact: that people not only get "high" in the Colorado Rockies, they get killed there, too, by rockslides, cold, and other *natural* phenomena. The point is that nature has two sides, creative *and* destructive. The great American novelist Herman Melville recognized this truth. In the following passage from his novel *The Confidence-Man,* a cynical Missourian and a miserly old man with tuberculosis argue over the merits of a cough medicine made out of natural "yarbs" (herbs):

> "Think it will cure me?" coughed the miser in echo; "why shouldn't it? The medicine is nat'ral yarbs, pure yarbs; yarbs must cure me."

> "Because a thing is nat'ral, as you call it, you think it must be good. But who gave you that cough? Was it, or was it not, nature?"

> "Sure, you don't think that natur, Dame natur, will hurt a body, do you?"

"Natur is good Queen Bess; but who's responsible for the cholera?"

"But yarbs, yarbs; yarbs are good?"

"What's deadly nightshade? Yarb, ain't it?"

"Oh, that a Christian man should speak agin natur and yarbs—ugh, ugh, ugh!—ain't sick men sent out into the country; sent out to natur and grass?"

"Aye, and poets send out the sick spirit to green pastures, like lame horses turned out unshod to the turf to renew their hoofs. A sort of yarb-doctors in their way, poets have it that for sore hearts, as for sore lungs, nature is the grand cure. But who froze to death my teamster on the prairie?"

The destructive side of "Dame nature" can also be seen in the big-budget disaster movies which were so popular several years ago and which all dealt with the same essential theme: the devastation of some supreme technological achievement (an unsinkable ship, a fireproof building, a modern city) by a natural force (such as a tidal wave, fire, or earthquake).

Disaster movies or movies which show doomed men adrift on a tiny raft in the midst of an immense, featureless sea, stories of pioneers whose farms are destroyed by drought or dust storm, express in concrete shape our instinctive knowledge that nature is a killer. That is to say, Mother Nature is not *just,* or always, a Good Mother; she is a Terrible Mother as well. She deals out death as abundantly as she gives life. As Erich Neumann reminds us, all things not only rise from the earth, but also sink back into it. Thus the female deities that represent earth are not only goddesses of fertility, they are goddesses of death, too. As is true of other archetypes we have looked at so far—the Shadow, for instance, and the Trickster—mythology reveals the Mother as having both a positive and negative side. Perhaps the most powerful mythic representation of the two-sided Mother is the Indian goddess Kali. In his book *Hero with a Thousand Faces* (1949), Joseph Campbell quotes the following passage from the gospels of the famous Indian mystic, Ramakrishna, which vividly illustrates Kali's contradictory character. It also serves as a terrifying parable of human existence: nature gives us life—briefly—and then takes it away again.

One quiet afternoon Ramakrishna beheld a beautiful woman ascend from the Ganges and approach the grove in which he was meditating. He perceived that she was about to give birth to a child. In a moment, the babe was born, and she gently nursed it. Presently, however, she assumed a horrible aspect, took the infant in her now ugly jaws and crushed it, chewed it. Swallowing it, she returned again to the Ganges, where she disappeared.

In fairy tales, the dualistic Mother archetype, by now more recognizably human, is often split into two figures, an evil stepmother and a helpful fairy godmother ("Cinderella" is a good example). Similarly, in the children's classic *The Wizard of Oz,* the bad and benign aspects of the Mother are embodied separately, in the Wicked Witch of the West and Glinda, Good Witch of the North.

World literature (as well as real life!) provides countless examples of both types of Mother. Good Earth Mothers—who are generally strong, buxom women notable for their sympathetic, nurturing, self-sacrificing qualities—include John Steinbeck's Ma Joad (*The Grapes of Wrath*), Kate Chopin's Madame Ratignolle (*The Awaken-*

ing), William Faulkner's Lena Grove (*Light in August*), and George Eliot's Mrs. Poyser (*Adam Bede*).

Literary incarnations of the Terrible Mother—the tyrannical woman who dominates or even destroys her children or dependents—include Charles Dickens' Mrs. Clennam (*Little Dorrit*), Charlotte Brontë's Mrs. Reed (*Jane Eyre*), Herman Melville's Mary Glendinning (*Pierre*), Washington Irving's Dame Van Winkle ("Rip Van Winkle"), Henry James' Madame de Bellegarde (*The American*), and Ken Kesey's Nurse Ratched (*One Flew Over the Cuckoo's Nest*).

Sometimes, as in the case of Kali, a single female figure incorporates both sides of the Mother archetype (a situation which occurs as often in fact as in fiction or myth). This is the sort of woman who, like Sophie Portnoy in Philip Roth's *Portnoy's Complaint*, protects her offspring to the point of suffocating them, whose love is so overpowering that her children can never break free.

ANONYMOUS

"Hymn to Demeter"

Among various poems which were, at one time, believed to be the work of Homer (see headnote for Circe, p. 119) are a group of thirty-four hymns to Apollo, Aphrodite, Demeter, Dionysus, Hermes, and other gods. Though often very beautiful, these so-called Homeric Hymns are primarily important as sources of information about ancient Greek mythology and religion.

The "Hymn to Demeter" tells the story of the Greek earth goddess Demeter and her search for her daughter Persephone, abducted by the god of the Underworld. The translation below is by Andrew Lang (1844–1912), the Scottish author and scholar, best known for his writings on myth (especially *Myth, Literature, and Religion*), his translations of *The Odyssey* and *The Iliad*, and his collections of children's fairy tales.

Of fair-tressed Demeter, Demeter holy Goddess, I begin to sing: of her and her slim-ankled daughter whom Hades snatched away, the gift of wide-beholding Zeus,[1] but Demeter knew it not, she that bears the Seasons, the giver of goodly crops. For her daughter was playing with the deep-bosomed maidens of Oceanus,[2] and was gathering flowers—roses, and crocuses, and fair violets in the soft meadow, and lilies, and hyacinths, and the narcissus which the earth brought forth as a snare to the fair-faced maiden, by the counsel of Zeus and to pleasure the Lord with many guests. Wondrously bloomed the flower, a marvel for all

From *The Homeric Hymns: A New Prose Translation, and Essays Literary and Mythological,* by Andrew Lang. Copyright 1899 by George Allen.

[1] The ruler of the ancient Greek gods, the "All-high." Among other functions, he controlled the wind, the clouds, the rain, and thunder.
[2] See footnote 1, p. 120.

to see, whether deathless gods or deathly men. From its root grew forth a hundred blossoms, and with its fragrant odour the wide heaven above and the whole earth laughed, and the salt wave of the sea. Then the maiden marvelled, and stretched forth both her hands to seize the fair plaything, but the wide-wayed earth gaped in the Nysian plain, and up rushed the Prince, the host of many guests, the many-named son of Cronos, with his immortal horses.[3] Maugre her will he seized her, and drave her off weeping in his golden chariot, but she shrilled aloud, calling on Father Cronides, the highest of gods and the best.[4]

But no immortal god or deathly man heard the voice of her, . . . save the daughter of Persæus, Hecate[5] of the shining head-tire, as she was thinking delicate thoughts, who heard the cry from her cave [and Prince Helios,[6] the glorious son of Hyperion], the maiden calling on Father Cronides. But he far off sat apart from the gods in his temple haunted by prayers, receiving goodly victims from mortal men. By the design of Zeus did the brother of Zeus lead the maiden away, the lord of many, the host of many guests, with his deathless horses; right sore against her will, even he of many names the son of Cronos. Now, so long as the Goddess beheld the earth, and the starry heaven, and the tide of the teeming sea, and the rays of the sun, and still hoped to behold her mother dear, and the tribes of the eternal gods; even so long, despite her sorrow, hope warmed her high heart; then rang the mountain peaks, and the depths of the sea to her immortal voice, and her lady mother heard her. Then sharp pain caught at her heart, and with her hands she tore the wimple about her ambrosial hair, and cast a dark veil about her shoulders, and then sped she like a bird over land and sea in her great yearning; but to her there was none that would tell the truth, none, either of Gods, or deathly men, nor even a bird came nigh her, a soothsaying messenger. Thereafter for nine days did Lady Deo roam the earth, with torches burning in her hands, nor ever in her sorrow tasted she of ambrosia and sweet nectar, nor laved her body in the baths. But when at last the tenth morn came to her with the light, Hecate met her, a torch in her hands, and spake a word of tidings, and said:

"Lady Demeter, thou that bringest the Seasons, thou giver of glad gifts, which of the heavenly gods or deathly men hath ravished away Persephone, and brought thee sorrow: for I heard a voice but I saw not who the ravisher might be? All this I say to thee for sooth."

So spake Hecate, and the daughter of fair-tressed Rheie[7] answered her not, but swiftly rushed on with her, bearing torches burning in her hands. So came they to Helios that watches both for gods and men, and stood before his car, and the lady Goddess questioned him:

"Helios, be pitiful on me that am a goddess, if ever by word or deed I gladdened thy heart. My daughter, whom I bore, a sweet plant and fair to see; it was her shrill voice I heard through the air unharvested, even as of one violently entreated, but I saw her not with my eyes. But do thou that lookest down with thy rays from the holy air upon all the land and sea, do thou tell me truly

[3] Hades, the Lord of the Underworld, son of the Titans Cronos and Rhea, brother of Zeus.
[4] Zeus ("son of Cronos").
[5] An Underworld goddess, associated with the moon, death, and night.
[6] See footnote 1, p. 120. In this selection, the lines that appear in brackets "state the probable meaning of a dilapidated passage" (translator's note).
[7] A Titaness, married to her brother Cronos, Rheie (or Rhea) was the mother of the great Greek gods, including Zeus, Hades, and Demeter.

concerning my dear child, if thou didst behold her; who it is that hath gone off and ravished her away from me against her will, who is it of gods or mortal men?"

"So spake she, and Hyperionides[8] answered her:

"Daughter of fair-tressed Rheia, Queen Demeter, thou shalt know it; for greatly do I pity and revere thee in thy sorrow for thy slim-ankled child. There is none other guilty of the Immortals but Zeus himself that gathereth the clouds, who gave thy daughter to Hades, his own brother, to be called his lovely wife; and Hades has ravished her away in his chariot, loudly shrilling, beneath the dusky gloom. But, Goddess, do thou cease from thy long lamenting. It behoves not thee thus vainly to cherish anger unassuaged. No unseemly lord for thy daughter among the Immortals is Aidoneus,[9] the lord of many, thine own brother and of one seed with thee, and for his honour he won, since when was made the threefold division, to be lord among those with whom he dwells."

So spake he, and called upon his horses, and at his call they swiftly bore the fleet chariot on like long-winged birds. But grief more dread and bitter fell upon her, and wroth thereafter was she with Cronion[10] that hath dark clouds for his dwelling. She held apart from the gathering of the Gods and from tall Olympus, and disfiguring her form for many days she went among the cities and rich fields of men.

• • •

Then the most dread and terrible of years did the Goddess bring for mortals upon the fruitful earth, nor did the earth send up the seed, for Demeter of the goodly garland concealed it. Many crooked ploughs did the oxen drag through the furrows in vain, and much white barley fell fruitless upon the land. Now would the whole race of mortal men have perished utterly from the stress of famine, and the Gods that hold mansions in Olympus[11] would have lost the share and renown of gift and sacrifice, if Zeus had not conceived a counsel within his heart.

First he roused Iris[12] of the golden wings to speed forth and call the fair-tressed Demeter, the lovesome in beauty. So spake Zeus, and Iris obeyed Zeus, the son of Cronos, who hath dark clouds for his tabernacle, and swiftly she sped adown the space between heaven and earth. Then came she to the citadel of fragrant Eleusis,[13] and in the temple she found Demeter clothed in dark raiment, and speaking wingèd words addressed her: "Demeter, Father Zeus, whose counsels are imperishable, bids thee back unto the tribes of the eternal Gods. Come thou, then, lest the word of Zeus be of no avail." So spake she in her prayer, but the Goddess yielded not. Thereafter the Father sent forth all the blessed Gods, all of the Immortals, and coming one by one they bade Demeter return, and gave her many splendid gifts, and all honours that she might choose among the immortal Gods. But none availed to persuade by turning her mind and her angry heart, so stubbornly she refused their sayings. For she deemed no more for ever to enter fragrant Olympus, and no more to allow the earth to bear her fruit, until

---

[8] "Son of Hyperion," i.e., Helios.
[9] An extended form of the name Hades.
[10] Zeus.
[11] See footnote 5, p. 123.
[12] The rainbow, a messenger for Zeus.
[13] A city near Athens which became the center for the worship of Demeter.

her eyes should behold her fair-faced daughter.

But when far-seeing Zeus, the lord of the thunder-peal, had heard the thing, he sent to Erebus the slayer of Argos, the God of the golden wand,[14] to win over Hades with soft words, and persuade him to bring up holy Persephone into the light, and among the Gods, from forth the murky gloom, that so her mother might behold her, and that her anger might relent. And Hermes disobeyed not, but straightway and speedily went forth beneath the hollow places of the earth, leaving the home of Olympus. That King he found within his dwelling, sitting on a couch with his chaste bedfellow, who sorely grieved for desire of her mother, that still was cherishing a fell design against the ill deeds of the Gods. Then the strong slayer of Argos drew near and spoke: "Hades of the dark locks, thou Prince of men out-worn, Father Zeus bade me bring the dread Persephone forth from Erebus[15] among the Gods, that her mother may behold her, and relent from her anger and terrible wrath against the Immortals, for now she contrives a mighty deed, to destroy the feeble tribes of earth-born men by withholding the seed under the earth. Thereby the honours of the Gods are minished, and fierce is her wrath, nor mingles she with the Gods, but sits apart within the fragrant temple in the steep citadel of Eleusis."

So spake he, and smiling were the brows of Aidoneus, Prince of the dead, nor did he disobey the commands of King Zeus, as speedily he bade the wise Persephone: "Go, Persephone, to thy dark-mantled mother, go with a gentle spirit in thy breast, nor be thou beyond all other folk disconsolate. Verily I shall be no unseemly lord of thine among the Immortals, I that am the brother of Father Zeus, and whilst thou art here shalt thou be mistress over all that lives and moves, but among the Immortals shalt thou have the greatest renown. Upon them that wrong thee shall vengeance be unceasing, upon them that solicit not thy power with sacrifice, and pious deeds, and every acceptable gift."

So spake he, and wise Persephone was glad; and joyously and swiftly she arose, but the God himself, stealthily looking around her, gave her sweet pomegranate seed to eat, and this he did that she might not abide for ever beside revered Demeter of the dark mantle.[16] Then openly did Aidoneus, the Prince of all, get ready the steeds beneath the golden chariot, and she climbed up into the golden chariot, and beside her the strong Slayer of Argos took reins and whip in hand, and drove forth from the halls, and gladly sped the horses twain. Speedily they devoured the long way; nor sea, nor rivers, nor grassy glades, nor cliffs, could stay the rush of the deathless horses; nay, far above them they cleft the deep air in their course. Before the fragrant temple he drove them, and checked them where dwelt Demeter of the goodly garland, who, when she beheld them, rushed forth like a Mænad down a dark mountain woodland.[17]

---

[14] A reference to Hermes (see footnote 4, p. 122, who, at Zeus' command, slew the hundred-eyed watchman Argos (or Argus). Zeus, surprised by his wife Hera while attempting to seduce the mortal woman Io, changed Io into a cow and claimed he had no idea where the animal had come from. Hera, undeceived, asked Zeus to make her a gift of the heifer and set Argos to stand guard over the beast.

[15] A region of the Underworld, usually used as a synonym for Hades.

[16] An universally diffused belief declares that whosoever tastes the food of the dead may never return to earth. [A. L.]

[17] Female followers of the wine-god Dionysus, the Maenads were, in the words of Edith Hamilton, "women frenzied with wine. They rushed through the woods and over mountains uttering sharp cries, waving pine-cone-tipped wands, swept away in a fierce ecstasy. Nothing could stop them. They would tear to pieces the wild creatures they met and devour the bloody shreds of flesh."

[But Persephone on the other side rejoiced to see her mother dear, and leaped to meet her; but the mother said, "Child, in Hades hast thou eaten any food? for if thou hast not] then with me and thy father the son of Cronos, who has dark clouds for his tabernacle, shalt thou ever dwell honoured among all the Immortals. But if thou hast tasted food, thou must return again, and beneath the hollows of the earth must dwell in Hades a third portion of the year; yet two parts of the year thou shalt abide with me and the other Immortals. When the earth blossoms with all manner of fragrant flowers, then from beneath the murky gloom shalt thou come again, a mighty marvel to Gods and to mortal men.

• • •

So the livelong day in oneness of heart did they cheer each other with love, and their minds ceased from sorrow, and great gladness did either win from other. Then came to them Hekatê of the fair wimple, and often did she kiss the holy daughter of Demeter, and from that day was her queenly comrade and handmaiden; but to them for a messenger did far-seeing Zeus of the loud thunder-peal send fair-tressed Rhea to bring dark-mantled Demeter among the Gods, with pledge of what honour she might choose among the Immortals. He vowed that her daughter, for the third part of the revolving year, should dwell beneath the murky gloom, but for the other two parts she should abide with her mother and the other gods.

Thus he spake, and the Goddess disobeyed not the commands of Zeus. Swiftly she sped down from the peaks of Olympus, and came to fertile Rarion; fertile of old, but now no longer fruitful; for fallow and leafless it lay, and hidden was the white barley grain by the device of fair-ankled Demeter. None the less with the growing of the Spring the land was to teem with tall ears of corn, and the rich furrows were to be heavy with corn, and the corn to be bound in sheaves. There first did she land from the unharvested ether, and gladly the Goddesses looked on each other, and rejoiced in heart, and thus first did Rhea of the fair wimple speak to Demeter:

"Hither, child; for he calleth thee, far-seeing Zeus, the lord of the deep thunder, to come among the Gods, and has promised thee such honours as thou wilt, and hath decreed that thy child, for the third of the rolling year, shall swell beneath the murky gloom, but the other two parts with her mother and the rest of the Immortals. So doth he promise that it shall be and thereto nods his head; but come, my child, obey, and be not too unrelenting against the Son of Cronos, the lord of the dark cloud. And anon do thou increase the grain that bringeth life to men."

So spake she, and Demeter of the fair garland obeyed. Speedily she sent up the grain from the rich glebe, and the wide earth was heavy with leaves and flowers.

QUESTIONS
Language

1. A characteristic of the writing in this work is the use of compound adjectives, or phrases used as adjectives, to modify nouns. Thus in the first line of the "Hymn to Demeter," the poet uses the compound adjective "fair-tressed" to modify the proper noun "Demeter"; and whenever we see that goddess' name, we are likely to see the same modifier.

Make a list of all the gods and goddesses who appear in the hymn and the words or phrases that typically describe them. What do these modifiers add to this poem?

2. Find the meaning of these words in a good dictionary: *maugre* (p. 163); *wimple* (p. 163); *ambrosial* (p. 163); *sooth-saying* (p. 163); *nectar* (p. 163); *lave* (p. 163); *unassuaged* (p. 164); *tabernacle* (p. 164); *citadel* (p. 164); *raiment* (p. 164); *imperishable* (p. 164); *mantle* (p. 165); *disconsolate* (p. 165); *fallow* (p. 166); *glebe* (p. 166).

3. Lang deliberately uses a number of *archaic*—ancient, not current—words in his translation of this hymn. Find these archaisms; what do you think they mean? (The *Oxford English Dictionary* will be helpful where you have difficulty.) Why does Lang use archaisms when he can use modern words?

4. Look at this sentence describing the narcissus, a flower especially loved by the lord of the Underworld: "From its roots grew forth a hundred blossoms, and with its fragrant odour the wide heaven above and the whole earth laughed, and the salt wave of the sea." How does the *syntax* of this sentence—the order of its words—differ from that of sentences you are accustomed to reading or writing? Can you find other sentences which depart from traditional English syntax? Why does Lang use this unconventional syntax?

Content

1. What happens to Persephone, Demeter's daughter, at the beginning of this myth? What is her mother's reaction?

2. Why won't any gods or men tell Demeter where her daughter is, or help to get her back? What does Helios finally counsel Demeter to do? What is her reaction? Why are the other gods alarmed by it?

3. Why must Persephone spend one-third of the year in the underworld with Aidoneus (Hades)? At what time of the year does she reemerge from the darkness?

4. The pomegranate was an ancient symbol of marriage. Explain how this fact helps illuminate the Demeter–Persephone myth.

Suggestions for Writing

1. Many modern people tend to think of myths as fanciful stories—fictions—which are entertaining but which don't make much sense. To the ancient people who believed in them, however, a myth such as this one, carefully recorded thousands of years after it was first uttered, was no fiction: it was absolute truth; it was reality. Every culture has—in addition to a mythology (such as a religious one) it may share with other cultures—a mythology peculiar to itself, more or less passionately believed in. With your classmates, try to step back for awhile from American culture. What are some of *our* myths; what are the "stories" we believe in and which influence our behavior? To help you discover them, try imagining yourself a stranger from a totally alien culture, observing the United States.

2. The "Hymn to Demeter" is one of a group of myths which express, in symbol and metaphor, the eternal cycle of nature, the death of all vegetation in the fall and its rebirth in the spring, as well as the human feelings of sorrow and joy, respectively, these natural phenomena inspire. Create a myth of your own which expresses the same extraordinary cycle. Be as imaginative as you can: try to capture the *feel* of the myths you've been reading in this book.

CHARLES PERRAULT

"Cinderella"

As psychologist Bruno Bettelheim points out in *The Uses of Enchantment* (see p. 433), "Cinderella" is probably the most popular and widely known of all fairy tales. Versions of it exist throughout the world; in 1893, the Victorian folklorist Marion R. Cox published a collection consisting of 345 variants of the tale. The earliest known written version comes from ninth-century China, while in the West, the story first appeared in print in *The Pentamerone of Giambattista Basile,* published in 1636.

The version best known today, however, is the one written by Charles Perrault (1628–1703), the "Father of the French Fairytale." After an early governmental career, Perrault turned to literature in 1683. During his own lifetime, he was most famous (or infamous) for his belief, set forth at length in his four-volume *Le Parallèle des anciens et des modernes* (1688–1696), that, in the realms of literature and art, modern men had far surpassed the achievements of the ancients.

His enduring reputation, however, rests on one slim volume, *Contes de ma mère l'Oye* (*Tales of Mother Goose*) in which the author wrote down eight fairy tales he had apparently learned from his son (who in turn had probably heard them from a nurse): "Sleeping Beauty," "Little Red Riding Hood," "Bluebeard," "Puss-in-Boots," "The Fairies," "Riquet of the Tuft," "Hop O' My Thumb," and "Cinderella."

Since Perrault's work was intended for a refined, aristocratic audience, he prettified the stories by eliminating or altering any detail he considered vulgar or overly brutal. In the version of "Cinderella" found in *Grimms' Fairy Tales,* for example, each of the wicked stepsisters attempts to fit her foot into the tiny slipper by mutilating herself (one slices off her big toe, the other her heel). And, whereas Perrault's Cinderella forgives her cold-hearted siblings, the stepsisters in the Grimm brothers' story are punished for their dreadful behavior by having their eyes pecked out by pigeons. It is also interesting to note that in no other version but Perrault's does Cinderella lose a *glass* slipper—a detail which may be the result of a misunderstanding on Perrault's part. Since the French words for fur (*vair*) and glass (*verre*) are so similar, it is possible that when Perrault first heard the story he mistook one word for the other and thus, as Bettelheim says, "changed a fur slipper into one made of glass." Finally, Perrault supplies his heroine with a fairy godmother who makes it possible for the young girl to attend the prince's ball. In earlier versions of the story, the supernatural assistance received by Cinderella comes from various Helpful Animals.

Once upon a time there was a gentleman who married, for his second wife, the proudest and most haughty woman that ever was seen. She had two daughters of her own, who were, indeed, exactly like her in all things. The gentleman

From *The Tales of Mother Goose,* translated by Charles Welsh. Copyright 1901 by D. C. Heath & Co.

had also a young daughter, of rare goodness and sweetness of temper, which she took from her mother, who was the best creature in the world.

The wedding was scarcely over, when the stepmother's bad temper began to show itself. She could not bear the goodness of this young girl, because it made her own daughters appear the more odious. The stepmother gave her the meanest work in the house to do; she had to scour the dishes, tables, etc., and to scrub the floors and clean out the bedrooms. The poor girl had to sleep in the garret, upon a wretched straw bed, while her sisters lay in fine rooms with inlaid floors, upon beds of the very newest fashion, and where they had looking-glasses so large that they might see themselves at their full length. The poor girl bore all patiently, and dared not complain to her father, who would have scolded her if she had done so, for his wife governed him entirely.

When she had done her work, she used to go into the chimney corner, and sit down among the cinders, hence she was called Cinderwench. The younger sister of the two, who was not so rude and uncivil as the elder, called her Cinderella. However, Cinderella, in spite of her mean apparel, was a hundred times more handsome than her sisters, though they were always richly dressed.

It happened that the King's son gave a ball, and invited to it all persons of fashion. Our young misses were also invited, for they cut a very grand figure among the people of the country-side. They were highly delighted with the invitation, and wonderfully busy in choosing the gowns, petticoats, and head-dresses which might best become them. This made Cinderella's lot still harder, for it was she who ironed her sisters' linen and plaited their ruffles. They talked all day long of nothing but how they should be dressed.

"For my part," said the elder, "I will wear my red velvet suit with French trimmings."

"And I," said the younger, "shall wear my usual skirt; but then, to make amends for that I will put on my gold-flowered mantle, and my diamond stomacher, which is far from being the most ordinary one in the world." They sent for the best hairdressers they could get to make up their hair in fashionable style, and bought patches for their cheeks. Cinderella was consulted in all these matters, for she had good taste. She advised them always for the best, and even offered her services to dress their hair, which they were very willing she should do.

As she was doing this, they said to her:—

"Cinderella, would you not be glad to go to the ball?"

"Young ladies," she said, "you only jeer at me: it is not for such as I am to go there."

"You are right," they replied; "people would laugh to see a Cinderwench at a ball."

Any one but Cinderella would have dressed their hair awry, but she was good-natured, and arranged it perfectly well. They were almost two days without eating, so much were they transported with joy. They broke above a dozen laces in trying to lace themselves right, that they might have a fine, slender shape, and they were continually at their looking-glass.

At last the happy day came; they went to Court, and Cinderella followed them with her eyes as long as she could, and when she had lost sight of them, she fell a-crying.

Her godmother, who saw her all in tears, asked her what was the matter.

"I wish I could—I wish I could—" but she could not finish for sobbing.

Her godmother, who was a fairy, said to her, "You wish you could go to the ball; is it not so?"

"Alas, yes," said Cinderella, sighing.

"Well," said her godmother, "be but a good girl, and I will see that you go." Then she took her into her chamber, and said to her, "Run into the garden, and bring me a pumpkin."

Cinderella went at once to gather the finest she could get, and brought it to her godmother, not being able to imagine how this pumpkin could help her to go to the ball. Her godmother scooped out all the inside of it, leaving nothing but the rind. Then she struck it with her wand, and the pumpkin was instantly turned into a fine gilded coach.

She then went to look into the mouse-trap, where she found six mice, all alive. She ordered Cinderella to lift the trap-door, when, giving each mouse, as it went out, a little tap with her wand, it was that moment turned into a fine horse, and the six mice made a fine set of six horses of a beautiful mouse-colored, dapple gray.

Being at a loss for a coachman, Cinderella said, "I will go and see if there is not a rat in the rat-trap—we may make a coachman of him."

"You are right," replied her godmother; "go and look."

Cinderella brought the rat-trap to her, and in it there were three huge rats. The fairy chose the one which had the largest beard, and, having touched him with her wand, he was turned into a fat coachman with the finest mustache and whiskers ever seen.

After that, she said to her:—

"Go into the garden, and you will find six lizards behind the watering-pot; bring them to me."

She had no sooner done so than her godmother turned them into six footmen, who skipped up immediately behind the coach, with their liveries all trimmed with gold and silver, and they held on as if they had done nothing else their whole lives.

The fairy then said to Cinderella, "Well, you see here a carriage fit to go to the ball in; are you not pleased with it?"

"Oh, yes!" she cried; "but must I go as I am in these rags?"

Her godmother simply touched her with her wand, and, at the same moment, her clothes were turned into cloth of gold and silver, all decked with jewels. This done, she gave her a pair of the prettiest glass slippers in the whole world. Being thus attired, she got into the carriage, her godmother commanding her, above all things, not to stay till after midnight, and telling her, at the same time, that if she stayed one moment longer, the coach would be a pumpkin again, her horses mice, her coachman a rat, her footmen lizards, and her clothes would become just as they were before.

She promised her godmother she would not fail to leave the ball before midnight. She drove away, scarce able to contain herself for joy. The King's son, who was told that a great princess, whom nobody knew, was come, ran out to receive her. He gave her his hand as she alighted from the coach, and led her into the hall where the company were assembled. There was at once a profound silence; every one left off dancing, and the violins ceased to play, so attracted was every one by the singular beauties of the unknown newcomer. Nothing was then heard but a confused sound of voices saying:—

"Ha! how beautiful she is! Ha! how beautiful she is!"

The King himself, old as he was, could not keep his eyes off her, and he told the Queen under his breath that it was a long time since he had seen so beautiful and lovely a creature.

All the ladies were busy studying her clothes and head-dress, so that they might have theirs made next day after the same pattern, provided they could meet with such fine materials and able hands to make them.

The King's son conducted her to the seat of honor, and afterwards took her out to dance with him. She danced so very gracefully that they all admired her more and more. A fine collation was served, but the young Prince ate not a morsel, so intently was he occupied with her.

She went and sat down beside her sisters, showing them a thousand civilities, and giving them among other things part of the oranges and citrons with which the Prince had regaled her. This very much surprised them, for they had not been presented to her.

Cinderella heard the clock strike a quarter to twelve. She at once made her adieus to the company and hastened away as fast as she could.

As soon as she got home, she ran to find her godmother, and, after having thanked her, she said she much wished she might go to the ball the next day, because the King's son had asked her to do so. As she was eagerly telling her godmother all that happened at the ball, her two sisters knocked at the door; Cinderella opened it. "How long you have stayed!" said she, yawning, rubbing her eyes, and stretching herself as if she had been just awakened. She had not, however, had any desire to sleep since they went from home.

"If you had been at the ball," said one of her sisters, "you would not have been tired with it. There came thither the finest princess, the most beautiful ever was seen with mortal eyes. She showed us a thousand civilities, and gave us oranges and citrons."

Cinderella did not show any pleasure at this. Indeed, she asked them the name of the princess; but they told her they did not know it, and that the King's son was very much concerned, and would give all the world to know who she was. At this Cinderella, smiling, replied:—

"Was she then so very beautiful? How fortunate you have been! Could I not see her? Ah! dear Miss Charlotte, do lend me your yellow suit of clothes which you wear every day."

"Ay, to be sure!" cried Miss Charlotte; "lend my clothes to such a dirty Cinderwench as thou art! I should be out of my mind to do so."

Cinderella, indeed, expected such an answer and was very glad of the refusal; for she would have been sadly troubled if her sister had lent her what she jestingly asked for. The next day the two sisters went to the ball, and so did Cinderella, but dressed more magnificently than before. The King's son was always by her side, and his pretty speeches to her never ceased. These by no means annoyed the young lady. Indeed, she quite forgot her godmother's orders to her, so that she heard the clock begin to strike twelve when she thought it could not be more than eleven. She then rose up and fled, as nimble as a deer. The Prince followed, but could not overtake her. She left behind one of her glass slippers, which the Prince took up most carefully. She got home, but quite out of breath, without her carriage, and in her old clothes, having nothing left her of all her finery but one of the little slippers, fellow to the one she had dropped. The guards at the palace gate were asked if they had not seen a princess go out, and they replied they had seen nobody go out but a young girl, very meanly dressed, and who had more the air of a poor country girl than of a young lady.

When the two sisters returned from the ball, Cinderella asked them if they had had a pleasant time, and if the fine lady had been there. They told her, yes; but that she hurried away the moment it struck twelve, and with so much haste that she dropped one of her little glass slippers, the prettiest in the world, which the King's son had taken up. They said, further, that he had done nothing but look at her all the time, and that most certainly he was very much in love with the beautiful owner of the glass slipper.

What they said was true; for a few days after the King's son caused it to be proclaimed, by sound of trumpet, that he would marry her whose foot this slipper would fit exactly. They began to try it on the princesses, then on the duchesses, and then on all the ladies of the Court; but in vain. It was brought to the two sisters, who did all they possibly could to thrust a foot into the slipper, but they could not succeed. Cinderella, who saw this, and knew her slipper, said to them, laughing:—

"Let me see if it will not fit me."

Her sisters burst out a-laughing, and began to banter her. The gentleman who was sent to try the slipper looked earnestly at Cinderella, and, finding her very handsome, said it was but just that she should try, and that he had orders to let every lady try it on.

He obliged Cinderella to sit down, and, putting the slipper to her little foot, he found it went on very easily, and fitted her as if it had been made of wax. The astonishment of her two sisters was great, but it was still greater when Cinderella pulled out of her pocket the other slipper and put it on her foot. Thereupon, in came her godmother, who, having touched Cinderella's clothes with her wand, made them more magnificent than those she had worn before.

And now her two sisters found her to be that beautiful lady they had seen at the ball. They threw themselves at her feet to beg pardon for all their ill treatment of her. Cinderella took them up, and, as she embraced them, said that she forgave them with all her heart, and begged them to love her always.

She was conducted to the young Prince, dressed as she was. He thought her more charming than ever, and, a few days after, married her. Cinderella, who was as good as she was beautiful, gave her two sisters a home in the palace, and that very same day married them to two great lords of the Court.

QUESTIONS

Language

1. Look up these words in a dictionary: *stomacher* (p. 169), *collation* (p. 171).
2. Are there any elements of humor in this version of "Cinderella"? What are they? Does Cinderella herself have a sense of humor?
3. Try to decide what Perrault's attitudes are toward the various members of Cinderella's family by looking at his *tone* when he speaks of them. For example, do you think he dislikes the stepsisters? How does he feel about the father?

Content

1. Describe Cinderella as completely as possible: consider her actions, her speeches, her private life. Do you like her as a character? Admire her?

2. What parts of this fairy tale would most appeal to children? Why?
3. What do you think the moral of ''Cinderella'' is? What does it teach the reader? What fantasies does it gratify?

Suggestions for Writing

1. Child psychologist Bruno Bettleheim has said, ''No other fairy tale renders so well as the 'Cinderella' stories the inner experiences of the young child in the throes of sibling rivalry, when he feels hopelessly outclassed by his brothers and sisters.'' Write an essay in which you explore how ''Cinderella'' represents the conflicts and pain of sibling rivalry. Be sure to write not just about Cinderella and her sisters but also about the parents and how they contribute to the situation.
2. We see nothing of Cinderella's real mother in Perrault's tale, but the fairy godmother is a symbolic representation of her. Write an essay in which you compare and contrast Cinderella's magical helper with her stepmother. Talk not only about each one's character and actions, but also about their feelings for the young girl who sits in the ashes of the hearth.
3. The Cinderella story is a perennial favorite and has been treated in a variety of ways. For example, the comedian Jerry Lewis starred in a movie called *Cinderfella* about a young man maltreated by the people he lives with. Write your own modern version of ''Cinderella,'' in which the central character is either a young man or a young woman. Your story can be humorous or serious. Change whatever details of the fairy tale you like. Your heroine or hero might have to work nights at a dingy diner while the brothers and sisters go out dancing at a fashionable disco. Be inventive. Later, read your stories in class. Whose version do you like best? Why?

COURTLAND N. SMITH

''The Greatest Mother in the World''

In his book *The Hundred Greatest Advertisements* (1949), Julian N. Watkins describes Courtland Smith's ''The Greatest Mother in the World'' as ''the most famous ad of the First World War.'' Created by Smith for the War Advertising Committee, the poster proved so effective that it was adopted by Great Britain for use in its own Red Cross drives—''the only instance,'' according to Watkins, ''where an American ad was accorded such an honor.''

The poster demonstrates the important interplay of artwork and copy (the written text) in advertising. Smith's idea of depicting the Red Cross as an ''allegorical figure typifying motherhood'' was brilliantly realized by artist A. E. Foringer. The figure's succoring, suppliant pose, its monumental size, the sculpted look of the long, flowing gown—all these features give the drawing the look of a Renaissance pietà (a statue or painting of the Virgin Mary cradling the dead body of Christ), thereby imparting a religious quality to the advertisement.

The GREATEST MOTHER in the WORLD

 Stretching forth her hands to all in need; to Jew or Gentile, black or white; knowing no favorite, yet favoring all.

Ready and eager to comfort at a time when comfort is most needed. Helping the little home that's crushed beneath an iron hand by showing mercy in a healthy, human way; rebuilding it, in fact, with stone on stone; replenishing empty bins and empty cupboards; bringing warmth to hearts and hearths too long neglected.

Seeing all things with a mother's sixth sense that's blind to jealousy and meanness; seeing men in their true light, as naughty children — snatching, biting, bitter—but with a hidden side that's quickest touched by mercy.

Reaching out her hands across the sea to No Man's land; to cheer with warmer comforts thousands who must stand and wait in stenched and crawling holes and water-soaked entrenchments where cold and wet bite deeper, so they write, than Boche steel or lead.

She's warming thousands, feeding thousands, healing thousands from her store; the Greatest Mother in the World—the RED CROSS.

Every Dollar of a Red Cross War Fund goes to War Relief

QUESTIONS

Language

1. One of the most useful techniques a writer employs is *parallelism* (see definition on p. 8): organizing and unifying a sentence, a paragraph, or an even larger unit of writing by repeating certain verbal patterns. Though parallelism, used in rather simple sentences, can be dull, it is, in long, complicated sentences and paragraphs, an effective way of controlling and organizing what you have to say. Find instances of parallelism in this advertisement. Are there sentences that don't fit the pattern? Why were they included?

2. What essential element does nearly every sentence in this ad lack? What is the effect of this?

3. With the exception of the second, every paragraph of the Red Cross ad consists of a single sentence. Why did the copywriter make these sentences so long? What effect is he striving for?

4. Why do advertisements and journalism use, in general, one- or two-sentence paragraphs? What are the disadvantages or limitations of this practice?

5. This ad utilizes—as does most good writing—both abstract and concrete language. Look up *concrete* and *abstract* in a good dictionary; discuss the distinctions between them in class. Then point out which language in the ad is abstract and which, concrete.

6. The adjective *stenched* in the fourth paragraph does not exist, though of course the noun *stench* does. Why did the copywriter make up a word like this?

Content

1. Look closely at this ad's physical layout, designed by artist A. E. Foringer. Look at the woman's size, her costume, her pose, the soldier, the stretcher on which he lies, and the design of the text or copy. What is each of these things supposed to suggest? What does each contribute? What effect is Foringer trying to achieve?

2. How do you respond to the woman's face? Does she look like a mother? What is her expression?

3. Why does the copywriter, Courtland Smith, establish immediately that "The Greatest Mother in the World" helps "Jew or Gentile, black or white"? Is it *necessary* to say this?

4. Do you think men are "naughty children—snatching, biting, bitter"? (And does Smith mean to include women here, too?) Does this seem a strange way to depict men, given the fact that Europe and America were both fighting one of the bloodiest, most devastating wars in human history?

5. Look up the word *sentimentality* in a good dictionary. Can you find sentimentality in this ad?

6. What does the word *Boche* mean? Why was this particular word chosen? What emotions does it appeal to?

Suggestions for Writing

1. The Red Cross is an enormous international organization, which, although it performs necessary and merciful social services, is very far removed from the one woman personally dispensing physical comfort pictured in this advertisement and praised in the copy. Why, then, was the ad so successful? Would it have appealed most to women or to men? In your opinion, how much did the religious associations (see the headnote) contribute? Write an essay analyzing the reasons for the advertisement's legendary success.

2. The Red Cross might have used other advertising strategies to attract donations during World War I. Compose one such alternative ad yourself. Briefly describe the illustration or photograph—if you choose to have one—and then write out the copy. Along with

the rest of your class, read your advertisement aloud. Which one do you like best? Why?

3. Define, in a short essay, one of the following words: *mercy; compassion; tenderness; tolerance; generosity; selflessness; understanding.* Consult a dictionary for the formal definition of the word you choose; then create your own definition. If you choose *selflessness,* for example, you might proceed by giving different examples of selfless behavior, by telling a story from your own experience which illustrates selflessness, or by contrasting your word with its opposite, selfishness.

ALMADÉN VINEYARDS

"Grapes, Like Children, Need Love and Affection"

The following advertisement, showing a rather sexy Earth Mother rocking her "baby" (a California vineyard) to sleep, was created for the Almadén Vineyards by the ad agency of Dancer Fitzgerald Sample Inc.

Reprinted with permission of Dancer Fitzgerald Sample Inc.

Grapes, like children, need love and affection.

Here in the Almadén Vineyards in Northern California we coddle and
protect our children, the grapes of Almadén.
The fruit of our efforts can be seen in our versatile Grenache Rosé.
Carefully nurtured from the descendants of the famed Grenache
grapes of Tavel, this Rosé is fruity, light and refreshing.
It's the perfect "goes with everything" wine.
Yes, we are proud parents.

Almadén Vineyards, Los Gatos and Paicines, California

Almadén

QUESTIONS

Language

1. Who is the speaker in this advertisement? What is the tone of the copy? What does the tone reveal about the attitude the advertiser—Almadén Vineyards—has toward its product? Toward us, the potential customers?
2. How would you characterize the diction—the kind of words—used in this advertisement? Is it formal or informal? Is the language basically concrete or abstract?
3. The headline of this ad contains a figure of speech. What is it? Point to every word in the copy which develops it.

Content

1. What kind of audience do you think this ad is addressed to? Describe the typical "target." Would he—or she—drink much wine? Be knowledgeable about wine? How do you know? Notice that the price of Grenache Rosé is never mentioned, even in the most general of terms. Why is this? After reading the ad, would you think the wine is inexpensive? Expensive? Why?
2. Besides selling wine, Almadén Vineyards is trying in this ad to project an image of itself. Or, put another way, the image is the vehicle through which the wine is sold. What is this image? How is it embodied in language and picture? Do you think this image corresponds to reality? (Remember that Almadén is one of the largest wine manufacturers in the United States.) How does the image help sell the product?
3. Every advertisement is aimed at certain needs and desires in its audience. In this case, what are they?
4. Study the illustration in this advertisement. Why would the advertisers choose such a young woman to serve as an Earth Mother? Why was such a low-cut dress chosen? Does this sexualize her? Is she a typical or atypical mother figure? Why are nearly all the lines in the picture curves? Why is the earth in the "cradle" rounded and swollen-looking? What other details do you notice?

Suggestions for Writing

1. Using the figure of the Good Mother, write an advertisement for some kind of food, either something that comes to us relatively straight from the earth, such as grapefruit or milk, or something considerably altered, pre-prepared, and packaged, such as TV dinners or breakfast cereals. Choose the advertiser for the product you try to sell (such as the Dairymen's Association or a division of a large food corporation) because you may want to mention it in your ad. Write the copy; describe the layout. Compare your ad with those of your classmates. Which uses the Good Mother most skillfully? What major differences do you see in the ads?
2. Discuss with your classmates, and then write an essay about, the kinds of products the Good Mother figure might profitably be used to advertise, and those for which this archetype is inappropriate. Why is the Good Mother figure wrong in some instances and right in others? Can you generalize about the merchandise and the people for whom the merchandise is intended? Would the images we unconsciously attach to some products—the preconceived attitudes we have toward them—influence an advertiser's decision to use this archetype?

JOHN LENNON AND PAUL MCCARTNEY

"Mother Nature's Son"

(as recorded by the Beatles)

Although John Lennon, Paul McCartney, and George Harrison had been playing music together since their school days in Liverpool, it was not until they recruited drummer Ringo Starr (whom they had met while performing at a nightclub in Hamburg, West Germany) and put themselves in the hands of manager Brian Epstein that the Beatles began to achieve large-scale popularity. Epstein took the four young musicians and completely transformed their image, getting rid of their tough, "rocker" look—black leather jackets, slicked-back "Elvis" hairdos—and substituting "mod" collarless suits and neatly trimmed (though, for their day, shockingly long) "bowl-cut" hairstyles. Thus, the "four mop-tops" were born. An expensive publicity campaign got Beatlemania going; but it was the talent of John, Paul, George, and Ringo that made the group a sixties phenomenon.

Though their early singles such as "She Loves You," "Please Please Me" and "I Want to Hold Your Hand" were simple, unsophisticated songs, they possessed a freshness and energy largely missing from the spiritless pop music of the early sixties. Between 1964 and 1967, the Beatles produced a string of extraordinarily popular albums, which displayed the group's growing musical inventiveness and culminated in the release, in June, 1967, of *Sergeant Pepper's Lonely Hearts Club Band,* considered by many to be the finest rock album ever made. The record proved to be not only a tremendous commercial success, but a critical triumph as well. Its release, however, also brought misfortune. Over the years, the group had come to depend less and less on their manager, and in August, 1967, while the Beatles were in Bangor, Wales, with their new guru, the Maharishi, Epstein took an overdose of drugs and died. The event was a traumatic blow for the Beatles; Lennon later remarked that "the Beatles broke up after Brian died." Though they continued to cut and release albums over the next few years, increasing discord within the band led to its eventual dissolution in 1970. Rumors of a reunion persist, but the four men seem intent on pursuing separate careers.

"Mother Nature's Son," from the so-called White Album of 1968, was a hit record in the early seventies for singer John Denver (see headnote for "Rocky Mountain High," p. 397).

"Mother Nature's Son"

Born a poor young country boy—
Mother Nature's son.
All day long I'm sitting singing songs for everyone.

"Mother Nature's Son" (John Lennon and Paul McCartney) Copyright © 1968 Northern Songs Limited. All rights for the U.S.A., Canada and Mexico controlled by Maclen Music, Inc. c/o ATV Music Corp. Used by permission, all rights reserved.

Sit beside a mountain stream—
see her waters rise.
Listen to the pretty sound of music as she flies.

Find me in my field of grass—
Mother Nature's son.
Swaying daisies sing a lazy song beneath the sun.

Mother Nature's son.

ERIC KAZ

"Mother Earth"

(as recorded by Tom Rush)

Eric Kaz's "Mother Earth" is a contemporary celebration of one of the world's oldest deities: the Great Mother goddess, source of nature's bounties. This song appears on the album *Merrimack County* by the singer Tom Rush, who rose to prominence during the "great American folk revival" of the early sixties. Rush, who began recording professionally while still a student at Harvard, is a reclusive and not particularly prolific artist. But, as rock scholars Nick Logan and Bob Woffinden point out in *The Illustrated Encyclopedia of Rock* (1977), he is highly regarded for his original compositions—the best-known of which is the song "No Regrets"— and is considered to be "one of the few authentic-sounding white interpreters of blues material." Besides *Merrimack County*, Rush's albums include *Tom Rush, Blues/Songs/Ballads, Take a Little Walk with Me, The Circle Game, Wrong End of the Rainbow,* and *Ladies Love Outlaws.*

"Mother Earth"

Mother Earth lives on the ocean
Mother Earth sails on the sea
I am blessed with her devotion
Mother Earth provides for me.

Now I am going on a journey
And I pray all things end well
While Mother Earth looks after me
I will follow faithfully

Green trees grow on mountain top
Birds still sing while morning come
Though I treat her carelessly
Mother Earth provides for me

Copyright © 1971 Willow Way Music. All rights administered by Unart Music Corporation.

When grasslands crave for water
And the harvest needs sunlight
These are times when I am helpless
Mother Earth makes all things right

Mother Earth lives on the ocean
Mother Earth sails on the sea
I am blessed with her devotion
Mother Earth provides for me

QUESTIONS

Language

1. Look at the *syntax* of these songs—that is, at the grammatical parts of each line and their arrangement—and describe what differences you find. What is the effect of the differences? For example, which song is more formal?
2. Notice in "Mother Earth" the composer deliberately says, in the third stanza, "mountain top," rather than "mountain tops," and the grammatically incorrect "morning come" rather than "comes." These things give the song a calypso flavor. How do they change the tone or mood of it?
3. There is considerable *alliteration* in the Beatles' song. (Alliteration is the repetition of the same sound in successive words, e.g., "*d*ull, *d*ark, and soun*d*less *d*ay.") Find the most commonly repeated sound in "Mother Nature's Son." What effect does it have on you as you say it aloud?

Content

1. In what respects is "Mother Earth" like a prayer?
2. Do you think the speakers of these two songs are very much alike? Describe them as well as you can after listening to their songs.
3. Is there some difference of emphasis in these two songs? Is the subject matter slightly different? Which song seems more "innocent"? Why?
4. Look at the first two lines of "Mother Earth." What do you think they mean?
5. In what respects is the figure of Mother Earth in Eric Kaz's song like a true god? In what respects like a human mother?

Suggestions for Writing

1. Write a second verse to the song "Mother Nature's Son." Try to capture the Beatles' tone; try to create as many vivid images as you can, if you decide to continue the praise of nature. Or you might like to supply a more detailed history of the singer, talk about how he sees his future, or imagine him in the middle of winter, finding things to praise even in that season.
2. Where would you prefer to live: in the city or in the country? Write an essay voicing and defending your choice.
3. Discuss with your classmates and then write an essay on what elements of these two songs would have made them especially popular with the so-called flower children of the late 1960s and early 1970s.
4. Who would be more likely to write songs like "Mother Nature's Son" and "Mother Earth": someone from a city who had little contact with nature, or someone raised in the country—perhaps a farmer's son or daughter—who lived in the midst of nature? Write an essay giving the reasons for your opinion. (You might start by considering how nature is portrayed in these songs, and what emotions it generates in the speaker.)

WALTER DONALDSON

"My Mom"

Although he never received any formal musical training, Walter Donaldson (1893–1947) was the composer of some of the best-loved songs in the history of American popular music. Briefly employed in a brokerage house after graduating from high school, Brooklyn-born Donaldson began his musical career as a "demonstration pianist" on Tin Pan Alley (the name given to an area in New York City which, beginning in the 1890s, became a center for songwriters and music publishers), and was soon composing his own tunes.

His most prolific period was the decade following the end of World War I when he was associated with the Irving Berlin Music Corporation. It was during this time that he composed "My Mammy" (1920), probably the most famous of all "mother songs" (a term applied to highly sentimental songs, particularly popular during the late nineteenth and early twentieth centuries, which exalted or gave thanks to an idealized mother figure). Though originally presented on stage by vaudevillian William Frawley (who was later to achieve television stardom in the role of Fred Mertz on the "I Love Lucy" show), the number was made famous by the celebrated entertainer Al Jolson, who performed it in the first "talkie" ever made, *The Jazz Singer* (1927). In 1928, Donaldson left the Berlin organization and founded his own music publishing house, serving as president until illness forced him to retire in 1946. Among his most memorable compositions are: "Carolina in the Morning," "Yes, Sir, That's My Baby," "Makin' Whoopee," "Love Me or Leave Me," "My Blue Heaven," and "Little White Lies."

"My Mom," another one of Donaldson's successful "mother songs," was first recorded by the famous "crooner" of the 1920s, Rudy Vallee.

"My Mom"

I've got one real friend,
More than a friend, I find,
The way I feel, friend,
She's all of this heart of mine.

I'm all for her and I know,
She'll always be for me.
I'm on my way, friend,
I'm going home to see.

Chorus:
My Mom, I love her,
My Mom, you'd love her,
Who wouldn't love her, my Mom!

Reprinted with permission of Traubner & Flynn and Bregman, Vocco & Conn, Inc. © 1932 by Bregman, Vocco & Conn, Inc. Copyright renewed 1959. All rights reserved. Used by permission.

That sweet somebody,
Thinks I'm somebody,
My Pal, My Buddy, My Mom!

Anything I do,
She's my only inspiration,
Anytime I'm blue,
She's my only consolation.

As years come on her,
I gaze upon her,
She's my Madonna,
My Mom! My Mom!

(*Chorus*)

QUESTIONS

Language

1. Look at the words used to describe the speaker's mother. Do any of them surprise you? Are you accustomed to hearing mothers described in this way? Would you use the same words to describe your own mother?
2. Do you think there's anything contradictory or confusing about having a mother called both a ''buddy'' or a ''pal'' *and* a ''madonna''?

Content

1. Of course you know what the subject of this song is when you glance at the title. But suppose you hadn't seen the title; suppose you had only heard the first six or seven lines of the song. Whom would you think the speaker was describing?
2. To whom is the speaker talking? What do you think the other person's reaction is? Or is there any way you can tell?
3. Can you imagine this song being sung by a young woman? How would the song be changed? Would your reaction to it be affected? How?

Suggestions for Writing

1. Do you think a contemporary composer—aiming at a mass audience—would write a song like this? Write an essay giving your opinion and supporting it with reasons. You might begin by considering whether we actually *feel* differently about ''Mother'' than this composer did, or, on the contrary, whether only our style of music has changed.
2. Write, in three different paragraphs, psychological profiles of the young man (the speaker of this song), his mother, and his father. Use the song to help you picture the son and the mother; picturing the father will require more imagination.
3. Look up the words *ideal* and *idealism* in a good dictionary. Write a brief essay, referring back to the definition to strengthen your argument, showing how this song idealizes mothers. You might like to discuss with your classmates what a *realistic* portrait of a mother might consist of.

JACK KIRBY

from "Sonny Sumo"

No one draws action comics better than Jack "King" Kirby (b. 1917), the undisputed master of the form. His superheroes have bodies that seem carved out of granite; their sledgehammer punches explode off the page. Beginning as a cartoon animator and newspaper comic strip illustrator, Kirby came into his own during the early 1940s when, along with his partner Joe Simon, he created the legendary Captain America, the greatest Nazi-fighter of World War II. Twenty years later, Kirby revived the character for Marvel Comics, for whom he also created, in collaboration with editor-in-chief Stan Lee, *The Mighty Thor* and *The Fantastic Four,* two of the titles that helped bring about the great comic book renaissance of the late 1960s.

Discord with Lee led Kirby to leave Marvel in 1970 and join National Periodical Publications, where, given full creative control, he produced what are perhaps his most strikingly original—and certainly his most ambitious—works: an interrelated trilogy of comic books, entitled *The New Gods, Mr. Miracle,* and *The Forever People.* In them, Kirby attempted nothing less than the invention of an entire mythology, dealing with the attempts of the evil lord Darkseid, dictator of Apokolips, to gain control of the universe by locating the "Anti-Life Equation." He is opposed in this terrible quest by the young gods of New Genesis, among whom are the Forever People: Big Bear, Serifan, Moonrider, Vykin, and Beautiful Dreamer. The Forever People are aided and protected by a mysterious but benevolent machine called a Mother Box. The following episode (from *The Forever People,* no. 5) shows Mother Box in action: with the Forever People in the clutches of Darkseid, she has sought someone to help rescue them and discovered the noble warrior Sonny Sumo. Here, she tends Sumo's wounds following his wrestling match with a killer robot. Kirby's is a fascinating, futuristic vision, in which technology has replaced nature in the role of Good Mother.

Forever People, © 1971 DC Comics Inc.

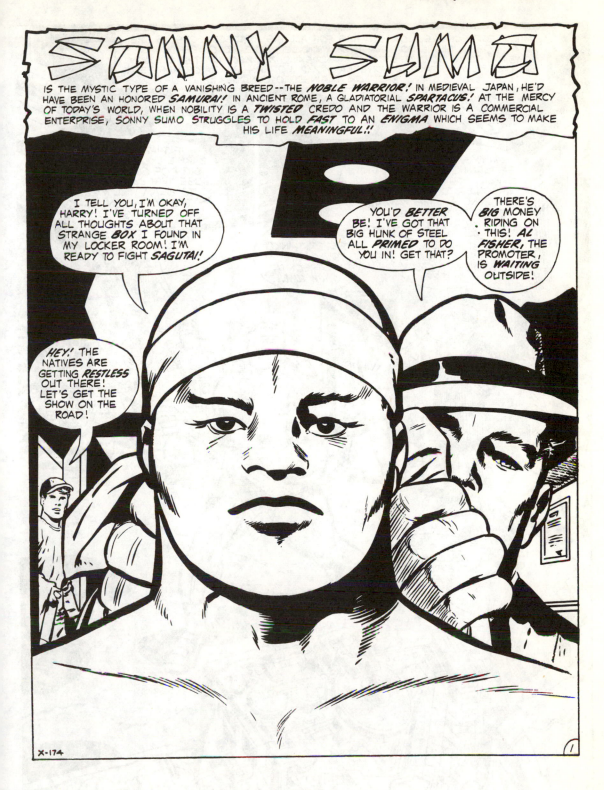

THE *UNCANNY* ROBOT SWIVELS WITH LIGHTNING MOTION AND *STUNS* SONNY WITH A *SAVAGE* KARATE CHOP!

ONLY HIS INCREDIBLE STRENGTH AND STAMINA SAVE SONNY FROM THE DESCENDING BLADES!! HE ROLLS OUT OF DANGER!!

AAAAAAA

BUT *NOT* QUICK ENOUGH TO *FULLY* AVOID THE TERRIBLE FLAME-THROWING FINGERS OF SAGUTAI'S *OTHER* HAND!

ARE YOU *NUTTY*, SHARP? DO YOU THINK I'D BACK *THIS* KIND OF STUNT? WHY, IT'S *MURDER!!* THE POOR GUY IS *DONE FOR!*

IT'S ROUGH! BUT IT'S *NOT* OVER! THERE'S AN *ANGLE* TO THIS ACT THAT YOU'LL HAVE TO *SEE* TO BELIEVE!

IT'S A KIND OF ORIENTAL THING--LIKE INVOKING A *MYSTIC* POWER IN THE MIND! SONNY'S GOING THROUGH THE *RITUAL* NOW! HE CALLS IT *"WOUND REJECTION"!*

DIE, SUMO! DIE!

FOR A FLEETING SECOND, SONNY'S SCORCHED FACE BECOMES A RIGID MASK OF CONCENTRATION!

INSIDE HIM, ANCIENT CENTURIES AND EVEN MORE ANCIENT PRACTICES COME ALIVE! EXPAND! TAKE HOLD!--AND DO THEIR WORK!!

THEN, QUICKLY, THE HEAD RISES! THE FACE IS *STRONG! CLEAN! UNMARKED* BY PAIN OR WOUND!

THEN, WITH AN ALMOST *DESPERATE* URGENCY, SONNY *ATTACKS* HIS MAMMOTH OPPONENT!

YOU'VE FOUGHT LIKE THE THING YOU *ARE,* SAGUTAI!

BUT I MUST *END* THE BATTLE!

KRAAASSH

9.

WHEN SONNY AND HIS TRAINER REACH THE LOCKER ROOM...

DON'T TELL ME WHAT'S UP! I *KNOW!* SAGUTAI GOT 'CHA REAL GOOD, *DIDN'T* HE!!

SURE! THAT *MUST* BE IT! YOUR "MIND-GIMMICK" *CAN'T* HOLD IT FOR LONG! THE WOUNDS ARE COMING *BACK!!*

DON'T STAND THERE, RAPPING! GET A DOCTOR-- HURRY!!

SAGUTAI WAS *GOOD* TONIGHT! THIS *WON'T--BE-- EASY-- TO-- HEAL--*

YOU *WON'T* BATTLE AN ORDINARY PRO!! OH, NO! YOU'RE A *SAMURAI!* YOU GOTTA HAVE BIG ODDS AGAINST YOU--

LEFT ALONE, SONNY *SINKS* WEAKLY TO HIS KNEES! HE ENDURES WHAT WOULD MAKE OTHERS CRY OUT!! SMALL WONDER HE *IGNORES* THE *STIRRING* IN THE *STRANGE* BOX IN HIS ROOM!

PING PING PING PING PING PING

10

MOTHER BOX *REACHES* OUT TO THE SENSITIVE MIND--*LINKS* WITH IT! WORKS WITH *ATOMS*! RESTRUCTURES--*REMOLDS*!--

THEN IT'S OVER! MOTHER HAS RESTORED! PRE-SERVED! AND ESTABLISHED *RAPPORT* WITH SONNY SUMO!!

Y-YOU'VE *HEALED* MY WOUNDS--!

I-I CAN LISTEN TO YOU AND *UNDERSTAND*!

YOU'RE *MOTHER BOX*!!

PING PING PING

YOU SOUGHT ME OUT!--ZEROED IN ON MY MIND!

--AND, NOW, YOU *NEED* MY SERVICES!--A MISSION *WORTHY* OF A SAMURAI!!

PING-PING-PING-PING-PING--

HOW CAN I *REFUSE* YOU, *MOTHER BOX*!? *LEAD ON*!!

PING-PING--PING-PING-PING--

MOTHER BOX AND SONNY SUMO GROW TRANSPARENT AND FADE--UNTIL THEY *VANISH* FROM THE ROOM!!

11

QUESTIONS

Language

1. Look at the various captions in the panels of this comic book story. What is the *tone* of the narrator's voice? Is it calm and businesslike? Does the narrator tell you just the facts? What do you think his attitude toward Sonny Sumo is?

2. Why is it necessary to have captions in this story? What do they add?

3. Look at the trainer's remarks to Sumo. Do you think he feels differently from Fisher or Sharp about the young fighter?

4. Why does the trainer call the fighting robot a "bull-dozing Barbie-Doll"? Does this seem an appropriate label?

Content

1. When do you think this story takes place? What aspects of it are futuristic? What aspects are contemporary? What sort of world does Sonny Sumo live in?

2. What is Sonny Sumo like? What sort of man is he linked with by the narrator in the caption of the first panel? How is he different from them? How do Al Fisher and Harry Sharp see him?

3. Does Sonny seem badly equipped to fight the mechanical monster Sagutai? Does this make his victory more impressive, or are you just surprised by the way he wins? What special talents does he have?

4. What do you think Jack Kirby's—the writer's—attitude toward machines is? How do the various people in the comic strip react to Sagutai? Does the appearance of the Mother Box suggest its power?

5. Just before the fight begins, Sonny Sumo discovers the strange red Mother Box inside his locker; he has no idea what it is. How then does he later come to understand it so quickly? Does he analyze it—try to comprehend it rationally?

6. What tasks does Mother Box perform that we usually associate with a good *human* mother?

Suggestions for Writing

1. Write an essay on how television, advertising, and elaborate promotion have affected sports and the athletes who perform in them. You might want to try to discover why professional sports have become such a big business in modern, urban America.

2. Rewrite the story you have just read in the form of a narrative, interspersing it with Kirby's, or your own rephrasing of Kirby's, original dialogue. Describe the action as vividly as you can. Along with your classmates, read your version aloud. What good things from the comic book, besides the pictures, have been lost? What has been gained? Whose story do you like best? Why?

3. Discuss in class the level of violence in the comics that appear in this book. Does such violence disturb you or are you accustomed to it from your personal reading or from watching television? In an essay, try to answer the question of why there is so much violence in American popular entertainment such as comic books.

IAN FLEMING

from *From Russia with Love*

Next to Beatlemania (see headnote on the Beatles, p. 179), the biggest craze of the mid-sixties was the one that revolved around the literary and cinematic exploits of James Bond, Secret Agent 007 (Bond's code name, signifying that he has a "license to kill"). The creation of English author Ian Fleming (1908–1964), the Bond adventures achieved their enormous success through a skillful blend of "sex, sadism, and snobbery." With one or two exceptions, the Bond books all follow the same formula: 007, a suave, "cruelly handsome" superspy, with a taste for fine wines, fancy cars, and beautiful women, travels to some exotic locale where he does battle with a criminal mastermind who usually possesses a bizarre name (Dr. No, Goldfinger, Hugo Drax) and a fiendish scheme which threatens the safety of the free world. The James Bond movies, like the novels, are slick, highly formulaic works, characterized by picturesque settings, stunning women, extreme violence, and a fascination with technological gadgetry.

The villain of *From Russia with Love* (1957), Fleming's fifth novel, is Rosa Klebb, a hideously ugly woman who heads Otdyel II, the "Operations and Executions" department of the Russian counterespionage organization SMERSH. The plot of the book concerns Klebb's diabolical (if thoroughly ridiculous) scheme to destroy England's most celebrated spy. Briefly, Klebb orders the lovely, loyal Tatiana Romanova to pose as a defector. The woman is told to contact the British Secret Service and say that she is ready to "come over" to the West and bring with her a top-secret Spektor decoding machine on the condition that Bond himself travel to Istanbul and fetch her. Klebb's intention is to have the girl seduce Bond while hidden agents photograph the sordid scene, and then—after Bond has been assassinated by SMERSH's chief executioner—to publish the "filthy pictures" in newspapers all over the world, thereby demolishing the reputations of both Bond and the British Secret Service. In addition, Klebb equips Tatiana with a fake, booby-trapped Spektor machine, rigged to explode when the British cipher experts examine it.

Needless to say, the Russian plot is foiled when Tatiana falls hopelessly in love with the dashing 007, and the SMERSH assassin (a homicidal maniac going by the name of Captain Nash) taunts his intended victim with the details of Klebb's scheme, only to be killed by Bond in a fierce battle aboard the Orient Express. Arriving in Paris, Bond installs Tatiana at the British Embassy and then goes off to confront Klebb who, in the closing moments of the book, makes one last desperate attempt to destroy her hated enemy.

LA TRICOTEUSE

The taxi drew up at the Rue Cambon entrance to the Ritz Hotel.

Bond looked at Nash's watch. 11.45. He must be dead punctual. He knew that if a Russian spy was even a few minutes early or late for a rendezvous the

Reprinted with permission of Macmillan Publishing Co., Inc. and Jonathan Cape Ltd. from *From Russia with Love* by Ian Fleming. Copyright 1957 by Glidrose Productions Limited.

rendezvous was automatically cancelled. He paid off the taxi and went through the door on the left that leads into the Ritz bar.

Bond ordered a double vodka martini. He drank it half down. He felt wonderful. Suddenly the last four days, and particularly last night, were washed off the calendar. Now he was on his own, having his private adventure. All his duties had been taken care of. The girl was sleeping in a bedroom at the Embassy. The Spektor, still pregnant with explosive, had been taken away by the bomb-disposal squad of the Deuxième Bureau. He had spoken to his old friend René Mathis, now head of the Deuxième, and the concierge at the Cambon entrance to the Ritz had been told to give him a pass-key and to ask no questions.

René had been delighted to find himself again involved with Bond in *une affaire noire*. 'Have confidence, *cher* James,' he had said. 'I will execute your mysteries. You can tell me the story afterwards. Two laundry-men with a large laundry basket will come to Room 204 at 12.15. I shall accompany them dressed as the driver of their camion. We are to fill the laundry basket and take it to Orly and await an R.A.F. Canberra which will arrive at two o'clock. We hand over the basket. Some dirty washing which was in France will be in England. Yes?'

Head of Station F had spoken to M. on the scrambler. He had passed over a short written report from Bond. He had asked for the Canberra. No, he had no idea what it was for. Bond had only shown up to deliver the girl and the Spektor. He had eaten a huge breakfast and had left the Embassy saying he would be back after lunch.

Bond looked again at the time. He finished his martini. He paid for it and walked out of the bar and up the steps to the concierge's lodge.

The concierge looked sharply at him and handed over a key. Bond walked over to the lift and got in and went up to the third floor.

The lift door clanged behind him. Bond walked softly down the corridor, looking at the numbers.

2.04. Bond put his right hand inside his coat and on to the taped butt of the Beretta. It was tucked into the waistband of his trousers. He could feel the metal of the silencer warm across his stomach.

He knocked once with his left hand.

'Come in.'

It was a quavering voice. An old woman's voice.

Bond tried the handle of the door. It was unlocked. He slipped the pass-key into his coat-pocket. He pushed the door open with one swift motion and stepped in and shut it behind him.

It was a typical Ritz sitting-room, extremely elegant, with good Empire furniture. The walls were white and the curtains and chair covers were of a small patterned chintz of red roses on white. The carpet was wine-red and close-fitted.

In a pool of sunshine, in a low armed chair beside a Directoire writing desk, a little old woman sat knitting.

The tinkle of the steel needles continued. The eyes behind light-blue tinted bi-focals examined Bond with polite curiosity.

'*Oui, Monsieur?*' The voice was deep and hoarse. The thickly powdered, rather puffy face under the white hair showed nothing but well-bred interest.

Bond's hand on the gun under his coat was taut as a steel spring. His half-closed eyes flickered round the room and back to the little old woman in the chair.

Had he made a mistake? Was this the wrong room? Should he apologize and get out? Could this woman possibly belong to SMERSH? She looked so exactly like the sort of respectable rich widow one would expect to find sitting by herself in the Ritz, whiling the time away with her knitting. The sort of woman who would have her own table, and her favourite waiter, in a corner of the restaurant downstairs—not, of course, the grill room. The sort of woman who would doze after lunch and then be fetched by an elegant black limousine with white side-walled tyres and be driven to the tea-room in the rue de Berri to meet some other rich crone. The old-fashioned black dress with the touch of lace at the throat and wrists, the thin gold chain that hung down over the shapeless bosom and ended in a folding lorgnette, the neat little feet in the sensible black-buttoned boots that barely touched the floor. It couldn't be Klebb! Bond had got the number of the room wrong. He could feel the perspiration under his arms. But now he would have to play the scene through.

'My name is Bond, James Bond.'

'And I, Monsieur, am the Comtesse Metterstein. What can I do for you?' The French was rather thick. She might be German Swiss. The needles tinkled busily.

'I am afraid Captain Nash has met with an accident. He won't be coming today. So I came instead.'

Did the eyes narrow a fraction behind the pale blue spectacles?

'I have not the pleasure of the Captain's acquaintance, Monsieur. Nor of yours. Please sit down and state your business.' The woman inclined her head an inch towards the high-backed chair beside the writing desk.

One couldn't fault her. The graciousness of it all was devastating. Bond walked across the room and sat down. Now he was about six feet away from her. The desk held nothing but a tall old-fashioned telephone with a receiver on a hook, and, within reach of her hand, an ivory-buttoned bellpush. The black mouth of the telephone yawned at Bond politely.

Bond stared rudely into the woman's face, examining it. It was an ugly face, toadlike, under the powder and the tight cottage-loaf of white hair. The eyes were so light brown as to be almost yellow. The pale lips were wet and blubbery below the fringe of nicotine-stained moustache. Nicotine? Where were her cigarettes? There was no ashtray—no smell of smoke in the room.

Bond's hand tightened again on his gun. He glanced down at the bag of knitting, at the shapeless length of small-denier beige wool the woman was working on. The steel needles. What was there odd about them? The ends were discoloured as if they had been held in fire. Did knitting needles ever look like that?

'*Eh bien, Monsieur?*' Was there an edge to the voice? Had she read something in his face?

Bond smiled. His muscles were tense, waiting for any movement, any trick. 'It's no use,' he said cheerfully, gambling. 'You are Rosa Klebb. And you are Head of Otdyel II of SMERSH. You are a torturer and a murderer. You wanted to kill me and the Romanov girl. I am very glad to meet you at last.'

The eyes had not changed. The harsh voice was patient and polite. The woman reached out her left hand towards the bellpush. 'Monsieur, I am afraid you are deranged. I must ring for the *valet de chambre* and have you shown to the door.'

Bond never knew what saved his life. Perhaps it was the flash of realization that no wires led from the bellpush to the wall or into the carpet. Perhaps it was the sudden memory of the English 'Come in' when the expected knock came on the door. But, as her finger reached the ivory knob, he hurled himself sideways out of the chair.

As Bond hit the ground there was a sharp noise of tearing calico. Splinters from the back of his chair sprayed around him. The chair crashed to the floor.

Bond twisted over, tugging at his gun. Out of the corner of his eye he noticed a curl of blue smoke coming from the mouth of the 'telephone.' Then the woman was on him, the knitting needles glinting in her clenched fists.

She stabbed downwards at his legs. Bond lashed out with his feet and hurled her sideways. She had aimed at his legs! As he got to one knee, Bond knew what the coloured tips of the needles meant. It was poison. Probably one of those German nerve poisons. All she had to do was scratch him, even through his clothes.

Bond was on his feet. She was coming at him again. He tugged furiously at his gun. The silencer had caught. There was a flash of light. Bond dodged. One of the needles rattled against the wall behind him and the dreadful chunk of woman, the white bun of wig askew on her head, the slimy lips drawn back from her teeth, was on top of him.

Bond, not daring to use his naked fists against the needles, vaulted sideways over the desk.

Panting and talking to herself in Russian, Rosa Klebb scuttled round the desk, the remaining needle held forward like a rapier. Bond backed away, working at the stuck gun. The back of his legs came against a small chair. He let go the gun and reached behind him and snatched it up. Holding it by the back, with its legs pointing like horns, he went round the desk to meet her. But she was beside the bogus telephone. She swept it up and aimed it. Her hand went to the button. Bond leapt forward. He crashed the chair down. Bullets sprayed into the ceiling and plaster pattered down on his head.

Bond lunged again. The legs of the chair clutched the woman round the waist and over her shoulders. God she was strong! She gave way, but only to the wall. There she held her ground, spitting at Bond over the top of the chair, while the knitting needle quested towards him like a long scorpion's sting.

Bond stood back a little, holding the chair at arms' length. He took aim and high-kicked at the probing wrist. The needle sailed away into the room and pinged down behind him.

Bond came in closer. He examined the position. Yes, the woman was held firmly against the wall by the four legs of the chair. There was no way she could get out of the cage except by brute force. Her arms and legs and head were free, but the body was pinned to the wall.

The woman hissed something in Russian. She spat at him over the chair. Bond bent his head and wiped his face against his sleeve. He looked up and into the mottled face.

'That's all, Rosa,' he said. 'The Deuxième will be here in a minute. In an hour or so you'll be in London. You won't be seen leaving the hotel. You won't be seen going into England. In fact very few people will see you again. From now on you're just a number on a secret file. By the time we've finished with you you'll be ready for the lunatic asylum.'

The face, a few feet away, was changing. Now the blood had drained out of it, and it was yellow. But not, thought Bond, with fear. The pale eyes looked levelly into his. They were not defeated.

The wet, shapeless mouth lengthened in a grin.

'And where will you be when I am in the asylum, Mister Bond?'

'Oh, getting on with my life.'

'I think not, *Angliski spion.*'

Bond hardly noticed the words. He had heard the click of the door opening. A burst of laughter came from the room behind him.

'*Eh bien,*' it was the voice of delight that Bond remembered so well. 'The 70th position! Now, at last, I have seen everything. And invented by an Englishman! James, this really is an insult to my countrymen.'

'I don't recommend it,' said Bond over his shoulder. 'It's too strenuous. Anyway, you can take over now. I'll introduce you. Her name's Rosa. You'll like her. She's a big noise in SMERSH—she looks after the murdering, as a matter of fact.'

Mathis came up. There were two laundry-men with him. The three of them stood and looked respectfully into the dreadful face.

'Rosa,' said Mathis thoughtfully. 'But, this time, a Rosa Malheur. Well, well! But I am sure she is uncomfortable in that position. You two, bring along the *panier de fleurs*—she will be more comfortable lying down.'

The two men walked to the door. Bond heard the creak of the laundry basket.

The woman's eyes were still locked in Bond's. She moved a little, shifting her weight. Out of Bond's sight, and not noticed by Mathis, who was still examining her face, the toe of one shiny buttoned boot pressed under the instep of the other. From the point of its toe there slid forward half an inch of thin knife blade. Like the knitting needles, the steel had a dirty bluish tinge.

The two men came up and put the big square basket down beside Mathis.

'Take her,' said Mathis. He bowed slightly to the woman. 'It has been an honour.'

'*Au revoir,* Rosa,' said Bond.

The yellow eyes blazed briefly.

'Farewell, Mister Bond.'

The boot, with its tiny steel tongue, flashed out.

Bond felt a sharp pain in his right calf. It was only the sort of pain you would get from a kick. He flinched and stepped back. The two men seized Rosa Klebb by the arms.

Mathis laughed. 'My poor James,' he said. 'Count on SMERSH to have the last word.'

The tongue of dirty steel had withdrawn into the leather. Now it was only a harmless bundle of old woman that was being lifted into the basket.

Mathis watched the lid being secured. He turned to Bond. 'It is a good day's work you have done, my friend,' he said. 'But you look tired. Go back to the Embassy and have a rest because this evening we must have dinner together. The best dinner in Paris. And I will find the loveliest girl to go with it.'

Numbness was creeping up Bond's body. He felt very cold. He lifted his hand to brush back the comma of hair over his right eyebrow. There was no feeling in his fingers. They seemed as big as cucumbers. His hand fell heavily to his side.

Breathing became difficult. Bond sighed to the depth of his lungs. He clenched his jaws and half closed his eyes, as people do when they want to hide their drunkenness.

Through his eyelashes he watched the basket being carried to the door. He prised his eyes open. Desperately he focused Mathis.

'I shan't need a girl, René,' he said thickly.

Now he had to gasp for breath. Again his hand moved up towards his cold face. He had an impression of Mathis starting towards him.

Bond felt his knees begin to buckle.

He said, or thought he said, 'I've already got the loveliest. . . .'

Bond pivoted slowly on his heel and crashed headlong to the wine-red floor.

QUESTIONS

Language

1. Look up these words in a dictionary: *crone* (p. 197); *lorgnette* (p. 197); *rapier* (p. 198); *bogus* (p. 198); *prise* (p. 200).
2. What sort of man does James Bond seem to be from the way he speaks? Does he sound the way you expect a killer to sound? Compare his speeches to Sam Spade's in *The Maltese Falcon* (p. 365). What differences do you see? How can you account for them?
3. Look at the paragraphs in which Fleming describes the physical struggle between Rosa Klebb and James Bond. Do you think they are exciting? How does Fleming achieve this excitement? Look carefully at his verbs. Are they vivid? Do they evoke the struggle for you? Pick out the sentences which you think are most vivid and evocative. What makes them so?

Content

1. Rosa Klebb is expecting a visit from one of her own agents—from Captain Nash (whom Bond has killed the night before), a Russian executioner who speaks English because he was born and raised in Ireland. Trace the process by which Bond guesses that the "little old woman" he finds in the Ritz Hotel is in fact the deadliest woman in Russia.
2. Why doesn't Bond recognize Rosa Klebb immediately? How does he describe her? Later on, when Klebb is unmasked, is she portrayed differently?
3. Are there any elements of humor in this excerpt from the Fleming novel? What are they? Is it a sophisticated kind of humor?
4. One ingredient of Fleming's Bond novels is, as we point out in the headnote, "snob appeal." What details in the chapter can you find to support this statement? What sort of person would be most impressed by these things?
5. *From Russia with Love* was the fifth James Bond novel; Fleming intended it to be his last—hence he has Bond poisoned at the end. (Public demand made Fleming later resurrect his hero.) How satisfactory an ending to the book is it? How satisfactory an ending to the 007 series?

Suggestions for Writing

1. What qualities does Bond possess that make him good at his job? Study the chapter carefully; look at everything Bond says, does, and thinks; then write an essay which analyzes why 007 is a successful spy.
2. Rosa Klebb dispenses murder with one hand and torture with the other; she enjoys her work. Discuss in class what effect the use of a woman as head of executions in the Russian secret service has on you. Why do you suppose Fleming *chose* a woman?

Do you find a woman believable in this role? Does Rosa Klebb repel you more than a man would in the same position? If so, why? Write an essay in which you describe as precisely as possible how reading about a woman in this role makes you feel; then analyze why you respond the way you do.

3. The Ian Fleming novels were extremely successful in the late fifties and sixties, but they were only the first of a number of spy novels that filled, and continue to fill in the seventies, the book stores. Write an essay in which you try to account for the popular appeal of the spy story or novel. (You might begin, if you like, with historical reasons: ask your parents what the international political climate of the 1950s and 1960s was like.) If you are familiar with any other spy novels, or with the movies that were and are often made from them, mention them and your reactions to them in your essay.

WILLA CATHER

from *My Ántonia*

When Willa Cather (1873–1947) was nine, her family moved from Virginia to the Nebraska prairie, where they homesteaded for a year before settling in the frontier town of Red Cloud. Until the age of seventeen, when she left home to attend school in Lincoln, her neighbors were the sturdy pioneer immigrants—Germans, Scandinavians, Russians—whose fortitude and spirit she later celebrated in her best-remembered works. After graduating from the University of Nebraska, she moved to Pittsburgh and worked for a time as a journalist and, later, as a high-school teacher. Her first collection of short stories, *The Troll Garden* (1905) won her the admiration of publisher S. S. McClure, who offered Cather an editorial position on his muckraking magazine *McClure's,* based in New York. Cather accepted the job, and served as the magazine's managing editor until 1912, when she left journalism entirely to devote all of her time to writing fiction. Between 1913 and 1918, she published three novels dealing with life on the Nebraska frontier: *O Pioneers!, My Ántonia,* and *The Song of the Lark.* Her 1922 novel, *One of Ours,* won the Pulitzer Prize (though contemporary critics tend not to regard it as one of her best books). Her other novels include: *A Lost Lady* (1923), *The Professor's House* (1925), *Death Comes to the Archbishop* (1927), *Shadows on the Rock* (1931), and *Lucy Gayheart* (1935).

My Ántonia is narrated by Jim Burden, who as a boy, following the death of his father and mother, is sent by relatives in Virginia to live with his grandparents on their Nebraska farm. The book takes the form of Burden's reminiscences, and is largely concerned with his memories of his childhood friend, Ántonia Shimerda, daughter of poor Bohemian immigrants who are struggling to make a life for themselves on a small, unyielding homestead. Later in life, Jim leaves Nebraska to attend Harvard University. In the following selection, having returned for a visit to his grandparents, he learns from a neighbor, the Widow Steavens, the unhappy

From *My Ántonia* by Willa Cather, "The Pioneer Woman's Story," pages 198–209. Copyright 1918, 1926, 1946 by Willa Sibert Cather. Copyright 1954 by Edith Lewis. Reprinted by permission of Houghton Mifflin Company.

story of Ántonia's betrayal by the railway conductor Larry Donovan—an experience which, like all the blows her hard life has dealt her, leaves the simple, courageous frontier woman "battered but not diminished."

On the first or second day of August I got a horse and cart and set out for the high country, to visit the Widow Steavens. The wheat harvest was over, and here and there along the horizon I could see black puffs of smoke from the steam threshing-machines. The old pasture land was now being broken up into wheatfields and cornfields, the red grass was disappearing, and the whole face of the country was changing. There were wooden houses where the old sod dwellings used to be, and little orchards, and big red barns; all this meant happy children, contented women, and men who saw their lives coming to a fortunate issue. The windy springs and the blazing summers, one after another, had enriched and mellowed that flat tableland; all the human effort that had gone into it was coming back in long, sweeping lines of fertility. The changes seemed beautiful and harmonious to me; it was like watching the growth of a great man or of a great idea. I recognized every tree and sandbank and rugged draw. I found that I remembered the conformation of the land as one remembers the modelling of human faces.

When I drew up to our old windmill, the Widow Steavens came out to meet me. She was brown as an Indian woman, tall, and very strong. When I was little, her massive head had always seemed to me like a Roman senator's. I told her at once why I had come.

'You'll stay the night with us, Jimmy? I'll talk to you after supper. I can take more interest when my work is off my mind. You've no prejudice against hot biscuit for supper? Some have, these days.'

While I was putting my horse away, I heard a rooster squawking. I looked at my watch and sighed; it was three o'clock, and I knew that I must eat him at six.

After supper Mrs. Steavens and I went upstairs to the old sitting-room, while her grave, silent brother remained in the basement to read his farm papers. All the windows were open. The white summer moon was shining outside, the windmill was pumping lazily in the light breeze. My hostess put the lamp on a stand in the corner, and turned it low because of the heat. She sat down in her favourite rocking-chair and settled a little stool comfortably under her tired feet. 'I'm troubled with calluses, Jim; getting old,' she sighed cheerfully. She crossed her hands in her lap and sat as if she were at a meeting of some kind.

'Now, it's about that dear Ántonia you want to know? Well, you've come to the right person. I've watched her like she'd been my own daughter.

'When she came home to do her sewing that summer before she was to be married, she was over here about every day. They've never had a sewing-machine at the Shimerdas', and she made all her things here. I taught her hem-stitching, and I helped her to cut and fit. She used to sit there at that machine by the window, pedalling the life out of it—she was so strong—and always singing them queer Bohemian songs, like she was the happiest thing in the world.

' "Ántonia," I used to say, "don't run that machine so fast. You won't hasten the day none that way."

'Then she'd laugh and slow down for a little, but she'd soon forget and begin to pedal and sing again. I never saw a girl work harder to go to housekeeping right and well-prepared. Lovely table-linen the Harlings had given her, and Lena Lingard had sent her nice things from Lincoln. We hemstitched all the tablecloths and pillow-cases, and some of the sheets. Old Mrs. Shimerda knit yards and yards of lace for her underclothes. Tony told me just how she meant to have everything in her house. She'd even bought silver spoons and forks, and kept them in her trunk. She was always coaxing brother to go to the post-office. Her young man did write her real often, from different towns along his run.

'The first thing that troubled her was when he wrote that his run had been changed, and they would likely have to live in Denver. "I'm a country girl," she said, "and I doubt if I'll be able to manage so well for him in a city. I was counting on keeping chickens, and maybe a cow." She soon cheered up, though.

'At last she got the letter telling her when to come. She was shaken by it; she broke the seal and read it in this room. I suspected then that she'd begun to get faint-hearted, waiting; though she'd never let me see it.

'Then there was a great time of packing. It was in March, if I remember rightly, and a terrible muddy, raw spell, with the roads bad for hauling her things to town. And here let me say, Ambrosch did the right thing. He went to Black Hawk and bought her a set of plated silver in a purple velvet box, good enough for her station. He gave her three hundred dollars in money; I saw the cheque. He'd collected her wages all those first years she worked out, and it was but right. I shook him by the hand in this room. "You're behaving like a man, Ambrosch," I said, "and I'm glad to see it, son."

' 'Twas a cold, raw day he drove her and her three trunks into Black Hawk to take the night train for Denver—the boxes had been shipped before. He stopped the wagon here, and she ran in to tell me good-bye. She threw her arms around me and kissed me, and thanked me for all I'd done for her. She was so happy she was crying and laughing at the same time, and her red checks was all wet with rain.

' "You're sure handsome enough for any man," I said, looking her over.

'She laughed kind of flighty like, and whispered, "Good-bye, dear house!" and then ran out to the wagon. I expect she meant that for you and your grandmother, as much as for me, so I'm particular to tell you. This house had always been a refuge to her.

'Well, in a few days we had a letter saying she got to Denver safe, and he was there to meet her. They were to be married in a few days. He was trying to get his promotion before he married, she said. I didn't like that, but I said nothing. The next week Yulka got a postal card, saying she was "well and happy." After that we heard nothing. A month went by, and old Mrs. Shimerda began to get fretful. Ambrosch was as sulky with me as if I'd picked out the man and arranged the match.[1]

'One night brother William came in and said that on his way back from the fields he had passed a livery team from town, driving fast out the west road. There was a trunk on the front seat with the driver, and another behind. In the back seat there was a woman all bundled up; but for all her veils, he thought 'twas Ántonia Shimerda, or Ántonia Donovan, as her name ought now to be.

'The next morning I got brother to drive me over. I can walk still, but my

---

[1] Yulka is Ántonia's younger sister; Ambrosch, her older brother.

feet ain't what they used to be, and I try to save myself. The lines outside the Shimerdas' house was full of washing, though it was the middle of the week. As we got nearer, I saw a sight that made my heart sink—all those underclothes we'd put so much work on, out there swinging in the wind. Yulka came bringing a dishpanful of wrung clothes, but she darted back into the house like she was loath to see us. When I went in, Ántonia was standing over the tubs, just finishing up a big washing. Mrs. Shimerda was going about her work, talking and scolding to herself. She didn't so much as raise her eyes. Tony wiped her hand on her apron and held it out to me, looking at me steady but mournful. When I took her in my arms she drew away. "Don't, Mrs. Steavens," she says, "you'll make me cry, and I don't want to."

'I whispered and asked her to come out-of-doors with me. I knew she couldn't talk free before her mother. She went out with me, bareheaded, and we walked up toward the garden.

' "I'm not married, Mrs. Steavens," she says to me very quiet and natural-like, "and I ought to be."

' "Oh, my child," says I, "what's happened to you? Don't be afraid to tell me!"

'She sat down on the draw-side, out of sight of the house. "He's run away from me," she said. "I don't know if he ever meant to marry me."

' "You mean he's thrown up his job and quit the country?" says I.

' "He didn't have any job. He'd been fired; blacklisted for knocking down fares. I didn't know. I thought he hadn't been treated right. He was sick when I got there. He'd just come out of the hospital. He lived with me till my money gave out, and afterward I found he hadn't really been hunting work at all. Then he just didn't come back. One nice fellow at the station told me, when I kept going to look for him, to give it up. He said he was afraid Larry'd gone bad and wouldn't come back any more. I guess he's gone to Old Mexico. The conductors get rich down there, collecting half-fares off the natives and robbing the company. He was always talking about fellows who had got ahead that way."

'I asked her, of course, why she didn't insist on a civil marriage at once—that would have given her some hold on him. She leaned her head on her hands, poor child, and said, "I just don't know, Mrs. Steavens. I guess my patience was wore out, waiting so long. I thought if he saw how well I could do for him, he'd want to stay with me."

'Jimmy, I sat right down on that bank beside her and made lament. I cried like a young thing. I couldn't help it. I was just about heart-broke. It was one of them lovely warm May days, and the wind was blowing and the colts jumping around in the pastures; but I felt bowed with despair. My Ántonia, that had so much good in her, had come home disgraced. And that Lena Lingard, that was always a bad one, say what you will, had turned out so well, and was coming home here every summer in her silks and her satins, and doing so much for her mother. I give credit where credit is due, but you know well enough, Jim Burden, there is a great difference in the principles of those two girls. And here it was the good one that had come to grief! I was poor comfort to her. I marvelled at her calm. As we went back to the house, she stopped to feel of her clothes to see if they was drying well, and seemed to take pride in their whiteness— she said she'd been living in a brick block, where she didn't have proper conveniences to wash them.

'The next time I saw Ántonia, she was out in the fields ploughing corn. All that spring and summer she did the work of a man on the farm; it seemed to be an understood thing. Ambrosch didn't get any other hand to help him. Poor Marek had got violent and been sent away to an institution a good while back. We never even saw any of Tony's pretty dresses. She didn't take them out of her trunks. She was quiet and steady. Folks respected her industry and tried to treat her as if nothing had happened. They talked, to be sure; but not like they would if she'd put on airs. She was so crushed and quiet that nobody seemed to want to humble her. She never went anywhere. All that summer she never once came to see me. At first I was hurt, but I got to feel that it was because this house reminded her of too much. I went over there when I could, but the times when she was in from the fields were the times when I was busiest here. She talked about the grain and the weather as if she'd never had another interest, and if I went over at night she always looked dead weary. She was afflicted with toothache; one tooth after another ulcerated, and she went about with her face swollen half the time. She wouldn't go to Black Hawk to a dentist for fear of meeting people she knew. Ambrosch had got over his good spell long ago, and was always surly. Once I told him he ought not to let Ántonia work so hard and pull herself down. He said, "If you put that in her head, you better stay home." And after that I did.

'Ántonia worked on through harvest and threshing, though she was too modest to go out threshing for the neighbours, like when she was young and free. I didn't see much of her until late that fall when she begun to herd Ambrosch's cattle in the open ground north of here, up toward the big dog-town. Sometimes she used to bring them over the west hill, there, and I would run to meet her and walk north a piece with her. She had thirty cattle in her bunch; it had been dry, and the pasture was short, or she wouldn't have brought them so far.

'It was a fine open fall, and she liked to be alone. While the steers grazed, she used to sit on them grassy banks along the draws and sun herself for hours. Sometimes I slipped up to visit with her, when she hadn't gone too far.

' "It does seem like I ought to make lace, or knit like Lena used to," she said one day, "but if I start to work, I look around and forget to go on. It seems such a little while ago when Jim Burden and I was playing all over this country. Up here I can pick out the very places where my father used to stand. Sometimes I feel like I'm not going to live very long, so I'm just enjoying every day of this fall."

'After the winter begun she wore a man's long overcoat and boots, and a man's felt hat with a wide brim. I used to watch her coming and going, and I could see that her steps were getting heavier. One day in December, the snow began to fall. Late in the afternoon I saw Ántonia driving her cattle homeward across the hill. The snow was flying round her and she bent to face it, looking more lonesome-like to me than usual. "Deary me," I says to myself, "the girl's stayed out too late. It'll be dark before she gets them cattle put into the corral." I seemed to sense she'd been feeling too miserable to get up and drive them.

'That very night, it happened. She got her cattle home, turned them into the corral, and went into the house, into her room behind the kitchen, and shut the door. There, without calling to anybody, without a groan, she lay down on the bed and bore her child.

'I was lifting supper when old Mrs. Shimerda came running down the base-ment stairs, out of breath and screeching:

' "Baby come, baby come!" she says. "Ambrosch much like devil!"

'Brother William is surely a patient man. He was just ready to sit down to a hot supper after a long day in the fields. Without a word he rose and went down to the barn and hooked up his team. He got us over there as quick as it was humanly possible. I went right in, and began to do for Ántonia; but she laid there with her eyes shut and took no account of me. The old woman got a tubful of warm water to wash the baby. I overlooked what she was doing and I said out loud: "Mrs. Shimerda, don't you put that strong yellow soap near that baby. You'll blister its little skin." I was indignant.

' "Mrs. Steavens," Ántonia said from the bed, "if you'll look in the top tray of my trunk, you'll see some fine soap." That was the first word she spoke.

'After I'd dressed the baby, I took it out to show it to Ambrosch. He was muttering behind the stove and wouldn't look at it.

' "You'd better put it out in the rain-barrel," he says.

' "Now, see here, Ambrosch," says I, "there's a law in this land, don't forget that. I stand here a witness that this baby has come into the world sound and strong, and I intend to keep an eye on what befalls it." I pride myself I cowed him.

'Well, I expect you're not much interested in babies, but Ántonia's got on fine. She loved it from the first as dearly as if she'd had a ring on her finger, and was never ashamed of it. It's a year and eight months old now, and no baby was ever better cared-for. Ántonia is a natural-born mother. I wish she could marry and raise a family, but I don't know as there's much chance now.'

I slept that night in the room I used to have when I was a little boy, with the summer wind blowing in at the windows, bringing the smell of the ripe fields. I lay awake and watched the moonlight shining over the barn and the stacks and the pond, and the windmill making its old dark shadow against the blue sky.

The next afternoon I walked over to the Shimerdas'. Yulka showed me the baby and told me that Ántonia was shocking wheat on the southwest quarter. I went down across the fields, and Tony saw me from a long way off. She stood still by her shocks, leaning on her pitchfork, watching me as I came. We met like the people in the old song, in silence, if not in tears. Her warm hand clasped mine.

'I thought you'd come, Jim. I heard you were at Mrs. Steavens's last night. I've been looking for you all day.'

She was thinner than I had ever seen her, and looked as Mrs. Steavens said, 'worked down,' but there was a new kind of strength in the gravity of her face, and her colour still gave her that look of deep-seated health and ardour. Still? Why, it flashed across me that though so much had happened in her life and in mine, she was barely twenty-four years old.

Ántonia stuck her fork in the ground, and instinctively we walked toward that unploughed patch at the crossing of the roads as the fittest place to talk to each other. We sat down outside the sagging wire fence that shut Mr. Shimerda's plot off from the rest of the world. The tall red grass had never been cut there. It had died down in winter and come up again in the spring until it was as thick and shrubby as some tropical garden-grass. I found myself telling her everything: why I had decided to study law and to go into the law office of one of my mother's relatives in New York City; about Gaston Cleric's death from pneumonia last winter, and the difference it had made in my life. She wanted to know about my friends, and my way of living, and my dearest hopes.

'Of course it means you are going away from us for good,' she said with a sigh. 'But that don't mean I'll lose you. Look at my papa here; he's been dead all these years, and yet he is more real to me than almost anybody else. He never goes out of my life. I talk to him and consult him all the time. The older I grow, the better I know him and the more I understand him.'

She asked me whether I had learned to like big cities. 'I'd always be miserable in a city. I'd die of lonesomeness. I like to be where I know every stack and tree, and where all the ground is friendly. I want to live and die here. Father Kelly says everybody's put into this world for something, and I know what I've got to do. I'm going to see that my little girl has a better chance than ever I had. I'm going to take care of that girl, Jim.'

I told her I knew she would. 'Do you know, Ántonia, since I've been away, I think of you more often than of anyone else in this part of the world. I'd have liked to have you for a sweetheart, or a wife, or my mother or my sister— anything that a woman can be to a man. The idea of you is a part of my mind; you influence my likes and dislikes, all my tastes, hundreds of times when I don't realize it. You really are a part of me.'

She turned her bright, believing eyes to me, and the tears came up in them slowly, 'How can it be like that, when you know so many people, and when I've disappointed you so? Ain't it wonderful, Jim, how much people can mean to each other? I'm so glad we had each other when we were little. I can't wait till my little girl's old enough to tell her about all the things we used to do. You'll always remember me when you think about old times, won't you? And I guess everybody thinks about old times, even the happiest people.'

As we walked homeward across the fields, the sun dropped and lay like a great golden globe in the low west. While it hung there, the moon rose in the east, as big as a cart-wheel, pale silver and streaked with rose colour, thin as a bubble or a ghost-moon. For five, perhaps ten minutes, the two luminaries confronted each other across the level land, resting on opposite edges of the world.

In that singular light every little tree and shock of wheat, every sunflower stalk and clump of snow-on-the-mountain, drew itself up high and pointed; the very clods and furrows in the fields seemed to stand up sharply. I felt the old pull of the earth, the solemn magic that comes out of those fields at nightfall. I wished I could be a little boy again, and that my way could end there.

We reached the edge of the field, where our ways parted. I took her hands and held them against my breast, feeling once more how strong and warm and good they were, those brown hands, and remembering how many kind things they had done for me. I held them now a long while, over my heart. About us it was growing darker and darker, and I had to look hard to see her face, which I meant always to carry with me; the closest, realest face, under all the shadows of women's faces, at the very bottom of my memory.

'I'll come back,' I said earnestly, through the soft, intrusive darkness.

'Perhaps you will'—I felt rather than saw her smile. 'But even if you don't, you're here, like my father. So I won't be lonesome.'

As I went back alone over that familiar road, I could almost believe that a boy and girl ran along beside me, as our shadows used to do, laughing and whispering to each other in the grass.

QUESTIONS

Language

1. The prairie residents in *My Ántonia* are simple, proud people—pioneer immigrants who, though intelligent, haven't had much schooling. Willa Cather has to suggest this simplicity, directness, and lack of formal education by their language. Find examples of incorrect grammar and of idiosyncratic phrasing in Mrs. Steavens' speeches. Is the old woman a good storyteller? Do these things contribute to her narrative power? Do you think Cather succeeds in capturing the speech of these midwestern pioneers?
2. Is it possible to tell from the language of this selection that the narrator who introduces it—the person who visits the Widow Steavens—is a man?

Content

1. Why does Willa Cather include the description of the countryside found in the first paragraph of this excerpt? What does it add to the story?
2. What kind of relationship does Ántonia have with Mrs. Steavens? With the narrator, Jim Burden?
3. Why doesn't Ántonia insist that Larry Donovan marry her? What do we learn about her character in the way she handles her betrayal and her pregnancy? How do her mother and her brother Ambrosch react to her misfortune?
4. Twice Ántonia says she couldn't live in a city. Why? Is this characteristic of hers significant? Explain.
5. How different will Jim Burden's life be from Ántonia's? Do you think they will stay friends? What does Jim mean when he says Ántonia's is the "realest face, under all the shadows of women's faces, at the very bottom of my memory"?

Suggestions for Writing

1. Walter Havighurst, in an introduction to *My Ántonia*, comments that Ántonia Shimerda was "the material out of which countries are made." Write an essay in which you point out what qualities in this young woman lead Havighurst to this conclusion. Do you see any of them displayed in this selection?
2. As we point out in the headnote, Willa Cather was raised in the empty prairie country she carefully recaptures in *My Ántonia*. In a descriptive essay, evoke the scenes of your own childhood, whether you grew up in city, suburb, or rural area. (If your family moved while you were a child, choose the place that meant most to you and that you remember most clearly.) Describe your house or apartment, your neighborhood or community, the countryside, the climate throughout the year, the people with whom you came in contact. Make your description as pictorial as possible, as though you were snapping photographs of childhood scenes.
3. Many years after the events narrated in this excerpt, Jim Burden returns to the prairie to seek Ántonia out. She has married and has had several children; her eldest daughter has just had a baby of her own. Burden says of his old friend, ". . . she still had that something which fires the imagination, could still stop one's breath for a moment by a

look or gesture that somehow revealed the meaning in common things. She had only to stand in the orchard, to put her hand on a little crab tree and look up at the apples, to make you feel the goodness of planting, of tending and harvesting. . . .'' Another ''common thing'' which plays a prominent role in this book is the land itself: the wild prairie slowly being cultivated by the pioneers. Write an essay in which you indicate the attitudes Jim and Ántonia (and through them, the author) have about the land. Then speculate why Cather has given it such a large part to play.

ADDITIONAL WRITING SUGGESTIONS FOR CHAPTER FOUR

1. In an essay, describe your mother as completely as you can. Avoid superficiality; try to make her come completely alive for your reader. Include information about her past, her early dreams, her disappointments, her hopes for the future, details about her character and personality, and so on. If there are things you don't know about her, interview her. Later, discuss in class how you selected and organized your material.

2. Look through some magazines like *Family Circle, McCall's, The Ladies Home Journal,* and *Woman's Day* for advertisements which use the Good Mother figure to sell their products. Then write an essay about some of these ads, describing the illustrations or photographs and pointing out those parts of the text or copy that refer to or capitalize on the Good Mother. Try to generalize about these ads and their appeal: are the products advertised similar to each other or in the same family; what things seem to be promised to the purchaser; what emotions are aroused in the reader?

3. Write an essay comparing and contrasting the Good Mother with the Temptress. Draw on any of the selections from this and the preceding section, as well as the chapter introductions, for your generalizations and examples. You may want to concentrate on only one aspect of the two figures: their sexuality, for example, or their private lives.

4. Nature has been and is today almost universally regarded as female, despite the fact that half ''her'' living creatures are male (and even plants have both male and female reproductive organs). In an essay, then, speculate about why human beings see nature as female and invariably personify it as a woman.

5. Most of us have vague notions of what constitutes an ideal mother and some of us have very clear ideas. As honestly and thoroughly as you can, describe your conception of the ideal mother. Then *criticize* that conception. (It might help, at this point, to imagine yourself as that mother: what is wrong with or unfair about the ideal laid out for you in this role?)

Five

The Wise Old Man

> "My dear child," said the old man. . . . "You can no longer turn back. Now that you have run away, you must seek a new future in the world. As I have neither house nor home, nor wife nor child, I can not take further care of you, but I will give you some good advice for nothing."
>
> —from an Estonian folktale, "How an Orphan Boy Unexpectedly Found His Luck"

The Wise Old Man is the masculine counterpart of the Good Mother archetype. When the protagonist of a fairy tale, for instance, is a girl (as in "Cinderella"), her guardian spirit is most likely to be female: a helpful fairy godmother. But when the main character is a boy, his supernatural helper is usually a little old man who provides guidance and good advice, or the clue to a baffling puzzle—in short, who offers some sort of wisdom. Unlike the Good Mother, the Wise Old Man is rarely a source of physical sustenance. While the Good Mother may give comfort and wise counsel to those in distress, she also gives food, shelter, and other forms of *material* support. (Indeed the words *maternal* and *material* are closely connected, both deriving from the Latin word *mater*.) The province of the Wise Old Man, however, is not matter (that is, all the visible, physical, tangible objects around us), but spirit—the things of the soul and the mind. Whatever form he assumes—seer, sage, prophet, priest, teacher, magician, or wizard—he is always the possessor of superior knowledge, the master of the spiritual or philosophical realm.

Like all archetypes, the image of the Wise Old Man occurs throughout history, always clothed in the cultural costume of a particular time and place—ancient Greece, medieval England, colonial America—but always displaying, despite every variation in outward appearance, the same underlying traits. One of these traits is exceptional insight. Perhaps the most famous Wise Old Man in Greek mythology is the blind Theban seer Teiresias, who figures so prominently in Sophocles' classical tragedy *Oedipus Rex.* Paradoxically, Teiresias' blindness is a symbol of his superior sight. Like the owl who sees best in the nighttime, Teiresias can see clearly into the darkness of the human soul; his blindness to the outer world only makes his "inner vision" more intense. Another blind man who possesses this kind of heightened perception, which allows him to penetrate the dark mysteries of the human heart and mind, is the sightless Shaolin priest in the popular television program of several years ago, "Kung Fu." Throughout this series, whenever the hero, Kwai Chang Caine, confronted a problem he could not solve, he would recall the wise teachings of his venerable master: "A good door is never locked, but still cannot be opened," "He who would lead must follow behind," and so on. (One of the obvious problems of this show was that, though these sayings were meant to sound like profound Zen paradoxes, they usually sounded more like the sort of messages found inside Chinese fortune cookies.)

In fairy tales, too, the Wise Old Man is commonly associated, if not with blindness, then with darkness and enveloping gloom. Often, for example, he appears in the form of a hermit who lives deep in a shadowy forest in which the hero has lost his way. The point is, once again, that the Wise Old Man is at home in the dark. As the psychologist C. G. Jung points out in his essay "The Phenomenology of the Spirit in Fairy Tales," the old man "sees through the gloomy situation of the hero who has got himself into trouble" and gives him "such information as will help him on his journey." He shows the hero the road he needs to follow to arrive at his goal. Though the sunlight never reaches the forest floor, the Wise Old Man, with his long white beard and long white robe, is himself the source of light (as the Mother is often the source of food). At times or in places of darkness, when it is difficult to know where to turn or how to proceed, he provides the necessary illumination and *enlightenment.* The black forest in which the hero is lost symbolizes the problem he has gotten himself into and cannot cope with on his own; the old man's familiarity with the woods and his ability to point to the path leading out symbolize, not only his greater knowledge, experience, and wisdom, but also (to quote Jung again) his "moral qualities, such as goodwill and readiness to help."

As the examples of both the television program and the fairy tale indicate, another characteristic of the Wise Old Man is that he nearly always appears in the company of a young and callow hero. Just as the Trickster cannot exist without a "sucker" to play his pranks on, nor a Temptress without a susceptible man to seduce, so the Wise Old Man requires an inexperienced companion who will profit from his insights and advice. In folklore and in the arts (both popular and high), the roles assumed by these two complementary characters—the Wise Old Man and the innocent young one—are extremely varied. Nevertheless, the *kind* of relationship they share is always, essentially, the same: the knowing teacher instructing the naive (but eager) student. Sometimes, the Wise Old Man literally *is* a teacher. A good example can be seen in the movie version of Jules Verne's *Journey to the Center of the Earth*—a popular fantasy film still often shown on television—in which James Mason plays the distinguished geology professor, Sir Oliver Lindenbrook, who makes a heroic descent to the earth's core accompanied by his worshipful pupil Alec (played by Pat Boone). But even when education is not the Wise Old Man's profession, he is still, in a very fundamental way, the teacher, the master of initiation who ushers the novice, the innocent and even ignorant youth, into unsuspected worlds of knowledge and power (since knowledge, as the saying goes, *is* power). "A Man of Knowledge" is, in fact, the name which don Juan, the Yaqui Indian shaman of Carlos Castaneda's books, gives to such a person; and for such a man, a primary purpose of life is not merely to utilize his knowledge for the benefit of others, but to pass it along to a worthy successor.

In general, therefore, the relationship between the experienced old man and the innocent youth is that of teacher to student, master to disciple, guide to follower, or father to son. While the two figures may be constant companions, with the aged counselor always at the young hero's side, it is also common for the Wise Old Man to appear mainly at moments of crisis, when the hero is (as Jung puts it) in "a hopeless and desperate situation from which only profound reflection or a lucky idea . . . can extricate him." Such a situation occurs several times in the enormously popular movie *Star Wars*. Here, the young and inexperienced hero, Luke Skywalker, is taken under the wings of "the last of the Jedi Knights," the sage and seasoned warrior Obi-wan Kenobi, who tutors Luke in the ways of "the force." It is significant that Obi-wan's first and last appearances in the film come at precisely those moments when Luke is in direct peril: we meet him first when he arrives, right in the nick of time, to rescue Luke from the clutches of the dreaded "Sandpeople." His final "appearance" in the film takes place during the climactic space battle, when Luke, now a rebel fighter-pilot attempting to blow up the enemy's "Death Star," becomes aware of Obi-wan's disembodied presence, counseling him to put aside his computerized crosshairs and "trust to the force." Up until this point, the rebel pilots, who have been relying solely on their sophisticated technological hardware to destroy the Death Star, have failed to score a hit. It is not until a desperate Luke heeds Obi-wan's advice and puts his faith in the force that he is able to accomplish his mission.

Besides being extremely suspenseful and exciting, there is a good deal of psychological wisdom in this episode from *Star Wars*. Indeed, it contains the same truth conveyed by all the fairy tales in which the hero unexpectedly meets an old man in the woods. What is this truth? It is that there are certain problems which our rational minds cannot deal with; that logic has its limitations and can carry us only so far (this is symbolized in *Star Wars* by the failure of the computers— those sophisticated, supremely logical machines—to help the rebel pilots hit the target). But there is another kind of knowledge, a "higher knowledge," which is available to us if we will only learn to trust in it, to leave ourselves open to it. It is an intuitive, completely *nonrational* type of wisdom or insight, which may come to us "out of the blue," giving us guidance when we least expect it but most desperately need it—in the nick of time (just as the voice of Obi-wan comes to Luke in the cockpit of his spacecraft, or as the old hermit of the fairy tales suddenly materializes out of the darkness of the woods).

This all sounds very mystical. (And indeed, the Wise Old Man, who is an embodiment of this intuitive power, this spiritual "force," is sometimes portrayed as a mystic. *Doctor Strange* comic books, for example, feature a character known as the "Ancient One," who is the hero's guru and a "Master of the Mystic Arts.") But in fact, such intuitive, nonrational insight has been documented throughout history. There are many famous cases of people who, while struggling with some apparently irresolvable dilemma, have had the solution suddenly present itself to them in a burst of inspiration at the most unexpected moment: when, for example, out of despair or exhaustion, they have given up on the problem and stopped thinking about it entirely. At times, the answer to a particularly difficult problem may even appear to us in a dream, when our logical processes have been totally (if temporarily) suspended. It seems that there is indeed a power inside each of us which can provide unlooked-for wisdom when the rational mind has reached the limit of what it can do. This is the "force" which not only Obi-wan Kenobi, but every Wise Old Man represents.

With his medieval costume of hooded cloak and shining sword, and his connection with a passing order of chivalric knights, Obi-wan is reminiscent of the most famous Wise Old Man in heroic legend: Merlin, the sorcerer and sage of Camelot and King Arthur's tutor. The wizard Merlin is, in fact, the model for many of the Wise Old Man figures in contemporary fantasy literature—a genre which has become increasingly popular in America over the past decade or so. Perhaps the best-known of these wizards is Gandalf the Grey, from J. R. R. Tolkien's *The Hobbit* and *Lord of the Rings* trilogy. Midway through the latter work, while defending his companions from a "dreadful spirit of the underworld" during a journey through the Mines of Moria, Gandalf plunges to his death in a black abyss, only to reappear to his friends later on in the work (typically, at a moment of crisis, as they wander uncertainly through a "dark and unknown forest") in the resurrected form of the "White Rider":

> They all gazed at him. His hair was white as snow in the sunshine, and gleaming white was his robe; the eyes under his deep brows were bright, piercing in the rays of the sun; power was in his hand. Between wonder, joy, and fear they stood and found no words to say.

As is true of Gandalf and other wizards of fantasy literature (Allanon, from Terry Brooks' novel *The Sword of Shannara,* is another example), the Wise Old Man often has not only great knowledge in his head, but also great "power . . . in his hand," power which usually displays itself, as we have seen in the case of Obi-wan and Luke, when the young hero is threatened by evil. Sometimes, this power is occult—sorcery or "white magic." At other times it is religious. The title character of William Peter Blatty's *The Exorcist* is the aging Catholic priest Lankester Merrin, a man of enormous wisdom and inner strength, who, as a soldier of Christ, does battle with a demon for the soul of young Regan MacNeil. A similar Wise Old Man is Dr. Van Helsing of Bram Stoker's *Dracula,* who, though a scientist and not a priest, uses sacred Christian objects—the Host and the Crucifix—in his fight against the king of the vampires. In more realistic art, however, the Wise Old Man ordinarily does not possess any special power and certainly has no magical or supernatural power. Rather, he is an "old-timer"; what he offers is the learning and experience acquired during a long and varied life. Examples of this sort of character include the canny Howard, from B. Traven's *The Treasure of the Sierra Madre,* who knows everything there is to know about prospecting, and cowboy Tiger Man McCool of Bobby Bare's country-western song "The Winner," who gently gives a belligerent, confused stranger a valuable lesson about empty victories. Often, the kind of wisdom the old-timer possesses is knowledge of the human heart. Sometimes he must teach the over-eager or arrogant hero that success, maturity, or whatever the young man is seeking is dependent on his developing a sympathetic, understanding, and respectful relationship with other people.

What are some of the other forms that the Wise Old Man archetype assumes? Really, they are almost endless, since every occupation, discipline, or field of knowledge has its own specialists and masters. Often, for instance, the Wise Old Man is a doctor. Television provides many examples: Doctors Zorba and Gillespie (from two extremely popular programs of the early sixties, "Ben Casey" and "Doctor Kildare"), Marcus Welby, M.D., and "Doc" (from "Gunsmoke"). The Wise Old Man may also appear as a lawyer, like Lawrence Pressman of "The Defenders" (another very successful television show of the sixties); a land baron, like Ben Cartwright, the patriarch of "Bonanza"; or the chief of a governmental agency, like "M," the head of the British Secret Service in the James Bond novels and movies. Whatever his profession, the Wise Old Man's main function in life (as we have seen) is to be a father figure to the young hero; and often, he will actually be the hero's father or some other elderly and respected male relative. Two of the examples already mentioned—Ben Cartwright and Lawrence Pressman—are cases in point. Others include Jim Anderson of television's "Father Knows Best," Grandpa Walton of "The Waltons," and Don Corleone, the title character of Mario Puzo's *The Godfather*.

The case of Don Corleone brings to light one final, significant feature of the Wise Old Man archetype: namely, its negative side. Don Corleone is, after all, a criminal. True, he is a sympathetic character in many respects and, to his family, a figure of great strength, authority, and wisdom—the protector and beloved patriarch of his clan. Nevertheless, he is also a gangster, a corrupt and quite dangerous man who orders people killed as a casual part of his "business." Just as the mother figure may have both a good and evil aspect, so may the father figure. In Tolkien's *Lord of the Rings* trilogy, for example, the benevolent Gandalf the Grey has a malevolent counterpart called Saruman the White. Similarly, Ira Levin's *Rosemary's Baby* contains a pair of elderly men, one good, one wicked: Rosemary's devoted friend Hutch, a "father-substitute" who is always "on hand for emergencies," and her sinister neighbor Roman Castevet, who turns out to be the leader of a Satan cult. Like the positive side of the archetype, the negative side takes various forms: instead of the kindly family physician, the diabolical witch doctor or the half-crazed old scientist; instead of a fount of wisdom, a pompous fool (like Polonius, in Shakespeare's play *Hamlet*); instead of a lovable, admired graybeard, a lecherous "dirty old man."

SOPHOCLES

"Teiresias the Seer" (from *Oedipus Rex*)

The great Greek tragic poet Sophocles (497– or 495–406 B.C.) wrote about 120 plays in his long and honored career. Only seven complete tragedies remain; *Oedipus Rex* is considered the finest of them.

When the play opens, Oedipus has been King of Thebes and married to Jocasta for fifteen years. His city is now suffering under a long famine, and he has recently learned that the plague has been visited on the Thebans because they have been harboring, unpunished, the murderer of their previous king, Laius.

What Oedipus does not know is that he himself is the criminal. He is actually the son of Jocasta and the dead Laius. Shortly after Oedipus' birth, his father cast him out into the wilderness to die because it had been prophesied that a son born to Jocasta would eventually murder Laius. But Oedipus was taken in by the king and queen of Corinth, who raised him as their son. Later, after learning from the oracle at Delphi that he would one day kill his father and marry his mother, Oedipus fled in horror from the people he believed to be his parents.

In the course of his journeys he came upon a stranger in a chariot, driven by a charioteer who ordered Oedipus to move out of the road. When Oedipus refused, the charioteer drove ahead and the passenger struck Oedipus on the head. Infuriated, Oedipus slew the charioteer and the rider who, unbeknownst to Oedipus, was King Laius of Thebes, his true father.

Arriving at Thebes, Oedipus found the city in thrall to a female monster called the Sphinx, who had been devouring the innocent citizens one by one. The Thebans had learned from the oracle that the only way to defeat the Sphinx was by answering her riddle, but so far no solution had been found. When Oedipus answered the riddle correctly, the Sphinx killed herself and Oedipus was rewarded with the kingship of Thebes and marriage to Laius' widow, Jocasta. Thus the terrible prophecy was fulfilled.

The city prospered for some time under Oedipus' rule. But now, fifteen years later, its citizens are again suffering grievously. In the scene reprinted below, Oedipus, in answer to the prayers of his people, promises to free them from their ordeal by discovering the killer of Laius. Launching his investigation, he sends first for the blind seer Teiresias, renowned for his wisdom.

Teiresias had gained his powers of knowledge and prophecy from Zeus, ruler of the gods of Olympus. In his youth, Teiresias had encountered a pair of coupling snakes and, upon slaying the female, was suddenly transformed into a woman. Coming upon another pair of snakes several years later, he killed the male and was instantly changed back into a man. Shortly after this second transformation,

Reprinted by permission of Penguin Books Ltd. from *King Oedipus* in *Sophocles: The Theban Plays*, translated by E. F. Watling (Penguin Classics, 1947) pages 30–38. Copyright © E. F. Watling, 1947. Renewal copyright by E. F. Watling, 1974.

Teiresias was called upon to resolve an argument between Zeus and his wife Hera over whether men or women find sex more enjoyable. When Teiresias answered that women do, the infuriated Hera struck him blind. Zeus, however, rewarded him with the gifts of prophecy and long life.

Enter OEDIPUS *from the Palace.*

OEDIPUS : You have prayed; and your prayers shall be answered with help and release
    If you will obey me, and are willing to put in hand
    The remedy your distress requires. I speak
    As a stranger, except by hearsay, to what has passed
    And the story that has been told—without this clue
    I should make but little headway in my search.
    Therefore, as a citizen newly received among you,
    It is to you, Thebans, I make this proclamation:
    If any one of you knows whose hand it was
    That killed Laius, the son of Labdacus,
    Let him declare it fully, now, to me.

(He pauses: there is silence.)

Or if any man's conscience is guilty, let him give himself up.
He will suffer the less. His fate will be nothing worse
Than banishment. No other harm will touch him.

(The hearers are still silent.)

Or, if some alien is known to have been the assassin,
Declare it. The informer shall have his reward of me,
As well as the thanks he will earn from all of you.

(Silence still.)

But—if you will not speak, and any man
Is found to be screening himself or another, in fear,
I here pronounce my sentence upon his head:
No matter who he may be, he is forbidden
Shelter or intercourse with any man
In all this country over which I rule;
From fellowship of prayer or sacrifice
Or lustral rite is excommunicated;
Expelled from every house, unclean, accursed,
In accordance with the word of the Pythian oracle.
Thus I shall have done my duty to the god,
And to the dead. And it is my solemn prayer
That the unknown murderer, and his accomplices,
If such there be, may wear the brand of shame
For their shameful act, unfriended, to their life's end.
Nor do I exempt myself from the imprecation:
If, with my knowledge, house or hearth of mine
Receive the guilty man, upon my head

Lie all the curses I have laid on others.
It is for you to see this faithfully carried out,
As in duty bound to me, and to the god,
And to our suffering plague-tormented country.
Indeed I am surprised that no purification was made,
Even without the express command of heaven.
The death of a man so worthy, and your King,
Should surely have been probed to the utmost. Be that as it may,
Now that I hold the place that he once held—
His bed, his wife—whose children, had fate so willed,
Would have grown to be another bond of blood between us—
And upon him, alas, has this disaster fallen;
I mean to fight for him now, as I would fight
For my own father, and leave no way untried
To bring to light the killer of Laius,
The son of Labdacus, the son of Polydorus, the son of Cadmus, the son
    of Agenor.
        The gods curse all that disobey this charge!
For them the earth be barren of harvest, for them
Women be childless; and may this present calamity,
And worse than this, pursue them to their death!
For the rest—you sons of Cadmus who are on my side—
May Justice and all the gods be with you for ever.

CHORUS : Under your curse, O King, I make bold to answer:
    I am not the man, nor can I point him out.
    The question came from Phoebus,[1] and he, if anyone,
    Could surely tell us who the offender is.

OEDIPUS : No doubt, but to compel a god to speak
    Against his will, is not in mortal power.

CHORUS : I have another thing to say.

OEDIPUS : Say on.
    Second, or third, thoughts—we will hear them all.

CHORUS : To the lord Phoebus the lord Teiresias
    Stands nearest, I would say, in divination.
    He is the one who could help us most in our search.

OEDIPUS : I have not overlooked it. I have sent for him—
    It was Creon's advice—twice I have sent for him,
    And am much surprised he is not already here.

CHORUS :
    There were rumours, of course; but mostly old wives' tales.

OEDIPUS : Rumours? What rumours? I must hear them all.

CHORUS :
    He was said to have been killed by travellers on the road.

OEDIPUS : So I have heard. But where are the witnesses?

CHORUS : He'd be a bold man, sir, that would pay no heed
    To such a curse as yours, when he had heard it.

---

[1] "The Bright One," an epithet for Apollo, God of Light and Truth. Prior to the start of the play, Oedipus had dispatched his brother-in-law, Creon, to Delphi to learn from Apollo's oracle how the curse could be lifted from Thebes. Creon has returned with the god's message that the city will be saved when Laius' murderer is found and punished.

OEDIPUS : Will he fear words, that did not shrink from the deed?

CHORUS :

There is one can find him out. They are bringing the prophet
In whom, of all men, lives the incarnate truth.

Enter TEIRESIAS, *blind, led by an attendant.*

OPEDIPUS :

Teiresias, we know there is nothing beyond your ken;
Lore sacred and profane, all heavenly and earthly knowledge
Are in your grasp. In your heart, if not with the eye,
You see our city's condition: we look to you
As our only help and protector. We have sent—
They may have told you—to Phoebus, and he has answered.
The only way of deliverance from our plague
Is for us to find out the killers of Laius
And kill or banish them.
Now, sir, spare not your skill
In bird-lore or whatever other arts
Of prophecy you profess. It is for yourself,
It is for Thebes, it is for me. Come, save us all,
Save all that is polluted by this death.
We look to you. To help his fellow-men
With all his power is man's most noble work.

TEIRESIAS :

Wise words; but O, when wisdom brings no profit,
To be wise is to suffer. And why did I forget this,
Who knew it well? I never should have come.

OEDIPUS : It seems you bring us little encouragement.

TEIRESIAS : Let me go home. It will be easier thus
For you to bear your burden, and me mine.

OEDIPUS :

Take care, sir. You show yourself no friend to Thebes,
Whose son you are, if you refuse to answer.

TEIRESIAS : It is because I see your words, sir, tending
To no good end; therefore I guard my own.

OEDIPUS :

By the gods! If you know, do not refuse to speak!
We all beseech you; we are all your suppliants.

TEIRESIAS : You are all deluded. I refuse to utter
The heavy secrets of my soul—and yours.

OEDIPUS :

What? Something you know, and will not tell? You mean
To fail us and to see your city perish?

TEIRESIAS : I mean to spare you, and myself. Ask me
No more. It is useless. I will tell you nothing.

OEDIPUS : Nothing? Insolent scoundrel, you would rouse
A stone to fury! Will you never speak?
You are determined to be obstinate to the end?

TEIRESIAS : Do not blame me; put your own house in order.

OEDIPUS : Hear him! Such words—such insults to the State
    Would move a saint to anger.
TEIRESIAS : What will be
    Will be, though I should never speak again.
OEDIPUS : What is to be, it is your trade to tell.
TEIRESIAS : I tell no more. Rage with what wrath you will.
OEDIPUS : I shall; and speak my mind unflinchingly.
    I tell you I do believe *you* had a hand
    In plotting, and all but doing, this very act.
    If you had eyes to see with, I would have said
    Your hand, and yours alone, had done it all.
TEIRESIAS : You would so? Then hear this: upon your head
    Is the ban your lips have uttered—from this day forth
    Never to speak to me or any here.
    You are the cursed polluter of this land.
OEDIPUS : You dare to say it! Have you no shame at all?
    And do you expect to escape the consequence?
TEIRESIAS : I have escaped. The truth is my defence.
OEDIPUS : Whose work is this? This is no soothsaying.
THEIRESIAS :
    You taught me. You made me say it against my will.
OEDIPUS : Say it again. Let there be no mistake.
TEIRESIAS :
    Was it not plain? Or will you tempt me further?
OEDIPUS : I would have it beyond all doubt. Say it again.
TEIRESIAS : I say that the killer you are seeking is yourself.
OEDIPUS : The second time. You shall be sorry for this.
TEIRESIAS : Will you have more, to feed your anger?
OEDIPUS: Yes!
    More, and more madness. Tell us all you know.
TEIRESIAS : I know, as you do not, that you are living
    In sinful union with the one you love,
    Living in ignorance of your own undoing.
OEDIPUS :
    Do you think you can say such things with impunity?
TEIRESIAS : I do—if truth has any power to save.
OEDIPUS : It has—but not for you; no, not for you,
    Shameless and brainless, sightless, senseless sot!
TEIRESIAS : You are to be pitied, uttering such taunts
    As all men's mouths must some day cast at *you*.
OEDIPUS : Living in perpetual night, you cannot harm
    Me, nor any man else that sees the light.
TEIRESIAS : No; it is not for me to bring you down.
    That is in Apollo's hands, and he will do it.
OEDIPUS (*scenting a possible connection with Creon's embassy*):
    Creon! Was this trick his, then, if not yours?
TEIRESIAS : Not Creon either. Your enemy is yourself.
OEDIPUS (*pursuing his own thought*):
    Ah, riches and royalty, and wit matched against wit

In the race of life, must they always be mated with envy?
Must Creon, so long my friend, my most trusted friend,
Stalk me by stealth, and study to dispossess me
Of the power this city has given me—freely given—
Not of my asking—setting this schemer on me,
This pedlar of fraudulent magical tricks, with eyes
Wide open for profit, but blind in prophecy?
(*To* TEIRESIAS) What was your vaunted seercraft ever worth?
And where were you, when the Dog-faced Witch[2] was here?
Had you any word of deliverance then for our people?
There was a riddle too deep for common wits;
A seer should have answered it; but answer came there none
From you; bird-lore and god-craft all were silent.
Until *I* came—I, ignorant Oedipus, came—
And stopped the riddler's mouth, guessing the truth
By mother-wit, not bird-lore. This is the man
Whom you would dispossess, hoping to stand
Nearest to Creon's throne. You shall repent,
You and your fellow-plotter, of your zeal
For scapegoat-hunting. Were you not as old
As you appear to be, sharp punishment
Would soon convince you of your wickedness.

CHORUS : Sir, to our thinking, both of you have spoken
In the heat of anger. Surely this is not well,
When all our thought should be, how to discharge
The god's command.

TEIRESIAS : King though you are, one right—
To answer—makes us equal; and I claim it.
It is not you, but Loxias,[3] whom I serve;
Nor am I bound to Creon's patronage.
You are pleased to mock my blindness. Have you eyes,
And do not see your own damnation? Eyes,
And cannot see what company you keep?
Whose son are you? I tell you, you have sinned—
And do not know it—against your own on earth
And in the grave. A swift and two-edged sword,
Your mother's and your father's curse, shall sweep you
Out of this land. Those now clear-seeing eyes
Shall then be darkened, then no place be deaf,
No corner of Cithaeron echoless,[4]
To your loud crying, when you learn the truth
Of that sweet marriage-song that hailed you home
To the fair-seeming haven of your hopes—

---

[2] A reference to the Sphinx, a female monster with the body of a winged lion and the face and breast of a woman.
[3] A title of Apollo.
[4] A mountain range which was the site of many legendary events. It was while walking on Mount Cithaeron that Teiresias came upon the coupling snakes and slew the female, an act which brought about his sexual transformation.

With more, more misery than you can guess,
To show you what you are, and who they are
That call you father. Rail as you will at Creon,
And at my speaking—you shall be trodden down
With fouler scorn than ever fell on man.

ODEIPUS : Shall I bear more of this? Out of my sight!
Go! Quickly, go! Back where you came from! Go!

TEIRESIAS : I will. It was your wish brought me here, not mine.

OEDIPUS : Had I known what madness I was to listen to,
I would have spared myself the trouble.

TEIRESIAS : Mad I may seem
To you. Your parents would not think me so.

OEDIPUS :
What's that? My parents? Who then . . . gave me birth?

TEIRESIAS :
This day brings you your birth; and brings you death.

OEDIPUS :
Man, must you still wrap up your words in riddles?

TEIRESIAS : Were you not famed for skill at solving riddles?

OEDIPUS : You taunt me with the gift that is my greatness?

TEIRESIAS : Your great misfortune, and your ruin.

OEDIPUS : No matter!
I have saved this land from ruin. I am content.

TEIRESIAS :
Well, I will go. Your hand, boy. Take me home.

OEDIPUS : We well can spare you. Let him take you home.

TEIRESIAS : When I have said my all. Thus, to your face,
Fearful of nothing you can do to me:
The man for whom you have ordered hue and cry,
The killer of Laius—that man is *here;*
Passing for an alien, a sojourner here among us;
But, as presently shall appear, a Theban born,
To his cost. He that came seeing, blind shall he go;
Rich now, then a beggar; stick-in-hand, groping his way
To a land of exile; brother, as it shall be shown,
And father at once, to the children he cherishes; son,
And husband, to the woman who bore him; father-killer,
And father-supplanter.
Go in, and think on this.
When you can prove me wrong, then call me blind.

Exeunt.

QUESTIONS

Language

1. How does Sophocles build up drama in Oedipus' long first speech? Where in this speech do you see irony?

2. When Oedipus begins speaking to Teiresias, what is his tone? When does the tone of his remarks start to change? Does his attitude toward Teiresias' skills as a seer change as well?

3. What is the tone of Teiresias' speeches at the beginning of his conversation with Oedipus? Toward the end?

4. What does Oedipus mean when he says he "stopped the riddler's mouth, . . . by mother-wit, not bird-lore"? And what is a scapegoat?

5. Teiresias' early answers to Oedipus' questions are quite plain and straightforward. But his last speech is a kind of riddle. Why do his replies get less clear as the scene goes on?

6. How do you interpret Oedipus' tone toward the end when he says to Teiresias, "No matter! I have saved this land from ruin. I am content."

Content

1. Describe Oedipus as fully as you can. Look at all his speeches: what do they reveal about his character? Do you feel he is a good king? Explain. Has he any faults?

2. What are the details of Oedipus' proclamation (which becomes a curse) against the unknown killer?

3. What does Teiresias mean when he says "when wisdom brings no profit, to be wise is to suffer"? And to whom is he speaking?

4. What makes Teiresias finally speak out? Does Oedipus understand what he tells him? How does the king of Thebes react to the seer's words?

5. Why does Teiresias say Oedipus' skill at solving riddles is his "misfortune," his "ruin"?

6. How does the chorus react to the exchange between Teiresias and Oedipus? The members of the chorus speak infrequently. What does their function seem to be?

Suggestions for Writing

1. Write an essay about the kind of wisdom—the kind of insight—Teiresias possesses and offers to Oedipus. Look at *all* the seer's speeches as a starting point.

2. Before Oedipus is even born, his father Laius is told that his unborn son will eventually grow up to murder his father. Later there is another prophecy concerning this unfortunate young man: that he will marry his mother. The play suggests that neither Oedipus nor any other human being can escape his fate. Do you think this is true? Do you think people are fated to do certain things, some to suffer in particular ways, and others to achieve victory after victory? Or do you think that we are completely responsible for everything that happens to us in life? Write an essay about this subject; be sure you know what the word *fate* means (a good dictionary is the answer). Avoid using abstract language only—a common trap in an essay like this. Find in your own experience (or invent) concrete examples to support your argument.

3. Oedipus prides himself on his riddling skills, but the tragic irony the play reveals is that he has no skills to solve the riddle of himself and his terrible history. Write an essay about self-knowledge. How important do you think it is to "know thyself"? Is self-knowledge something you take seriously, or do you never think about it? Do you feel you do know yourself? What sorts of things can happen to a person who does not know himself very well?

ANONYMOUS

"The Hare Herd"

As we indicate in our headnote to "The Singing Bone" (p. 9), *Grimm's Fairy Tales* is regarded as a pioneering work of folklore scholarship because its authors were the first collectors of folktales to reproduce with accuracy the speech of the common people, to record these stories more or less precisely as they were told by the unlettered peasants of the German countryside. In later editions of their famous book, however, the Grimm brothers departed from this method, substituting their own polished, stylistically refined stories for the verbatim versions in the original collection. As the American folklorist Richard Dorson puts it, the Grimms gradually "abandoned the *Volksmärchen* or true folktale collected exactly from the lips of the storyteller for the *Buchmärchen* or literary version shaped by the editor."

The following story is from a volume entitled *Folktales of Germany*, which Dorson describes as "the first major collection of German folktales to appear in English since the translation of the Grimm's *Kinder- und Hausmärchen.*" The volume is edited by Kurt Ranke, Germany's leading authority on folklore and a severe critic of the Grimms' method of "*märchen*-polishing." Unlike the consciously crafted stories in the Grimm brothers' later collections, all of the tales in Ranke's volume, including "The Hare Herd," are "genuine *Volksmärchen.*"

There was a king who had only one daughter. She fell ill, and nobody could help her. It was made known that whoever was able to cure her should marry her, even if he were a poor fellow. First of all there came the kings, princes, baronets, and other people of high rank with their medicine. It was no use; she did not recover. Then the rich people were asked to come. But she still did not feel better. Finally it was proclaimed that anybody might come, no matter if he were a peasant or an artisan, if only he could help her.

There was a very poor man. He had three sons. His wife knew how to make all sorts of medicines. Their eldest son, who was a neat fellow, said, "Mother, make a medicine ready for me; everybody is allowed to go there." His mother prepared a medicine for him. She also gave him a loaf of white bread for the journey. Then he left.

On his way he met an old gray man who said, "Well, my child, where are you going? What are you carrying with you?"

"Why do you ask, you old cur?" he said. "Pig dirt!" He then walked off insolently, convinced that the princess would be his. When he got there, the guard searched him and asked him what he was carrying and why he had come. He really had pig dirt! They saw it at once and locked him up. Instead of being brought to the princess, he was imprisoned for three months. Afterward they sent him home. At home everybody thought that he would bring the princess,

Reprinted with permission of The University of Chicago Press from *Folktales of Germany* by Kurt Ranke. Copyright 1966.

since he had been away for such a long time. They asked him what had happened to him. He said to his mother, "On the way I met an old man who asked me what I was carrying. I told him it was pig dirt. And when I got to the king, it really was pig dirt. Instead of leading me to the princess, they locked me up."

Now the second son said, "Mother, make a medicine ready for me. I will try, too." His mother prepared a medicine, and he left. On his way he met the old gray man, too. He asked again, "Well, my child, where are you going?"

He said, "Why do you ask, you old cur? Are you trying to do what you have done to my brother?"

"What have you got?"

"Pig dirt," he said. Before getting to the royal entrance door, he looked at it again. Well, I have still got my medicine, he thought. It is not pig dirt. I have been on my guard; the old chap dared not do it with me. When he entered, he was searched by the guard and now he had pig dirt, too. He was arrested, got a sound beating, and was locked up for six months because he was the second one to come with pig dirt. At home they thought that the medicine worked, since he did not come back. When he came home, his mother said, "Has it worked?"

He said, "Things have gone even worse with me than with my brother; I have been locked up for six months."

Now the youngest one, who was believed to be stupid, said, "Mother, make a medicine ready for me, too; now I am going to try."

The others said, "We have not succeeded, and you, fool, think you can cure her?" They laughed at him.

He said, "Mother, please! I want to try. Let me go." Now she made a medicine, but she only gave him a little loaf of brown bread for the journey. On his way he met the old man, too.

"Well, my child, where are you going and what are you carrying here?"

"Oh," he said, "where am I going? I am going very far. Let's sit down, I shall tell you. You see, the princess is ill, and he who can cure her will marry her. I want to try."

The other one said, "Where is your medicine? Let me see."

He said, "It's in this glass here. My mother has prepared it. I don't know whether it will be any good or not." The old man took the medicine and blessed it.

After this the fellow said, "I am hungry; you can eat with me." He took his loaf of brown bread, and they ate together. After the meal, he wanted to leave.

The old man said, "My child, here is a little flute. If you are in trouble, you blow it and you will be helped." He took the flute and went on. The old man left, too.

After a while he came across two ants who had a stick. One pulled it to one side, the other one to the other side. He took the stick, broke it in two, and gave half to each of them. The two ants happened to be ant kings. After this he went on.

At last he came to the castle. The guards searched him. They declared the medicine to be good and led him inside. He went to the princess and gave her some of the medicine. She immediately felt better. She talked more than she had for a long time. When she took the medicine for the third time, she was all right again. She went for a walk in the garden.

When the king saw it, he felt sorry, for he did not want to give his daughter to this simpleton. He sent for his councilors and asked them what he should do. The fellow really was too stupid to be king. They told him that there was only one thing to be done. He should set another task for him. He should mix a quarter of poppy seeds with a quarter of ashes, and if the lad was not able to pick them out in one night, then he would not get the princess.

They put the poppy seeds and the ashes into a dark room, and he was told to pick the poppy seeds out in the dark.

My God, he thought, now I have cured her and shall not get her after all! How shall I do this work in the dark? I could not do it even in broad daylight. While he was sitting there and thinking it all over, with the moon looking into the room, the ant kings came, each with a crowd of ants. They started picking out the seeds, and the work was soon done.

In the morning the councilors came to see. They told the king, "It's neat work, as if the pigeons had done it. Excellent!" The king sent for the fellow and asked him how he had done it. He told the king not to worry about that, since the work was properly done. The king did not know what to do next. He sent for his councilors again and told them that he was at his wits' end. They told him to give the lad 300 woodland hares to tend. If he was not able to do so, he could not marry the princess.

It was proclaimed that the king would buy living woodland hares. Everybody caught hares, and within one day there were enough of them brought to the king. Now the fellow was told to tend the 300 hares. People gathered in the streets to watch the hares leaving their cages. There was a great fuss, but nobody could catch them again. The poor fellow stood there all alone. Then he plucked up his courage and went out of town, while everybody laughed at him. Walking along, he suddenly thought of the little flute that the gray old man had given him. When he was out of town, he started blowing it. The hares immediately came running along and remained by his side. The king had a big pasture, and he led them to it. There he drilled them; they were like soldiers.

Before an hour was over, the king knew all about it. "Well," he said, "what am I going to do with this fellow? I am afraid I shall have to give him my daughter."

Toward noon his daughter said, "Mother, give me the clothes of a servant. I am going to bring him his lunch." She brought him his lunch and ate with him. Then she told him to give her a hare for the king, for he would like to have one for supper. He said that he would gladly give her one, but that before he did she would have to go with him behind the bushes. He knew quite well that she was the princess. She thought that nobody would see her and that if he gave her a hare, he would never marry her. After playing around with her, he caught a hare and gave it to her.

She put it into her basket and thought, well, I have got the hare; so he will not bring them all back, and we shall not get married. She left. After a while he blew the flute, and the hare jumped out of the basket and came running back to the others. When the princess got home, her mother asked her, "Have you got a hare?"

"No," she said, "I haven't got any."

"Didn't he give you one?"

She said, "Yes he did, but when I had left, the hare jumped out of the basket and ran back."

The queen said, "Tomorrow I will go myself; I shall be more skillful and bring one home."

The next day the old queen dressed like a servant and brought him his lunch. She told him that His Majesty asked him to send a hare for his supper. "Why not?" he said. "I have got enough. But you will have to go behind the bushes with me." She looked round and thought, nobody can see me, and I shall not have to give him my daughter.

Afterward she took a thread and tied the hare's legs together. In this way it will not jump out, she thought. However, after a short while the hare tumbled out of the basket and rolled back, and the fellow untied it. So he had all his hares again. I have not been any more successful than my daughter, she thought.

When she came back, the king asked, "Have you got the hare?"

"Oh well," she said, "it overturned the basket and started tumbling back."

On the third day, they did not know what to do. Finally the king said, "Now I will bring him his lunch." He took a bag with him. When the fellow had eaten, the king told him, "The king sends you his respects and asks you to send him a hare, for he would like to eat one."

"With great pleasure. But behind this bush there is a dead ass. You must lick its arse three times. Then you can take a hare." The king did not like it at all. He looked around. Then he thought, Nobody can see me, so I will do it and then I will not have to give him my daughter. After having done it, he got a hare. He put it into his bag and tied it well. Then he put the bag on his shoulder and left. After a little while the hare started jumping up and down on his back until the bag fell down and the hare rolled back in the bag. The king remained there for a long while, but he was too ashamed to go back. When he reached home, he knew that now he had to give his daughter to the fellow. But perhaps there was still something to be done? He sent for his councilors again and told them, "Tonight he will come with the hares, for he has all of them. What am I to do? I do not want to give him my daughter!"

At night the fellow came with all his hares. What could be done about it? The councilors told the lad that he had to talk three bags full. They prepared a big scaffold, and he started talking. "Well," he said, "the first day when I was tending the hares, the princess brought me my lunch. After the meal she told me that His Majesty the king asked me to send him a hare. I said, 'Why not? But . . .'"

At this moment the princess cried, "Tie the bag up; it is full!"

He went on, "On the second day the old queen brought my lunch. After the meal she said that His Majesty the king would like me to send him a hare. 'Well,' I said, 'with pleasure.'" At this moment the old queen cried, "Tie up; the bag is full!" She did not even let him go on as far as her daughter had.

He went on, "On the third day His Royal Majesty brought my lunch. After the meal he asked me to give him a hare."

The king cried, "Tie the bag up; it is full!" For he was afraid that everything would be made public.

Now there was nothing to be done about it. She had to marry him. They prepared the feast but with little pleasure. He became a very valorous king. He ruled the country so well that nobody else, not even a person of high birth, would have done better. Thus the simpleton was king, and his brothers became even poorer. If they have not died, they are alive to this very day.

QUESTIONS

Language

1. Look at the encounters between the oldest two brothers and the old man. What seems to be his attitude toward them as he questions them? How do they answer? Why do they respond as they do?
2. What do you think "to talk a bag full" means?
3. Were you surprised by the vulgarity of this fairy tale? Are some crude episodes handled delicately?

Content

1. How is the youngest son's attitude and behavior on the way to court different from that of his older brothers? How would his family interpret the incident with the ants?
2. How is the young hero viewed by everyone else in the fairy tale?
3. What powers does the old man have? Why does he decide to use them to benefit the third son?
4. The narrator of this tale informs us that the youngest son "was believed to be stupid." Do you think he is stupid? And is there more to him than innocence and goodness?
5. Who is handled most roughly by the hero (and the narrator)—the princess, the queen, or the king? Why do you think this character receives the roughest treatment?

Suggestions for Writing

1. Three is a magical number in fairy tales; it appears repeatedly. In "The Hare Herd," "The Queen Bee" (p. 273), and "The Water of Life" (p. 333), there are three brothers, two evil and one good, while in "Cinderella" (p. 168), there are three sisters. In "The Juniper Tree" (p. 388), the bird visits the homes of three tradesmen and sings its song at each. In "The Queen Bee," there are three tasks to perform. "The Hare Herd" contains several references to the number three. Clearly, there is some special significance to this number, as there is to others: seven is considered lucky, thirteen, unlucky. Many people have their own individual lucky or unlucky numbers. Do you have a magical number (lucky or unlucky), or a number that has some special significance to you? If so, write an essay in which you explain what your special number is, why it is meaningful to you, and how it has brought you either good or bad fortune.
2. Do the king, the queen, their daughter, and their councilors behave as you expect leaders, people with power, to behave? How would you characterize their actions? Write an essay in which you argue that the royal family in this fairy tale is typical or atypical of the rulers or political leaders of a country. Give reasons for your opinion.
3. There are many things to be learned from this fairy tale. Discuss with your classmates and then write an essay about what it seems to say or prove to the reader.

C. C. BECK AND DENNY O'NEIL

"In the Beginning"

The creation of writer Bill Parker and artist C. C. Beck, Captain Marvel made his first appearance in *Whiz Comics* No. 2 (1940) and soon became the most popular of the costumed superheroes. The World's Mightiest Mortal (as he was called, though his enemies were more likely to refer to him scornfully as the Big Red Cheese), Captain Marvel was, in reality, newsboy Billy Batson, who could transform himself into the Herculean hero simply by uttering the magic word SHAZAM (the meaning of which is explained in the story below). Despite—or rather because of—his popularity, Captain Marvel disappeared from the comic book scene in the mid-1950s, the victim, not of his archfoe, the notorious Dr. Sivana (the World's Wickedest Scientist), but of his prototype and prime competitor in the comic book marketplace, Superman. Piqued by the success of the Captain Marvel stories (which were issued by Fawcett), the publishers of *Superman,* National Comics, sued Fawcett for copyright infringement. The case dragged on for years (with renowned lawyer Louis Nizer representing Superman's side) until Fawcett, in an out-of-court settlement, agreed to discontinue the Captain Marvel adventures.

Ironically, the character was revived twenty years later in a magazine called *SHA-ZAM!,* published by none other than National Comics. The following retelling of the origin of Captain Marvel, written by Denny O'Neil and drawn by the original artist, is from *SHAZAM!* no. 1 (1972). Though, in a subsequent story, Billy explains that he has been missing for two decades because the villainous Dr. Sivana captured him and placed him in suspended animation, the real, and far more prosaic, reason for Captain Marvel's "exile" is that he was taken to court by Superman.

SHAZAM!, © 1972 DC Comics Inc.

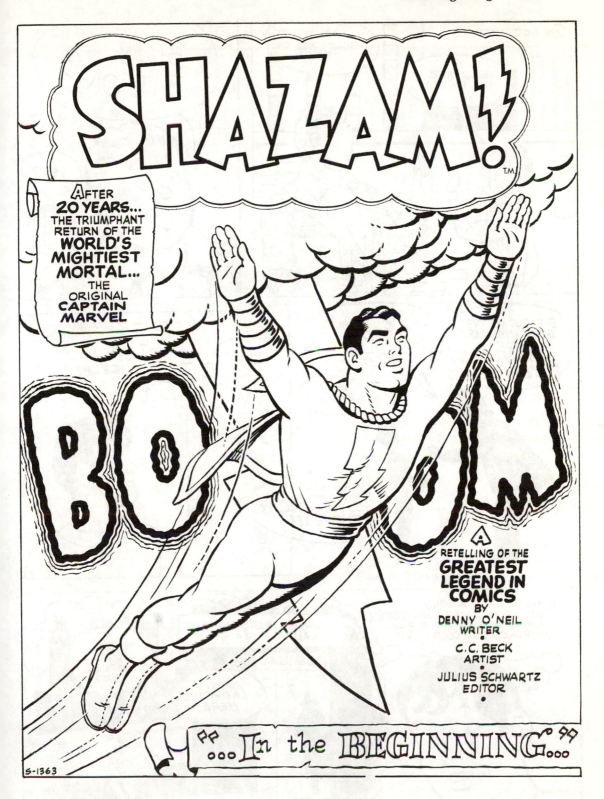

NO, SON. BUT IT'S LATE! WHY AREN'T YOU HOME IN BED?

I HAVE NO HOME, SIR! I SLEEP IN THE SUB-WAY STATION. IT'S WARM THERE!

FOLLOW ME!

"THE MYSTERIOUS FIGURE LED ME INTO A MURKY, ABANDONED TUNNEL..."

"SUDDENLY, A STRANGE SUBWAY CAR, WITH HEADLIGHTS GLEAMING LIKE A DRAGON'S EYES, ROARED INTO THE STATION AND STOPPED--- ALTHOUGH *NO ONE WAS DRIVING IT!* "

HAVE NO FEAR! A MYSTIC POWER WILL GUIDE US SAFELY!

ENTER!

"WE TRAVELED TO THE END OF THE LINE, WHERE MY STRANGE COMPANION LED ME INTO THE MOUTH OF A CAVERN..."

"SUDDENLY I FOUND MYSELF IN AN ANCIENT UNDERGROUND HALL, CARVED OUT OF SOLID ROCK AND LIT BY FLARING TORCHES...! "

THE SEVEN DEADLY ENEMIES OF MAN

PRIDE   ENVY   GREED   HATRED   SELFISHNESS   LAZINESS   INJUSTICE

3

SNAP!

"AND IN THE SAME UNBELIEVABLE INSTANT, THE BLOCK OF STONE THAT HAD HUNG BY A THREAD ABOVE THE WIZARD'S THRONE CRASHED DOWNWARD!"

SO IT IS WRITTEN THAT I MUST GO!

KRASSSSHH

H-HOLY MOLEY!

P-POOR OLD GUY...

OH, DO NOT MOURN FOR ME!

ALTHOUGH MY BODY IS NO MORE, MY SPIRIT LIVES ON IN ETHEREAL FORM!

SHOULD YOU EVER NEED ME, YOU HAVE ONLY TO LIGHT THIS BRAZIER AND I SHALL RETURN!

5

QUESTIONS

Language

1. What kind of boy is Billy Batson? Is there any hint in the way he talks that he is the perfect candidate to become Captain Marvel? Do his manner of speaking and his tone of voice change when he is transformed into the superhero? Can you imagine him ever becoming another aged wizard like Shazam?

Content

1. Discuss the dreamlike elements of this story. If, as some psychologists say, dreams are fantasies which fulfill our secret wishes, what kind of wish-fulfillment can you see in the story?
2. Look at the picture of Captain Marvel on p. 234. On the face of it, nothing could be sillier than a big, burly man who looks like a football player, wearing a skin-tight red leotard with a white satin cape, edged with flowers, draped over one shoulder. Yet such outlandish costumes are a standard feature of superheroes. Think of Superman, for example, or the Lone Ranger, who rides around the Wild West in a skin-tight silver suit, high-heeled boots, a black mask, and matching silver-mounted pistols. What is the appeal of the superhero's costume? Think of other costumed heroes from popular culture. In what sense do even realistic heroes like Tony Manero in the movie *Saturday Night Fever* wear distinctive outfits that confer special powers or status on them?
3. How "Egyptian" does Shazam look? Why does the writer make him an ancient Egyptian?

Suggestions for Writing

1. Rock singer Ken Weaver once remarked that as a child he imagined God looked like Shazam. Look at the tunnel leading to Shazam's throne room, the room's furnishings, his activities, his transformation into pure spirit, even the derivation of his name. Write an essay about the godlike properties of Shazam, as well as all Wise Old Man figures.
2. Often in fairy tales or other children's literature, the young hero or heroine is either an orphan or homeless. This condition—being alone and cut loose from family ties and support—would seem to be very threatening to the young reader. Yet there is obviously something about this imaginary situation which appeals to children. Write an essay in which you explore the reasons for this. Were there any times during your own childhood when the thought of being without parents or far from home and family was attractive?
3. This comic story was originally published in 1940; the version you see here has been redrawn but follows the same plot as the original. In many respects Billy Batson seems an old-fashioned boy. What qualities or characteristics of his are old-fashioned? (You might, for example, consider his extreme politeness.) Write an essay comparing him to children of a similar age, eleven or twelve, whom you know.

SHEL SILVERSTEIN

"The Winner"

(as recorded by Bobby Bare)

Shel Silverstein, humorist and songwriter, has been a cartoonist for *Playboy* magazine, a successful author of children's books, and the composer of several country-flavored hit tunes, among them "A Boy Named Sue," a Grammy award-winner for singer Johnny Cash; "Sylvia's Mother" and "The Cover of *Rolling Stone*," both written for the country-rock band, Dr. Hook & the Medicine Show; and "The Winner." Silverstein has also recorded several albums of his own compositions, including *Hairy Jazz, A Boy Named Sue, Freakin' at the Freakers' Ball*, and *Inside*.

"The Winner" was a best-selling song for country singer Bobby Bare and appears on his album *The Winner and Other Losers*.

"The Winner"

The hulk of a man with the beer in his hand, he looked like a drunk old fool,
And I knew if I hit him right, why, I could knock him off-a that stool.
But ev'rybody, they said, "Watch out, hey, that's Tiger Man McCool,
He's had a whole lot of fights and he's always come out the winner. (Yeah,
   he's a winner.)

But I'd had myself about five too many, and I walked up tall and proud,
I faced his back and I faced the fact that he had never stooped or bowed;
I said, "Tiger Man, you're a pussy cat," and a hush fell on the crowd,
I said, "Let's you and me go outside and see who's a winner."

Well, he gripped the bar with one big hairy hand and he braced against the
   wall,
He slowly looked up from his beer, My God, that man was tall;
He said, "Boy I see you're a scrapper, so just before you fall,
I'm gonna tell you just a little about what it means to be a winner."

(He said,) "Now, you see these bright white smilin' teeth, you know they ain't
   my own,
Mine rolled away like chiclets down a street in San Antone;
But I left that person cursin', nursin' seven broken bones,
And he only broke three of mine and that makes me the winner."

(He said,) "Now, behind this grin I got a steel pin that holds my jaw in place,
A trophy of my most successful motorcycle race;
And each mornin' when I wake and touch this scar across my face,
It reminds me of all I got by bein' a winner."

"The Winner." Words and music by Shel Silverstein. © Copyright 1973 Evil Eye Music, Inc., New York, N.Y. Used by permission.

"Now, this broken back was the dyin' act of a handsome Harry Clay,
That sticky Cincinnati night I stole his wife away;
But that woman she gets uglier and she gets meaner every day,
But I got her, boy, and that's what makes me a winner."

(He said,) "You gotta speak loud when you challenge me, son, 'cause it's hard
for me to hear,
With this twisted neck and these migraine pains and this big old cauliflower
ear;
Now, if it wasn't for this glass eye of mine, why, I'd shed a happy tear,
To think of all that you're gonna get by bein' a winner."

"I got 'arthuritic' elbows, boy, I got dislocated knees
From pickin' fights with thunderstorms and chargin' into trees;
And my nose been broke so often, I might lose it if I sneeze,
And, son, you say you still wanna be a winner?"

"Now you remind me a lot of my younger days with your knuckles clenchin'
white,
But, boy, I'm gonna sit right here and sip this beer all night;
And if there's somethin' that you gotta gain to prove by winnin' some silly
fight,
Well, O.K., I quit, I lose, you're the winner."

Oh, I stumbled from that barroom, not so tall and not so proud,
And behind I still hear the hoots o' laughter of the crowd;
But my eyes still see and my nose still works and my teeth are still in my mouth,
And y'know, I guess that makes me the winner!

QUESTIONS

Language

1. Look up the word *irony* in a good dictionary; then talk about all the places in this song where you find irony.
2. Why does the aged "winner" say he has been "pickin' fights with thunderstorms and chargin' into trees"? What is this kind of language called?
3. Does the line "And if there's somethin' that you gotta gain to prove by winnin' some silly fight" sound awkward to you? Rewrite it.

Content

1. Why does the younger man want to fight with Tiger Man McCool? What does his desire tell us about him?
2. How does the challenger look and feel at the beginning of the song? At the end?
3. What is Tiger Man McCool's attitude toward the younger man? Is it different from the one held by the other men in the bar?
4. Given McCool's appearance and personal history, is he the sort of man we expect to be wise? Why or why not?
5. What other victory, besides retaining intact all his teeth, organs, and bones, does the young man in this song achieve?

Suggestions for Writing

1. Write an essay about a "victory" you once had that turned out later not to be a victory at all. Describe the event, your feelings at the time, and your reflections about it later.
2. The situation presented in this song is one that has occurred in countless Western movies and television shows: a young man steps into a bar and challenges an older man to a fight of some sort. But does "The Winner" end the same way as all those other confrontations? Write an essay comparing and contrasting the situation in this song with the classic Western scene. Don't neglect the *characters* of the two combatants.
3. Write an essay about how this song comments on changing ideas of what it means to be a man, on how a man ought to behave, and related issues (such as "proving one's manhood"). You might like to discuss this with your classmates or friends first. It might also be helpful to question an older man about the subject—your father, for instance, or other male relatives of a comparable age.
4. Describe a *major* fight that you have had with a friend or enemy. It need not have led to blows, but must have been a very serious fight. What led up to it? What happened? Was anyone else present? What did you learn from this fight? Try to make your essay as dramatic as possible; you will probably want to include some dialogue.

WILLIAM PETER BLATTY

from *The Exorcist*

A fascinating, though sometimes frightening, development of recent years has been America's growing interest in such occult phenomena as magic, astrology, parapsychology, and, most disturbing of all, witchcraft and satanism. As *Time* magazine reported in a cover story, "The Occult Revival" (June 19, 1972), the late sixties witnessed an unsettling proliferation of witches' covens and devil cults. To be sure, some of these were nothing more than groups of bored suburbanites trying to add some excitement to their lives by toying with the forbidden. But others—most notoriously the demoniac family headed by Charles Manson—paid terrifying tribute to the Prince of Darkness.

In the popular arts, Lucifer suddenly became a hot property, a media superstar. At the height of their success, for example, the Rolling Stones began posing as "Their Satanic Majesties," and Mick Jagger's rendition of "Sympathy for the Devil" at the infamous concert at Altamont drove some of the audience into a murderous frenzy. In fiction, Ira Levin's *Rosemary's Baby* sold millions of copies and the movie version, directed by Roman Polanski, was equally successful. But it was William Peter Blatty's *The Exorcist* which affected the public most deeply. The film version of the best-selling novel produced, not only unprecedented profits, but a kind of mass hysteria. Moviegoers fainted and had to be carried from the theaters, while newspapers reported a nationwide outbreak of demonic possession.

Blatty's story concerns the movie actress Chris MacNeil, whose daughter Regan (nicknamed "Rags") suddenly and horrendously falls victim to the demon Pazuzu.

From pp. 289–301 (hard cover edition) in *The Exorcist* by William Peter Blatty, Harper & Row, Publishers, Inc. Copyright © 1971 by William Peter Blatty.

In desperation, Chris turns to Father Damien Karras, a young priest who is passing through a crisis of faith. Karras, after resisting the notion, is finally convinced that Regan is indeed possessed, and sends for the aged priest Lankester Merrin, who has battled, and bested, Pazuzu in a previous encounter. In the following scene, Father Merrin arrives at the MacNeil home, where he is greeted by Chris, Karras, Sharon (Chris' secretary), Karl, the family butler, and Willie, his wife.

Karras sat alone and sipped bleakly at his coffee. He felt warm in the sweater that he wore beneath his cassock; felt weak in his failure to have given Chris comfort. Then a memory of childhood shimmered up sadly, a memory of Ginger, his mongrel dog, growing skeletal and dazed in a box in the apartment; Ginger shivering with fever and vomiting while Karras covered her with towels, tried to make her drink warm milk, until a neighbor came by and saw it was distemper, shook his head and said, "Your dog needed shots right away." Then dismissed from school one afternoon . . . to the street . . . in columns of twos to the corner . . . his mother there to meet him . . . unexpected . . . looking sad . . . and then taking his hand to press a shiny half-dollar piece into it . . . elation . . . so much money! . . . then her voice, soft and tender, "Gingie die. . . ."

He looked down at the steaming, bitter blackness in his cup and felt his hands empty of comfort or of cure.

". . . pious bastard!"

The demon. Still raging.

"Your dog needed shots right away. . . ."

Quickly he returned to Regan's bedroom, where he held her while Sharon administered the Librium injection that now brought the total dosage up to five hundred milligrams.

Sharon was swabbing the needle puncture while Karras watched Regan, puzzled. The frenzied obscenities seemed to be directed at no one in the room, but rather at someone unseen—or not present.

He dismissed the thought. "I'll be back," he told Sharon.

Concerned about Chris, he went down to the kitchen, where again he found her sitting alone at the table. She was pouring brandy into her coffee. "Are you sure you wouldn't like some, Father?" she asked.

Shaking his head, he came over to the table and sat down wearily. He stared at the floor. Heard porcelain clicks of a spoon stirring coffee. "Have you talked to her father?" he asked.

"Yes. Yes, he called." A pause. "He wanted to talk to Rags."

"And what did you tell him?"

A pause. Then, "I told him she was out at a party."

Silence. Karras heard no more clicks. He looked up and saw her staring at the ceiling. And then he noticed it too: the shouts above had finally ceased.

"I guess the Librium took hold," he said gratefully.

Chiming of the doorbell. He glanced toward the sound; then at Chris, who met his look of surmise with a questioning, apprehensive lifting of an eyebrow.

Kinderman?[1]

Seconds. Ticking. They waited. Willie was resting. Sharon and Karl were

---

[1] Lieutenant Kinderman is a police detective investigating the grotesque murder of Chris' friend, movie director Burke Dennings.

still upstairs. No one coming to answer. Tense, Chris got up abruptly from the table and went to the living room. Kneeling on a sofa, she parted a curtain and peered furtively through the window at her caller. *Thank God!* Not Kinderman. She was looking, instead, at a tall old man in a threadbare raincoat, his head bowed patiently in the rain. He carried a worn, old-fashioned valise. For an instant, a buckle gleamed in street-lamp glow as the bag shifted slightly in his grip.

The doorbell chimed again.

Who is that?

Puzzled, Chris got down off the sofa and walked to the entry hall. She opened the door only slightly, squinting out into darkness as a fine mist of rain brushed her eyes. The man's hat brim obscured his face. "Yes, hello; can I help you?"

"Mrs. MacNeil?" came a voice from the shadows. It was gentle, refined, yet as full as a harvest.

As he reached for his hat, Chris was nodding her head, and then suddenly she was looking into eyes that overwhelmed her, that shone with intelligence and kindly understanding, with serenity that poured from them into her being like the waters of a warm and healing river whose source was both in him yet somehow beyond him; whose flow was contained and yet headlong and endless.

"I'm Father Merrin."

For a moment she looked blank as she stared at the lean and ascetic face, at the sculptured cheekbones, polished like soapstone; then quickly she flung wide the door. "Oh, my gosh, please come *in!* Oh, come *in!* Gee, I'm . . . *Honestly!* I don't know where my . . ."

He entered and she closed the door.

"I mean, I didn't expect you until tomorrow!"

"Yes, I know," she heard him saying.

As she turned around to face him, she saw him standing with his head angled sideways, glancing upward, as if he were listening—no, more like *feeling,* she thought—for some presence out of sight . . . some distant vibration that was known and familiar. Puzzled, she watched him. His skin seemed weathered by alien winds, by a sun that shone elsewhere, somewhere remote from her time and her place.

What's he doing?

"Can I take that bag for you, Father? It must weigh a ton by now."

"It's all right," he said softly. Still feeling. Still probing. "It's like part of my arm: very old . . . very battered." He looked down with a warm, tired smile in his eyes. "I'm accustomed to the weight. . . . Is Father Karras here?" he asked.

"Yes, he is. He's in the kitchen. Have you had any dinner, incidentally, Father?"

He flicked his glance upward at the sound of a door being opened. "Yes, I had some on the train."

\ "Are you sure you wouldn't like something else?"

A moment. Then sound of the door being closed. He glanced down. "No, thank you."

"Gee, all of this rain," she protested, still flustered. "If I'd known you were coming, I could have met you at the station."

"It's all right."

"Did you have to wait long for a cab?"

"A few minutes."

"I take that, Father!"

Karl. He'd descended the stairs very quickly and now slipped the bag from the priest's easy grip and took it off down the hall.

"We've put a bed in the study for you, Father." Chris was fidgeting. "It's really very comfortable and I thought you'd like the privacy. I'll show you where it is." She'd started moving, then stopped. "Or would you like to say hello to Father Karras?"

"I should like to see your daughter first," said Merrin.

She looked puzzled. "Right now, you mean, Father?"

He glanced upward again with that distant attentiveness. "Yes, now—I think now."

"Gee, I'm sure she's asleep."

"I think not."

"Well, if—"

Suddenly, Chris flinched at a sound from above, at the voice of the demon, booming and yet muffled, croaking, like amplified premature burial.

"Merriiiiinnnnnn!"

Then the massive and shiveringly hollow jolt of a single blow against the bedroom wall.

"*God almighty!*" Chris breathed as she clutched a pale hand against her chest. Stunned, she looked at Merrin. The priest hadn't moved. He was still staring upward, intense and yet serene, and in his eyes there was not even a hint of surprise. It was more, Chris thought, like recognition.

Another blow shook the walls.

Merriiiiinnnnnnnnnnn!"

The Jesuit moved slowly forward, oblivious of Chris, who was gaping in wonder; of Karl, stepping lithe and incredulous from the study; of Karras, emerging bewildered from the kitchen while the nightmarish poundings and croakings continued. He went calmly up the staircase, slender hand like alabaster sliding upward on the banister.

Karras came up beside Chris, and together they watched from below as Merrin entered Regan's bedroom and closed the door behind him. For a time there was silence. Then abruptly the demon laughed hideously and Merrin came out. He closed the door and started down the hall. Behind him, the bedroom door opened again and Sharon poked her head out, staring after him, an odd expression on her face.

The Jesuit descended the staircase rapidly and put out his hand to the waiting Karras.

"Father Karras . . ."

"Hello, Father."

Merrin had clasped the other priest's hand in both of his; he was squeezing it, searching Karras' face with a look of gravity and concern, while upstairs the laughter turned to vicious obscenities directed at Merrin. "You look terribly tired," he said. "Are you tired?"

"Not at all. Why do you ask?"

"Do you have your raincoat with you?"

Karras shook his head and said, "No."

"Then here, take mine," said the gray-haired Jesuit, unbuttoning the coat.
"I should like you to go to the residence, Damien, and gather up a cassock for myself, two surplices, a purple stole, some holy water and two copies of *The Roman Ritual.*" He handed the raincoat to the puzzled Karras. "I believe we should begin."

Karras frowned. "You mean now? Right away?"

"Yes, I think so."

"Don't you want to hear the background of the case first, Father?"

"Why?"

Merrin's brows were knitted in earnestness.

Karras realized that he had no answer. He averted his gaze from those disconcerting eyes. "Right," he said. He was slipping on the raincoat and turning away. "I'll go and get the things."

Karl made a dash across the room, got ahead of Karras and pulled the front door open for him. They exchanged brief glances, and then Karras stepped out into the rainy night. Merrin glanced back to Chris. "You don't mind if we begin right away?" he asked softly.

She'd been watching him, glowing with relief at the feeling of decision and direction and command rushing in like a shout in sunlit day. "No, I'm glad," she said gratefully. "You must be tired, though, Father."

He saw her anxious gaze flick upward toward the raging of the demon.

"Would you like a cup of coffee?" she was asking. "It's fresh." Insistent. Faintly pleading. "It's hot. Wouldn't you like some, Father?"

He saw the hands lightly clasping, unclasping; the deep caverns of her eyes. "Yes, I would," he said warmly. "Thank you." Something heavy had been gently brushed aside; told to wait. "If you're sure it's no trouble . . ."

She led him to the kitchen and soon he was leaning against the stove with a mug of black coffee in his hand.

"Want some brandy in it, Father?" Chris held up the bottle.

He bent his head and looked down into the mug without expression. "Well, the doctors say I shouldn't," he said. And then he held out the mug. "But thank God, my will is weak."

Chris paused for a moment, unsure, then saw the smile in his eyes as he lifted his head.

She poured.

"What a lovely name you have," he told her. "Chris MacNeil. It's not a stage name?"

Chris trickled brandy into her coffee and shook her head. "No, I'm really not Esmerelda Glutz."

"Thank God for *that,*" murmured Merrin.

Chris smiled and sat down. "And what's Lankester, Father? So unusual. Were you named after someone?"

"A cargo ship," he murmured as he stared absently and put the mug to his lips. He sipped. "Or a bridge. Yes, I suppose it was a bridge." He looked rueful. "Now, Damien," he went on, "how I wish I had a name like Damien. So lovely."

"Where does that come from, Father? That name?"

"Damien?" He looked down at his cup. "It was the name of a priest who devoted his life to taking care of the lepers on the island of Molokai. He finally caught the disease himself." He paused. "Lovely name," he said again. "I believe that with a first name like Damien, I might even be content with the last name Glutz."

Chris chuckled. She unwound. Felt easier. And for minutes, she and Merrin spoke of homely things, little things. Finally, Sharon appeared in the kitchen, and only then did Merrin move to leave. It was as if he had been waiting for her arrival, for immediately he carried his mug to the sink, rinsed it out and placed it carefully in the dish rack. "That was good; that was just what I wanted," he said.

Chris got up and said, "I'll take you to your room."

He thanked her and followed her to the door of the study. "If there's anything you need, Father," she said, "let me know."

He put his hand on her shoulder and squeezed it reassuringly. Chris felt a power and warmth flowing into her. Peace. She felt peace. And an odd sense of . . . safety? she wondered.

"You're very kind." His eyes smiled. "Thank you."

He removed his hand and watched her walk away. As soon as she was gone, a tightening pain seemed to clutch at his face. He entered the study and closed the door. From a pocket of his trousers, he slipped out a tin marked *Bayer Aspirin,* opened it, extracted a nitroglycerin pill and placed it carefully under his tongue.

Chris entered the kitchen. Pausing by the door, she looked at Sharon, who was standing by the stove, the palm of her hand against the percolator as she waited for the coffee to reheat.

Chris went over to her, concerned. "Hey, honey," she said softly. "Why don't you get a little rest?"

No response. Sharon seemed lost in thought. Then she turned and stared blankly at Chris. "I'm sorry. Did you say something?"

Chris studied the tightness in her face, the distant look. "What happened up there, Sharon?" she asked.

"Happened where?"

"When Father Merrin walked in upstairs."

"Oh, yes . . ." Sharon frowned. She shifted her faraway gaze to a point in space between doubt and remembrance. "Yes. It was funny."

"Funny?"

"Strange. They only . . ." She paused. "Well, they only just stared at each other for a while, and then Regan—that thing—it said . . ."

"Said what?"

"It said, 'This time, you're going to lose.' "

Chris stared at her, waiting. "And then?"

"That was it," Sharon answered. "Father Merrin turned around and walked out of the room."

"And how did he look?" Chris asked her.

"Funny."

"Oh, Christ, Sharon, think of some other word!" snapped Chris, and was about to say something else when she noticed that Sharon had angled her head up, to the side, abstracted, as if she were listening.

Chris glanced upward and heard it too: the silence; the sudden cessation of the raging of the demon; yet something more . . . something . . . and growing.

The women flicked sidelong stares at each other.

"You feel it too?" asked Sharon quietly.

Chris nodded. The house. Something in the house. A tension. A gradual thickening of the air. A pulsing, like energies slowly building up.

The lilting of the door chimes sounded unreal.

Sharon turned away. "I'll get it."

She walked to the entry hall and opened the door. It was Karras. He was carrying a cardboard laundry box. "Thank you, Sharon."

"Father Merrin's in the study," she told him.

Karras moved quickly to the study, tapped lightly and cursorily at the door and then entered with the box. "Sorry, Father," he was saying, "I had a little—"

Karras stopped short. Merrin, in trousers and T-shirt, kneeled in prayer beside the rented bed, his forehead bent low to his tight-clasped hands. Karras stood rooted for a moment, as if he had casually rounded a corner and suddenly encountered his boyhood self with an altar boy's cassock draped over an arm, hurrying by without a glance of recognition.

Karras shifted his eyes to the open laundry box, to speckles of rain on starch. Then slowly, with his gaze still averted, he moved to the sofa and soundlessly laid out the contents of the box. When he finished, he took off the raincoat and draped it carefully over a chair. As he glanced back toward Merrin, he saw the priest blessing himself and he hastily looked away, reaching down for the larger of the white cotton surplices. He began to put it on over his cassock. He heard Merrin rising, and then, "Thank you, Damien." Karras turned to face him, tugging down the surplice while Merrin came over in front of the sofa, his eyes brushing tenderly over its contents.

Karras reached for a sweater. "I thought you might wear this under your cassock, Father," he told Merrin as he handed it over. "The room gets cold at times."

Merrin touched the sweater lightly with his hands. "That was thoughtful of you, Damien."

Karras picked up Merrin's cassock from the sofa, and watched him pull the sweater down over his head, and only now, and very suddenly, while watching this homely, prosaic action, did Karras feel the staggering impact of the man; of the moment; of a stillness in the house, crushing down on him, choking off breath.

He came back to awareness with the feeling of the cassock being tugged from his hands. Merrin. He was slipping it on. "You're familiar with the rules concerning exorcism, Damien?"

"Yes, I am," answered Karras.

Merrin began buttoning up the cassock. "Especially important is the warning to avoid conversations with the demon. . . ."

The demon. He'd said it so matter-of-factly, thought Karras. It jarred him.

"We may ask what is relevant," said Merrin as he buttoned the collar of the cassock. "But anything beyond that is dangerous. Extremely." He lifted the surplice from Karras' hands and began to slip it over the cassock. "Especially, do not listen to anything he says. The demon is a liar. He will lie to confuse us; but he will also mix lies with the truth to attack us. The attack is psychological, Damien. And powerful. Do not listen. Remember that. Do not listen."

As Karras handed him the stole, the exorcist added, "Is there anything at all you would like to ask now, Damien?"

Karras shook his head. "No. But I think it might be helpful if I gave you some background on the different personalities that Regan has manifested. So far, there seem to be three."

"There is only one," said Merrin softly, slipping the stole around his shoulders. For a moment, he gripped it and stood unmoving as a haunted expression came into his eyes. Then he reached for the copies of *The Roman Ritual* and gave one to Karras. "We will skip the Litany of the Saints. You have the holy water?"

Karras slipped the slender, cork-tipped vial from his pocket. Merrin took it, then nodded serenely toward the door. "If you will lead, please, Damien."

Upstairs, by the door to Regan's bedroom, Sharon and Chris stood tense and waiting. They were bundled in heavy sweaters and jackets. At the sound of a door coming open, they turned and looked below and saw Karras and Merrin come down the hall to the stairs in solemn procession. Tall: how tall they were, thought Chris; and Karras: the dark of that rock-chipped face above the innocent, altar-boy white of the surplice. Watching them steadily ascending the staircase, Chris felt deeply and strangely moved. *Here comes my big brother to beat your brains in, creep!* It was a feeling, she thought, much like that. She could feel her heart begin to beat faster.

At the door of the room, the Jesuits stopped. Karras frowned at the sweater and jacket Chris wore. "You're coming in?"

"Well, I really thought I should."

"Please don't," he urged her. "Don't. You'd be making a great mistake."

Chris turned questioningly to Merrin.

"Father Karras knows best," said the exorcist quietly.

Christ looked to Karras again. Dropped her head. "Okay," she said despondently. She leaned against the wall. "I'll wait out here."

"What is your daughter's middle name?" asked Merrin.

"Teresa."

"What a lovely name," said Merrin warmly. He held her gaze for a moment, reassuring. Then he looked at the door, and again Chris felt it: that tension; that thickening of coiled darkness. Inside. In the bedroom. Beyond that door. Karras felt it too, she noticed, and Sharon.

Merrin nodded. "All right," he said softly.

Karras opened the door, and almost reeled back from the blast of stench and icy cold. In a corner of the room, Karl sat huddled in a chair. He was dressed in a faded olive green hunting jacket and turned expectantly to Karras. The Jesuit quickly flicked his glance to the demon in the bed. Its gleaming eyes stared beyond him to the hall. They were fixed on Merrin.

Karras moved forward to the foot of the bed while Merrin walked slowly, tall and erect, to the side. There he stopped and looked down into hate.

A smothering stillness hung over the room. Then Regan licked a wolfish, blackened tongue across her cracked and swollen lips. It sounded like a hand smoothing crumpled parchment. "Well, proud scum!" croaked the demon. "At last! At last you've come!"

QUESTIONS

Language

1. Look at all of Lankester Merrin's conversations with Chris MacNeil and Father Karras. What do they reveal about the kind of man he is?
2. Blatty describes the atmosphere beyond the closed door to Regan's room as a "thickening of coiled darkness." Is this a very *precise* description? Is it effective?
3. When Karras and Merrin ascend the stairs to begin the exorcism, Chris MacNeil feels, we are told, "deeply and strangely moved. *Here comes my big brother to beat your brains in, creep!* It was a feeling, she thought, much like that." Do you think the italicized words are appropriate to the situation? To the tone of the entire selection?
4. What is the purpose of the conversation MacNeil has with Merrin over coffee? Why would the author include it?

Content

1. The devil is conventionally portrayed as a spirit from a place of perpetual fire. Why, then, does Blatty make Regan's room "icy cold"?
2. Why does Merrin tell Karras there's no reason to hear the "background of the case"? Do the two priests seem to have different attitudes toward the demon?
3. What special powers does Merrin have? How does Blatty make him seem different from ordinary men? How does he establish Merrin's *link* with ordinary men?
4. Do the demon and Merrin share any characteristics?
5. How old does Chris MacNeil seem in this scene? Does she act or talk like a woman in her middle thirties who is a world-famous actress?
6. For what purpose does Blatty include the incident about Karras' childhood dog, Ginger?
7. *The Exorcist* is an extremely suspenseful book. How does Blatty build suspense even in this brief scene?

Suggestions for Writing

1. Discuss with your classmates and then write about the sudden growth of interest in the occult, the supernatural, in the late 1960s and early 1970s. What did such things as the Vietnam War, all the mass protest movements, the "counterculture," and the experimentation with drugs have to do with this interest? Was there a corresponding flowering of new religions? Do you see any evidence of renewed participation in religion today? You may want to write about only the *causes* of the new interest in the occult and the supernatural, or, alternatively, only about the *results* of it.
2. Starting as early as the late 1950s with *The Bad Seed,* a movie about a young girl who, though innocent-looking, murders people close to her, American novelists and filmmakers have created a number of evil or demon-possessed children. After *Rosemary's Baby* in the late 1960s, there were *The Exorcist,* Tom Tryon's *The Other*—the possessed child in this book kills four people and attempts to kill, but only paralyzes, his mother— the sequence of *Omen* movies, and the improbable *It's Alive* films. How do you account for the creation of these evil, demon-ridden youngsters? Explore in an essay what this phenomenon reveals about America's hidden attitudes toward children over the past two decades.
3. Since long before the dawn of recorded history, men and women have believed in gods, in good and evil spirits, dangerous, potent, awe-inspiring supernatural beings. Many people in modern America, however, scoff at these notions as primitive superstitions. Express your own personal theology—your belief or lack of belief in gods and devils—in an essay.

CARLOS CASTANEDA

from *The Teachings of Don Juan: A Yaqui Way of Knowledge*

Little is known about Carlos Castaneda. Although he is a literary celebrity whose books have sold millions of copies, he remains a mysterious figure. Born in São Paulo, Brazil, in 1931, he studied anthropology at the University of California, Los Angeles, where he obtained his B.A. (1962), M.A. (1964), and Ph.D. (1970). In 1961, while doing research in the Southwest on the medicinal plants of that area, he was introduced by a friend to a Yaqui Indian *brujo,* or sorcerer, named don Juan, who undertook to initiate Castaneda into the mysteries of a world radically different from the one we normally inhabit. Guided by his Indian master, Castaneda entered this world of "nonordinary reality" (as he terms it) through the ritual use of various hallucinogenic drugs: peyote ("Mescalito"), jimson weed, and the mushroom *psilocyba mexicana.* His account of his five-year apprenticeship to the sorcerer, *The Teachings of Don Juan: A Yaqui Way of Knowledge,* served as his master's thesis and was later published as a book (1968). Written in lean, vigorous prose and filled with vivid evocations of his psychedelic experiences, it became a campus best-seller and its author a counterculture hero. Further accounts of his progress along the Yaqui path of enlightenment followed: *A Separate Reality* (1971), *Journey to Ixtlan* (1972), *Tales of Power* (1974), and *The Second Ring of Power* (1978). Partly because these books read like novels and partly because of Castaneda's penchant for privacy—his secretiveness and refusal to answer questions about don Juan (whose existence remains undocumented, since there are no photographs or tape recordings of him)—the authenticity of Castaneda's work has been called into question. Nevertheless, whether factual or not, the books are an impressive achievement.

Friday, June 23, 1961

"Would you teach me about peyote, don Juan?"

"Why would you like to undertake such learning?"

"I really would like to know about it. Is not just to want to know a good reason?"

"No! You must search in your heart and find out why a young man like you wants to undertake such a task of learning."

"Why did you learn about it yourself, don Juan?"

"Why do you ask that?"

"Maybe we both have the same reasons."

"I doubt that. I am an Indian. We don't have the same paths."

"The only reason I have is that I *want* to learn about it, just to know. But I assure you, don Juan, my intentions are not bad."

"I believe you. I've smoked you."

Copyright 1968 by The Regents of the University of California; reprinted by permission of the University of California Press.

"I beg your pardon!"

"It doesn't matter now. I know your intentions."

"Do you mean you saw through me?"

"You could put it that way."

"Will you teach me, then?"

"No!"

"Is it because I'm not an Indian?"

"No. It is because you don't know your heart. What is important is that you know exactly why you want to involve yourself. Learning about 'Mescalito' is a most serious act. If you were an Indian your desire alone would be sufficient. Very few Indians have such a desire."

Sunday, June 25, 1961

I stayed with don Juan all afternoon on Friday. I was going to leave about 7 P.M. We were sitting on the porch in front of his house and I decided to ask him once more about the teaching. It was almost a routine question and I expected him to refuse again. I asked him if there was a way in which he could accept just my desire to learn, as if I were an Indian. He took a long time to answer. I was compelled to stay because he seemed to be trying to decide something.

Finally he told me that there was a way, and proceeded to delineate a problem. He pointed out that I was very tired sitting on the floor, and that the proper thing to do was to find a "spot" (*sitio*) on the floor where I could sit without fatigue. I had been sitting with my knees up against my chest and my arms locked around my calves. When he said I was tired, I realized that my back ached and that I was quite exhausted.

I waited for him to explain what he meant by a "spot," but he made no overt attempt to elucidate the point. I thought that perhaps he meant that I should change positions, so I got up and sat closer to him. He protested my movement and clearly emphasized that a spot meant a place where a man could feel naturally happy and strong. He patted the place where he sat and said it was his own spot, adding that he had posed a riddle I had to solve by myself without any further deliberation.

What he had posed as a problem to be solved was certainly a riddle. I had no idea how to begin or even what he had in mind. Several times I asked for a clue, or at least a hint, as to how to proceed in locating a point where I felt happy and strong. I insisted and argued that I had no idea what he really meant because I couldn't conceive the problem. He suggested I walk around the porch until I found the spot.

I got up and began to pace the floor. I felt silly and sat down in front of him.

He became very annoyed with me and accused me of not listening, saying that perhaps I did not want to learn. After a while he calmed down and explained to me that not every place was good to sit or be on, and that within the confines of the porch there was one spot that was unique, a spot where I could be at my very best. It was my task to distinguish it from all the other places. The general pattern was that I had to "feel" all the possible spots that were accessible until I could determine without a doubt which was the right one.

I argued that although the porch was not too large (12 x 8 feet), the number of possible spots was overwhelming, and it would take me a very long time to check all of them, and that since he had not specified the size of the spot, the possibilities might be infinite. My arguments were futile. He got up and very sternly warned me that it might take me days to figure it out, but that if I did not solve the problem, I might as well leave because he would have nothing to say to me. He emphasized that he knew where my spot was, and that therefore I could not lie to him; he said this was the only way he could accept my desire to learn about Mescalito as a valid reason. He added that nothing is his world was a gift, that whatever there was to learn had to be learned the hard way.

He went around the house to the chaparral to urinate. He returned directly into his house through the back.

I thought the assignment to find the alleged spot of happiness was his own way of dismissing me, but I got up and started to pace back and forth. The sky was clear. I could see everything on and near the porch. I must have paced for an hour or more, but nothing happened to reveal the location of the spot. I got tired of walking and sat down; after a few minutes I sat somewhere else, and then at another place, until I had covered the whole floor in a semisystematic fashion. I deliberately tried to "feel" differences between places, but I lacked the criteria for differentiation. I felt I was wasting my time, but I stayed. My rationalization was that I had come a long way just to see don Juan, and I really had nothing else to do.

I lay down on my back and put my hands under my head like a pillow. Then I rolled over and lay on my stomach for a while. I repeated this rolling process over the entire floor. For the first time I thought I had stumbled upon a vague criterion. I felt warmer when I lay on my back.

I rolled again, this time in the opposite direction, and again covered the length of the floor, lying face down on all the places where I had lain face up during my first rolling tour. I experienced the same warm and cold sensations, depending on my position, but there was no difference between spots.

Then an idea occurred to me which I thought to be brilliant: don Juan's spot! I sat there, and then lay, face down at first, and later on my back, but the place was just like all the others. I stood up. I had had enough. I wanted to say good-bye to don Juan, but I was embarrassed to wake him up. I looked at my watch. It was two o'clock in the morning! I had been rolling for six hours.

At that moment don Juan came out and went around the house to the chaparral. He came back and stood at the door. I felt utterly dejected, and I wanted to say something nasty to him and leave. But I realized that it was not his fault; that it was my own choice to go through all that nonsense. I told him I had failed; I had been rolling on his floor like an idiot all night and still couldn't make any sense of his riddle.

He laughed and said that it did not surprise him because I had not proceeded correctly. I had not been using my eyes. That was true, yet I was very sure he had said to feel the difference. I brought that point up, but he argued that one can feel with the eyes, when the eyes are not looking right into things. As far as I was concerned, he said, I had no other means to solve this problem but to use all I had—my eyes.

He went inside. I was certain that he had been watching me. I thought there was no other way for him to know that I had not been using my eyes.

I began to roll again, because that was the most comfortable procedure.

This time, however, I rested my chin on my hands and looked at every detail.

After an interval the darkness around me changed. When I focused on the point directly in front of me, the whole peripheral area of my field of vision became brilliantly colored with a homogeneous greenish yellow. The effect was startling. I kept my eyes fixed on the point in front of me and began to crawl sideways on my stomach, one foot at a time.

Suddenly, at a point near the middle of the floor, I became aware of another change in hue. At a place to my right, still in the periphery of my field of vision, the greenish yellow became intensely purple. I concentrated my attention on it. The purple faded into a pale, but still brilliant, color which remained steady for the time I kept my attention on it.

I marked the place with my jacket, and called don Juan. He came out to the porch. I was truly excited; I had actually seen the change in hues. He seemed unimpressed, but told me to sit on the spot and report to him what kind of feeling I had.

I sat down and then lay on my back. He stood by me and asked me repeatedly how I felt; but I did not feel anything different. For about fifteen minutes I tried to feel or to see a difference, while don Juan stood by me patiently. I felt disgusted. I had a metallic taste in my mouth. Suddenly I had developed a headache. I was about to get sick. The thought of my nonsensical endeavors irritated me to a point of fury. I got up.

Don Juan must have noticed my profound frustration. He did not laugh, but very seriously stated that I had to be inflexible with myself if I wanted to learn. Only two choices were open to me, he said: either to quit and go home, in which case I would never learn, or to solve the riddle.

He went inside again. I wanted to leave immediately, but I was too tired to drive; besides, perceiving the hues had been so startling that I was sure it was a criterion of some sort, and perhaps there were other changes to be detected. Anyway, it was too late to leave. So I sat down, stretched my legs back, and began all over again.

During this round I moved rapidly through each place, passing don Juan's spot, to the end of the floor, and then turned around to cover the outer edge. When I reached the center, I realized that another change in coloration was taking place, again on the edge of my field of vision. The uniform chartreuse I was seeing all over the area turned, at one spot to my right, into a sharp verdigris. It remained for a moment and then abruptly metamorphosed into another steady hue, different from the other one I had detected earlier. I took off one of my shoes and marked the point, and kept on rolling until I had covered the floor in all possible directions. No other change of coloration took place.

I came back to the point marked with my shoe, and examined it. It was located five to six feet away from the spot marked by my jacket, in a southeasterly direction. There was a large rock next to it. I lay down there for quite some time trying to find clues, looking at every detail, but I did not feel anything different.

I decided to try the other spot. I quickly pivoted on my knees and was about to lie down on my jacket when I felt an unusual apprehension. It was more like a physical sensation of something actually pushing on my stomach. I jumped up and retreated in one movement. The hair on my neck pricked up.

My legs had arched slightly, my trunk was bent forward, and my arms stuck out in front of me rigidly with my fingers contracted like a claw. I took notice of my strange posture and my fright increased.

I walked back involuntarily and sat down on the rock next to my shoe. From the rock, I slumped to the floor. I tried to figure out what had happened to cause me such a fright. I thought it must have been the fatigue I was experiencing. It was nearly daytime. I felt silly and embarrassed. Yet I had no way to explain what had frightened me, nor had I figured out what don Juan wanted.

I decided to give it one last try. I got up and slowly approached the place marked by my jacket, and again I felt the same apprehension. This time I made a strong effort to control myself. I sat down, and then knelt in order to lie face down, but I could not lie in spite of my will. I put my hands on the floor in front of me. My breathing accelerated; my stomach was upset. I had a clear sensation of panic, and fought not to run away. I thought don Juan was perhaps watching me. Slowly I crawled back to the other spot and propped my back against the rock. I wanted to rest for a while to organize my thoughts, but I fell asleep.

I heard don Juan talking and laughing above my head. I woke up.

"You have found the spot," he said.

I did not understand him at first, but he assured me again that the place where I had fallen asleep was the spot in question. He again asked me how I felt lying there. I told him I really did not notice any difference.

He asked me to compare my feelings at that moment with what I had felt while lying on the other spot. For the first time it occurred to me that I could not possibly explain my apprehension of the preceding night. He urged me in a kind of challenging way to sit on the other spot. For some inexplicable reason I was actually afraid of the other place, and did not sit on it. He asserted that only a fool could fail to see the difference.

I asked him if each of the two spots had a special name. He said that the good one was called the *sitio* and the bad one the enemy; he said these two places were the key to a man's well-being, especially for a man who was pursuing knowledge. The sheer act of sitting on one's spot created superior strength; on the other hand, the enemy weakened a man and could even cause his death. He said I had replenished my energy, which I had spent lavishly the night before, by taking a nap on my spot.

He also said that the colors I had seen in association with each specific spot had the same overall effect either of giving strength or of curtailing it.

I asked him if there were other spots for me like the two I had found, and how I should go about finding them. He said that many places in the world would be comparable to those two, and that the best way to find them was by detecting their respective colors.

It was not clear to me whether or not I had solved the problem, and in fact I was not even convinced that there had been a problem; I could not avoid feeling that the whole experience was forced and arbitrary. I was certain that don Juan had watched me all night and then proceeded to humor me by saying that wherever I had fallen asleep *was* the place I was looking for. Yet I failed to see a logical reason for such an act, and when he challenged me to sit on the other spot I could not do it. There was a strange cleavage between my pragmatic experience of fearing the "other spot" and my rational deliberations about the total event.

Don Juan, on the other hand, was very sure I had succeeded, and, acting in accordance with my success, let me know he was going to teach me about peyote.

"You asked me to teach you about Mescalito," he said. "I wanted to find out if you had enough backbone to meet him face to face. Mescalito is not something to make fun of. You must have command over your resources. Now I know I can take your desire alone as a good reason to learn."

"You really are going to teach me about peyote?"

"I prefer to call him Mescalito. Do the same."

"When are you going to start?"

"It is not so simple as that. You must be ready first."

"I think I am ready."

"This is not a joke. You must wait until there is no doubt, and then you will meet him."

"Do I have to prepare myself?"

"No. You simply have to wait. You may give up the whole idea after a while. You get tired easily. Last night you were ready to quit as soon as it got difficult. Mescalito requires a very serious intent."

QUESTIONS

Language

1. Castaneda's prose is, for the most part, direct, plain, unemotional, and factual. Given the kinds of experiences he is trying to write about, why is it a good strategy to use this kind of prose?
2. *The Teachings of Don Juan* was Castaneda's master's thesis in anthropology at UCLA. Can you find evidence in his prose of the scientific, scholarly observer and recorder of experience? (Look for places where his actions and feelings have been phrased in formal, "academic" language.)

Content

1. Why is Castaneda assigned the task of finding his special spot? Why does he try? Does he think he will be successful?
2. Why does don Juan say that if Castaneda were an Indian, his desire to learn about peyote "alone would be sufficient"? What difference between Indians and other people is here implied?
3. What does Castaneda mean when, after he has been asked to find the *sitio*, he says "I couldn't conceive the problem"?
4. What kinds of wisdom does don Juan display in this scene? Is any of it useful?
5. What do you make of the fact that Castaneda is at one time able to sit calmly on the first special spot he finds, but later is so repelled by it he can't get close to it? What has happened to him?
6. How does don Juan refute Castaneda's insistence that he can't feel any differences between the *sitio* and any other place?
7. Discuss the different roles that *reason*, or *rationality*, plays in Castaneda's and don Juan's worlds.

Suggestions for Writing

1. Castaneda is a student and don Juan, a teacher. In an essay define, as comprehensively as possible, what it is that don Juan teaches his student in this scene.

2. In a short essay, describe in detail the *process* by which Castaneda discovers his *sitio*.

3. Most of us neither believe in nor ever encounter ideas such as don Juan's: he lives in a world remote from ours in every respect. What, then, is the value of his teaching, the value of that world? Is there any truth at all to what he says? Write an essay exploring these questions. Before you begin to write, describe to yourself the Yaqui sorcerer's world and define the lesson he teaches Castaneda.

4. Discuss with your class and then write an essay about what appeal Castaneda's books have to modern America, which is, after all, industrialized, largely urban, technologically sophisticated, pragmatic and rational in temper, and scientifically oriented.

5. As we point out in the headnote, some of Castaneda's critics have questioned the authenticity of his supposedly factual experiences. Assume the book is fiction, a product of the author's imagination. Argue in an essay that as a fictional creation, don Juan is even more impressive.

George Lucas

from *Star Wars*

Written and directed by George Lucas (who had a previous hit with the film *American Graffiti*), *Star Wars* broke all box office records when it opened in 1977. A highly entertaining "space fantasy" drawing on various elements of American pop mythology—from John Ford Westerns to *The Wizard of Oz, Flash Gordon* serials to *Fantastic Four* comic books—the movie features spectacular visual effects; a fast-paced, action-packed story; sensational "intergalactic" settings; clean-cut heroes, black-hearted villains, and a damsel in distress; a delightful collection of alien creatures (Jawas, Banthas, Wookies); and an endearing pair of comical robots, named Artoo Deetoo and See Threepio.

The hero of the film is young Luke Skywalker, a twenty-year-old farm boy from the planet Tatooine, who, along with his mentor Obi-wan ("Ben") Kenobi—"the last of the Jedi Knights"—set out to rescue Princess Leia Organa of Alderaan from the clutches of the evil lord, Darth Vader. The princess, who is in league with the rebel forces that are attempting to overthrow the tyrannical Galactic Empire, has been captured while smuggling top-secret plans of the Death Star, the enemy's ultimate weapon, to her comrades on the planet Yevin. In their efforts to save her, Luke and Ben enlist the services of the swaggering Corellian pirate Han Solo and his faithful Wookie companion, Chewbacca. The following scene, from Lucas' novelization of the film, takes place on board Solo's ship, the *Millennium Falcon*, which has just made a breathtaking escape from pursuing Imperial spacecraft.

From *Star Wars: From the Adventures of Luke Skywalker,* by George Lucas. Copyright © 1976 by The Star Wars Corporation. Reprinted by permission of Ballantine Books, a Division of Random House, Inc.

A moment of relative calm ensues, during which Obi-wan instructs Luke in the ways of the mystical power known as the force.

Solo was busily checking readouts from gauges and dials in the hold area. Occasionally he would pass a small box across various sensors, study the result, and cluck with pleasure.

"You can stop worrying about your Imperial friends," he told Luke and Ben. "They'll never be able to track us now. Told you I'd lose them."

Kenobi might have nodded briefly in response, but he was engaged in explaining something to Luke.

"Don't everybody thank me at once," Solo grunted, slightly miffed. "Anyway, navigation computer calculates our arrival in Alderaan orbit at oh-two-hundred. I'm afraid after this little adventure I'll have to forge a new registration."

He returned to his checking, passing in front of a small circular table. The top was covered with small squares lit from beneath, while computer monitors were set into each side. Tiny three-dimensional figures were projected above the tabletop from various squares.

Chewbacca sat hunched over one side of the table, his chin resting in massive hands. His great eyes glowing and facial whiskers wrinkled upward, he gave every sign of being well pleased with himself.

At least, he did until Artoo Detoo reached up with a stubby clawed limb across from him and tapped his own computer monitor. One of the figures walked abruptly across the board to a new square and stopped there.

An expression of puzzlement, then anger crossed the Wookie's face as he studied the new configuration. Glaring up and over the table, he vented a stream of abusive gibberish on the inoffensive machine. Artoo could only beep in reply, but Threepio soon interceded on behalf of his less eloquent companion and began arguing with the hulking anthropoid.

"He executed a fair move. Screaming about it won't help you."

Attracted by the commotion, Solo looked back over his shoulder, frowning slightly. "Let him have it. Your friend's way ahead anyhow. It's not wise to upset a Wookie."

"I can sympathize with that opinion, sir," Threepio countered, "but there is principle at stake here. There are certain standards any sentient creature must hold to. If one compromises them for any reason, including intimidation, then one is abrogating his right to be called intelligent."

"I hope you'll both remember that," Solo advised him, "when Chewbacca is pulling the arms off you and your little friend."

"Besides that, however," Threepio continued without missing a beat, "being greedy or taking advantage of someone in a weakened position is a clear sign of poor sportsmanship."

That elicited a beep of outrage from Artoo, and the two robots were soon engaged in violent electronic argument while Chewbacca continued jabbering at each in turn, occasionally waving at them through the translucent pieces waiting patiently on the board.

Oblivious to the altercation, Luke stood frozen in the middle of the hold. He held an activated lightsaber in position over his head. A low hum came from the ancient instrument while Luke lunged and parried under Ben Kenobi's instructive gaze. As Solo glanced from time to time at Luke's awkward movements, his lean features were sprinkled with smugness.

"No, Luke, your cuts should flow, not be so choppy," Kenobi instructed gently. "Remember, the force is omnipresent. It envelops you as it radiates from you. A Jedi warrior can actually feel the force as a physical thing."

"It is an energy field, then?" Luke inquired.

"It is an energy field and something more," Kenobi went on, almost mystically. "An aura that at once controls and obeys. It is a nothingness that can accomplish miracles." He looked thoughtful for a moment.

"No one, not even the Jedi scientists, were able to truly define the force. Possibly no one ever will. Sometimes there is as much magic as science in the explanations of the force. Yet what is a magician but a practicing theorist? Now, let's try again."

The old man was hefting a silvery globe about the size of a man's fist. It was covered with fine antennae, some as delicate as those of a moth. He flipped it toward Luke and watched as it halted a couple of meters away from the boy's face.

Luke readied himself as the ball circled him slowly, turning to face it as it assumed a new position. Abruptly it executed a lightning-swift lunge, only to freeze about a meter away. Luke failed to succumb to the feint, and the ball soon backed off.

Moving slowly to one side in an effort to get around the ball's fore sensors, Luke drew the saber back preparatory to striking. As he did so the ball darted in behind *him.* A thin pencil of red light jumped from one of the antennae to the back of Luke's thigh, knocking him to the deck even as he was bringing his saber around—too late.

Rubbing at his tingling, sleeping leg, Luke tried to ignore the burst of accusing laughter from Solo. "Hocus-pocus religions and archaic weapons are no substitute for a good blaster at your side," the pilot sneered.

"You don't believe in the force?" asked Luke, struggling back to his feet. The numbing effect of the beam wore off quickly.

"I've been from one end of this galaxy to the other," the pilot boasted, "and I've seen a lot of strange things. Too many to believe there couldn't be something like this 'force.' Too many to think that there could be some such controlling one's actions. *I* determine my destiny—not some half-mystical energy field." He gestured toward Kenobi. "I wouldn't follow him so blindly, if I were you. He's a clever old man, full of simple tricks and mischief. He might be using you for his own ends."

Kenobi only smiled gently, then turned back to face Luke. "I suggest you try it again, Luke," he said soothingly. "You must try to divorce your actions from conscious control. Try not to focus on anything concrete, visually or mentally. You must let your mind drift, drift; only then can you use the force. You have to enter a state in which you act on what you sense, not on what you think beforehand. You must cease cogitation, relax, stop thinking . . . let yourself drift . . . free . . . free . . ."

The old man's voice had dropped to a mesmerizing buzz. As he finished, the chrome bulb darted at Luke. Dazed by Kenobi's hypnotic tone, Luke didn't see it charge. It's doubtful he saw much of anything with clarity. But as the ball neared, he whirled with amazing speed, the saber arcing up and out in a peculiar fashion. The red beam that the globe emitted was neatly deflected to one side. Its humming stopped and the ball bounced to the deck, all animation gone.

Blinking as if coming awake from a short nap, Luke stared in absolute astonishment at the inert remote.

"You see, you can do it," Kenobi told him. "One can teach only so much. Now you must learn to admit the force when you want it, so that you can learn to control it consciously."

Moving to one side, Kenobi took a large helmet from behind a locker and walked over to Luke. Placing the helmet over his head effectively eliminated the boy's vision.

"I can't see," Luke muttered, turning around and forcing Kenobi to step back out of range of the dangerously wavering saber. "How can I fight?"

"With the force," old Ben explained. "You didn't really 'see' the seeker when it went for your legs the last time, and yet you parried its beam. Try to let that sensation flow within you again."

"I *can't* do it," Luke moaned. "I'll get hit again."

"Not if you let yourself trust *you,*" Kenobi insisted, none too convincingly for Luke. "This is the only way to be certain you're relying wholly on the force."

Noticing that the skeptical Corellian had turned to watch, Kenobi hesitated momentarily. It did Luke no good to have the self-assured pilot laugh every time a mistake was made. But coddling the boy would do him no good either, and there was no time for it anyway. Throw him in and hope he floats, Ben instructed himself firmly.

Bending over the chrome globe, he touched a control at its side. Then he tossed it straight up. It arched toward Luke. Braking in midfall, the ball plummeted stonelike toward the deck. Luke swung the saber at it. While it was a commendable try, it wasn't nearly fast enough. Once again the little antenna glowed. This time the crimson needle hit Luke square on the seat of his pants. Though it wasn't an incapacitating blow, it felt like one; and Luke let out a yelp of pain as he spun, trying to strike his invisible tormentor.

"Relax!" old Ben urged him. "Be free. You're trying to use your eyes and ears. Stop predicting and use the rest of your mind."

Suddenly the youth stopped, wavering slightly. The seeker was still behind him. Changing direction again, it made another dive and fired.

Simultaneously the lightsaber jerked around, as accurate as it was awkward in its motion, to deflect the bolt. This time the ball didn't fall motionless to the deck. Instead it backed up three meters and remained there, hovering.

Aware that the drone of the seeker remote no longer assaulted his ears, a cautious Luke peeked out from under the helmet. Sweat and exhaustion competed for space on his face.

"Did I—?"

"I told you you could," Kenobi informed him with pleasure. "Once you start to trust your inner self there'll be no stopping you. I told you there was much of your father in you."

"I'd call it luck," snorted Solo as he concluded his examination of the read-outs.

"In my experience there is no such thing as luck, my young friend—only highly favorable adjustments of multiple factors to incline events in one's favor."

"Call it what you like," the Corellian sniffed indifferently, "but good against a mechanical remote is one thing. Good against a living menace is another."

As he was speaking a small telltale light on the far side of the hold had began flashing. Chewbacca noticed it and called out to him.

Solo glanced at the board, then informed his passengers, "We're coming up on Alderaan. We'll be slowing down shortly and going back under lightspeed. Come on, Chewie."

Rising from the game table, the Wookie followed his partner toward the cockpit. Luke watched them depart, but his mind wasn't on their imminent arrival at Alderaan. It was burning with something else, something that seemed to grow and mature at the back of his brain as he dwelt on it.

"You know," he murmured, "I did feel something. I could almost 'see' the outlines of the remote." He gestured at the hovering device behind him.

Kenobi's voice when he replied was solemn. "Luke, you've taken the first step into a larger universe."

QUESTIONS

Language

1. Is this novelization of the movie *Star Wars* as effective as the film? Do you think that George Lucas is as talented and resourceful a novelist as he is a director and filmmaker? Find evidence in the selection to support your view.
2. See Threepio, unlike Artoo Deetoo, has been programmed for human speech. Does he sound like the human beings around him? How does his speech compare, for example, to Kenobi's? To Han Solo's?
3. Do you understand what the force is after reading Kenobi's explanation of it? Why hasn't Lucas made Kenobi's description more precise?

Content

1. In terms of the story, what is the purpose of the chess game scene? The scene with Luke and the lightsaber? Do both advance the plot?
2. How does Solo feel about the force? About Kenobi? Why would Lucas include an unbeliever on Kenobi's "team"?
3. What is the proper way, according to Kenobi, of fighting with the lightsaber? What must Luke do?
4. What kind of relationship do Luke and Kenobi have? Describe it.
5. How does Solo explain Luke's success with the lightsaber? What does Solo warn Luke about?

Suggestions for Writing

1. In describing the force to Luke, Kenobi says, "You have to enter a state in which you act on what you sense, not on what you think beforehand." Have you ever found yourself faced with a decision you were unable to think through, or a problem you couldn't solve by using logic alone? Describe a situation in which you let yourself be guided by instinct or intuition, and say what the outcome of the situation was.
2. "Hocus-pocus religions," says Solo, ". . . are no substitute for a good blaster at your side." Solo is skeptical about the existence of the force; for him, reality consists of

things a person can see and feel, things, like a "good blaster," that a man can wrap his hand around. Do you believe that there are unseen forces in the universe which affect our lives, even "determine our destinies"? Or are you, like Solo, skeptical of the existence of such things?

3. According to its creator, George Lucas, *Star Wars* "is a movie for the kid in all of us." As Lucas has pointed out on numerous occasions, *Star Wars* is a re-creation of his own child's fantasy world, a world woven out of various threads—old Westerns, war movies, outer space adventure serials like *Flash Gordon* and *Buck Rogers.* Most children escape from bouts of boredom by imagining glamorous or exciting adventures for themselves, which are often based on books they have read or movies and television shows they have seen. Did you have a favorite fantasy or daydream as a child? Describe it in an essay.

Benjamin Franklin

from *Father Abraham's Speech*

Benjamin Franklin (1706–1790) was the quintessential Yankee; his rise from rags to riches is the original American success story. He began his career as a penniless runaway, arriving in Philadelphia at the age of seventeen with nothing but the clothes on his back and enough cash to purchase a bit of bread. By the time he was forty-two he had made enough money as a printer to retire from business and devote the rest of his long life to the service of humanity and of the new nation he helped found.

This rise from poverty and obscurity to fortune and fame was, Franklin asserted, the result of his diligence and thrift, and throughout his career, he strove to instill these virtues in his fellow Americans, both through his own example and through the shrewd maxims and sayings he included in *Poor Richard's Almanack.* This popular work, which Franklin published annually for twenty-five years (1733–1758), was intended to be both "entertaining and useful." "I considered it," Franklin writes in his classic *Autobiography,* "as a proper vehicle for conveying instruction among the common people, who bought scarce any other books. I therefore filled all the little spaces that occurred between the remarkable days in the calendar with proverbial sentences, chiefly such as inculcated industry and frugality as the means of procuring wealth and thereby securing virtue—it being more difficult for a man in want to act always honestly, as (to use here one of those proverbs) 'it is for an empty sack to stand upright.' "

For the preface to the 1758 edition of the almanac, Franklin assembled Poor Richard's proverbs and made them into a single, continuous lecture, which he put into the mouth of one "Father Abraham," a Wise Old Man addressing a group of people at an auction. Reprinted innumerable times throughout the world, *Father Abraham's Speech* (also known as *The Way to Wealth*) is, as Donald McQuade and Robert Atwan say in *Popular Writing in America* (1974), "a storehouse of . . . American folk wisdom."

Courteous Reader,

I have heard that nothing gives an Author so great Pleasure, as to find his Works respectfully quoted by other learned Authors. This Pleasure I have seldom enjoyed; for tho' I have been, if I may say it without Vanity, an *eminent Author* of Almanacks annually now a full Quarter of a Century, my Brother Authors in the same Way, for what Reason I know not, have ever been very sparing in their Applauses; and no other Author has taken the least Notice of me, so that did not my Writings produce me some solid *Pudding,* the great Deficiency of *Praise* would have quite discouraged me.

I concluded at length, that the People were the best Judges of my Merit; for they buy my Works; and besides, in my Rambles, where I am not personally known, I have frequently heard one or other of my Adages repeated, with, *as Poor Richard says,* at the End on't; this gave me some Satisfaction, as it showed not only that my Instructions were regarded, but discovered likewise some Respect for my Authority; and I own, that to encourage the Practice of remembering and repeating those wise Sentences, I have sometimes *quoted myself* with great Gravity.

Judge then how much I must have been gratified by an Incident I am going to relate to you. I stopt my Horse lately where a great Number of People were collected at a Vendue of Merchant Goods. The Hour of Sale, not being come, they were conversing on the Badness of the Times, and one of the Company call'd to a plain clean old Man, with white Locks, *Pray, Father Abraham, what think you of the Times? Won't these heavy Taxes quite ruin the Country? How shall we be ever able to pay them? What would you advise us to?*—Father Abraham stood up, and reply'd, If you'd have my Advice, I'll give it you in short, for a *Word to the Wise is enough,* and *many Words won't fill a Bushel,* as *Poor Richard says.* They join'd in desiring him to speak his Mind, and gathering round him, he proceeded as follows;

"Friends, says he, and Neighbours, the Taxes are indeed very heavy, and if those laid on by the Government were the only Ones we had to pay, we might more easily discharge them; but we have many others, and much more grievous to some of us. We are taxed twice as much by our *Idleness,* three times as much by our *Pride,* and four times as much by our *Folly,* and from these Taxes the Commissioners cannot ease or deliver us by allowing an Abatement. However let us hearken to good Advice, and something may be done for us; *God helps them that help themselves,* as Poor Richard says, in his Almanack of 1733.

It would be thought a hard Government that should tax its People one tenth Part of their *Time,* to be employed in its Service. But *Idleness* taxes many of us much more, if we reckon all that is spent in absolute *Sloth,* or doing of nothing, with that which is spent in idle Employments or Amusements, that amount to nothing. *Sloth,* by bringing on Diseases, absolutely shortens Life. *Sloth, like Rust, consumes faster than Labour wears, while the used Key is always bright,* as Poor Richard says. But *dost thou love Life, then do not squander Time, for that's the Stuff Life is made of,* as Poor Richard says. How much more than is necessary do we spend in Sleep! forgetting that *The sleeping Fox catches no Poultry,* and that *there will be sleeping enough in the Grave,* as Poor Richard says. If Time be of all Things the most precious, *wasting Time* must be, as Poor Richard says, *the greatest Prodigality,* since, as he elsewhere tells us, *Lost Time is never found again;* and what we call *Time-enough, always proves little enough:* Let us then be up and be doing, and doing to the Purpose; so by Diligence shall we do more with less Perplexity. *Sloth makes all Things difficult, but Industry all easy,* as Poor Richard says; and *He that riseth late, must trot all Day, and shall scarce overtake his Business at Night.* While *Laziness travels so slowly, that Poverty soon overtakes him,* as we read in Poor Richard, who adds, *Drive thy Business, let not that drive thee;* and *Early to Bed, and early to rise, makes a Man healthy, wealthy and wise.*

So what signifies *wishing* and *hoping* for better Times. We may make these Times better if we bestir ourselves. *Industry need not wish,* as Poor Richard says, and *He that lives upon Hope will die fasting. There are no Gains, without Pains;* then *Help Hands, for I have no Lands,* or if I have, they are smartly taxed. And, as Poor Richard likewise observes, *He that hath a Trade hath an Estate,* and *He that hath a Calling hath an Office of Profit and Honour,* but then the *Trade* must be worked at, and the *Calling* well followed, or neither the *Estate,* nor the *Office,* will enable us to pay our Taxes. If we are industrious we shall never starve; for, as Poor Richard says, *At the working Man's House Hunger looks in, but dares not enter.* Nor will the Bailiff nor the Constable enter, for *Industry pays Debts, while Despair encreaseth them,* says Poor Richard. What though you have found no Treasure, nor has any rich Relation left you a Legacy, *Diligence is the Mother of Good luck,* as Poor Richard says, and *God gives all Things to Industry.* Then *plough deep, while Sluggards sleep, and you shall have Corn to sell and to keep,* says Poor Dick. Work while it is called To-day for you know not how much you may be hindered To-morrow, which makes Poor Richard say, *One To-day is worth two To-morrows;* and farther, *Have you somewhat to do To-morrow, do it To-day.* If you were a Servant, would you not be ashamed that a good Master should catch you idle? Are you then your own Master, be ashamed to catch yourself idle, as Poor Dick says. When there is so much to be done for yourself, your Family, your Country, and your gracious King, be up by Peep of Day; *Let not the Sun look down and say, Inglorious here he lies.* Handle your Tools without Mittens; remember that *the Cat in Gloves catches no Mice,* as Poor Richard says. 'Tis true there is much to be done, and perhaps you are weak handed, but stick to it steadily, and you will see great Effects, for *constant Dropping wears away Stones,* and by *Diligence and Patience the Mouse ate in two the Cable;* and *little Strokes fell great Oaks,* as Poor Richard says in his Almanack, the Year I cannot just now remember.

Methinks I hear some of you say, *Must a Man afford himself no Leisure?* I will tell thee, my Friend, what Poor Richard says, *Employ thy Time well if thou meanest to gain Leisure;* and, *since thou art not sure of a Minute, throw not away an Hour.* Leisure, is Time for doing something useful; this Leisure the diligent Man will obtain, but the lazy Man never; so that, as Poor Richard says, a *Life of Leisure and a Life of Laziness are two Things.* Do you imagine that Sloth will afford you more Comfort than Labour? No, for as Poor Richard says, *Trouble springs from Idleness, and grievous Toil from needless Ease. Many without Labour, would live by their* Wits *only, but they break for want of Stock.* Whereas Industry gives Comfort, and Plenty, and Respect: *Fly Pleasures, and they'll follow you. The diligent Spinner has a large Shift;* and *now I have a*

Sheep and a Cow, every Body bids me Good morrow; all which is well said by
Poor Richard.

But with our Industry, we must likewise be *steady, settled* and *careful,*
and oversee our own Affairs *with our own Eyes,* and not trust too much to
others; for, as Poor Richard says,

> *I never saw an oft removed Tree,*
> *Nor yet an oft removed Family,*
> *That throve so well as those that settled be.*

And again, *Three Removes is as bad as a Fire;* and again, *Keep thy Shop,
and thy Shop will keep thee;* and again, *If you would have your Business done,
go; If not, send.* And again,

> *He that by the Plough would thrive,*
> *Himself must either hold or drive.*

And again, *The Eye of a Master will do more Work than both his Hands;*
and again, *Want of Care does us more Damage than Want of Knowledge;* and
again, *Not to oversee Workmen, is to leave them your Purse open.* Trusting
too much to others Care is the Ruin of many; for, as the Almanack says, *In the
Affairs of this World, Men are saved, not by Faith, but by the Want of it;* but
a Man's own Care is profitable; for, saith Poor Dick, *Learning is to the Studious,*
and *Riches to the Careful,* as well as *Power to the Bold,* and *Heaven to the
Virtuous.* And farther, *If you would have a faithful Servant, and one that you
like, serve yourself.* And again, he adviseth to Circumspection and Care, even
in the smallest Matters, because sometimes *a little Neglect may breed great Mischief;* adding, *For want of a Nail the Shoe was lost; for want of a Shoe the
Horse was lost; and for want of a Horse the Rider was lost,* being overtaken
and slain by the Enemy, all for want of Care about a Horse-shoe Nail.

So much for Industry, my Friends, and Attention to one's own Business;
but to these we must add *Frugality,* if we would make our *Industry* more certainly
successful. A Man may, if he knows not how to save as he gets, *keep his Nose
all his Life to the Grindstone,* and die not worth a *Groat* at last. *A fat Kitchen
makes a lean Will,* as Poor Richard says; and,

> *Many Estates are spent in the Getting,*
> *Since Women for Tea forsook Spinning and Knitting,*
> *And Men for Punch forsook Hewing and Splitting.*

If you would be wealthy, says he, in another Almanack, *think of Saving as well
as of Getting: The Indies have not made Spain rich, because her* Outgoes *are
greater than her* Incomes. Away then with your expensive Follies, and you will
not have so much Cause to complain of hard Times, heavy Taxes, and chargeable
Families; for, as Poor Dick says,

> *Women and Wine, Game and Deceit,*
> *Make the Wealth small, and the Wants great,*

And farther, *What maintains one Vice, would bring up two Children.* You may
think perhaps, That a *little* Tea, or a *little* Punch now and then, Diet a *little*
more costly, Clothes a *little* finer, and a *little* Entertainment now and then, can
be no *great* Matter; but remember what Poor Richard says, *Many* a Little *makes*

a Mickle; and farther, *Beware of* little *Expenses; a small Leak will sink a great Ship;* and again, *Who Dainties love, shall Beggars prove;* and moreover, *Fools make Feasts, and wise Men eat them.*

. . .

And now to conclude, *Experience keeps a dear School, but Fools will learn in no other, and scarce in that;* for it is true, *we may give Advice, but we cannot give Conduct,* as Poor Richard says: However, remember this, *They that won't be counselled, can't be helped,* as Poor Richard says: And farther, That *if you will not hear Reason, she'll surely rap your Knuckles.*

Thus the old Gentleman ended his Harangue. The People heard it, and approved the Doctrine, and immediately practised the contrary, just as if it had been a common Sermon; for the Vendue opened, and they began to buy extravagantly, notwithstanding all his Cautions, and their own Fear of Taxes. I found the good Man had thoroughly studied my Almanacks, and digested all I had dropt on those Topicks during the Course of Five-and-twenty Years. The frequent Mention he made of me must have tired any one else, but my Vanity was wonderfully delighted with it, though I was conscious that not a tenth Part of the Wisdom was my own which he ascribed to me, but rather the *Gleanings* I had made of the Sense of all Ages and Nations. However, I resolved to be the better for the Echo of it; and though I had at first determined to buy Stuff for a new Coat, I went away resolved to wear my old One a little longer. *Reader,* if thou wilt do the same, thy Profit will be as great as mine. I am, as ever, Thine to serve thee,

RICHARD SAUNDERS.

July 7, 1757.

QUESTIONS

Language

1. In writing his famous almanacs, Benjamin Franklin adopted the guise of Poor Richard, a "shrewd tradesman" of homely sayings and a "full pocketbook" (as historian Russel B. Nye describes him). Like his creator, Poor Richard is saved from taking his fame too seriously by an ability to poke gentle fun at himself. What instances of such humor can you find in the opening paragraphs of this selection?

2. Many of Poor Richard's sayings employ the device of *personification.* Look up personification; then find examples of it in *Father Abraham's Speech.* Why does Franklin use it so frequently in his proverbs?

3. Select several of Poor Richard's proverbs and analyze their language in an attempt to discover what makes them so effective. How does Franklin manage to compress so much meaning into such short sentences? How does he make his sayings memorable? What use does he make of such things as vivid images, simple words, and clever rhymes?

Content

1. Father Abraham delivers his speech to a crowd that is milling around, waiting for an auction to begin. Given the subject of the lecture, what makes this group of people such an appropriate audience?

2. Why do you think Franklin chose to assemble his famous proverbs in this particular form? He might just as easily have issued them as a collection of inspirational sayings: ''The Wit and Wisdom of Poor Richard.'' What is gained by putting them in the framework of a story?

3. Imagine a person who faithfully followed all of Poor Richard's advice. What sort of life do you think such a person would lead? Do you think he or she would be happy? Are there things in life—important things—which are omitted from Poor Richard's philosophy?

Suggestions for Writing

1. Do you believe, as Franklin did, that by working hard and being frugal anyone in America can rise from poverty to wealth? Write an essay explaining why you either do or do not believe this is true.

2. Do you believe that the ''American dream'' of going from ''rags to riches'' is easier or more difficult to achieve today than it was in the past? Explain your opinion in an essay.

3. Select one of Poor Richard's sayings—''Early to bed and early to rise makes a man healthy, wealthy, and wise''; ''A stitch in time saves nine''; ''A word to the wise is sufficient''; etc.—and explain why you either agree or disagree with it. You might support your argument by describing a personal experience which either proves or disproves the validity of the proverb.

4. Franklin's sayings use images which the readers of his time could easily relate to: images drawn from the countryside, the farm, the rustic household. Take several of the sayings and try to rewrite them using modern, up-to-date images, drawn from the world of twentieth-century America. Alternatively, try to create your own, original proverbs, in which you compress general truths into short, clever, memorable sentences.

ADDITIONAL WRITING SUGGESTIONS FOR CHAPTER FIVE

1. Describe your father, grandfather or any older male relative who is very close to you. Draw as complete a picture as you can, paying particular attention to how well—or how poorly—your father or his substitute embodies the qualities of the Wise Old Man. For example, you might try to remember conversations you have had in which he gave you advice. How helpful was it, how just, how true? Include as many details as you need to make your points clear and your essay interesting, but be sure to generalize sufficiently, too.

2. Look back through some of the selections in this chapter and the Mother chapter. Then, using these selections as your evidence, write an essay comparing and contrasting the *kinds* of advice and support offered by the Wise Old Man and the Good Mother. Are they different? Arrive at a decision; support that decision with examples.

3. Write an essay about anyone who has played the role of a Wise Old Man in your life. This might be a teacher, coach, camp counselor, doctor, neighbor, police officer, priest, minister, rabbi, or an employer. Describe what kinds of assistance this person gave you, what you learned, how you felt about him, whether the relationship continues to this day, and why you needed assistance at the time he provided it.

4. Look back at the Wise Old Man figures in this chapter. Usually they are treated with respect, even reverence (and when they are not, we realize this disrespect is misguided and, sometimes, dangerous, as in *Oedipus Rex* and ''The Hare Herd''). In most cultures, older people have historically been treated with respect and reverence, because they are assumed to have purchased with their white hairs a wisdom valuable to the community. Is this true in modern America? Write an essay about how we treat old people in America, and what this treatment says about how we value them and what we think of them.

5. Discuss with your classmates the sorts of assistance and advice provided by the Good Mother and the Wise Old Man. Can you think of cultural and historical reasons for the roles they have traditionally played? Do you think that these roles are likely to change as men and women participate more equally, regardless of their sex, in all aspects of life? Or do you think they will remain essentially unchanged? After your discussion, write an essay expressing and supporting one position or the other.

6. Imagine for yourself the ideal Wise Old Man figure. You have been granted the special favor of a conversation with him. You can ask him for any kind of advice, assistance, wisdom. Choose carefully. Write up, in the form of a dialogue, your conversation with him. Alternatively, since inventing responses for the Wise Old Man is very difficult, write a short essay indicating what you intend to ask, justifying your choices. Later, talk in class about the kinds of things you asked, or planned to ask, of him. Do some chances seem wasted? Are some requests for help better than others? Why?

The Helpful Animal
and the Holy Fool

"Polulu!" cried Bomba, as he recognized the giant puma that was struggling with the jaguar. "Good Polulu! He has come to the help of Bomba when Bomba most needed a friend."

—Roy Rockwood, *Bomba the Jungle Boy on Terror Trail*

It is customary to associate wisdom with age and dignity; we expect good advice and useful knowledge from a person who has lived a long and estimable life. But myths and fairy tales teach us that, sometimes, wisdom may be forthcoming from very surprising sources: not from those figures we tend to respect—the understanding mother and knowing old man—but from figures we tend to ignore, look down upon, or even laugh at. Two of these figures, frequently met with in folklore and mythology, are the Helpful Animal and the Holy Fool.

In fairy tales the Helpful Animal, like the Wise Old Man, often appears when the hero has reached an impasse and cannot see a way out of his dilemma. Simpleton, for example, the protagonist of the Grimm Brothers' story "The Queen Bee," must perform three impossible deeds to deliver a castle from enchantment. He gives way to despair, until a group of grateful creatures whose lives he has previously saved arrives to assist him in his tasks. Similarly, the hero of the fairy tale "The Three Feathers" (whose name is also Simpleton) finds himself faced with three hopeless challenges: to bring his father, the king, the most beautiful carpet, ring, and woman in the world, and thereby inherit the kingdom. Like his namesake in "The Queen Bee," young Simpleton sits down sadly and utterly at a loss, only to discover a trapdoor in the ground leading down to the dwelling place of a "great, fat toad," who magically supplies him with the treasures he seeks.

As these and other fairy tales reveal, the Helpful Animal may be a member of virtually any species. Miraculous creatures of every variety abound in the folktales of all nations, as well as in world mythology and the popular arts: cats, cows, goats, gulls, ravens, eagles, bears, bees, fish, foxes, ducks, deer, and many more. Sometimes, of course, the kind of Helpful Animal found in a work will depend on the story's locale. In such jungle tales as the Tarzan and Bomba series, for example, the Helpful Animals are, predictably, elephants, chimps, and lions; while in works which take place in domestic settings, the animal is bound to be a house pet—most likely a dog. Popular culture in particular is filled with canines whose courage and resourcefulness far surpass those of most human beings. Lassie, Rin Tin Tin, Rex the Wonder Dog, Old Yeller, Old Blue, and Benji are just a few well-known examples. Even Toto, the pup who accompanies Dorothy on her magical journey to Oz, turns out—despite his tiny size and frailty—to be an exceptional creature: he saves his mistress' life by leading her three friends, the Scarecrow, Tin Woodman, and Cowardly Lion, to the Wicked Witch's castle, where Dorothy is being held prisoner.

But of all Helpful Animals (as the folklorist Stith Thompson points out in his book *The Folktale* [1946]), "none has been so popular with tale tellers as the horse." In world literature, stories of magical horses have been told for thousands of years. Ancient Greek myths, for example, tell of the winged steed Pegasus, who carried the hero Bellerophon through the sky and could create a mountain spring just by "stamping his moon-shaped hoof" on the ground. Similarly, in the fantasy world of the fairy tale, we frequently meet horses that possess miraculous powers, can fly, speak, or gallop up glass mountains. In more recent times, such marvelous creatures are generally found in the popular arts. Black Beauty is one famous example; others include Fury, My Friend Flicka, Old Stewball, Mr. Ed ("The Talking Horse") and, from Tolkien's trilogy, Gandalf the Grey's incomparable steed Shadowfax (". . . tireless, swift as the flowing wind. . . . By day his coat glistens like silver; and by night it is like a shade, and he passes unseen").

But the pop genre containing more of these animals than any other is, of course, the Western. Throughout the thirties, forties, and fifties, nearly all the cowboy heroes in movies and on television rode "wonderhorses": creatures that could outrun locomotives, untie knots with their teeth, and understand every word spoken to them by their masters. Between the cowboy star and his mount there was always perfect communication. They were an inseparable couple. Indeed, it is hard to think of one without the other: Roy Rogers and Trigger, Gene Autry and Champion, the Lone Ranger and Silver, Hopalong Cassidy and Topper, the Cisco Kid and Diablo. Though the figure of the wonderhorse is at least as old as ancient Greece, its American version—the Western supersteed—dates back to the nineteenth century, when tales of the Wild West first achieved great popularity in this country, in the form of newspaper stories, magazine articles, and "dime novels." The February 1867 issue of *Harper's New Monthly Magazine,* for example, contains an "Interview with Wild Bill Hickock," which portrays Hickock's horse, Black Nell, as a creature of uncanny endowments. The author, George Ward Nichols, is standing in the lobby of the Springfield (Missouri) Hotel, when he sees "Wild Bill riding up the street at a swift gallop":

> Arrived opposite to the hotel, he swung his right arm around with a circular motion. Black Nell instantly stopped and dropped to the ground as if a cannon-ball had knocked the life out of her. Bill left her there, stretched upon the ground, and joined the group of observers on the porch.

"Black Nell hasn't forgot her old tricks," said one of them.

"No," answered the scout. "God bless her! she is wiser and truer than most men I know of. That mare will do anything for me. Won't you, Nelly?"

The mare winked affirmatively the only eye we could see.

.   .   .

"Black Nell has carried me along through many a tight place," said the scout, . . . "That trick of dropping quick which you saw has saved my life time and again. When I have been out scouting on the prarer or in the woods I have come across parties of rebels, and have dropped out of sight in the tall grass before they saw us. . . . The mare will come at my whistle and foller me about just like a dog. She won't mind any one else, nor allow them to mount her, . . ."

Black Nell's behavior, as described in this piece (which obviously owes more to fantasy than to fact), is typical of the Helpful Animal. Not only does she understand Wild Bill perfectly when he speaks to her, she even responds to him in a remarkably human way, "winking affirmatively" in reply to a question. She is "wiser . . . than most men"; in fact, Bill later informs us, "she knows more than a judge." And she has saved his life "time and again." Like the Wise Old Man, the Helpful Animal often intervenes when the hero's life is in danger and rescues him from certain death. When Lassie, Rin Tin Tin, and Rex the Wonder Dog are not busy dragging unconscious people from burning houses, they can usually be found fighting off the hosts of killer beasts—alligators, wild boars, mountain lions, and so on—their young masters keep running afoul of. In *Bomba the Jungle Boy on Terror Trail,* the title character is "snatched from destruction" when his old friend, Pololu the Puma, suddenly arrives on the scene and throws himself in the path of an oncoming jaguar. And whenever Tarzan of the Apes finds himself in peril— a captive of the evil Gomangani tribe, for example—he lets off his famous jungle cry, which brings a herd of bull elephants charging to the rescue, like the cavalry in the old-time cowboy-and-Indian movies.

Another sign of the Helpful Animal's superiority—besides its bravery and ability to understand human speech—is its skill as a guide. Always good in emergencies, the Helpful Animal can lead the trapped or hopelessly lost hero out of most of the tight spots he lands in: dungeons, dark forests, enchanted castles, caves. In fairy tales, where the laws of reality are suspended and creatures themselves can talk, the Helpful Animal may *tell* the hero (or heroine) the way to escape. At other times, the animal will lead the hero to safety, *show* him the path that he seeks. The film version of Jules Verne's *Journey to the Center of the Earth* provides a good example. At the very start of the trip, Professor Lindenbrook, the leader of the expedition, stands on a ledge inside a volcanic crater, completely at a loss. He cannot locate the concealed opening in the mountainside which will give him access to the earth's interior. Suddenly, Gertrude, the pet duck of one of the explorers and the expedition's mascot, wanders away from the rest of the company and waddles into a small opening in the rock. Needless to say, Gertrude has discovered the hidden entrance, and Lindenbrook joyfully follows her.

This episode from the movie illustrates a very significant point: namely, that the Helpful Animal can be a wonderful ally, but only of those who are willing to pay attention to it. And conversely, one of the marks of the true hero is precisely his willingness to follow the animal's guidance—to accept its "advice." Lindenbrook, the world-famous scientist, succeeds not only because he is a brilliant thinker, but also because he respects and heeds the "wisdom" of a lowly creature like Gertrude the duck. He succeeds, in short, because he combines both *intellect* and *instinct.* This combination is what the hero and his animal companion *always* represent. From the Lone Ranger and Silver, to Lindenbrook and Gertrude, to Tarzan and his chimpanzee sidekick Cheetah, the two figures, human and animal, form a single unit—a unit which stands for the fusion of the "higher human faculties," such as reason and morality, with the "lower," animal level of our nature. Thus, the hero is the complete human being, the "integrated personality": neither spineless "egghead" nor mindless brute, but a healthy combination of intelligence, virtue, and animal spirits. Too often, society encourages us to develop our rationality at the expense of our vitality (as C. G. Jung puts it), to regard the earthy, physical, instinctual side of our nature as lowly or inferior (hence, this part of ourselves is symbolized in fairy tales, films, and so forth by the "lowly" animal). The hero, however, recognizes the value of this "inferior" side. He understands not only that instinct is sometimes a more reliable guide than pure reason, but also that it can be a source of great strength. Far from despising the animal side of himself, he respects it, befriends it. And in turn, like the grateful animals of the Grimms' stories, it repays him with its energies and powers.

Of course, the person who prizes something that the common run of humanity holds in contempt is himself in danger of becoming an object of scorn. The two elder brothers in "The Queen Bee" are selfish, callous men who look at a living duck and see a meal for their table. Their younger brother, however, respects the creature. He saves it from destruction (along with the ants and bees his brothers also want to kill) and, as a result, is rewarded by the animals. At the same time, precisely because he is the kind of sensitive person who cares so much about the fate of "insignificant" insects and birds, he is regarded as a fool, and called Simpleton. This kind of character, known variously as the Holy Fool, the Holy Innocent, or the Wise Fool, is an archetypal figure found in myths and literature all over the world.

The Holy Fool is a person who goes against the "wisdom" of the world. He or she does not operate by the usual standards of profit and practicality, which would insist emphatically that a duck is good for nothing *but* to be eaten. Rather, the Wise Fool lives according to other, *higher* laws and values. He does not care about "getting ahead" or "making it"; he has a childlike innocence and simplicity in his dealings with the world. As a result, he is totally unsuited to the "serious" business of society. Instead of following the dictates of a culture which puts a premium on material advancement and financial success, he may, for example, spend his time in such "idle" pursuits as contemplation and communion with nature. While such behavior makes him an object of scorn to those many members of society proud of their common sense and "tough-mindedness," it also puts him in touch with a more spiritual order of truth.

The notion that the sayings of the fool are divinely inspired—that, in the words of the poet Emily Dickinson, his "madness is divinest sense"—is extremely ancient and widespread. The Bible, for example, tells us that "God hath chosen the foolish things of the world to confound the wise" (1 Cor. 1:27). During the Middle Ages, professional court jesters often acted out the part of the Wise Fool. These jesters were usually given a licence in their speech forbidden to other retainers. Like the fool in Shakespeare's *King Lear,* who couches his bitter truths in puns and witticisms, they were allowed to speak words to their rulers for which other people would have been beheaded. Similarly, among many tribes of North American Indians, the mad were accorded special consideration. In *The Deerslayer,* James Fenimore Cooper's classic novel of the American frontier, the hero explains the Indian attitude toward such people to a companion:

> "Them are beings that the Lord has in his special care," said Deerslayer solemnly, "for he looks carefully to all who fall short of their proper share of reason. The Redskins honor and respect them who are so gifted, knowing that the Evil Spirit delights more to dwell in an artful body than in one that has no cunning to work upon."

One of the characters in *The Deerslayer,* a girl named Hetty Hutter, is a perfect representation of the Holy Innocent archetype. Though she is "feeble-minded," her "perception of the right," we are told, seems "intuitive." Her face is marked by a "calm, almost holy expression." Indeed, despite her intellectual limitations, she is so pure that she appears to be a person "superior to human infirmities. Guileless, innocent, and without distrust . . . Providence had nevertheless shielded her from harm by a halo of moral light."

Besides Hetty Hutter and Shakespeare's fool, there are many examples of Holy Innocents in world literature and popular culture. In "The Fool on the Hill," the Beatles sing of a man whom nobody likes or listens to—"they can see that he's just a fool." But the "fool" himself sits serenely on a hill, removed from the wearying conflicts and cares of the workaday world, contemplating the simple beauty of a sunset. Similarly, the narrator of Richard Brautigan's book *A Confederate General from Big Sur* retreats to the country, where his only desire is to "stay put and watch the world go round." Brautigan and the Beatles remind us that a fool, cut off from "common sense," can sometimes see crucial things about life that the worldly businessman, for instance, cannot.

The Wise Fool has also been a perennial favorite of humorists. Indeed, like the medieval jesters, many satirists have, in their writings, deliberately adopted the role of the harmless fool—a ploy which permits them to poke fun at sacred cows with impunity. This tradition is particularly prevalent in American humor. The innocent "country bumpkin" who turns out to be a great deal wiser than the educated "city slicker" is a figure that has been popular throughout our history, from Benjamin Franklin's Poor Richard, to Charles Farrar Browne's Artemus Ward, to Al Capp's Li'l Abner.

Other well-known examples of the Holy Fool archetype include Isaac Bashevis Singer's Gimpel the Fool, Fyodor Dostoyevsky's Prince Myshkin (from *The Idiot*), Mark Twain's Huckleberry Finn, J. D. Salinger's Holden Caulfield (from *The Catcher in the Rye*), Kurt Vonnegut's Billy Pilgrim (from *Slaughterhouse-Five*), and Pip the cabin boy, from Herman Melville's *Moby-Dick.* During a frantic chase after a whale, Pip falls overboard, and, floating alone on a vast sea, becomes mentally unhinged. At the same time, however, his mind is opened up to profound spiritual mysteries. Behind all the apparent randomness and confusion of the world, he suddenly sees a divine plan: "He saw God's foot upon the treadle of the loom, and spoke it; and therefore his shipmates called him mad." From the hour of his accident on, the rest of the crew considers Pip an idiot; but what they regard as his "absurd and frantic" reason is really, the author tells us, "celestial thought." "So man's insanity is heaven's sense," concludes Melville, summing up in a sentence the regrettable truth that, in our world of "getting and spending," spiritual insight is all too often mistaken for madness.

EDITH HAMILTON

"Pegasus and Bellerophon"

During her distinguished career, Edith Hamilton (1867–1963) did more than any other modern classicist to introduce the American reading public to the cultures of ancient Greece and Rome. After graduating from Bryn Mawr College, where she received her B.A. and M.A. degrees, Hamilton was awarded a European fellowship, and spent a year of study in Germany at the universities of Leipzig and Munich, becoming the first female student ever admitted to the latter. Returning to the United States in 1896, she assumed the post of headmistress of the Bryn Mawr preparatory school in Baltimore, Maryland, a position she held until 1922, when she left teaching to devote her time to writing. Her most famous book, *The Greek Way*, appeared in 1930, and was followed two years later by *The Roman Way* (both works later becoming Book-of-the-Month Club selections). Her other major writings on ancient civilizations include *The Prophets of Israel* (1936), *Mythology* (1946), and *The Echo of Greece* (1957). She was the recipient of many awards, including honorary Doctor of Letters degrees from several major universities and—the honor she cherished most—the Cross of the Order of Benefaction, bestowed on her by King Paul of Greece in a 1957 ceremony held at the foot of the Acropolis in Athens.

The story of Pegasus and Bellerophon is from Hamilton's *Mythology*, her popular retelling of the ancient Greek myths.

In Ephyre, the city later called Corinth, Glaucus was King. He was the son of Sisyphus who in Hades must forever try to roll a stone uphill because he once betrayed a secret of Zeus. Glaucus, too, drew down on himself the displeasure of heaven. He was a great horseman and he fed his horses human flesh to make them fierce in battle. Such monstrous deeds always angered the gods and they served him as he had served others. He was thrown from his chariot and his horses tore him to pieces and devoured him.

In the city a bold and beautiful young man named Bellerophon was generally held to be his son. It was rumored, however, that Bellerophon had a mightier father, Poseidon himself, the Ruler of the Sea, and the youth's surpassing gifts

Copyright 1942, by Edith Hamilton; Copyright © renewed 1969 by Dorian Fielding Reid; © renewed 1969 by Doris Fielding Reid, Executrix of the will of Edith Hamilton. From *Mythology* by Edith Hamilton, by permission of Little, Brown and Co.

of spirit and body made this account of his birth seem likely. Moreover his mother, Eurynome, although a mortal, had been taught by Athena[1] until in wit and wisdom she was the peer of the gods. It was only to be expected on all scores that Bellerophon should seem less mortal than divine. Great adventures would call to such a one as he and no peril would ever hold him back. And yet the deed for which he is best known needed no courage at all, no effort, even. Indeed, it proved that

> What man would swear cannot be done,—
> Must not be hoped for,—the great Power on high
> Can give into his hand, in easy mastery.

More than anything on earth Bellerophon wanted Pegasus, a marvelous horse which had sprung from the Gorgon's blood when Perseus killed her.[2] He was

> A winged steed, unwearying of flight,
> Sweeping through air swift as a gale of wind.

Wonders attended him. The spring beloved of poets, Hippocrene, on Helicon, the Muses' mountain, had sprung up where his hoof had struck the earth. Who could catch and tame such a creature? Bellerophon suffered from hopeless longing.

The wise seer of Ephyre (Corinth), Polyidus, to whom he told his desperate desire, advised him to go to Athena's temple and sleep there. The gods often spoke to men in their dreams. So Bellerophon went to the holy place and when he was lying deep in slumber beside the altar he seemed to see the goddess standing before him with some golden thing in her hand. She said to him, "Asleep? Nay, wake. Here is what will charm the steed you covet." He sprang to his feet. No goddess was there, but a marvelous object lay in front of him, a bridle all of gold, such as never had been seen before. Hopeful at last with it in his hand, he hurried out to the fields to find Pegasus. He caught sight of him, drinking from the far-famed spring of Corinth, Pirene; and he drew gently near. The horse looked at him tranquilly, neither startled nor afraid, and suffered himself to be bridled without the least trouble. Athena's charm had worked. Bellerophon was master of the glorious creature.

In his full suit of bronze armor he leaped upon his back and put him through his paces, the horse seeming to delight in the sport as much as he himself. Now he was lord of the air, flying wherever he would, envied of all. As matters turned out, Pegasus was not only a joy, but a help in time of need as well, for hard trials lay before Bellerophon.

In some way, we are not told how except that it was purely through accident, he killed his brother; and he went to Argos where the King, Proetus, purified him. There his trials began and his great deeds as well. Anteia, the wife of Proetus, fell in love with him, and when he turned from her and would have nothing

---

[1] Zeus' favorite child, who sprang fully grown and fully armored from his head. Athena was the virgin goddess of war, wisdom, and the arts. Her symbol was the owl.

[2] The hero Perseus was the son of Danaë, a mortal woman, and the god Zeus, who came to her in a shower of gold. Perseus' great deed was the slaying of Medusa, one of the three Gorgons. These female monsters had bronze hands, golden wings, and teeth like the tusks of swine. Their heads were covered with living snakes. They were so hideous that a single glance at them would turn a man to stone.

to do with her, in her bitter anger she told her husband that his guest had wronged her and must die. Enraged though he was, Proetus would not kill him. Bellerophon had eaten at his table; he could not bring himself to use violence against him. However, he made a plan which seemed certain to have the same result. He asked the youth to take a letter to the King of Lycia in Asia and Bellerophon easily agreed. Long journeys meant nothing to him on Pegasus' back. The Lycian king received him with antique hospitality and entertained him splendidly for nine days before he asked to see the letter. Then he read that Proetus wanted the young man killed.

He did not care to do so, for the same reason that had made Proetus unwilling: Zeus's well-known hostility to those who broke the bond between host and guest. There could be no objection, however, to sending the stranger on an adventure, him and his winged horse. So he asked him to go and slay the Chimaera, feeling quite assured that he would never come back. The Chimaera was held to be unconquerable. She was a most singular portent, a lion in front, a serpent behind, a goat in between—

A fearful creature, great and swift of foot and strong,
Whose breath was flame unquenchable.

But for Bellerophon riding Pegasus there was no need to come anywhere near the flaming monster. He soared up over her and shot her with his arrows at no risk to himself.

When he went back to Proetus, the latter had to think out other ways of disposing of him. He got him to go on an expedition, against the Solymi, mighty warriors; and then when Bellerophon had succeeded in conquering these, on another against the Amazons, where he did equally well. Finally Proetus was won over by his courage and his good fortune, too; he became friends with him and gave him his daughter to marry.

He lived happily thus for a long time; then he made the gods angry. His eager ambition along with his great success led him to think "thoughts too great for man," the thing of all others the gods objected to. He tried to ride Pegasus up to Olympus. He believed he could take his place there with the immortals. The horse was wiser. He would not try the flight, and he threw his rider. Thereafter Bellerophon, hated of the gods, wandered alone, devouring his own soul and avoiding the paths of men until he died.

Pegasus found shelter in the heavenly stalls of Olympus where the steeds of Zeus were cared for. Of them all he was foremost, as was proved by the extraordinary fact the poets report, that when Zeus wished to use his thunderbolt, it was Pegasus who brought the thunder and lightning to him.

QUESTIONS

Language

1. Look at the language of this selection and pick out sentences and phrases which give the story a sense of majesty and stateliness appropriate to the heroic subject matter. Describing Bellerophon, for example, Hamilton writes, "Great adventure would call to such a one as he." What effect is created by such diction? How would the story be different if Hamilton had written, "He would have many adventures?"

Content

1. Two famous old sayings are relevant to this story: "Hell hath no fury like a woman scorned" and "Pride goeth before a fall." What episodes in this myth illustrate these sayings? Do you think these sayings are generally valid?
2. Describe what happens to Bellerophon in Athena's temple.
3. From this myth, what can you deduce about the importance of hospitality in ancient Greek culture?
4. Though he is "bold and beautiful," Bellerophon comes to a bad end, wandering alone, "devouring his own soul and avoiding the paths of men" until he dies. From what you are told about him in the story, do you think he deserves such a fate? Did you find him, in general, an attractive or unattractive figure? Explain.
5. Explain the meaning of the three lines of verse which appear at the end of paragraph two.

Suggestions for Writing

1. Hamilton relates the major events of Bellerophon's life, though she does not describe them in great detail. Look over the passage in which she recounts his battle with the Chimaera, a fire-breathing monster with the head of a lion, the body of a goat, and the tail of a serpent. Then, imagining this incident for yourself, write a description of it from the hero's point of view, as—mounted on the back of his winged steed, Pegasus—he approaches the fearful Chimaera.
2. Though the stories of mythology are obviously impossible, people have always believed in them. Even in our own, seemingly scientific age, myths survive in the form of figures like the Bionic Man (a contemporary Hercules) and of stories such as *2001* (a science fiction *Odyssey;* see p. 412). Write an essay in which you attempt to explain the appeal of myths for human beings—why people seem to *need* myths. Discuss this question in class before you begin writing. You might also, in this connection, take a look at Alan McGlashan's essay "Daily Paper Pantheon" (p. 448) and the selection from Robert Jewett and John Shelton Lawrence's book *The American Monomyth* (p. 437).

THE BROTHERS GRIMM

"The Queen Bee"

As Bruno Bettelheim points out in *The Uses of Enchantment* (see p. 433), fairy tales operate by communicating messages to the unconscious minds of their young audience, helping children to "cope with the psychological problems of growing up and integrating their personalities." In the introduction to his book, Bettelheim quotes an intriguing remark by the German poet Schiller: "Deeper meaning resides in the fairy tales told to me in my childhood than in the truth that is taught by life."

From *The Complete Grimm's Fairy Tales,* by Jakob Ludwig and Wilhelm Karl Grimm, translated by Margaret Hunt and James Stern. Copyright 1944 by Pantheon Books and renewed 1972 by Random House, Inc. Reprinted by permission of Pantheon Books, a Division of Random House, Inc.

Though relatively obscure, the story "The Queen Bee" contains a good deal of psychological wisdom. Its hero, a Holy Fool character named Simpleton, succeeds in his seemingly impossible tasks by rescuing a series of Helpful Animals who later come to his aid. According to Bettelheim, this tale teaches children the importance of befriending their "animal natures," of bringing the disparate parts of the personality "into accord" with each other. "After we have thus achieved an integrated personality," he writes, "we can accomplish what seem like miracles."

Two kings' sons once went out in search of adventures, and fell into a wild, disorderly way of living, so that they never came home again. The youngest, who was called Simpleton, set out to seek his brothers, but when at length he found them they mocked him for thinking that he with his simplicity could get through the world, when they two could not make their way, and yet were so much cleverer. They all three traveled away together, and came to an anthill. The two elder wanted to destroy it, to see the little ants creeping about in their terror, and carrying their eggs away, but Simpleton said: "Leave the creatures in peace; I will not allow you to disturb them." Then they went onwards and came to a lake, on which a great number of ducks were swimming. The two brothers wanted to catch a couple and roast them, but Simpleton would not permit it, and said: "Leave the creatures in peace, I will not suffer you to kill them." At length they came to a bee's nest, in which there was so much honey that it ran out of the trunk of the tree where it was. The two wanted to make a fire beneath the tree, and suffocate the bees in order to take away the honey, but Simpleton again stopped them and said: "Leave the creatures in peace, I will not allow you to burn them." At length the two brothers arrived at a castle where stone horses were standing in the stables, and no human being was to be seen, and they went through all the halls until, quite at the end, they came to a door in which were three locks. In the middle of the door, however, there was a little pane, through which they could see into the room. There they saw a little grey man, who was sitting at a table. They called him, once, twice, but he did not hear; at last they called him for the third time, when he got up, opened the locks, and came out. He said nothing, however, but conducted them to a handsomely-spread table, and when they had eaten and drunk, he took each of them to a bedroom. Next morning the little grey man came to the eldest, beckoned to him, and conducted him to a stone table, on which were inscribed three tasks, by the performance of which the castle could be delivered from enchantment. The first was that in the forest, beneath the moss, lay the princess's pearls, a thousand in number, which must be picked up, and if by sunset one single pearl was missing, he who had looked for them would be turned to stone. The eldest went thither, and sought the whole day, but when it came to an end, he had only found one hundred, and what was written on the table came true, and he was turned into stone. Next day, the second brother undertook the adventure; but it did not fare much better with him than with the eldest; he did not find more than two hundred pearls, and was changed to stone. At last it was Simpleton's turn to seek in the moss; but it was so difficult for him to find the pearls, and he got on so slowly, that he seated himself on a stone, and wept. And while he was thus sitting, the King of the ants whose life he had once saved, came with five thousand ants, and before long the little creatures had got all the pearls together, and laid them in a heap. The second task, however, was to fetch out of the lake the key of the King's daughter's bed-chamber. When Simpleton came to the lake, the ducks which he had saved, swam up to him, dived down, and brought the key out of the water. But the third task was the most difficult; from amongst the three sleeping daughters of the King was the youngest and dearest to be sought out. They, however, resembled each other exactly, and were only to be distinguished by their having eaten different sweet-meats before they fell asleep: the eldest a bit of sugar; the second a little syrup; and the youngest a spoonful of honey. Then the Queen of the bees, whom Simpleton had protected from the fire, came and tasted the lips of all three, and at last she remained sitting on the mouth which had eaten honey, and thus the King's son recognized the right princess. Then the enchantment was at an end; everything was delivered from sleep, and those who had been turned to stone received once more their natural forms. Simpleton married the youngest and sweet-est princess, and after her father's death became King, and his two brothers received the two other sisters.

QUESTIONS

Language

1. This fairy tale has been stripped down to its bare essentials; the only details given are those necessary to the unfolding of the plot. Find places in ''The Queen Bee'' where elaboration seems natural and would be easy. What would you add?
2. Note that this tale consists of one long paragraph. Point out those places where new paragraphs might begin.

Content

1. Why do the two oldest brothers in this fairy tale want to destroy the ants, the ducks, and the bees? What do these incidents tell us about them?
2. Describe the youngest brother, Simpleton, as completely as you can. What is he like; what kind of relationship does he have with his brothers?
3. Unlike his brothers, Simpleton bursts into tears when he discovers how poorly he is performing the first task. Do you think this incident is significant? What does it say about him?
4. The two oldest brothers are turned into stone because of their failure to collect the pearls. In *The Uses of Enchantment*, Bruno Bettelheim says that being turned into stone is not a symbol of death; ''rather it stands for a lack of true humanity, an inability to respond to higher values, so that the person, being dead to what life is all about in the best sense, might as well be made of stone.'' What ''higher values'' are the brothers ignorant of? And why are they released from their stony prisons at the end?
5. What do you think this fairy tale is trying to ''teach'' the reader? Why is Simpleton the one person to free the castle of its dreadful enchantment?

Suggestions for Writing

1. Have you ever been assigned a task or job so difficult that you despaired of ever complet-ing it? Describe in an essay what the job was, whether you needed to ask for help, what your emotional reactions were, and what you learned about your own strengths and perseverance or, conversely, what you learned from your discouragement and defeat.
2. Write your own fairy tale in which an animal comes to the aid of a beleaguered hero or heroine.

BOB HANEY, GIL KANE, AND BERNARD SACHS

"The Secret of the Golden Crocodile"

The following story, starring Rex the Wonder Dog—a Helpful Animal in the mold of Lassie and Rin Tin Tin—was written by Bob Haney and first appeared in 1957. The primary artwork is by the distinguished comic book illustrator Gil Kane (b. 1926). Born Eric Katz in Riga, Latvia, Kane began his career in this country at the age of sixteen, and throughout the forties and fifties worked on assorted action comics for various publishers. It was not until the 1960s, however, while drawing such superhero series as *Green Lantern* and *The Atom,* that he perfected the elegant, fluid style he is known for. After working for Marvel Comics in the late sixties, Kane left to create his own publication, a black-and-white comic in a large-size, magazine format, called *His Name Is Savage.* The magazine was discontinued after one issue, partly because the actor Lee Marvin, whose face Kane used as the model for the cover portrait of his fictional character Savage, sued the artist. In 1971, after Kane had returned to Marvel, Bantam Books issued his adventure saga *Blackmark,* a "sword-and-sorcery" comic strip in the format of a paperback novel. Kane's more recent work includes the daily newspaper strip *Star Hawks,* one of several space adventure comics that followed in the wake of the movie *Star Wars.*

Rex, The Wonder Dog, © 1957 DC Comics Inc.

THE ADVENTURES OF

REX

THE Wonder DOG

K-1273

COPYRIGHT © 1957 by NATIONAL COMICS PUBLICATIONS, INC.

STORY BY: BOB HANEY
ART BY: GIL KANE & BERNARD SACHS

DANNY DENNIS WAS DISAPPOINTED! HE THOUGHT THE **REAL** AFRICA--IN WHICH PERIL LURKED BEHIND EVERY BUSH--WAS DREAMED UP IN THE MOVIES! BUT THAT WAS BEFORE HE AND HIS *WONDER DOG*, REX, STUMBLED UPON...

The Secret Of The GOLDEN CROCODILE!

On a plane speeding high over the ocean is the Dennis family...

SOON WE'LL BE IN MYSTERIOUS AFRICA-- LOOKING FOR THAT *GOLDEN CROCODILE* FOR THE ZOO!

WE HAVEN'T MUCH TO GO ON, DANNY! JUST NATIVE RUMORS OF A *GOLDEN CROCODILE*-- SOMEWHERE ALONG THE NILE!

Shortly after the plane lands...

SKYSCRAPERS IN AFRICA? WHERE IS THE MYSTERIOUS JUNGLE, DAD? WHERE ARE THE LIONS AND ELEPHANTS AND CROCODILES I TOLD *REX* ABOUT?

Later, as the trio leaves the city...

GOSH, DAD! CALL *THIS* A SAFARI? I THOUGHT WE'D BE WALKING ON FOOT--ALONG A JUNGLE PATH-- *NOT RIDING IN A JEEP!*

After camp is made...

CALL *THIS* ROUGHING IT IN DARKEST AFRICA-- WITH YOU SHAVING WITH AN ELECTRIC RAZOR?

RRRRR!

LOOK AT THEM! INSTEAD OF DOING TRIBAL DANCES WITH DRUMS AND SPEARS-- THEY'RE JITTERBUGGING TO RADIO MUSIC!

Day after day passes...

NOT A SIGN OF THAT *GOLDEN CROCODILE!* MAYBE WE'LL HAVE BETTER LUCK AT THE NEXT CAMP, DANNY!

THAT *GOLDEN CROCODILE* MUST HAVE BEEN DREAMED UP BY SOME MOVIE WRITER TOO, DAD! ALONG WITH DARKEST AFRICA--THE CONTINENT OF MYSTERY, PERIL, SUSPENSE!

The next day...along the river bank...

BE CAREFUL, DANNY!

DON'T WORRY, DAD! WE'RE JUST GOING FOR A LITTLE RIDE! THE ONLY DANGER WE MIGHT RUN INTO-- IS GETTING OUR NOSES SUN-BURNED!

CONTINUED ON 3RD PAGE FOLLOWING.

2

SLOWLY, THE YOUTH AND HIS *WONDER DOG* PADDLE ALONG THE RIVER ...

POOR DAD! WE'LL NEVER FIND THAT *GOLDEN CROCODILE--!*

ANYMORE THAN WE'LL FIND THE UNTAMED AFRICA WE SAW IN THE MOVIES!

SUDDENLY... STARTLED BY THAT BUMP, REX? IT'S NOTHING!

BUMP!

JUST A FLOATING LOG OR SOMETHING LIKE THAT WE'RE BUMPING ACROSS!

BUMP!

BUMP!

THE NEXT MOMENT, A HUGE, SCALY FIGURE HURTLES UP FROM THE DANK WATERS AND...

CROCODILE--! THE BOAT'S GOING OVER...!

WITH INCREDIBLE AGILITY, *REX* FAIRLY LEAPS OUT OF THE WATER...

CHOMP!

ENRAGED, THE MONSTER'S MASSIVE JAWS CLASH A FRACTION OF AN INCH AWAY FROM THE *WONDER DOG*...

INFURIATED BEYOND REASON, THE SLIMY BEAST DIVES AND TWISTS AND TURNS IN THE MURKY DEPTHS ... IN A MADDENED EFFORT TO DISLODGE THE COURAGEOUS CANINE ...

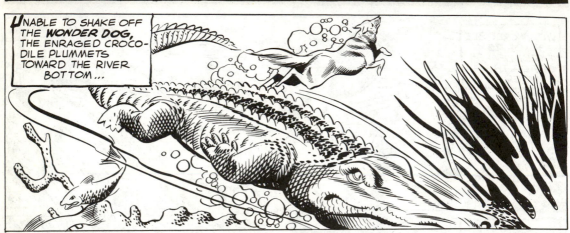

UNABLE TO SHAKE OFF THE **WONDER DOG**, THE ENRAGED CROCODILE PLUMMETS TOWARD THE RIVER BOTTOM...

THE EX-WAR DOG EMERGES NEAR HIS YOUNG MASTER AND...

WELL-- WE SAW A CROCODILE, **REX**! BUT IT CERTAINLY WASN'T GOLD! I'M AFRAID DAD WILL NEVER FIND WHAT HE'S LOOKING FOR!

THAT HASSLE WITH THE CROCODILE WILL PROBABLY BE OUR FIRST AND ONLY TASTE OF WILD AFRICA-- **REX**!--WHAT ARE YOU LOOKING AT?

THE AGILE **REX** HURLS HIMSELF BACKWARD AS A STEEL-NAILED PAW SLASHES THE AIR IN FRONT OF HIM...

LION--!

RRR!

AS THE BEAST HURLS ANOTHER CRUSHING BLOW AT THE YOUTH AND HIS AMAZING DOG...

ONLY SAFE PLACE AWAY FROM THOSE CLAWS OF DEATH--IS UNDERWATER, REX!

RROWRR!

BUT AS THE FEARLESS DOG DIVES UNDERWATER WITH HIS YOUNG MASTER...

REX'S WONDER MUSCLES TOW DANNY THROUGH THE WATER AT TOP SPEED--

I CAN'T OUTSPEED OUR PURSUER! I'LL HAVE TO GET US ONTO LAND!

EMERGING FROM THE WATER, THE BOY AND HIS DOG FIND...

REX! THE LION FOLLOWED US! LET'S GET BACK INTO THE WATER!

RRR!

GROWR!

WE'RE CUT OFF ON BOTH SIDES!

HSSSS!

WITHOUT HESITATION, THE EX-WAR DOG HURLS HIMSELF UPON THE STARTLED LION...

RROWR!

WITH INCREDIBLE COURAGE BORN OF HIS LOYALTY TO HIS YOUNG MASTER, *REX* LEAPS AGAIN AND AGAIN AT THE STARTLED LION...

AND THEN...

BUT, DANNY'S FRANTIC SHOUTS CUT THROUGH THE BATTLE HAZE SURROUNDING *REX* UNTIL...

AN AGILE LEAP LIFTS THE *WONDER DOG* OUT OF REACH OF THE MASSIVE BEASTS... UPWARD--UPWARD HE LIGHTLY SPRINGS...

REX! THEY'RE KNOCKING OVER THE SMALLER TREES! COME UP HERE TO MINE -- IT'S TOO BIG FOR THEM!

BUT EVEN THE MIGHTY TREE ON WHICH *REX* JOINS HIS YOUNG MASTER BEGINS TO SWAY UNDER THE ONSLAUGHT OF THE THUNDERING ELEPHANT HERD... UNTIL...

THE TREE'S CRACKING!

KRAACK!

TORN LOOSE FROM THEIR PERCH, THE DARING DUO LEAPS FOR A MOUNTAINOUS BACK...

REX! SOMETHING TELLS ME WE'VE LEAPED FROM THE FRYING PAN-- INTO THE FIRE!

EEEE!

ENRAGED BY THE PIGMIES CLINGING TO IT, THE ELEPHANT RUSHES AWAY FROM THE REST OF THE HERD...

REX! HE'S TRYING TO SWEEP US OFF!

EEE!

FINALLY, A LOW-HANGING BOUGH SWEEPS *REX* AND HIS YOUNG MASTER OFF THE MADDENED ELEPHANT'S BACK...

WE'VE GOT TO GET OUT OF THAT BEAST'S SIGHT OR SCENT--OR HE'LL TRAMPLE ON US--ONCE HE STOPS AND TURNS AROUND!

BUT, AS THE DARING DUO TUMBLES TO THE ROTTING FLOOR OF THE JUNGLE...

*REX--*THE GROUND'S GIVING WAY UNDER US!

INTO AN UNDERGROUND CAVE, THE BOY AND HIS DOG ARE SOMER-SAULTED...

REX! WE'VE LANDED RIGHT IN THE LAP OF A TREASURE CAVE! WHAT DIFFERENCE DOES IT MAKE NOW--IF WE NEVER FIND THAT *GOLDEN CROCODILE!* *REX--* WHAT ARE YOU LOOKING AT?

REX! YOU'VE FOUND IT! THE *GOLDEN CROCODILE!* WE WERE MISTAKEN THINKING IT WAS A *LIVE ONE!* IT'S *REALLY* GOLD!

LATER, THE *WONDER DOG* LEADS DANNY BACK TO CAMP WHERE...

WELL, DANNY, MAYBE YOU'RE RIGHT! MAYBE THE *GOLDEN CROCODILE IS* JUST A FAIRY TALE! AND THE AFRICA OF LIONS AND ELEPHANTS IS SOMETHING DREAMED UP IN THE MOVIES! NOTHING EXCITING HAS HAPPENED TO COMPARE WITH THE WORLD SERIES!

SAY--WHAT ARE YOU TWO LAUGHING AT?

The End

QUESTIONS

Language

1. Look at the captions of this comic. What attitude does the narrator have toward his story? How would you characterize his style, his tone? Does the writer strive for dramatic variety—in Danny's speeches, for example, or in the action of the comic?
2. What speeches in this story are ironic? Why?

Content

1. What are Danny and his father doing in Africa? Do you approve of their mission? What do you think will happen after Danny reveals his discovery of the treasure?
2. Why is Danny so disappointed in Africa? What had he expected? What is his father's attitude toward the country they visit?
3. How is Rex treated by Danny? Is the dog depicted realistically? Is the story in general realistic?
4. What do we learn about Danny from his response to the discovery of the treasure in the cave?
5. How much of a barrier is there between Danny and Rex? In what ways do they function as a unit?
6. This comic was written in 1957. Are there ways you would have known it wasn't written more recently—last year, for example?

Suggestions for Writing

1. Write an essay about why the dog is a perfect Helpful Animal. What qualities does the dog possess that make it possible for us to imagine it in this role? Why not have a story about Rex the Wonder Cat? Alternatively, write a story about Rex the Wonder Cat, or Rex the Wonder Parakeet. You will probably want to make your story humorous.
2. Have you ever intensely longed to go to a special place only to get there and find it shorn of mystery and appeal? Write an essay about such an experience, comparing and contrasting what you had expected of this place with what it was like in reality. How did you feel about your discovery? Or, write an essay about a place you have always, intensely, wanted to go to. Describe it as you imagine it; then analyze why you want to go there and what it means to you.
3. Many of us have some sort of fantasy vision of Africa; it is a place, like the American West, which has a kind of mythic identity in addition to historical identity. Describe your vision of Africa. Then try to account for your picture: where did you get your ideas about that continent? How do you suppose the real Africa compares?

FRAN STRIKER

from *The Lone Ranger*

Play the *William Tell Overture* for most Americans and they will probably picture a costumed cowboy astride a dazzling white horse and hear a deep-voiced announcer cry, "A cloud of dust, a fiery horse with the speed of light, a hearty Hi-Yo Silver. The Lone Ranger rides again!"

Copyright © 1936 by The Lone Ranger, Inc.; copyright renewed 1964 by Wrather Corporation.

Although later generations know him primarily as a television character, the "masked rider of the plains"—with his silver bullets, snowy steed, and faithful Indian companion Tonto—was originally the hero of a highly popular radio series. Broadcast between 1933 and 1954, the show was created by George W. Trendle, head of station WXYZ in Detroit, and scriptwriter Fran Striker.

The following chapter is from Striker's 1938 novel, *The Lone Ranger,* based on the radio program. The story focuses on Dave Walton, an earnest young engineer charged with overseeing the construction of "the first railroad ever laid across the great American desert." Walton is working against a deadline: if he does not complete the job within a certain time, it will be awarded to a rival contractor. Attempting to prevent Walton from meeting his deadline is the villainous Colton J. Glencoe, who has been hired by the rival contractor to sabotage Walton's efforts. One of Glencoe's evil schemes is to instigate a mutiny among Walton's workers by arranging for their payroll to be robbed. By bribing the crew of a special train (which consists of a single car attached to a steam engine), Glencoe ensures that it will be left unguarded. His plan is to sneak into the unattended cab of the engine and throw the throttle, thereby sending the special train hurtling down the tracks, where it will collide with the oncoming pay train. In the ensuing confusion, a band of drunken Indians, led by three of Glencoe's slimy associates (including his right-hand man, Maxim Gunner, alias Slotkin) is to steal the camp's payroll. In the chapter below, the Lone Ranger and Silver attempt to thwart Glencoe's nefarious plan. Other characters who appear in the chapter include Kate Stevens, a young woman from the East who has fallen in love with Dave Walton, and a crusty but lovable old codger named Clem—Striker's conception of a colorful, authentic western type.

THE PAY TRAIN

Clem's yelp of profane disgust was cut short by a sharp hiss from the rider standing outside. "Come out of there, you old whiskered Gila-monster, and don't make any noise doing it!"

Clem's frowsy whiskers and sleep-bleared, angry eyes popped out suddenly between the tent flaps. "What in time is your idea haulin' me out of bed again in the middle of the night? Ranger, don't you *never* keep human hours? It must be nigh three o'clock in the mornin'."

"Sometimes I do, but I'll probably never get the habit of it," the rider laughed softly. "The point of our keeping quiet now is that our little friend Maxim-Slotkin and his pals are sneaking into camp to lift a load of liquor out of the store-tent of the bar. I just a little prefer that they didn't know we're awake."

"Prefer! Why, don't you want to stop the dirty sons-of-so-and-so's? Jest wait till I get my gun and I'll be right with you!" The old man would have ducked back into his tent if the Ranger's strong hand had not seized and stopped him.

"Sh-h! Hold on a minute, Old Timer! I'm perfectly willing they should take the liquor and get away with it. It would spoil my plans later if they were scared off now. I just came to ask you if you can get together a few sticks of dynamite and a couple of dozen red flares, the same number of detonating caps, and six feet of fuse. Pack them up in one bundle, and send them up to my hideout east of camp by Tonto some time after sunrise. How about it? I'll tell you later what all the fun's about."

"Humph," the old plainsman grumbled. "What's that you've got on your saddle? Looks like an Injun bow and arry. Are those some more of your little playthings, along with the dynamite and the rest of it?"

"You guessed it, Old Timer," replied the Ranger good-naturedly. "But how about getting those things I asked you for?"

Old Clem clawed at his whiskers as he looked dourly up at the Ranger's shadowed features. "All right, all right," he muttered. "I'll git 'em from Dave Walton before breakfast and send them by Tonto. If you won't spill what's on your mind, I suppose there's no use askin' questions. If you're goin' to play alone, you'll play alone, and that's all there is to it. Only," the old man snarled like a dyspeptic wildcat, "don't you dare wake me up again to-night!" The whiskers disappeared suddenly inside the tent flaps, and the Lone Ranger rode silently away, his grin hidden by the darkness that preceded a desert dawn.

When young Dave heard of Old Clem's midnight visitor and his strange request for explosives, a worried scowl grew on his already care-marked features. "Of course our friend can have what he wants, Clem," the young man answered. "He could have anything in camp, so far as I'm concerned,—except Miss Kate! Lord! Think of all that man has done for us, just out of generosity and his own love of adventure. He has the spirit of an old-time knight-errant, along with the keen wits and cleverness that only this new, brave country can produce!

"But speaking of Miss Kate, Clem, I'm worried about her staying on here in this rough-and-tumble railroad camp. I have a hunch that more dirty work may be tried before long by Glencoe and his crowd. That means more danger to every one in camp, and who knows when Kate may be involved, despite everything you and I might do to protect her? She ought to go back East immediately. Much as I shall miss her, I've got to persuade her to do it. There's a special car leaving camp to-night with those four divisional officers who are here to-day. They'll be only too glad to have her ride with them.

"Another thing, Clem,—this whole camp is to be broken up and moved forty miles ahead. Much equipment is already on the way to the new campsite, as you know. To-morrow morning the tents will come down and the men will leave here in box-cars. So if Kate can pack up and leave tonight, she'll escape all that confusion.

"Clem, can you persuade her to drop in here at the Engineer's Office Tent some time this morning? I must talk to her!"

The old timer shrugged, and pulled at his tobacco-stained moustache. "They won't be no trouble gittin' her to come for a pow-wow with you," he replied, his old eyes twinkling. "Good heavens to Betsey! She ain't done nothin' but talk to me *about* you all the time she's been here, since your daddy died! But as for persuadin' that gal to pick up and go home just because things is maybe gittin' a little lively in camp,—wa—ll, son, you'll have to be *some* good persuader. You see, if things go right, another month will see the hull job completed, the rails from the West meetin' ours from the East, and the first cross-continent railroad in operation. Miss Kate somehow considers that will be your personal and private triumph, son; and she's set her mind on bein' on the job to witness it. If you kin change her mind, you're a better arguer than me, that's all!"

On leaving the Office Tent with an order on the Supplies Tent for certain explosives, the old man attended first to this business, then dispatched Tonto with the package for the Lone Ranger, and finally returned with Dave's message to Kate Stevens. Before noon, the girl appeared at the door of Dave's tent, flushed with pretty excitement and with the eager light of battle in her eyes.

Seating herself at Dave's embarrassed invitation, she proceeded to stare the young man out of countenance. He dropped his eyes to the desk, cleared his throat several times, and floundered helplessly for a way to open the conversation. It was not easy to tell the girl with whom he had fallen really in love, to leave and go back home, probably against her own choice.

All at once Kate broke into a merry laugh. "I don't wonder you feel foolish, Dave Walton," she said regaining a tone of mock severity. "You want to send me away like a bad little girl so that I won't be a nuisance to you any more. You want to tell me that a rough railroad camp is not place for a young lady, especially in all the confusion of moving to a new campsite. That you have had enough to think about without protecting me and keeping track of my where-abouts every minute of the day; and that you'll be very much relieved, the sooner I am out of sight on my way back East. There! Now I've said it all for you, haven't I? So why don't you sit up and say thank you?"

Dave's jaw dropped lower and lower with consternation, until his pipe fell out and bounced from the desk to the ground. "You—you've been pumping Clem, I see," he managed to choke out.

"Exactly," tittered the girl, pushing back a stray lock of her brown hair. "I can always pump him dry without the slightest effort. So I know, young man, what all your plans are regarding me. I know, too, that you're afraid of more trouble from Glencoe and his crowd, and that you feel that is all the more reason for my leaving camp to-night on the same train with the divisional inspec-tors. You want me to go right back now to my tent and spend the day packing my bags; and then you'll come around after supper and tell me how sorry you are to have me go, how I have been an angel of goodness, an inspiration to you in your work, and so forth, and how you are going to miss me.

"But it won't work, Dave Walton, it won't work at all! I'm not such a tender child as you think, and I'm no 'fraidy-cat, in *spite* of what you may think. In one more month the rails from the East and from the West are going to meet, and it will all be due to you, Dave, that they do meet on time. That will be your triumph, and I intend to be here to see it,—yes, and to stand by you through all the dangers and hardships during the coming month while you're winning your great fight.

"You can't keep me away, Dave! And if you could and did, I should never forgive you!"

The young engineer drew a long breath, and sank back into his chair. For a moment he stared wonderingly at the determined young person in front of him, and then surrendered. "All right Kate," he agreed, "I guess you win!" The red blood surged up through his face to the very roots of his hair. "I—I didn't dream that you cared so much!"

Kate's blush answered his own. "But now that you see that I do, Dave," she whispered, "you will let me stay, won't you?"

Dave threw her a glance full of admiration. "I shouldn't, of course," he smiled, "but I guess you've won the trick. You can stay, and I'll admit that in my heart I'm more than glad!

"But how are you going to travel, Kate, to the new campsite? The only trains are flat cars and box-cars filled with rough, sweaty laborers and their equipment. You can't ride with them."

"Why, we'll ride our horses!" the girl exclaimed, her eyes shining. "A forty-mile ride will be a wonderful outing, the first real outing I've had since coming here. Old Clem can go with me to see that no Indians take my scalp. You yourself, I suppose, will have to ride on the train with your old laborers,—"

"Indeed I won't, Kate! If you travel on horse-back, you'll travel with me beside you, and Old Clem can ride with us, of course. We'll keep close to the tracks, with the work-trains always in sight, as they'll move slowly, and it's not likely the redskins will bother us at all,—

"Well, that's settled, young lady, and I'm glad of it. So now you can go and pack your things anyhow. But save out what you need for the day's ride to-morrow. The rest of it will be carried safely on one of the trains."

Meanwhile at the little clearing in the jack-pines, the Lone Ranger was busy removing the heads of the arrows he had filched from the Indian camp, and doing curious things with his knife, some thick paper, glue, and stout thread, to the contents of the package which Tonto had brought him early that morning. After their work was finished, he cut up a small roll of canvas into two parts, and fashioned them into crude, wide-mouthed sacks with straps to sling them from his shoulders. When he had padded the sacks well with soft grass and filled them with his altered arrows, they looked like big, clumsy quivers for ammunition such as had never been seen before.

"It's a mighty good thing," chuckled the Ranger as he filled the last sack and tested the length of its strap over his shoulder, "it's a mighty good thing that I learned how to handle a bow and arrow when I was a boy. It's been useful more than once, but never so useful as it's going to be to-night." He glanced up at the setting sun. "Silver Horse, it's about time we were getting started. Just a bite of supper, and then we'll hit back toward the camp to start our little game."

After a supper consisting of fried sage-chicken, camp biscuits, and strong tea, Silver's master saddled him and mounted, with the strange canvas quivers hanging just below each elbow. Then, with plenty of time to spare, they ambled slowly toward camp through the gathering twilight. Had the Ranger guessed that Glencoe had set the time for action half an hour earlier than originally planned, Silver's gait would not have been the slow trot that he maintained until well within sight of the railroad.

It was the former's plan to lie in wait near the special train until the instant that the bribed engine-crew had disappeared,—then to slip into the cab before Glencoe could arrive, and to damage or remove certain necessary parts of the engine's more delicate machinery. This would prevent both the wreck and the hold-up, though the Ranger planned to gallop on to the scene of the proposed Indian ambush, prepared to spoil any rash attack by the drink-crazed Indians on the speeding pay-train.

However, as the dim outline of the camp and railroad embankment loomed into sight, a shock of alarm coursed through the Ranger's brain. *The special train was in motion.* Though its headlight had been extinguished, the moving shape of the engine and the single car was visible against the evening sky. The exhaust, slow and muffled as it was, could be heard as the train crept furtively from its siding on to the main track.

Silver bounded forward under the touch of his rider's heels, but even as he did so, the engine reached the main right-of-way, the sound of its exhaust quickened, a low rumbling filled the air as the train picked up speed under open throttle, and a tiny human figure dropped from the engine's cab, to disappear into the prairie dusk.

Grinding his teeth with anger and with fear for the lives threatened by a head-on collision between the pay-train and the runaway steel horse, the Lone Ranger urged his mount towards the limit of his magnificent speed. "Hi-Yo, Silver Horse," he gritted. "If you step in a prairie-dog hole now, there'll be more besides you and me to suffer!"

But there was no cause for such worry,—no chance that the great brute whose whole life had been spent on the pathless desert, who had raced over far worse country than this and on far darker nights with the wild horses that he led and ruled,—there was no fear that Silver now would lose his sureness of foot or fail his rider. Slowly but surely he gained upon the snorting engine, which was an ancient wood-burning type with a top speed of twenty miles an hour. Slowly but surely he narrowed the angle between its course and his own, until he was racing parallel with the tracks and overtaking the man-made monster.

Hope lifted in the Ranger's heart. If he could force Silver close enough to the rocking engine so as to leap from the saddle into its steel cab, he could still save the situation by stopping the train completely. After that, the warning of the pay train would be a simple matter by planting a red flare some distance up the tracks.

But in the end, it was the half-wild stallion himself who made this plan impossible. Overtake the rushing train he would and did, but approach it closely he would not. The snort of the exhaust, the grinding of the iron wheels, the fiery glow coming from firebox and smoke-stack,—all caused a terror in the stallion's mighty breast, which nothing living could ever do. Thirty feet from the iron monster was the nearest he would go, and then only by the sharpest urging. The Ranger groaned bitterly as he realized this,—that the one safe, sure way of averting a wreck was closed to him. But not yet did he give up all hope. His mind, racing ahead over the few possibilities remaining, and the lessening minutes before the crash would be inevitable, made and cast aside one mad plan after another.

Suddenly his chin came up, his form straightened in the saddle. Then, leaning forward, he touched the silver horse for the first time in his life with the spurs.

A shock seemed to strike the great beast's body. The stallion crouched in his stride, then leaped forward at a great speed that not even he had ever known. Darkness, sage-brush, hollows in the desert floor, all seemed smoothed to a perfect level beneath his flying feet. The runaway train dropped behind as if it were barely crawling. Three hundred yards, six hundred yards, a quarter of a mile stretched out between the horse of the desert and the steel horse of the rails. The Ranger, glancing over his shoulder, muttered fiercely, "We can do it, Silver Horse, we have lead enough now! If only that pay-train doesn't get here too soon,—"

Far down the track a single spark of light winked into being, disappeared, winked again, and grew into a steady gleaming eye. Headlight aglow, the pay-train was coming to its rendezvous. But hardly had its light appeared when the Ranger pulled Silver to a sliding, dusty stop, threw himself from the saddle, and snatching his rifle from its leather boot, leaped toward the tracks.

A desperate moment passed as the Ranger searched up and down the dim rails; then with a shout of relief he bounded toward a switch that led from the main track on to an old siding. There, jamming the muzzle of his rifle into the opening beside the steel "frog," he braced himself and pried with straining muscles. The frog, long disused, was rusty, clogged with sand. It did not budge. With breath whistling through his clenched teeth, the Ranger heaved again. The gun muzzle bent, snapped off. The broken end was jammed again into the frog. Another heave on the creaking stock,—and gratingly the frog moved into place.

The Ranger jumped back, sweat streaming down his face and soaking his clothing. But as he jumped, he noted with a quick satisfied glance, that the eastern end of the old siding had been torn up, so that its track broke off abruptly into the desert sand.

An instant later, the runaway engine passed him, plunging its single car over the switch, onto the siding, and off the tracks, where it seemed to stumble, and then topple slowly on to its side, well away from the main track.

The Lone Ranger paused hardly an instant before racing back to where Silver awaited him, flanks still heaving after his desperate run. Once in the saddle, his rider urged him again at a swift canter down the track, while he made certain preparations involving the bow and the strangely-tipped arrows in their canvas quivers.

There would be no collision now, no halting of the pay-car in a jumbled pile of smashed steel and broken bodies, no massacre of the stunned guards, no easy looting of the train whose gleaming headlight showed brighter and nearer every second. But the Ranger's work was not yet done. The drink-mad savages might still attack, pouring bullets and arrows into the train windows and perhaps wounding the engine-crew with a lucky shot. That must be prevented if possible.

As the Ranger galloped onward through the night, his Indian bow ready-strung for use, he finished his preparations by drawing a cigar from his breast-pocket and lighting it with an old-fashioned sulphur match, which even the wind of his passage could not blow out.

As he had suspected would happen, a pandemonium of yells and shouts broke out suddenly beside the oncoming train a quarter of a mile away. Even at that distance, the Lone Ranger could make out a dim blot of shadow keeping pace with the headlight, and knew it to be the mob of mounted savages. He pulled Silver's head sharply to the right, away from the tracks, drew the great horse down to a slow canter, and extracting a bulky-headed arrow from his right-hand quiver, touched the middle section of it to his glowing cigar. The instant it sputtered, he nocked it to the bowstring and shot it in a long, descending curve. Striking the ground at a point not far from the rails, the "arrow" burst into flaming red light. A dozen more followed it, striking at various places in the path of the approaching raiders. Sometimes the red flare broke out in mid-air before it struck the earth, and there continued to light up the ground for many yards about.

The Ranger's next move was to ride still closer to the already alarmed raiders. Galloping parallel with them now, but still far enough out to be hidden by dark-ness, he began to draw arrows from the left-hand quiver, and after touching each fuse briefly to his glowing cigar tip, to shoot them over the heads of the bewildered savages. One after another, white lights exploded in ear-shattering thunder over their heads.

The short-fused dynamite fastened to the Ranger's arrowheads gave the effect of an artillery bombardment. Once or twice the improvised bombs exploded almost in the middle of the redskins' party. Horses leaped, bucked, and screamed. Their riders, as often as not, dropped rifle or hunting bow and rode madly, regardless of direction. Several redskins were thrown by their frantic beasts and left to make their way home on foot. In five minutes after its beginning, the drunken but dangerous raid on the pay-train had been demoralized, scattered, and changed into separate units of half-deafened, thoroughly scared Indians, whose one idea was to put more and more landscape between themselves and the train which they had hoped to rob. The three "white" outlaws who had led the raid were more angry than scared, to be sure, yet they had no choice except to follow their red friends' flight.

The pay-train rolled onward at half speed, its crew realizing the danger of halting when attacked unless some obstacle thrown across the rails were barring the way. The fact that no such obstacle existed was revealed not only by the glow of the headlight but by the light of the still-burning flares which the Ranger had shot into the ground. When the last red flare was passed the puzzled but relieved engine-man re-opened his throttle to full speed, the payroll guards laid aside their rifles and stared at one another with bewildered expressions, the wheels beneath them beat a swifter, more confident rhythm upon the steel rails; and the pay-train, with only a few broken windows to show for its narrow escape, rushed safely toward its destination.

Somewhere out on the prairie, a dusty rider on a panting, sweat-streaked silver horse, gazed after the vanishing tail-light, and laughed silently, "Thanks to you, Silver Pony, there's another good job done, and done to the Queen's taste,—though probably Gunner Maxim & Company won't see it quite that way. Hi-Yo, Silver, away!"

QUESTIONS

Language

1. What do these words and expressions mean: *dyspeptic* (p. 289); *knight-errant* (p. 289); *stared out of countenance* (p. 290).
2. What is Striker's attitude toward the Indians (excluding Tonto) in this excerpt from the novel? Look at the language with which the author describes and refers to them on p. 293.
3. Twice the Ranger refers to the action he's going to take as "our little game" and "fun"; Clem calls the hero's equipment "playthings." What does this choice of words and the Ranger's secrecy about his plans tell us about him? Does Dave see him differently?
4. Look at the conversations between the Ranger and Clem, Clem and Dave, and Dave and Kate. How well does Striker handle dialogue? Is the dialogue fresh, interesting, lively, *natural?* Explain.
5. Sometimes a writer must repeat or recapitulate portions of his story to remind readers of important events. It must be done in such a way that it seems a natural part of the story; the readers must not think it is aimed directly at them. The dialogue between Clem and Dave about Kate (see p. 289) is an example of recapitulation. Is it skillfully done? Justify your opinion.

Content

1. Does Clem seem realistically drawn to you? How about Dave and Kate? Explain.
2. Why won't Silver approach the "iron monster"? Do you find yourself disappointed in the horse? Why would Striker choose to have the horse balk at this crucial moment?
3. Why doesn't Striker spend more time on the "love scene" between Dave and Kate? Why don't they declare their love more openly and with greater emotion? Do Kate and Dave seem well matched? Do you think they will be happy together? Explain.
4. Why do you think the Lone Ranger never takes any public credit for his heroic actions?

Suggestions for Writing

1. Can you think of any current analogies to the Lone Ranger? (They need not necessarily be cowboys or Wild West lawmen.) Take your examples from films, television, comics, and novels; then write an essay about these contemporary Lone Rangers, saying in what respects they are similar to him. Consider their personality and moral character, their relationship to and their function within a community, their adversaries, their actions, and their rewards.
2. Write an essay about the appeal of the cowboy to Americans. Fran Striker's Lone Ranger first thundered across the airwaves in 1933, long after the West was settled, paved, and "citified." America invented the Western movie; one of the advertising industry's most successful—and longest-running—campaigns is Marlboro's poetic evocation of cowboy life. What about the cowboy is so attractive to us? What do you think he symbolizes for us?
3. Describe the typical cowboy in as much detail as possible—his looks, his speech and manners, his actions, his values, his domestic arrangements, and so on. Then compare your description to those of your classmates. Discuss what differences and similarities you find. Where did your ideas come from? Whose picture is clearest and best brings the cowboy to life? Why?

GEORGE HERRIMAN

Krazy Kat

The son of a Los Angeles baker, George Herriman (1880–1944) managed to get himself thrown out of his unhappy home at an early age by pulling pranks which would have made Peck's Bad Boy proud: inserting dead mice in bread loaves, covering dozens of donuts with salt. Out on his own, he turned to a career in cartooning. After producing a string of newspaper strips during the first decade of the 1900s, he had his first real success with *The Dingbat Family,* the saga of a hapless little clerk and his wife, whose lives are made endlessly miserable by the noisy, never-seen neighbors in the apartment above their own. As the strip progressed, however, its real focal point became, not the goings-on over the Dingbats' heads, but the action beneath their feet, for, beginning in 1910, Herriman introduced a little cartoon, running parallel to and below the main story, which focused on the antics of the family's pet cat and a brick-wielding mouse named Ignatz. This strip proved so popular with the public that, in 1913, it was made into a separate feature entitled *Krazy Kat.*

The central situation of *Krazy Kat* (which is generally regarded as the greatest comic strip ever created) has a kind of classic simplicity. Krazy—a cat of ambiguous gender, though seemingly female—is madly in love with Ignatz Mouse who, however, has nothing but contempt for Krazy, a feeling he expresses by hurling a brick at her head at every available opportunity. Meanwhile, the staunch, though sentimental, Offissa Pup, who adores the Kat, spends every waking moment trying to prevent Ignatz from clobbering Krazy. Krazy, however, *wants* Ignatz to smash her; as Barbara Gelman writes, the Kat "lives to be beaned with that omnipresent brick. To our heroine—or hero—it is a sign that her 'li'l angil' Ignatz is constant and true: 'He neva fah-gets,' as Krazy puts it.'' Around this unconventional lovers' triangle, Herriman constructed the enchanted universe of Coconino County and populated it with a host of marvelous characters: Joe Stork, Katbird and the Krazy Katfish, Mock Duck, Don Kiyote, Sancho Pansy, and others. Sweetly surrealistic (the background landscapes, for example, are in a state of constant flux, magically shifting from panel to panel), the strip is full of verbal and visual poetry. Most of all, it is pervaded by the spirit of its saintly hero/heroine, the invincibly innocent Krazy.

© King Features Syndicate, Inc.

QUESTIONS

Language

1. Consult a dictionary for the meaning of these words: *nefarious; coup;* to *couch; susceptible; infamy; marauder; propound; ingrate; purveyor; progeny; proletariat.*
2. What is Herriman's *tone* when he says, in the first comic, "We are moist with tears of pity"? What kind of relationship is he trying to establish with the reader in this and the other comic?
3. Look at the way Krazy speaks. Is her English grammatical? Does her *syntax*—the way in which she combines words to form sentences—seem unusual?
4. What does Herriman gain by his idiosyncratic spelling?
5. There are many elements of humor in these comics. Do you feel that the narrator's and his characters' *language* contribute to the humorous effect? Explain.

Content

1. What do you think Herriman's attitude is toward his characters Krazy Kat and Ignatz Mouse? In the first comic he calls Ignatz evil, infamous, and nefarious. Do you think Herriman really feels this way? How do you know?
2. Describe Krazy. Do we see different aspects of her in each comic? Which comic best illustrates her innocence?
3. Define the word *improbability.* Where do you find improbability in these comics? How does it contribute to their humor?
4. Discuss how Herriman's artwork contributes to the comic effect of his stories.
5. Do you think another animal—a dog, for example—would better fit the role the artist assigns to Krazy?

Suggestions for Writing

1. What is the point of each of these comics? What does each of them mean? Write an essay comparing and contrasting what each of these comics is trying to say to us.
2. Although Krazy never gets her mouse—never gets anything at all from Ignatz except hundreds of bone-splitting bricks—poet e.e. cummings says, in an essay on the Herriman comic strip, "If you're going to pity anyone, the last anyone to pity is our loving heroine, Krazy Kat. . . . The person to really pity (if really pity you must) is Ignatz. Poor villain!" In an essay, agree or disagree with e.e. cummings. (It might help to imagine two human beings in essentially the same kind of relationship.)
3. As we point out in our headnote, Krazy is of indeterminate sex: Herriman himself treated her sometimes as male, sometimes as female. Yet most people have persistently imagined her as female. Write an essay analyzing the reasons for this. Is there something in Krazy's behavior or situation that seems "female"?
4. Have you ever been deeply attracted or devoted to someone who didn't return your affection at all? Or, have you ever tried, without much initial success, to discourage the affections of a person you disliked? Describe the experience—the emotions you felt, some of your typical encounters with the other person—and indicate what you learned from it.

L. FRANK BAUM

from *The Wonderful Wizard of Oz*

Considering that Lewis Frank Baum (1856–1919) was afflicted from childhood on with a serious heart ailment and suffered recurrent debilitating attacks of the disease, his life was exceptionally active. In his early years, he worked at a remarkable variety of jobs: newspaper publisher, poultry breeder, actor, general store owner, salesman, opera house manager. He also tried his hand at writing, turning out plays, newspaper articles, and "how-to" books on subjects ranging from chicken raising to the art of shop window decoration.

According to legend, it was his mother-in-law, the prominent suffragette, Mathilda Joslyn Gage, who first encouraged Baum to write down the fairy tales she heard him tell to his children. In any event, the publication of *Father Goose: His Book* in 1899 and *The Wonderful Wizard of Oz* in 1900 brought Baum his first real success, both books becoming immediate children's best-sellers. In 1902, a "musical extravaganza" based on *The Wonderful Wizard of Oz* opened in Chicago and was a hit, moving to New York in 1903 and running for nine years.

Baum, however, was afflicted with more than a heart disease. Like many of his contemporaries in turn-of-the-century America, he was a compulsive quester for instantaneous wealth, filled with innumerable get-rich-quick schemes: theatrical sequels to the stage version of *The Wonderful Wizard of Oz,* a grandiose slide show called the "Fairylogue," movie versions of his stories, plans for an elaborate amusement park. Most of these ventures ended disastrously, and Baum fell back on his storytelling gifts to recoup his losses. His most successful works and the ones he is best remembered for are the fourteen novels in the Oz series.

The Wonderful Wizard of Oz, the basis of the famous 1939 MGM movie starring Judy Garland, concerns the adventures of Dorothy, a young girl transported by a tornado from her drab Kansas farm, where she lives with her Aunt Em and Uncle Henry, to the magical land of Oz. Arriving in the country of the Munchkins with her dog Toto, she learns that the only person who might be able to help her return home is the marvelous Wizard who lives in the Emerald City. And so she sets off along the Yellow Brick Road. Before she gets very far, she comes upon a Scarecrow with no brains, who decides to accompany her on her quest in the hope that the Wizard will provide him with the wisdom he believes he lacks. Later, Dorothy and the Scarecrow are joined by two more questers: a Tin Woodman who is seeking a heart and a Cowardly Lion who hopes to acquire some courage.

HOW DOROTHY SAVED THE SCARECROW

There were several roads near by, but it did not take her long to find the one paved with yellow brick. Within a short time she was walking briskly toward the Emerald City, her silver shoes tinkling merrily on the hard, yellow roadbed.

The sun shone bright and the birds sang sweet and Dorothy did not feel nearly as bad as you might think a little girl would who had been suddenly whisked away from her own country and set down in the midst of a strange land.

She was surprised, as she walked along, to see how pretty the country was about her. There were neat fences at the sides of the road, painted a dainty blue color, and beyond them were fields of grain and vegetables in abundance. Evidently the Munchkins were good farmers and able to raise large crops. Once in a while she would pass a house, and the people came out to look at her and bow low as she went by; for everyone knew she had been the means of destroying the wicked witch and setting them free from bondage. The houses of the Munchkins were odd looking dwellings, for each was round, with a big dome for a roof. All were painted blue, for in this country of the East blue was the favorite color.

When she had gone several miles she thought she would stop to rest, and so climbed to the top of the fence beside the road and sat down. There was a great cornfield beyond the fence, and not far away she saw a Scarecrow, placed high on a pole to keep the birds from the ripe corn.

Dorothy leaned her chin upon her hand and gazed thoughtfully at the Scarecrow. Its head was a small sack stuffed with straw, with eyes, nose and mouth painted on it to represent a face. An old, pointed blue hat, that had belonged to some Munchkin, was perched on this head, and the rest of the figure was a blue suit of clothes, worn and faded, which had also been stuffed with straw. On the feet were some old boots with blue tops, such as every man wore in this country, and the figure was raised above the stalks of corn by means of the pole stuck up its back.

While Dorothy was looking earnestly into the queer, painted face of the Scarecrow, she was surprised to see one of the eyes slowly wink at her. She thought she must have been mistaken, at first, for none of the scarecrows in Kansas ever wink; but presently the figure nodded its head to her in a friendly way. Then she climbed down from the fence and walked up to it, while Toto ran around the pole and barked.

"Good day," said the Scarecrow, in a rather husky voice.

"Did you speak?" asked the girl, in wonder.

"Certainly," answered the Scarecrow; "how do you do?"

"I'm pretty well, thank you," replied Dorothy, politely; "how do you do?"

"I'm not feeling well," said the Scarecrow, with a smile, "for it is very tedious being perched up here night and day to scare away crows."

"Can't you get down?" asked Dorothy.

"No, for this pole is stuck up my back. If you will please take away the pole I shall be greatly obliged to you."

Dorothy reached up both arms and lifted the figure off the pole; for, being stuffed with straw, it was quite light.

"Thank you very much," said the Scarecrow, when he had been set down on the ground. "I feel like a new man."

Dorothy was puzzled at this, for it sounded queer to hear a stuffed man speak, and to see him bow and walk along beside her.

"Who are you?" asked the Scarecrow, when he had stretched himself and yawned, "and where are you going?"

"My name is Dorothy," said the girl, "and I am going to the Emerald City, to ask the great Oz to send me back to Kansas."

"Where is the Emerald City?" he enquired; "and who is Oz?"

"Why, don't you know?" she returned, in surprise.

"No, indeed; I don't know anything. You see, I am stuffed, so I have no brains at all," he answered, sadly.

"Oh," said Dorothy; "I'm awfully sorry for you."

"Do you think," he asked, "if I go to the Emerald City with you, that the great Oz would give me some brains?"

"I cannot tell," she returned; "but you may come with me, if you like. If Oz will not give you any brains you will be no worse off than you are now."

"That is true," said the Scarecrow. "You see," he continued, confidentially, "I don't mind my legs and arms and body being stuffed, because I cannot get hurt. If anyone treads on my toes or sticks a pin into me, it doesn't matter, for I can't feel it. But I do not want people to call me a fool, and if my head stays stuffed with straw instead of with brains, as yours is, how am I ever to know anything?"

"I understand how you feel," said the little girl, who was truly sorry for him. "If you will come with me I'll ask Oz to do all he can for you."

"Thank you," he answered, gratefully.

They walked back to the road, Dorothy helped him over the fence, and they started along the path of yellow brick for the Emerald City.

Toto did not like this addition to the party, at first. He smelled around the stuffed man as if he suspected there might be a nest of rats in the straw, and he often growled in an unfriendly way at the Scarecrow.

"Don't mind Toto," said Dorothy, to her new friend; "he never bites."

"Oh, I'm not afraid," replied the Scarecrow, "he can't hurt the straw. Do let me carry that basket for you. I shall not mind it, for I can't get tired. I'll tell you a secret," he continued, as he walked along; "there is only one thing in the world I am afraid of."

"What is that?" asked Dorothy; "the Munchkin farmer who made you?"

"No," answered the Scarecrow; "it's a lighted match."

THE ROAD THROUGH THE FOREST

After a few hours the road began to be rough, and the walking grew so difficult that the Scarecrow often stumbled over the yellow brick, which were here very uneven. Sometimes, indeed, they were broken or missing altogether, leaving holes that Toto jumped across and Dorothy walked around. As for the Scarecrow, having no brains he walked straight ahead, and so stepped into the holes and fell at full length on the hard bricks. It never hurt him, however, and Dorothy would pick him up and set him upon his feet again, while he joined her in laughing merrily at his own mishap.

The farms were not nearly so well cared for here as they were farther back. There were fewer houses and fewer fruit trees, and the farther they went the more dismal and lonesome the country became.

At noon they sat down by the roadside, near a little brook, and Dorothy opened her basket and got out some bread. She offered a piece to the Scarecrow, but he refused.

"I am never hungry," he said; "and it is a lucky thing I am not. For my mouth is only painted, and if I should cut a hole in it so I could eat, the straw I am stuffed with would come out, and that would spoil the shape of my head."

Dorothy saw at once that this was true, so she only nodded and went on eating her bread.

"Tell me something about yourself, and the country you came from," said the Scarecrow, when she had finished her dinner. So she told him all about Kansas, and how gray everything was there, and how the cyclone had carried her to this queer land of Oz. The Scarecrow listened carefully, and said,

"I cannot understand why you should wish to leave this beautiful country and go back to the dry, gray place you call Kansas."

"That is because you have no brains," answered the girl. "No matter how dreary and gray our homes are, we people of flesh and blood would rather live there than in any other country, be it ever so beautiful. There is no place like home."

The Scarecrow sighed.

"Of course I cannot understand it," he said. "If your heads were stuffed with straw, like mine, you would probably all live in the beautiful places, and then Kansas would have no people at all. It is fortunate for Kansas that you have brains."

"Won't you tell me a story, while we are resting?" asked the child.

The Scarecrow looked at her reproachfully, and answered,

"My life has been so short that I really know nothing whatever. I was only made day before yesterday. What happened in the world before that time is all unknown to me. Luckily, when the farmer made my head, one of the first things he did was to paint my ears, so that I heard what was going on. There was another Munchkin with him, and the first thing I heard was the farmer saying,

" 'How do you like those ears?'

" 'They aren't straight,' answered the other.

" 'Never mind,' said the farmer; 'they are ears just the same,' which was true enough.

" 'Now I'll make the eyes,' said the farmer. So he painted my right eye, and as soon as it was finished I found myself looking at him and at everything around me with a great deal of curiosity, for this was my first glimpse of the world.

" 'That's a rather pretty eye,' remarked the Munchkin who was watching the farmer; 'blue paint is just the color for eyes.'

" 'I think I'll make the other a little bigger,' said the farmer; and when the second eye was done I could see much better than before. Then he made my nose and my mouth; but I did not speak, because at that time I didn't know what a mouth was for. I had the fun of watching them make my body and my arms and legs; and when they fastened on my head, at last, I felt very proud, for I thought I was just as good a man as anyone.

" 'This fellow will scare the crows fast enough,' said the farmer; 'he looks just like a man.'

" 'Why, he is a man,' said the other, and I quite agreed with him. The farmer carried me under his arm to the cornfield, and set me up on a tall stick, where you found me. He and his friend soon after walked away and left me alone.

"I did not like to be deserted this way; so I tried to walk after them, but my feet would not touch the ground, and I was forced to stay on that pole. It was a lonely life to lead, for I had nothing to think of, having been made such a little while before. Many crows and other birds flew into the cornfield, but as soon as they saw me they flew away again, thinking I was a Munchkin; and this pleased me and made me feel that I was quite an important person. By and by an old crow flew near me, and after looking at me carefully he perched upon my shoulder and said,

" 'I wonder if that farmer thought to fool me in this clumsy manner. Any crow of sense could see that you are only stuffed with straw.' Then he hopped down at my feet and ate all the corn he wanted. The other birds, seeing he was not harmed by me, came to eat the corn too, so in a short time there was a great flock of them about me.

"I felt sad at this, for it showed I was not such a good Scarecrow after all; but the old crow comforted me, saying: 'If you only had brains in your head you would be as good a man as any of them, and a better man than some of them. Brains are the only things worth having in this world, no matter whether one is a crow or a man.'

"After the crows had gone I thought this over, and decided I would try hard to get some brains. By good luck, you came along and pulled me off the stake, and from what you say I am sure the great Oz will give me brains as soon as we get to the Emerald City."

"I hope so," said Dorothy, earnestly, "since you seem anxious to have them."

"Oh yes; I am anxious," returned the Scarecrow. "It is such an uncomfortable feeling to know one is a fool."

"Well," said the girl, "let us go." And she handed the basket to the Scarecrow.

There were no fences at all by the road side now, and the land was rough and untilled. Towards evening they came to a great forest, where the trees grew so big and close together that their branches met over the road of yellow brick. It was almost dark under the trees, for the branches shut out the daylight; but the travellers did not stop, and went on into the forest.

"If this road goes in, it must come out," said the Scarecrow, "and as the Emerald City is at the other end of the road, we must go wherever it leads us."

"Anyone would know that," said Dorothy.

"Certainly; that is why I know it," returned the Scarecow. "If it required brains to figure it out, I never should have said it."

After an hour or so the light faded away, and they found themselves stumbling along in the darkness. Dorothy could not see at all, but Toto could, for some dogs see very well in the dark; and the Scarecrow declared he could see as well as by day. So she took hold of his arm, and managed to get along fairly well.

"If you see any house, or any place where we can pass the night," she said, "you must tell me; for it is very uncomfortable walking in the dark."

Soon after the Scarecrow stopped.

"I see a little cottage at the right of us," he said, "built of logs and branches. Shall we go there?"

"Yes, indeed;" answered the child. "I am all tired out."

So the Scarecrow led her through the trees until they reached the cottage, and Dorothy entered and found a bed of dried leaves in one corner. She lay down at once, and with Toto beside her soon fell into a sound sleep. The Scarecrow, who was never tired, stood up in another corner and waited patiently until morning came.

Questions

Language

1. Part of the charm of *The Wonderful Wizard of Oz* lies in its language; Baum skillfully captures the sound of a parent telling a story to his child. Analyze how Baum achieves this effect. Point to specific examples.

Content

1. Describe the Scarecrow's personality. What kind of fellow does he seem to be? Does he react to the new world he is born into the way a human infant would?
2. What does the Scarecrow's first day of work in the cornfield teach him?
3. The Scarecrow is missing a number of things human beings possess. Why does he long only for brains?
4. In some ways, the Scarecrow really does suffer for lack of a brain; he falls into holes in the yellow brick road, for instance, that a three-year-old child would avoid. Point out three or four other places, though, where he proves he is quite wise and perceptive.

Suggestions for Writing

1. The Scarecrow, who can ask Oz for anything in the world, plans simply to ask him for brains, so that he can think, so that he can acquire knowledge and, perhaps, wisdom. How important are learning and knowledge to you? What sorts of things do you want to know? Why? Are you content to know only what you need to know to "get through" college or, afterwards, earn a comfortable income? Does learning bore you? Do you find it exciting? Write an essay indicating what place learning and knowledge have in your life.
2. When Dorothy first lands in Oz, she is not surprised by the magical things she sees— witches, tiny strange people, an endless yellow brick road—and no matter how many marvels she encounters in Oz, she seems able to believe in them all, instantly: her imagination is large enough to accommodate extraordinary things. Do you think a person's imagination becomes less rich and fertile as he or she grows older? Do children seem to you to have more imagination than adults? Write an essay in which you argue either that the adult imagination is richer than the child's, or that it is poorer; give evidence that supports your opinion; and, if you decide that the adult imagination is the less rich, try to explain the reasons for this phenomenon.

JOHN LENNON AND PAUL McCARTNEY

"The Fool on the Hill"

(as recorded by the Beatles)

The Beatles (see headnote for "Mother Nature's Son," p. 179) were not only recording stars but movie stars as well. Their first two films, *A Hard Day's Night* (1964) and *Help!* (1965), both directed by Richard Lester, drew huge audiences and generally glowing reviews. Witty, ebullient, full of slapstick comedy, sight gags, and innocent charm, the movies perfectly captured the spirit of the four musicians whom rock critic Richard Goldstein has called the "clown-gurus of the sixties."

During the latter half of the decade, however, the Beatles—by then the most phenomenally successful entertainers in the history of show business—began to show signs of hubris, an overconfidence, even arrogance, that resulted in some severe errors of judgment. These included John Lennon's comment that the Beatles were more popular than Jesus Christ (a remark which touched off an international uproar); the creation of an unwieldy business organization called Apple; and the production of their third film, *Magical Mystery Tour*, which the Beatles made entirely by themselves. A one-hour movie produced for television, *Magical Mystery Tour* was a sloppy, sophomoric, self-indulgent affair. It was so savagely attacked by critics after its British premier that plans to broadcast it in the United States were scrapped. But, though the film was a fiasco, much of its music was first-rate. "The Fool on the Hill," from the soundtrack of *Magical Mystery Tour*, is the purest expression in rock music of the Holy Fool sensibility.

"The Fool on the Hill"

Day after day, alone on a hill, the man with the foolish grin is keeping perfectly
    still.
But nobody wants to know him, they can see that he's just a fool and he never
    gives an answer
But the fool on the hill sees the sun going down
And the eyes in his head see the world spinning round.
Well on the way, head in a cloud, the man of a thousand voices talking perfectly
    loud.
But nobody ever hears him or the sound he appears to make and he never seems
    to notice
But the fool on the hill sees the sun going down
And the eyes in his head see the world spinning round.
And nobody seems to like him, they can tell what he wants to do
And he never shows his feelings but the fool on the hill
Sees the sun going down and the eyes in his head see the world spinning round.
He never listens to them, he knows that they're the fools.

"The Fool on the Hill" (John Lennon and Paul McCartney). Copyright © 1967 Northern Songs Limited. All rights for the U.S.A., Canada and Mexico controlled by Comet Music Corp. c/o ATV Music Corp. Used by permission, all rights reserved.

They don't like him
The fool on the hill sees the sun going down
And the eyes in his head see the world spinning round.

QUESTIONS

Language

1. Why do the Beatles call the grin of the man on the hill "foolish"? Does the vantage point or the perspective of the speaker or singer have something to do with it?

2. When the speaker says that the fool watches "the world spinning round," does he mean the physical world only? And why does he say the fool has a "thousand voices"?

3. Other people don't like the man on the hill because "they can tell what he wants to do." What do you think this means? Are there some lines of this song that elude understanding?

Content

1. Why do people think the man on the hill is a fool? Is it because of what he does or what he fails to do?

2. Why do you think the fool considers the other people mentioned in the song to be the real fools? Where do the songwriters stand on this question?

3. Describe the fool. What is he like? What does he do all day? How would you be likely to react if *you* saw him?

4. What is it, exactly, that the fool on the hill knows? How large a claim are the Beatles making for him? Why aren't they more specific about his powers and wisdom?

Suggestions for Writing

1. Because the man on the hill refuses to conform to the rest of society—because his values and behavior are antithetical to his community—he is despised and laughed at. Write an essay about conformity or noncomformity; begin by defining the one word or the other.

2. Have you ever found yourself in opposition to a group of friends, classmates, or relatives over some issue? Describe the experience in detail, your emotions at the time, the treatment you received from the other people, and indicate whether you were forced to change your position on the issue.

3. The figure of the Holy Fool was popular in the 1960s, partly because it embodies the notion of "dropping out" from a society whose values are seen as corrupt or misguided. Do you agree with the point of view expressed by the Beatles' song that the best way to deal with the perceived ills of society is to remove oneself from society entirely? Write an essay giving and supporting your opinion.

ISAAC BASHEVIS SINGER

"Gimpel the Fool"

The grandson and son of rabbis, Isaac Bashevis Singer was born in Poland in 1904 and emigrated to America in 1935. He is widely regarded as the most important of modern Yiddish authors, and in 1978 was awarded the Nobel Prize in literature. The world he recreates in his fiction is that of the small Jewish villages (or *shtetls*) of eastern Europe—a world steeped in the demonic and divine. Like the novels and stories of Nathaniel Hawthorne, a writer to whom he has sometimes been compared, Singer's fiction is filled with mystical and supernatural occurrences. "What gives his stories their strength," writes a reviewer for the *Times Literary Supplement,* "is a quality common to all folk literature: an exact literalness about the visible combined with an unquestioned acceptance of the invisible." Singer is, in many ways, an old-fashioned storyteller who writes in a straightforward, vigorous style evocative of the oral tale. "When I tell a story, I tell a story," he once remarked in an interview. "I don't try to discuss, criticize, or analyze my characters." His major works include *The Family Moskat, Satan in Goray and Other Stories, In My Father's Court, Gimpel the Fool and Other Stories, The Spinoza of Market Street, The Magician of Lublin,* and *Shosha.*

The following translation of "Gimpel the Fool" is by another Nobel Prize-winning author, Saul Bellow.

1.

I am Gimpel the fool. I don't think myself a fool. On the contrary. But that's what folks call me. They gave me the name while I was still in school. I had seven names in all: imbecile, donkey, flax-head, dope, glump, ninny, and fool. The last name stuck. What did my foolishness consist of? I was easy to take in. They said, "Gimpel, you know the rabbi's wife has been brought to childbed?" So I skipped school. Well, it turned out to be a lie. How was I supposed to know? She hadn't had a big belly. But I never looked at her belly. Was that really so foolish? The gang laughed and hee-hawed, stomped and danced and chanted a good-night prayer. And instead of the raisins they give when a woman's lying in, they stuffed my hand full of goat turds. I was no weakling. If I slapped someone he'd see all the way to Cracow. But I'm really not a slugger by nature. I think to myself, Let it pass. So they take advantage of me.

I was coming home from school and heard a dog barking. I'm not afraid of dogs, but of course I never want to start up with them. One of them may be mad, and if he bites there's not a Tartar in the world who can help you. So I made tracks. Then I looked around and saw the whole market place wild with laughter. It was no dog at all but Wolf-Leib the thief. How was I supposed to know it was he? It sounded like a howling bitch.

When the pranksters and leg-pullers found that I was easy to fool, every one of them tried his luck with me. "Gimpel, the Czar is coming to Frampol;

From *A Treasury of Yiddish Stories* edited by Irving Howe and Eliezer Greenberg. Copyright 1953 by Isaac Bashevis Singer. Reprinted by permission of The Viking Press.

Gimpel, the moon fell down in Turbeen; Gimpel, little Hodel Furpiece found a treasure behind the bathhouse." And I like a *golem*[1] believed everyone. In the first place, everything is possible, as it is written in the Wisdom of the Fathers, I've forgotten just how. Second, I had to believe when the whole town came down on me! If I ever dared to say, "Ah, you're kidding!" there was trouble. People got angry. "What do you mean! You want to call everyone a liar?" What was I to do? I believed them, and I hope at least that did them some good.

I was an orphan. My grandfather who brought me up was already bent toward the grave. So they turned me over to a baker, and what a time they gave me there! Every woman or girl who came to bake a pan of cookies or dry a batch of noodles had to fool me at least once. "Gimpel, there's a fair in heaven; Gimpel, the rabbi gave birth to a calf in the seventh month; Gimpel, a cow flew over the roof and laid brass eggs." A student from the yeshiva came once to buy a roll, and he said, "You, Gimpel, while you stand here scraping with your baker's shovel the Messiah has come. The dead have arisen." "What do you mean?" I said. "I heard no one blowing the ram's horn!" He said, "Are you deaf?" And all began to cry, "We heard it, we heard!" Then in came Reitze the candle-dipper and called out in her hoarse voice, "Gimpel, your father and mother have stood up from the grave. They're looking for you."

To tell the truth, I knew very well that nothing of the sort had happened, but all the same, as folks were talking, I threw on my wool vest and went out. Maybe something had happened. What did I stand to lose by looking? Well, what a cat music went up! And then I took a vow to believe nothing more. But that was no go either. They confused me so that I didn't know the big end from the small.

I went to the rabbi to get some advice. He said, "It is written, better to be a fool all your days than for one hour to be evil. You are not a fool. They are the fools. For he who causes his neighbor to feel shame loses Paradise himself." Nevertheless the rabbi's daughter took me in. As I left the rabbinical court she said, "Have you kissed the wall yet?" I said, "No; what for?" She answered, "It's a law; you've got to do it after every visit." Well, there didn't seem to be any harm in it. And she burst out laughing. It was a fine trick. She put one over on me, all right.

I wanted to go off to another town, but then everyone got busy matchmaking, and they were after me so they nearly tore my coat tails off. They talked at me and talked until I got water on the ear. She was no chaste maiden, but they told me she was virgin pure. She had a limp, and they said it was deliberate, from coyness. She had a bastard, and they told me the child was her little brother. I cried, "You're wasting your time. I'll never marry that whore." But they said indignantly, "What a way to talk! Aren't you ashamed of yourself? We can take you to the rabbi and have you fined for giving her a bad name." I saw then that I wouldn't escape them so easily and I thought, They're set on making me their butt. But when you're married the husband's the master, and if that's all right with her it's agreeable to me too. Besides, you can't pass through life unscathed, nor expect to.

I went to her clay house, which was built on the sand, and the whole gang, hollering and chorusing, came after me. They acted like bear-baiters. When

---

[1] In Jewish folklore, a Frankenstein-like being artificially created by magic.

we came to the well they stopped all the same. They were afraid to start anything with Elka. Her mouth would open as if it were on a hinge, and she had a fierce tongue. I entered the house. Lines were strung from wall to wall and clothes were drying. Barefoot she stood by the tub, doing the wash. She was dressed in a worn hand-me-down gown of plush. She had her hair put up in braids and pinned across her head. It took my breath away, almost, the reek of it all.

Evidently she knew who I was. She took a look at me and said, "Look who's here! He's come, the drip. Grab a seat."

I told her all; I denied nothing. "Tell me the truth," I said, "are you really a virgin, and is that mischievous Yechiel actually your little brother? Don't be deceitful with me, for I'm an orphan."

"I'm an orphan myself," she answered, "and whoever tries to twist you up, may the end of his nose take a twist. But don't let them think they can take advantage of me. I want a dowry of fifty guilders, and let them take up a collection besides. Otherwise they can kiss my you-know-what." She was very plainspoken. I said, "It's the bride and not the groom who gives a dowry." Then she said, "Don't bargain with me. Either a flat 'yes' or a flat 'no'—go back where you came from."

I thought, No bread will ever be baked from *this* dough. But ours is not a poor town. They consented to everything and proceeded with the wedding. It so happened that there was a dysentery epidemic at the time. The ceremony was held at the cemetery gates, near the little corpse-washing hut. The fellows got drunk. While the marriage contract was being drawn up I heard the most pious high rabbi ask, "Is the bride a widow or a divorced woman?" And the sexton's wife answered for her, "Both a widow and divorced." It was a black moment for me. But what was I to do, run away from under the marriage canopy?

There was singing and dancing. An old granny danced opposite me, hugging a braided white *chalah*.[2] The master of revels made a "God 'a mercy" in memory of the bride's parents. The schoolboys threw burrs, as on *Tishe b'Av* fast day.[3] There were a lot of gifts after the sermon: a noodle board, a kneading trough, a bucket, brooms, ladles, household articles galore. Then I took a look and saw two strapping young men carrying a crib. "What do we need this for?" I asked. So they said, "Don't rack your brains about it. It's all right, it'll come in handy." I realized I was going to be rooked. Take it another way though, what did I stand to lose? I reflected, I'll see what comes of it. A whole town can't go altogether crazy.

2.

At night I came where my wife lay, but she wouldn't let me in. "Say, look here, is this what they married us for?" I said. And she said, "My monthly has come." "But yesterday they took you to the ritual bath, and that's afterward, isn't it supposed to be?" "Today isn't yesterday," said she, "and yesterday's not today. You can beat it if you don't like it." In short, I waited.

Not four months later she was in childbed. The townsfolk hid their laughter

---

[2] A loaf of white egg bread traditionally eaten by Jews on the Sabbath and holidays.
[3] The ninth day of the Hebrew month of *Av.* A day of mourning (which usually falls during August), it commemorates the date of the destruction of the Second Temple in Jerusalem by the Romans in 70 A.D.

with their knuckles. But what could I do? She suffered intolerable pains and clawed at the walls. "Gimpel," she cried, "I'm going. Forgive me!" The house filled with women. They were boiling pans of water. The screams rose to the welkin.

The thing to do was to go to the House of Prayer to repeat Psalms, and that was what I did.

The townsfolk liked that, all right. I stood in a corner saying Psalms and prayers, and they shook their heads at me. "Pray, pray!" they told me. "Prayer never made any woman pregnant." One of the congregation put a straw to my mouth and said, "Hay for the cows." There was something to that too, by God!

She gave birth to a boy. Friday at the synagogue the sexton stood up before the Ark, pounded on the reading table, and announced, "The wealthy Reb Gimpel invites the congregation to a feast in honor of the birth of a son." The whole House of Prayer rang with laughter. My face was flaming. But there was nothing I could do. After all, I *was* the one responsible for the circumcision honors and rituals.

Half the town came running. You couldn't wedge another soul in. Women brought peppered chick-peas, and there was a keg of beer from the tavern. I ate and drank as much as anyone, and they all congratulated me. Then there was a circumcision, and I named the boy after my father, may he rest in peace. When all were gone and I was left with my wife alone, she thrust her head through the bed-curtain and called me to her.

"Gimpel," said she, "why are you silent? Has your ship gone and sunk?"

"What shall I say?" I answered. "A fine thing you've done to me! If my mother had known of it she'd have died a second time."

She said, "Are you crazy, or what?"

"How can you make such a fool," I said, "of one who should be the lord and master?"

"What's the matter with you?" she said. "What have you taken it into your head to imagine?"

I saw that I must speak bluntly and openly. "Do you think this is the way to use an orphan?" I said. "You have borne a bastard."

She answered, "Drive this foolishness out of your head. The child is yours."

"How can he be mine?" I argued. "He was born seventeen weeks after the wedding."

She told me then that he was premature. I said, "Isn't he a little too premature?" She said she had had a grandmother who carried just as short a time and she resembled this grandmother of hers as one drop of water does another. She swore to it with such oaths that you would have believed a peasant at the fair if he had used them. To tell the plain truth, I didn't believe her; but when I talked it over the next day with the schoolmaster he told me that the very same thing had happened to Adam and Eve. Two they went up to bed, and four they descended.

"There isn't a woman in the world who is not the granddaughter of Eve," he said.

That was how it was—they argued me dumb. But then, who really knows how such things are?

I began to forget my sorrow. I loved the child madly, and he loved me too. As soon as he saw me he'd wave his little hands and want me to pick him up, and when he was colicky I was the only one who could pacify him. I bought him a little bone teething ring and a little gilded cap. He was forever catching the evil eye from someone, and then I had to run to get one of those abracadabras for him that would get him out of it. I worked like an ox. You know how expenses go up when there's an infant in the house. I don't want to lie about it; I didn't dislike Elka either, for that matter. She swore at me and cursed, and I couldn't get enough of her. What strength she had! One of her looks could rob you of the power of speech. And her orations! Pitch and sulphur, that's what they were full of, and yet somehow also full of charm. I adored her every word. She gave me bloody wounds though.

In the evening I brought her a white loaf as well as a dark one, and also poppyseed rolls I baked myself. I thieved because of her and swiped everything I could lay hands on, macaroons, raisins, almonds, cakes. I hope I may be forgiven for stealing from the Saturday pots the women left to warm in the baker's oven. I would take out scraps of meat, a chunk of pudding, a chicken leg or head, a piece of tripe, whatever I could nip quickly. She ate and became fat and handsome.

I had to sleep away from home all during the week, at the bakery. On Friday nights when I got home she always made an excuse of some sort. Either she had heartburn, or a stitch in the side, or hiccups, or headaches. You know what women's excuses are. I had a bitter time of it. It was rough. To add to it, this little brother of hers, the bastard, was growing bigger. He'd put lumps on me, and when I wanted to hit back she'd open her mouth and curse so powerfully I saw a green haze floating before my eyes. Ten times a day she threatened to divorce me. Another man in my place would have taken French leave and disappeared. But I'm the type that bears it and says nothing. What's one to do? Shoulders are from God, and burdens too.

One night there was a calamity in the bakery; the oven burst, and we almost had a fire. There was nothing to do but go home, so I went home. Let me, I thought, also taste the joy of sleeping in bed in midweek. I didn't want to wake the sleeping mite and tiptoed into the house. Coming in, it seemed to me that I heard not the snoring of one but, as it were, a double snore, one a thin enough snore and the other like the snoring of a slaughtered ox. Oh, I didn't like that! I didn't like it at all. I went up to the bed, and things suddenly turned black. Next to Elka lay a man's form. Another in my place would have made an uproar, and enough noise to rouse the whole town, but the thought occurred to me that I might wake the child. A little thing like that—why frighten a little swallow like that, I thought. All right then, I went back to the bakery and stretched out on a sack of flour, and till morning I never shut an eye. I shivered as if I had had malaria. "Enough of being a donkey," I said to myself. "Gimpel isn't going to be a sucker all his life. There's a limit even to the foolishness of a fool like Gimpel."

In the morning I went to the rabbi to get advice, and it made a great commotion in the town. They sent the beadle for Elka right away. She came, carrying the child. And what do you think she did? She denied it, denied everything, bone and stone! "He's out of his head," she said. "I know nothing of dreams or divinations." They yelled at her, warned her, hammered on the table, but she stuck to her guns: it was a false accusation, she said.

The butchers and the horse-traders took her part. One of the lads from the slaughterhouse came by and said to me, "We've got our eye on you, you're a marked man." Meanwhile the child started to bear down and soiled itself. In the rabbinical court there was an Ark of the Covenant, and they couldn't allow that, so they sent Elka away.

I said to the rabbi, "What shall I do?"

"You must divorce her at once," said he.

"And what if she refuses?" I asked.

He said, "You must serve the divorce, that's all you'll have to do."

I said, "Well, all right, Rabbi. Let me think about it."

"There's nothing to think about," said he. "You mustn't remain under the same roof with her."

"And if I want to see the child?" I asked.

"Let her go, the harlot," said he, "and her brood of bastards with her."

The verdict he gave was that I mustn't even cross her threshold—never again, as long as I should live.

During the day it didn't bother me so much. I thought, It was bound to happen, the abscess had to burst. But at night when I stretched out upon the sacks I felt it all very bitterly. A longing took me, for her and for the child. I wanted to be angry, but that's my misfortune exactly, I don't have it in me to be really angry. In the first place—this was how my thoughts went—there's bound to be a slip sometimes. You can't live without errors. Probably that lad who was with her led her on and gave her presents and what not, and women are often long on hair and short on sense, and so he got around her. And then since she denies it so, maybe I was only seeing things? Hallucinations do happen. You see a figure or a mannikin or something, but when you come up closer it's nothing, there's not a thing there. And if that's so, I'm doing her an injustice. And when I got so far in my thoughts I started to weep. I sobbed so that I wet the flour where I lay. In the morning I went to the rabbi and told him that I had made a mistake. The rabbi wrote on with his quill, and he said that if that were so he would have to reconsider the whole case. Until he had finished I wasn't to go near my wife, but I might send her bread and money by messenger.

3.

Nine months passed before all the rabbis could come to an agreement. Letters went back and forth. I hadn't realized that there could be so much erudition about a matter like this.

Meantime Elka gave birth to still another child, a girl this time. On the Sabbath I went to the synagogue and invoked a blessing on her. They called me up to the Torah,[4] and I named the child for my mother-in-law, may she rest in peace. The louts and loudmouths of the town who came into the bakery gave me a going over. All Frampol refreshed its spirits because of my trouble and grief. However, I resolved that I would always believe what I was told. What's the good of *not* believing? Today it's your wife you don't believe; tomorrow it's God Himself you won't take stock in.

By an apprentice who was her neighbor I sent her daily a corn or a wheat loaf, or a piece of pastry, rolls or bagels, or, when I got the chance, a slab of pudding, a slice of honeycake, or wedding strudel—whatever came my way. The apprentice was a goodhearted lad, and more than once he added something on

---

[4] The scroll of parchment on which the Pentateuch (the first five books of the Bible) is written.

his own. He had formerly annoyed me a lot, plucking my nose and digging me in the ribs, but when he started to be a visitor to my house he became kind and friendly. "Hey, you, Gimpel," he said to me, "you have a very decent little wife and two fine kids. You don't deserve them."

"But the things people say about her," I said.

"Well, they have long tongues," he said, "and nothing to do with them but babble. Ignore it as you ignore the cold of last winter."

One day the rabbi sent for me and said, "Are you certain, Gimpel, that you were wrong about your wife?"

I said, "I'm certain."

"Why, but look here! You yourself saw it."

"It must have been a shadow," I said.

"The shadow of what?"

"Just of one of the beams, I think."

"You can go home then. You owe thanks to the Yanover rabbi. He found an obscure reference in Maimonides[5] that favored you."

I seized the rabbi's hand and kissed it.

I wanted to run home immediately. It's no small thing to be separated for so long a time from wife and child. Then I reflected, I'd better go back to work now, and go home in the evening. I said nothing to anyone, although as far as my heart was concerned it was like one of the Holy Days. The women teased and twitted me as they did every day, but my thought was, Go on, with your loose talk. The truth is out, like the oil upon the water. Maimonides says it's right, and therefore it is right!

At night, when I had covered the dough to let it rise, I took my share of bread and a little sack of flour and started homeward. The moon was full and the stars were glistening, something to terrify the soul. I hurried onward, and before me darted a long shadow. It was winter, and a fresh snow had fallen. I had a mind to sing, but it was growing late and I didn't want to wake the householders. Then I felt like whistling, but remembered that you don't whistle at night because it brings the demons out. So I was silent and walked as fast as I could.

Dogs in the Christian yards barked at me when I passed, but I thought, Bark your teeth out! What are you but mere dogs? Whereas I am a man, the husband of a fine wife, the father of promising children.

As I approached the house my heart started to pound as though it were the heart of a criminal. I felt no fear, but my heart went thump! thump! Well, no drawing back. I quietly lifted the latch and went in. Elka was asleep. I looked at the infant's cradle. The shutter was closed, but the moon forced its way through the cracks. I saw the newborn child's face and loved it as soon as I saw it—immediately—each tiny bone.

Then I came nearer to the bed. And what did I see but the apprentice lying there beside Elka. The moon went out all at once. It was utterly black, and I trembled. My teeth chattered. The bread fell from my hands and my wife waked and said, "Who is that, ah?"

I muttered, "It's me."

"Gimpel?" she asked. "How come you're here? I thought it was forbidden."

---

[5] Rabbi Moses ben Maimon (1135–1204), a Spanish-born Jewish philosopher and physician.

"The rabbi said," I answered and shook as with a fever.

"Listen to me, Gimpel," she said, "go out to the shed and see if the goat's all right. It seems she's been sick." I have forgotten to say that we had a goat. When I heard she was unwell I went into the yard. The nannygoat was a good little creature. I had a nearly human feeling for her.

With hesitant steps I went up to the shed and opened the door. The goat stood there on her four feet. I felt her everywhere, drew her by the horns, examined her udders, and found nothing wrong. She had probably eaten too much bark. "Good night, little goat," I said. "Keep well." And the little beast answered with a "Maa" as though to thank me for the good will.

I went back. The apprentice had vanished.

"Where," I asked, "is the lad?"

"What lad?" my wife answered.

"What do you mean?" I said. "The apprentice. You were sleeping with him."

"The things I have dreamed this night and the night before," she said, "may they come true and lay you low, body and soul! An evil spirit has taken root in you and dazzles your sight." She screamed out, "You hateful creature! You moon calf! You spook! You uncouth mane! Get out, or I'll scream all Frampol out of bed!"

Before I could move, her brother sprang out from behind the oven and struck me a blow on the back of the head. I thought he had broken my neck. I felt that something about me was deeply wrong, and I said, "Don't make a scandal. All that's needed now is that people should accuse me of raising spooks and *dybbuks.*"[6] For that was what she had meant. "No one will touch bread of my baking."

In short, I somehow calmed her.

"Well," she said, "that's enough. Lie down, and be shattered by wheels."

Next morning I called the apprentice aside. "Listen here, brother!" I said. And so on and so forth. "What do you say?" He stared at me as though I had dropped from the roof or something.

"I swear," he said, "you'd better go to an herb doctor or some healer. I'm afraid you have a screw loose, but I'll hush it up for you." And that's how the thing stood.

To make a long story short, I lived twenty years with my wife. She bore me six children, four daughters, and two sons. All kinds of things happened, but I neither saw nor heard. I believed, and that's all. The rabbi recently said to me, "Belief in itself is beneficial. It is written that a good man lives by his faith."

Suddenly my wife took sick. It began with a trifle, a little growth upon the breast. But she evidently was not destined to live long; she had no years. I spent a fortune on her. I have forgotten to say that by this time I had a bakery of my own and in Frampol was considered to be something of a rich man. Daily the healer came, and every witch doctor in the neighborhood was brought. They decided to use leeches, and after that to try cupping. They even called a doctor from Lublin, but it was too late. Before she died she called me to her bed and said, "Forgive me, Gimpel."

---

[6] Demons.

I said, "What is there to forgive? You have been a good and faithful wife."

"Woe, Gimpel!" she said. "It was ugly how I deceived you all these years. I want to go clean to my Maker, and so I have to tell you that the children are not yours."

If I had been clouted on the head with a piece of wood it couldn't have bewildered me more.

"Whose are they?" I asked.

"I don't know," she said, "there were a lot. . . . But they're not yours." And as she spoke she tossed her head to the side, her eyes turned glassy, and it was all up with Elka. On her whitened lips there remained a smile.

I imagined that, dead as she was, she was saying, "I deceived Gimpel. That was the meaning of my brief life."

4.

One night, when the period of mourning was done, as I lay dreaming on the flour sacks, there came the Spirit of Evil himself and said to me, "Gimpel, why do you sleep?"

I said, "What should I be doing? Eating *kreplach?*"[7]

"The whole world deceives you," he said, "and you ought to deceive the world in your turn."

"How can I deceive all the world?" I asked him.

He answered, "You might accumulate a bucket of urine every day and at night pour it into the dough. Let the sages of Frampol eat filth."

"What about judgment in the world to come?" I said.

"There is no world to come," he said. "They've sold you a bill of goods and talked you into believing you carried a cat in your belly. What nonsense!"

"Well then," I said, "and is there a God?"

He answered, "There is no God either."

"What," I said, "*is* there, then?"

"A thick mire."

He stood before my eyes with a goatish beard and horns, long-toothed, and with a tail. Hearing such words, I wanted to snatch him by the tail, but I tumbled from the flour sacks and nearly broke a rib. Then it happened that I had to answer the call of nature, and, passing, I saw the risen dough, which seemed to say to me, "Do it!" In brief, I let myself be persuaded.

At dawn the apprentice came. We kneaded the bread, scattered caraway seeds on it, and set it to bake. Then the apprentice went away, and I was left sitting in the little trench by the oven, on a pile of rags. Well, Gimpel, I thought, you've revenged yourself on them for all the shame they've put on you. Outside the frost glittered, but it was warm beside the oven. The flames heated my face. I bent my head and fell into a doze.

I saw in a dream, at once, Elka in her shroud. She called to me, "What have you done, Gimpel?"

I said to her, "It's all your fault," and started to cry.

"You fool!" she said. "You fool! Because I was false is everything false too? I never deceived anyone but myself. I'm paying for it all, Gimpel. They spare you nothing here."

---

[7] A dumpling, often stuffed with meat.

I looked at her face. It was black. I was startled and waked, and remained sitting dumb. I sensed that everything hung in the balance. A false step now and I'd lose Eternal Life. But God gave me His help. I seized the long shovel and took out the loaves, carried them into the yard, and started to dig a hole in the frozen earth.

My apprentice came back as I was doing it. "What are you doing, boss?" he said, and grew pale as a corpse.

"I know what I'm doing," I said, and I buried it all before his very eyes.

Then I went home, took my hoard from its hiding place, and divided it among the children. "I saw your mother tonight," I said. "She's turning black, poor thing."

They were so astounded they couldn't speak a word.

"Be well," I said, "and forget that such a one as Gimpel ever existed." I put on my short coat, a pair of boots, took the bag that held my prayer shawl in one hand, my stick in the other, and kissed the *mezzuzah*.[8] When people saw me in the street they were greatly surprised.

"Where are you going?" they said.

I answered, "Into the world." And so I departed from Frampol.

I wandered over the land, and good people did not neglect me. After many years I became old and white; I heard a great deal, many lies and falsehoods, but the longer I lived the more I understood that there were really no lies. Whatever doesn't really happen is dreamed at night. It happens to one if it doesn't happen to another, tomorrow if not today, or a century hence if not next year. What difference can it make? Often I heard tales of which I said, "Now this is a thing that cannot happen." But before a year had elapsed I heard that it actually had come to pass somewhere.

Going from place to place, eating at strange tables, it often happens that I spin yarns—improbable things that could never have happened—about devils, magicians, windmills, and the like. The children run after me, calling, "Grandfather, tell us a story." Sometimes they ask for particular stories, and I try to please them. A fat young boy once said to me, "Grandfather, it's the same story you told us before." The little rogue, he was right.

So it is with dreams too. It is many years since I left Frampol, but as soon as I shut my eyes I am there again. And whom do you think I see? Elka. She is standing by the washtub, as at our first encounter, but her face is shining and her eyes are as radiant as the eyes of a saint, and she speaks outlandish words to me, strange things. When I wake I have forgotten it all. But while the dream lasts I am comforted. She answers all my queries, and what comes out is that all is right. I weep and implore, "Let me be with you." And she consoles me and tells me to be patient. The time is nearer than it is far. Sometimes she strokes and kisses me and weeps upon my face. When I awaken I feel her lips and taste the salt of her tears.

No doubt the world is entirely an imaginary world, but it is only once removed from the true world. At the door of the hovel where I lie, there stands the plank on which the dead are taken away. The grave-digger Jew has his spade

---

[8] A small container of wood, metal, or stone, marked with the word *Shaddai* (Almighty) and holding a rolled piece of parchment inscribed with biblical passages (*Deuteronomy* 6:4–9 and 11:13–21). The mezzuzah is attached to the doorpost of Jewish homes; it is also sometimes worn around the neck as an amulet.

ready. The grave waits and the worms are hungry; the shrouds are prepared—I carry them in my beggar's sack. Another *shnorrer*[9] is waiting to inherit my bed of straw. When the time comes I will go joyfully. Whatever may be there, it will be real, without complication, without ridicule, without deception. God be praised: there even Gimpel cannot be deceived.

QUESTIONS

Language

1. Consult a good dictionary for the meaning of these words: *bear-baiter* (p. 309); *welkin* (p. 311); *tripe* (p. 312); *beadle* (p. 312); *divination* (p. 312).
2. How would you characterize Gimpel's tone in this story? What kind of relationship does he try to establish with his readers? What is the effect of his addressing us directly (as in "You know how expenses go up . . .")? Is he a good storyteller?
3. The *American Heritage Dictionary* defines as aphorism as "a brief statement of a principle; a tersely phrased statement of a truth or opinion; maxim; an adage." Find as many of Gimpel's aphorisms as you can. What do you tell us about the way Gimpel thinks?

Content

1. Why does Gimpel believe everything that is told him? Do his reasons change as the story progresses?
2. What is Gimpel's relationship to his community? How do the villagers treat him; how does he regard them? Is he supported by anyone in Frampol?
3. Describe Gimpel's relationship with his wife. How is she able to deceive him for so many years? How does she finally make amends? Why does she?
4. Look at the scene in which Gimpel discovers Elka in bed with his bakery apprentice, beginning with Gimpel's decision to go home unexpectedly. What details does Singer add to increase the pathos of this part of the story; how does he make us feel even more sympathy for his hero than we ordinarily might?
5. What happens in the dreams or visions that Gimpel has? How are they related to the central themes of the story?
6. Why does Gimpel divide his fortune among "his" children, leave Frampol, and wander over the countryside as a beggar? Does he tell us how he is treated by the people he meets?
7. Gimpel says at the end of the story, "No doubt the world is entirely an imaginary world, but it is only once removed from the true world." Discuss in class what you think he means by this. How has he been moving toward this conviction throughout the story? Why does he look forward so to death?

Suggestions for Writing

1. What sort of man is Gimpel the fool? In an essay, characterize him as fully as you can. Consider his actions and his private reflections, his relationship to his wife, children, and community, and the things he values and believes in.
2. Gimpel imagines, when his wife is dying, that she is thinking, "I deceived Gimpel. That was the meaning of my brief life." Write an essay in which you discuss what the meaning of Gimpel's life was.

[9] A freeloader.

3. Gimpel is persecuted by his community not because of his race or religion or sex, but solely because he is different: he is "simple-minded." Have you ever been the object of prejudice, persecution, or dislike by a group of people because you were different from them in some way that mattered to them? Describe the experience, your feelings, and what you learned. Has it continued to affect your life? Alternatively, if you have ever been one of a group of people who persecuted someone *else*, write an essay about what led up to the incident, what emotions you had at the time, and how you viewed it later. What has it taught you?

ADDITIONAL WRITING SUGGESTIONS FOR CHAPTER SIX

1. Have you ever had a special pet, a dog or a cat, for example? Describe your pet, working in stories of its exploits and incidents that illustrate its personality. What did it mean to you or give to you? Was it ever a Helpful Animal in any way?

2. Every society expects its members to act in certain ways, to value particular things, to strive for certain goals; a man or woman who doesn't conform to these expectations risks, depending upon the extent of the nonconformity and the intolerance of society, varying degrees of social displeasure and contempt. (Sometimes what is denounced in one country is applauded in another.) Before you begin to write the essay explained below, ask yourself these questions: What kinds of things are we supposed to value in America? What are our goals supposed to be? What sort of life are we expected to strive for? Once you've explored these questions, write an essay which paints a portrait of the kind of man or woman most likely to be denounced as a fool by his or her fellow Americans. Remember that this person will not value the same things as his neighbors, will not strive for the same goals, will not even try to live up to society's expectations. He or she will have different values, dreams, and goals; what they *are* is up to you to decide.

3. Argue in an essay (it can be humorous or serious) that one of the following creatures makes a better pet than any other: a dog, cat, fish, turtle, duck, snake, bird, lizard, or frog. Give reasons for your choice.

4. Choose one of the following quotes and write an essay about it. What does the quote mean? Do you agree or disagree with it? Use your personal experiences, observations, and so on to support your position.

a. " 'Tis an old saw, Children and fooles speake true."—John Lyly, *Endymion*

b. "God hath chosen the foolish things of the world to confound the wise; and God hath chosen the weak things of the world to confound the things which are mighty."—1 Cor. 1:27

c. "The fool doth think he is wise, but the wise man knows himself to be a fool."—William Shakespeare, *As You Like It*

5. Have you ever deliberately played the fool or the Holy Innocent to get yourself out of a very bad or dangerous situation? Write a narrative—complete with dialogue—showing the events that led up to your predicament and your means of escape. Don't leave the drama and fear out of your story.

Seven

The Quest

motifs

"At least none can foretell what will come to pass, if we take this road or that. But it seems to me now clear which is the road that we must take. . . . Now at this last we must take a hard road, a road unforeseen. There lies our hope, if hope it be. To walk into peril. . . .

—J. R. R. Tolkien, *The Fellowship of the Ring*

The Quest is the most ancient and universal story known to us. It is a story which reflects our sense of human life as a journey from the womb to the tomb (or perhaps even beyond the tomb, to some unknown, everlasting realm), and as a continuing process of growth and discovery. This journey is, in a sense, a circular one, beginning and ending (depending upon one's religious or philosophical outlook) in either nothingness or eternity. And within that circle, the whole of human experience is contained—all of life's changes, adventures, successes, and setbacks. Few of us, of course, make this journey without having a purpose or goal in mind, for it is a characteristic of human beings that we are constantly looking for something in life, always engaged in a search. The objects we seek may vary widely; indeed they may change any number of times in the course of a single life, so that one person may spend his days steadfastly pursuing a particular goal, whereas another may attain the end he has striven for, only to find after a while that he now desires something new. But in either case, questing—for money, power, love, or meaning—is what the individual's life consists of. In fact, this search for things not necessary to our biological survival is an activity which, perhaps more than any other, *defines* us as human beings. For this reason, the Quest can be considered the single most important of all archetypal patterns.

Like the other archetypes we have looked at, that of the Quest comes in various forms, all, however, sharing certain features. These features have been identified by Joseph Campbell in his classic work *Hero with a Thousand Faces* (1949).

First, there is the character of the Quester. The title of Campbell's study tells us two important facts about this central figure. On the other hand, he appears in innumerable shapes and sizes, from the lowly fairy tale hero, like the humble young son of "The Water of Life," who searches for the magic elixir, to the great mythological heroes like Odysseus, Hercules, and Gilgamesh. Every culture imagines its own version of the hero. In Greek mythology, for instance, he might appear as a bearded demigod draped in a lion skin and bearing a club, whereas a nineteenth-century American hero might be a lanky frontiersman dressed in buckskin and toting a Kentucky long-rifle. Even within a single society, the hero might wear a number of different "faces" or forms. In our own culture, the "all-American hero" might be a cowboy, cop, or private eye. But whatever costume he is wearing, the man beneath it is always, essentially, the same. The heroic characters portrayed by John Wayne, for example, hardly vary at all from movie to movie, except for their wardrobes.

And this is the second point of Campbell's title: that despite all superficial differences in "cultural overlay," the fundamental traits of the hero remain universal and unchanging. He is the person blessed with special attributes—courage, imagination, fortitude, resolution, strength, dedication. In short, he is the embodiment of those qualities which all of us must display if we are to succeed in our searches and win the difficult prizes we seek.

We ought to say at this point that, just as Western culture, because of its masculine orientation, creates intensely negative fantasy images of women, portraying them as vampires and sirens, so it imagines its heroes as men. Throughout history, that is to say, nearly all the great heroes of legend and myth have been males. Reflecting this regrettable but inescapable fact, our discussion in this section will likewise focus on male heroes, though it should be noted that, as a result of the women's movement, female heroes like the Bionic Woman, Charlie's Angels, and Ms. Marvel are becoming more common in the popular arts.

The hero's Quest always begins with a "call"—a summons which rouses him from the comfortable routines of his life and sets him on the road to adventure. The call can come in many forms. Sometimes, a "herald" will arrive at the hero's abode and beg his assistance in, or dare him to undertake, a perilous enterprise. This is a tradition that runs through heroic literature. The action of the medieval Quest romance, *Sir Gawain and the Green Knight,* for example, is set in motion when a fearsome green giant interrupts the Christmas festivities at King Arthur's court and issues a challenge, which the noble Sir Gawain accepts. Similarly, the Red Crosse Knight of Edmund Spenser's Renaissance epic *The Faerie Queene,* is launched on *his* great adventure when a lovely maiden named Una appears at the court of Queen Gloriana, pleading for a champion who will journey to her parents' kingdom and free it from a dragon that is ravaging the land. The call can also be found in many works of contemporary popular culture. We see it clearly, for instance, in the cowboy movie *The Magnificent Seven,* in which the aid of a gallant band of gunslingers is sought by some poor Mexican farmers, whose village, like Una's homeland, is being terrorized by an evil power (although in this case it is a gang of outlaws instead of a dragon).

The herald, however, does not always assume human form. At times it might appear, not as messenger, challenger, or supplicant, but as something completely out of the ordinary—an object or incident which unexpectedly disrupts the day-to-day existence of the hero. In *Star Wars,* for instance, young Luke Skywalker's intergalactic exploits begin with the sudden appearance, at his uncle's "moisture farm," of a strange little robot carrying a cryptic message. Sometimes, in modern works of literature or popular art, the call may take the form of an actual telephone call or telegram. Almost all the episodes of the popular television Western of the sixties, *Have Gun, Will Travel,* opened with a similar scene: its hero, a suave soldier of fortune named Paladin, would receive a telegraph message, calling him away from his luxurious life at the Hotel Carleton, San Francisco, to rescue someone in distress. Many detective novels also start in this way. Sitting in his shabby office, the private eye suddenly receives an urgent phone call—a murder has been committed, a husband has dropped out of sight, a blackmail threat has been received—and all at once the hero is off on his Quest for the solution to the mystery.

There are also occasions when the "call to adventure" is nothing external at all, but rather a feeling *within* the hero, an impulse to action, a craving for excitement. At the very start of the greatest Quest story in American literature, Herman Melville's *Moby-Dick,* we are introduced to Ishmael, the book's narrator, who tells us that he is suffering from an acute case of the "hypos"—a severe depression which he feels he may cure by leaving the monotony of his shore life and setting forth on an ocean adventure. In a sense, Ishmael's experience at the beginning of *Moby-Dick* is typical of that of all heroes, for the call, no matter what its source, outside the hero or within, always means the same thing: that the hero's present situation has grown stale, unrewarding, even deadening. The call is the sign that—whether he is a private eye sitting with his feet propped on his desk, hoping for a client, a knight of the Round Table feeling restless after a prolonged holiday, or a young farmer in a far-off galaxy dreaming of the day when he will be sent to the Space Academy—the hero is in need of a change, ready to move on to something new, unknown, and exciting.

Having responded to the call, the hero leaves his familiar surroundings and enters a different world: he "crosses the threshold" into a region of mystery and danger. The fairy tale hero travels away from his father's cottage and finds himself in an enchanted forest; Kull, the warrior-king of Valusia, journeys from his palace to the forbidden swamp of the Serpent-men; J. R. R. Tolkien's Frodo the Hobbit, on his mission to destroy the evil Ring of Power, abandons the domestic comforts of his dwelling in Hobbiton and passes into the Land of Shadow; and the private eye, from Phillip Marlowe to Mike Hammer, sets out from the safety of his office or apartment to pursue his investigations in a dark, criminal underworld.

It is within this alien realm that the hero's adventures begin in earnest—adventures which usually involve his encounter with the other archetypal figures. We have said that the Quest can be considered the single most important of the archetypes, and this is true partly because the Quest *encompasses* the others. On his journey, for example, the hero may be accompanied by a Shadow figure in the shape of a servant, sidekick, or "lower man." Gilgamesh undertakes the early parts of his Quest with the savage hill-man Enkidu at his side; King Kull is accompanied on his adventures by Brule the Spear-slayer, a "barbarian from the Pictish Isles and now Kull's most trusted friend"; and Frodo's inseparable companion in *The*

Lord of the Rings is the faithful Sam Gamgee, who is prepared to follow his master to "the very crack of Doom" and die with him, if need be. Again, at some point in his Quest, the hero may be seduced from his task by a Temptress. The Renaissance poet Samuel Daniel describes just such a situation in his poem "Ulysses and the Siren," in which the "delicious nymph" attempts to persuade the legendary hero to forego his sea-quest and tarry with her on land:

> Come, worthy Greek, Ulysses, come,
> Possess these shores with me;
> The winds and seas are troublesome,
> And here we may be free.
> Here we may sit and view their toil
> That travail in the deep,
> And joy the day in mirth the while,
> And spend the night in sleep.

True hero that he is, however, Ulysses resists the Siren's enticing words, telling her that fame and honor cannot "be attained with ease," but must be energetically pursued in the world of action and danger.

Because the world he enters *is* so full of danger, the hero, as we have seen in previous sections, is often assisted in his adventure by various helpful beings. He may be aided, as Danny Dennis is in his search for the "golden crocodile" (see Chapter Six), by a miraculous animal, like Rex the Wonder Dog. Or he may be given guidance by a Wise Old Man like Gandalf the Grey, who leads Frodo and his comrades through the dismal Mines of Moria. Or a Good Mother figure may provide the hero with a magical, protective amulet. Frodo, for instance, is assisted in his perilous journey, not only by Gandalf, but by the Elf-Queen Galadriel, who furnishes him with a small crystal phial filled with star-light—a gift to guide him "in dark places, when all other lights go out." And in the film version of *The Wizard of Oz* (an example of a hero's Quest which features a female as its leading figure), Dorothy is protected on her trip to the Emerald City by the charmed Ruby Slippers, which Glinda, Good Witch of the North, magically transfers from the feet of the dead Wicked Witch onto those of the young girl.

The hero, it is clear, needs all the help he can get on the Quest, for wherever it leads him—bewitched forest, evil kingdom, subterranean city, or open sea—his journey is always, in a sense, a voyage to hell, a descent into a nightmarish landscape where he must survive a series of ordeals. He may have to slay a dragon, do battle with an army of demons, defeat a giant or a wicked witch, scale a treacherous mountain, cross a bridge as narrow as a knife blade, or, in more realistic fiction, defy angry authorities or the threats of an entire community. Although the trials he must undergo are infinitely varied, they all stand for the same thing—the difficulties involved in reaching any goal. For the message of the hero's Quest is the one we learn from life: that the prize worth pursuing is never easy to attain, and the more valuable the object, the more arduous is the path to its achievement.

Hence the goal of the hero's Quest, the object he seeks, is known, in mythological terms, as "the treasure hard to attain," and like the ordeals which lead up to it, it assumes an almost limitless variety of forms. It may be a pirate chest, silver mine, fabled diamond, fountain of youth, plant of immortality, holy grail, heart of

D. H. Lawrence.

gold, sleeping princess, long-lost sibling, great white whale, or golden crocodile. Or it may be the proof of innocence the detective seeks, or the punishment for guilt a cowboy inflicts on a villain who has long eluded him. At times, the hero is shown searching for some legendary place: the center of the earth, the Blessed Isles, Shangri-la, or the lost city of Atlantis. And sometimes, particularly in more realistic or psychologically oriented literature, the hero is looking for some quality, condition, or emotion which he feels his life lacks—happiness, love, serenity, wisdom, or meaning.

The great variety of these treasures reflects a fundamental fact of human experience, not only because different people have different objects in life, but also because the things we find important, the goals we regard as most desirable, often change as we advance through the years on our own individual journeys. During the first half of life, most of us engage in a Quest for those external, material objects which will, we believe, secure our happiness and physical comfort. We search for the treasure of wealth in the form of a high-salaried job; for the fairy tale princess (or prince) in the form of a mate who will awaken to our gestures of love, and return them; for our own private Shangri-las in the form of a dream house or country retreat. In later years, however, our values may well undergo a major transformation. Frequently, people who have attained all the prizes they've striven for—a rewarding career, a family, a house full of precious possessions— suddenly realize that the treasures most worth seeking are the ones that can be found, not in society, but within themselves: maturity, inner strength, self-knowledge. To achieve *these* goals they must undertake the hardest journey of all, the one that requires their most heroic efforts—the Quest of self-discovery.

This is the difficult Quest which leads down into the darkness of our own personalities, into the depths of our unexplored interiors. It is here, in this alien world within, known to most of us only in our dreams (our nightly "descents" into the realm of the subconscious) that we must confront and learn to accept the concealed and unpleasant parts of ourselves (our Shadow sides). Here we must come to terms with our hidden and sometimes negative attitudes toward the opposite sex (symbolized, in masculine literature, by the meeting with the Temptress, and, in feminine literature, by the seductive, yet ruinous, Don Juan) and toward our parents (the Mother, the Old Man). And here we must discover our primitive connection with the world of animal instinct (as represented by the Helpful Animal). Compared to such an inner exploration, the search for buried treasure is child's play, for the personality traits we must confront on this Quest for the real self are often extremely painful or terrifying to face (which is why we keep them hidden from other people and even ourselves in the first place). "Explore thyself," wrote the great American author Henry David Thoreau in his masterpiece *Walden*. "Herein are demanded the eye and the nerve."

For those with "the nerve," those who are brave enough and strong enough to accomplish such a journey, there awaits a treasure which is literally priceless: self-realization, the fulfillment of all our latent psychological powers. Scientists report that during our waking hours most of us utilize only a small fraction of our potential mental abilities. The rest remain blocked off, buried deep within our psyches. "All the life-potentialities that we never managed to bring to adult realization" (in the words of Joseph Campbell) are still with us, in the dark realm of our subconscious minds. "If only a portion of that lost totality could be dredged up into the light of day," writes Campbell, "we should experience a marvelous expansion of our powers, a vivid renewal of life. We should tower in stature." Having dived to the ocean floor and discovered a sunken Spanish ship, the treasure-seeker returns to the surface with a chest full of gold doubloons—fortune enough for him to afford all the luxuries of life: a new house, a fancy car, and so forth. The superficial circumstances of his life are completely changed. But those people who dive into themselves and gain possession of the powers and resources which lie buried there undergo a transformation which is far more profound. It is not their property which grows larger but their whole personalities. For those depressed by the sense that their lives are reaching a dead end, those who feel that they have betrayed their youthful promise or that life itself is dreary, monotonous, and unrewarding, the Quest for self-knowledge can bring about a change so dramatic that, as we will see in the following chapter, they may feel themselves reborn.

ANONYMOUS

from *The Epic of Gilgamesh*

The Epic of Gilgamesh is a very ancient Middle Eastern poem, dating back in written form to the beginning of the second millennium B.C., and in oral tradition to the previous millennium. It predates Homer's *Odyssey* by at least 1500 years. Originally written in the Sumerian language, the epic comes down to us in its most complete form translated into Akkadian on clay tablets. The translation was completed in the seventh century B.C. Some 100 years later, the tablets were buried under the rubble of war, not to be unearthed until the middle of the nineteenth century by English and American archeologists.

The name Gilgamesh, which has been variously translated as "father, hero" and "the old one, the hero," belonged to a historical king who ruled an ancient city in Sumer (a region that is now part of Iraq) around 2700 B.C. Other than the fact that he was a great builder, not much is known about him. He was supposed to have reigned for some 126 years, but his son and all succeeding kings ruled only ordinary human terms.

The Gilgamesh of the epic, writes translator N. K. Sandars, inherited from his mother, a goddess, "beauty, strength and restlessness." His father, a king, bequeathed him mortality. It is this gift which haunts Gilgamesh. From the very beginning of the epic we see in him, says Sandars, "an overriding preoccupation with fame, reputation, and the revolt of mortal man against the laws of separation and death." When Gilgamesh's faithful friend Enkidu falls ill, dreams of the "house of dust" which awaits him, and dies, Gilgamesh's terror of mortality forces him

Reprinted by permission of Penguin Books Ltd. from *The Epic of Gilgamesh* translated by N. K. Sandars (Penguin Classics, 1972) pp. 97–99, 99–103, 105, 106–107, 114–117. Copyright © N. K. Sandars, 1960, 1964, 1972.

to undertake a Quest to the ends of the earth. He searches for Utnapishtim, who, rumor has it, has been granted the gift of eternal life by the gods. The result of his journey makes him, in Sandars' words, if "not the first human hero," then the "first tragic hero of whom anything is known."

THE SEARCH FOR EVERLASTING LIFE

Bitterly Gilgamesh wept for his friend Enkidu; he wandered over the wilderness as a hunter, he roamed over the plains; in his bitterness he cried, 'How can I rest, how can I be at peace? Despair is in my heart. What my brother is now, that shall I be when I am dead. Because I am afraid of death I will go as best I can to find Utnapishtim whom they call the Faraway, for he has entered the assembly of the gods.' So Gilgamesh travelled over the wilderness, he wandered over the grasslands, a long journey, in search of Utnapishtim, whom the gods took after the deluge; and they set him to live in the land of Dilmun,[1] in the garden of the sun; and to him alone of men they gave everlasting life.

At night when he came to the mountain passes Gilgamesh prayed: 'In these mountain passes long ago I saw lions, I was afraid and I lifted my eyes to the moon; I prayed and my prayers went up to the gods, so now, O moon god Sin, protect me.' When he had prayed he lay down to sleep, until he was woken from out of a dream. He saw the lions around him glorying in life; then he took his axe in his hand, he drew his sword from his belt, and he fell upon them like an arrow from the string, and struck and destroyed and scattered them.

So at length Gilgamesh came to Mashu, the great mountains about which he had heard many things, which guard the rising and the setting sun. Its twin peaks are as high as the wall of heaven and its paps reach down to the underworld. At its gate the Scorpions stand guard, half man and half dragon; their glory is terrifying, their stare strikes death into men, their shimmering halo sweeps the mountains that guard the rising sun. When Gilgamesh saw them he shielded his eyes for the length of a moment only; then he took courage and approached. When they saw him so undismayed the Man-Scorpion called to his mate, 'This one who comes to us now is flesh of the gods.' The mate of the Man-Scorpion answered, 'Two thirds is god but one third is man.'

Then he called to the man Gilgamesh, he called to the child of the gods: 'Why have you come so great a journey; for what have you travelled so far, crossing the dangerous waters; tell me the reason for your coming?' Gilgamesh answered, 'For Enkidu; I loved him dearly, together we endured all kinds of hardships; on his account I have come, for the common lot of man has taken him. I have wept for him day and night, I would not give up his body for burial, I thought my friend would come back because of my weeping. Since he went, my life is nothing; that is why I have travelled here in search of Utnapishtim my father; for men say he has entered the assembly of the gods, and has found everlasting life. I have a desire to question him concerning the living and the dead.' The Man-Scorpion opened his mouth and said, speaking to Gilgamesh, 'No man born of woman has done what you have asked, no mortal man has

---

[1] The "Sumerian island paradise . . . in the midst of the primeval sea" (Joseph Campbell, *The Masks of God: Occidental Mythology*).

gone into the mountain; the length of it is twelve leagues of darkness; in it there is no light, but the heart is oppressed with darkness. From the rising of the sun to the setting of the sun there is no light.' Gilgamesh said, 'Although I should go in sorrow and in pain, with sighing and with weeping, still I must go. Open the gate of the mountain.' And the Man-Scorpion said, 'Go, Gilgamesh, I permit you to pass through the mountain of Mashu and through the high ranges; may your feet carry you safely home. The gate of the mountain is open.'

When Gilgamesh heard this he did as the Man-Scorpion had said, he followed the sun's road to his rising, through the mountain. When he had gone one league the darkness became thick around him, for there was no light, he could see nothing ahead and nothing behind him. After two leagues the darkness was thick and there was no light, he could see nothing ahead and nothing behind him. . . . After ten leagues the end was near. After eleven leagues the dawn light appeared. At the end of twelve leagues the sun streamed out.

There was the garden of the gods; all round him stood bushes bearing gems. Seeing it he went down at once, for there was fruit of carnelian with the vine hanging from it, beautiful to look at; lapis lazuli leaves hung thick with fruit, sweet to see. For thorns and thistles there were haematite and rare stones, agate, and pearls from out of the sea. While Gilgamesh walked in the garden by the edge of the sea Shamash[2] saw him, and he saw that he was dressed in the skins of animals and ate their flesh. He was distressed, and he spoke and said, 'No mortal man has gone this way before, nor will, as long as the winds drive over the sea.' And to Gilgamesh he said, 'You will never find the life for which you are searching.' Gilgamesh said to glorious Shamash, 'Now that I have toiled and strayed so far over the wilderness, am I to sleep, and let the earth cover my head for ever? Let my eyes see the sun until they are dazzled with looking. Although I am no better than a dead man, still let me see the light of the sun.'

Beside the sea she lives, the woman of the vine, the maker of wine; Siduri[3] sits in the garden at the edge of the sea, with the golden bowl and the golden vats that the gods gave her. She is covered with a veil; and where she sits she sees Gilgamesh coming towards her, wearing skins, the flesh of the gods in his body, but despair in his heart, and his face like the face of one who has made a long journey. She looked, and as she scanned the distance she said in her own heart, 'Surely this is some felon; where is he going now?' And she barred her gate against him with the cross-bar and shot home the bolt. But Gilgamesh, hearing the sound of the bolt, threw up his head and lodged his foot in the gate; he called to her, 'Young woman, maker of wine, why do you bolt your door; what did you see that made you bar your gate? I will break in your door and burst in your gate, for I am Gilgamesh who seized and killed the Bull of Heaven, I killed the watchman of the cedar forest, I overthrew Humbaba[4] who lived in the forest, and I killed the lions in the passes of the mountain.'

Then Siduri said to him, 'If you are that Gilgamesh who seized and killed the Bull of Heaven, who killed the watchman of the cedar forest, who overthrew Humbaba that lived in the forest, and killed the lions in the passes of the mountain,

[2] Shamash is the name of the Assyro-Babylonian sun god. He was worshiped as a god of justice and divination.
[3] The goddess Siduri was also known as Sabitu, "the inn-keeper." N. K. Sandars compares her to Circe (see p. 119): "Like Circe . . . Siduri dispenses the 'philosophy' of eat, drink, and be merry."
[4] In Assyro-Babylonian mythology, an evil giant who guards the forest.

why are your cheeks so starved and why is your face so drawn? Why is despair in your heart and your face like the face of one who has made a long journey? Yes, why is your face burned from heat and cold, and why do you come here wandering over the pastures in search of the wind?'

Gilgamesh answered her, 'And why should not my cheeks be starved and my face drawn? Despair is in my heart and my face is the face of one who has made a long journey, it was burned with heat and with cold. Why should I not wander over the pastures in search of the wind? My friend, my younger brother, he who hunted the wild ass of the wilderness and the panther of the plains, my friend, my younger brother who seized and killed the Bull of Heaven and overthrew Humbaba in the cedar forest, my friend who was very dear to me and who endured dangers beside me, Enkidu my brother, whom I loved, the end of mortality has overtaken him. I wept for him seven days and nights till the worm fastened on him. Because of my brother I am afraid of death, because of my brother I stray through the wilderness and cannot rest. But now, young woman, maker of wine, since I have seen your face do not let me see the face of death which I dread so much.'

She answered, 'Gilgamesh, where are you hurrying to? You will never find that life for which you are looking. When the gods created man they allotted to him death, but life they retained in their own keeping. As for you, Gilgamesh, fill your belly with good things; day and night, night and day, dance and be merry, feast and rejoice. Let your clothes be fresh, bathe yourself in water, cherish the little child that holds your hand, and make your wife happy in your embrace; for this too is the lot of man.'

But Gilgamesh said to Siduri, the young woman, 'How can I be silent, how can I rest, when Enkidu whom I love is dust, and I too shall die and be laid in the earth. You live by the sea-shore and look into the heart of it; young woman, tell me now, which is the way to Utnapishtim, the son of Ubara-Tutu? What directions are there for the passage; give me, oh, give me directions. I will cross the Ocean if it is possible; if it is not I will wander still farther in the wilderness.' The wine-maker said to him, 'Gilgamesh, there is no crossing the Ocean; whoever has come, since the days of old, has not been able to pass that sea. The Sun in his glory crosses the Ocean, but who beside Shamash has ever crossed it? The place and the passage are difficult, and the waters of death are deep which flow between. Gilgamesh, how will you cross the Ocean? When you come to the waters of death what will you do? But Gilgamesh, down in the woods you will find Urshanabi, the ferryman of Upnapishtim; with him are the holy things, the things of stone. He is fashioning the serpent prow of the boat. Look at him well, and if it is possible, perhaps you will cross the waters with him; but if it is not possible, then you must go back.'

[Angered at Siduri's discouraging words, Gilgamesh destroys the sacred stones and the tackle to Urshanabi's boat with axe and javelin, then tells the ferryman his story. Urshanabi informs Gilgamesh that when he smashed the stones, he robbed the boat of its power to pass safely over the waters of death. Nonetheless the hero and his guide manage the crossing, though toward the end Gilgamesh must strip himself of his clothes and, after hanging them from his outstretched arms, serve as mast and sail.]

. . . So Urshanabi the ferryman brought Gilgamesh to Upnapishtim, whom they call the Faraway, who lives in Dilmun at the place of the sun's transit, eastward of the mountain. To him alone of men the gods had given everlasting life.

Now Utnapishtim, where he lay at ease, looked into the distance and he said in his heart, musing to himself, 'Why does the boat sail here without tackle and mast; why are the sacred stones destroyed, and why does the master not sail the boat? That man who comes is none of mine; where I look I see a man whose body is covered with skins of beasts. Who is this who walks up the shore behind Urshanabi, for surely he is no man of mine?' So Utnapishtim looked at him and said, 'What is your name, you who come here wearing the skins of beasts, with your cheeks starved and your face drawn? Where are you hurrying to now? For what reason have you made this great journey, crossing the seas whose passage is difficult? Tell me the reason for your coming.'

[Gilgamesh repeats to Utnapishtim the same story he has told to others, and concludes:] '. . . Because of my brother I am afraid of death; because of my brother I stray through the wilderness. His fate lies heavy upon me. How can I be silent, how can I rest? He is dust and I shall die also and be laid in the earth for ever.' Again Gilgamesh said, speaking to Utnapishtim, 'It is to see Utnapishtim whom we call the Faraway that I have come this journey. For this I have wandered over the world, I have crossed many difficult ranges, I have crossed the seas, I have wearied myself with travelling; my joints are aching, and I have lost acquaintance with sleep which is sweet. My clothes were worn out before I came to the house of Siduri. I have killed the bear and hyena, the lion and panther, the tiger, the stag and the ibex, all sorts of wild game and the small creatures of the pastures. I ate their flesh and I wore their skins; and that was how I came to the gate of the young woman, the maker of wine, who barred her gate of pitch and bitumen against me. But from her I had news of the journey; so then I came to Urshanabi the ferryman, and with him I crossed over the waters of death. Oh, father Utnapishtim, you who have entered the assembly of the gods, I wish to question you concerning the living and the dead, how shall I find the life for which I am searching?'

Utnapishtim said, 'There is no permanence. Do we build a house to stand for ever, do we seal a contract to hold for all time? Do brothers divide an inheritance to keep for ever, does the flood-time of rivers endure? It is only the nymph of the dragon-fly who sheds her larva and sees the sun in his glory. From the days of old there is no permanence. The sleeping and the dead, how alike they are, they are like a painted death. What is there between the master and the servant when both have fulfilled their doom? When the Anunnaki, the judges, come together, and Mammetun the mother of destinies, together they decree the fates of men. Life and death they allot but the day of death they do not disclose.'

[Utnapishtim tells Gilgamesh of his own trying history: how, preserving in a boat the seed of all living creatures, he endured for six days and nights raging tempests and world-wide floods. He doubts that Gilgamesh has as much strength.] '. . . But if you wish, come and put it to the test: only prevail against sleep for six days and seven nights.' But while Gilgamesh sat there resting on his haunches, a mist of sleep like soft wool teased from the fleece drifted over him, and Utnapishtim said to his wife, 'Look at him now, the strong man who would have everlasting life, even now the mists of sleep are drifting over him.' His wife replied, 'Touch the man to wake him, so that he may return to his own land in peace, going back through the gate by which he came.' Utnapishtim said to his wife, 'All men are deceivers, even you he will attempt to deceive; therefore bake loaves of bread, each day one loaf, and put it beside his head; and make a mark on the wall to number the days he has slept.'

So she baked loaves of bread, each day one loaf, and put it beside his head, and she marked on the wall the days that he slept; and there came a day when the first loaf was hard, the second loaf was like leather, the third was soggy, the crust of the fourth had mould, the fifth was mildewed, the sixth was fresh, and the seventh was still on the embers. Then Utnapishtim touched him and he woke. Gilgamesh said to Utnapishtim the Faraway, 'I hardly slept when you touched and roused me.' But Utnapishtim said, 'Count these loaves and learn how many days you slept, for your first is hard, your second like leather, your third is soggy, the crust of your fourth has mould, your fifth is mildewed, your sixth is fresh and your seventh was still over the glowing embers when I touched and woke you.' Gilgamesh said, 'What shall I do, O Utnapishtim, where shall I go? Already the thief in the night has hold of my limbs, death inhabits my room; wherever my foot rests, there I find death.'

Then Utnapishtim spoke to Urshanabi the ferryman: 'Woe to you Urshanabi, now and for ever more you have become hateful to this harbourage; it is not for you, nor for you are the crossings of this sea. Go now, banished from the shore. But this man before whom you walked, bringing him here, whose body is covered with foulness and the grace of whose limbs has been spoiled by wild skins, take him to the washing-place. There he shall wash his long hair clean as snow in the water, he shall throw off his skins and let the sea carry them away, and the beauty of his body shall be shown, the fillet on his forehead shall be renewed, and he shall be given clothes to cover his nakedness. Till he reaches his own city and his journey is accomplished, these clothes will show no sign of age, they will wear like a new garment.' So Urshanabi took Gilgamesh and led him to the washing-place, he washed his long hair as clean as snow in the water, he threw off his skins, which the sea carried away, and showed the beauty of his body. He renewed the fillet on his forehead, and to cover his nakedness gave him clothes which would show no sign of age, but would wear like a new garment till he reached his own city, and his journey was accomplished.

Then Gilgamesh and Urshanabi launched the boat on to the water and boarded it, and they made ready to sail away; but the wife of Utnapishtim the Faraway said to him, 'Gilgamesh came here wearied out, he is worn out; what will you give him to carry him back to his own country?' So Utnapishtim spoke, and Gilgamesh took a pole and brought the boat in to the bank. 'Gilgamesh, you came here a man wearied out, you have worn yourself out; what shall I give you to carry you back to your own country? Gilgamesh, I shall reveal a secret thing, it is a mystery of the gods that I am telling you. There is a plant that grows under the water, it has a prickle like a thorn, like a rose; it will wound your hands, but if you succeed in taking it, then your hands will hold that which restores his lost youth to a man.'

When Gilgamesh heard this he opened the sluices so that a sweet-water current might carry him out to the deepest channel; he tied heavy stones to his feet and they dragged him down to the water-bed. There he saw the plant growing; although it pricked him he took it in his hands; then he cut the heavy stones from his feet, and the sea carried him and threw him on to the shore. Gilgamesh said to Urshanabi the ferryman, 'Come here, and see this marvellous plant. By its virture a man may win back all his former strength. I will take it to Uruk of the strong walls; there I will give it to the old men to eat. Its name shall be "The Old Men Are Young Again"; and at last I shall eat it myself and have back all my lost youth.' So Gilgamesh returned by the gate through which he had come, Gilgamesh and Urshanabi went together. They travelled their twenty leagues and then they broke their fast; after thirty leagues they stopped for the night.

Gilgamesh saw a well of cool water and he went down and bathed; but deep in the pool there was lying a serpent, and the serpent sensed the sweetness of the flower. It rose out of the water and snatched it away, and immediately it sloughed its skin and returned to the well. Then Gilgamesh sat down and wept, the tears ran down his face, and he took the hand of Urshanabi; 'O Urshanabi, was it for this that I toiled with my hands, is it for this I have wrung out my heart's blood? For myself I have gained nothing; not I, but the beast of the earth has joy of it now. Already the stream has carried it twenty leagues back to the channels where I found it. I found a sign and now I have lost it. Let us leave the boat on the bank and go.'

QUESTIONS

Language

1. Look up the meaning of these words in a good dictionary: *carnelian* (p. 327); *lapis lazuli* (p. 327); *haematite* (p. 327); *bitumen* (p. 329); *ibex* (p. 329); *pitch* (p. 329); *fillet* (p. 330); *sluice* (p. 330); *slough* (p. 331).
2. Look at Utnapishtim's reply to Gilgamesh's request for everlasting life on p. 329. What are the various images the old man uses to convince the young hero that human life is always at the mercy of time? Can you make up some images of your own?
3. Note that Gilgamesh repeats the full story of the reason for his journey, with some variations, each time he is asked. Why wouldn't the original recorders of this myth merely have summarized his story?
4. Examine Gilgamesh's lament on p. 331 after he has lost the plant that restores youth. It is one of the shortest speeches he makes. Do you think it is anticlimactic or do you admire its simplicity? How does it make you feel about him? Does he seem different from the desperate young man of the earlier speeches? Explain.

Content

1. Describe Gilgamesh as completely as you can. What are his strengths? His weaknesses?
2. What is the object of Gilgamesh's Quest? What things led up to it? Do the reasons he gives for going on his long journey change slightly as he goes along?
3. In this myth we not only see the world as Gilgamesh perceives it during his journey, we also see him as he is perceived by others. How do these others react to his Quest? What do they think of him? Why are Siduri and Utnapishtim surprised as Gilgamesh's unhappiness?
4. In what sense is Gilgamesh's journey a road of trials? What must he overcome? Describe the garden of the gods he passes through; what is its function in the narrative? What role does the woman Siduri play?
5. Why do you think Utnapishtim is so angry at Urshanabi?
6. Although there is some disagreement as to the meaning of the underwater plant Utnapish-

tim gives to Gilgamesh, many critics believe that it represents the immortality the hero has been seeking. If this is so, why does Utnapishtim, who believes the young man unworthy, tell him how to find it?

Suggestions for Writing

1. Siduri's advice to Gilgamesh is to forget his impossible Quest and instead "eat, drink, and be merry," to enjoy the material things of life and the simple pleasures of home, of children, of loved ones. But Gilgamesh refuses to settle for the common lot of ordinary people; he vigorously pursues a higher goal. Words like Siduri's are frequently offered to idealistic young men and women who, in the service of one cause or another, are forced to give up the riches and pleasures their friends enjoy. With your classmates, discuss the value of Siduri's words. Is she right or wrong? Think of examples of men and women who have given up all the ordinary joys and sometimes even their lives to serve other people. Are they right or wrong? After your discussion, write a paper expressing your idea of what people should do with their lives.

2. Gilgamesh is propelled into his desperate search for everlasting life by the death of Enkidu (in a sense, Gilgamesh also mourns his own coming death in his laments over his friend). Death terrifies Gilgamesh. Write a personal essay about your own feelings about death, your fears or acceptance of it. Include any past experiences that have influenced your attitude. Alternatively, write an essay analyzing, in general terms, America's attitude toward death. Do you think Americans by and large easily accept death and dying? Some things you might want to consider in arriving at an opinion are: our treatment of old people; our emphasis on youth as a standard of beauty; our multibillion dollar cosmetics industry to help us stay young; plastic surgery (face-lifting, etc.) for men and women; medicine's attempts to prolong life, especially in the hospital; funeral and burial customs.

3. John Donne concludes his seventeenth-century sonnet "Death Be Not Proud" with these words:

   One short sleep past, we wake eternally
   And death shall be no more; Death, thou shalt die.

Donne felt no fear of death and could declare that death is not "mighty and dreadful," because, as a believing Christian, he knew that eternal life begins immediately after our last, painful moments on earth. Gilgamesh had no such religious tradition to guarantee him everlasting life and the peace that accompanies it—hence his arduous and dangerous search for someone who could grant him immortality. Write an essay about your own ideas about life after death.

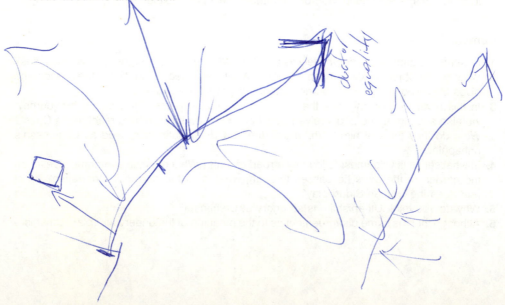

THE BROTHERS GRIMM

"The Water of Life"

"The Water of Life," another story from the Brothers Grimm, is a virtual anthology of fairy tale and mythological themes. It includes such typical characters and motifs as: an ailing king, who can only be healed by a magical elixir; a Wise Old Man who points the way to the cure; three brothers, two proud and treacherous, the youngest noble and unselfish; a perilous Quest, filled with trials the hero must undergo; a supernatural helper who provides the hero with protective charms; a captive princess; an enchanted castle; a task which must be accomplished before the clock strikes twelve; a noble huntsman, ordered to slay the hero but too soft-hearted to carry out the command; and the hero's final reward, his triumphant marriage to the beautiful princess.

There was once a King who had an illness, and no one believed that he would come out of it with his life. He had three sons who were much distressed about it, and went down into the palace-garden and wept. There they met an old man who inquired as to the cause of their grief. They told him that their father was so ill that he would most certainly die, for nothing seemed to cure him. Then the old man said: "I know of one more remedy; and that is the water of life; if he drinks of it he will become well again; but it is hard to find." The eldest said: "I will manage to find it," and went to the sick King, and begged to be allowed to go forth in search of the water of life, for that alone could save him. "No," said the King, "the danger of it is too great. I would rather die." But he begged so long that the King consented. The prince thought in his heart: "If I bring the water, then I shall be best beloved of my father, and shall inherit the kingdom." So he set out, and when he had ridden forth a little distance, a dwarf stood there in the road who called to him and said: "Whither away so fast?" "Silly shrimp," said the prince, very haughtily, "it is nothing to do with you," and rode on. But the little dwarf had grown angry, and had wished an evil wish. Soon after this the prince entered a ravine, and the further he rode the closer the mountains drew together, and at last the road became so narrow that he could not advance a step further; it was impossible either to turn his horse or to dismount from the saddle, and he was shut in there as if in prison. The sick King waited long for him, but he came not. Then the second son said: "Father, let me go forth to seek the water," and thought to himself: "If my brother is dead, then the kingdom will fall to me." At first the King would not allow him to go either, but at last he yielded, so the prince set out on the same road that his brother had taken, and he too met the dwarf, who stopped him to ask, whither he was going in such haste. "Little shrimp," said the prince, "that is nothing to do with you," and rode on without giving him another look. But the dwarf bewitched him, and he, like the other, rode into a ravine, and could neither go forwards nor backwards. So fare haughty people.

From *The Complete Grimm's Fairy Tales*, by Jakob Ludwig and Wilhelm Karl Grimm, translated by Margaret Hunt and James Stern. Copyright 1944 by Pantheon Books and renewed 1972 by Random House, Inc. Reprinted by permission of Pantheon Books, a Division of Random House, Inc.

As the second son also remained away, the youngest begged to be allowed to go forth to fetch the water, and at last the King was obliged to let him go. When he met the dwarf and the latter asked him whither he was going in such haste, he stopped, gave him an explanation, and said: "I am seeking the water of life, for my father is sick unto death." "Do you know, then, where that is to be found?" "No," said the prince. "As you have borne yourself as is seemly, and not haughtily like your false brothers, I will give you the information and tell you how you may obtain the water of life. It springs from a fountain in the courtyard of an enchanted castle, but you will not be able to make your way to it, if I do not give you an iron wand and two small loaves of bread. Strike thrice with the wand on the iron door of the castle, and it will spring open: inside lie two lions with gaping jaws, but if you throw a loaf to each of them, they will be quieted. Then hasten to fetch some of the water of life before the clock strikes twelve, else the door will shut again, and you will be imprisoned." The prince thanked him, took the wand and the bread, and set out on his way. When he arrived, everything was as the dwarf had said. The door sprang open at the third stroke of the wand, and when he had appeased the lions with the bread, he entered the castle, and came to a large and splendid hall, wherein sat some enchanted princes whose rings he drew off their fingers. A sword and a loaf of bread were lying there, which he carried away. After this, he entered a chamber, in which was a beautiful maiden who rejoiced when she saw him, kissed him, and told him that he had set her free, and should have the whole of her kingdom, and that if he would return in a year their wedding should be celebrated; likewise she told him where the spring of the water of life was, and that he was to hasten and draw some of it before the clock struck twelve. Then he went onwards, and at last entered a room where there was a beautiful newly-made bed, and as he was very weary, he felt inclined to rest a little. So he lay down and fell asleep. When he awoke, it was striking a quarter to twelve. He sprang up in fright, ran to the spring, drew some water in a cup which stood near, and hastened away. But just as he was passing through the iron door, the clock struck twelve, and the door fell to with such violence that it carried away a piece of his heel.

He, however, rejoicing at having obtained the water of life, went homewards, and again passed the dwarf. When the latter saw the sword and the loaf, he said: "With these you have won great wealth; with the sword you can slay whole armies, and the bread will never come to an end." But the prince would not go home to his father without his brothers, and said: "Dear dwarf, can you not tell me where my two brothers are? They went out before I did in search of the water of life, and have not returned."

"They are imprisoned between two mountains," said the dwarf. "I have condemned them to stay there, because they were so haughty." Then the prince begged until the dwarf released them, but he warned him and said: "Beware of them, for they have bad hearts." When his brothers came, he rejoiced, and told them how things had gone with him, that he had found the water of life, and had brought a cupful away with him, and had rescued a beautiful princess, who was willing to wait a year for him, and then their wedding was to be celebrated, and he would obtain a great kingdom. After that they rode on together, and chanced upon a land where war and famine reigned, and the King already thought he must perish, for the scarcity was so great. Then the prince went to him and gave him the loaf, wherewith he fed and satisfied the whole of his kingdom, and then the prince gave him the sword also, wherewith he slew the hosts of his enemies, and could now live in rest and peace. The prince then took back his loaf and his sword, and the three brothers rode on. But after this they entered two more countries where war and famine reigned, and each time the prince gave his loaf and his sword to the Kings, and had now delivered three kingdoms, and after that they went on board a ship and sailed over the sea. During the passage, the two eldest conversed apart and said: "The youngest has found the water of life and not we, for that our father will give him the kingdom,—the kingdom which belongs to us, and he will rob us of all our fortune." They then began to seek revenge, and plotted with each other to destroy him. They waited until they found him fast asleep, then they poured the water of life out of the cup, and took it for themselves, but into the cup they poured salt sea-water.

Now therefore, when they arrived home, the youngest took his cup to the sick King in order that he might drink out of it, and be cured. But scarcely had he drunk a very little of the salt sea-water than he became still worse than before. And as he was lamenting over this, the two eldest brothers came, and accused the youngest of having intended to poison him, and said that they had brought him the true water of life, and handed it to him. He had scarcely tasted it, when he felt his sickness departing, and became strong and healthy as in the days of his youth. After that they both went to the youngest, mocked him, and said: "You certainly found the water of life, but you have had the pain, and we the gain; you should have been cleverer, and should have kept your eyes open. We took it from you whilst you were asleep at sea, and when a year is over, one of us will go and fetch the beautiful princess. But beware that you do not disclose aught of this to our father; indeed he does not trust you, and if you say a single word, you shall lose your life into the bargain, but if you keep silent, you shall have it as a gift."

The old King was angry with his youngest son, and thought he had plotted against his life. So he summoned the court together, and had sentence pronounced upon his son, that he should be secretly shot. And once when the prince was riding forth to the chase, suspecting no evil, the King's huntsman was told to go with him, and when they were quite alone in the forest, the huntsman looked so sorrowful that the prince said to him: "Dear huntsman, what ails you?" The huntsman said: "I cannot tell you, and yet I ought." Then the prince said: "Say openly what it is, I will pardon you." "Alas!" said the huntsman, "I am to shoot you dead, the King has ordered me to do it." Then the prince was shocked, and said: "Dear huntsman, let me live; there, I give you my royal garments; give me your common ones in their stead." The huntsman said: "I will willingly do that, indeed I would not have been able to shoot you." Then they exchanged clothes, and the huntsman returned home, while the prince went further into the forest. After a time three waggons of gold and precious stones came to the King for his youngest son, which were sent by the three Kings who had slain their enemies with the prince's sword, and maintained their people with his bread, and who wished to show their gratitude for it. The old King then thought: "Can my son have been innocent?" and said to his people: "Would that he were still alive, how it grieves me that I have suffered him to be killed!" "He still lives," said the huntsman, "I could not find it in my heart to carry out your command," and told the King how it had happened. Then a stone fell from the King's heart, and he had it proclaimed in every country that his son might return and be taken into favor again.

The princess, however, had a road made up to her palace which was quite bright and golden, and told her people that whosoever came riding straight along it to her, would be the right one and was to be admitted, and whoever rode by the side of it, was not the right one, and was not to be admitted. As the time was now close at hand, the eldest thought he would hasten to go to the King's daughter, and give himself out as her rescuer, and thus win her for his bride, and the kingdom to boot. Therefore he rode forth, and when he arrived in front of the palace, and saw the splendid golden road, he thought: "It would be a sin and a shame if I were to ride over that," and turned aside, and rode on the right side of it. But when he came to the door, the servants told him that he was not the right one, and was to go away again. Soon after this the second prince set out, and when he came to the golden road, and his horse had put one foot on it, he thought: "It would be a sin and a shame, a piece might be trodden off," and he turned aside and rode on the left side of it, and when he reached the door, the attendants told him he was not the right one, and he was to go away again. When at last the year had entirely expired, the third son likewise wished to ride out of the forest to his beloved, and with her forget his sorrows. So he set out and thought of her so incessantly, and wished to be with her so much, that he never noticed the golden road at all. So his horse rode onwards up the middle of it, and when he came to the door, it was opened and the princess received him with joy, and said he was her savior, and lord of the kingdom, and their wedding was celebrated with great rejoicing. When it was over she told him that his father invited him to come to him, and had forgiven him. So he rode thither, and told him everything; how his brothers had betrayed him, and how he had nevertheless kept silence. The old King wished to punish them, but they had put to sea, and never came back as long as they lived.

QUESTIONS

Language

1. Often, in literary works, dialogue is used as a means of characterization. Do the different characters in this fairy tale have different ways of speaking? Can they be distinguished from each other by their speech? Does the king speak like a king, the old man like an old man, the princess like a princess?

2. Is there much descriptive language in this fairy tale? Without looking back at the story, describe the old man; the dwarf; the enchanted castle; the princess; the huntsman; the hero. Now, reread the story and see if the written descriptions match your own. Do your think that this story would have been better if the settings, characters, and actions had been described in greater detail? Would you have been able to visualize the story more clearly?

Content

1. Why—and how—does the dwarf help the youngest son? What does he give him?

2. What happens to the good son at midnight in the enchanted castle? In what way is this incident reminiscent of "Cinderella"? Does this story bear similarities to any other fairy tales in this book besides "Cinderella"?

3. What are the two evil brothers like? How do they differ from the youngest son?

4. Describe the test contrived by the princess to discover the identity of the true prince.

Suggestions for Writing

1. In this fairy tale, the youngest son goes on a Quest to find the magic remedy which will cure his father's fatal illness. Fortunately, few of us ever find ourselves in a parallel situation: our parents' lives are rarely in our hands. But their happiness or financial security sometimes is. Many people, that is to say, strive to please their parents or to provide them with a degree of material comfort. Do you believe that children should feel obligated to please or give financial support to their parents, even at the possible cost of their own comfort or happiness? Write an essay in which you explain and defend your views on this question.

2. As in many fairy tales, the hero of ''The Water of Life'' rescues a princess who immediately falls in love with him and promises to be his bride. Based on your own experience or your observation of other people, explain why you either do or do not believe in such a thing as ''love at first sight.''

3. In his book *The Uses of Enchantment* (see p. 433), Bruno Bettelheim laments the fact that few modern parents tell their children traditional fairy tales. Basing your answer on the fairy tales you have read in this book, explain why you are either sympathetic or not to Bettelheim's position: that is, why you feel that fairy tales are either a valuable or worthless form of children's literature.

J. R. ROBERTSON

''The Weight''

(as recorded by The Band)

Though the songs of the rock group known as The Band are deeply rooted in the music of the American South—blues, country, and ''rockabilly''—only one of its members, Arkansan Levon Helm, hails from that region. The other members of the group—Robbie Robertson, Rick Danko, Richard Manuel, and Garth Hudson—are all Canadians by birth. Originally known as the Hawks, the group got its start in the early sixties playing seedy nightclubs and bars throughout the Deep South and up into Ontario as the back-up band for rock singer Ronnie Hawkins. In 1965, Bob Dylan (see following selection), who was then in the process of switching from folk to rock music, invited the Hawks to play back-up in a concert at the Hollywood Bowl and, later, to accompany him on an international tour. When Dylan, following a serious motorcycle accident, went into seclusion in the small, pastoral town of Woodstock, in upstate New York, the five musicians settled there, too. Soon, they became known simply as The Band, and their reputation began to build as other musicians who heard them play—including such rock luminaries as Eric Clapton and Beatle George Harrison—spread the word about their music. Their first two albums, *Music from Big Pink* and *The Band,* are remarkable achievements, containing songs which (as rock critic Greil Marcus writes in

''The Weight,'' Copyright © 1968, by Dwarf Music. Used by permission. All rights reserved.

his book *Mystery Train* [1974]) manage ''to bring to life the fragments of experience, legend, and artifact every American has inherited as the legacy of a mythical past.'' The Band's subsequent releases, however, never matched the brilliance of their earlier albums, and in 1976, after sixteen years together on the road, the group decided to disband, marking the occasion with a farewell concert (called ''The Last Waltz'') held at Winterland in San Francisco.

''The Weight'' is a kind of seriocomic parable, the tale of a hapless wanderer and his cryptic encounters with a string of strange characters who take endless advantage of him. The song first appeared on the group's debut album, the 1968 *Music from Big Pink*, and was also featured on the soundtrack of Peter Fonda and Dennis Hopper's famous motorcycle movie, *Easy Rider*.

''The Weight''

I pulled into Nazareth, was feeling 'bout half past dead,
I just need some place where I can lay my head.
Hey, Mister, can you tell me where a man might find a bed,
He just grinned and shook my hand, and ''no'' was all he said.

Chorus :

Take a load off Fanny, Take a load for free,
Take a load off Fanny, And——you put the load right on me.

I picked up my bag, I went lookin' for a place to hide
When I saw Carmen and the devil walkin' side by side
I said, ''Hey, Carmen, come on, let's go downtown''
She said, ''I gotta go, but my friend can stick around.''

(Chorus)

Go down, Miss Moses, there's nothing you can say
It's just old Luke, and Luke's waitin' on the Judgement Day
Well, Luke my friend, what about young Anna Lee?
He said, ''Do me a favor, son, won't you stay and keep Anna Lee company.''

(Chorus)

Crazy Chester followed me and he caught me in the fog
He said, ''I'll fix your rack if you'll just jack my dog.''
I said, ''Wait a minute, Chester, you know, I'm a peaceful man.''
He said, ''That's okay, boy, won't you feed him when you can.''

(Chorus)

Catch a cannonball, now take me down the line
My bag is sinkin' low and I do believe it's time
To get back to Miss Fanny, you know she's the only one
Who sent me here with her regards for everyone.

(Chorus)

QUESTIONS

Language

1. Find examples of biblical or religious references in this song. What effect is created by the use of such references?
2. Can you find any examples of humor in this song, or is it completely serious?
3. Some parts of this song are difficult to understand. Point to lines in which the meaning is unclear to you and discuss possible interpretations with your classmates. Why might the songwriter have made his lyrics intentionally obscure?

Content

1. Describe the speaker. What kind of person is he? Go over the song stanza by stanza and describe what happens to him.
2. What kind of Quest is the narrator on? What is he looking for? Does he find it?
3. Who is Fanny?
4. Why is this song called "The Weight"?

Suggestions for Writing

1. Have you ever felt that people were taking unfair advantage of you? Or, conversely, have you ever taken advantage of a good-natured (or weak-willed) friend? Think of an example, either from the recent past or from your childhood, and describe it in a detailed personal experience paper.
2. When the narrator arrives at Nazareth, he is feeling "'bout half past dead." Describe a time when you've felt like the narrator.
3. Rewrite this song as a story. Put yourself in the narrator's shoes (that is, use the first person voice). Describe what happens to you in detail. Describe the setting, the different people you meet, how you feel, what you'd like to do, and so on.

BOB DYLAN

"A Hard Rain's A-Gonna Fall"

Along with the Beatles, Bob Dylan was the major musical force of the 1960s. It was Dylan who introduced the complexities of modern poetry to the rock lyric (which before him had always been very simple and often extremely inane), thereby revolutionizing the art of popular songwriting. Born Robert Allen Zimmerman in Duluth, Minnesota in 1941, he adopted the name Dylan—presumably because of his admiration for the Welsh poet Dylan Thomas—while a student at the University of Minnesota, which he entered in 1959. After leaving college the following year, he journeyed east, partly to make a pilgrimage to the New Jersey hospital where his idol, Woody Guthrie, the great folksinger of the 1930s, lay dying. Mostly, however, Dylan was eager to make a name for himself in the burgeoning folk music community centered around New York City's Greenwich Village. Within a few

© 1963 Warner Bros. Inc. All rights reserved. Used by permission.

years, on the strength of several remarkable albums, Dylan had become the poet laureate of the folk-protest movement: his song "Blowin' in the Wind" became the battle hymn of the civil rights struggle, while a whole generation of young Americans adopted "The Times They are A-Changin' " as their own countercultural anthem.

As an artist, however, Dylan himself was rapidly changing; by the middle of the decade he had moved from political protest lyrics, sung to the accompaniment of an acoustic guitar, to dark, highly suggestive, surrealistic verses set to the driving rhythms of rock. Dylan's rock music phase—which outraged his early followers, who considered his shift to electric music a terrible betrayal—culminated in the release of the album *Blonde on Blonde,* which is generally regarded as his masterpiece. Shortly after its release, though, he suddenly withdrew from the public eye; presumably, he had suffered a serious motorcycle accident and required a long period of recovery at his home in Woodstock, New York. (It is indicative of the air of mystery and legend which has always surrounded Dylan, however, that even such authoritative rock scholars as Nick Logan and Bob Woffinden, compilers of *The Illustrated Encyclopedia of Rock,* are unsure of the truth of this story.) In any event, when Dylan emerged from this period of retirement, his music had undergone yet another dramatic change: his harsh, nasal delivery was considerably more mellow, his lyrics were far less savage (indeed, they now often verged on the sentimental), and his melodies were decidedly country-flavored. More recently, Dylan has managed to recapture some of the toughness and brilliance of his early recordings, particularly on the 1975 album *Blood on the Tracks.* Though his newer compositions are of uneven quality, he remains a vital and intriguing artist.

"A Hard Rain's A-Gonna Fall," from Dylan's second album, *The Freewheelin' Bob Dylan,* takes its form from the famous English ballad "Lord Randal."

"A Hard Rain's A-Gonna Fall"

Oh where have you been, my blue-eyed son?
Oh where have you been, my darling young one?
I've stumbled on the side of twelve misty mountains,
I've walked and I've crawled on six crooked highways,
I've stepped in the middle of seven sad forests,
I've been out in front of a dozen dead oceans,
I've been ten thousand miles in the mouth of a graveyard,
And it's a hard, it's a hard, it's a hard, it's a hard,
It's a hard rain gonna fall.

Oh what did you see, my blue-eyed son?
Oh what did you see, my darling young one?
I saw a newborn baby with wild wolves all around it,
I saw a highway of diamonds with nobody on it,
I saw a black branch with blood that kept dripping,
I saw a roomful of men with their hammers a-breakin'
I saw a white ladder all covered with water,

I saw ten thousand talkers whose tongues were all broken,
I saw guns and sharp swords in the hands of young children,
And it's a hard, it's a hard, it's a hard, it's a hard,
It's a hard rain gonna fall.

And what did you hear, my blue-eyed son?
And what did you hear, my darling young one?
I heard the sound of a thunder, it roared out a warnin',
I heard the roar of a wave that could drown the whole world,
Heard one hundred drummers whose hands were a-blazin',
Heard ten thousand whisperin' and nobody listenin',
Heard one person starve, I heard many people laughin',
Heard the song of a poet who died in the gutter,
Heard the sound of a clown that cried in the alley,
And it's a hard, it's a hard, it's a hard, it's a hard,
It's a hard rain gonna fall.

Oh who did you meet, my blue-eyed son?
Who did you meet, my darling young one?
I met a young child beside a dead pony,
I met a white man who walked a black dog,
I met a young woman whose body was burning,
I met a young girl, she gave me a rainbow,
I met a young man who was wounded in love,
I met another man who was wounded with hatred,
And it's a hard, it's a hard, it's a hard, it's a hard,
It's a hard rain gonna fall.

Oh what'll you do now, my blue-eyed son?
And what'll you do now, my darling young one?
I'm a-goin' back out 'fore the rain starts a-fallin'
I'll walk to the depths of the deepest black forest,
Where the people are many and their hands are all empty,
Where the pellets of poison are flooding their waters,
Where the executioner's face is always well hidden,
Where hunger is ugly, where souls are forgotten,
Where black is the color, where none is the number,
And I'll tell it and think it and speak it and breathe it,
And reflect it from the mountain for all souls to see it,
Then I'll stand on the ocean until I start sinkin',
But I'll know my song well before I start singin',
And it's a hard, it's a hard, it's a hard, it's a hard,
It's a hard rain gonna fall.

QUESTIONS

Language

1. This song consists of a series of images which more or less form the unexpected answers to the questions the parent asks. What is the *overall* emotional effect Dylan is trying to achieve with these images? Are there any which arouse a different emotion?

2. What kinds of things do you notice about the sentence structure in this song? If you wrote an essay following the same patterns, what would be the effect? What variations in the pattern do you see in "A Hard Rain's A-Gonna Fall"?

3. In the first stanza of this song, the speaker or singer says "I've stumbled on the side of twelve misty mountains" and "I've crawled on six crooked highways." Why does he choose the verbs *stumbled* and *crawled?* What is their effect?

Content

1. The young man in this song has been on a long journey looking at America. What, essentially, has he seen? Is his America a country you recognize? Why or why not?

2. Having seen what he has, the speaker or singer of this song decides to go "back out 'fore the rain starts a-fallin'." Why? What do we know about him because he makes this decision?

3. Are there some images in this song that are less clear, or less comprehensible, than others? What are they? What do you think Dylan might mean by each of them?

4. What is Dylan trying to say in his refrain at the end of each stanza? Is the refrain to be interpreted literally?

Suggestions for Writing

1. "A Hard Rain's A-Gonna Fall" attempts, through an accretion of detail, a piling up of images, to describe America and at the same time to arouse certain emotions—two are fear and dread—in the listener. Write a descriptive essay picturing the America you see (or, alternatively, your city or town). But use the same technique: create images, as Dylan has done, which convey your emotional response to what you observe.

2. In addition to painting America in rather bleak colors, Dylan predicts dire things for America's future (though these things are merely suggested, not fully drawn, by his repeated warning "It's a hard rain gonna fall"). Remember that this famous song was written in the early 1960s. Write an essay arguing that it accurately predicted what would happen to this country over the next ten years. *Did* a "hard rain" fall on America? Support your argument. Alternatively, make your own predictions for this country; in an essay, imagine America's future.

3. Write an essay comparing this song to a sermon you might hear in a church or a synagogue. A discussion with your classmates before you begin to write should help you formulate ideas. Consider such things as syntax, repetition and emphasis of certain words, exaggeration, mood or tone, "message," imagery, and the attitude of the speaker toward what he has seen and toward his audience.

ROY THOMAS AND
MARIE AND JOHN SEVERIN

"The Forbidden Swamp"

Robert Ervin Howard (1906–1936) was a prolific writer of action stories for the pulp magazines of the 1930s. Although he turned out tales in a variety of genres—Western, detective, ghost, sport, Oriental adventure—he is best remembered today for his "sword-and-sorcery" fiction: lurid fantasies, set in dark, imaginary worlds and starring "brawny barbarians" who, with battle ax or broad sword in hand and scantily clad "slave wenches" clinging helplessly to their sides, hack and cleave their way through legions of supernatural foes. Given the he-man quality of his fiction, it is perhaps worth noting that Howard lived with his parents all his life and was—in the words of fellow fantasy writer L. Sprague de Camp—"excessively devoted" to his mother, who, in her early sixties, developed terminal cancer. The day before her death, Howard visited her in the hospital. Upon hearing from a nurse that his mother had no chance of recovery, the thirty-year-old author went out to his car, took a pistol from the glove compartment, and shot himself in the head.

Howard's most popular creations are the barbarians Conan the Cimmerian and King Kull of Valusia. In the following story (a Marvel Comic, drawn by Marie and John Severin, written by Roy Thomas, and based on Howard's characters), King Kull, determined to rid his land of the monstrous Serpent-men, undertakes an expedition to their sinister stronghold deep in the heart of the Forbidden Swamp. He is accompanied on this perilous Quest by seven stout warriors, including his faithful follower, Brule the Spear-Slayer.

Copyright © 1972 by Marvel Comics Group. All rights reserved.

THEY RIDE IN SILENCE, **WEAPONS** AT THE READY: **KING KULL**, REARED IN THE WILD HILL-COUNTRY OF DISTANT ATLANTIS, NOW RISEN TO THE THRONE OF ANCIENT, DECADENT VALUSIA... **BRULE**, CALLED THE **SPEAR-SLAYER**, BARBARIAN FROM THE PICTISH ISLES AND NOW KULL'S MOST TRUSTED FRIEND... AND **SIX RED SLAYERS**, MIGHTIEST MEN-AT-ARMS OF THE PROUDEST SOLDIERY IN ALL THE WORLD.

AYE, THEY RIDE IN STONY **SILENCE** THRU THE STEAMY VASTNESS, THE BROODING WILDERNESS WHICH MEN CALL...

the FORBIDDEN SWAMP

...AND, WHEN THE **AMBUSH** IS LAUNCHED...IT IS WELL MET...!

DEATH TO THEM, LADS!

DEATH TO THE **SERPENTS** WHO WALK LIKE **MEN**!

Stan Lee ✱ Roy Thomas
EDITOR   WRITER

Marie and John Severin
ARTISTS

Artie Simek
LETTERER

BASED ON CHARACTERS CREATED BY:
Robert E. Howard

"IT IS *OVER*."

"BUT *FEAR NOT*, DURON... FOR SOON, YOUR SPIRIT SHALL REST *EASY*...YOUR NOBLE DEATH BE *AVENGED*..."

"...WHEN THE *SERPENT TEMPLE*, 'CROSS YON RIVER, RUNS RED WITH *REPTILIAN BLOOD*."

THEN, AS TWELVE STRONG HANDS PREPARE A MAKESHIFT RAFT, THE BARBARIAN-BECOMING-MONARCH DRAWS FORTH A GLEAMING JEWEL...AND GAZES DEEP INTO IT...

WHAT SEES KING KULL WITHIN THE MANY-FACETED RECESSES OF THE SERPENT-EYE GEM, STOLEN YEARS AGONE BY PICTS FROM THE GRIM TEMPLE WHICH LOOMS BEYOND THE WRITHING WATERS?

DOES HE VIEW THE SLOW INROADS MADE BY THE SNAKE-HEADED DEMI-MEN IN HIS KINGDOM, ERE HE ROSE TO THWART THEM AND ANNIHILATE THEM?

DOES HE GLIMPSE HINTS, MAYHAP, OF THE DARK ROAD WHICH LIES BEYOND THE END OF THIS DAY'S PATH?

OR DOES HE SEE---NOTHING--?

--NOTHING SAVE THE COMBAT AND CARNAGE OF THAT DAY WHEN HE FIRST STOOD AGAINST THEM--

*--THE LOYAL BRULE AT HIS SIDE.**

**AS PORTRAYED IN KULL #2. --STAN.*

ALAS, WE NE'ER SHALL KNOW...FOR, NOW...

"YOU'VE BUILT A *STURDY* RAFT THIS DAY, RED SLAYERS."

"BUT, WHY DO YOU *DRAW IN YOUR BREATH* SO, ALECTO?"

"DON'T YOU *HEAR*, SIRE? SOUNDS...A WEIRD *CHANTING*....!?"

"AYE... AND I DO *MORE* THAN HEAR..."

"I SEE *THREE HOODED FIGURES* EMERGE FROM YON TEMPLE...NO DOUBT THE VERY *PRIESTS* WHO DARED COVET THE *TOPAZ THRONE*."

"THE *CHANT*, I TROW, IS MEANT AS A CHARM TO *WARD* US OFF."

"BUT, THEY'LL FIND IT TAKES MORE THAN *HYMNS* TO SAVE THEM FROM THE *KING'S JUSTICE!*"

3

AYE, AND NOT MERE LOGS ALONE...

...BUT ALSO MEN'S LIVES ARE SNAPPED LIKE TWIGS BETWEEN THE MONSTER'S SLAVERING JAWS...

YET, TWO FORMS DO NOT FLAIL ABOUT IN WILD-EYED TERROR... BUT DIVE BENEATH THE SURGING WATERS...

KULL IS FIRST TO STRIKE....!

THEN, EVEN AS THAT PRIMAL WOUND MAKES THE SWAMP-DRAGON WRITHE IN BITTER PAIN...

...THE WILY PICT, SPEAR IN HAND, DIVES E'EN DEEPER INTO THE FROTHING MURK...

...AND LO, EVEN THE BEAST-THING'S TINY BRAIN WILL LONG REMEMBER THIS DAY AMONG DAYS!

ARE YOU-- WELL, MY LIEGE?

I FEARED THAT-- ENCUMBERED AS YOU BE BY ARMOR--YOU MIGHT HAVE--

HARBOR NO FEAR FOR MY LIFE, BRULE.

BUT SHANNA, HERE, IS BRAVEST AMONG THE RED SLAYERS--AND IF HE SHOULD PERISH--

--NOT ALL THE SWAMP-DRAGONS FROM HERE TO THE LEMURIAN SEA SHALL KEEP ME FROM MY VENGEANCE!

5

BUT, IF I AM TRULY *ENCHANTED*, I NEED THIS *ARMOR* NO LONGER.

YOUR *SLAYERS*, KULL, ARE *VALUSIANS* AND *MERCENARIES*-- YOURS TO *COMMAND*.

STAY *HERE*, BRULE-- WHILE I VENTURE *WITHIN* THE *ACCURSED* TEMPLE.

BRULE GOES WHERE HE *WILLS!*

*N*O WORD OF KING OR COURTIER CAN SWAY THE MIND OF THE WILLFUL *PICT*--AND SO, TWO MEN SET FORTH, IN SEARCH OF AUGHT WHICH MAY *LIVE WITHIN*--

--*B*UT NEARLY FIND *DEATH*, INSTEAD!

KULL! THE *FLOOR*--IT DROPS AWAY BENEATH OUR *FEET*--!

I HAVE THE *LEDGE*, BRULE--AND YOU HAVE *ME*.

NO *NEED*, THEN, FOR *HISSING* TO ESCAPE YOUR *LIPS*.

IT WAS NOT *MY* HISSING YOU HEARD--

--BUT *THEIRS!*

BRULE--GO BACK AND *WARN* MY MEN NOT TO FOLLOW US. MY MAGIC CHARM, IT SEEMS, DOES NOT EXTEND TO *OTHERS*.

GO--OR WE'LL HAVE IT OUT *HERE*, WITH *SWORDS*

NO PURPOSE WILL *THAT* SERVE.

THUS-- I *GO*.

*T*HEN, ALONE, THE ONCE-SAVAGE KULL WANDERS *DEEPER* INTO THE DARKNESS --THE SERPENT-SCENT NEARLY CHOKING HIM NOW-- UNTIL--

VALKA!

*H*IS KEEN SENSES SURVEY THE SCENE IN A MOMENT: A GROTESQUE CARVEN *IDOL*--AND BEFORE IT, A SWATHED *FIGURE*, UPON AN ALTAR--AND ABOVE THAT FORM, *ANOTHER*--!

YOU THERE-- *SNAKE-PRIEST!*

TURN-- FOR *VENGEANCE* STALKS YOUR FETID HALLS THIS DAY!

7

STAY YOUR VENGEANCE, KULL OF VALUSIA! 'TIS NO ACCURSED SERPENT PRIEST YOU SEE BEFORE YOU...

...BUT A MAN OF SCIENCE, AS MUCH THEIR FOEMAN AS YOURSELF.

TO PROVE MY HUMANITY, I SPEAK THE WORDS NO SNAKE-MAN CAN SAY...

"KA NAMA KAA LA JERAMA!"

WELL SAID! YOU'VE SAVED YOUR LIFE WITH THOSE MOUTHINGS.

YET, SPEAK AGAIN-- TO TELL ME WHO YOU ARE.

I AM...THULSA DOOM.

"FROM FAR-DISTANT GRONDAR I HAIL, ON A MISSION OF REVENGE NO LESS SACRED THAN YOUR OWN... FOR, THE SERPENT-MEN DID STEAL AWAY MY BETROTHED..!

"THRU GLOOMY, ADDER-HAUNTED SWAMPS I TRACKED THEM--READY TO TRADE MY LIFE FOR THAT OF THE WOMAN I LOVED...

...BUT, I WAS TOO LATE!

THE PRIEST-THINGS KNEW YOU WERE COMING, KING... AND, RATHER THAN FACE THEIR DEATHS WITH ONE FINAL ACT OF MERCY...

...THEY CHOSE TO SLAY HER, LIKE SOME ANIMAL ON THEIR UNHOLY ALTAR.

THEN SAD I AM, THULSA DOOM, THAT WE ARRIVED NOT A FEW MOMENTS SOONER.

HOLD! THE GEMS WHICH ONCE WERE THAT STATUE'S EYES...THEY BOTH ARE GONE!

BOTH STOLEN LONG SINCE, FOR THEIR MAGICAL POWERS.

NAY, MAN. ONLY ONE IS TRULY LOST...

8

"FOR, IT WAS A SAVAGE *PICT* WHO *PURLOINED* ONE OF THEM, YEARS *AGONE*...

...WHENCE IT FELL INTO *MY* HANDS...

...FOR ALL THE *GOOD* IT DOES *MY* SWORD-ARM.

"STILL, THE *LEGENDS* SAY THAT HE WHO HOLDS BOTH STONES *TOGETHER*... POSSESSES POWER WITHOUT. *EQUAL.*

*T*HUS LOST IN MUSING, THE *ATLANTEAN* DOES NOT TAKE NOTE OF THE SOLEMN *STRANGER,* RECLINING HIS *HEAD* UPON THE ALTAR IN SOB-WRACKED GRIEF...

*N*OR DOES HE SEE A SHINY *BAUBLE* LIFTED *GENTLY,* FURTIVELY FROM THE *DEAD* GIRL'S *TRESSES...*

*T*HEN, BREAKING THE OMINOUS *SILENCE*...

ENOUGH! THIS *TEMPLE* HAS STOOD FOR *CENTURIES.*

THIS DAY...AN *END!*

KULL--*WHAT?* WHO IS--?

WORDS SHALL COME *LATER.* NOW STAND YE *BACK,* ALL--

--FOR *FLAMING* OILS FILL YON *MONUMENT* TO EVIL--

--AND, LIKE A THING WHICH ONCE DID *LIVE--* IT SHALL *DIE!!*

THE NOXIOUS *VAPORS* OF THE PLACE MUST HAVE MIXED *UNTIMELY* WITH THE FLAMES. BUT HOW DID YOU *KNOW--?*

I--SIMPLY *KNEW,* AS CLEARLY AS IF A *VOICE* DID WHISPER IN MY EAR!

BY THE BYE, BRULE ...THIS IS *THULSA DOOM,* OF *GRONDAR.*

THE FAME OF EVEN KING KULL'S *UNDERLINGS* HAS SPREAD TO MY LAND.

AND *I* HAVE HEARD FEARFUL WHISPERS OF ONE CALLED *THULSA DOOM...*

YET, IT WAS FROM THE INHUMAN WASTES TO THE *SOUTH* THE MURMURS CAME ...NOT FROM *GRONDAR.*

THE RAIN GROWS *COLD,* KULL...

SHOULD WE NOT RETURN TO YOUR *CITY OF WONDERS?*

9

AND DEPART THEY DO, PAUSING FIRST TO GATHER THEIR WOUNDED...

M-MAJESTY... GOMAR STANDS READY TO SERVE YOU...

YOU ARE HURT. IT IS RATHER WE WHO SHOULD CARRY YOU BACK.

YOU'RE FAR TOO ILL TO GUARD EITHER KULL, OR OUR HONORED GUEST...

GUEST? WHY-- TH-THAT--

BEWARE, MY LORD! B-BEEEEEEE

LOOK OUT! GOMAR TOPPLES FROM HIS MOUNT --!

HE IS-- DEAD. HIS WOUNDS WERE MORE MORTAL THAN HE SUPPOSED.

PERHAPS...

BUT SOON, AS THE SPEAR-SLAYER CRAVES THE KING'S EAR IN PRIVATE...

THERE IS SORCERY HERE, KULL. THAT MAN DOOM...

...IS OUR GUEST, BRULE, TILL HE PROVES TO BE OTHER THAN HE CLAIMS.

UNTIL THAT TIME... YOU WILL TREAT HIM AS SUCH!

KULL HAS SPOKEN!

THEN, BECAUSE VALUSIA'S BARBARIAN KING IS UNYIELDING AS STONE, THE PICT FALLS INTO A COWED, YET SOMBRE SILENCE...

...A SILENCE WHICH ENDURES THE LENGTH AND BREADTH OF THE ONCE FORBIDDEN SWAMP...

...AND WHICH THRIVES, UNSHATTERED, TILL THE CITY OF WONDERS HEAVES INTO VIEW AMID THE RUMBLINGS OF THUNDER AND THE FAINT, IMAGINED STIRRINGS OF THE EARTH ITSELF...

YET IS IT MERE IMAGINATION WHICH MAKES KULL, AND BRULE, AND ALL OF THEM TO HALF-GLIMPSE, AMID A MOMENT'S LIGHTNING-FLASH...

...A GLEAMING DEATH'S HEAD, BROODING ABOVE THOSE PROUD SPIRES...?

AND IS IT THAT WHICH CAUSES THULSA DOOM TO...SMILE...?

NEXT: **A VIPER IN OUR MIDST!**

QUESTIONS

Language

1. This story is obviously set sometime in a mythical past. How does the dialogue—the way the characters talk—help create a sense of antiquity? Point out specific examples of words and sentence constructions which contribute to this sense.
2. Take a look at the short narrative and descriptive passages which appear in the narrow boxes along the edges of the individual panels. How important are they? What do they contribute to the story?

Content

1. Who is King Kull? Brule? Who are the Red Slayers?
2. What is their mission?
3. Who are the Snakemen? Describe them.
4. Why isn't Kull hurt by the Snakemen's "fire-venom"?
5. Describe Thulsa Doom. How does Brule feel about him?
6. What is the significance of the words "Ka Nama Kaa La Jerama"?

Suggestions for Writing

1. To whom would this comic book appeal more—men or women? Why? Write an essay in which you express your opinion on this question and support it with specific references to the story. Try to explain why this type of story (commonly called "sword-and-sorcery" fantasy) is so appealing to so many people.
2. In this story, different creatures are associated with different qualities: the tiger with ferocity and courage, the snake with evil. Think of examples of animals that represent specific qualities. Then, write an essay in which you classify animals according to the traits they represent. For example, you might have a paragraph on animals that symbolize strength, a paragraph on animals that symbolize cowardice, a paragraph on animals that stand for innocence, and so on. Try to explain *why* the animals you choose have come to stand for specific qualities.

J. R. R. TOLKIEN

from *The Fellowship of the Ring*

Throughout his childhood, John Ronald Reuel Tolkien (1892–1973) was fascinated by the look and sound of foreign languages. Like many children, he had, as a boy, amused himself by making up nonsense words, but during his adolescence he began experimenting seriously with the invention of his own original language. This linguistic interest led Tolkien to specialize in philology during his college years at Oxford. And his attempt to create an entire language—which came to be called *Quenya* or High-Elven—developed into an all-consuming hobby which occupied him throughout his life and became the basis for his best-known writings.

This selection is reprinted from *The Fellowship of the Ring* by J. R. R. Tolkien. Copyright © 1965 by J. R. R. Tolkien. Used by permission of Houghton Mifflin Company and George Allen & Unwin Ltd.

During his convalescence from the "trench fever" he developed while serving in France during World War I, Tolkien decided to supply a history for the language he was in the process of inventing by writing a collection of myths set in the imaginary landscape of Middle-earth. He considered this collection, later entitled *The Silmarillion* and published posthumously in 1977, his most important creation; throughout his career as a university professor (first at Leeds, then at Oxford), he worked on the book.

The work which first brought him popular success, however, was *The Hobbit,* originally a story Tolkien told to his children. Its hero and title character (hobbits are merry little people, distinguished by their large, furry feet and love of domestic comfort) is Bilbo Baggins, who accompanies the wizard Gandalf and a party of dwarves on a treasure-quest, in the course of which Bilbo finds a magic ring which renders its wearer invisible. The book sold well upon its publication in 1937, though it wasn't until thirty years later that it, along with its sequel *The Lord of the Rings,* became the object of a fanatical following among American college students and others.

The Lord of the Rings, published in three volumes—*The Fellowship of the Ring, The Two Towers,* and *The Return of the King*—between 1954 and 1955, and considered by many to be the greatest work of fantasy literature ever written, concerns Frodo Baggins, Bilbo's nephew and heir. Frodo learns from Gandalf that the ring Bilbo discovered during his Quest and later bequeathed to his nephew is actually the One Ring—ruler of the ancient Rings of Power—which is being sought by Sauron, the Dark Lord of Mordor. The plot of the trilogy involves Frodo's Quest to destroy the Ring by casting it into the Cracks of Doom in the depths of the Fiery Mountain. He is accompanied on this perilous mission by his faithful servant, Sam, and friends Merry and Pippin; the wizard Gandalf; the noble Aragorn, heir of the Kings of the West; Boromir, son of the Lord of Gondor; the Elf-prince Legolas; and Gimli the Dwarf. In the following episode from *The Fellowship of the Ring,* Frodo and company arrive at the gates of the dismal Mines of Moria.

The night was old, and westward the waning moon was setting, gleaming fitfully through the breaking clouds. Suddenly Frodo started from sleep. Without warning a storm of howls broke out fierce and wild all about the camp. A great host of Wargs had gathered silently and was now attacking them from every side at once.

'Fling fuel on the fire!' cried Gandalf to the hobbits. 'Draw your blades, and stand back to back!'

In the leaping light, as the fresh wood blazed up, Frodo saw many grey shapes spring over the ring of stones. More and more followed. Through the throat of one huge leader Aragorn passed his sword with a thrust; with a great sweep Boromir hewed the head off another. Beside them Gimli stood with his stout legs apart, wielding his dwarf-axe. The bow of Legolas was singing.

In the wavering firelight Gandalf seemed suddenly to grow: he rose up, a great menacing shape like the monument of some ancient king of stone set upon a hill. Stooping like a cloud, he lifted a burning branch and strode to meet the wolves. They gave back before him. High in the air he tossed the blazing brand. It flared with a sudden white radiance like lightning; and his voice rolled like thunder.

'Naur an edraith ammen! Naur dan i ngaurhoth!' he cried.

There was a roar and a crackle, and the tree above him burst into a leaf and bloom of blinding flame. The fire leapt from tree-top to tree-top. The whole hill was crowned with dazzling light. The swords and knives of the defenders shone and flickered. The last arrow of Legolas kindled in the air as it flew, and plunged burning into the heart of a great wolf-chieftain. All the others fled.

Slowly the fire died till nothing was left but falling ash and sparks; a bitter smoke curled above the burned tree-stumps, and blew darkly from the hill, as the first light of dawn came dimly in the sky. Their enemies were routed and did not return.

'What did I tell you, Mr. Pippin?' said Sam, sheathing his sword. 'Wolves won't get him. That was an eye-opener, and no mistake! Nearly singed the hair off my head!'

When the full light of the morning came no signs of the wolves were to be found, and they looked in vain for the bodies of the dead. No trace of the fight remained but the charred trees and the arrows of Legolas lying on the hill-top. All were undamaged save one of which only the point was left.

'It is as I feared,' said Gandalf. 'These were no ordinary wolves hunting for food in the wilderness. Let us eat quickly and go!'

That day the weather changed again, almost as if it was to the command of some power that had no longer any use for snow, since they had retreated from the pass, a power that wished now to have a clear light in which things that moved in the wild could be seen from far away. The wind had been turning through north to north-west during the night, and now it failed. The clouds vanished southwards and the sky was opened, high and blue. As they stood upon the hill side, ready to depart, a pale sunlight gleamed over the mountain-tops.

'We must reach the doors before sunset,' said Gandalf, 'or I fear we shall not reach them at all. It is not far, but our path may be winding, for here Aragorn cannot guide us; he has seldom walked in this country, and only once have I been under the west wall of Moria, and that was long ago.

'There it lies,' he said, pointing away south-eastwards to where the mountains' sides fell sheer into the shadows at their feet. In the distance could be dimly seen a line of bare cliffs, and in their midst, taller than the rest, one great grey wall. 'When we left the pass I led you southwards, and not back to our starting point, as some of you may have noticed. It is well that I did so, for now we have several miles less to cross, and haste is needed. Let us go!'

'I do not know which to hope,' said Boromir grimly: 'that Gandalf will find what he seeks, or that coming to the cliff we shall find the gates lost for ever. All choices seem ill, and to be caught between wolves and the wall the likeliest chance. Lead on!'

Gimli now walked ahead by the wizard's side, so eager was he to come to Moria. Together they led the Company back towards the mountains. The only road of old to Moria from the west had lain along the course of a stream, the Sirannon, that ran out from the feet of the cliffs near where the doors had stood. But either Gandalf was astray, or else the land had changed in recent years; for he did not strike the stream where he looked to find it, only a few miles southwards from their start.

The morning was passing towards noon, and still the Company wandered and scrambled in a barren country of red stones. Nowhere could they see any gleam of water or hear any sound of it. All was bleak and dry. Their hearts sank. They saw no living thing, and not a bird was in the sky; but what the night would bring, if it caught them in that lost land, none of them cared to think.

Suddenly Gimli, who had pressed on ahead, called back to them. He was standing on a knoll and pointing to the right. Hurrying up they saw below them a deep and narrow channel. It was empty and silent, and hardly a trickle of water flowed among the brown and red-stained stones of its bed; but on the near side there was a path, much broken and decayed, that wound its way among the ruined walls and paving-stones of an ancient highroad.

'Ah! Here it is at last!' said Gandalf. 'This is where the stream ran: Sirannon, the Gate-stream, they used to call it. But what has happened to the water, I cannot guess; it used to be swift and noisy. Come! We must hurry on. We are late.'

The Company were footsore and tired; but they trudged doggedly along the rough and winding track for many miles. The sun turned from the noon and began to go west. After a brief halt and a hasty meal they went on again. Before them the mountains frowned, but their path lay in a deep trough of land and they could see only the higher shoulders and the far eastward peaks.

At length they came to a sharp bend. There the road, which had been veering southwards between the brink of the channel and a steep fall of the land to the left, turned and went due east again. Rounding the corner they saw before them a low cliff, some five fathoms high, with a broken and jagged top. Over it a trickling water dripped, through a wide cleft that seemed to have been carved out by a fall that had once been strong and full.

'Indeed things have changed!' said Gandalf. 'But there is no mistaking the place. There is all that remains of the Stair Falls. If I remember right, there was a flight of steps cut in the rock at their side, but the main road wound away left and climbed with several loops up to the level ground at the top. There used to be a shallow valley beyond the falls right up to the Walls of Moria, and the Sirannon flowed through it with the road beside it. Let us go and see what things are like now!'

They found the stone steps without difficulty, and Gimli sprang swiftly up them, followed by Gandalf and Frodo. When they reached the top they saw that they could go no further that way, and the reason for the drying up of the Gate-stream was revealed. Behind them the sinking Sun filled the cool western sky with glimmering gold. Before them stretched a dark still lake. Neither sky nor sunset was reflected on its sullen surface. The Sirannon had been dammed and had filled all the valley. Beyond the ominous water were reared vast cliffs, their stern faces pallid in the fading light: final and impassable. No sign of gate or entrance, not a fissure or crack could Frodo see in the frowning stone.

'There are the Walls of Moria,' said Gandalf, pointing across the water. 'And there the Gate stood once upon a time, the Elven Door at the end of the road from Hollin by which we have come. But this way is blocked. None of the Company, I guess, will wish to swim this gloomy water at the end of the day. It has an unwholesome look.'

'We must find a way round the northern edge,' said Gimli. 'The first thing

for the Company to do is to climb up by the main path and see where that
will lead us. Even if there were no lake, we could not get our baggage-pony up
this stair.'

'But in any case we cannot take the poor beast into the Mines,' said Gandalf.
'The road under the mountains is a dark road, and there are places narrow and
steep which he cannot tread, even if we can.'

'Poor old Bill!' said Frodo. 'I had not thought of that. And poor Sam! I
wonder what he will say?'

'I am sorry,' said Gandalf. 'Poor Bill has been a useful companion, and it
goes to my heart to turn him adrift now. I would have travelled lighter and
brought no animal, least of all this one that Sam is fond of, if I had had my
way. I feared all along that we should be obliged to take this road.'

The day was drawing to its end, and cold stars were glinting in the sky
high above the sunset, when the Company, with all the speed they could, climbed
up the slopes and reached the side of the lake. In breadth it looked to be no
more than two or three furlongs at the widest point. How far it stretched away
southward they could not see in the failing light; but its northern end was no
more than half a mile from where they stood, and between the stony ridges
that enclosed the valley and the water's edge there was a rim of open ground.
They hurried forward, for they had still a mile or two to go before they could
reach the point on the far shore that Gandalf was making for; and then he had
still to find the doors.

When they came to the northernmost corner of the lake they found a narrow
creek that barred their way. It was green and stagnant, thrust out like a slimy
arm towards the enclosing hills. Gimli strode forward undeterred, and found
that the water was shallow, no more than ankle-deep at the edge. Behind him
they walked in file, threading their way with care, for under the weedy pools
were sliding and greasy stones, and footing was treacherous. Frodo shuddered
with disgust at the touch of the dark unclean water on his feet.

As Sam, the last of the Company, led Bill up on to the dry ground on the
far side, there came a soft sound: a swish, followed by a plop, as if a fish had
disturbed the still surface of the water. Turning quickly they saw ripples, black-
edged with shadow in the waning light: great rings were widening outwards
from a point far out in the lake. There was a bubbling noise, and then silence.
The dusk deepened, and the last gleams of the sunset were veiled in cloud.

Gandalf now pressed on at a great pace, and the others followed as quickly
as they could. They reached the strip of dry land between the lake and the
cliffs: it was narrow, often hardly a dozen yards across, and encumbered with
fallen rock and stones; but they found a way, hugging the cliff, and keeping as
far from the dark water as they might. A mile southwards along the shore they
came upon holly trees. Stumps and dead boughs were rotting in the shallows,
the remains it seemed of old thickets, or of a hedge that had once lined the
road across the drowned valley. But close under the cliff there stood, still strong
and living, two tall trees, larger than any trees of holly that Frodo had ever
seen or imagined. Their great roots spread from the wall to the water. Under
the looming cliffs they had looked like mere bushes, when seen far off from
the top of the Stair; but now they towered overhead, stiff, dark, and silent, throwing deep night-shadows about their feet, standing like sentinel pillars at the end
of the road.

'Well, here we are at last!' said Gandalf. 'Here the Elven-way from Hollin ended. Holly was the token of the people of that land, and they planted it here to mark the end of their domain; for the West-door was made chiefly for their use in their traffic with the Lords of Moria. Those were happier days, when there was still close friendship at times between folk of different race, even between Dwarves and Elves.'

'It was not the fault of the Dwarves that the friendship waned,' said Gimli.

'I have not heard that it was the fault of the Elves,' said Legolas.

'I have heard both,' said Gandalf; 'and I will not give judgement now. But I beg you two, Legolas and Gimli, at least to be friends, and to help me. I need you both. The doors are shut and hidden, and the sooner we find them the better. Night is at hand!'

Turning to the others he said: 'While I am searching, will you each make ready to enter the Mines? For here I fear we must say farewell to our good beast of burden. You must lay aside much of the stuff that we brought against bitter weather: you will not need it inside, nor, I hope, when we come through and journey on down into the South. Instead each of us must take a share of what the pony carried, especially the food and the water-skins.'

'But you can't leave poor old Bill behind in this forsaken place, Mr. Gandalf!' cried Sam, angry and distressed. 'I won't have it, and that's flat. After he has come so far and all!'

'I am sorry, Sam,' said the wizard. 'But when the Door opens I do not think you will be able to drag your Bill inside, into the long dark of Moria. You will have to choose between Bill and your master.'

'He'd follow Mr. Frodo into a dragon's den, if I led him,' protested Sam. 'It'd be nothing short of murder to turn him loose with all these wolves about.'

'It will be short of murder, I hope,' said Gandalf. He laid his hand on the pony's head, and spoke in a low voice. 'Go with words of guard and guiding on you,' he said. 'You are a wise beast, and have learned much in Rivendell. Make your ways to places where you can find grass, and so come in time to Elrond's house, or wherever you wish to go.'

'There, Sam! He will have quite as much chance of escaping wolves and getting home as we have.'

Sam stood sullenly by the pony and returned no answer. Bill, seeming to understand well what was going on, nuzzled up to him, putting his nose to Sam's ear. Sam burst into tears, and fumbled with the straps, unlading all the pony's packs and throwing them on the ground. The others sorted out the goods, making a pile of all that could be left behind, and dividing up the rest.

When this was done they turned to watch Gandalf. He appeared to have done nothing. He was standing between the two trees gazing at the blank wall of the cliff, as if he would bore a hole into it with his eyes. Gimli was wandering about, tapping the stone here and there with his axe. Legolas was pressed against the rock, as if listening.

'Well, here we are and all ready,' said Merry; 'but where are the Doors? I can't see any sign of them.'

'Dwarf-doors are not made to be seen when shut,' said Gimli. 'They are invisible, and their own masters cannot find them or open them, if their secret is forgotten.'

'But this Door was not made to be a secret known only to Dwarves,' said

Gandalf, coming suddenly to life and turning round. 'Unless things are altogether changed, eyes that know what to look for may discover the signs.'

He walked forward to the wall. Right between the shadow of the trees there was a smooth space, and over this he passed his hands to and fro, muttering words under his breath. Then he stepped back.

'Look!' he said. 'Can you see anything now?'

The Moon now shone upon the grey face of the rock; but they could see nothing else for a while. Then slowly on the surface, where the wizard's hands had passed, faint lines appeared, like slender veins of silver running in the stone. At first they were no more than pale gossamer-threads, so fine that they only twinkled fitfully where the Moon caught them, but steadily they grew broader and clearer, until their design could be guessed.

At the top, as high as Gandalf could reach, was an arch of interlacing letters in an Elvish character. Below, though the threads were in places blurred or broken, the outline could be seen of an anvil and a hammer surmounted by a crown with seven stars. Beneath these again were two trees, each bearing crescent moons. More clearly than all else there shone forth in the middle of the door a single star with many rays.

'There are the emblems of Durin!' cried Gimli.

'And there is the Tree of the High Elves!' said Legolas.

'And the Star of the House of Fëanor,' said Gandalf. 'They are wrought of *ithildin* that mirrors only starlight and moonlight, and sleeps until it is touched by one who speaks words now long forgotten in Middle-earth. It is long since I heard them, and I thought deeply before I could recall them to my mind.'

'What does the writing say?' asked Frodo, who was trying to decipher the inscription on the arch. 'I thought I knew the elf-letters, but I cannot read these.'

'The words are in the elven-tongue of the West of Middle-earth in the Elder Days,' answered Gandalf. 'But they do not say anything of importance to us. They say only: *The Doors of Durin, Lord of Moria. Speak, friend, and enter.* And underneath small and faint is written: *I, Narvi, made them. Celebrimbor of Hollin drew these signs.*'

'What does it mean by *speak, friend, and enter?*' asked Merry.

'That is plain enough,' said Gimli. 'If you are a friend, speak the password, and the doors will open, and you can enter.'

'Yes,' said Gandalf, 'these doors are probably governed by words. Some dwarf-gates will open only at special times, or for particular persons; and some have locks and keys that are still needed when all necessary times and words are known. These doors have no key. In the days of Durin they were not secret. They usually stood open and doorwards sat here. But if they were shut, any who knew the opening word could speak it and pass in. At least so it is recorded, is it not, Gimli?'

'It is,' said the dwarf. 'But what the word was is not remembered. Narvi and his craft and all his kindred have vanished from the earth.'

'But do not *you* know the word, Gandalf?' asked Boromir in surprise.

'No!' said the wizard.

The others looked dismayed; only Aragorn, who knew Gandalf well, remained silent and unmoved.

'Then what was the use of bringing us to this accursed spot?' cried Boromir, glancing back with a shudder at the dark water. 'You told us that you have

Here is written in the Fëanorian characters according-
ing to the mode of Beleriand: Ennyn Durin Aran
Moria: pedo mellon a minno. Im Narvi hain ech-
ant: Celebrimbor o Eregion teithant i thiw hin.

once passed through the Mines. How could that be, if you did not know how to enter?'

'The answer to your first question, Boromir,' said the wizard, 'is that I do not know the word—yet. But we shall soon see. And,' he added, with a glint in his eyes under their bristling brows, 'you may ask what is the use of my deeds when they are proved useless. As for your other question: do you doubt my tale? Or have you no wits left? I did not enter this way. I came from the East.

'If you wish to know, I will tell you that these doors open outwards. From the inside you may thrust them open with your hands. From the outside nothing will move them save the spell of command. They cannot be forced inwards.'

'What are you going to do then?' asked Pippin, undaunted by the wizard's bristling brows.

'Knock on the doors with your head, Peregrin Took,' said Gandalf. 'But if that does not shatter them, and I am allowed a little peace from foolish questions, I will seek for the opening words.

'I once knew every spell in all the tongues of Elves or Men or Orcs, that was ever used for such a purpose. I can still remember ten score of them without searching in my mind. But only a few trials, I think, will be needed; and I shall not have to call on Gimli for words of the secret dwarf-tongue that they teach to none. The opening words were Elvish, like the writing on the arch: that seems certain.'

He stepped up to the rock again, and lightly touched with his staff the silver star in the middle beneath the sign of the anvil.

Annon edhellen, edro hi ammen!
Fennas nogothrim, lasto beth lammen!

he said in a commanding voice. The silver lines faded, but the blank grey stone did not stir.

Many times he repeated these words in different order, or varied them. Then he tried other spells, one after another, speaking now faster and louder, now soft and slow. Then he spoke many single words of Elvish speech. Nothing happened. The cliff towered into the night, the countless stars were kindled, the wind blew cold, and the doors stood fast.

Again Gandalf approached the wall, and lifting up his arms he spoke in tones of command and rising wrath. *Edro, edro!* he cried, and struck the rock with his staff. *Open open!* he shouted, and followed it with the same command in every language that had ever been spoken in the West of Middle-earth. Then he threw his staff on the ground, and sat down in silence.

At that moment from far off the wind bore to their listening ears the howling of wolves. Bill the pony started in fear, and Sam sprang to his side and whispered softly to him.

'Do not let him run away!' said Boromir. 'It seems that we shall need him still, if the wolves do not find us. How I hate this foul pool!' He stooped and picking up a large stone he cast it far into the dark water.

The stone vanished with a soft slap; but at the same instant there was a swish and a bubble. Great rippling rings formed on the surface out beyond where the stone had fallen, and they moved slowly towards the foot of the cliff.

'Why did you do that, Boromir?' said Frodo. 'I hate this place, too, and I am afraid. I don't know of what: not of wolves, or the dark behind the doors, but of something else. I am afraid of the pool. Don't disturb it!'

'I wish we could get away!' said Merry.

'Why doesn't Gandalf do something quick?' said Pippin.

Gandalf took no notice of them. He sat with his head bowed, either in despair or in anxious thought. The mournful howling of the wolves was heard again. The ripples on the water grew and came closer; some were already lapping on the shore.

With a suddenness that startled them all the wizard sprang to his feet. He was laughing! 'I have it!' he cried. 'Of course, of course! Absurdly simple, like most riddles when you see the answer.'

Picking up his staff he stood before the rock and said in a clear voice: *Mellon!*

The star shone out briefly and faded again. Then silently a great doorway was outlined, though not a crack or joint had been visible before. Slowly it divided in the middle and swung outwards inch by inch, until both doors lay back against the wall. Through the opening a shadowy stair could be seen climbing steeply up; but beyond the lower steps the darkness was deeper than the night. The Company stared in wonder.

'I was wrong after all,' said Gandalf, 'and Gimli too. Merry, of all people, was on the right track. The opening word was inscribed on the archway all the time! The translation should have been: *Say "Friend" and enter.* I had only to speak the Elvish word for *friend* and the doors opened. Quite simple. Too simple for a learned lore-master in these suspicious days. Those were happier times. Now let us go!'

He strode forward and set his foot on the lowest step. But at that moment several things happened. Frodo felt something seize him by the ankle, and he fell with a cry. Bill the pony gave a wild neigh of fear, and turned tail and dashed away along the lakeside into the darkness. Sam leaped after him, and then hearing Frodo's cry he ran back again, weeping and cursing. The others swung round and saw the waters of the lake seething, as if a host of snakes were swimming up from the southern end.

Out from the water a long sinuous tentacle had crawled; it was pale-green and luminous and wet. Its fingered end had hold of Frodo's foot, and was dragging him into the water. Sam on his knees was now slashing at it with a knife.

The arm let go of Frodo, and Sam pulled him away, crying out for help. Twenty other arms came rippling out. The dark water boiled, and there was a hideous stench.

'Into the gateway! Up the stairs! Quick!' shouted Gandalf leaping back. Rousing them from the horror that seemed to have rooted all but Sam to the ground where they stood, he drove them forward.

They were just in time. Sam and Frodo were only a few steps up, and Gandalf had just begun to climb, when the groping tentacles writhed across the narrow shore and fingered the cliff-wall and the doors. One came wriggling over the threshold, glistening in the starlight. Gandalf turned and paused. If he was considering what word would close the gate again from within, there was no need. Many coiling arms seized the doors on either side, and with horrible strength, swung them round. With a shattering echo they slammed, and all light was lost. A noise of rending and crashing came dully through the ponderous stone.

Sam, clinging to Frodo's arm, collapsed on a step in the black darkness. 'Poor old Bill!' he said in a choking voice. 'Poor old Bill! Wolves and snakes! But the snakes were too much for him. I had to choose, Mr. Frodo. I had to come with you.'

They heard Gandalf go back down the steps and thrust his staff against the doors. There was a quiver in the stone and the stairs trembled, but the doors did not open.

'Well, well!' said the wizard. 'The passage is blocked behind us now, and there is only one way out—on the other side of the mountains. I fear from the sounds that boulders have been piled up, and the trees uprooted and thrown across the gate. I am sorry; for the trees were beautiful, and had stood so long.'

'I felt that something horrible was near from the moment that my foot first touched the water,' said Frodo. 'What was the thing, or were there many of them?'

'I do not know,' answered Gandalf; 'but the arms were all guided by one purpose. Something has crept, or has been driven out of dark waters under the mountains. There are older and fouler things than Orcs in the deep places of the world.' He did not speak aloud his thought that whatever it was that dwelt in the lake, it had seized on Frodo first among all the Company.

Boromir muttered under his breath, but the echoing stone magnified the sound to a hoarse whisper that all could hear: 'In the deep places of the world! And thither we are going against my wish. Who will lead us now in this deadly dark?'

'I will,' said Gandalf, 'and Gimli shall walk with me. Follow my staff!'

QUESTIONS

Language

1. As we point out in the headnote to this selection, J. R. R. Tolkien had a lifelong fascination with language, and his famous fantasy books, *The Hobbit* and *The Lord of the Rings*, had their roots in the author's invention of his own original language, *Quenya*. Find examples of invented names, words, and phrases in this selection. Do you think that they are an important element of the world Tolkien creates in his fiction? Why or why not?
2. This selection contains highly detailed descriptions of the landscape the Company must pass through on its Quest. What do these passages contribute to the story? Do you think the story would be stronger or weaker without them?

Content

1. What are Wargs?
2. Describe Sam. How is he different from the other Questers? How is Boromir different?
3. Do you detect any signs of strain or enmity between Gimli the Dwarf and Legolas the Elf? Describe them.
4. What sort of world does this story seem to be set in? What are its characteristics? Does it seem believable to you? Why or why not?

Suggestions for Writing

1. As we indicate in our introduction to Chapter Five, Gandalf the Grey is an example of the Wise Old Man. Write an essay in which you show how Gandalf exemplifies this archetype. Support your paper with specific references to the selection above. You might also want to compare Gandalf to other Wise Old Man figures in this book.

2. One of the reasons for the great popularity of Tolkien's books is that they allow readers to enter a fabulous world filled with excitement and wonder. It has been said that most people lead such dull lives nowadays that they desperately need the kind of escape from reality which books like Tolkien's provide. Write a paper in which you either agree or disagree with this view of modern life and explain the reasons for your opinion.

3. In this selection, the wizard Gandalf is faced with an apparently insoluble riddle which, however, turns out to have a simple answer. Have you ever found yourself in a similar situation: namely, confronted by a problem, puzzle, or mystery which seemed impossible to figure out but which, in the end, proved to have a very obvious solution? If you have ever had such an experience, describe it in detail.

DASHIELL HAMMETT

from *The Maltese Falcon*

One of the masters of the detective novel, Dashiell Hammett (1894–1961) spent eight years working as a Pinkerton detective himself, an experience which provided material for much of his fiction. As a sergeant during World War I, he contracted tuberculosis and, though he returned briefly to "sleuthing" following his discharge from the army, his poor health forced him to abandon that profession. He turned to writing, contributing detective stories to such publications as *Argosy, Esquire,* and the popular pulp magazine *Black Mask.* His reputation rests on the five novels he published between 1929 and 1932: *Red Harvest, The Dain Curse, The Maltese Falcon, The Glass Key,* and *The Thin Man.* During World War II, though he was a middle-aged man with tuberculosis-scarred lungs, he reenlisted as a sergeant in the army, serving for two years in the Aleutians. He was a man of great integrity: called before the House Un-American Activities Committee during the McCarthy era, he—along with two other trustees of the bail bond fund of the Civil Rights Congress—refused to reveal the names of contributors and was imprisoned for contempt. The experience brought financial ruin and further damage to his health. He died of lung cancer in 1961.

The Maltese Falcon (the basis of the famous 1941 movie starring Humphrey Bogart) is considered Hammett's masterpiece. Its hero is Sam Spade—like his creator, a man of tough integrity—who, through a beautiful but treacherous female client named Brigid O'Shaughnessy, gets caught up in a Quest for a priceless statuette in the shape of a falcon. Several people besides Brigid have been trying to get their hands on the "black bird," including Joel Cairo, an oily, somewhat effeminate

From *The Maltese Falcon,* by Dashiell Hammett. Copyright 1929, 1930 by Alfred A. Knopf, Inc. and renewed 1957, 1958 by Dashiell Hammett. Reprinted by permission of Alfred A. Knopf, Inc.

individual, and a jovial, sinister "fat man" named Gutman. In the following scene, Spade, having just disarmed Gutman's young henchman, Wilmer, learns from the "fat man" the history of the Maltese falcon.

THE EMPEROR'S GIFT

Gutman opened the door. A glad smile lighted his fat face. He held out a hand and said: "Ah, come in, sir! Thank you for coming. Come in."

Spade shook the hand and entered. The boy went in behind him. The fat man shut the door. Spade took the boy's pistols from his pockets and held them out to Gutman. "Here. You shouldn't let him run around with these. He'll get himself hurt."

The fat man laughed merrily and took the pistols. "Well, well," he said, "what's this?" He looked from Spade to the boy.

Spade said: "A crippled newsie took them away from him, but I made him give them back."

The white-faced boy took the pistols out of Gutman's hands and pocketed them. The boy did not speak. Gutman laughed again. "By Gad, sir," he told Spade, "you're a chap worth knowing, an amazing character. Come in. Sit down. Give me your hat." The boy left the room by the door to the right of the entrance.

The fat man installed Spade in a green plush chair by the table, pressed a cigar upon him, held a light to it, mixed whiskey and carbonated water, put one glass in Spade's hand, and, holding the other, sat down facing Spade. "Now, sir, I hope you'll let me apologize for—"

"Never mind that," Spade said. "Let's talk about the black bird."

The fat man cocked his head to the left and regarded Spade with fond eyes. "All right, sir," he agreed. "Let's." He took a sip from the glass in his hand. "This is going to be the most astounding thing you've ever heard of, sir, and I say that knowing that a man of your caliber in your profession must have known some astounding things in his time."

Spade nodded politely. The fat man screwed up his eyes and asked: "What do you know, sir, about the Order of the Hospital of St. John of Jerusalem, later called the Knights of Rhodes and other things?"

Spade waved his cigar. "Not much—only what I remember from history in school—Crusaders or something."

"Very good. Now you don't remember that Suleiman the Magnificent chased them out of Rhodes in 1523?"

"No."

"Well, sir, he did, and they settled in Crete. And they stayed there for seven years, until 1530 when they persuaded the Emperor Charles V to give them"—Gutman held up three puffy fingers and counted them—"Malta, Gozo, and Tripoli."

"Yes."

"Yes, sir, but with these conditions: they were to pay the Emperor each year the tribute of one"—he held up a finger—"falcon in acknowledgment that Malta was still under Spain, and if they ever left the island it was to revert to Spain. Understand? He was giving it to them, but not unless they used it, and they couldn't give or sell it to anybody else."

"Yes."

The fat man looked over his shoulder at the three closed doors, hunched his chair a few inches nearer Spade's, and reduced his voice to a husky whisper: "Have you any conception of the extreme, the immeasurable, wealth of the Order at that time?"

"If I remember," Spade said, "they were pretty well fixed."

Gutman smiled indulgently. "Pretty well, sir, is putting it mildly." His whisper became lower and more purring. "They were rolling in wealth, sir. You've no idea. None of us has any idea. For years they had preyed on the Saracens, had taken nobody knows what spoils of gems, precious metals, silks, ivories— the cream of the cream of the East. That is history, sir. We all know that the Holy Wars to them, as to the Templars, were largely a matter of loot. Well, now, the Emperor Charles has given them Malta, and all the rent he asks is one insignificant bird per annum, just as a matter of form. What could be more natural than for these immeasurably wealthy Knights to look around for some way of expressing their gratitude? Well, sir, that's exactly what they did, and they hit on the happy thought of sending Charles for the first year's tribute, not an insignificant live bird, but a glorious golden falcon encrusted from head to foot with the finest jewels in their coffers. And—remember, sir—they had fine ones, the finest out of Asia." Gutman stopped whispering. His sleek dark eyes examined Spade's face, which was placid. The fat man asked: "Well, sir, what do you think of that?"

"I don't know."

The fat man smiled complacently. "These are facts, historical facts, not schoolbook history, not Mr. Wells's history, but history nevertheless." He leaned forward. "The archives of the Order from the twelfth century on are still at Malta. They are not intact, but what is there holds no less than three"—he held up three fingers—"references that can't be to anything else but this jeweled falcon. In J. Delaville LeRoulx's *Les Archives de l'Ordre de Saint-Jean* there is a reference to it—oblique to be sure, but a reference still. And the unpublished—because unfinished at the time of his death—supplement to Paoli's *Dell' origine ed instituto del sacro militar ordine* has a clear and unmistakable statement of the facts I am telling you."

"All right," Spade said.

"All right, sir. Grand Master Villiers de L'Isle Adam had this foot-high jeweled bird made by Turkish slaves in the castle of St. Angelo and sent it to Charles, who was in Spain. He sent it in a galley commanded by a French knight named Cormier or Corvere, a member of the Order." His voice dropped to a whisper again. "It never reached Spain." He smiled with compressed lips and asked: "You know of Barbarossa, Redbeard, Khaired-Din? No? A famous admiral of buccaneers sailing out of Algiers then. Well, sir, he took the knight's galley and he took the bird. The bird went to Algiers. That's a fact. That's a fact that the French historian Pierre Dan put in one of his letters from Algiers. He wrote that the bird had been there for more than a hundred years, until it was carried away by Sir Francis Verney, the English adventurer who was with the Algerian buccaneers for a while. Maybe it wasn't, but Pierre Dan believed it was, and that's good enough for me.

"There's nothing said about the bird in Lady Frances Verney's *Memoirs of the Verney Family during the Seventeenth Century,* to be sure. I looked. And it's pretty certain that Sir Francis didn't have the bird when he died in a Messina hospital in 1615. He was stony broke. But, sir, there's no denying that the bird *did* go to Sicily. It was there and it came into the possession there of Victor Armadeus II some time after he became king in 1713, and it was one of his gifts to his wife when he married in Chambéry after abdicating. That is a fact, sir. Carutti, the author of *Storia del Regno di Vittorio Amadeo II,* himself vouched for it.

"Maybe they—Amadeo and his wife—took it along with them to Turin when he tried to revoke his abdication. Be that as it may, it turned up next in the possession of a Spaniard who had been with the army that took Naples in 1734—the father of Don José Monino y Redondo, Count of Floridablanca, who was Charles III's chief minister. There's nothing to show that it didn't stay in that family until at least the end of the Carlist War in '40. Then it appeared in Paris at just about the time that Paris was full of Carlists who had had to get out of Spain. One of them must have brought it with him, but, whoever he was, it's likely he knew nothing about its real value. It had been—no doubt as a precaution during the Carlist trouble in Spain—painted or enameled over to look like nothing more than a fairly interesting black statuette. And in that disguise, sir, it was, you might say, kicked around Paris for seventy years by private owners and dealers too stupid to see what it was under the skin."

The fat man paused to smile and shake his head regretfully. Then he went on: "For seventy years, sir, this marvelous item was, as you might say, a football in the gutters of Paris—until 1931 when a Greek dealer named Charilaos Konstantinides found it in an obscure shop. It didn't take Charilaos long to learn what it was and to acquire it. No thickness of enamel could conceal value from his eyes and nose. Well, sir, Charilaos was the man who traced most of its history and who identified it as what it actually was. I got wind of it and finally forced most of the history out of him, though I've been able to add a few details since. Charilaos was in no hurry to convert his find into money at once. He knew that—enormous as its intrinsic value was—a far higher, a terrific, price could be obtained for it once its authenticity was established beyond doubt. Possibly he planned to do business with one of the modern descendants of the old Order—the English Order of St. John of Jerusalem, the Prussian Johanniterorden, or the Italian or German *Langues* of the Sovereign Order of Malta—all wealthy orders." The fat man raised his glass, smiled at its emptiness, and rose to fill it and Spade's. "You begin to believe me a little?" he asked as he worked the siphon.

"I haven't said I didn't."

"No," Gutman chuckled. "But how you looked." He sat down, drank generously, and patted his mouth with a white handkerchief. "Well, sir, to hold it safe while pursuing his researches into its history, Charilaos had re-enameled the bird, apparently just as it is now. One year to the very day after he had acquired it—that was possibly three months after I'd made him confess to me—I picked up the *Times* in London and read that his establishment had been burglarized and he had been murdered. I was in Paris the next day." He shook his head sadly. "The bird was gone. By Gad, sir, I was wild. I didn't believe anybody else knew what it was. I didn't believe he had told anybody but me. A great quantity of stuff had been stolen. That made me think that the thief had simply taken the bird along with the rest of his plunder, not knowing what it was. Because I assure you that a thief who knew its value would not burden himself with anything else—no, sir—at least not anything less than crown jewels."

He shut his eyes and smiled complacently at an inner thought. He opened his eyes and said: "That was seventeen years ago. Well, sir, it took me seventeen years to locate the bird, but I did it. I wanted it, and I'm not a man that's easily discouraged when he wants something." His smile grew broad. "I wanted it and I found it. I want it and I'm going to have it." He drained his glass, dried his lips again, and returned his handkerchief to his pocket. "I traced it to the home of a Russian general—one Kemidov—in a Constantinople suburb. He didn't know a thing about it. It was nothing but a black enameled figure to him, but his natural contrariness—the natural contrariness of a Russian general—kept him from selling it to me when I made him an offer. Perhaps in my eagerness I was a little unskillful, though not very. I don't know about that. But I did know I wanted it and I was afraid this stupid soldier might begin to investigate his property, might chip off some of the enamel. So I sent some—ah—agents to get it. Well, sir, they got it and I haven't got it." He stood up and carried his empty glass to the table. "But I'm going to. Your glass, sir."

"Then the bird doesn't belong to any of you?" Spade asked, "but to a General Kemidov?"

"Belong?" the fat man said jovially. "Well, sir, you might say it belonged to the King of Spain, but I don't see how you can honestly grant anybody else clear title to it—except by right of possession." He clucked. "An article of that value that has passed from hand to hand by such means is clearly the property of whoever can get hold of it."

"Then it's Miss O'Shaughnessy's now?"

"No, sir, except as my agent."

Spade said, "Oh," ironically.

Gutman, looking thoughtfully at the stopper of the whiskey-bottle in his hand, asked: "There's no doubt that she's got it now?"

"Not much."

"Where?"

"I don't know exactly."

The fat man set the bottle on the table with a bang. "But you said you did," he protested.

Spade made a careless gesture with one hand. "I meant to say I know where to get it when the time comes."

The pink bulbs of Gutman's face arranged themselves more happily. "And you do?" he asked.

"Yes."

"Where?"

Spade grinned and said: "Leave that to me."

"When?"

"When I'm ready."

The fat man pursed his lips and, smiling with only slight uneasiness, asked: "Mr. Spade, where is Miss O'Shaughnessy now?"

"In my hands, safely tucked away."

Gutman smiled with approval. "Trust you for that, sir," he said. "Well now, sir, before we sit down to talk prices, answer me this: how soon can you—or how soon are you willing to—produce the falcon?"

"A couple of days."

The fat man nodded. "That is satisfactory. We— But I forget our nourishment." He turned to the table, poured whiskey, squirted charged water into it, set a glass at Spade's elbow and held his own aloft. "Well, sir, here's to a fair bargain and profits large enough for both of us."

They drank. The fat man sat down. Spade asked: "What's your idea of a fair bargain?"

Gutman held his glass up to the light, looked affectionately at it, took another long drink, and said: "I have two proposals to make, sir, and either is fair. Take your choice. I will give you twenty-five thousand dollars when you deliver the falcon to me, and another twenty-five thousand as soon as I get to New York; or I will give you one quarter—twenty-five per cent—of what I realize on the falcon. There you are, sir: an almost immediate fifty thousand dollars or a vastly greater sum within, say, a couple of months."

Spade drank and asked: "How much greater?"

"Vastly," the fat man repeated. "Who knows how much greater? Shall I say a hundred thousand, or a quarter of a million? Will you believe me if I name the sum that seems the probable minimum?"

"Why not?"

The fat man smacked his lips and lowered his voice to a purring murmur. "What would you say, sir, to half a million?"

Spade narrowed his eyes. "Then you think the dingus is worth two million?"

Gutman smiled serenely. "In your own words, why not?" he asked.

Spade emptied his glass and set it on the table. He put his cigar in his mouth, took it out, looked at it, and put it back in. His yellow-grey eyes were faintly muddy. He said: "That's a hell of a lot of dough."

The fat man agreed: "That's a hell of a lot of dough." He leaned forward and patted Spade's knee. "That is the absolute rock-bottom minimum—or Charilaos Konstantinides was a blithering idiot—and he wasn't."

Spade removed the cigar from his mouth again, frowned at it with distaste, and put it on the smoking-stand. He shut his eyes hard, opened them again. Their muddiness had thickened. He said: "The—the minimum, huh? And the maximum?" An unmistakable *sh* followed the x in maximum as he said it.

"The maximum?" Gutman held his empty hand out, palm up. "I refuse to guess. You'd think me crazy. I don't know. There's no telling how high it could go, sir, and that's the one and the only truth about it."

Spade pulled his sagging lower lip tight against the upper. He shook his head impatiently. A sharp frightened gleam awoke in his eyes—and was smothered by the deepening muddiness. He stood up, helping himself up with his hands on the arms of his chair. He shook his head again and took an uncertain step forward. He laughed thickly and muttered: "Damn you."

Gutman jumped up and pushed his chair back. His fat globes jiggled. His eyes were dark holes in an oily pink face. Spade swung his head from side to side until his dull eyes were pointed at—if not focused on—the door. He took another uncertain step. The fat man called sharply: "Wilmer!" A door opened and the boy came in.

Spade took a third step. His face was grey now, with jaw-muscles standing out like tumors under his ears. His legs did not straighten again after his fourth step and his muddy eyes were almost covered by their lids. He took his fifth step. The boy walked over and stood close to Spade, a little in front of him, but not directly between Spade and the door. The boy's right hand was inside his coat over his heart. The corners of his mouth twitched. Spade essayed his sixth step. The boy's leg darted out across Spade's leg, in front. Spade tripped over the interfering leg and crashed face-down on the floor. The boy, keeping his right hand under his coat, looked down at Spade. Spade tried to get up. The boy drew his right foot far back and kicked Spade's temple. The kick rolled Spade over on his side. Once more he tried to get up, could not, and went to sleep.

QUESTIONS

Language

1. Gutman has a very distinctive way of talking. Describe his speech mannerisms. Judging from his language alone, what sort of person does he seem to be?
2. Sam Spade is an example—one of the most famous in literature—of the tough-talking, "hard-boiled" private eye. Does his toughness come through in his comments to Gutman? Point to examples in the selection to support your opinion.
3. Take a look at Hammett's description of Spade's actions after the detective has been drugged, beginning with the sentence, "Spade pulled his sagging lower lip tight against the upper." What do you notice about the individual sentences in this passage? How would you characterize the author's literary style? Does it seem well suited to the subject matter?

Content

1. How did the Maltese falcon come into existence? Who made it?
2. How did Gutman learn the history of the falcon?
3. How did the falcon come to be, in Gutman's words, "a football in the gutters of Paris"?
4. Who is Wilmer? Describe him.

Suggestions for Writing

1. "Well, sir," says Gutman to Spade, "it took me seventeen years to locate the bird, but I did it. I wanted it, and I'm not a man that's easily discouraged when he wants something." Have you ever wanted something so badly that you couldn't stop thinking about it? If you have ever had such an experience, describe it in detail. What was the object of your obsession? Did you face many difficulties in trying to obtain what you were seeking? Were you successful?
2. Although Gutman repeatedly insists that the details of his narrative are facts, the story of the Maltese falcon is, of course, fiction, an invention of the author, Dashiell Hammett. Write a paper in which you invent your own story of a legendary lost treasure—a hoard of jewels, a priceless object, or something similar. Tell how the treasure came into being, describe the original owner, and trace its history up to the present.
3. This chapter, "The Emperor's Gift," ends at a very suspenseful moment: having been drugged by Gutman, Sam Spade is knocked unconscious by the psychopathic killer Wilmer—who hates the detective—and now lies helpless at his enemies' feet. What do you think happens next? Write a paper in which you continue the story from the point at which it breaks off in the selection above. Try to keep your style as close to Hammett's as possible.
4. At the end of *The Maltese Falcon*, Spade explains to the beautiful Brigid O'Shaughnessy—

who has murdered Spade's partner, Miles Archer—why he must turn her in to the police, despite his love for her and despite the fact that he could never stand Archer. "When a man's partner is killed," says Spade, "he's supposed to do something about it. It doesn't make any difference what you thought of him. He was your partner and you're supposed to do something about it." Spade, though he is not above "milking" a rich client of money, nevertheless lives by a strict, if unconventional, code of conduct. There are certain things he will do and certain things he absolutely will not. Do you have such a code—that is to say, do you conduct your life according to rules of behavior from which you refuse to deviate? Are there certain standards you set for yourself which you won't compromise under any circumstances? If so, describe your code. If not, explain why you don't think such a code is necessary for you.

HERMAN MELVILLE

from *Moby-Dick*

Herman Melville (1819–1891) was the son of an educated gentleman and businessman who died, after suffering severe financial setbacks, when the boy was twelve. His wife and eight children were left nearly destitute. Three years later, the writer's formal education ended, and during the next decade he practiced a variety of trades on land and at sea. For his first few novels, exciting stories of adventure in exotic settings, Melville, who loved the sea, drew on his experience as a sailor. But readers began to lose interest in his books with the publication of the difficult and ambitious *Moby-Dick* (1851), considered today a masterpiece of American literature. In the next six years, Melville wrote three more novels and a fine collection of short fiction, *The Piazza Tales.* With the exception of the novelette *Billy Budd,* written shortly before his death, Melville, defeated by public indifference, wrote no more prose after 1857, turning instead to poetry. In order to support his family, he moved from his Massachusetts farm to New York City, where he took an ill-paying customs inspector's position. Few people noticed his death in 1891. Not until the 1920s was this monumental figure in American letters rediscovered by literary scholars and posthumously accorded the recognition he deserved.

Moby-Dick, a novel based on Melville's early experiences on a whaling ship, is the story of Captain Ahab, a "grand, godlike, ungodly old man," and his mad search for the whale that he has come to see as the symbol of all evil. The tale is told by one Ishmael, a restless, discontented young man who signs aboard the whaler *Pequod.* The ship is shrouded in mystery; dark rumors about it circulate throughout the Nantucket port. Not until the *Pequod* is well-distanced from shore does Ahab emerge from below deck to explain the real purpose of the voyage: to hunt down and kill the great white whale, Moby Dick, which tore off his leg in a previous encounter. In this scene, Ahab strives to inflame his crew—which includes the chief mate, Starbuck, the second mate, Stubb, the third mate, Flask, and the harpooneers Queequeg, Daggoo, and Tashtego—with his own fierce hatred of the White Whale.

THE QUARTER-DECK

(Enter Ahab: Then, all)

It was not a great while after the affair of the pipe, that one morning shortly after breakfast, Ahab, as was his wont, ascended the cabin-gangway to the deck. There most sea-captains usually walk at that hour, as country gentlemen, after the same meal, take a few turns in the garden.

Soon his steady, ivory stride was heard, as to and fro he paced his old rounds, upon planks so familiar to his tread, that they were all over dented, like geological stones, with the peculiar mark of his walk. Did you fixedly gaze, too, upon that ribbed and dented brow; there also, you would see still stranger footprints—the footprints of his one unsleeping, ever-pacing thought.

But on the occasion in question, those dents looked deeper, even as his nervous step that morning left a deeper mark. And, so full of his thought was Ahab, that at every uniform turn that he made, now at the main-mast and now at the binnacle, you could almost see that thought turn in him as he turned, and pace in him as he paced; so completely possessing him, indeed, that it all but seemed the inward mold of every outer movement.

"D'ye mark him, Flask?" whispered Stubb; "the chick that's in him pecks the shell. 'Twill soon be out."

The hours wore on—Ahab now shut up within his cabin; anon, pacing the deck, with the same intense bigotry of purpose in his aspect.

It drew near the close of day. Suddenly he came to a halt by the bulwarks, and inserting his bone leg into the auger-hole there, and with one hand grasping a shroud, he ordered Starbuck to send everybody aft.

"Sir!" said the mate, astonished at an order seldom or never given on shipboard except in some extraordinary case.

"Send everybody aft," repeated Ahab. "Mast-heads, there! come down!"

When the entire ship's company was assembled, and with curious and not wholly unapprehensive faces, were eyeing him, for he looked not unlike the weather horizon when a storm is coming up, Ahab, after rapidly glancing over the bulwarks, and then darting his eyes among the crew, started from his standpoint; and as though not a soul were nigh him resumed his heavy turns upon the deck. With bent head and half-slouched hat he continued to pace, unmindful of the wondering whispering among the men; till Stubb cautiously whispered to Flask, that Ahab must have summoned them there for the purpose of witnessing a pedestrian feat. But this did not last long. Vehemently pausing he cried:

"What do ye do when ye see a whale, men?"

"Sing out for him!" was the impulsive rejoinder from a score of clubbed voices.

"Good!" cried Ahab, with a wild approval in his tones; observing the hearty animation into which his unexpected question had so magnetically thrown them.

"And what do ye next, men?"

"Lower away, and after him!"

"And what tune is it ye pull to, men?"

"A dead whale or a stove boat!"

More and more strangely and fiercely glad and approving, grew the countenance of the old man at every shout; while the mariners began to gaze curiously at each other, as if marveling how it was that they themselves became so excited at such seemingly purposeless questions.

But, they were all eagerness again, as Ahab, now half-revolving in his pivot-hole, with one hand reaching high up a shroud, and tightly, almost convulsively grasping it, addressed them thus:

"All ye mast-headers have before now heard me give orders about a white whale. Look ye! d'ye see this Spanish ounce of gold?"—holding up a broad bright coin to the sun—"it is a sixteen dollar piece, men. D'ye see it? Mr. Starbuck, hand me yon top-maul."

While the mate was getting the hammer, Ahab, without speaking, was slowly rubbing the gold piece against the skirts of his jacket, as if to heighten its luster, and without using any words was meanwhile lowly humming to himself, producing a sound so strangely muffled and inarticulate that it seemed the mechanical humming of the wheels of his vitality in him.

Receiving the top-maul from Starbuck, he advanced toward the main-mast with the hammer uplifted in one hand, exhibiting the gold with the other, and with a high raised voice exclaiming: "Whosoever of ye raises me a white-headed whale with a wrinkled brow and a crooked jaw; whosoever of ye raises me that white-headed whale, with three holes punctured in his starboard fluke—look ye, whosoever of ye raises me that same White Whale, he shall have this gold ounce, my boys!"

"Huzza! huzza!" cried the seamen, as with swinging tarpaulins they hailed the act of nailing the gold to the mast.

"It's a white whale, I say," resumed Ahab, as he threw down the top-maul: "a white whale. Skin your eyes for him, men; look sharp for white water; if ye see but a bubble, sing out."

All this while Tashtego, Daggoo, and Queequeg had looked on with even more intense interest and surprise than the rest, and at the mention of the wrinkled brow and crooked jaw they had started as if each was separately touched by some specific recollection.

"Captain Ahab," said Tashtego, "that White Whale must be the same that some call Moby Dick."

"Moby Dick?" shouted Ahab. "Do ye know the White Whale then, Tash?"

"Does he fan-tail a little curious, sir, before he goes down?" said the Gay-Header deliberately.

"And has he a curious spout, too," said Daggoo, "very bushy, even for a parmacetty, and mighty quick, Captain Ahab?"

"And he have one, two, tree—oh! good many iron in him hide, too, Captain," cried Queequeg disjointedly, "all twiske-tee be-twisk, like him—him—" faltering hard for a word, and screwing his hand round and round as though uncorking a bottle—"like him—him—"

"Corkscrew!" cried Ahab, "aye, Queequeg, the harpoons lie all twisted and wrenched in him; aye, Daggoo, his spout is a big one, like a whole shock of wheat, and white as a pile of our Nantucket wool after the great annual sheep-shearing; aye, Tashtego, and he fan-tails like a split jib in a squall. Death and devils! men, it is Moby Dick ye have seen—Moby Dick—Moby Dick!"

"Captain Ahab," said Starbuck, who, with Stubb and Flask, had thus far been eyeing his superior with increasing surprise, but at last seemed struck with a thought which somewhat explained all the wonder. "Captain Ahab, I have heard of Moby Dick—but it was not Moby Dick that took off thy leg?"

"Who told thee that?" cried Ahab; then pausing, "Aye, Starbuck; aye, my hearties all round; it was Moby Dick that dismasted me; Moby Dick that brought me to this dead stump I stand on now. Aye, aye," he shouted with a terrific, loud, animal sob, like that of a heart-stricken moose; "Aye, aye! it was that accursed White Whale that razeed me; made a poor pegging lubber of me forever and a day!" Then tossing both arms, with measureless imprecations he shouted out: "Aye, aye! and I'll chase him round Good Hope, and round the Horn, and round the Norway Maelstrom, and round perdition's flames before I give him up. And this is what ye have shipped for, men! to chase that White Whale on both sides of land, and over all sides of earth, till he spouts black blood and rolls fin out. What say ye, men, will ye splice hands on it, now? I think ye do look brave."

"Aye, aye!" shouted the harpooneers and seamen, running closer to the excited old man: "A sharp eye for the White Whale; a sharp lance for Moby Dick!"

"God bless ye," he seemed to half sob and half shout. "God bless ye, men. Steward! go draw the great measure of grog. But what's this long face about, Mr. Starbuck; wilt thou not chase the White Whale? art not game for Moby Dick?"

"I am game for his crooked jaw, and for the jaws of Death too, Captain Ahab, if it fairly comes in the way of the business we follow; but I came here to hunt whales, not my commander's vengeance. How many barrels will thy vengeance yield thee even if thou gettest it, Captain Ahab? it will not fetch thee much in our Nantucket market."

"Nantucket market! Hoot! But come closer, Starbuck; thou requirest a little lower layer. If money's to be the measurer, man, and the accountants have computed their great counting-house the globe, by girdling it with guineas, one to every three parts of an inch; then, let me tell thee, that my vengeance will fetch a great premium *here!*"

"He smites his chest," whispered Stubb, "what's that for? methinks it rings most vast, but hollow."

"Vengeance on a dumb brute!" cried Starbuck, "that simply smote thee from blindest instinct! Madness! To be enraged with a dumb thing, Captain Ahab, seems blasphemous."

"Hark ye yet again—the little lower layer. All visible objects, man, are but as pasteboard masks. But in each event—in the living act, the undoubted deed—there, some unknown but still reasoning thing puts forth the moldings of its features from behind the unreasoning mask. If man will strike, strike through the mask! How can the prisoner reach outside except by thrusting through the wall? To me, the White Whale is that wall, shoved near to me. Sometimes I think there's naught beyond. But 'tis enough. He tasks me; he heaps me; I see in him outrageous strength, with an inscrutable malice sinewing it. That inscrutable thing is chiefly what I hate; and be the White Whale agent, or be the White Whale principal, I will wreak that hate upon him. Talk not to me of blasphemy, man; I'd strike the sun if it insulted me. For could the sun do that, then could I do the other; since there is ever a sort of fair play herein, jealousy presiding over all creations. But not my master, man, is even that fair play. Who's over

me? Truth hath no confines. Take off thine eye! more intolerable than fiends'
glarings is a doltish stare! So, so; thou reddenest and palest; my heat has melted
thee to anger-glow. But look ye, Starbuck, what is said in heat, that thing unsays
itself. There are men from whom warm words are small indignity. I meant not
to incense thee. Let it go. Look! see yonder Turkish cheeks of spotted tawn—
living, breathing pictures painted by the sun. The Pagan leopards—the unrecking
and unworshiping things, that live; and seek, and give no reasons for the torrid
life they feel! The crew, man, the crew! Are they not one and all with Ahab, in
this matter of the whale? See Stubb! he laughs! See yonder Chilean! he snorts
to think of it. Stand up amid the general hurricane, thy one tost sapling cannot,
Starbuck! And what is it? Reckon it. 'Tis but to help strike a fin; no wondrous
feat for Starbuck. What is it more? From this one poor hunt, then, the best
lance out of all Nantucket, surely he will not hang back, when every foremast-
hand has clutched a whetstone. Ah! constrainings seize thee; I see! the billow
lifts thee! Speak, but speak!—Aye, aye! thy silence, then, *that* voices thee. *(Aside)*
Something shot from my dilated nostrils, he has inhaled it in his lungs. Starbuck
now is mine; cannot oppose me now, without rebellion."

"God keep me!—keep us all!" murmured Starbuck, lowly.

But in his joy at the enchanted, tacit acquiescence of the mate, Ahab did
not hear his foreboding invocation; nor yet the low laugh from the hold; nor
yet the presaging vibrations of the winds in the cordage; nor yet the hollow
flap of the sails against the masts, as for a moment their hearts sank in. For
again Starbuck's downcast eyes lighted up with the stubbornness of life; the
subterranean laugh died away; the winds blew on; the sails filled out; the ship
heaved and rolled as before. Ah, ye admonitions and warnings! why stay ye
not when ye come? But rather are ye predictions than warnings, ye shadows!
Yet not so much predictions from without, as verifications of the foregoing things
within. For with little external to constrain us, the innermost necessities in our
being, these still drive us on.

"The measure! the measure!" cried Ahab.

Receiving the brimming pewter, and turning to the harpooneers, he ordered
them to produce their weapons. Then ranging them before him near the capstan,
with their harpoons in their hands, while his three mates stood at his side with
their lances, and the rest of the ship's company formed a circle round the group;
he stood for an instant searchingly eyeing every man of his crew. But those
wild eyes met his, as the bloodshot eyes of the prairie wolves meet the eye of
their leader, ere he rushes on at their head in the trail of the bison; but, alas!
only to fall into the hidden snare of the Indian.

"Drink and pass!" he cried, handing the heavy charged flagon to the nearest
seamen. "The crew alone now drink. Round with it, round! Short draughts—
long swallows, men; 'tis hot as Satan's hoof. So, so; it goes round excellently. It
spiralizes in ye; forks out at the serpent-snapping eye. Well done; almost drained.
That way it went, this way it comes. Hand it me—here's a hollow! Men, ye
seem the years; so brimming life is gulped and gone. Steward, refill!

"Attend now, my braves. I have mustered ye all round this capstan; and
ye mates, flank me with your lances; and ye harpooneers, stand there with your
irons; and ye, stout mariners, ring me in, that I may in some sort revive a noble
custom of my fishermen fathers before me. O men, you will yet see that— Ha!
boy, come back? bad pennies come not sooner. Hand it me. Why, now, this

pewter had run brimming again, wer't not thou St. Vitus' imp—away, thou ague!

"Advance, ye mates! Cross your lances full before me. Well done! Let me touch the axis." So saying, with extended arm, he grasped the three level, radiating lances at their crossed center; while so doing, suddenly and nervously twitched them; meanwhile glancing intently from Starbuck to Stubb; from Stubb to Flask. It seemed as though, by some nameless, interior volition, he would fain have shocked into them the same fiery emotion accumulated within the Leyden jar of his own magnetic life. The three mates quailed before his strong, sustained, and mystic aspect. Stubb and Flask looked sideways from him; the honest eye of Starbuck fell downright.

"In vain!" cried Ahab; "but, maybe, 'tis well. For did ye three but once take the full-forced shock, then mine own electric thing, *that* had perhaps expired from out me. Perchance, too, it would have dropped ye dead. Perchance ye need it not. Down lances! And now, ye mates, I do appoint ye three cupbearers to my three pagan kinsmen there—yon three most honorable gentlemen and noble-men, my valiant harpooneers. Disdain the task? What, when the great Pope washes the feet of beggars, using his tiara for ewer? Oh, my sweet cardinals! your own condescension, *that* shall bend ye to it. I do not order ye; ye will it. Cut your seizings and draw the poles, ye harpooneers!"

Silently obeying the order, the three harpooneers now stood with the de-tached iron part of their harpoons, some three feet long, held, barbs up, before him.

"Stab me not with that keen steel! Cant them; cant them over! know ye not the goblet end? Turn up the socket! So, so; now, ye cupbearers, advance. The irons! take them; hold them while I fill!" Forthwith, slowly going from one officer to the other, he brimmed the harpoon sockets with the fiery waters from the pewter.

"Now, three to three, ye stand. Commend the murderous chalices! Bestow them, ye who are now made parties to this indissoluble league. Ha! Starbuck! but the deed is done! Yon ratifying sun now waits to sit upon it. Drink, ye harpooneers! drink and swear, ye men that man the deathful whaleboat's bow—Death to Moby Dick! God hunt us all, if we do not hunt Moby Dick to his death!" The long, barbed steel goblets were lifted; and to cries and maledictions against the white whale, the spirits were simultaneously quaffed down with a hiss. Starbuck paled, and turned, and shivered. Once more, and finally, the replen-ished pewter went the rounds among the frantic crew; when, waving his free hand to them, they all dispersed; and Ahab retired within his cabin.

QUESTIONS

Language

1. Underline the words in this selection that are unfamiliar to you; then look them up in a good dictionary. How do you respond to reading prose like Melville's, which displays such a rich and extensive vocabulary? Does such writing seem enriching, challenging, or discouraging to you?

2. *Moby-Dick* is narrated by a man who calls himself Ishmael. In this particular chapter, do you have the sense that one of the crew members of the *Pequod* is telling the story? Why or why not?

3. Ahab's speech is highly metaphorical. Find all of the metaphors used by Ahab, members

of the crew, and the narrator. Rephrase some of them into ordinary language. How does your paraphrase compare to the original? Is anything lost in the translation of Melville's words into your own?

4. Look at Ahab's speeches to his men. What tactics does he use to sway them to his course? Does he use a different approach with Starbuck? Is Ahab's relationship with Starbuck different from his relationship with the rest of the crew?

Content

1. As he watches Captain Ahab pace the deck, Stubb whispers to Flask, "the chick that's in him pecks the shell. 'Twill soon be out" (p. 373). What does Stubb mean? To what is he referring?
2. Describe Ahab's behavior in this scene. What sort of man does he seem to be?
3. How is Moby Dick described?
4. Why does Ahab hate the White Whale so fiercely?
5. Describe the harpooneer's pledge at the end of this chapter. What do they drink out of?

Suggestions for Writing

1. *Moby-Dick* is a book about a man, Captain Ahab, who seeks vengeance on the white whale that has maimed him. Write an essay in which you explain your feelings about *revenge*. Do you believe in the law of "eye for eye; tooth for tooth"? Or do you believe instead in "turning the other cheek"? Explain the reasons for your belief, drawing, if you wish, on personal experience.
2. In "The Quarter Deck," Captain Ahab—using what one critic, Richard B. Sewall, calls "demonic eloquence"—convinces the crew of the *Pequod* to follow him on his mad hunt for Moby Dick. Have you ever heard a speaker who had a similar power over an audience, who could stir people up, move them deeply with his or her words? Write an essay describing the speaker, what he said, and the response of the listeners. Examples might include a preacher, a politician, an athletic coach giving a pep talk, a lawyer addressing a jury, a speaker at a graduation exercise, or just a friend with the ability to persuade people to do things his way.
3. One definition of *nemesis* is someone or something that continually plagues us, a rival whom we can never seem to get the better of—the "bane of our existence." In this sense, Moby Dick is Ahab's nemesis. Write a paper in which you describe *your* nemesis.

ADDITIONAL WRITING SUGGESTIONS FOR CHAPTER SEVEN

1. As we say in the introduction to this chapter, few people go through life without having a purpose or goal in mind, for it is characteristic of human beings that we are always looking for something, always engaged in a search. Write an essay in which you describe your present goal in life—what it is you are searching for. Is the object of your Quest different from what it was when you were younger? What path must you follow to attain it? What kinds of obstacles stand in your way? Why do you want to attain this particular object or goal? Why is it so important to you?

2. Choose one of the following selections from previous chapters and, in a well-organized essay, explain why it can be considered a Quest story: "The Open Sea" (p. 29); "The Birthmark" (p. 45); "Hymn to Demeter" (p. 162); "The Queen Bee" (p. 273); "The Secret of the Golden Crocodile" (p. 276); "I've Been Born Again" (p. 395). Describe the Quester. What is he or she searching for? What trials must be faced and overcome? Is this person successful?

3. In their book *The World of the Short Story: Archetypes in Action* (1971), Oliver Evans and Harry Finestone write that a person who has achieved his goal may end up disillusioned, for he may find "that he has deceived himself—that this, after all, is not what he was really looking for." Have you ever had the experience of yearning for something, struggling to attain it, and then discovering that it wasn't what you had expected it to be, wasn't what you wanted after all? Describe such an experience in an essay.

4. "A man who was not searching for something," write Evans and Finestone, "would truly be a monster." In a well-organized thesis-and-support essay, either defend or take issue with this statement. (The quote is meant to apply equally well to women.)

5. Write your own story—science fiction, "sword-and-sorcery" fantasy, cowboy, pirate, romance—centering around a Quest. Try to include all the classical elements of the Quest: describe the hero or heroine, the call to adventure, the helpers encountered, the "unknown region" that must be entered, the ordeals which must be overcome, the goal of the Quest, and so on.

6. Write an interpretation of the following poem by the great American writer Walt Whitman (1819–1892):

Darest Thou Now O Soul

Darest thou now O soul,
Walk out with me toward the unknown region,
Where neither ground is for the feet nor any path to follow?

No map there, nor guide,
Nor voice sounding, nor touch of human hand,
Nor face with blooming flesh, nor lips, nor eyes, are in that land.

I know it not O soul,
Nor dost thou, all is a blank before us,
All waits undream'd of in that region, that inaccessible land.

Till when the ties loosen,
All but the ties eternal, Time and Space,
Nor darkness, gravitation, sense, nor any bounds bounding us.

Then we burst forth, we float,
In Time and Space O soul, prepared for them,
Equal, equipt at last, (O joy! O fruit of all!) them to fulfil O soul.

What is the nature of the speaker's Quest? To what "unknown region" is he going? What does he expect to find there? How would you describe his mood? Why does he feel this way?

Eight

Rebirth

But if they was joyful, it warn't nothing to what I was; for it was like being born again.

—Mark Twain, *The Adventures of Huckleberry Finn*

The idea of rebirth, of leaving one kind of life behind and passing on to a new existence, is central to many religions, both ancient and modern. This idea takes different forms. Hindus and Buddhists, for instance, believe in the theory of reincarnation, which holds that when a person dies, the soul returns briefly to its original, otherwordly source before being sent back to earth to inhabit another body, usually (though not necessarily) human. How the soul is re-embodied—what particular shape it takes—is dependent on the person's conduct in his previous existence, so that, while a virtuous man might come back as a prince, a criminal might be reborn as a rodent. According to this view, life is a process of spiritual evolution, in which the soul passes through successive incarnations, learning a bit more during each one, until it achieves that level of purity which will allow it to merge for all time with its divine source. Thus, human life is seen as an ongoing series of births, deaths, and rebirths.

Another type of rebirth, of particular importance to Christianity, is resurrection—the raising of the body after death. Christians believe both in the resurrection of the dead on Judgment Day, when God will raise them up to stand trial before Him, and in the resurrection of Jesus—his return to life three days after his crucifixion. The fact that Jesus was resurrected in the spring is significant, since it suggests that, to some extent, Christianity was influenced by earlier Near Eastern religions which also featured a god who died and was reborn in the springtime. Worshiped under various names in different places—as Attis in ancient Phrygia, Osiris in Egypt, and Tammuz in Babylonia (who was later adopted by the Greeks and renamed Adonis)—this deity was essentially a nature or vegetation god, whose death and rebirth were intimately bound up with the annual cycle of the seasons.

Though the myths about this "year god" vary somewhat in details, in accordance with cultural distinctions, the story is always essentially the same: that of a young male diety whose tragic (and usually violent) death brings a loss of fertility to the natural world. Attis castrates himself in a fit of madness and dies from his wounds; Adonis is gored by a wild boar; Osiris is dismembered by his evil brother Set. Each of these deities is mourned by a goddess—Cybele, Aphrodite, or Isis— who either journeys to the underworld to retrieve the slain god or restores his dismembered body to wholeness. And just as his death brings barrenness to the land, so his return to the world restores it to fruitfulness. Since the growth of the crops was believed to depend on the resurrection of the dying god, his worship was always attended by yearly celebrations held in the spring—the season of his (and of nature's) miraculous revival. Thus, in the religions of the ancient Near East, the idea of resurrection tended to be connected, not, as in Christianity, with a concern over the human soul's fate after death, but with the perception of the cyclical processes of growth, decay, and rebirth in the natural world.

The process of rebirth, however, is restricted neither to the natural nor to the supernatural worlds; it is not something that happens only to plants in the spring and souls after death. Rather, it is an experience which may occur to any human being in the course of his or her existence. The sensation of being reborn, of beginning life anew, can have many different sources. Sometimes, it can come upon us when we emerge from a period of bad luck, illness, or depression and are filled with new hope, a feeling summed up in a popular slogan of the 1960s: "Today is the first day of the rest of your life." Sometimes, the feeling of rebirth may be produced by a religious conversion. In evangelical Christianity, for instance, a repentant sinner, filled with God's love, may feel that he has been "born again," cleansed of corruption, "raised from being dead in sin to a state of new . . . life" (to quote the great eighteenth-century Puritan minister Jonathan Edwards). Human love, too, can have the effect of making us "feel like new." In Johnnie Taylor's pop song "I've Been Born Again," for instance, the speaker's promiscuous life is totally transformed by the love of "one special woman":

> I've been born again
> I've been born again
> I'm not a Casanova
> My playing days are over.

In D. H. Lawrence's famous and frequently anthologized short story, "The Horse-Dealer's Daughter," the title character, a woman named Mabel Pervin, is also born again through the power of love. Driven by her extreme loneliness to attempt suicide, she is saved by young Dr. Fergusson, whose human touch not only restores her to life but awakens her long-suppressed passions. Lawrence's use of imagery in this story—his skillful shift of scenery from the gray, dead, wintry landscape in which Mabel tries to kill herself to the hot, firelit room in which she is brought back to life—reinforces the theme of his heroine's rebirth, of her transformation from a morbid young woman, with a face as immobile as a death mask, to a vibrant and fiery creature. In Henry James' *The American,* the hero's rebirth is similarly symbolized by a change in locale, as Christopher Newman travels by coach from the gloomy district of New York City's Wall Street to the green world of the Long Island countryside.

In both Lawrence's work and James', the authors artistically use the landscape as a symbol of death and rebirth. In John Denver's enormously popular "Rocky Mountain High," on the other hand, the landscape is the *cause* of the singer's rebirth. As we saw in Chapter Four ("The Mother"), it has become increasingly common in our mechanized, technologized society for people, and particularly city dwellers, to long for greater contact with nature. The success of Denver's music attests to the strength of that longing. For years, he has given voice to it in his songs. In "Rocky Mountain High," the singer's climb up the "cathedral mountains" of the Colorado Rockies leads to a profound—even a religious—experience: he is "born again," has visions of fire raining from the sky, converses with God. Though the description of this experience seems somewhat overstated (more applicable to Moses' ascent of Mount Sinai than to a backpacking trip in Colorado), it is nevertheless true that a change of scenery, especially a change from the closed, concrete world of the city to the wide-open spaces of the West, can work deep psychological and physical changes and be enormously reinvigorating.

In one sense, Denver's "Rocky Mountain High" is a very typical American work, not only because it is set in a uniquely American landscape, but also because the dream it expresses—of leaving civilization behind, journeying into the wilderness, and there being transformed into a new person—is at the very heart of our national experience. Our country, after all, was originally colonized by people who abandoned European civilization to seek a new existence in this vast, alien, unspoiled land. And ever since the time of the earliest settlers, America has always represented, for immigrants, a place where a second chance is possible, where they can start life anew and be, in a sense, reborn. As early as 1782, the writer St. Jean de Crèvecoeur attempted to define the typical inhabitant of this country in an essay entitled "What Is an American." Once established in this land, with its boundless natural resources and endless opportunities, the downtrodden European immigrant "begins to feel the effects of a sort of resurrection," says Crèvecoeur. Thus, the answer to the question which he poses in his title is "The American is a new man." A hundred years later, the great American author Henry James arrives at the same conclusion. The hero of his novel *The American*—which, like Crèvecoeur's essay, attempts to portray the "national type"—is a lanky Westerner with the significant name of Newman (new man). For writers from St. Jean de Crèvecoeur to John Denver, therefore, the "American dream" can be defined as the search for a new and better life: a social, economic, or spiritual rebirth.

The search for rebirth, however, is by no means unique to our culture. On the contrary, every hero's Quest involves a kind of rebirth. As we saw in the previous chapter, the hero is the person who leaves his outworn or empty existence behind, travels into a hellish place—a literal or figurative underworld—and, if he is successful, returns with a treasure which completely transforms his life. This transformation is, in effect, a rebirth. The hero's descent into darkness and danger represents what amounts to his death, or, more precisely, the death of his previous existence. *All* rebirths require a death; we cannot begin a new life until the old is dead and gone. Casting off established patterns of behavior—leaving behind those habits and routines which, no matter how humdrum they may seem, provide us with a deep sense of security and stability—is a difficult, even frightening, undertaking for many people. To contemplate the passage from the familiar to the unknown (even when the familiar seems cramped or unfulfilling) is often unnerving. But those individuals who can courageously accomplish this passage, who can, in disregard of convention, comfort, and safety, plunge into a darkness that may at times seem as dark and terrifying as a tomb's, often discover at the end of their journeys a way of life far more satisfying than the one they left behind. What looked like a tomb may in fact turn out to be a kind of womb, a place which marks, not only the end of an old mode of existence, but also the start of a new.

In some of the selections which follow ("Rocky Mountain High," for example), only the moment of renewal is shown. Others, however, portray the entire process of death and rebirth. This is true, as we have seen, of the myth of the "dying and reviving god," as well as of James' *The American,* in which the hero's awakening to a new life is preceded by a symbolic death, as the sleeping Newman is carried by coach through the city streets like a corpse in a hearse. The same pattern of death and rebirth can also be seen in Will Eisner's comic strip "Life Below." Here, Eisner's detective hero, the Spirit, in pursuit of a murderer believed to be long dead, descends into a dark and terrifying realm—the city's sewer system, now serving as the subterranean hideout for a group of desperate criminals. Interestingly, at the very moment the Spirit enters this dismal underworld, a terrible snowstorm begins to fall on the city, and when, after finding the man he seeks, he emerges again into the daylight, the snow melts and life begins "to regain its tempo." Like the nature or vegetation god's passage after death from the earth to the gloomy realm below, which brings the processes of nature to a standstill, the Spirit's disappearance from the surface produces a temporary suspension of aboveground activity, while his return (again like that of the vegetation god) restores energy and vitality to the world.

In our earlier discussion of the hero myth, we pointed out that one of the things it stands for, one of the purposes of the Quest, is the achievement of self-knowledge. This kind of Quest also involves a death and rebirth. In an essay entitled "Concerning Rebirth," C. G. Jung describes the process of self-realization as one of "inner transformation and rebirth into another being. This 'other being' is the other person in ourselves—that larger and greater personality maturing within us." As we undergo this process of inner development, we leave our old personalities behind. We begin to see that there is more to life and to ourselves than we had suspected. Our horizons expand; our old attitudes and assumptions suddenly seem insufficient, and we leave them behind, cast them off like the slough of a snake, the old skin which can no longer contain the creature's growing body.

Anthropologists have discovered that, in primitive societies, this process of maturation is literally acted out in those tribal ceremonies commonly known as puberty or initiation rites. Although initiation rites for women exist, such ceremonies are far more frequent among males; in fact, male puberty rituals are virtually universal among primitive people, and, whether performed in Africa, Australia, or South America, always follow the same essential pattern. The youth to be initiated is taken from home and mother by a group of men who carry him to some isolated spot—a dark hut or a special clearing in the forest—where he is subjected to various ordeals: beatings, deprivation of food, water, and sleep, even bodily mutilation. At the end of these tortures, the youth is tutored in tribal lore: he receives religious instruction, is taught how to hunt, and learns what will be expected of him as a man. Finally, he is given a new name, his *man's* name, and is returned to the tribe, where he is now to take a bride and assume the duties and obligations of an adult. The purpose of these rites is, very simply, to transform the boy into a man; the process they represent is the death of the initiate's childhood (his removal from the security of home and the protection of mother, the symbolic "killing" of his old self through beatings, starvation, etc.) and his rebirth as a mature and responsible adult. In our own time and place, we see the echoes of these ancient ceremonies in the Christian rite of confirmation for adolescent boys and girls, the Jewish *bar mitzvah,* and even in such procedures as fraternity and sorority initiations, which confer a new, special status upon those people who have passed through the required tests or hazing.

Another interesting modern version of the ancient mythic pattern of death and rebirth is the so-called "Paul McCartney death rumor." One of the well-known stories of the classical world (set down by the Roman poet Ovid in his book the *Metamorphoses*) is the myth of the beautiful youth Hyacinth, a very literal flower-child, who was accidentally slain and subsequently resurrected in the form of the blossom which bears his name. Nearly two thousand years after Ovid, a whole generation of flower-children, members of the counterculture and other rock music fans, were suddenly gripped by the strange conviction that one of *their* heroes, the Beatle Paul McCartney, had been killed in an accident and then miraculously resurrected. More recently, another rock demigod, Elvis Presley, has been "reborn" in the form of various imitators and look-alikes (one of whom even went to the length of having himself surgically transformed to resemble "the King"). We should not be surprised, however, to see the same archetype of death and rebirth appearing both in ancient Greece and modern America. As we started this book by saying, the archetype is a pattern which is basic to human experience and can be found throughout history and in all societies. It is an eternal image which is present in every area of our lives, not only in folklore, classic literature, and popular art, but in the things we believe and the ways we behave.

OVID

"The Story of Apollo and Hyacinthus"

"My intention is to tell of bodies changed to different forms." So begins the *Metamorphoses* (*Transformations*), the best-known work of the Roman poet Ovid (43 B.C.–17 A.D.). Born to a family of wealthy landowners in the small town of Sulmo, high in the Apennine mountains, Publius Ovidius Naso was educated at Rome in preparation for a public career. After holding some minor official posts, however, he chose to devote himself to poetry. Ovid's great theme is love, passion, the

From Ovid, *Metamorphoses,* translated by Rolfe Humphries, copyright 1955 by Indiana University Press. Reprinted by permission of the publisher.

erotic. His early works include the *Amores* (*Loves*), dealing with a love affair, probably imaginary, between the poet and a woman called Corinna; *Heroides* (*Heroines*), consisting of a series of love letters sent by fifteen famous women to their paramours; *Ars Amatoria* (*The Art of Love*) and *Remedia Amators* (*The Cure for Love*), two treatises offering witty advice on such matters as adultery and seduction; and *De Medicamina Faciei* (*On Make-up*), a verse manual on the use of cosmetics.

His masterpiece, however, is the *Metamorphoses*, a collection of mythological stories, in fifteen books, dealing with various types of transformation, from the creation of the world (the metamorphosis of chaos into order) to the deification of Julius Caesar (the metamorphosis of a mortal into a god). Though Ovid uses the image of transformation to tie together the many different tales in the collection, his main concern is once again the power of passion. During the Middle Ages and the Renaissance, the *Metamorphoses* was the major sourcebook of classical mythology, and exerted an enormous influence on such writers as Petrarch, Chaucer, Marlowe, Spenser, Shakespeare, and Milton.

With its publication in 8 A.D., Ovid had reached the peak of his poetic career, but was soon cast down from this height by the Emperor Augustus, a staunch moral reformer. Augustus, who had long been irritated by the cheery amorality of Ovid's work, was now driven to the limits of his tolerance by a mysterious offense which Ovid, in his later writings, speaks of as an "indiscretion," though he never specifies its nature. As a punishment for his crime, the poet was banished to Tomis, a bleak, semicivilized outpost on the very edge of the Roman Empire. There, while his devoted third wife remained in Rome, guarding his property and working for his return, Ovid wrote poetic appeals to the emperor for a pardon which was never granted. He died in Tomis in 17 A.D.

The story of Hyacinthus, reprinted below, is taken from Book Ten of the *Metamorphoses*, as translated by Rolfe Humphries.

The Story of Apollo and Hyacinthus

There was another boy, who might have had
A place in Heaven, at Apollo's order,[1]
Had Fate seen fit to give him time, and still
He is, in his own fashion, an immortal.
Whenever spring drives winter out, and the Ram
Succeeds the wintry Fish, he springs to blossom
On the green turf. My father loved him dearly,
This Hyacinthus, and left Delphi for him,
Outward from the world's center, on to Sparta,
The town that has no walls, and Eurotas River.
Quiver and lyre were nothing to him there,

---

[1] The god Apollo (also called Phoebus, "The Bright One") is, in Edith Hamilton's words, "the master musician who delights Olympos as he plays on his golden lyre; the lord of the silver bow, the Archer-god, far-shooting; the Healer, as well, who first taught men the healing art. Even more than of these good and lovely endowments, he is the God of Light, in whom is no darkness at all, and so he is the God of Truth."

No more than his own dignity; he carried
The nets for fellows hunting, and held the dogs
In leash for them, and with them roamed the trails
Of the rough mountain ridges. In their train
He fed the fire with long association.
It was noon one day: Apollo, Hyacinthus,
Stripped, rubbed themselves with oil, and tried their skill
At discus-throwing. Apollo sent the missile
Far through the air, so far it pierced the clouds,
A long time coming down, and when it fell
Proved both his strength and skill, and Hyacinthus,
All eager for his turn, heedless of danger,
Went running to pick it up, before it settled
Fully to earth. It bounded once and struck him
Full in the face, and he grew deadly pale
As the pale god caught up the huddled body,
Trying to warm the dreadful chill that held it,
Trying to staunch the wound, to keep the spirit
With healing herbs, but all the arts were useless,
The wound was past all cure. So, in a garden,
If one breaks off a violet or poppy
Or lilies, bristling with their yellow stamens,
And they droop over, and cannot raise their heads,
But look on earth, so sank the dying features,
The neck, its strength all gone, lolled on the shoulder.
'Fallen before your time, O Hyacinthus,'
Apollo cried, 'I see your wound, my crime:
You are my sorrow, my reproach; my hand
Has been your murderer. But how am I
To blame? Where is my guilt, except in playing
With you, in loving you? I cannot die
For you, or with you either; the law of Fate
Keeps us apart: it shall not! You will be
With me forever, and my songs and music
Will tell of you, and you will be reborn
As a new flower whose markings will spell out
My cries of grief, and there will come a time
When a great hero's name will be the same[2]
As this flower's markings.' So Apollo spoke,
And it was truth he told, for on the ground
The blood was blood no longer; in its place
A flower grew, brighter than any crimson,
Like lilies with their silver changed to crimson.
That was not all; Apollo kept the promise
About the markings, and inscribed the flower
With his own grieving words: *Ai, Ai*

---

[2] A reference to Ajax, a hero the Trojan War, whose Greek name (Aias) contains the markings on
the hyacinth petals.

The petals say, Greek for *Alas!* In Sparta,
Even to this day, they hold their son in honor,
And when the day comes round, they celebrate
The rites for Hyacinthus, as did their fathers.

QUESTIONS

Language

1. What device does Ovid use in the beginning of his narrative to represent the passage of time? Why doesn't he simply say "spring follows winter"?
2. What metaphor does Ovid use to tell us how badly hurt Hyacinthus is? Why would he use this particular metaphor?
3. Ovid tells us that Apollo gathered up Hyacinthus' "huddled body,/Trying to warm the dreadful chill that held it,/Trying to staunch the wound, . . ." What is the effect of these lines? What effect is achieved by the repetition of the word *all* in the following: ". . . all the arts were useless,/The wound was past all cure"?

Content

1. When Ovid says "my father loved . . ./This Hyacinthus, and left Delphi for him," who is the father he refers to?
2. The central transformation of Ovid's story is of course the metamorphosis of the mortal youth Hyacinthus into an "immortal" flower. But the god Apollo is also transformed in the story. How and why?
3. Why does Apollo cause Hyacinthus to be reborn as a flower? As a god, why doesn't he simply restore his human life?
4. "The Story of Apollo and Hyacinthus" follows the traditional narrative pattern: an introduction establishes the context of the story; next, the events of this story are recited; and finally, the writer briefly comments on the tale in the conclusion. Find this tripartite division in Ovid's narrative. What details in his introduction establish the context of the story? What words mark the start of the body of the tale? What words, the conclusion? Is the narrative ordered chronologically from beginning to end?

Suggestions for Writing

1. In *The Uses of Enchantment*, Bruno Bettelheim comments that one of the significant differences between a myth and a fairy tale is that "the myth is pessimistic, while the fairy story is optimistic." We see this, he says, most clearly in their endings: the myth ends tragically and the fairy tale, happily. Using the myths and fairy tales in this book as your evidence, argue in support of or against Bettelheim's thesis.
2. Though the transformations that take place in Ovid's *Metamorphoses* and throughout classical mythology usually involve dramatic physical alterations—a young woman is turned into a tree, a young man into a stag—they symbolize something that happens, on a more ordinary level, to most of us at least once during our lives. We change; we become something we never thought we could become; we cease to be something we once were. Sometimes we actively work for this change; in other cases, it just seems to happen to us. Using the formula "Once I was . . . but now I am . . ." to provide a structure for your writing, write an essay comparing and contrasting your past self with your present self. (The transformation, by the way, need not be a positive one.)

3. Apollo is deeply devoted to his friend Hyacinthus. Write an essay explaining what part friendship plays in your own life. How highly do you value it? Do you have many friends but few close ones; few but very intimate friends; or are you a "loner"? What things do you expect from your friends? What things do you give? Do you wish you had more friends or could make friends more easily?

THE BROTHERS GRIMM

"The Juniper Tree"

"The Juniper Tree," a story of haunting beauty, contains powerful mythic elements. Two images of rebirth stand out: the coming of spring at the start of the tale, accompanied by the sudden fertility of the rich man's first wife; and the resurrection of the murdered son, who first rises phoenix-like in the shape of a marvelous bird and is later restored to his human shape. As in many fairy tales, we find two opposing images of motherhood—the familiar wicked stepmother and the loving natural mother, whose symbol is the sheltering juniper tree. (Some folklore scholars explain the maternal significance of the juniper tree by pointing out its association with Juno, the Roman goddess of marriage and childbirth.) Finally, there is the gruesome scene in which the father unknowingly dines on the "black-puddings" made from the body of his slain boy—an episode reminiscent of several Greek myths. (There is the story of Atreus, for example, who avenged himself on his brother Thyestes by killing the latter's sons, cutting them into pieces, and then serving them to Thyestes at a feast. Tereus, the king of Thrace, was punished in a similar way by his wife, Procne.)

It is now long ago, quite two thousand years, since there was a rich man who had a beautiful and pious wife, and they loved each other dearly. They had, however, no children, though they wished for them very much, and the woman prayed for them day and night, but still they had none. Now there was a court-yard in front of their house in which was a juniper tree, and one day in winter the woman was standing beneath it, paring herself an apple, and while she was paring herself the apple she cut her finger, and the blood fell on the snow. "Ah," said the woman, and sighed right heavily, and looked at the blood before her, and was most unhappy, "ah, if I had but a child as red as blood and as white as snow!" And while she thus spoke, she became quite happy in her mind, and felt just as if that were going to happen. Then she went into the house, and a month went by and the snow was gone, and two months, and then everything was green, and three months, and then all the flowers came out of the earth, and four months, and then all the trees in the wood grew thicker, and the green branches were all closely entwined, and the birds sang until the wood resounded

From *The Complete Grimm's Fairy Tales,* by Jakob Ludwig and Wilhelm Karl Grimm, translated by Margaret Hunt and James Stern. Copyright 1944 by Pantheon Books and renewed 1972 by Random House, Inc. Reprinted by permission of Pantheon Books, a Division of Random House, Inc.

and the blossoms fell from the trees, then the fifth month passed away and she stood under the juniper tree, which smelt so sweetly that her heart leapt, and she fell on her knees and was beside herself with joy, and when the sixth month was over the fruit was large and fine, and then she was quite still, and the seventh month she snatched at the juniper-berries and ate them greedily, then she grew sick and sorrowful, then the eighth month passed, and she called her husband to her, and wept and said: "If I die, then bury me beneath the juniper tree." Then she was quite comforted and happy until the next month was over, and then she had a child as white as snow and as red as blood, and when she beheld it she was so delighted that she died.

Then her husband buried her beneath the juniper tree, and he began to weep sore; after some time he was more at ease, and though he still wept he could bear it, and after some time longer he took another wife.

By the second wife he had a daughter, but the first wife's child was a little son, and he was as red as blood and as white as snow. When the woman looked at her daughter she loved her very much, but then she looked at the little boy and it seemed to cut her to the heart, for the thought came into her mind that he would always stand in her way, and she was for ever thinking how she could get all the fortune for her daughter, and the Evil One filled her mind with this till she was quite wroth with the little boy and she pushed him from one corner to the other and slapped him here and cuffed him there, until the poor child was in continual terror, for when he came out of school he had no peace in any place.

One day the woman had gone upstairs to her room, and her little daughter went up too, and said: "Mother, give me an apple." "Yes, my child," said the woman, and gave her a fine apple out of the chest, but the chest had a great heavy lid with a great sharp iron lock. "Mother," said the little daughter, "is brother not to have one too?" This made the woman angry, but she said: "Yes, when he comes out of school." And when she saw from the window that he was coming, it was just as if the Devil entered into her, and she snatched at the apple and took it away again from her daughter, and said: "You shall not have one before your brother." Then she threw the apple into the chest, and shut it. Then the little boy came in at the door, and the Devil made her say to him kindly: "My son, will you have an apple?" and she looked wickedly at him. "Mother," said the little boy, "how dreadful you look! Yes, give me an apple." Then it seemed to her as if she were forced to say to him: "Come with me," and she opened the lid of the chest and said: "Take out an apple for yourself," and while the little boy was stooping inside, the Devil prompted her, and crash! she shut the lid down, and his head flew off and fell among the red apples. Then she was overwhelmed with terror, and thought: "If I could but make them think that is was not done by me!" So she went upstairs to her room to her chest of drawers, and took a white handkerchief out of the top drawer, and set the head on the neck again, and folded the handkerchief so that nothing could be seen, and she set him on a chair in front of the door, and put the apple in his hand.

After this Marlinchen came into the kitchen to her mother, who was standing by the fire with a pan of hot water before her which she was constantly stirring round. "Mother," said Marlinchen, "brother is sitting at the door, and he looks quite white, and has an apple in his hand. I asked him to give me the apple, but he did not answer me, and I was quite frightened." "Go back to him," said her mother, "and if he will not answer you, give him a box on the ear." So Marlinchen went to him and said: "Brother, give me the apple." But he was silent, and she gave him a box on the ear, whereupon his head fell off. Marlinchen was terrified, and began crying and screaming, and ran to her mother, and said: "Alas, mother, I have knocked my brother's head off!" and she wept and wept and could not be comforted. "Marlinchen," said the mother, "what have you done? but be quiet and let no one know it; it cannot be helped now, we will make him into black-puddings." Then the mother took the little boy and chopped him in pieces, put him into the pan and made him into black-puddings; but Marlinchen stood by weeping and weeping, and all her tears fell into the pan and there was no need of any salt.

Then the father came home, and sat down to dinner and said: "But where is my son?" And the mother served up a great dish of black-puddings, and Marlinchen wept and could not leave off. Then the father again said: "But where is my son?" "Ah," said the mother, "he has gone across the country to his mother's great uncle; he will stay there awhile." "And what is he going to do there? He did not even say good-bye to me."

"Oh, he wanted to go, and asked me if he might stay six weeks, he is well taken care of there." "Ah," said the man, "I feel so unhappy lest all should not be right. He ought to have said good-bye to me." With that he began to eat and said: "Marlinchen, why are you crying? Your brother will certainly come back." Then he said: "Ah, wife, how delicious this food is, give me some more." And the more he ate the more he wanted to have, and he said: "Give me some more, you shall have none of it. It seems to me as if it were all mine." And he ate and ate and threw all the bones under the table, until he had finished the whole. But Marlinchen went away to her chest of drawers, and took her best silk handkerchief out of the bottom drawer, and got all the bones from beneath the table, and tied them up in her silk handkerchief, and carried them outside the door, weeping tears of blood. Then she lay down under the juniper tree on the green grass, and after she had lain down there, she suddenly felt light-hearted and did not cry any more. Then the juniper tree began to stir itself, and the branches parted asunder, and moved together again, just as if someone were rejoicing and clapping his hands. At the same time a mist seemed to arise from the tree, and in the centre of this mist it burned like a fire, and a beautiful bird flew out of the fire singing magnificently, and he flew high up in the air, and when he was gone, the juniper tree was just as it had been before, and the handkerchief with the bones was no longer there. Marlinchen, however, was as gay and happy as if her brother were still alive. And she went merrily into the house, and sat down to dinner and ate.

But the bird flew away and lighted on a goldsmith's house, and began to sing:

"My mother she killed me,
My father he ate me,
My sister, little Marlinchen,
Gathered together all my bones,
Tied them in a silken handkerchief,
Laid them beneath the juniper tree,
Kywitt, kywitt, what a beautiful bird am I!"

The goldsmith was sitting in his workshop making a golden chain, when he heard the bird which was sitting singing on his roof, and very beautiful the song seemed to him. He stood up, but as he crossed the threshold he lost one of his slippers. But he went away right up the middle of the street with one shoe on and one sock; he had his apron on, and in one hand he had the golden chain and in the other the pincers, and the sun was shining brightly on the street. Then he went right on and stood still, and said to the bird: "Bird," said he then, "how beautifully you can sing! Sing me that piece again." "No," said the bird, "I'll not sing it twice for nothing! Give me the golden chain, and then I will sing it again for you." "There," said the goldsmith, "there is the golden chain for you, now sing me that song again." Then the bird came and took the golden chain in his right claw, and went and sat in front of the goldsmith, and sang:

"My mother she killed me,
My father he ate me,
My sister, little Marlinchen,
Gathered together all my bones,
Tied them in a silken handkerchief,
Laid them beneath the juniper tree,
Kywitt, kywitt, what a beautiful bird am I!"

Then the bird flew away to a shoemaker, and lighted on his roof and sang:

"My mother she killed me,
My father he ate me,
My sister, little Marlinchen,
Gathered together all my bones,
Tied them in a silken handkerchief,
Laid them beneath the juniper tree,
Kywitt, kywitt, what a beautiful bird am I!"

The shoemaker heard that and ran out of doors in his shirt sleeves, and looked up at his roof, and was forced to hold his hand before his eyes lest the sun should blind him. "Bird," said he, "how beautifully you can sing!" Then he called in at his door: "Wife, just come outside, there is a bird, look at that bird, he certainly can sing." Then he called his daughter and children, and apprentices, boys and girls, and they all came up the street and looked at the bird and saw how beautiful he was, and what fine red and green feathers he had, and how like real gold his neck was, and how the eyes in his head shone like stars. "Bird," said the shoemaker, "now sing me that song again." "Nay," said the bird, "I do not sing twice for nothing; you must give me something." "Wife," said the man, "go to the garret, upon the top shelf there stands a pair of red shoes, bring them down." Then the wife went and brought the shoes. "There, bird," said the man, "now sing me that piece again." Then the bird came and took the shoes in his left claw, and flew back on the roof, and sang:

"My mother she killed me,
My father he ate me,
My sister, little Marlinchen,
Gathered together all my bones,
Tied them in a silken handkerchief,
Laid them beneath the juniper tree,
Kywitt, kywitt, what a beautiful bird am I!"

And when he had finished his song he flew away. In his right claw he had the chain and in his left the shoes, and he flew far away to a mill, and the mill went "klipp klapp, klipp klapp, klipp klapp," and in the mill sat twenty miller's men hewing a stone, and cutting, hick hack, hick hack, hick hack, and the mill went klipp klapp, klipp klapp, klipp klapp. Then the bird went and sat on a lime-tree which stood in front of the mill, and sang:

"My mother she killed me,"

Then one of them stopped working,

"My father he ate me,"

Then two more stopped working and listened to that,

"My sister, little Marlinchen,"

Then four more stopped,

"Gathered together all my bones,
  Tied them in a silken handkerchief,"

Now eight only were hewing,

"Laid them beneath"

Now only five,

"The juniper tree,"

And now only one,

"Kywitt, kywitt, what a beautiful bird am I!"

Then the last stopped also, and heard the last words. "Bird," said he, "how beautifully you sing! Let me, too, hear that. Sing that once more for me."

"Nay," said the bird, "I will not sing twice for nothing. Give me the millstone, and then I will sing it again."

"Yes," said he, "if it belonged to me only, you should have it."

"Yes," said the others, "if he sings again he shall have it." Then the bird came down, and the twenty millers all set to work with a beam and raised the stone up. And the bird stuck his neck through the hole, and put the stone on as if it were a collar, and flew on to the tree again, and sang:

"My mother she killed me,
  My father he ate me,
  My sister, little Marlinchen,
  Gathered together all my bones,
  Tied them in a silken handkerchief,
  Laid them beneath the juniper tree,
  Kywitt, kywitt, what a beautiful bird am I!"

And when he had done singing, he spread his wings, and in his right claw he had the chain, and in his left the shoes, and round his neck the millstone, and he flew far away to his father's house.

In the room sat the father, the mother, and Marlinchen at dinner, and the father said: "How light-hearted I feel, how happy I am!" "Nay," said the mother, "I feel so uneasy, just as if a heavy storm were coming." Marlinchen, however, sat weeping and weeping, and then came the bird flying, and as it seated itself on the roof the father said: "Ah, I feel so truly happy, and the sun is shining so beautifully outside, I feel just as if I were about to see some old friend again." "Nay," said the woman, "I feel so anxious, my teeth chatter, and I seem to have fire in my veins." And she tore her stays open, but Marlinchen sat in a corner crying, and held her plate before her eyes and cried till it was quite wet. Then the bird sat on the juniper tree, and sang:

"My mother she killed me,"

Then the mother stopped her ears, and shut her eyes, and would not see or hear, but there was a roaring in her ears like the most violent storm, and her eyes burnt and flashed like lightning:

"My father he ate me,"

"Ah, mother," says the man, "that is a beautiful bird! He sings so splendidly, and the sun shines so warm, and there is a smell just like cinnamon."

"My sister, little Marlinchen,"

Then Marlinchen laid her head on her knees and wept without ceasing, but the man said: "I am going out, I must see the bird quite close." "Oh, don't go," said the woman, "I feel as if the whole house were shaking and on fire." But the man went out and looked at the bird:

"Gathered together all my bones,
  Tied them in a silken handkerchief,
  Laid them beneath the juniper tree,
  Kywitt, kywitt, what a beautiful bird am I!"

On this the bird let the golden chain fall, and it fell exactly round the man's neck, and so exactly round it that it fitted beautifully. Then he went in and said: "Just look what a fine bird that is, and what a handsome golden chain he has given me, and how pretty he is!" But the woman was terrified, and fell down on the floor in the room, and her cap fell off her head. Then sang the bird once more:

"My mother she killed me,"

"Would that I were a thousand feet beneath the earth so as not to hear that!"

"My father he ate me,"

Then the woman fell down again as if dead.

"My sister, little Marlinchen,"

"Ah," said Marlinchen, "I too will go out and see if the bird will give me anything," and she went out.

"Gathered together all my bones,
  Tied them in a silken handkerchief,"

Then he threw down the shoes to her.

"Laid them beneath the juniper tree,
  Kywitt, kywitt, what a beautiful bird am I!"

Then she was light-hearted and joyous, and she put on the new red shoes, and danced and leaped into the house. "Ah," said she, "I was so sad when I went out and now I am so light-hearted; that is a splendid bird, he has given me a pair of red shoes!" "Well," said the woman, and sprang to her feet and her hair stood up like flames of fire, "I feel as if the world were coming to an end! I, too, will go out and see if my heart feels lighter." And as she went out at the door, crash! the bird threw down the millstone on her head, and she was entirely crushed by it. The father and Marlinchen heard what had happened and went out, and smoke, flames and fire were rising from the place, and when that was over, there stood the little brother, and he took his father and Marlinchen by the hand, and all three were right glad, and they went into the house to dinner, and ate.

QUESTIONS

Language

1. In several places, the storyteller describes the son as a child who is "as red as blood and as white as snow." What does this mean? Where else in the story do the colors red and white appear? Can you find other places where bright colors appear? What effect is created by this use of color imagery?
2. Take a careful look at the first paragraph of the story describing the birth of the son. In what way can the details of the natural world, the outer world—the drop of blood on the snow, the coming of spring, the growth of the juniper tree—be seen as a metaphor for the biological process (i.e., pregnancy) taking place *within* the woman?
3. In their *Handbook to Literature,* Thrall and Hibbard define the term *onomatopoeia* as the "use of words which in their pronunciation suggest their meaning. Some onomatopoeic words are 'hiss,' 'slam,' 'buzz,' 'whirr,' 'sizzle.' " Point to examples of onomatopoeic words in "The Juniper Tree." Can you think of any others?

Content

1. Why does the first mother die?
2. Why does the stepmother hate the son so fiercely?
3. Describe Marlinchen. What kind of person is she?
4. Why does the father find his wife's "black-puddings" so delicious? How do you explain his voracious appetite?
5. How do the various tradesmen—the goldsmith, shoemaker, and miller's men—respond to the bird's song?
6. How does the stepmother react when she hears the bird's song?

Suggestions for Writing

1. Like many of the Grimm brothers' stories, "The Juniper Tree" contains some very gruesome elements: cannibalism, decapitation, bloody revenge. To protect their children from such violent matters, parents often recite censored versions of these stories. The question of how children are affected by images of violence in the things they hear or read (including comic books), the television shows or movies they watch, and the music they listen to has been a subject of concern among parents, educators, and psychologists for many years. Write an essay in which you either defend or refute the argument that children should not be exposed to images of violence in the mass media—that such

images have a harmful effect on young children. Support your argument with examples drawn from movies, television shows, comic books, and so on.

2. Compare "The Juniper Tree" to the other fairy tales in this book. What features do they share? Do they contain similar language, characters, incidents? Based on similarities you discern, write a definition of the fairy tale as a literary form. Try to get at the essential traits of the fairy tale, as if you were telling someone who had never heard of fairy tales exactly what they are.

3. The term *reincarnation* refers to the widespread belief that, after death, the soul is reborn into a new body, sometimes that of an animal. In "The Juniper Tree," the murdered son returns in the shape of a beautiful bird. If you were to be reincarnated after death, what animal would you like to come back as? Write an essay explaining your choice.

JAMES DEAN AND DON DAVIS

"I've Been Born Again"

(as recorded by Johnnie Taylor)

Born in Crawfordsville, Alabama in 1938, Johnnie Taylor began his career singing gospel music but later switched to soul. A popular and prolific performer, he has cut more than thirty albums, the majority of them for the Stax record company. "I've Been Born Again" was a hit single for Taylor in the summer of 1974. According to Clive Anderson, one of the authors of *The Soul Book* (1975), this song—a "soul-blues opus" about a man who finds "love, miraculously, amid the harsh urban lifestyle suggested by the music"—represents the singer's "artistic zenith." Taylor has recently gained an even wider audience as a performer of disco songs. Among his many albums are *Disco 9000, Eargasm, Ever Ready, Super Taylor, Rated Extraordinaire,* and *Reflections.*

"I've Been Born Again"

I've been born again
I'm a brand new man
I've been born again
Saturday night in the city
Parties on every block
It's a temptation for a man who loves to party

But my party days had to stop
So fellows you can keep your street life
Changing women like you change your clothes
Every woman I need is wrapped up in one
Our love just grows and grows.

Copyright © 1974 by Groovesville Music. Used by permission. All rights reserved.

A whole lotta women is an ego trip
I rather spend my time kissing my baby's sweet lips
I've been born again
I've been born again

I've been born again
I've been born again
I'm not a Casanova
My playing days are over.

I think I'm going to start me a fire
I've got my match box in my hand
Burning up the pages in my little black book
Start my life all over again

I don't need no women in excess
Can't afford to spread my lovin' around
When my woman needs me by her side
I just don't want to let her down.

I don't need a lot of women just to prove my manhood
I've got me one special woman
So I can be the man I should.

QUESTIONS

Language

1. Discuss the use of informal, colloquial speech in the lyrics of this song. Point to examples. What effect does such diction create? How does the singer's *way* of talking (as opposed to *what* he says) convey an impression of the kind of person he is?
2. Define the term *ego trip*. What kind of ego trip is the singer referring to in this song? Describe some other kinds of ego trips.

Content

1. What picture of street life, of male-female relationships in the big city, does this song portray?
2. As you read the lyrics of this song, what kind of person do you picture in your imagination? Describe him in detail.
3. Why does the singer decide to devote himself to just one woman?

Suggestions for Writing

1. Write an essay in which you describe a love affair, or any important relationship, which transformed your life (either for better or worse). What kind of change took place? Did it last?
2. This song suggests that, in order to "prove their manhood," most men "need a lot of women." Do you think that this is generally true of men? Write an essay in which you either agree or disagree with this assertion.
3. How are women treated in this song? Write an essay in which you explain why you either do or do not feel that "I've Been Born Again" accurately represents male attitudes toward women.

JOHN DENVER AND MIKE TAYLOR

"Rocky Mountain High"

John Denver (b. 1943) began life as John Henry Deutschendorf, taking his professional name from the capital of Colorado, his adopted state, whose beauty he celebrates in many of his songs, including the one reprinted here. During the folk music boom of the 1960s, he achieved a degree of success as a composer and performer: his song "Leaving on a Jet Plane" was a hit for folksingers Peter, Paul and Mary, and Denver himself toured and recorded with another popular group of the time, the Chad Mitchell Trio, after the lead singer left to pursue a solo career.

Denver's own solo career started slowly until he underwent a transformation—brought about either by the quasi-religious experience described in the lyrics below or by the advice of a clever manager—and began projecting a new image. With the release of "Take Me Home Country Roads" in 1971, the collegiate "folkie" of the Mitchell Trio suddenly became Mother Nature's son: a clean-cut, all-American boy, comfortably old-fashioned despite the touches of the flower-child about him (rimless eyeglasses, Beatle-style, bowl-cut hair), whose songs extolled the splendors of the Western wilderness and the homely virtues of the country way of life. Denver's music—sunny, reassuring, sentimental—struck a responsive chord in millions of listeners at a time when many Americans, fatigued by the social turmoil of the 1960s and increasingly distrustful of urban sophistication, seemed to crave for a return to "the good old days," when the world was supposedly a simpler, stabler, more "natural" place. Songs like "Thank God I'm a Country Boy," "Back Home Again," and "Sunshine on My Shoulder" appealed to this deeply felt yearning, and Denver soon achieved superstar status; his 1975 television special, "Rocky Mountain Christmas," drew an audience of over 30 million viewers and his *Greatest Hits* album remained on the best-seller charts for more than two years. His other albums include *Rhymes & Reasons, Take Me to Tomorrow, Poems, Prayers & Promises, Aerie, Farewell Andromeda, Windsong,* and *Spirit.*

"Rocky Mountain High"

He was born in the summer of his twenty-seventh year
Comin' home to a place he'd never been before

He left yesterday behind him
You might say he was born again
You might say he found a key for every door

When he first came to the mountains
His life was far away on the road and hangin' by a song

"Rocky Mountain High" by John Denver and Mike Taylor. © Copyright 1972 Cherry Lane Music Co. International copyright secured. All rights reserved. Used by permission.

But the string's already broken and he doesn't really care
It keeps changin' fast and it don't last for long
But the Colorado Rocky Mountain High

I've seen it rainin' fire in the sky
The shadow from the starlight is softer than a lullaby
Rocky Mountain High Colorado, Rocky Mountain High Colorado.

He climbed cathedral mountains, he saw silver clouds below
He saw everything as far as you can see
And they say that he got crazy once
And he tried to touch the sun
And he lost a friend but kept his memory

Now he walks in quiet solitude the forests and the streams
Seeking grace in every step he takes

His sight has turned inside himself to try and understand
The serenity of a clear blue mountain lake

And the Colorado Rocky Mountain High
I've seen it rainin' fire in the sky
You can talk to God and listen to the casual reply
Rocky Mountain High.

Now his life is full of wonder
But his heart still knows some fear
Of a simple thing he cannot comprehend

Why they try to tear the mountains down
To bring in a couple more

More people, more scars upon the land
And the Colorado Rocky Mountain High
I've seen it rainin' fire in the sky
I know he'd be a poorer man if he never saw an eagle fly
Rocky Mountain High
It's a Colorado Rocky Mountain High
I've seen it rainin' fire in the sky
Friends around the campfire and everybody's high
Rocky Mountain High.

QUESTIONS
Language
1. Discuss the use of religious imagery and language in this song. Why does Denver use such imagery? What is he trying to say about the experience described in the song?
2. Why does Denver alternate between the third person ("he") and the first ("I")? Who *is* the "he" in the song? How do you know?

Content
1. This song is about a person who has had a profoundly significant experience high in the Colorado Rockies. What was this person's life like before the experience? What,

for example, did he do for a living?

2. How old was he when the experience happened?

3. What does Denver mean when he says, in the first stanza, that this man came "home to a place he'd never been before"?

4. Describe the precise nature of the experience. What happened, exactly?

5. How has the man changed?

6. What is the one "simple thing" that he "cannot comprehend"?

Suggestions for Writing

1. Over the past few years, many Americans have been seized by a desire to "get back to nature." One sign of this desire has been the growing popularity of such outdoor activities as camping, backpacking, and mountain climbing. Do you enjoy being in the wilderness? Based on your personal experiences, write an essay describing your feelings about being in the wilderness, about camping out in the woods, taking long hikes, and so forth. If you've never done these things, write an essay explaining why you feel you either would or would not enjoy them.

2. Because his songs appeal to the widespread desire among modern Americans to enjoy nature, John Denver has been one of the most popular singers of recent years. Write an essay in which you explain why you either do or do not like the music of Denver. If you are not familiar enough with his songs (or are completely indifferent to them), write an essay in which you describe your favorite singer and explain why you like his or her music so much.

3. In the last stanza of this song, Denver criticizes the destruction of the American wilderness by the forces of "progress." The growing ecology movement in this country (of which Denver may be said to be the minstrel) struggles to preserve our vanishing wilderness from those technological powers that wish to deplete it of its remaining natural resources. Where do you stand on this issue? Which, in other words, do you feel is more important: to save the wilderness or to use its materials—timber, coal, oil, metals of various kinds— for industrial purposes?

WILL EISNER

"Life Below"

Born in New York City in 1917, William Erwin Eisner studied at the Art Students' League before beginning his career as a cartoonist in the 1930s. After some early work on a comic book entitled *Wow, What a Magazine,* he opened his own studio in 1937 and turned out a string of action-adventure features, including *Muss 'Em Up Donovan,* a detective comic which he drew under the pseudonym Willis Rensie (Eisner spelled backwards), and the pirate strip *Hawk of the Seas.*

Eisner's most famous creation, however, is *The Spirit,* which appeared first on June 2, 1940, as part of a sixteen-page Sunday newspaper supplement. He drew the strip until he was drafted in 1942; four years later, following his discharge from the army, he returned to his work on *The Spirit* (which had been taken over in his absence by another artist), but gave it up for good in 1950.

The Spirit is the alter ego of detective Denny Colt, who, fittingly enough (since he is believed to be dead), has his headquarters in Wildwood Cemetery. Unlike other comic book crime fighters, the Spirit wears no outlandish costume, but rather an ordinary business suit, a wide-brimmed hat, and a miniature eye mask behind which he hides his real identity. What truly distinguishes *The Spirit,* however, is not the hero's outfit, but the excellence of its storylines and artwork. Comic book fans and fellow cartoonists alike hold Eisner in high esteem, both for his writing abilities and for his artistic innovations. It was Eisner, for example, who took the visual techniques and atmospheric effects of the 1940s detective film and introduced them into the comics. This aspect of Eisner's art is perhaps best summed up by writer/cartoonist Jules Feiffer in his book *The Great Comic Book Heroes* (1965). Speaking of *Muss 'Em Up Donovan* (though the description applies equally well to *The Spirit*), Feiffer writes that it "was full of dark shadows, creepy angle shots, graphic close-ups of violence and terror. Eisner's world seemed more real than the world of other comic book men because it looked that much more like a movie."

The following story—set, like most of Eisner's strips in Central City (his fantasy version of New York)—was first published on February 22, 1949.

Copyright 1974 Will Eisner, reprinted by permission.

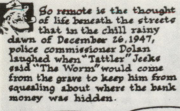

So remote is the thought of life beneath the streets that in the chill rainy dawn of December 26, 1947, police commissioner Dolan laughed when "Tattler" Jeeks said "The Worm" would come from the grave to keep him from squealing about where the bank money was hidden.

NOTHING TO FEAR, TATTLER...YOU'RE IN THE POLICE HEADQUARTERS COURTYARD!

I..I..I K-KNOW.. B-BUT THE WOIM AIN'T DEAD.. HE'LL COME FROM BELOW... TO GET ME...

NONSENSE! THE WORM WAS SHOT MONTHS AGO, AND POLICE SAW HIM FALL INTO A SEWER...HE WAS WASHED OUT TO SEA! BESIDES, THE AREA IS SURROUNDED.. A FLY COULDN'T GET AT YOU..

B-B-BUT A W-WOIM COULD!

BRRR.. ACHOO! IT'S RAINING AGAIN... LET'S TAKE A STAFF CAR TO THE CELLS, DOLAN.

YEAH...HEY, KLINK... GET US A STAFF CAR.. WE'RE TAKING TATTLER TO CELL BLOCK 10 FOR FINGERPRINTING... HURRY..THIS RAIN IS SOAKING ME!

YES, SIR.

?

HA HA HA HA..

TH' WOIM! ...BUT WHERE?

HA HA HA.. TATTLER, I'M GONNA KILL YA...

SO Y'R GONNA TELL, EH?

BANG

BANG

BANG

CLANCY...BERRY... GEEZ! WHERE'D THOSE SHOTS COME FROM?... KILLED RIGHT UNDER YOUR NOSES.. DOPES!

BUT, SIR..IT'S IMPOSSIBLE! NO ONE IS WITHIN SHOOTIN' DISTANCE!

THERE AIN'T EVEN A WINDOW FACIN' THIS COURT...

HMM.. SHOT FROM BELOW...

HEY, SPIRIT.. SPIRIT! CONFOUND IT, WHAT'S GOIN' ON AROUND HERE.. HE'S GONE..

HE RAN DOWN THE STREET, SIR.

And so began the day... the temperature was dropping, and the rain was now snow, falling in heavy flakes....

BOY, IS OL' MAN DOLAN SORE...FIRST HIS STAR WITNESS IS SHOT UNDER HIS NOSE...NOW HE CAN'T FIND THE SPIRIT...

HO-HUM.. LOOKS LIKE I'LL BE BELLY-WHOPPIN' WITH ME KID TOMORROW IF THIS SNOW KEEPS UP...

...And so...
in the silence of
the city beneath....

OOF..

HELLO, MR. WORM... MY GUESS WAS RIGHT... YOU SHOT HIM FROM THE SEWER DRAIN IN THE COURTYARD... TATTLER IS DEAD...

NOW AIN'T THAT TOO BAD... HA HA HA HA HA HA

YES.. AND A JURY WILL AGREE, I'M SURE...

YOU'LL HAVE TO CATCH ME FIRST, SPIRIT...

YEOW! OUCH..

UGH!

EEEEP

THIS IS MY WORLD DOWN HERE... HERE IN THE PIPES AND CATACOMBS WE GOT ONLY ONE LAW... SURVIVAL! THE JUDGE AND JURY IS DEATH..... YEAH, THE TABLES IS TOINED, SPIRIT... HA HA HA...

HEH HEH

WELCOME TO OUR FAIR CITY, SON...

CACKLE

COUGH.. HAK.. COUGH.. WHAT NEWS FROM THE UPPER CITY?.. TELL ME...

SPIRIT.. REMEMBER ME.. KNIFE SCHNITZEL?

HOLY COW... YOU! CROAKER! 'SHADOW! YOU'RE ALL HERE... LIVING DOWN HERE..

YEAH.. COUGH.. WHEEZE AND THE COPS ALL THINK WE'RE **DEAD!**

TELL ME.. WHAT IS IT LIKE... THE FRESH AIR.. TREES.. PARKS.. IS IT ALL THE SAME?

YES... IT'S WINTER UP THERE NOW... HOW LONG HAVE YOU BEEN DOWN HERE, SWIPER?

6 YEARS.. 6 YEARS... **SIX LONG, WET, SLIMY, SMELLY, YEARS** ..BAW!

GOOD GRIEF...

YOU WERE A FOOL TO RUN AWAY, SWIPER..IF YOU COME BACK AND PAY THE PENALTY FOR THAT THEFT, YOU'LL BE OUT IN TWO YEARS. **FREE** TO LIVE IN THE COUNTRY.

..SIGH..SOB.. THE COUNTRY... THE GRASS... **TAKE ME BACK UP WITH YOU, SPIRIT..** PLEASE.. PLEASE...

DON'T BE FOOLS!

DON'T LET HIM GO... THE SPIRIT WORKS WITH THE COPS... HE'LL BRING 'EM DOWN AFTER US....

SCREECH! HA HA HA HA FEED HIM TO THE RATS...

KILL HIM

STAY THERE, AMELIA..I'LL GET YOU YOUR SUPPER... MASKED CRIMEFIGHTER ON TOAST.. HAK HAK HAK!

OOF!

WE'RE GOING BACK, MR.. WORM, AND YOU'LL **PAY** FOR YOUR CRIME.

It was now midnight of the 26th of December, 1947...a snowfall greater than the blizzard of '88 had fallen and the city lay prostrate under 25.8 inches of snow...railroads were halted...power lines down...cars and trucks lay abandoned in the streets...the once-busy metropolis lay inert and silent under a shroud of white. Atop the manhole cover stands a 2½ ton truck...immovable...

PUFF
PUFF
IT'S
PUFF
HOPELESS

NO NO NO!
IT CAN'T BE...
IT'S GOT TO
OPEN!

THUD

MY
LAST
CHANCE...
THIS
CAN'T
HAPPEN
NOW!

THUD
THUD

THUD
THUD

UGH

SWIPER!

HA HA
SWIPER
KNOCKED
HIMSELF
OUT!

NOT
QUITE...
HE'S
DEAD..

HAW!
THAT'S
A BREAK FOR
ME...I'M LEAVIN'
YA...YA'LL NEVER
FIND ME WITHOUT
HIS HELP...

WORM..
LOOK OUT...
THAT WATER
MAIN IS
CRACKING!

TH-THANKS...
Y-Y'SAVED ME
F'UM DROWNIN'..

IT WAS NOT A
PLEASURE, I
ASSURE YOU!
HMM...NOW WE'RE
STUCK HERE...
WONDER WHAT
COULD BE HOLDING
DOWN THE LID...

G...G...DO SOMETHIN'
SPIRIT...I...I'M FREEZIN'
T'DEATH!

...I GET IT NOW...ICE..
THAT WATER MAIN
BURST BECAUSE IT WAS
OVERTAXED...MELTING ICE
...ONLY A HEAVY SNOW
COULD HAVE DONE
THAT...

TWO WATER
MAINS HAVE BURST,
SIR...AND WE'RE OPENING
THE POLICE DORMITORIES
TO STRANDED
COMMUTERS.

FINE, KLINK...
HO·HUM.. GET ME
A COT...I CAN'T
GET HOME
EITHER!

On the morning of the 27th, the city with military precision moved huge equipment into the streets and began the million-dollar job of snow removal ... life began to regain its tempo, and things long buried under the drifts began to move ....

Within 48 hours the temperature dropped ... a soft rain melted the snow, saving the city millions of dollars...

.... and all was normal above...

... and below the city..

QUESTIONS

Language

1. What metaphor does Eisner use to describe the city in the small inset panel which appears on the title page?

2. Take a close look at the "dialogue balloons" which contain the characters' words. How does Eisner create a sense of authentic human speech? What devices does he use to let the reader know what tone of voice a particular character is using at any moment? Find examples of dialogue expressing fear, suspicion, malice, despair, hope.

Content

1. Describe "life below." How have the criminal inhabitants of the sewer system managed to survive for so long? What, for example, do they eat?

2. In what way can the catacombs under the city be said to resemble Hell? Are there any panels in which the inhabitants appear to be inhuman, even demonic, creatures?

3. Why does Swiper agree to guide the Spirit back to the surface?

4. Will Eisner is one of the most highly regarded of all comic book artists. Basing your answer on "Life Below," how would you define the distinctive features of his work? In what ways does this story *look* different from other comics? (You might want to compare the drawing style in "Life Below" to that in some of the other comics reprinted in this book.) How does Eisner manage to combine drama and humor? In what way does this comic seem somewhat more *serious* than others you are familiar with?

Suggestions for Writing

1. Write a paper analyzing "Life Below" as a traditional Quest story. Point to the different elements of the hero's Quest (described in the introduction to the previous chapter) as they appear in this comic—the call to adventure, the descent into the underworld, the road of trials, etc.

2. As we indicate in our introduction to this section, the Spirit's return to the surface at the end of this story is accompanied by a break in the bad weather, a hint of the coming of spring. Traditionally, the spring has been thought of as a time of rebirth or resurrection. Write an essay in which you try to account for this association between spring and the idea of rebirth.

3. As we suggest in Contents question 2, the catacombs portrayed in this story represent a vision of Hell. Write an essay in which you describe in detail your personal vision of both Heaven and Hell.

4. Several "morals" can be drawn from this story—morals concerning human nature, crime, courage, survival, suffering, hope, and degradation. Write an essay in which you state what you think the moral of this story is, and then support your statement with specific references to the comic.

ALPHA KERI BATH OIL

"The Age-Old Secret of Younger Looking Skin"

Created by the agency of Stern Walters/Earle Ludgin, the following advertisement for Alpha Keri Bath Oil—a skin moisturizer for women—is meant to make consumers feel that, by using the product, they will be rejuvenated; indeed, that they will experience a return, not merely to youth, but to the protected world of mother's womb.

Reprinted by permission of Stern Walters/Earle Ludgin, Inc.

The age-old secret of younger looking skin.

Mother Nature knows. Skin needs protection. Which is why she gave you a protective coating while you were still in the womb.

That was then. You're all grown up now. But that doesn't mean your skin doesn't still need protection.

From the wind.

From the weather.

From the water.

Alpha Keri* helps to give you that kind of protection.

It works in the bath to help soften and smooth your dry skin. And Alpha Keri mixes completely with water to moisturize and protect every inch of you. So, long after you bathe, your skin still feels rich and silky.

Not slick and greasy.

Not dry and flaky.

Well, now you know. It's no big secret after all. For skin to stay younger looking it needs protection. Like doctor recommended Alpha Keri Bath Oil. The kind of protection Mother would want for your skin.

Bathe in moisture. Alpha Keri Bath Oil.

©1978 WESTWOOD PHARMACEUTICALS INC.

QUESTIONS

Language

1. How would you describe the speaker's tone of voice? How old a person does the speaker seem to be addressing? How is the copy (the written text) supposed to make the reader feel?
2. The written part of this ad contains several incomplete sentences—sentence fragments. Point them out. Why does the writer use them? What effect do they create?

Content

1. Discuss the pose of the model in this advertisement. What is it meant to suggest?
2. Discuss the use of *lighting* in the photograph. How does the movement from darkness to light reinforce the *theme* of this ad?

Suggestions for Writing

1. It is often said that America is a youth-oriented culture, that we are obsessed with looking young and terrified of old age. Do you agree with this assessment of Americans? What examples can you find either to support or refute it? Write an essay expressing your opinion. (You might consider such things as the kinds of clothes people wear, the celebrities we admire, the growing popularity of cosmetic surgery, our treatment of the elderly, etc.)
2. Almost all of us have been moved, at one time or another, to buy something because we have been convinced by a billboard, television commercial, or magazine advertisement that, if we owned a particular product, our lives would be significantly improved—that we would find love, success, and happiness if only we drove this car, smoked that cigarette, or regularly gargled with a mint-flavored mouthwash. Write a personal experience paper in which you describe a time when an ad or a commercial convinced you to purchase something by creating a fantasy of how wonderful your life would be once you owned it. Describe what happened after you bought the object. Were your fantasies fulfilled? What did you learn from this experience?
3. Write an essay in which you either support or disagree with the argument that advertisements like the one for Alpha Keri Bath Oil serve to keep women in a subordinate position in society by encouraging them to think of themselves as helpless babies whose sole purpose in life is to look soft and appealing and who require constant comfort, care, and protection.
4. Have you ever purchased a product that made you feel like a new person, that made you feel healthier, happier, or more confident? If so, write a personal experience paper in which you describe the product and the way it made you feel.

ARTHUR C. CLARKE

from *2001: A Space Odyssey*

When Stanley Kubrick's film *2001: A Space Odyssey* opened in 1968, most reviewers reacted with either bafflement or outright hostility. All agreed that the movie was visually stunning, a technical *tour de force;* at the same time, they tended to feel that it was slow-paced, plotless, and pretentious. Audiences, however—particularly college-age viewers—responded very differently. To many, *2001* was a deeply moving, almost religious work of art. And soon, many critics, too, began to revise their initial opinions. In August, 1968, for example, *Time* magazine judged the work a dramatic failure with an "obscure" message. By the following year, the same publication was describing *2001* as an "epic film about a voyage to Jupiter that assumes awesome metaphysical consequences."

2001 traces the development of the human race from prehistoric creature to futuristic "star-child," an evolutionary process monitored, and perhaps even directed, by a mysterious, towering black tablet placed on earth by an extraterrestrial intelligence. The movie opens at that moment, four million years in the past, when, under the guidance of this unearthly monolith, a group of our ape-like ancestors discovers the use of weapons. Suddenly, the film shifts to the year 2001. A second black monolith, identical to the first, has been uncovered on the moon by a team of American explorers. As scientists examine the strange, rectangular object (which, in the interest of secrecy, they have code-named TMA-1), it begins to emit a piercing radio signal in the direction of the planet Jupiter. The third segment of the film concerns the voyage of the spaceship *Discovery,* which has been dispatched to Jupiter with a five-man crew, led by astronauts Dave Bowman and Frank Poole. Their mission is to seek out the beings that, millions of years earlier, planted the black slab on the moon. Along the way, however, the expedition is sabotaged by a malfunctioning (though engagingly human) computer named Hal, who murders all the crew members except Bowman. After dismantling Hal, Bowman continues with the mission by himself. The film's climax comes when the lone astronaut, exploring the planet's surface in his "space pod," is suddenly swept through a "star gate" and hurled into a region "beyond the infinite." Bowman's psychedelic voyage ends in a brightly lit, beautifully furnished room where, within the space of a few minutes, he passes from youth to extreme old age. As he lies on his deathbed, another monolith appears in the room, and at that moment Bowman is mystically reborn as a glowing, celestial star-child. The final shot of the movie shows him orbiting the earth, the first member, presumably, of a new and higher race of beings.

Kubrick's movie is based on a short story called "The Sentinel" by the English science fiction writer Arthur C. Clarke (b. 1917). Clarke—whose books, including *Childhood's End*, *Prelude to Space*, and *Rendezvous with Rama*, have sold more

Reprinted by permission of the author and the author's agents, Scott Meredith Literary Agency, Inc., 845 Third Avenue, New York, New York 10022. From *2001: A Space Odyssey,* by Arthur C. Clarke. Copyright 1968 by Arthur C. Clarke and Polaris Productions, Inc. Published by The New American Library, Inc.

than five million copies in twenty different languages—co-wrote the screenplay for *2001* with Kubrick, and is the author of the novel from which the following selection is taken. In addition to *2001*, Kubrick's movies include *Paths of Glory*, *Lolita*, *Dr. Strangelove*, *A Clockwork Orange*, and *Barry Lyndon*.

RECEPTION

The pillar of fire was marching over the edge of the sun, like a storm passing beyond the horizon. The scurrying flecks of light no longer moved across the redly glowing starscape still thousands of miles below. Inside his space pod, protected from an environment that could annihilate him within a millisecond, David Bowman awaited whatever had been prepared.

The White Dwarf was sinking fast as it hurtled along its orbit; presently it touched the horizon, set it aflame, and disappeared. A false twilight fell upon the inferno beneath, and in the sudden change of illumination Bowman became aware that something was happening in the space around him.

The world of the red sun seemed to ripple, as if he were looking at it through running water. For a moment he wondered if this was some refractive effect, perhaps caused by the passage of an unusually violent shock wave through the tortured atmosphere in which he was immersed.

The light was fading; it seemed that a second twilight was about to fall. Involuntarily, Bowman looked upward, then checked himself sheepishly, as he remembered that here the main source of light was not the sky, but the blazing world below.

It seemed as if walls of some material like smoked glass were thickening around him, cutting out the red glow and obscuring the view. It became darker and darker; the faint roar of the stellar hurricanes also faded out. The space pod was floating in silence, and in night. A moment later, there was the softest of bumps as it settled on some hard surface, and came to rest.

To rest on *what?* Bowman asked himself incredulously. Then light returned; and incredulity gave way to a heart-sinking despair—for as he saw what lay around him, he knew that he must be mad.

He was prepared, he thought, for any wonder. The only thing he had never expected was the utterly commonplace.

The space pod was resting on the polished floor of an elegant, anonymous hotel suite that might have been in any large city on Earth. He was staring into a living room with a coffee table, a divan, a dozen chairs, a writing desk, various lamps, a half-filled bookcase with some magazines lying on it, and even a bowl of flowers. Van Gogh's *Bridge at Arles* was hanging on one wall—Wyeth's *Christina's World* on another. He felt confident that when he pulled open the drawer of that desk, he would find a Gideon Bible inside it. . . .

If he was indeed mad, his delusions were beautifully organized. Everything was perfectly real; nothing vanished when he turned his back. The only incongruous element in the scene—and that certainly a major one—was the space pod itself.

For many minutes, Bowman did not move from his seat. He half expected the vision around him to go away, but it remained as solid as anything he had ever seen in his life.

It *was* real—or else a phantom of the senses so superbly contrived that there was no way of distinguishing it from reality. Perhaps it was some kind of test; if so, not only his fate but that of the human race might well depend upon his actions in the next few minutes.

He could sit here and wait for something to happen, or he could open the pod and step outside to challenge the reality of the scene around him. The floor appeared to be solid; at least, it was bearing the weight of the space pod. He was not likely to fall through it—whatever "it" might really be.

But there was still the question of air; for all that he could tell, this room might be in vacuum, or might contain a poisonous atmosphere. He thought it very unlikely—no one would go to all this trouble without attending to such an essential detail—but he did not propose to take unnecessary risks. In any event, his years of training made him wary of contamination; he was reluctant to expose himself to an unknown environment until he knew that there was no alternative. This place *looked* like a hotel room somewhere in the United States. That did not alter the fact that in reality he must be hundreds of light-years from the Solar System.

He closed the helmet of his suit, sealing himself in, and actuated the hatch of the space pod. There was a brief hiss of pressure equalization; then he stepped out into the room.

As far as he could tell, he was in a perfectly normal gravity field. He raised one arm, then let it fall freely. It flopped to his side in less than a second.

This made everything seem doubly unreal. Here he was wearing a spacesuit, standing—when he should have been floating—outside a vehicle which could only function properly in the absence of gravity. All his normal astronaut's reflexes were upset; he had to think before he made every movement.

Like a man in a trance he walked slowly from his bare, unfurnished half of the room toward the hotel suite. It did not, as he had almost expected, disappear as he approached, but remained perfectly real—and apparently perfectly solid.

He stopped beside the coffee table. On it sat a conventional Bell System vision-phone, complete with the local directory. He bent down and picked up the volume with his clumsy, gloved hands.

It bore, in the familiar type he had seen thousands of times, the name: WASHINGTON, D.C.

Then he looked more closely; and for the first time, he had objective proof that, although all this might be real, he was not on Earth.

He could read only the word *Washington;* the rest of the printing was a blur, as if it had been copied from a newspaper photograph. He opened the book at random and riffled through the pages. They were all blank sheets of crisp white material which was certainly not paper, though it looked very much like it.

He lifted the telephone receiver and pressed it against the plastic of his helmet. If there had been a dialing sound he could have heard it through the conducting material. But, as he had expected, there was only silence.

So—it was all a fake, though a fantastically careful one. And it was clearly not intended to deceive but rather—he hoped—to reassure. That was a very comforting thought; nevertheless he would not remove his suit until he had completed his voyage of exploration.

All the furniture seemed sound and solid enough; he tried the chairs, and they supported his weight. But the drawers in the desk would not open; they were dummies.

So were the books and magazines; like the telephone directory, only the titles were readable. They formed an odd selection—mostly rather trashy best sellers, a few sensational works of nonfiction, and some well-publicized autobiographies. There was nothing less than three years old, and little of any intellectual content. Not that it mattered, for the books could not even be taken down from the shelves.

There were two doors that opened readily enough. The first one took him into a small but comfortable bedroom, fitted with a bed, bureau, two chairs, light switches that actually worked, and a clothes closet. He opened this, and found himself looking at four suits, a dressing gown, a dozen white shirts, and several sets of underwear, all neatly draped from hangers.

He took down one of the suits, and inspected it carefully. As far as his gloved hands could judge, it was made of material that was more like fur than wool. It was also a little out of style; on Earth, no one had been wearing single-breasted suits for at least four years.

Next to the bedroom was a bathroom, complete with fittings which, he was relieved to note, were not dummies, but worked in a perfectly normal manner. And after that was a kitchenette, with electric cooker, refrigerator, storage cupboards, crockery and cutlery, sink, table, and chairs. Bowman began to explore this not only with curiosity, but with mounting hunger.

First he opened the refrigerator, and a wave of cold mist rolled out. The shelves were well stocked with packages and cans, all of them looking perfectly familiar from a distance, though at close quarters their proprietary labels were blurred and unreadable. However, there was a notable absence of eggs, milk, butter, meat, fruit, or any other unprocessed food; the refrigerator held only items that had already been packaged in some way.

Bowman picked up a carton of a familiar breakfast cereal, thinking as he did so that it was odd to keep this frozen. The moment he lifted the package, he knew that it certainly did *not* contain cornflakes; it was much too heavy.

He ripped open the lid, and examined the contents. The box contained a slightly moist blue substance, of about the weight and texture of bread pudding. Apart from its odd color, it looked quite appetizing.

But this is ridiculous, Bowman told himself. I am almost certainly being watched, and I must look an idiot wearing this suit. If this is some kind of intelligence test, I've probably failed already. Without further hesitation, he walked back into the bedroom and began to undo the clamp of his helmet. When it was loose, he lifted the helmet a fraction of an inch, cracked the seal and took a cautious sniff. As far as he could tell, he was breathing perfectly normal air.

He dropped the helmet on the bed, and began thankfully—and rather stiffly—to divest himself of this suit. When he had finished, he stretched, took a few deep breaths, and carefully hung the spacesuit up among the more conventional articles of clothing in the closet. It looked rather odd there, but the compulsive tidiness that Bowman shared with all astronauts would never have allowed him to leave it anywhere else.

Then he walked quickly back into the kitchen and began to inspect the "cereal" box at closer quarters.

The blue bread pudding had a faint, spicy smell, something like a macaroon. Bowman weighed it in his hand, then broke off a piece and cautiously sniffed at it. Though he felt sure now that there would be no deliberate attempt to poison him, there was always the possibility of mistakes—especially in a matter so complex as biochemistry.

He nibbled at a few crumbs, then chewed and swallowed the fragment of food; it was excellent, though the flavor was so elusive as to be almost indescribable. If he closed his eyes, he could imagine it was meat, or wholemeal bread, or even dried fruit. Unless there were unexpected aftereffects, he had no cause to fear starvation.

When he had eaten just a few mouthfuls of the substance, and already felt quite satisfied, he looked for something to drink. There were half a dozen cans of beer—again of a famous brand—at the back of the refrigerator, and he pressed the tab on one of them to open it.

The prestressed metal lid popped off along its strain lines, exactly as usual. But the can did not contain beer; to Bowman's surprised disappointment, it held more of the blue food.

In a few seconds he had opened half a dozen of the other packages and cans. Whatever their labels, their contents were the same; it seemed that his diet was going to be a little monotonous, and that he would have nothing but water to drink. He filled a glass from the kitchen faucet and sipped at it cautiously.

He spat out the first few drops at once; the taste was terrible. Then, rather ashamed of his instinctive reaction, he forced himself to drink the rest.

That first sip had been enough to identify the liquid. It tasted terrible because it had no taste at all; the faucet was supplying pure, distilled water. His unknown hosts were obviously taking no chances with his health.

Feeling much refreshed, he then had a quick shower. There was no soap, which was another minor inconvenience, but there was a very efficient hot-air drier in which he luxuriated for a while before trying on underpants, vest, and dressing gown from the clothes closet. After that, he lay down on the bed, stared up at the ceiling, and tried to make sense of this fantastic situation.

He had made little progress when he was distracted by another line of thought. Immediately above the bed was the usual hotel-type ceiling TV screen; he had assumed that, like the telephone and books, it was a dummy.

But the control unit on its swinging bedside arm looked so realistic that he could not resist playing with it; and as his fingers touched the ON sensor disk, the screen lit up.

Feverishly, he started to tap out channel selector codes at random, and almost at once he got his first picture.

It was a well-known African news commentator, discussing the attempts being made to preserve the last remnants of his country's wild life. Bowman listened for a few seconds, so captivated by the sound of a human voice that he did not in the least care what it was talking about. Then he changed channels.

In the next five minutes, he got a symphony orchestra playing Walton's *Violin Concerto,* a discussion on the sad state of the legitimate theater, a western, a demonstration of a new headache cure, a panel game in some Oriental language, a psychodrama, three news commentaries, a football game, a lecture on solid geometry (in Russian), and several tuning signals and data transmissions. It was, in fact, a perfectly normal selection from the world's TV programs, and apart from the psychological uplift it gave him, it confirmed one suspicion that had already been forming in his mind.

All the programs were about two years old. That was around the time TMA-1 had been discovered, and it was hard to believe that this was a pure coincidence. Something had been monitoring the radio waves; that ebon block had been busier than men had suspected.

He continued to wander across the spectrum, and suddenly recognized a familiar scene. Here was this very suite, now occupied by a celebrated actor who was furiously denouncing an unfaithful mistress. Bowman looked with a shock of recognition upon the living room he had just left—and when the camera followed the indignant couple toward the bedroom, he involuntarily looked toward the door to see if anyone was entering.

So that was how this reception area had been prepared for him; his hosts had based their ideas of terrestrial living upon TV programs. His feeling that he was inside a movie set was almost literally true.

He had learned all that he wished to for the moment, and turned off the set. What do I do now? he asked himself, locking his fingers behind his head and staring up at the blank screen.

He was physically and emotionally exhausted, yet it seemed impossible that one could sleep in such fantastic surroundings, and farther from Earth than any man in history had ever been. But the comfortable bed, and the instinctive wisdom of the body, conspired together against his will.

He fumbled for the light switch, and the room was plunged into darkness. Within seconds, he had passed beyond the reach of dreams.

So, for the last time, David Bowman slept.

RECAPITULATION

There being no further use for it, the furniture of the suite dissolved back into the mind of its creator. Only the bed remained—and the walls, shielding this fragile organism from the energies it could not yet control.

In his sleep, David Bowman stirred restlessly. He did not wake, nor did he dream, but he was no longer wholly unconscious. Like a fog creeping through a forest, something invaded his mind. He sensed it only dimly, for the full impact would have destroyed him as surely as the fires raging beyond these walls. Beneath that dispassionate scrutiny, he felt neither hope nor fear; all emotion had been leached away.

He seemed to be floating in free space, while around him stretched, in all directions, an infinite geometrical grid of dark lines or threads, along which moved tiny nodes of light—some slowly, some at dazzling speed. Once he had peered through a microscope at a cross-section of a human brain, and in its network of nerve fibers had glimpsed the same labyrinthine complexity. But that had been dead and static, whereas this transcended life itself. He knew—or believed he knew—that he was watching the operation of some gigantic mind, contemplating the universe of which he was so tiny a part.

The vision, or illusion, lasted only a moment. Then the crystalline planes and lattices, and the interlocking perspectives of moving light, flickered out of existence, as David Bowman moved into a realm of consciousness that no man had experienced before.

At first, it seemed that Time itself was running backward. Even this marvel he was prepared to accept, before he realized the subtler truth.

The springs of memory were being tapped; in controlled recollection, he was reliving the past. There was the hotel suite—there the space pod—there the burning starscapes of the red sun—there the shining core of the galaxy—there the gateway through which he had re-emerged into the universe. And not only vision, but all the sense impressions, and all the emotions he had felt at the time, were racing past, more and more swiftly. His life was unreeling like a tape recorder playing back at ever-increasing speed.

Now he was once more aboard the *Discovery* and the rings of Saturn filled the sky. Before that, he was repeating his final dialogue with Hal; he was seeing Frank Poole leave on his last mission; he was hearing the voice of Earth, assuring him that all was well.

And even as he relived these events, he knew that all indeed was well. He was retrogressing down the corridors of time, being drained of knowledge and experience as he swept back toward his childhood. But nothing was being lost; all that he had ever been, at every moment of his life, was being transferred to safer keeping. Even as one David Bowman ceased to exist, another became immortal.

Faster, faster he moved back into forgotten years, and into a simpler world. Faces he had once loved, and had thought lost beyond recall, smiled at him sweetly. He smiled back with fondness, and without pain.

Now, at last, the headlong regression was slackening; the wells of memory were nearly dry. Time flowed more and more sluggishly, approaching a moment of stasis—as a swinging pendulum, at the limit of its arc, seems frozen for one eternal instant, before the next cycle begins.

The timeless instant passed; the pendulum reversed its swing. In an empty room, floating amid the fires of a double star twenty thousand light-years from Earth, a baby opened its eyes and began to cry.

TRANSFORMATION

Then it became silent, as it saw that it was no longer alone.

A ghostly, glimmering rectangle had formed in the empty air. It solidified into a crystal tablet, lost its transparency, and became suffused with a pale, milky luminescence. Tantalizing, ill-defined phantoms moved across its surface and in its depths. They coalesced into bars of lights and shadow, then formed intermeshing, spoked patterns that began slowly to rotate, in time with the pulsing rhythm that now seemed to fill the whole of space.

It was a spectacle to grasp and hold the attention of any child—or of any man-ape. But, as it had been three million years before, it was only the outward manifestation of forces too subtle to be consciously perceived. It was merely a toy to distract the senses, while the real processing was carried out at far deeper levels of the mind.

This time, the processing was swift and certain, as the new design was woven. For in the eons since their last meeting, much had been learned by the weaver; and the material on which he practiced his art was now of an infinitely finer texture. But whether it should be permitted to form part of his still-growing tapestry, only the future could tell.

With eyes that already held more than human intentness, the baby stared into the depths of the crystal monolith, seeing—but not yet understanding—the mysteries that lay beyond. It knew that it had come home, that here was the origin of many races besides its own; but it knew also that it could not stay. Beyond this moment lay another birth, stranger than any in the past.

Now the moment had come; the glowing patterns no longer echoed the secrets in the crystal's heart. As they died, so too the protective walls faded back into the nonexistence from which they had briefly emerged, and the red sun filled the sky.

The metal and plastic of the forgotten space pod, and the clothing once worn by an entity who had called himself David Bowman, flashed into flame. The last links with Earth were gone, resolved back into their component atoms.

But the child scarcely noticed, as he adjusted himself to the comfortable glow of his new environment. He still needed, for a little while, this shell of matter as the focus of his powers. His indestructible body was his mind's present image of itself; and for all his powers, he knew that he was still a baby. So he would remain until he had decided on a new form, or had passed beyond the necessities of matter.

And now it was time to go—though in one sense he would never leave this place where he had been reborn, for he would always be part of the entity that used this double star for its unfathomable purposes. The direction, though not the nature, of his destiny was clear before him, and there was no need to trace the devious path by which he had come. With the instincts of three million years, he now perceived that there were more ways than one behind the back of space. The ancient mechanisms of the Star Gate had served him well, but he would not need them again.

The glimmering rectangular shape that had once seemed no more than a slab of crystal still floated before him, indifferent as he was to the harmless flames of the inferno beneath. It encapsulated yet unfathomed secrets of space and time, but some at least he now understood and was able to command. How obvious—how *necessary*—was that mathematical ratio of its sides, the quadratic sequence 1 : 4 : 9! And how naïve to have imagined that the series ended at this point, in only three dimensions!

He focused his mind upon these geometrical simplicities, and as his thoughts brushed against it, the empty framework filled with the darkness of the interstellar night. The glow of the red sun faded—or, rather, seemed to recede in all directions at once; and there before him was the luminous whirlpool of the galaxy.

It might have been some beautiful, incredibly detailed model, embedded in a block of plastic. But it was the reality, grasped as a whole with senses now more subtle than vision. If he wished, he could focus his attention upon any one of its hundred billion stars; and he could do much more than that.

Here he was, adrift in this great river of suns, halfway between the banked fires of the galactic core and the lonely, scattered sentinel stars of the rim. And *here* he wished to be, on the far side of this chasm in the sky, this serpentine band of darkness, empty of all stars. He knew that this formless chaos, visible only by the glow that limned its edges from fire-mists far beyond, was the still unused stuff of creation, the raw material of evolutions yet to be. Here, Time had not begun; not until the suns that now burned were long since dead would light and life reshape this void.

Unwittingly, he had crossed it once; now he must cross it again—this time, of his own volition. The thought filled him with a sudden, freezing terror, so that for a moment he was wholly disoriented, and his new vision of the universe trembled and threatened to shatter into a thousand fragments.

It was not fear of the galactic gulfs that chilled his soul, but a more profound disquiet, stemming from the unborn future. For he had left behind the time scales of his human origin; now, as he contemplated that band of starless night, he knew his first intimations of the Eternity that yawned before him.

Then he remembered that he would never be alone, and his panic slowly ebbed. The crystal-clear perception of the universe was restored to him—not, he knew, wholly by his own efforts. When he needed guidance in his first faltering steps, it would be there.

Confident once more, like a high diver who had regained his nerve, he launched himself across the light-years. The galaxy burst forth from the mental frame in which he had enclosed it; stars and nebulae poured past him in an illusion of infinite speed. Phantom suns exploded and fell behind as he slipped like a shadow through their cores; the cold, dark waste of cosmic dust which he had once feared seemed no more than the beat of a raven's wing across the face of the Sun.

The stars were thinning out; the glare of the Milky Way was dimming into a pale ghost of the glory he had known—and, when he was ready, would know again.

He was back, precisely where he wished to be, in the space that men called real.

QUESTIONS

Language

1. Why does Clarke provide such a minutely detailed description of the room in which Bowman finds himself?
2. Compare and contrast the description of the room in the chapter "Reception" to the description of what Bowman sees inside the crystal tablet in the third chapter, "Transformation." Which of these passages is easier for you to understand? Why? How successful is Clarke in creating a description of phenomena beyond the grasp of human understanding? What techniques of description does the author use to evoke or suggest such things?
3. Clarke is a writer with a wide knowledge of science. How much technical, scientific language can you find in this section? Point to examples. Do you feel Clarke relies too heavily on such language? Or do you feel that his vocabulary is not technical enough?

Content

1. Describe the room Bowman lands in. Who has prepared or created it? Why don't the books have printing inside? Why do all the food cans, boxes, and packages contain the same blue substance? What is the room modeled on?
2. What happens to Bowman in the room?

3. What is the crystal tablet that appears in the room?

4. Why is this book (and the movie on which it is based) subtitled *A Space Odyssey?*

Suggestions for Writing

1. Science fiction books, movies, and television shows have never been more popular in this country than they are now. Write an essay in which you attempt to explain America's current fascination with science fiction.

2. A phenomenon related to the burgeoning popularity of science fiction is the growing belief in the existence of flying saucers or UFOs (unidentified flying objects). Do you believe that flying saucers from outer space exist and have visited our planet? Write an essay explaining why you do or why you do not.

3. Write a story in which you describe an imaginary encounter with alien beings from outer space. Describe the circumstances of the encounter, where it takes place, what the aliens look like, how they behave, your reactions, etc.

4. The film versions of *2001* and *Star Wars* are two of the best-known science fiction works of recent years. They are, however, very different in terms of plot, character, and incident. Write an essay in which you compare and contrast the chapters from *2001* reprinted above with the selection from *Star Wars* found in Chapter Five. How do the two selections differ? What features do they share? What, in short, makes them both *science fiction?* Which do you think is a better work of science fiction? Which do you think is a better piece of writing? Why?

5. Do you believe, as *2001* suggests, that the process of evolution which raised us from apes to human beings is still going on, and that we will evolve eventually into an even higher form of life? Or do you believe instead that we are gradually degenerating, that human beings are growing worse, not better? Write an essay in which you argue one or the other of these positions. Explain the reasons for your opinion and include a description of your conception of the man and woman of the future.

HENRY JAMES

from *The American*

Henry James was born in New York City in 1843, although his earliest memories were of Paris. His father, a cosmopolitan man with a profound interest in philosophy, wanted to expose his sons to the cultural wealth of the Old World and provide them with a sense of life's possibilities; accordingly, James—along with his three brothers (including the eldest, William, who was to win fame himself as a philosopher-psychologist)—was educated in a very unconventional way, moving from tutor to tutor (so that his developing intellect would not fall under the sway of any one individual or system) and from America to Europe and back again. After a brief period of study at Harvard Law School, James began his career as an author, writing reviews and short stories for various literary magazines. He made lengthy trips to Europe in 1864 and again in 1872–1874; by 1876, he had settled permanently in England.

His first important novel, *The American,* appeared in 1877. The following year, he won wide popularity with the publication of "Daisy Miller," the story of a vivacious American girl whose naiveté brings her into conflict with the rigid conventions of European society. His major works of the 1880s include *Washington Square, The Portrait of a Lady, The Princess Casamassima, The Aspern Papers,* and *The Turn of the Screw.* During the following decade, declining sales of his fiction led him to try his hand at writing plays, but the attempt proved ill-fated. After suffering a terrible public humiliation (at the end of the opening night performance of one of his plays, he walked out on stage when the audience called for the author, only to be greated by catcalls and hisses), he returned to fiction, producing the three great novels of his "late period": *The Wings of the Dove* (1902), *The Ambassadors* (1903), and *The Golden Bowl* (1905). In 1915, as a protest against America's reluctance to enter the war and as a gesture of support for his adopted homeland, he became a British subject. A month before his death (by a stroke) in February, 1916, he was awarded the Order of Merit by King George V.

Most of James' fiction deals with what is known as "the international theme": the confrontation between the cultures of the Old World and the New. *The American* is his first major treatment of this theme. Its hero, Christopher Newman (the name is revealing), is meant to be a "national type," an archetypal New World man— shrewd, good-humored, self-reliant, unsophisticated. Having made a fortune in business, Newman has come to Europe to acquire all those things he has never had time for: an appreciation of art, an understanding of history, and a beautiful wife. The plot concerns Newman's involvement with the lovely Claire de Cintré, the daughter of an aristocratic French family, whose haughty, iron-willed matriarch at first approves and then later, after finding that she cannot reconcile herself to her daughter's marriage to a "commercial person," seeks to prevent the alliance. In the following passage, Newman, seated at a sidewalk cafe in Paris with Tom Tristram, an old acquaintance he has not seen for years, briefly recounts his "intensely Western story."

"And now," began Mr. Tristram, when they had tasted the decoction which he had caused to be served to them, "now just give an account of yourself. What are your ideas, what are your plans, where have you come from and where are you going? In the first place, where are you staying?"

"At the Grand Hotel," said Newman.

Mr. Tristram puckered his plump visage. "That won't do! You must change."

"Change?" demanded Newman. "Why, it's the finest hotel I ever was in."

"You don't want a 'fine' hotel; you want something small and quiet and elegant, where your bell is answered and your—your person is recognised."

"They keep running to see if I have rung before I have touched the bell," said Newman, "and as for my person, they are always bowing and scraping to it."

"I suppose you are always tipping them. That's very bad style."

"Always? By no means. A man brought me something yesterday, and then stood loafing about in a beggarly manner. I offered him a chair and asked him if he wouldn't sit down. Was that bad style?"

"Very!"

"But he bolted, instantly. At any rate, the place amuses me. Hang your elegance, if it bores me. I sat in the court of the Grand Hotel last night until two o'clock in the morning, watching the coming and going, and the people knocking about."

"You're easily pleased. But you can do as you choose—a man in your shoes. You have made a pile of money, eh?"

"I have made enough."

"Happy the man who can say that! Enough for what?"

"Enough to rest a while, to forget the confounded thing, to look about me, to see the world, to have a good time, to improve my mind, and, if the fancy takes me, to marry a wife." Newman spoke slowly, with a certain dryness of accent and with frequent pauses. This was his habitual mode of utterance, but it was especially marked in the words I have just quoted.

"Jupiter! There's a programme!" cried Mr. Tristram. "Certainly, all that takes money, especially the wife; unless indeed she gives it, as mine did. And what's the story? How have you done it?"

Newman had pushed his hat back from his forehead, folded his arms, and stretched his legs. He listened to the music, he looked about him at the bustling crowd, at the plashing fountains, at the nurses and the babies. "I have worked!" he answered at last.

Tristram looked at him for some moments, and allowed his placid eyes to measure his friend's generous longitude and rest upon his comfortably contemplative face. "What have you worked at?" he asked.

"Oh, at several things."

"I suppose you're a smart fellow, eh?"

Newman continued to look at the nurses and babies; they imparted to the scene a kind of primordial, pastoral simplicity. "Yes," he said at last, "I suppose I am." And then, in answer to his companion's inquiries, he related briefly his history since their last meeting. It was an intensely Western story, and it dealt with enterprises which it will be needless to introduce to the reader in detail. Newman had come out of the war with a brevet of brigadier-general, an honour which in this case—without invidious comparisons—had lighted upon shoulders amply competent to bear it. But though he could manage a fight, when need was, Newman heartily disliked the business; his four years in the army had left him with an angry, bitter sense of the waste of precious things—life and time and money and "smartness" and the early freshness of purpose; and he had addressed himself to the pursuits of peace with passionate zest and energy. He was of course as penniless when he plucked off his shoulder-straps as when he put them on, and the only capital at his disposal was his dogged resolution and his lively perception of ends and means. Exertion and action were as natural to him as respiration; a more completely healthy mortal had never trod the elastic soil of the West. His experience, moreover, was as wide as his capacity; when he was fourteen years old, necessity had taken him by his slim young shoulders and pushed him into the street, to earn that night's supper. He had not earned it; but he had earned the next night's, and afterwards, whenever he had had none, it was because he had gone without it to use the money for something else, a keener pleasure or a finer profit. He had turned his hand, with his brain in it, to many things; he had been enterprising, in an eminent sense of the term; he had been adventurous and even reckless, and he had known bitter failure as well as brilliant success; but he was a born experimentalist, and he had always found something to enjoy in the pressure of necessity, even when it was as irritating as the haircloth shirt of the mediaeval monk. At one time failure seemed inexorably his portion; ill-luck became his bed-fellow, and whatever he touched he turned, not to gold, but to ashes. His most vivid conception of a supernatural element in the world's affairs had come to him once when this pertinacity of misfortune was at its climax: there seemed to him something stronger in life than his own will. But the mysterious something could only be the devil, and he was accordingly seized with an intense personal enmity to this impertinent force. He had known what it was to have utterly exhausted his credit, to be unable to raise a dollar, and to find himself at nightfall in a strange city, without a penny to mitigate its strangeness. It was under these circumstances that he made his entrance into San Francisco, the scene, subsequently, of his happiest strokes of fortune. If he did not, like Dr. Franklin in Philadelphia, march along the street munching a penny loaf, it was only because he had not the penny loaf necessary to the performance. In his darkest days he had had but one simple, practical impulse—the desire, as he would have phrased it, to see the thing through. He did so at last, buffeted his way into smooth waters, and made money largely. It must be admitted, rather nakedly, that Christopher Newman's sole aim in life had been to make money; what he had been placed in the world for was, to his own perception, simply to wrest a fortune, the bigger the better, from defiant opportunity. This idea completely filled his horizon and satisfied his imagination. Upon the uses of money, upon what one might do with a life into which one had succeeded in injecting the golden stream, he had up to his thirty-fifth year very scantily reflected. Life had been for him an open game, and he had played for high stakes. He had won at last and carried off his winnings; and now what was he to do with them? He was a man to whom, sooner or later, the question was sure to present itself, and the answer to it belongs to our story. A vague sense that more answers were possible than his philosophy had hitherto dreamt of had already taken possession of him, and it seemed softly and agreeably to deepen as he lounged in this brilliant corner of Paris with his friend.

"I must confess," he presently went on, "that here I don't feel at all smart. My remarkable talents seem of no use. I feel as simple as a little child, and a little child might take me by the hand and lead me about."

"Oh, I'll be your little child," said Tristram, jovially; "I'll take you by the hand. Trust yourself to me."

"I am a good worker," Newman continued, "but I rather think I am a poor loafer. I have come abroad to amuse myself, but I doubt whether I know how."

"Oh, that's easily learned."

"Well, I may perhaps learn it, but I am afraid I shall never do it by rote. I have the best will in the world about it, but my genius doesn't lie in that direction. As a loafer I shall never be original, as I take it that you are."

"Yes," said Tristram, "I suppose I am original; like all those immoral pictures in the Louvre."

"Besides," Newman continued, "I don't want to work at pleasure, any more than I played at work. I want to take it easily. I feel deliciously lazy, and I should like to spend six months as I am now, sitting under a tree and listening to a band. There's only one thing; I want to hear some good music."

"Music and pictures! Lord, what refined tastes! You are what my wife calls intellectual. I ain't, a bit. But we can find something better for you to do than to sit under a tree. To begin with, you must come to the club."

"What club?"

"The Occidental. You will see all the Americans there; all the best of them, at least. Of course you play poker?"

"Oh, I say," cried Newman, with energy, "you are not going to lock me up in a club and stick me down at a card-table! I haven't come all this way for that."

"What the deuce *have* you come for! You were glad enough to play poker in St. Louis, I recollect, when you cleaned me out."

"I have come to see Europe, to get the best out of it I can. I want to see all the great things, and do what the clever people do."

"The clever people? Much obliged. You set me down as a blockhead, then?"

Newman was sitting sidewise in his chair, with his elbow on the back and his head leaning on his hand. Without moving he looked awhile at his companion, with his dry, guarded, half-inscrutable, and yet altogether good-natured smile. "Introduce me to your wife!" he said at last.

Tristram bounced about in his chair. "Upon my word, I won't. She doesn't want any help to turn up her nose at me, nor do you, either!"

"I don't turn up my nose at you, my dear fellow; nor at anyone, or anything. I'm not proud, I assure you I'm not proud. That's why I am willing to take example by the clever people."

"Well, if I'm not the rose, as they say here, I have lived near it. I can show you some clever people, too. Do you know General Packard? Do you know C. P. Hatch? Do you know Miss Kitty Upjohn?"

"I shall be happy to make their acquaintance; I want to cultivate society."

Tristram seemed restless and suspicious; he eyed his friend askance, and then: "What are you up to, any way?" he demanded. "Are you going to write a book?"

Christopher Newman twisted one end of his moustache awhile, in silence, and at last he made answer. "One day, a couple of months ago, something very curious happened to me. I had come on to New York on some important business; it was rather a long story—a question of getting ahead of another party, in a certain particular way, in the stock-market. This other party had once played me a very mean trick. I owed him a grudge, I felt awfully savage at the time, and I vowed that, when I got a chance, I would, figuratively speaking, put his nose out of joint. There was a matter of some sixty thousand dollars at stake. If I put it out of his way, it was a blow the fellow would feel, and he really deserved no quarter. I jumped into a hack and went about my business, and it was in this hack—this immortal, historical hack—that the curious thing I speak of occurred. It was a hack like any other, only a trifle dirtier, with a greasy line along the top of the drab cushions, as if it had been used for a great many Irish funerals. It is possible I took a nap; I had been travelling all night, and though I was excited with my errand, I felt the want of sleep. At all events I woke up suddenly, from a sleep or from a kind of a reverie, with the most extraordinary feeling in the world—a mortal disgust for the thing I was going to do. It came upon me like *that!*"—and he snapped his fingers—"as abruptly as an old wound that begins to ache. I couldn't tell the meaning of it; I only felt that I loathed the whole business and wanted to wash my hands of it. The idea of losing that sixty thousand dollars, of letting it utterly slide and scuttle and never hearing of it again, seemed the sweetest thing in the world. And all this took place quite independently of my will, and I sat watching it as if it were a play at the theatre. I could feel it going on inside of me. You may depend upon it that there are things going on inside of us that we understand mighty little about."

"Jupiter! you make my flesh creep!" cried Tristram. "And while you sat in your hack, watching the play, as you call it, the other man marched in and bagged your sixty thousand dollars?"

"I have not the least idea. I hope so, poor devil! but I never found out. We pulled up in front of the place I was going to in Wall Street, but I sat still in the carriage, and at last the driver scrambled down off his seat to see whether his carriage had not turned into a hearse. I couldn't have got out, any more than if I had been a corpse. What was the matter with me? Momentary idiocy, you'll say. What I wanted to get out of was Wall Street. I told the man to drive down to the Brooklyn ferry and to cross over. When we were over, I told him to drive me out into the country. As I had told him originally to drive for dear life down town, I suppose he thought me insane. Perhaps I was, but in that case I am insane still. I spent the morning looking at the first green leaves on Long Island. I was sick of business; I wanted to throw it all up and break off short; I had money enough, or if I hadn't I ought to have. I seemed to feel a new man inside my old skin, and I longed for a new world. When you want a thing so very badly you had better treat yourself to it. I didn't understand the matter, not in the least; but I gave the old horse the bridle and let him find his way. As soon as I could get out of the game I sailed for Europe. That is how I come to be sitting here."

"You ought to have bought up that hack," said Tristram; "It isn't a safe vehicle to have about. And you have really sold out, then; you have retired from business?"

"I have made over my hand to a friend; when I feel disposed, I can take up the cards again. I daresay that a twelvemonth hence the operation will be reversed. The pendulum will swing back again. I shall be sitting in the gondola or on a dromedary, and all of a sudden I shall want to clear out. But for the present I am perfectly free. I have even bargained that I am to receive no business letters."

"Oh, it's a real *caprice de prince,*" said Tristram. "I back out; a poor devil like me can't help you to spend such very magnificent leisure as that. You should get introduced to the crowned heads."

Newman looked at him a moment, and then, with his easy smile: "How does one do it?" he asked.

"Come, I like that!" cried Tristram. "It shows you are in earnest."

"Of course I am in earnest. Didn't I say I wanted the best? I know the best can't be had for mere money, but I rather think money will do a good deal. In addition, I am willing to take a good deal of trouble."

"You are not bashful, eh?"

"I haven't the least idea. I want the biggest kind of entertainment a man can get. People, places, art, nature, everything! I want to see the tallest mountains, and the bluest lakes, and the finest pictures, and the handsomest churches, and the most celebrated men, and the most beautiful women."

"Settle down in Paris, then. There are no mountains that I know of, and the only lake is in the Bois de Boulogne, and not particularly blue. But there is everything else: plenty of pictures and churches, no end of celebrated men, and several beautiful women."

"But I can't settle down in Paris at this season, just as summer is coming on."

"Oh, for the summer go up to Trouville."

"What is Trouville?"

"The French Newport. Half the Americans go."

"Is it anywhere near the Alps?"

"About as near as Newport is to the Rocky Mountains."

"Oh, I want to see Mont Blanc," said Newman, "and Amsterdam, and the Rhine, and a lot of places. Venice in particular. I have great ideas about Venice."

"Ah," said Mr. Tristram, rising, "I see I shall have to introduce you to my wife!"

QUESTIONS

Language

1. Look at the first sentence of this selection. What does the word *decoction* mean? (Use a dictionary to find out, if you do not know the definition.) What decoction are Tristram and Newman probably tasting? Why does James use this particular word instead of naming the substance? What is the effect of such diction?
2. What does James mean when he says that Tristram looked at Newman and "allowed his placid eyes to measure his friend's generous longitude" (p. 423)?
3. Why does James summarize Newman's "history"—the story of his rise from rags to riches—instead of having the character tell it himself in his own words?
4. Look at Newman's long speech in which he recounts the "extraordinary" experience which led him to put aside his old life and come to Europe to take up a new one. How is the language of this passage different from that of the section in which James recounts Newman's earlier history?
5. Again, looking closely at Newman's long speech, point out the words and images related to death and oldness. Now point out the words and images related to birth and newness. In what sense does Newman undergo a kind of "death" in this scene? What part of him "dies"? In what sense is he reborn, transformed into a new man?

Content

1. What does James mean when he calls Newman's life "an intensely Western story"?
2. Describe Tristram. What is his attitude toward "culture"? How does Newman seem to feel about him?
3. Why has Newman come to Europe? What is he seeking?
4. What sort of man does Newman seem to be? In what way is he typical? In what way is he exceptional?
5. Describe the experience that led Newman to give up his business pursuits and travel to Europe.
6. What keeps Newman from following through on his impulse to take revenge on the man who had once played him "a very mean trick"?

7. At the start of the novel, James describes Newman as a singular blend of "innocence and experience." Find examples in this selection of Newman's innocence, his naiveté. What evidence of experience, knowledge, shrewdness, even toughness, can you find?

8. Why does James compare Newman to Dr. Franklin (that is, Benjamin Franklin)? It might be useful, in answering this question, to look over Franklin's *Father Abraham's Speech* (p. 258).

Suggestions for Writing

1. Telling Tristram about the experience which caused him to put aside his business and come to Europe, Newman explains that he "seemed to feel a new man inside his old skin." Do you believe that people can experience such a transformation, undergo a kind of rebirth, give up an old and established way of life and suddenly take up a new one? Or do people remain basically the same from childhood or adolescence on? Write an essay expressing your opinion on this question. Support your thesis with examples from your own experience and observation of others.

2. Newman has spent his early years earning a fortune and is now taking a break from business to spend his money. Imagine that you suddenly became very rich. Write an essay in which you describe what you would do with your money.

3. "It must be admitted, rather nakedly," writes James, "that Christopher Newman's sole aim in life had been to make money." Do you believe that making money is a worthy "aim in life"? Or do you think that people should have other, "higher" goals? Write an essay explaining your opinion.

4. On his way to avenge himself on the man who had once played him a "very mean trick," Newman falls asleep and suddenly awakens "with the most extraordinary feeling— a mortal disgust for the thing I was going to do." Have you ever had a similar experience; that is, have you ever set out to do something and then, repelled at what you intended to do, changed your mind? If so, describe the experience in a detailed autobiographical essay.

ADDITIONAL WRITING SUGGESTIONS FOR CHAPTER EIGHT

1. As we mention in the introduction to this section, a popular slogan of the late 1960s, which appeared on many posters, greeting cards, and buttons, was "Today is the first day of the rest of your life." Write an essay in which you explain the meaning of this saying. Why do you think it appealed to so many people? Give concrete examples of the ways in which people reading this slogan might respond to—or act on—its message. How does it make *you* feel?

2. Stories about the "fountain of youth," whose waters possess the power to rejuvenate those who drink from or bathe in them, are very ancient and widespread, and throughout history, people of many cultures have tried to find this legendary fountain. The Spanish explorer Ponce de León, for example, discovered Florida while searching for the fountain of youth. Write a story, set in modern-day America, in which you describe what happens when the fountain of youth is suddenly discovered in some previously unexplored place— an island located deep in the Florida Everglades, for instance, or a cave in the Colorado Rockies.

3. It can be argued that many people, without necessarily being aware of the fact, still believe in some form of the fountain of youth—that is, they are convinced (on some level of their minds) that substances exist which have the power to magically rejuvenate them, make them young again. Madison Avenue appeals to such fantasies in ads like the one for Alpha Keri Bath Oil, which subtly suggests, through the skillful combination of illustration and text, that the product will turn a mature person back into a child. Write an essay in which you analyze examples of other products which promise, through advertisements or commercials, to make people feel, look, or act young again—products, that is to say, which appeal to what might be called the "fountain of youth fantasy." Examples of such products might include certain kinds of clothing, cosmetics, cars, hair dyes, vitamins, etc. Be specific. Describe the product, the advertisement (or commercial) and how the advertisement *works*—that is, how it creates a "fountain of youth fantasy."

4. In the introduction to this chapter, we discuss different forms of rebirth: physical, spiritual, emotional, economic. It is possible to think of other forms as well. A person, for example, can "die" and be reborn in terms of his profession or career. For example, after "dying"— that is, giving a poorly received performance—during his debut appearance on national television, a young stand-up comedian may disappear for awhile, only to make a stunning comeback a year later. Similarly, a baseball, basketball, or football team might be "counted out" at midseason only to "spring back to life" and end up winning the championship. Can you think of other kinds of rebirths? Write an essay in which you *classify* different types of rebirth and provide examples of each type. Use the categories we have mentioned so far and add others that occur to you. Use examples from your own experience, as well as from your outside reading, television watching, movie-going, etc.

Appendix
Critical Essays

BRUNO BETTELHEIM

from *The Uses of Enchantment*

Renowned child psychologist Bruno Bettelheim was born in Vienna in 1903 and received his doctorate from the University of Vienna in 1938. He emigrated to the United States in 1939, following a year of imprisonment in the Nazi concentration camps of Dachau and Buchenwald. Distinguished Professor of Education and Professor of Psychology and Psychiatry at the University of Chicago, he is known principally for his pioneering work with autistic children. Among his many books are: *Love Is Not Enough* (1950), *Truants from Life* (1955), *The Informed Heart* (1960), *The Empty Fortress* (1967), and *Children of the Dream* (1969).

The Uses of Enchantment is, as its subtitle indicates, a study of the psychological "meaning and importance of fairy tales." It was first published in 1976.

LIFE DIVINED FROM THE INSIDE

"Little Red Riding Hood was my first love. I felt that if I could have married Little Red Riding Hood, I should have known perfect bliss." This statement by Charles Dickens indicates that he, like untold millions of children all over the world throughout the ages, was enchanted by fairy tales. Even when world-famous, Dickens acknowledged the deep formative impact that the wondrous figures and events of fairy tales had had on him and his creative genius. He repeatedly expressed scorn for those who, motivated by an uninformed and petty rationality, insisted on rationalizing, bowdlerizing, or outlawing these stories, and thus robbed children of the important contributions fairy tales could make to their lives. Dickens understood that the imagery of fairy tales helps children better than anything else in their most difficult and yet most important and satisfying task: achieving a more mature consciousness to civilize the chaotic pressures of their unconscious.

Today, as in the past, the minds of both creative and average children can be opened to an appreciation of all the higher things in life by fairy tales, from which they can move easily to enjoying the greatest works of literature and art. The poet Louis MacNeice, for example, tells that "Real fairy stories always meant much to me as a person, even when I was at a public school where to admit this meant losing face. Contrary to what many people say even now, a fairy story, at least of the classical folk variety, is a much more solid affair than the average naturalistic novel, whose hooks go little deeper than a gossip column. From folk tales and sophisticated fairy tales such as Hans Andersen's or Norse mythology and stories like the *Alice* books and *Water Babies* I graduated, at about the age of twelve, to the *Faerie Queene*." Literary critics such as G. K. Chesterton and C. S. Lewis felt that fairy stories are "spiritual explorations"

From *The Uses of Enchantment: The Meaning and Importance of Fairy Tales,* by Bruno Bettelheim. Copyright © 1976 by Bruno Bettelheim. Reprinted by permission of Alfred A. Knopf, Inc. Portions of this book originally appeared in *The New Yorker.*

and hence "the most life-like" since they reveal "human life as seen, or felt, or divined from the inside."

Fairy tales, unlike any other form of literature, direct the child to discover his identity and calling, and they also suggest what experiences are needed to develop his character further. Fairy tales intimate that a rewarding, good life is within one's reach despite adversity—but only if one does not shy away from the hazardous struggles without which one can never achieve true identity. These stories promise that if a child dares to engage in this fearsome and taxing search, benevolent powers will come to his aid, and he will succeed. The stories also warn that those who are too timorous and narrow-minded to risk themselves in finding themselves must settle down to a humdrum existence—if an even worse fate does not befall them.

Past generations of children who loved and felt the importance of fairy tales were subjected to the scorn only of pedants, as happened to MacNeice. Today many of our children are far more grievously bereaved—because they are deprived of the chance to know fairy stories at all. Most children now meet fairy tales only in prettified and simplified versions which subdue their meaning and rob them of all deeper significance—versions such as those on films and TV shows, where fairy tales are turned into empty-minded entertainment.

Through most of man's history, a child's intellectual life, apart from immediate experiences within the family, depended on mythical and religious stories and on fairy tales. This traditional literature fed the child's imagination and stimulated his fantasizing. Simultaneously, since these stories answered the child's most important questions, they were a major agent of his socialization. Myths and closely related religious legends offered material from which children formed their concepts of the world's origin and purpose, and of the social ideals a child could pattern himself after. These were the images of the unconquered hero Achilles and wily Odysseus; of Hercules, whose life history showed that it is not beneath the dignity of the strongest man to clean the filthiest stable; of St. Martin, who cut his coat in half to clothe a poor beggar. It is not just since Freud that the myth of Oedipus has become the image by which we understand the ever new but age-old problems posed to us by our complex and ambivalent feelings about our parents. Freud referred to his ancient story to make us aware of the inescapable cauldron of emotions which every child, in his own way, has to manage at a certain age.

In the Hindu civilization, the story of Rama and Sita (part of the *Ramayana*), which tells of their peaceable courage and their passionate devotion to each other, is the prototype of love and marriage relationships. The culture, moreover, enjoins everyone to try to relive this myth in his or her own life; every Hindu bride is called Sita, and as part of her wedding ceremony she acts out certain episodes of the myth.

In a fairy tale, internal processes are externalized and become comprehensible as represented by the figures of the story and its events. This is the reason why in traditional Hindu medicine a fairy tale giving form to his particular problem was offered to a psychically disoriented person, for his meditation. It was expected that through contemplating the story the disturbed person would be led to visualize both the nature of the impasse in living from which he suffered, and the possibility of its resolution. From what a particular tale implied about man's despair, hopes, and methods of overcoming tribulations, the patient could discover not only a way out of his distress but also a way to find himself, as the hero of the story did.

But the paramount importance of fairy tales for the growing individual resides in something other than teachings about correct ways of behaving in this world—such wisdom is plentifully supplied in religion, myths, and fables. Fairy stories do not pretend to describe the world as it is, nor do they advise what one ought to do. If they did, the Hindu patient would be induced to follow an imposed pattern of behavior—which is not just bad therapy, but the opposite of therapy. The fairy tale is therapeutic because the patient finds his *own* solutions, through contemplating what the story seems to imply about him and his inner conflicts at this moment in his life. The content of the chosen tale usually has nothing to do with the patient's external life, but much to do with his inner problems, which seem incomprehensible and hence unsolvable. The fairy tale clearly does not refer to the outer world, although it may begin realistically enough and have everyday features woven into it. The unrealistic nature of these tales (which narrow-minded rationalists object to) is an important device, because it makes obvious that the fairy tales' concern is not useful information about the external world, but the inner processes taking place in an individual.

In most cultures, there is no clear line separating myth from folk or fairy tale; all these together form the literature of preliterate societies. The Nordic languages have only one word for both: *saga*. German has retained the word *Sage* for myths, while fairy stories are called *Märchen*. It is unfortunate that both the English and French names for these stories emphasize the role of fairies in them—because in most, no fairies appear. Myths and fairy tales alike attain a definite form only when they are committed to writing and are no longer subject to continuous change. Before being written down, these stories were either condensed or vastly elaborated in the retelling over the centuries; some stories merged with others. All became modified by what the teller thought was of greatest interest to his listeners, by what his concerns of the moment or the special problems of his era were.

Some fairy and folk stories evolved out of myths; others were incorporated into them. Both forms embodied the cumulative experience of a society as men wished to recall past wisdom for themselves and transmit it to future generations. These tales are the purveyors of deep insights that have sustained mankind through the long vicissitudes of its existence, a heritage that is not revealed in any other form as simply and directly, or as accessibly, to children.

Myths and fairy tales have much in common. But in myths, much more than in fairy stories, the culture hero is presented to the listener as a figure he ought to emulate in his own life, as far as possible.

A myth, like a fairy tale, may express an inner conflict in symbolic form and suggest how it may be solved—but this is not necessarily the myth's central concern. The myth presents its theme in a majestic way; it carries spiritual force; and the divine is present and is experienced in the form of superhuman heroes who make constant demands on mere mortals. Much as we, the mortals, may strive to be like these heroes, we will remain always and obviously inferior to them.

The figures and events of fairy tales also personify and illustrate inner conflicts, but they suggest ever so subtly how these conflicts may be solved, and what the next steps in the development toward a higher humanity might be. The fairy tale is presented in a simple, homely way; no demands are made on the listener. This prevents even the smallest child from feeling compelled to act in specific ways, and he is never made to feel inferior. Far from making demands, the fairy tale reassures, gives hope for the future, and holds out the promise of a happy ending. That is why Lewis Carroll called it a "love-gift"—a term hardly applicable to a myth.[1]

Obviously, not every story contained in a collection called "Fairy Tales" meets these criteria. Many of these stories are simply diversions, cautionary tales, or fables. If they are fables, they tell by means of words, actions, or events— fabulous though these may be—what one ought to do. Fables demand and threaten—they are moralistic—or they just entertain. To decide whether a story is a fairy tale or something entirely different, one might ask whether it could rightly be called a love-gift to a child. That is not a bad way to arrive at a classification.

To understand how a child views fairy tales, let us consider as examples the many fairy stories in which a child outwits a giant who scares him or even threatens his life. That children intuitively understand what these "giants" stand for is illustrated by the spontaneous reaction of a five-year-old.

Encouraged by discussion about the importance fairy tales have for children, a mother overcame her hesitation about telling such "gory and threatening" stories to her son. From her conversations with him, she knew that her son already had fantasies about eating people, or people getting eaten. So she told him the tale of "Jack the Giant Killer." His response at the end of the story was: "There aren't any such things as giants, are there?" Before the mother could give her son the reassuring reply which was on her tongue—and which would have destroyed the value of the story for him—he continued, "But there are such things as grownups, and they're like giants." At the ripe old age of five, he understood the encouraging message of the story: although adults can be experienced as frightening giants, a little boy with cunning can get the better of them.

This remark reveals one source of adult reluctance to tell fairy stories: we are not comfortable with the thought that occasionally we look like threatening giants to our children, although we do. Nor do we want to accept how easy they think it is to fool us, or to make fools of us, and how delighted they are by this idea. But whether or not we tell fairy tales to them, we do—as the example of this little boy proves—appear to them as selfish giants who wish to keep to ourselves all the wonderful things which give us power. Fairy stories provide reassurance to children that they can eventually get the better of the giant— i.e., they can grow up to be like the giant and acquire the same powers. These are "the mighty hopes that make us men."

Most significantly, if we parents tell such fairy stories to our children, we can give them the most important reassurance of all: that we approve of their

---

[1] Child of the pure unclouded brow
  And dreaming eyes of wonder!
  Though time be fleet, and I and thou
  Are half a life asunder,
  Thy loving smile will surely hail
  The love-gift of a fairy-tale.

—C. L. Dodgson (Lewis Carroll), in *Through the Looking-Glass.* [Bettelheim's note.]

playing with the idea of getting the better of these giants. Here reading is not the same as being told the story, because while reading alone the child may think that only some stranger—the person who wrote the story or arranged the book—approves of outwitting and cutting down the giant. But when his parents *tell* him the story, a child can be sure that they approve of his retaliating in fantasy for the threat which adult dominance entails.

ROBERT JEWETT AND
JOHN SHELTON LAWRENCE

from *The American Monomyth*

The American Monomyth, a study of our nation's popular arts, attempts to show that a single central myth lies beneath the surface of our favorite movies, television shows, comic books, etc. This myth portrays an Edenic society rescued from evil by a selfless and celibate redeemer-hero who enters the community, rids it of corruption, and then "recedes into obscurity." The following selection from the book focuses on the popular television show "Star Trek." The authors argue that, despite this program's scientific trappings and its denigration of myths, its stories nevertheless follow distinctly mythic patterns.

Professor of Religious Studies at Morningside College in Sioux City, Iowa, Robert Jewett is the author of numerous articles and several books, including *The Captain America Complex.* John Shelton Lawrence is Professor of Philosophy at Morningside College. Besides his co-authorship of *The American Monomyth*, he is the editor, along with Bernard Timberg, of *Fair Use and Free Inquiry: Copyright Law and the New Media.*

At the surface level *Star Trek* stories seem to defy interpretation as mythic material with powerful unconscious appeal. The entire series takes a singularly dim view of myths, not to speak of legends, fables, and their primitive religious accouterments. *Star Trek* celebrates the freeing of the human spirit from superstition and narrow-mindedness. It wears the cloak of empirical science. It purports to be a future chapter in what Joseph Campbell called "the wonder story of mankind's coming to maturity." Campbell, the famous historian of world myths, argues that with the coming of the scientific age, mankind has been set free from myths. "The spell of the past, the bondage of tradition, was shattered with sure and mighty strokes. The dream-web of myth fell away; the mind opened to full waking consciousness; and modern man emerged from ancient ignorance, like a butterfly from its cocoon, or like the sun at dawn from the womb of mother night." Producer Gene Roddenberry would surely agree. The antimythic bias in *Star Trek* is clearly visible in the following episode.

Excerpted from *The American Monomyth* by Robert Jewett and John Shelton Lawrence. Copyright © 1977 by Robert Jewett and John Shelton Lawrence. Reprinted by permission of Doubleday & Company, Inc.

"Who Mourns for Adonais?"

The U.S.S. *Enterprise* is approaching an unexplored M Class planet when an immense, masculine face appears on the scanner screen and stops the ship in midspace by a tremendous exertion of energy. Captain Kirk leads the exploration party of Spock, Chekov, McCoy, Scott, and the ravishingly beautiful archaeologist Carolyn Palamas. They find themselves in a Greek-like temple complex. A magnificent, muscular man whose face they had seen on the scanner rises to greet them with the words, "I am Apollo. . . . You are here to worship me as your fathers worshipped me before you." When Kirk asks what he requires, he insists he is Apollo and demands "loyalty," "tribute," and "worship" in return for a "human life as simple and pleasureful as it was those thousands of years ago on our beautiful Earth so far away." Kirk replies, "We're not in the habit of bending our knees to everyone we meet with a bag of tricks." When they refuse obeisance, Apollo's wrath melts their phaser guns and injures Scott, who has attempted to protect Carolyn from amorous advances. She volunteers to go with Apollo and quickly falls in love with him.

Captain Kirk theorizes that an unknown race capable of space travel had come to ancient Greece with the ability ". . . to alter their shapes at will and command great energy." This theory is corroborated by Apollo's explanation to Carolyn:

"Your fathers turned away from us until we were only memories. A god cannot survive as a memory. We need awe, worship. We need love."

Carolyn replies, "You really consider yourself to be a god?"

He laughs, ". . . In a real sense we were gods. The power of life and death was ours. When men turned from us, we could have struck down from Olympus and destroyed them. But we had no wish to destroy. So we came back to the stars again."

After making love to Carolyn, Apollo returns to the other members of the crew. The enraged Scott attacks him, only to be struck down with the blue-hot streak that lashed from Apollo's finger. This provokes Kirk to declare war on the god, and Kirk too is struck down. When Apollo disappears to recharge his power source, they decide to attack him in hopes of wearing him down. The *Enterprise* crew meanwhile prepares to fire phasers against Apollo's force field. When Carolyn appears again, Kirk tries to cope with her infatuation.

The lovely archaeologist relates Apollo's message, "He wants to guard . . . and provide for us the rest of our lives. He can do it."

Kirk reminds her, "You've got work to do."

"Work?" Carolyn replies.

Kirk insists, "He thrives on love, on worship. . . . We can't give him worship. None of us, especially you. . . . Reject him! You must!"

"I love him!"

"All our lives, here and on the ship, depend on you."

"No! Not on me."

"On you, Lieutenant. Accept him—and you condemn the crew of the *Enterprise* to slavery!"

She stares at him blankly.

Kirk pleads with her to remember ". . . what you are! A bit of flesh and blood afloat in illimitable space. The only thing that is truly yours is this small moment of time you share with the rest of humanity. . . . That's where our duty lies. . . . Do you understand me?"

Carolyn comes to her senses when she discovers Apollo will not accept her liberated intellectual interests. This time the god lashes out in fury at her. But the incandescing phaser beams from the *Enterprise* strike his power source just in time, reducing him to a "man-size being."

"I would have loved you as a father his children," Apollo says, in anguish. "Did I ask so much of you?"

Kirk's reply is gentle. "We have outgrown you," he says. "You asked for what we can no longer give."

Denied the worship so necessary for his being, Apollo's body begins to lose substance, and for the first time he admits the time of the gods "is gone. Take me home to the stars on the wind."

This episode bears a clear message that the era of myths is over, that retreating into slavery to the gods of the past would be terrible. Moreover, the episode suggests that the ancient myths can be scientifically explained by assuming that space travelers played the role of gods. This theme has enormous appeal, judging from the popularity of works such as *Chariots of the Gods.* The episode implies that meaning is purely of this world, any threshold to mysterious, transcendent reality firmly denied. In contrast to the illusive message of myths and religions, the meaning of Carolyn Palamas' life is simply her "duty" to the only reality of which she can be sure, the "humanity" she shares. This conviction of Captain Kirk fits the spirit of the entire series. It is unthinkable that he or his crew, not to speak of the strictly scientific Spock, would give credence to myths for a moment.

Yet the story line of this and other episodes follows a mythic pattern. David Gerrold, one of the writers of *Star Trek* scripts, defined *Star Trek* as ". . . a set of fables—morality plays, entertainments, and diversions about contemporary man, but set against a science-fiction background. *The background is subordinate to the fable.*" This can be documented at those points in which dramatic coherence—that is, hewing to the mythic story line—caused scriptwriters to depart from the standards of scientific accuracy. For instance, the attractive young crew of the *Enterprise* never ages despite journeys through the light-year distances of outer space. Members of the bridge crew are regularly shaken off their seats by enemy torpedoes despite the fact that shock waves would not carry past a spaceship's artificial-gravity field. The scientific liberties are taken for dramatic effect, creating ". . . action, adventure, fun, entertainment, and thought-provoking statements." These are actually mythical elements that appeal to an audience schooled in a particular mythical tradition.

When one compares the themes of the series with the content of classical myths, similarities are immediately apparent. Isolating such content from the genesis and function of myths, we mention three patterns visible in "Who Mourns for Adonais?" The first is *saga,* which features a protagonist journeying to unknown and dangerous regions, undergoing trials to test his strength and wit. In the classical monomyth delineated by Joseph Campbell, a journey is undertaken in response to the requirement for each human to move from childhood to maturity through "the crooked lanes of his own spiritual labyrinth." But in materials embodying the American monomyth, the saga of maturation tends to be replaced by the defense against malevolent attacks upon innocent communities. Gene Roddenberry's original prospectus for *Star Trek*, featuring the format of "Wagon Train to the Stars," aims at saga. He planned the series to be ". . . built around characters who travel to other worlds and meet the jeopardy and adventure which become our stories." This correlates with the announcement at the beginning of *Star Trek* programs, that the mission of the *Enterprise* is ". . . to explore strange new worlds, to seek out new civilizations, to boldly go where no man has gone before." Thus in the saga of Apollo's planet, the *Enterprise* had to be mortally endangered by the gigantic face on the scanner, and it was essential for the protagonists Kirk and Spock to leave their command post and come face to face with the foe. It was obviously bad military and space-travel strategy, as many critics have pointed out. No sensible commander would send himself and the key technical officers on a landing party like this. But it is essential to the saga format and thus is characteristic of almost every episode.

The second mythic pattern visible in *Star Trek* is *sexual renunciation*. The protagonist in some mythical sagas must renounce previous sexual ties for the sake of his trials. He must avoid entanglements and temptations that inevitably arise from Sirens or Loreleis in the course of his travels. Thus Lieutenant Palamas is tested in the episode with Apollo, her sexual liaison endangering the survival of the *Enterprise*. After she renounces her passion, the saga can get back on course. In the classical monomyth this theme plays a subsidiary role in the initiation or testing phase. The protagonist may encounter sexual temptation symbolizing ". . . that pushing, self-protective, malodorous, carnivorous, lecherous fever which is the very nature of the organic cell," as Campbell points out. Yet the "ultimate adventure" is the ". . . mystical marriage . . . of the triumphant hero-soul with the Queen Goddess" of knowledge. In the current American embodiments of mythic renunciation there is a curious rejection of sexual union as a primary value.

In *Star Trek* each hero is locked into a renunciatory pattern closely related to the mission. On long expeditions in outer space, there is, for example, no intrinsic reason why the captain would not be accompanied by his wife and family. This was customary for the masters of some large sailing vessels in the era of extended voyages. But that would violate the mythic paradigm. So Roddenberry describes the renunciation pattern: "Long ago Captain Kirk consciously ruled out any possibility of any romantic interest while aboard the ship. It is an involvement he feels he simply could never risk. In a very real sense he is 'married' to his ship and his responsibilities as captain of her." In numerous episodes Kirk is in the situation Carolyn Palamas faced, forced to choose between an attractive sexual partner and his sense of duty to his mission. The authors of *Star Trek Lives!* report that female fans

> . . . vicariously thrill to Kirk's sexual exploits with gorgeous females of every size, shape and type—from the stunning lady lawyers, biologists and doctors who have loved him, to the vicious and breath-taking Elaan of Troyius, who ruled a planet but was willing to risk destroying her entire solar system for him. . . . Many see Kirk's loves as having a tragic element. There is affection and warmth in his response, and evidently the capacity for deep love. But very often the situation is impossible. He loses not through his faults but through his virtues, because of the demanding life he has chosen.

They go on to describe the renunciation of sexual bonds for the sake of loyalty to the *Enterprise* and its crew. "Time and again, he had to make a choice between a woman and his ship—and his ship always won."

This renunciation of sexual love for the sake of loyalty to one's comrades goes far beyond the classical monomyth. It is seen perhaps most clearly in the person of Spock. He is loyal to Kirk and his comrades at the expense of risking his life for them again and again, but he persistently resists the temptation of entanglements with the opposite sex. Nurse Christine Chapel, a beautiful, talented crew member who is hopelessly in love with Spock, receives the cold shoulder in story after story. Here is a man ". . . capable of the prodigious outpouring of passion triggered by the irresistible *pon farr* and yet incapable of lasting emotional ties" with women. Sex is an autonomous force here, distinct from Spock's personality and capable of destroying his ability to reason. Since he cannot integrate it with his personality, it must be rigidly repressed until it overpowers him in the rutting season. Spock bears within his person the temptation threatening every saga with disaster—it must be fiercely renounced for the mission to succeed. Such a motif may not be true to life, and it is certainly improbable that there are sophisticated planets with *pon farr* rites derived from Puritan fantasies, but it is true to the mythic paradigm.

•   •   •

The third mythical pattern in *Star Trek* is *redemption*. In the classical monomyth the beautiful maiden must be redeemed from the clutches of the sea monster, the endangered city spared from its peril, and the protagonist redeemed by fateful interventions in the nick of time. This pattern is much more diffuse in the classical monomyth than in modern materials standing closer to the American pattern. The classical hero may experience supernatural aid as he crosses the threshold into the realm of initiatory adventure and then returns, and he may confront trials embodying the redemption of others. But his own redemption takes the form of gaining mature wisdom, achieving atonement with his father, enjoying union with the goddess, and returning home with benefits for his people. The redemption scheme in materials like *Star Trek* has nothing to do with the maturation process. It fits rather the pattern of selfless crusading to redeem others. This form of selfless idealism has been elaborated most extensively by Ernest Tuveson in *Redeemer Nation*. As so frequently in American history, the *Enterprise* sense of high calling leads to violations of its "noninterference directive." If Kirk and his crew encounter an endangered planet, their sense of duty impels them to intervene. It may not be legal, or right, or even sensible, but the zealous imperative to redeem is all-pervasive. While Gerrold may have overstated in claiming that among the seventy-nine *Star Trek* episodes, ". . . there never was a script in which the *Enterprise*'s mission or goals were questioned," he has accurately described the series as a whole.

While the *Enterprise* regularly plays the mythic redeemer role, Mr. Spock embodies it in a particularly powerful way. His half Vulcan origin makes him a godlike figure, peculiarly capable of effecting redemption. Spock consults his computer with superhuman speed to devise the technique of saving galaxies and men from prodigious threats, leading the audience to view him with a kind of reverence that traditionally has been reserved for gods. Leonard Nimoy's interview, approvingly cited by the authors of *Star Trek Lives!*, points toward audience yearnings for an omniscient redeemer. The viewer sees Spock as someone

> . . . who knows something about me that nobody else knows. Here's a person that *understands* me in a way that nobody else understands me. Here's a person that I'd like to be able to spend time with and talk to because *he would know what I mean when I tell him how I feel*. He would have insight that nobody else seems to have. . . .

In short, Spock is perceived as a god, which matches the requirements of the mythical pattern, namely that without a superhuman agency of some sort, there is no true redemption.

        •   •   •

These mythical themes help us to focus sharply on a paradox evident in *Star Trek*. While its themes occasionally contest the mythical world view, its format and stories are thoroughly mythical. To use Joseph Campbell's terms, it is as if space-age man, having emerged from the "cocoon" of mythic ignorance, awoke to find himself still enmeshed "in the dream-web of myth." This paradox of *Star Trek* reveals a *myth of mythlessness*. Its implicit claim to be antimythical and purely scientific is itself a myth—that is, a set of unconsciously held, unexamined premises. The *Star Trek* format may be a new set of wineskins, but the mythic fermentation within is as old as Apollo.

URSULA K. LE GUIN

"Myth and Archetype in Science Fiction"

In addition to her novels, Ursula K. Le Guin (see headnote, p. 29) has written several lively theoretical essays on science fiction and mythology. The article reprinted below was first published in the fall 1976 issue of the magazine *Parabola: Myth and the Quest for Meaning*.

"Science fiction is the mythology of the modern world." It's a good slogan, and a useful one when you're faced with people ignorant and contemptuous of science fiction, for it makes them stop and think. But like all slogans it's a half-truth, and when used carelessly, as a whole truth, can cause all kinds of confusion.

    Where care must be taken is with that complex word, "mythology." What is a myth?

    "Myth is an attempt to explain, in rational terms, facts not yet rationally understood." That is the definition provided by the reductive, scientistic mentality of the first half of the twentieth century, and still accepted by many. According to this definition, the god Apollo "is merely" an inadequate effort made by primitive minds to explain and systematise the nature and behavior of the Sun. As

Copyright © 1976 by Ursula K. Le Guin; first appeared in *Parabola*.

soon as the Sun is rationally understood to be a ball of fire much larger than the Earth, and its behavior has been described by a system of scientific laws, the old mythological pseudoexplanation is left empty. The fiery horses and the golden chariot vanish, the god is dethroned, and his exploits remain only a pretty tale for children. According to this view, the advance of science is a progressive draining dry of the content of mythology.[1] And, in so far as the content of myth is rational and the function of myth is explanatory, this definition is suitable. However, the rational and explanatory is only one function of the myth. Myth is an expression of one of the several ways the human being, body/psyche, perceives, understands, and relates to the world. Like science, it is a product of a basic human mode of apprehension. To pretend that it can be replaced by abstract or quantitative cognition is to assert that the human being is, potentially or ideally, a creature of pure reason, a disembodied Mind. It might, indeed, be nice if we were all little bubbles of pure reason floating on the stream of time; but we aren't. We are rational beings, but we are also sensual, emotional, appetitive, ethical beings, driven by needs and reaching out for satisfactions which the intellect alone cannot provide. Where these other modes of being and doing are inadequate, the intellect should prevail. Where the intellect fails, and must always fail, unless we become disembodied bubbles, then one of the other modes must take over. The myth, mythological insight, is one of these. Supremely effective in its area of function, it needs no replacement. Only the schizoid arrogance of modern scientism pretends that it ought to be replaced, and that pretension is pretty easily deflated. For example, does our scientific understanding of the nature and behavior of the Sun explain (let alone explain away) Apollo's remarkable sex life, or his role as the god of music and of the divine harmony? No, it has nothing whatever to do with all that; it has nothing to do with sex, or music, or harmony, or divinity; nor, as science, did it ever pretend to—only scientism made the claim. Apollo is not the Sun, and never was. The Sun, in fact, "is merely" one of the names of Apollo.

Reductionism cuts both ways, after all.

So long, then, as we don't claim either that the science in science fiction replaces the "old, false" mythologies, or that the fiction in science fiction is a mere attempt to explain what science hasn't yet got around to explaining, we can use the slogan. Science fiction is the mythology of the modern world—or one of its mythologies—even though it is a highly intellectual form of art, and mythology is a non-intellectual mode of apprehension. For science fiction does use the mythmaking faculty to apprehend the world we live in, a world profoundly shaped and changed by science and technology; and its originality is that it uses the mythmaking faculty on new material.

But there's another catch to look out for. The presence of mythic material in a story does not mean that the mythmaking faculty is being used.

Here is a science fiction story: its plot is modelled directly upon that of an ancient myth, or there are characters in it modelled upon certain gods or heroes of legend. Is it, therefore, a myth? Not necessarily; in fact, probably not.

---

[1] This schema is reproduced in Freudian psychology, where the myth or symbol is considered to be a disguise, and the raising into consciousness of unconscious contents leads to a progressive emptying or draining dry of the unconscious: in contrast to the schema followed by Jung and others, where the emphasis is on the irreducibility of symbol, and the compensatory, mutually creative relationship between the conscious and the unconscious. [Le Guin's note.]

No mythmaking is involved: just theft.

Theft is an integral function of a healthy literature. It's much easier to steal a good plot from some old book than to invent one. Anyhow, after you've sweated to invent an original plot, it very often turns out to be a perfect parallel to one of the old stories (more on this curious fact later). And since there are beautiful and powerful stories all through world legendry, and since stories need retelling from generation to generation, why not steal them? I'm certainly not the one to condemn the practice; parts of my first novel were lifted wholesale from the Norse mythos (Brisingamen, Freya's necklace, and episodes in the life of Odin). My version isn't a patch on the original, of course, but I think I did the gods of Asgard no harm, and they did my book some good. This sort of pilfering goes on all the time, and produces many pleasant works of art, though it does not lead to any truly new creations or cognitions.

There is a more self-conscious form of thievery which is both more destructive and more self-destructive. In many college English courses the words "myth" and "symbol" are given a tremendous charge of significance. You just ain't no good unless you can see a symbol hiding, like a scared gerbil, under every page. And in many creative writing courses the little beasts multiply, the place swarms with them. What does this Mean? What does that Symbolise? What is the Underlying Mythos? Kids come lurching out of such courses with a brain full of gerbils. And they sit down and write a lot of empty pomposity, under the impression that that's how Melville did it.

Even when they begin to realise that art is not something produced for critics, but for other human beings, some of them retain the over-intellectualising bent. They still do not realize that a symbol is not a sign of something known, but an indicator of something not known and not expressible otherwise than symbolically. They mistake symbol (living meaning) for allegory (dead equivalence). So they use mythology in an arrogant fashion, rationalising it, condescending to it. They take plots and characters from it, not in the healthily furtive fashion of the literary sneakthief, but in a posturing, showy way. Such use of myth does real disservice to the original, by trivialising it, and no good at all to the story. The shallowness of its origin is often betrayed either by an elaborate vocabulary and ostentatiously cryptic style, or by a kind of jocose, chatty discomfort in the tone. Watch me up here on Olympus, you peasants, being fresh with Aphrodite. Look at me juggling symbols, folks! We sophisticates, we know how to handle these old archetypes.

But Zeus always gets 'em. ZAP!

So far I have been talking as if all mythologies the writer might use were dead—that is, not believed in with some degree of emotion, other than aesthetic appreciation, by the writer and his community. Of course this is far from being the case. It's easy to get fresh with Aphrodite. Who believes in some old Greek goddess, anyhow? But there are living mythologies, after all. Consider the Virgin Mary; or the State.

For an example of the use of science fiction of a living religious mythos one may turn to the work of Cordwainer Smith, whose Christian beliefs are evident, I think, all through his work, in such motifs as the savior, the martyr, rebirth, the "underpeople." Whether or not one is a Christian, one may admire wholeheartedly the strength and passion given the works by the author's living belief. In general, however, I think the critics' search for Christian themes in science fiction is sterile and misleading. For the majority of science-fiction writers, the themes of Christianity are dead signs, not living symbols, and those who use them do so all too often in order to get an easy emotional charge without working for it. They take a free ride on the crucifix, just as many now cash in cynically on the current occultist fad. The difference between this sort of thing and the genuine, naive mysticism of an Arthur Clarke, struggling to express his own, living symbol of rebirth, is all the difference in the world.

Beyond and beneath the great living mythologies of religion and power there is another region into which science fiction enters. I would call it the area of the Submyth: by which I mean those images, figures, and motifs which have no religious or moral resonance and no intellectual or aesthetic value, but which are vigorously alive and powerful, so that they cannot be dismissed as mere stereotypes. They are shared by all of us; they are genuinely collective. Superman is a submyth. His father was Nietzsche and his mother was a funnybook, and he is alive and well in the mind of every ten-year-old—and millions of others. Other science-fictional submyths are the blond heroes of sword and sorcery, with their unusual weapons; insane or self-deifying computers; mad scientists; benevolent dictators; detectives who find out who done it; capitalists who buy and sell galaxies; brave starship captains and/or troopers; evil aliens; good aliens; and every pointy-breasted brainless young woman who was ever rescued from monsters, lectured to, patronised, or, in recent years, raped, by one of the afore-mentioned heroes.

It hurts to call these creatures mythological. It is a noble word, and they are so grotty. But they are alive, in books, magazines, pictures, movies, advertising, and our own minds. Their roots are the roots of myth, are in our unconscious—that vast dim region of the psyche and perhaps beyond the psyche, which Jung called "collective" because it is similar in all of us, just as our bodies are basically similar. Their vigor comes from there, and so they cannot be dismissed as unimportant. Not when they can help motivate a world movement such as Fascism!—But neither can they furnish materials useful to art. They have the vitality of the collective unconscious, but nothing else, no ethical, aesthetic, or intellectual value. They have no element of the true myth except its emotive, irrational "thereness." The artist who deliberately submits his work to them has forfeited the right to call his work science fiction; he's just a pop-cultist cashing in.

True myth may serve for thousands of years as an inexhaustible source of intellectual speculation, religious joy, ethical inquiry, and artistic renewal. The real mystery is not destroyed by reason. The fake one is. You look at it and it vanishes. You look at the Blond Hero—really look—and he turns into a gerbil. But you look at Apollo, and he looks back at you.

The poet Rilke looked at a statue of Apollo about fifty years ago, and Apollo spoke to him. "You must change your life," he said.

When the genuine myth rises into consciousness, that is always its message. You must change your life.

The way of art, after all, is neither to cut adrift from the emotions, the senses, the body, etc., and sail off into the void of pure meaning, nor to blind the mind's eye and wallow in irrational, amoral meaninglessness—but to keep open the tenuous, difficult, essential connections between the two extremes. To connect. To connect idea with value, sensation with intuition, cortex with cerebellum. . . .

The true myth is precisely one of these connections.

Like any artist, the science fiction writer is trying to make and use such a connection or bridge between the conscious and the unconscious—so that his readers can make the journey too. If the only tool he uses is the intellect, he will produce only lifeless copies or parodies of the archetypes that live in his own deeper mind and in the great works of art and mythology. If he abandons intellect, he's likely to submerge his own personality and talent in a stew of mindless submyths, themselves coarse, feeble parodies of their archetypal origins. The only way to the truly collective, to the image that is alive and meaningful in all of us, seems to be through the truly personal. Not the impersonality of pure reason; not the impersonality of "the masses"; but the irreducibly personal— the self. To reach the others, the artist goes into himself. Using reason, he deliberately enters the irrational. The farther he goes into himself, the closer he comes to the other.

If this seems a paradox it is only because our culture overvalues abstraction and extraversion. Pain, for instance, can work the same way. Nothing is more personal, more unshareable, than pain; the worst thing about suffering is that you suffer alone. Yet those who have not suffered, or will not admit that they suffer, are those who are cut off in cold isolation from their fellow men. Pain, the loneliest experience, gives rise to sympathy, to love: the bridge between self and other, the means of communion. So with art. The artist who goes into himself most deeply—and it is a painful journey—is the artist who touches us most closely, speaks to us most clearly.

Of all the great psychologists, Jung best explains this process, by stressing the existence, not of an isolated "id," but a "collective unconscious." He reminds us that the region of the mind/body that lies beyond the narrow, brightly lit domain of consciousness is very much the same in all of us. This does not imply a devaluing of consciousness or of reason. The achievement of individual consciousness, which Jung calls "differentiation," is to him a great achievement, civilisation's highest achievement, the hope of our future. But the tree grows only from deep roots.

So it would seem that true myth arises only in the process of connecting the conscious and the unconscious realms. I won't find a living archetype in my bookcase or my television set. I will find it only in myself: in that core of individuality lying in the heart of the common darkness. Only the individual can get up and go to the window of his house, and draw back the curtains, and look out into the dark.

Sometimes it takes considerable courage to do that. When you open the curtains you don't know what may be out there in the night. Maybe starlight; maybe dragons; maybe the secret police. Maybe the grace of God; maybe the horror of death. They're all there. For all of us.

The writer who draws not upon the works and thoughts of others, but upon his own thoughts and his own deep being, will inevitably hit upon common material. The more original his work, the more imperiously *recognisable* it will be. "Yes, of course!" says the reader, recognising himself, his dreams, his nightmares. The characters, figures, images, motifs, plots, events of the story may be obvious parallels, even seemingly reproductions, of the material of myth and legend. There will be—openly in fantasy, covertly in naturalism—dragons, heroes, quests, objects of power, voyages at night and under sea, and so forth. In narrative, as in painting, certain familiar patterns will become visible.

This again is no paradox, if Jung is right, and we all have the same kind of dragons in our psyche, just as we all have the same kind of heart and lungs in our body. It does imply that nobody can invent an archetype by taking thought, any more than he can invent a new organ in his body. But this is no loss: rather a gain. It means that we can communicate, that alienation isn't the final human condition, since there is a vast common ground on which we can meet, not only rationally, but aesthetically, intuitively, emotionally.

A dragon, not a dragon cleverly copied or massproduced, but a creature of evil who crawls up, threatening and inexplicable, out of the artist's own unconscious, is alive: terribly alive. It frightens little children, and the artist, and the rest of us. It frightens us because it is part of us, and the artist forces us to admit it. We have met the enemy, as Pogo remarked, and he is us.

"What do you mean? There aren't any dragons in my living room, dragons are extinct, dragons aren't real. . . ."

"Look out of the window. . . . Look into the mirror. . . ."

The artist who works from the center of his own being will find archetypal images and release them into consciousness. The first science fiction writer to do so was Mary Shelley. She let Frankenstein's monster loose. Nobody has been able to shut him out again, either. There he is, sitting in the corner of our lovely modern glass and plastic living room, right on the tubular steel contour chair, big as life and twice as ugly. Edgar Rice Burroughs did it, though with infinitely less power and originality—Tarzan is a true myth-figure, though not a particularly relevant one to modern ethical/emotional dilemmas, as Frankenstein's monster is. Čapek did it, largely by *naming* something (a very important aspect of archetypizing): "Robots," he called them. They have walked among us ever since. Tolkien did it; he found a ring, a ring which we keep trying to lose. . . .

Scholars can have great fun, and can strengthen the effect of such figures, by showing their relationship to other manifestations of the archetype in myth, legend, dogma, and art.[2] These linkages can be highly illuminating. Frankenstein's monster is related to the Golem; to Jesus; to Prometheus. Tarzan is a direct descendant of the Wolfchild/Noble Savage on one side, and every child's fantasy of the Orphan-of-High-Estate on the other. The robot may be seen as the modern ego's fear of the body, after the crippling division of "mind" and "body," "ghost" and "machine," enforced by post-Renaissance mechanistic thought. In "The Time Machine" there is one of the great visions of the End, an archetype of eschatology comparable to any religious vision of the day of judgment. In "Nightfall" there is the fundamental opposition of dark and light, playing on the fear of darkness that we share with our cousins the great apes. Through Philip K. Dick's work one can follow an exploration of the ancient themes of identity and alienation, and the sense of the fragmentation of the ego. In Stanislaw Lem's works there seems to be a similarly complex and subtle exploration of the archetypal Other, the alien.

[2] Note that a manifestation is all we ever get; the archetype itself is beyond the reach of reason, art, or even madness. It is not a thing, an object, but is rather, Jung guessed, a psychic modality, a function, comparable to a function/limitation such as the visual range of the human eye, which, by limiting our perception of electromagnetic vibrations to a certain range, enables us to see. The archetypes "do not in any sense represent things as they are in themselves, but rather the forms in which things can be perceived and conceived." They are "*a priori* structural forms of the stuff of consciousness." (Jung: *Memories, Dreams, Reflections,* p. 347.) [Le Guin's note.]

Such myths, symbols, images do not disappear under the scrutiny of the intellect, nor does an ethical, or aesthetic, or even religious examination of them make them shrink and vanish. On the contrary: the more you look, the more there they are. And the more you think, the more they mean.

On this level, science fiction deserves the title of a modern mythology.

Most science fiction doesn't, of course, and never will. There are never very many artists around. No doubt we'll continue most of the time to get rewarmed leftovers from Babylon and Northrop Frye served up by earnest snobs, and hordes of brawny Gerbilmen ground out by hacks. But there will be mythmakers, too. Even now—who knows?—the next Mary Shelley may be lying quietly in her tower-top room, just waiting for a thunderstorm.

ALAN McGLASHAN

"Daily Paper Pantheon"

Alan McGlashan, a London psychiatrist, was educated at Epsom College and Clare College, Cambridge—where he took an Arts degree—and at St. George's Hospital, London. A Royal Air Force pilot during World War II, he was honored with several decorations, including the *Croix de Querre*. He has also been an officer on a tramp steamer, a drama critic, and a country doctor. His books include *St. George and the Dragon, Gravity and Levity*, and *Savage and Beautiful Country*, from which the following article is taken.

At heart modern man is lonely: isolated from all earlier generations by the brilliance, the power, the sheer mass of his own discoveries. Each new invention—drastically altering his life or dramatically changing his environment—fascinates him, yet leaves him secretly dismayed. He finds himself menaced by problems, undeniably of his own making, that are too large for him to handle. Looking round for reassurance, he discovers an almost total lack of guiding precedents, an almost total loss of the stabilizing sense of continuity with the past. In his haste to master new skills he has forgotten more than he can afford to forget.

In such a situation it may be well to look again at the contemporary scene, not—for once—in order to deplore or celebrate what is new, but to make a sustained attempt to reconnect with the past, to reestablish the sense of continuity.

So to look is to make an immediate discovery: the world of today is suddenly seen to be infiltrated in all directions with customs, ideas and beliefs which it

From *Savage and Beautiful Country* by Alan McGlashan. Copyright © 1966, 1967 by Alan McGlashan. Reprinted by permission of Chatto and Windus Ltd.

fancied it had long outgrown. Contemporary man, in fact, is by no means cut off. Between himself and men of earlier times pass a thousand delicate threads of mutual meaning. He is not even cut off from Nature—in spite of the violent efforts of the neo-abstractionists to disown the natural world. Between his own bold gambles with space and time, and the patient experiments of Nature itself through an unimaginable past, there stretch, as will be shown in later chapters, unbroken lines of descent, not so much evolutionary as recurrent. It is a clue which begins to make sense of the modern world.

To trace these lines, however, it is necessary to develop a sunny disregard concerning the current hierarchies of value. For over the unnumbered centuries there have been some astonishing reversals of form. Ideas and movements which engaged the finest intelligences of their age have swiftly sunk to the level of peasant "superstition," or dropped into empty vulgarities; while others, disregarded for millennia, have as swiftly emerged to be the hallmark of a whole civilization. The status accorded to an idea at any particular time is a historical accident, and is irrelevant to the question of its descent. It need therefore occasion no surprise that in this and the following chapters matters which are presently regarded either as vitally important or as entirely negligible are given equal space and consideration.

We are often told that if God did not exist it would be necessary to invent him. But this is true of many other and lesser things. If, for example, so quaint a creature as the Loch Ness Monster did not already exist as a possibility, it would have to be invented. And if the monster were fished out of the loch tomorrow and *proved* to exist, it would be urgently necessary to find a similar phenomenon somewhere else. For the mythic monster in the still waters of the Highland loch carries, however crudely, an intuition of something that is frighteningly real—the image of destructive dragon powers within himself which man has always known to be hidden there. It really seems as if man needs an image of this kind. The Loch Ness Monster is the latest of a long line of hair-raising creatures, half mocked at, half believed in: Roman Cerberus and Briareus, Anubis the dog-headed death-bringer of Egypt, the savage Fenris-Wolf that roamed the Nordic world, his cousins the werewolves of medieval Britain; these and a hundred others bear the burden of man's knowledge that crouched in the heart, biding its time, lies a ruthless predator. Even in so slight and recent a tale as *The Hound of the Baskervilles* the image was at once accepted in popular imagination, and outlives its author. In every age the more sophisticated have laughed at such things, but at the back of their laughter is often detectable a faint *frisson* of unease. And even by the hard-headed standards of Fleet Street, claims, however unauthentic, of having glimpsed the monster in the loch are eagerly accepted as news.

But there is more to read in the newspapers than news. Precisely because of the breakneck speed at which they are run off the presses, the hour-by-hour datelines which have to be met, certain concepts slip through—echoes of a remote past, intimations of things not yet known—that could never survive a more leisured and intellectual approach. There are ideas so dangerous and revolutionary that only in a naïve form can they be suffered to approach the human mind. All these "eyewitness" accounts of flying saucers, for instance, all these endless funny—but slightly hair-raising—stories of earth-visiting Martians . . . can this be a dramatization and projection onto images which we understand and can handle, of an idea which is invading our minds from somewhere beyond our familiar three-dimensional world, *an idea from psychological outer space,* as it were, which we *don't* understand and *can't* handle? Could it be that these feeble images and jokes are the nearest we can get to expressing our thrilled awareness of something "altogether other" on the verge of bursting through to us—something that may give the human mind a revised relationship to the external world? Is it the ferment in our souls that creates these childish visions in the sky?

Echoes of the long-forgotten past are to be found in the daily press even more frequently than intimations of the future. Nowhere is this more clear than in that curious and worldwide phenomenon the comic strip cartoon. Millions of adults read the comic strips in the daily papers. Those who do not are amused, baffled or exasperated by those who do. Unhappily addicts are either dumb (in both senses) or evasive, and they never seem able to give valid reasons for their semi-secret vice. It is a minor sociological mystery, inviting minor research.

Even a first glance shows something interesting. Comic strips for adults, an offshoot from children's comic papers, are not homogeneous: they fall into three groups. Two of the groups, whose puppets satirically reflect the modern scene, are different in nature from the third, but nevertheless have their own compulsive attraction, and their own faithful, furtive band of addicts.

The first is nothing more than a tabloid version of the ever-popular thriller. In the second group, much favored in the U.S.A., the intention cuts deeper, and a mordant image of contemporary society is projected, either directly in the squabbles and adventures of a typical young couple such as the Bumsteads, or indirectly through the eyes of a child or an animal—both being, of course, Everyman in an easily penetrated disguise. Perhaps the two best-loved of all American strip characters in this group are Charlie Brown, that endearingly bewildered infant, and Pogo, an appealing little creature of indefinable zoological status. Both Charlie Brown and Pogo are simple quixotic characters who wander in the modern jungle of hideous opportunity, frustrated by either the malicious and the corrupt or by the self-righteous and the ineffably stupid.

Charlie Brown can be counted on to take the responsibility that none will take, and to fail miserably, humiliatingly in every pinch. He is the common man, and his Lucy is the common man's Everywoman. In Lucy, a grim picture of a sexless life of unlove and mental tyranny is shown—woman, the ever-present executive assistant of life, undisturbed by the cancer of logic or the paralysis of doubt, who knows that she can do the job better. It is an unkind, unfair caricature—but recognizable.

Pogo, too, is an Everyman, adrift in a world too much for him. There are few problems in American life that he does not encounter. Pogo has been beset in his day by a wildcat, which bore a remarkable resemblance to Senator McCarthy, and a bear which dropped out of a plane and looked quite exactly like Khrushchev. There is Miz Beaver, who represents everything a man does not want in a woman, and Miss Mamselle, a juvenile skunk with a French accent, who is everything he does want—soft, eternally ingenuous, innocently sure that Pogo is good (as, of course, he is) and can in a crisis protect her from all harm. In this type of comic strip American society is laughing at itself, cynically and healthily.

But in the third group the comic strip moves into a new dimension, and draws its images from a more mysterious source. Distinguishable always by the presence of an element of the miraculous or magical, this form of strip has an attraction subtly compulsive, altogether different.

Examples of this third kind occur everywhere. For convenience may be cited a single British newspaper, the *Daily Mirror,* where till recently no less than four out of its six comic strips unmistakably belonged to it. These four comic strip characters have strikingly different personalities, and their adventures follow entirely different patterns. The first is *Garth,* a huge, honest, bull-necked fellow whose constant role is rescuing people and overcoming apparently hopeless odds by sheer physical strength. Then there is *Jane,* a highly seductive young woman who escapes by a hair's breadth—usually with the loss of most of her clothes—from a series of compromising situations. The third character is a gambling, drinking, rip-roaring, rather attractive scoundrel, *Captain Reilly-Ffoull,* whose exploits, however promisingly they begin, always end in his own discomfiture. Finally there is *Jimpy,* a curious little boy whose extreme politeness and humility conceal a startling capacity to work magic at just those moments when he and his companions are faced by disaster.

Garth and Jane, Jimpy and Captain Reilly-Ffoull: is it possible that someone on the staff of the *Daily Mirror* chose these grotesques with full understanding of what he was doing? It is wildly unlikely. Yet beyond this and the even less likely theory of coincidence there lies only one other possibility—that they were chosen by the uncannily accurate processes of unconscious selection, operating at the deepest level of the human psyche. If this fantastic hypothesis were true, they would be found to exert a curiously compulsive power, overriding rational repudiation, on the minds of multitudes. Which is precisely what they do.

For these figures are no casual products of the imagination. Faintly through all their exploits, vulgar and puerile as these usually are, sounds an echo of something unimaginably archaic: the adventure cycles of the early gods. The famous mythologist, Kerenyi, latest among many, has shown with high probability that such adventure cycles are the basic themes of human mental activity as far back as it can be traced, recurring endlessly in the likeliest and most unlikely places, the noblest and most degenerate forms.

Consider *Garth,* that beefy and bewildered giant, long-suffering, virtuous, strong, faced by a never-ending series of heroic tasks. Is there not more than an echo here of Hercules and his labors, much-enduring, far-traveled Ulysses, blinded Samson, Noah, Gilgamesh . . . and behind these the timeless image of the heroic principle in man, aided magically by Heaven in reward of faith and valor?

Garth, for all his crudity, is a hero in the classic sense. He uses his miraculous strength only to restore the balance of things disturbed by evil forces. If he were a Leader it would be of nothing more sinister than a Boy Scout patrol. He is a "verray parfit gentil knight." Indeed, with women his unwearying chivalry puts to shame many of the accepted heroes in their weaker moments. Calypso would have had no chance with Garth; Delilah would have charmed in vain. Even the colorless girl-companion of Garth's adventures, Dawn, is only there on sufferance, a sort of little sister allowed under strict rules—which she is always breaking—to share her brother's manly expeditions. To friendly ears it may be whispered that here lies the clue to this almost dismaying chastity: Garth's life is bounded by the simple certainties of pre-adolescence; he has never reached the mental age at which woman becomes a sweet temptation.

Woman as temptress: the image leads straight to another strip character, the often excruciating *Jane,* beautiful but virginal, constantly wooed but never wed. Above her—far, far above—does there not float, as on vaulted ceilings of Venetian palaces, a company of bright figures? Hainuwele the moon maiden, irresistible Helen, Aphrodite from the wine-dark sea, flower-gathering Persephone, and all the countless images of Kore the maiden goddess—"La Belle Dame sans Merci," the unpossessable yet eternally nubile she, whose golden promises invest with a brief splendor the too credulous heart of man. Does not Jane in *Fritzy* the dachshund even possess her appropriate animal attribute, as Diana has her hound, and Cynthia her hare?

In *Captain Reilly-Ffoull* the echoing image is at once more immediate and more remote. His life of shameless gusto, full of shady triumphs and richly earned humiliations, rouses in us secret sympathies; for here is the renegade, the lame god, our shadow-self, the dark and unacknowledged side of brindled human nature. Even the quaint title of his moated and battlemented country residence— Arntwee Hall—hints at his common humanity, and is clearly more than accident. Here is a god so close to us that even the shallowest modern still hears his bold licentious whispers, yet so remote in origin that without experience of him Man would not be Man.

Older than all these are the dim unfocusable forms that throng "like pageantry of mist on an autumnal stream" behind the enigmatic figure of young *Jimpy.* These dim shapes are indeed the Early Gods, older far than "the bright static hierarchy of Olympus," older perhaps than Time itself. They reach back, these primal figures, to those fluid ever-changing changeless archetypes that gloom and glow in the depths of the archaic psyche. Incredibly, little Jimpy is of their company. Eternally childlike, vague of parentage, he displays with startling fidelity the attributes of weakness and insignificance combined with mysterious power possessed by the dawn-image of God in the human mind. At one point in the Jimpy cycle an adult character says to him, "Is it true, then, you must always remain a boy?" It would be hard to devise a clearer modern evocation of the *Puer Aeternus.*

Perhaps the key to the whole mystery of the comic strip's compulsive force lies in this Jimpian paradox of weakness and smallness combined with magical, boundless power. For paradox itself, that disquieting insult to received opinion, is usually a pointer to the heart of things. The approaches to wisdom are paved with prickly paradox; hard going for bare rational feet.

"Smaller than small, yet bigger than big." In these apparently senseless words are expressed the earliest concepts of the Divine in the history of the human mind: the Little Copper Man, for instance, of the Finnish *Kalevala,* "no bigger than the thumb and no higher than an oxhoof," who yet could fell the giant oak tree that covered the sun and moon with its branches, with the happy result that "the sun shone again and the dear moon glimmered pleasantly, the clouds sailed far and wide and the rainbow spanned the heavens"; or *Narayana,* the little Hindu boy asleep in the branches of the nyagrodha tree, in whose belly lay "the whole world with its lands and cities, with the Ganges and the other rivers and the Sea"; or, a more familiar image, *the Babe* laid in a Manger, in whose praise the morning stars sang together and all the sons of God shouted for joy. In widely differing cultures the same paradoxical weakness and strength is visualized: in David with his sling, Hercules strangling serpents in his cradle, Eros armed with fatal arrows, and—little Jimpy, deferential to adults but gifted with his magic powers.

There is, of course, something both offensive and outrageous in these parallels of the sublime with the degenerate-ridiculous. The association is lunatic and the rational mind recoils from it at first in repulsion and disgust. The rational mind should calm itself. There have been in myth and legend many such divine *bouleversements;* as of Jove, Lord of an antique Heaven, dwindling down to bottle-nosed Father Christmas among the kitchen pots and pans; though later, it is true, promoted to reindeers and a fur coat. That these cheap and paltry images in the corner of a popular newspaper should have spiritual significance remains, nevertheless, a thing painful to contemplate. And yet, if accepted, it emerges as but one more illustration of a phenomenon to which, perhaps, the universe is subject: *enantiodromia,* the incessant inevitable turning of all things into their opposites. Heraclitus, as Jung points out, was first of European minds to express this concept philosophically, but it owns a far more ancient parentage. The *Tai-gi-tu,* Chinese symbol of unguessed age, conveys the same concept with incomparable wholeness and precision. A white fish with a seed of blackness at its center curves into a black fish with a seed of whiteness, to form a perfect circle; each fish changes eternally into its opposite. What was important carried within itself the seed of its own destruction, and is slowly emptied of meaning; what was derided carried a forgotten truth, and leads to a new valuation.

Seen by this light the values we now neglect, the stone which the builders have rejected, should be looked for in exactly such a place, in a despised, unhonored corner of daily life. It is a measure of our neglect that these values are forced to put on so mean a mask in order to reenter human consciousness. The comic strip by its very bathos and infantilism, by the derision it arouses, by its astonishing universality of appeal and crude vitality, fulfills the historic conditions for "the return of the repressed." The comic strip is, in fact, a ludicrous but valid symptom of our disease. For in one form or another "the return of the repressed" is precisely what is making the present century rock and quiver with premonitions of eruption.

Unpalatable though it may be to modern taste, the truth is that we cannot live without the Early Gods. It was said of Nature that even if you throw her out with a pitchfork she nevertheless comes back. So do the Gods. If cast out in the forms of Man's profoundest apprehensions of them—if Christ and Buddha and Mithra, if Ashtaroth and Pan are disowned—they nevertheless come back. However meanly and unrecognizably, they come back to the human heart whose inevictable tenants they are. And "there all smothered up in shade" they sit, radiating that strange compelling power which is Man's unconscious tribute to the Unknowable. In the comic strip may be concealed the indestructible germ of natural religion.

ROGER B. ROLLIN

from "Beowulf to Batman"

Professor of English at Clemson University in Clemson, South Carolina, Roger Rollin received his doctorate from Yale in 1960. He is the author of numerous articles on popular culture, seventeenth-century British literature, critical theory, and education. Among the books he has either written or edited are *Robert Herrick* and *Hero/Anti-hero*. "Beowulf to Batman: The Epic Hero and Pop Culture," a section of which is reprinted below, originally appeared in the journal *College English* (February, 1970).

> . . . the student's unmediated responses are to his comic books and television programs, while his response to *Macbeth* has every conceivable kind of inhibition attached to it.
>
> —Northrop Frye, "Reflections in a Mirror"

Many a teacher of English views with trepidation the prospect of introducing members of the present student generation to the study of *Beowulf, The Faerie Queene,* or *Paradise Lost.* The poems themselves have always posed enough scholarly and critical problems to make teaching them a problem, but nowadays the students themselves seem to make that pedagogy still more difficult. Many of them, more than is sometimes realized, are deeply concerned about the race problem in America or are involved in it, have fought in Viet Nam or fought going there, have demonstrated against the brutality of police or of college administrators, have been actively engaged in politics or social work, have complained about their education's lack of relevance, or have tried to do something about it. For such students the great old poems of the Anglo-Saxon *scop,* of Spenser, and of Milton may well seem not merely remote, but irrelevant. Even the best among them, those who despite their other real concerns can still be responsive to esthetic or scholarly appeals, may feel that reading the great English epics is reading only for art's or history's sake. Encountering Spenser's proud claim in his letter to Raleigh that "The generall end thereof of [*The Faerie Queene*] is to fashion a gentleman or noble person in vertuous and gentle discipline . . . ," they may at worst scorn or at best savor what seems to be the poet's quaintly Elizabethan squareness.

Yet these same serious students, when they temporarily put aside their sociopolitical and academic cares, will watch television programs like *Mission Impossible* or *Star Trek,* will follow installments of *Steve Canyon* or *Batman* in the comics, or will read Ian Fleming or attend "James Bond" films, all of which—as this paper will contend—have a "generall end" similar to Spenser's: "to fashion a gentlemen or noble person" for the age. The students themselves, however (and not a few of their teachers), think of such extra-curricular, extra-political activities as "escape."

But what is "escape"? If it means a temporary psychological and intellectual

From "Beowulf to Batman: The Epic Hero and Pop Culture" by Roger B. Rollin, *College English* 31:3 (February 1970). Copyright © 1970 by the National Council of Teachers of English. Reprinted by permission of the publisher and the author.

disengagement from the tensions and problems of "real" life, the type of entertainment referred to above will not serve. For "pop romance" (a term that will be used throughout this paper to designate television programs, films, and comic strips in the adventure category) is typically replete with tensions and problems, and those not usually very far removed from present reality. A few years ago it might have been argued that the frequent threats and acts of violence to be found in pop romance made the genre escapist by virtue of sheer hyperbole, but our growing awareness of how violent our reality actually is weakens that case.

It might better be argued that the "escapism" of pop romance resides paradoxically in the security it generates: we know, deep down in our hearts, that Batman will not be turned into a human shish kabob by "The Joker," that Steve Canyon will in the end foil the attempt of the Chinese Reds to defoliate Central Park. If this argument has some validity, it follows that the "escapism" provided by pop romance involves not only emotional catharsis, the purgation of pity and fear, but also what might be called "value satisfaction," that confirmation or reaffirmation of our value system which results from our seeing this value system threatened, but ultimately triumphant. For at least one of the things that happens when a hero like Batman or Steve Canyon wins out in the end—and not the least important thing—is that we experience *at some level* the defeat of Evil (as we imagine it) by the Good (as we have learned it). Even though we consciously are aware that such victories do not always occur in reality, there is a part of us which very much wants them to occur. We are of course unwilling to have such victories take place too easily, as the epic poets well realized, for an easy victory not only lacks dramatic force but paradoxically cheapens the value system the victory is to affirm by making it almost irrelevant.

"Escapism" then, connoting a retreat to a state of mindlessness or euphoria, may well be the wrong term to use to justify or to attack anyone's involvement in pop romance. Though adventure films, television programs and comic strips (*Cahiers du Cinema* and Roy Lichtenstein notwithstanding) may be only pseudo-art or semi-art, they need not be more "escapist" than "true" art. Or, as W. R. Robinson claims in his defense of films, "escape" (into the higher reality of moral truth) can be seen as a function of all forms of art:

> The more persistent and unjust criticism leveled at the movies has been that they are *sui generis* "escapist." But this critical term, the nastiest epithet conceivable within a very narrow-minded aesthetic of truth which sprung up alongside realism, absurdly distorts our sense of what art is or should be. It implies that only an art as grim and dour as the realist thought life to be under the aegis of materialism can qualify as serious aesthetic achievement. . . . Yet even in the dourest realistic view truth is a human triumph; through it man transcends suffering and determinism. Nikolai Berdyaev saw this clearly when he argued that all art is a victory over heaviness. It is always escape.[1]

Even popular art forms, Robinson continues, "are a part of man's intellectual armament in this war to liberate himself from heaviness . . . ," for "by incarnating the Good, a spiritual entity, in a concrete form, art frees it to be" (pp. 118–19).

That even pop romance is concerned with moral truth—by "incarnating

---

[1] W. R. Robinson, "The Movies Too, Will Make You Free," *Man and the Movies,* ed. W. R. Robinson (Baton Rouge, La., 1967), pp. 117–18.

the Good" in its hero figures—is easily shown. The more primitive films, television programs, and comics—those produced mainly for children—explicitly purport to be morality tales: The Lone Ranger is identified as a "champion of justice,"[2] for example, and Batman is plainly if infelicitously described as "fighting for righteousness and apprehending the wrong-doer."[3]

In more sophisticated pop romance the same process is handled more subtly and may even result in the establishment of fairly complex levels of meaning. Steve Canyon, for example, is clearly an incarnation of moral Good but he is also the means by which Milton Caniff, his creator, idealizes and glorifies the military, devalues civilians and civilian life, advances a Dullesian posture on international affairs, and in general espouses a conservative socio-political philosophy. Though Caniff is hardly less didactic than Spenser or Milton, and the thrust of his didacticism is such that he too invariably alienates some readers, he, like these poets, makes complete rejection of his "art" almost impossible by incorporating his specific socio-political views within the general framework of the Judeo-Christian value system. Left with a choice between desiring a victory for militantly militarist Steve Canyon (and Western Civilization) and a victory for The Other Side, only the most resolute radical has a real alternative.

There is still another level at which pop romance, both primitive and sophisticated, incarnates the Good. This is the level where personal ethics and ego meet to define individual spiritual and material aspirations. We tend to admire and identify with Batman, for example, not only because he is clean, upright, reverent, etc., an adult Boy Scout, square but undeniably *good*—all the things we should be—but also because he is handsome, athletic, intelligent, and rich—all the things we would like to be. He is the fulfillment of our fantasies as well as of our moral sense. And though Freudian psychology may lead us to expect that the former function is more crucial, this does not seem to be the case: a hero figure may be ugly or poor (and some are) but he can still be acceptable; if he should fail to honor his father and mother or if he should covet his neighbor's wife he will not be. Whatever different values may be stressed in various heroes of pop romance (and there is some variation), they tend to have the basic values of our culture in common. Thus their repeated triumphs, whether we are fully conscious of it or not, can help to reinforce our confidence in our value system and to encourage our conformity to it.

Clearly, his readers' conformity to the values he anatomized in *The Faerie Queene* was one of the main effects Spenser hoped to achieve through his art. But if the Instruction that effects moral conformity was his main purpose, Spenser, like all makers of fiction, also recognized that "the most part of men delight to read, rather for variety of matter, then for the profit of the ensample"; therefore, as he explained to Raleigh, instead of having "good discipline delivered plainly in way of precepts, or sermoned at large," he wrote an epic poem, in which the Instruction was "most plausible and pleasing, being coloured with an historicall fiction. . . ." It is of course far more likely that Delight rather than Instruction is the main conscious intent of most of the creators of pop romance. It is Delight that brings in the dollars. But to succeed in delighting a whole culture or even a sizeable portion of it is neither automatic nor easy. The chances for such success

[2] Quoted in Jim Harmon, *The Great Radio Heroes* (Garden City, N.Y., 1967), p. 203.
[3] Quoted in Jules Feiffer, *The Great Comic Book Heroes* (New York, 1965), p. 26

for example are diminished considerably if the Delight comes at the expense of the culture's value system. Thus neither epic poets nor the creators of pop culture are true cultural revolutionaries. (Even devout Royalists could accept *Paradise Lost.*) Whether Delight or Instruction then is uppermost in the mind of the creator of the fiction, if the fiction is successful the results will likely be the same: the culture will find reiterated in that fiction most of the values it passed on to the creator in the first place. It is almost inevitable therefore that pop romance, for example, instruct in spite of itself.

Milton Caniff has said: "The American hero lives in all of us . . . and if we are not all heroes, we are all hero ridden. Descendants of a legend, we persist in identifying with it." [4] To summarize the argument of this paper, if today's students can be made conscious of this truth about themselves by having their attention called to their involvement in pop romance, and if, by analyzing the nature and functions of the hero in pop romance and epic poems, they can begin to perceive significant esthetic and intellectual parallels between the popular and the classic, then their heightened awareness of the unity and the relevance of all art will help to make their study of literature easier, more enjoyable, and more pointed. To some extent Marshall McLuhan has made even the ordinary student more receptive to such an approach than he might have been a few years ago, and Northrop Frye of course has done even more for the well-read student. And Frye, in addition, is helpful in providing some guidelines by which such an approach can to an extent be systematized.

1

In *Anatomy of Criticism* (Princeton, N.J., 1957), Frye classifies five types of fictive hero, each type being determined "by the hero's power of action, which may be greater than ours, less, or roughly the same" (p. 33). (Frye's fourth type, the hero "superior neither to other men or to his environment" (p. 34) and his fifth type, the hero who is "inferior in power or intelligence to ourselves" (p. 34), do not concern us here, though they would if the limits of this essay extended beyond the literary epic and the pop romance.)

Type I. "If superior in *kind* both to other men and to the environment of other men, the hero is a divine being, and the story about him will be a *myth* in the common sense of a story about a god." (p. 33). Frye adds that "Such stories have an important place in literature, but are as a rule found outside the normal literary categories," but as we shall see, *Paradise Lost* is a noteworthy exception to this rule, as is, less obviously, *The Faerie Queene.* The pop hero who best illustrates Type I is Superman, who to all intent and purposes is absolute in his power, his glory, and his goodness. Superman, like other such mythic figures, is not only perfect, but is capable of donning imperfection—of voluntarily assuming a human role, in the playing of which he suffers what Jules Feiffer has called his "discreet martyrdom." [5]

Type II. "If superior in *degree* to other men and to his environment, the hero is the typical hero of *romance,* whose actions are marvellous but who is

---

[4] Quoted in David Manning White and Robert Abel, "Comic Strips and American Culture," *The Funnies: An American Idiom,* eds. David Manning White and Robert Abel (New York, 1963), p. 33.

[5] Feiffer, p. 19.

himself identified as a human being. The hero of romance moves in a world in which the ordinary laws of nature are slightly suspended . . ." (p. 33). The fact that these laws frequently seem to be suspended by the hero himself gives the Type II figure a semi-divine aura even though he is of earthly mold. Though limited, he is still overwhelmingly powerful and overwhelmingly virtuous. He is, however, capable of error (though seldom of crime or serious sin) and ultimately he is vulnerable. In pop romance Batman is a familiar example of this type.

Type III. "If superior in degree to other men but not to his natural environment, the hero is a leader. He has authority, passions, and powers of expression far greater than ours but . . . is subject both to social criticism and to the order of nature" (pp. 33–34). Although a number of pop heroes are of this type, Steve Canyon is fairly representative. He is a leader, an Air Force lieutenant colonel, passionate about the U.S. Air Force, the U.S., and—occasionally—a female (in that order), but what he does is sometimes criticized (most often by ignorant or malicious civilians) and the jet planes he flies are subject to the laws of physics. He is vulnerable, not only physically but also intellectually and psychologically, and he is capable, of, though not prone to, error.

The Type I hero is what we would all like to be ("faster than a speeding bullet," having "X-ray vision," capable of flying), but outside of our dreams of wish fulfillment, we recognize that we could not possibly be him. The Type II hero, being more human that superhuman, is a more attainable ideal, but again our conscious selves will acknowledge that we can never have all the powers and virtues he possesses nor have them to the degree that he does. The Type III hero is also greater in the sum total of his powers and virtues than we could be, but because he shares with the rest of humanity certain limitations upon his embodiment and exercise of these powers and virtues, some of them are at least theoretically within our reach and in a few we could even exceed him: we could conceivably fly airplanes as well as Lt. Col. Canyon; we might even become generals.

All of these heroes are larger than life; some are merely larger than others. But what the hero is and does in terms of objective reality are less important than what he represents to our inner reality. The local man who saves a child from drowning is of less enduring interest to us than our fictive or historical heroes: the former wants symbolism, and unless local mythopoeia provides him with it, we tend to displace him in our consciousness with the more value-charged heroes we seem to need. The heroes of the great English epics represent attempts by poets of genius to fulfill that need for their own times. In our time, supposedly the age of the "anti-hero," the writers of pop romance knowingly or unknowingly fulfill the same need. Thus, what Northrop Frye claims about popular literature in general is particularly true of pop romance: it is "literature which affords an almost unobstructed view of archetypes" (p. 116).

Specific illustrations of how the analogies between epic and pop heroes can be used to provide one kind of approach to *Beowulf, The Faerie Queene,* and *Paradise Lost* comprise the next three sections of this paper. The focus will be on the hero figures and the value systems in which they are involved rather than upon structure or imagery or the like. Nor will any attempt be made to justify on esthetic grounds the examples of pop romance considered. Whether primitive or slick, they seldom even approach the threshold of what is generally regarded as "art"—although they do qualify if we accept Norman Holland's definition of art as that which exists for our pleasure, requires us to suspend disbelief in order to experience that pleasure, and gives us that pleasure by "managing" or "controlling" our fantasies and feelings.[6] But whether they are regarded as "art" or not, pop romances can shed light on art and on our responses to it, as both Holland and Frye have suggested.[7] The same conclusion is arrived at by a student of the comic strip phenomenon, Kenneth E. Eble, even though he rejects the comics as an art form:

> The comics fail badly as art despite their pretension to seriousness—or perhaps because of it. They have about the same relation to serious art that a tract like *Pierce Pennilesse* has to *Paradise Lost*. . . . As objects of serious study, they rank considerably higher. They will offer much information to future historians as to how we lived, how we acted, and, in a large sense, how we (the thickening mass) responded. . . . As factors in shaping a nation's emotional and intellectual responses, they deserve much more study than they have yet received.[8]

2

In his consideration of "The Primitive Heroic Ideal," E. Talbot Donaldson says: "put most simply, the heroic ideal was excellence. The hero-kings strove to do better than anyone else the things that an essentially migratory life demanded. . . ." [9] Fighting was of course the primary activity, as it is so often in pop romance, and it is on those few violent hours in Beowulf's life when he wins his three great victories that the Anglo-Saxon *scop* concentrates rather than upon his youth or years of kingship. Violence, it might be added, is also a preoccupation of Spenser in *The Faerie Queene,* and it gets its due in *Paradise Lost* as well, in spite of Milton's intention to frame a "higher Argument" (IX, 42). Pop romance is frequently attacked for its own preoccupation with violence, but its critics do not always recognize that violence is seldom gratuitous; as in epic poems it is usually if not always effectively moralized: the resounding "Pow!" as Batman's fist connects with the Joker's jaw signals not only retribution but the re-establishment of moral order.

The plot of the first section of *Beowulf*—the bringing of order to the chaos that is Heorot through the deeds of the stranger-hero, and thus bringing stability and security to a community near collapse—has been utilized so often as to seem formula by now. The Western, of course, employs it over and over again. In a popular television series of a few years back, *Have Gun, Will Travel,* this formula shaped almost every episode. The hero, a gun-fighter-knight-errant (appropriately named Paladin), continually rode out to rid a variety of communities of a variety of Grendels. A typical episode begins in San Francisco, where Paladin lives like royalty, surrounded by retainers male and female. When the call comes, however, he abandons his sybaritic life without hesitation and exchanges his foppish apparel for a basic black Western outfit symbolic of his deadly role. Although he usually rides alone, he is often joined by a decent citizen or two who serve as his temporary retainers. Upon these retainers and the community he succors Paladin bestows

---

[6] Norman N. Holland, *The Dynamics of Literary Response* (New York, 1968), pp. 74–75.
[7] Holland, pp. xiii–xiv; Frye, *Anatomy of Criticism,* pp. 104, 116–17.
[8] "Our Serious Comics," *The Funnies,* p. 109.
[9] In *The Norton Anthology of English Literature,* gen. ed. M. H. Abrams, rev. ed. (New York, 1968), I, 3.

something of the courtesy that Beowulf shows to Hrothgar and the Geats. The rewards Paladin receives for his victories are, like Beowulf's, commensurate with the grave risks he takes, but he too is capable of exercising his talents for violence on the strength of a friendship or a principle, receiving for his victories only renewed fame.

The series which fixed the stranger-saviour most firmly in the imagination of mid-twentieth century America was of course *The Lone Ranger.* Conceived for juveniles, this series was so well received that it has appeared in all of the popular media. It is possible that the messianic overtones of the formula which *The Lone Ranger* so obviously played upon were partly responsible for its wide appeal: in times of crisis we look for a deliverer, a Beowulf or a Lone Ranger. The vague origins and the sudden departures of such heroes also serve to enhance their legends. These legends in time take on almost religious status, becoming myths which provide the communities not only with models for conduct but with the kind of heightened shared experiences which inspire and unify their members.

The final sequence of *Beowulf,* the hero's fight with the dragon, embodies still another formulaic plot, that of the resident-hero who champions the community in its struggle for self-preservation. This hero may or may not be the titular leader of the community, but he is always the *present* exemplification of the primitive kingly ideal (Hrothgar's heroism was in the past). "Dodge City," the archetypal community of the television Western, *Gunsmoke,* has a mayor, but it is the city's marshal, Matt Dillon, who guarantees its stability and security. "Gotham" not only has a mayor, but a police commissioner, a police chief, and squads of officers, but it is Batman who defeats the city's dragons. The ineffectuality of the forces of law and order and of the law itself seems almost a basic assumption both of epics and of pop romance.

The law frequently appears to be too complex or too cumbersome to deal with crises, so the hero, whether he is a real or titular king, becomes a law unto himself. Ian Fleming's "James Bond," a true primitive hero updated to espionage agent, is "licensed to kill." He is above the law not only of his own community but of the international community as well. So too are the agents featured in the television series, *Mission Impossible.* Unlike the individualistic Bond they operate in concert (the committee-as-hero?) and their numbers include the mandatory black man (a modern Tonto?) and the mandatory beautiful woman (a modern Britomart?). In their adventures these organization-man-heroes so frequently and blithely violate not only laws but human rights that they are warned before every mission that, if captured, they will be disavowed by the very national community which sends them forth. The legal and moral assumptions behind their activities are seldom questioned because these heroes, like Beowulf, are understood to be "on God's side," i.e., the community's. (It is only in the "low mimetic" and "ironic" modes that the question of whether God is on our side or on that of the big battalions can be entertained.)

The hero's antagonists, on the other hand, are depicted as being unresponsive to the community and the community's values, even if they happen to be residents. The antagonist may represent an alien community or only the community of the self, but the fact that he acts as a law unto himself is *not* glossed over. The *Beowulf*-poet stresses this: Grendel is of the exiled race of Cain, he inhabits that no-man's land where the influence of the community ends and what is in effect the jungle begins, and from that dark region he peers at the community and envies its happiness. Though he comes within the pale of the community by gaining control of Heorot, if only during the night, his natural element, his means of doing so puts him beyond the pale. The rules therefore need not apply to him: the only good renegade is a dead renegade.

Primitive heroes do not, however, have *carte blanche.* Although the community may be quite willing to waive *all* of its laws to ensure the defeat of its enemy, the hero cannot, for otherwise he loses face and his force as the repository of the community's values (which supposedly he is struggling to preserve). For heroes there seems to be a law of diminishing legal returns. He can violate some laws—against illegal search and seizure, for example—but he cannot violate others, particularly the unwritten laws of the community: killing the villain can eliminate the expense and delay in the community's vengeance entailed by the observation of due process, but the execution must take the form of a sword point or a bullet in the villain's chest, not in his back. It is to such a "code of the West" that Beowulf conforms when he undertakes to battle Grendel with his bare hands and Grendel's dam with a sword (a compensation for the disadvantage of fighting under water). This form of chivalry only allows for "equalizers"—in the "shoot-down" it must be .38 against .38. Of course this code is binding upon heroes only; it is one of the crosses they bear but without which they might be difficult to distinguish from their codeless antagonists, the merely instinctual Grendels and cattle-rustlers.

In spite of the fact that the community itself is usually inferior in the quality of its collective life to the life of the hero, it is still in some sense above him. Its survival is the *summum bonum,* and the issue of community survival is one which can conveniently be invoked in any crisis in order to justify its actions, even the sacrifice of its best, the hero himself. For the community in both epic and pop romance is not only a social unit but a quasi-religious one. It is that which nurtures, controls, and protects the non-heroes who comprise it: the community giveth and the community taketh away. Its wars are holy wars and its champions, as noted above, become quasi-religious figures. Thus the Unferths or the cowardly shopkeepers whose action or inaction undermines the hero (and thus the community) come close to being not only traitors but apostates.

Invariably this community religion becomes cosmic: in Hrothgar's view Beowulf has been divinely sent to deliver his people from a monster who is "at war with God" (although he appears to give real trouble only to the Geats). And Beowulf himself feels that he is under God's protection. His status as a messiah-figure receives the heaviest stress in the poem's climactic sequence, the fight with the dragon. This "worm" that flies by night, that is associated with fire, that lives somewhere below, shares at least in the archetype of Satan, whom Milton (in the "Nativity Ode") called "the old dragon underground." Beowulf's determination to save his people single-handedly, his going-forth with a band of twelve, one of whom initiated the chain of events which will lead to his death, and the *scop's* final description of him—"of world-kings the mildest of men and the gentlest"—all suggest an imitation of Christ. The image of the hero as gentle man which seems almost an afterthought in *Beowulf* is close to the formula in pop romance. "Clark Kent" is always "the mild-mannered reporter," and Steve Canyon's pipe-smoking is an obvious clue to his character. The image thrives too in the Western, the classic example being the mild hero (played by

Gary Cooper) of the film, *High Noon.*

Heroes cannot, however, remain lambs: crises call for lions. And whether they take place in epics or in pop romance, crises usually require violent solutions. Violence indeed seems to be the reality of their worlds and it is in violent situations that the heroes are defined. Superman is somehow more "real" than the mousey "Clark Kent," Batman more "real" than the do-gooder "Bruce Wayne." Indeed, in this "civilian" alter ego, each of these heroes is suspected of being, like the youthful Beowulf, "slack, a young man unbold."

Beowulf must, in spite of his divine aura, be classified as a Type II hero. He is "of mankind . . . the strongest of might," a prestigious swimmer, a supreme fighter, yet if you cut him, he bleeds. He belongs to the company of Batman and Paladin. One significant difference, however, between *Beowulf* and romance, pop or otherwise (and to some extent between *Beowulf* and *The Faerie Queene*), is the distinction between mortality and vulnerability. Spenser's heroes, like Batman and Paladin, are always being threatened with death but never die (or even age), whereas Beowulf not only ages but dies. And, unlike these other heroes he is intensely aware of fate and almost preoccupied with death. Transiency is his reality and this gives his story an additional dimension. The world of *The Faerie Queene* and, frequently, of the American Western, is largely static, a version of pastoral. "The Wild West," which existed for only a heartbeat in history, in fiction seems to exist out of time. Marshall Dillon's Dodge City resembles the town on Keats' Grecian urn, fixed forever. (This is very much the case with Spenser's "Faerie Lond" and Batman's "Gotham" as well.) Though populated, these places do not change nor does their populace. Only their heroes seem quite alive—and their villains also, who come and go and occasionally die. This tendency moves a romance-epic like *The Faerie Queene* and pop romance toward comedy while *Beowulf* approaches tragedy. And even though *Paradise Lost* involves tragic action in its story of Satan, the to-be-continued story of Adam and Eve takes the shape of elevated tragi-comedy, and the poem as a whole, with its promise of good coming out of evil, takes on the form of a history-play which is also a divine comedy.

3

In spite of the New Morality, the New Theology, and all of the other forces which are said to be radically altering American society, it is possible to question whether real changes have taken place on all of the levels at which that society responds to art. If, for example, a social scientist were to perform a study to determine which are the twelve moral virtues of most importance to Americans, is it necessarily the case that he would come up with a list that would differ significantly from that of Edmund Spenser? The answer would seem to be "No," if one can trust the impressions one receives from editorials and letters-to-the-editor, from high-circulation magazines ranging from *Life* and the *Reader's Digest* to *Playboy,* from pulpits and from the soap boxes of television news and documentaries. Additional evidence to validate this hypothesis can be extracted from an examination of the heroes of pop romance, in whom the virtues treated by Spenser in *The Faerie Queene,* for example, live still.

While the main task of these heroes is to insure that Justice is done (American justice, community justice), in the process of doing so they, like Sir Calidore, exhibit Courtesy (in the narrow sense of chivalric manners and in the broad sense of integrity); they exemplify Friendship's highest ideal, *agape*, by being willing to lay down their lives for their friends; and finally, although some might deviate slightly from Temperance conceived of in terms of wine and women (though even this is not usual), the life of moderation is generally their way of life. Even the virtues of Chastity and Holiness, whose very naming can elicit smiles from the God-Is-Dead, Sexual Freedom generation, seem deeply rooted in the consciousness of even the young. Holiness may perhaps be redefined in terms of Zen or drug-expanded awareness or Peace Corps-type service, and Chastity in terms of "I-Thou" relationships for sexual partners, but the spirit of the ideal still moves among us.

In pop romance, it is true, Holiness is something of a negative virtue. Men of the cloth and other pious folk are treated deferentially by a Superman, a Batman, or a Steve Canyon, but these heroes do not themselves espouse patently ecclesiastical causes. Churches remain sacred places and church-goers are often depicted as that segment of the populace which requires and merits secular as well as divine protection. Villains in pop romance, on the other hand, not infrequently appear as false religious figures (heirs of Archimago and Duessa), whether they be the phoney parsons of Westerns, the leaders of obscure and evil cults in modern adventures, or atheistic Communists of the type that Steve Canyon battles. Thus, although the heroes of pop romance appear to be essentially secular figures—and their creators take pains to avoid obvious religious controversy— they are in fact modern exemplars of Holiness, in the broad sense of having respect for religion, of being virtuous, and of being "on God's side." While they are not Christian militants, for the Word they spread is not the Gospel but "Justice" or "America," many pop heroes are not very far removed from the Puritan heroes of the seventeenth century. They are by implication and by default Protestants— there are rarely any Catholics, Jews, Muslims, or atheists in the foxholes of the fictive war against evil. And in his dogged and irresistible militancy on behalf of his cause, each pop hero resembles a one-man New Model Army.

Although their Chastity, like their Holiness, is more often implicit than explicit, the majority of the heroes of pop romance are still in the Spenserian tradition. Some viewers of *Gunsmoke* have long suspected that Miss Kitty, proprietress of the Dodge City saloon that Matt Dillon frequents, is no better than she should be, but the sexual overtones of their relationship remain muted. It is a standing joke among cinema buffs that the "Code of the West" permits the cowboy to kiss only his horse, but even today, in an era of attempts at making "realistic" Westerns, the hero is seldom permitted to be a rake. A really strong interest in sex is, in Westerns as in *The Faerie Queene*, usually reserved for villains.

Spenser's heroes are attractive to women, good and bad, and are sometimes attracted to women as other than objects of chivalric fulfillment. They are not professional virgins, even Britomart, but sex without full ecclesiastical and social sanctions is denied them. This is likewise the case with many of the heroes of pop romance; here as in most pastorals, sex is often portrayed as an intrusive force, leading the hero to unaccustomed excess and interfering with his performance of his duties. The male hero's dilemma is perfectly symbolized in the plight of Superman, who is forever having to rescue Lois Lane and forever rejecting her advances, but who, as "Clark Kent," degrades himself by making advances which she always spurns. Spenser's creation of the magnificent Bower of Bliss and his ruthless destruction of it show hardly more rigor than the tendency of the creators of pop romance to condemn their heroes to a largely sexless and even loveless existence. An exception to this tendency is to be found in recent "swinging" versions of the espionage-romance genre. Spy-heroes like James Bond and "Napoleon Solo," title-figure of the television series, *The Man from UNCLE,* who, as noted above, are already to a great extent outside both the law and the culture, apparently have licenses to fornicate as well as to kill. They are hedonist-heroes of the New Morality. Yet their popularity, enormous for a year or two, already seems on the wane, which may indicate that Spenser's ideal of Chastity is still operative beneath the surface of our supposedly liberated culture.

Spenser's very idealism makes the classification of his hero-types difficult. The deliberately non-realistic world he creates complicates the establishment of correspondences with our own world by which the hero is partially defined. The world of *The Faerie Queene,* being itself supernatural, is sometimes superior to the heroes and sometimes not. Since this world does not operate according to natural law in the first place, it seemingly cannot accommodate the Type III hero at all. Furthermore, Spenser's heroes themselves, informed as they are by so many levels of allegorical meaning but so little characterization, cannot readily be distinguished from each other. "Ordinary" human characters (like Colin Cloute perhaps), who might establish some kind of norm by which the heroes might be measured are relatively few and far between. "Faerye Land" seems to be populated mainly by heroes and villains. The majority of the former are clearly Type II heroes; in a few cases, however, there is another possibility.

As Spenser's letter to Raleigh explains, Prince Arthur is "perfected in the twelve private morall vertues, as Aristotle hath devised." Such perfection, summarized in the supreme virtue of Magnanimity, makes him "superior in *kind"* to even the other great heroes in the poem, and he is also superior to them in that he possesses a shield whose powers go beyond even the supernatural. This being the case, he is also superior to his "environment," the supernatural land of Faerie. Spenser does not call him a god, for this would compromise the Christian level of his allegory, but he gives the impression of being one. He is the deliverer, one who comes in glory, and will come again. Thus, along with his beloved, "That greatest glorious queene," Gloriana, the descendent of "either spright/Or angell" (II.10.lxxi), Arthur can be considered a Type I hero.

Two other possibilities for this classification present themselves. Although Talus, the "yron man" of Book V, is Artegall's squire, like God he is "Immoveable, resistlesse, without end," and, like Christ he "thresht out falshood, and did truth unfould" (V.1.xii). In his inhumanity—or more precisely, his ahumanity—he foreshadows Superman, whose human traits really emerge only when he is "Clark Kent." In Talus and in Superman the *deus ex machina* has become "the machine god," but in the case of the latter a poetic fantasy has been replaced by a technical fantasy; Superman, the man of tomorrow, "is the promise that each and every world problem will be solved by the technical trick." [10]

The mechanical savagery of Talus in some respects has its counterpart in

[10] Heinz Politzer, "From Little Nemo to Li'l Abner," *The Funnies,* p. 51.

the "natural" savagery of Calepine's rescuer (Book VI). Although he is, like Talus, a minor character, the "salvage man" is very close at least to being a Type I hero for he is quintessentially good, invincible, and rendered invulnerable through "magicke leare" (VI.4.iv). A Superman *sans* cape and leotards, he is also a "Clark Kent," capable of being "enmoved" to feel compassion. Without losing his god-like powers or his identity he can exhibit "milde humanity and perfect gentle mynd" (VI.5.xxix). His case is an example of how in its smallest as well as its largest developments Spenser's poem moves toward unity and identity whereas Superman's illustrates what seems to be the schizoid tendency of twentieth-century imaginings.

Although a Redcrosse or a Britomart is so far above us that we may be lulled into thinking of them as gods, if we remain responsive to Spenser's descriptions and his narrative it is evident that they are Type II heroes. Like Batman they are vulnerable and capable of error, though Batman's errors tend to be tactical, theirs human or moral; they can be overpowered by human, natural, or supernatural forces (technological forces in the case of Batman). Their human weaknesses get them into difficulties from which neither their physical nor their moral strength can extricate them. Unlike Adam they are not "sufficient": all Type II and Type III heroes are in fact fallen men. Being fallen and thus incomplete they frequently need assistance. Indeed assistants are a fixture of Type II heroes: as Redcrosse has his Una, Britomart her Glauce, and Artegall his Talus, so Batman has his Robin. Assistants come in handy for purposes of plot: they can be separated from the hero and become involved in sub-plots of their own, from which they may need to be rescued by the hero; or the separation which weakens the hero, can create a crisis in his own plot from which the assistant can extricate him. An assistant can serve as confidant or as foil to the hero. As foils they are both like the hero and unlike him—Una's Revealed Truth complements the Holiness of Redcrosse as Robin's boyish exuberance complements Batman's mature energy. In general assistants are inferior both physically and mentally to the Type II hero, but together, as a "dynamic duo," they approach the perfection of the Type I hero. Nonetheless, they still lack his invulnerability.

In a sense it is mankind's very vulnerability as well as his virtues and powers that is as much a major theme of *The Faerie Queene* as it is of *Beowulf.* . . .

Index

Achilles, 434
"Acid Queen, The," 118
Adam, 116, 462, 465
Adam Bede (Eliot), 162
Adonis, 5, 9, 380
Adventures of Huckleberry Finn, The (Twain), 60, 70, 108–114, 269
Adventures of Tom Sawyer, The (Twain), 60
Aesop, 66
"Age-Old Secret of Younger Looking Skin, The" (Alpha Keri Bath Oil), 409–411
"Ahab" (character), 1, 372–378
Ajax, 386
Aldrich, Thomas Bailey, 60
"Allanon" (character), 213
Alpha Keri Bath Oil, 409
Almadén Vineyards, 176
"Ambassador Trentino" (character), 60, 101–108
American, The (James), 162, 381, 382, 421–428
American Monomyth, The (Jewett and Lawrence), 437–442
Anatomy of Criticism (Frye), 457–458
"Ancient One, The" (character), 212
Andersen, Hans Christian, 433
Anderson, Clive, 395
Andy's Gang, 61
Antony and Cleopatra (Shakespeare), 117
Anubis, 449
Aphrodite, 444, 452
Apollo (Phoebus), 217, 218, 219, 384–388, 438–440, 442, 443, 445
Archetypes, 1–2, 442–448 passim, 452, 458
   Helpful Animal, 265–268, 323, 324
   Hero, 320–325, 382, 451–452, 454–465

Holy Fool, 265, 268–270
Mother, 158–162, 210, 265, 323, 324
Puer Aeternus, 452
Quest, 320–325, 382, 383
Rebirth, 5, 9, 380–384
Shadow, 1–4, 115, 161, 322, 324, 452
Temptress, 115–119, 158, 323, 324, 452
Trickster, 58–62, 115, 161
Wise Old Man, 210–214, 265, 267, 323, 324, 333, 365
"Archetypes of the Collective Unconscious" (Jung), 119
"Archimego" (character), 463
Argos, 165
"Artegall" (character), 464, 465
"Arthur Holmwood" (character), 116
Asgard, 444
Ashtaroth, 453
As You Like It (Shakespeare), 319
Athena, 271
Atlantis, 324
Atreus, 388
Attis, 5, 380
Atwan, Robert, 258
"Aunt Jemima," 160
Autobiography (Franklin), 258
Autrey, Gene, 266
Awakening, The (Chopin), 161

"Back-to-nature" movement, 159–160, 399
"Ballad of Two Brothers," 3
Bancroft, Anne, 118
Band, The (group), 337–338
Band, The (album), 338
Bandy, Moe, 118, 130

ndy the Rodeo Clown" (Shafer and Frizzell), 118, 130–131
Bara, Theda, 117
Bare, Bobby, 213, 236
Batman, 60, 454
"Batman" (character), 455–464 *passim*
Baum, L. Frank, 300
Beatles, The, 118, 179–180, 181, 195, 269, 306–307, 384
Beck, C. C., 228
Bellerophon. *See* Pegasus
"Ben Cartwright" (character), 214
"Ben Casey," 214
"Benjamin Braddock" (character), 118
"Benji" (character), 266
Beowulf, 454–462 *passim,* 465
"Beowulf" (character), 459–462
"Beowulf to Batman" (Rollin), 454–465
Bettelheim, Bruno, 273, 275, 337, 387, 433
"Betty Crocker," 160
"Bionic Woman" (character), 4, 321
"Birthmark, The" (Hawthorne), 45–57
"Billy Pilgrim" (character), 269
"Bizarro" (character), 4
"Black Beauty" (character), 266
"Black Nell" (character), 266–267
Blatty, William Peter, 213, 238
Blessed Isles, 324
Blonde on Blonde (Dylan), 340
Blood on the Tracks (Dylan), 340
Blood, Sweat and Tears, 118
"Blowin' in the Wind," 340
Blue Angel, The, 117, 118
Bogart, Humphrey, 365
"Bomba" (character), 266
Bomba the Jungle Boy on Terror Trail (Rockwood), 267
"Bonanza," 214
Boone, Pat, 211
Brautigan, Richard, 269
"Brer Rabbit" (character), 69–70, 74
Briareus, 449
Brisingamen, 444
"Britomart" (character), 460, 463, 465
Brontë, Charlotte, 162
Brooks, Terry, 213
"Bruce Wayne" (character), 462
"Brule the Spear-Slayer" (character), 343
Buddha, 453
Bugs Bunny, 60, 74–85
Browne, Charles Farrar, 269
"Bumsteads" (characters), 450

Burroughs, Edgar Rice, 136, 447
Busch, Wilhelm, 92

Cahiers du Cinema, 455
Cain, 9, 460
"Caliban" (character), 4
Calypso, 451
Campbell, Joseph
on fairy tales, 9
Hero with a Thousand Faces, 58–59, 161, 320–321, 324–325
on Trickster, 62
on "monomyth," 437, 439, 440, 442
Caniff, Milton, 456, 457
Čapek, Karel, 447
Capp, Al, 269
"Captain America" (character), 184
Captain and the Kids, The (Dirks), 92
"Captain Kirk" (character), 4, 438–441 *passim*
"Captain Marvel" (character), 228–235
"Captain Reilly-Ffoull" (character), 451, 452
Carradine, David, 12
Carroll, Lewis, 436
Cash, Johnny, 236
Castaneda, Carlos, 212, 247
Catcher in the Rye, The (Salinger), 269
Cather, Willa, 201
"Cathy's Clown," 118
Caxton, William, 66
Cerberus, 449
Chad Mitchell Trio, 397
"Champion" (character), 266
Chariots of the Gods (von Däniken), 439
"Charlie Brown" (character), 450
"Charlie's Angels" (characters), 321
Chaucer, Geoffrey, 385
"Cheetah" (character), 268
Chesterton, G. K., 433
Chopin, Kate, 161
Christ, 380, 447, 453, 461
"Christopher Newman" (character), 381, 382, 383, 422–428
"Cinderella" (Grimm), 168
"Cinderella" (Perrault), 161, 168–173, 210
Circe, 117
"Cisco Kid" (character), 266
Clapton, Eric, 337
Clarke, Arthur C., 412–413, 445
"Clark Kent" (character), 461, 464
Clemens, Samuel Langhorne. *See* Twain, Mark

Cleopatra, 117, 118
"Colin Cloute" (character), 464
Collective unconscious, 446
"Colonel J. T. Hall" (character), 61
"Commandant Klink" (character), 61
Conan the Barbarian, 4, 119, 343
"Concerning Rebirth" (Jung), 383
Confederate General from Big Sur, A (Brautigan), 269
Confidence-Man, The (Melville), 160–161
Conrad, Joseph, 3
Contes de ma mere l'Oye. See Tales of Mother Goose
Cooper, Gary, 462
Cooper, James Fenimore, 269
Corinthians, 268, 319
Cosmopolitan, 118
"Cowardly Lion" (character), 266, 300
Cox, Marion R., 168
Cronos, 162–166 *passim*
Creepy, 116
Crumb, Robert, 3, 37, 59, 86
cummings, e. e., 299
Cybele, 381
Cyclops, 121
Cynthia, 452

"Daily Paper Pantheon" (McGlashan), 448–453
"Daisy Miller" (James), 422
Dalton, Cal, 74
"Danny Dennis" (character), 277–286, 323
"Dame Van Winkle" (character), 162
Daniel, Samuel, 323
D'Arcy, H. Antoine, 117, 141
"Darest Thou Now O Soul" (Whitman), 379
David, 453
Davis, Don, 395
Dean, James, 395
"Death Be Not Proud" (Donne), 332
de Camp, L. Sprague, 343
de Crèvecoeur, St. Jean, 382
Deerslayer, The (Cooper), 269
"Defenders, The," 214
Delilah, 117, 451
Deliverance (Dickey), 3
Demeter, 159, 162–167
"Dennis the Menace" (character), 58, 60
Denver, John, 160, 179, 397, 399
de Palma, Brian, 115
"Devil Woman," 118
"Diablo" (character), 266

Diana, 159, 452
Dick, Philip K., 448
Dickens, Charles, 162, 433
Dickey, James, 3
Dickinson, Emily, 268
Dietrich, Marlene, 117
Dingbat Family, The (Herriman), 296
Dionysus, 5
Dirks, Rudolph, 92
Disaster movies, 161
"Doc" (character), 214
"Dr. Fergusson" (character), 381
"Doctor Gillespie" (character), 214
"Dr. Jekyll" (character), 4
Dr. Jekyll and Mr. Hyde (Stevenson), 4
"Doctor Kildare," 214
Doctor Strange, 212
"Dr. Van Helsing" (character), 116, 213
"Doctor Zorba" (character), 214
"Dolores" (Swinburne), 116
Donaldson, E. Talbot, 459
Donaldson, Walter, 182
"Don Corleone" (character), 214
"Don Juan" (character), 212, 247–253
Donne, John, 332
Doors, The, 118
Doppelgänger, 3
Dorey, Jacques, 66
"Dorothy" (character), 266, 300–305, 323
Dorson, Richard, 61, 223
Dostoyevsky, Fyodor, 3, 269
"Double, The" (Dostoyevsky), 3
Dracula (Stoker), 116, 144–148, 213
Duck Soup (Marx Brothers), 60, 101–108
Duel in the Sun, 2, 25
"Duessa" (character), 463
Dunaway, Faye, 118
Dylan, Bob, 118, 337, 339–340

Eagles, The, 118, 134
Earth Mother, 159–162 *passim*
Easy Rider, 338
Eble, Kenneth E., 459
"Ed Gentry" (character), 3
Edshu, 58–59, 60
Edwards, Jonathan, 381
Eisner, Will, 383, 400
Eleusis, 164
Eliot, George, 162
Eliot, T. S., 5
"Elmer Fudd" (character), 60
"Elsie the Cow," 160
Endymion (Keats), 154

Endymion (Lyly), 319
Englehart, Steve, 12
Enkidu, 322, 325–332 *passim*
Epic of the Beasts, 66
Epic of Gilgamesh, The, 325–332
Epstein, Brian, 179
Eros, 453
Evans, Oliver, 379
Eve, 117, 462
Everly Brothers, 118
Exorcist, The (Blatty), 213, 238–246

"Face on the Barroom Floor, The," 141
"Face Upon the Floor, The" (D'Arcy), 117, 141–143
Faerie Queene, The (Spenser), 321, 433, 454–465 *passim*
Fairy godmother, 161, 210
Fantastic Four, The, 184, 253
Father Christmas, 453
Father Abraham's Speech (Franklin), 258–263
Father Goose: His Book (Baum), 300
"Father Knows Best," 214
Faulkner, William, 162
Feiffer, Jules, 400, 456
Fellowship of the Ring, The (Tolkien), 354–365
Feminist movement, 118, 321
Femme fatale, 115–119 *passim*
Fenris-Wolf, 449
Finestone, Harry, 379
"Flash Gordon" (character), 253
Fleming, Ian, 195, 454, 460
"Flicka" (character), 266
Folktale, The (Thompson), 266
Folktales of Germany (Ranke), 223
"Fool on the Hill, The" (Lennon and McCartney), 269, 306–307
"Forbidden Swamp, The" (Thomas and Severin), 343–354
Ford, Henry, 1
Ford, John, 253
Forever People, The (Kirby), 184
Foringer, A. E., 173
Foster, Hal, 136
"Frankenstein" (character), 447
Franklin, Benjamin, 258, 269
Frawley, William, 182
Frazer, Sir James, 5
Freud, Sigmund, 434, 443n, 456
Freya, 444
Frizzell, Lefty, 130
"Frodo" (character), 322, 323, 355–364
"Froggy the Gremlin" (character), 61

From Russia with Love (Fleming), 195–201
Frye, Northrop, 448, 457–459
"Fury" (character), 266

Gage, Mathilda Joslyn, 300
"Galadriel" (character), 323
"Gandalf the Grey" (character), 213, 214, 266, 323, 355–365
Garland, Judy, 300
"Garth" (character), 451–452
Gawain and the Green Knight, Sir, 321
"Ged" (character), 4, 29–36
Gelman, Barbara, 296
"Gertrude the Duck" (character), 267–268
Gilgamesh, 321, 322, 325–332, 451
"Gimpel the Fool" (Singer), 269, 308–319
"Glauce" (character), 465
"Glinda, Good Witch of the North" (character), 161, 323
"Gloriana" (character), 321, 464
Godfather, The (Puzo), 214
Goethe, Johann Wolfgang von, 66
Golden Bough, The (Frazer), 5–9
Goldstein, Richard, 306
Golem, 309, 447
"Goofus and Gallant" (Myers and Hammel), 3, 25–29
Graduate, The, 118
"Grandpa Walton" (character), 214
"Grapes, Like Children, Need Love and Affection" (Almadén Vineyards), 176–178
Grapes of Wrath, The (Steinbeck), 161
Great Comic Book Heroes, The (Feiffer), 400
Great Mother, The (Neumann), 159
"Greatest Mother in the World, The" (Smith), 158–159, 173–176
"Green Goblin, The" (character), 60
"Grendel" (character), 460, 461
Grimm Brothers
  their career, 9
  their methods, 9, 223
  Tales: "Cinderella," 168; "The Juniper Tree," 388–395; "The Nixie of the Mill-Pond," 126–130; "The Queen Bee," 265, 268, 273–275; "The Singing Bone," 9–11; "The Three Feathers," 265; "The Water of Life," 333–337
"Gunsmoke," 214, 460, 463

Hades, 120, 162–166 *passim*
Haggard, H. Rider, 148–149
Hainuwele, 452

Hamilton, Edith, 165n, 270, 385n
Hamlet (Shakespeare), 214
Hammel, Marion Hull, 25
Hammett, Dashiell, 365
Haney, Bob, 276
Hans and Fritz (Dirks), 92
Hardaway, Ben, 74
Hard Day's Night, A, 306
"Hard Rain's A-Gonna Fall, A" (Dylan), 339–342
"Hare Herd, The" (Ranke), 223–227
Harris, Joel Chandler, 69–70
Harrison, George, 179, 337. *See also* Beatles
Hathor, 160
"Have Gun, Will Travel," 332, 459
Hawthorne, Nathaniel, 3, 45, 117, 308
Hearst, William Randolph, 92
Hecate, 163, 166
"Heckle and Jeckle" (characters), 60
Helen, 452
Helios, 120, 163, 164
Help!, 306
Helpful Animal, the, 265–268, 323, 324
Hemingway, Ernest, 117
Henley, Don, 134
"Henry Tremblechin" (character), 115
Hera, 216
Heraclitus, 453
Hercules, 321, 434, 451
Hermes, 2, 122, 165
Hero, 1, 320–325, 382, 451–452, 454–465
Hero with a Thousand Faces (Campbell), 58–59, 161, 320–321, 324–325
Herriman, George, 296
"Hetty Hutter" (character), 269
Hickock, Wild Bill, 266–267
Highlights for Children, 3, 25
High Noon, 462
"His Pa Stabbed" (Peck), 97–101
Historie of Reynart the Foxe (Caxton), 66
Hobbit, The (Tolkien), 213, 355
Hoffman, Dustin, 118
Hoffman, E. T. A., 3
"Hogan's Heroes" (characters), 61
"Holden Caulfield" (character), 269
Holden, William, 118
Holland, Norman, 459
Holy Fool, the, 265, 268–270
Homer, 117, 119, 162, 325
"Hopalong Cassidy" (character), 266
"Horla, The" (Maupassant), 3
"Horse Dealer's Daughter, The" (Lawrence), 381

Hound of the Baskervilles, The (Conan Doyle), 449
"Howard" (character), 213
"How Master Renard Enticed Ysengrin to Eat the Moon and How He Was Judged by the Court of the Lion" (Dorey), 66–69
Howard, Robert Ervin, 343
Howells, William Dean, 108
"Hrothgar" (character), 460, 461
Humphries, Rolfe, 385
"Hutch" (character), 214
Hyacinthus, 384, 385–388
"Hymn to Demeter," 162–167

"Iago" (character), 59–60
Id, 446
Idiot, The (Dostoyevsky), 269
"Ignatz the Mouse" (character), 60, 296–299
Iliad (Homer), 119
Illustrated Encyclopedia of Rock, The (Logan and Woffinden), 340
"I Love Lucy," 182
"Immanuel Rath" (character), 117
"Imp of the Perverse, The" (Poe), 62
Initiation rites, 383–384
"In the Beginning" (Beck and O'Neil), 228–235
Iris, 164
Irving, Washington, 162
"Ishmael" (character), 372, 377
Ishtar, 159
Isis, 5–8, 159, 381
"I've Been Born Again" (Dean and Davis), 381, 395–396

"Jack the Giant Killer," 436
"James Bond" (character), 195–201, 214, 454, 460, 464
James, Henry, 3, 162, 381, 382, 383, 421–422
"Jane" (character), 451, 452
Jane Eyre (Brontë), 162
Jaws, 1
Jazz Singer, The, 182
"Jesse McCanles" (character), 2
Jesus Christ. *See* Christ
Jewett, Robert, 437
"Jim Anderson" (character), 214
"Jimpy" (character), 451, 452–453
Joel, Billy, 43
"John Seward" (character), 116

"Joker" (character), 60, 455, 459
"Jolly Corner, The" (James), 3
Jolson, Al, 182
Journey to the Center of the Earth (Verne), 211, 267–268
Jove, 453
Joyce, James, 10
Jung, Carl Gustav
    on archetypes and the collective unconscious, 446, 447
    on "differentiation," 446
    on *enantiodromia*, 453
    on rationality and instinct, 268
    on the Shadow, 2
    on symbol, 443n
    on the Temptress, 119
    on the Trickster, 59
    on the Wise Old Man, 211
    Works: "Archetypes of the Collective Unconscious," 119; "Concerning Rebirth," 383; "The Phenomenology of the Spirit in Fairy Tales," 211
"Juniper Tree, The," 388–395
Juno, 388

Kalevala, 452
Kali, 161, 162
Kane, Gil, 376
Katzenjammer Kids, The (Dirks), 60, 92–97, 115
Kaz, Eric, 180
Keats, John, 154, 462
Kerenyi, Karl, 451
Kesey, Ken, 162
Kinder-und Hausmärchen (Grimm's Fairy Tales). See Grimm Brothers
"King Kull" (character), 322, 343–354
King Lear (Shakespeare), 269
King Solomon's Mines (Haggard), 148
Kirby, Jack, 184
Knerr, Harold, 92
Kobra, 3
Kore, 452
Krazy Kat (Herriman), 60, 296–299
Kubrick, Stanley, 412–413
"Kung Fu," 12, 211
"Kwai Chang Caine" (character), 211

LaBelle, 118
"La Belle Dame sans Merci" (Keats), 154–157, 452
"Lady Marmalade," 118
Laistrygonians, 121

Lamia, Isabella, The Eve of St. Agnes and Other Poems (Keats), 154
Lang, Andrew, 162
"Lankester Merrin" (character), 213, 239–246
"Lassie" (character), 266, 267
"Last Waltz, The," 338
Lawrence, D. H., 5, 381
Lawrence, John Shelton, 437
"Lawrence Pressman" (character), 214
Leadon, Bernie, 134
"Leaving on a Jet Plane," 397
Lee, Bruce, 12
Lee, Stan, 184
Le Guin, Ursula K., 4, 29, 442
Lem, Stanislaw, 448
"Lena Grove" (character), 162
Lennon, John, 179, 306. *See also* Beatles
Lester, Richard, 306
Levin, Ira, 214, 238
Lewis, C. S., 433
"Lewt McCanles" (character), 2
"Lex Luthor" (character), 4
Lichtenstein, Roy, 455
"Life Below" (Eisner), 383, 400–408
Life, 462
Light in August (Faulkner), 162
"Li'l Abner" (character), 269
Lilith, 116
Little Dorrit (Dickens), 162
"Little Iodine" (character), 115
Loch Ness Monster, 449
Logan, Nick, 340
"Lois Lane" (character), 464
Loki, 58
"Lola" (character), 117
Lone Ranger, The (Striker), 287–295, 460
"Lone Ranger, The" (character), 235, 266, 268, 287–295, 460
Looney Tunes & Merry Melodies, 74
Lord of the Rings, The (Tolkien), 213, 214, 323, 355
"Lord Randal," 340
Lorelei, 119, 126
Lucas, George, 253, 258
"Lucretia MacEvil," 118
"Lucy Westenra" (character), 116
"Luke Skywalker" (character), 212, 253–257, 322
Lyly, John, 319

"M" (character), 214
"Mabel Pervin" (character), 381

McCartney, Paul, 179, 306, 384. *See also* Beatles
McGlashan, Alan, 448
McLuhan, Marshall, 457
MacNeice, Louis, 433, 434
McQuade, Donald, 258
"Madame de Bellegard" (character), 162
"Madame Ratignolle" (character), 161
Maenad, 165
Magical Mystery Tour, 306
Magnificent Seven, The, 321
"Ma Joad" (character), 161
Maltese Falcon, The, 365–372
"Mama Celeste," 160
"Man from U.N.C.L.E., The," 464
Man, Myth, and Magic, 159
Manson, Charles, 238
Marcus, Greil, 338
Marlowe, Christopher, 385
Martin, Saint, 434
Marx Brothers, 60, 101–108
"Mary Glendinning" (character), 162
Mason, James, 211
Master of Kung-Fu, 2, 12
"Matt Dillion" (character), 460, 462
"Matthew Merygreeke" (character), 59
Maupassant, Guy de, 3
Max und Moritz (Busch), 92
Mayauel, 159
Melville, Herman, 444
    Works: *Billy Budd,* 372; *The Confidence-Man,*
    60, 160–161; *Moby-Dick,* 1, 269, 322,
    372–378; *Piazza Tales,* 372; *Pierre,* 162
"Merlin" (character), 213
Metamorphoses (Ovid), 384–385
"Midnight" (character), 3, 12–24
"Midnight Brings Dark Death" (Englehart
    and Starlin), 12–24
Mighty Thor, The, 184
"Mike Hammer" (character), 322
Milton, John, 454, 456, 459, 461
"Mission Impossible," 454, 460
"Miss Kitty" (character), 463
Moby-Dick (Melville), 1, 269, 322, 372–378
"Monsieur du Miroir" (Hawthorne), 3
Mother, the, 158–162, 210, 265, 323, 324
"Mother Earth" (Kaz), 180–181
Mother Nature, 159–161 *passim*
"Mother Nature's Son" (Lennon and
    McCartney), 179–180
"Mother songs," 182
"Mother Tums," 160
"Mr. Ed" (character), 266

Mr. Miracle, 184
"Mrs. Butterworth," 160
"Mrs. Clennam" (character), 162
"Mrs. Paul," 160
"Mrs. Poyser" (character), 162
"Mrs. Reed" (character), 292
"Mrs. Robinson" (character), 118
"Mrs. Smith," 160
"Ms. Marvel" (character), 321
Music from Big Pink (The Band), 338
Muss 'Em Up Donovan (Eisner), 400
My Ántonia (Cather), 201–209
Myers, Gary Cleveland, 25
"My Mammy," 182
Mithra, 453
"My Mom" (Donaldson), 182–183
"Myth and Archetype in Science Fiction"
    (Le Guin), 442–448
"Myth of Osiris, The" (Frazer), 5–9
Mythology (Hamilton), 270

"Napoleon Solo" (character), 464
Narayana, 452
Network, 118
Neumann, Erich, 159, 160, 161
New Gods, The, 184
Nichols, George Ward, 266
Nietzsche, Friedrich, 445
"Nightfall," 447
Nimoy, Leonard, 441
Nixie, 119, 126–130
"Nixie of the Mill-Pond, The" (Grimm
    Brothers), 126–130
Noah, 451
"Nurse Ratched" (character), 162
Nye, Russel B., 262

"Obi-Wan Kenobi" (character), 212–213,
    253–257 *passim*
Oceanus, 120, 162
Odin, 444
Odysseus, 119–126, 321, 434, 451
Odyssey (Homer), 117, 119–126, 325
Oedipus, 215–222, 434
Oedipus Rex (Sophocles), 211, 215–222
"Old Blue" (character), 266
"Old Stewball" (character), 266
"Old Yeller" (character), 266
Olympus, 123, 164–166 *passim*
One Flew Over the Cuckoo's Nest (Kesey), 162
O'Neil, Denny, 228
"Open Sea, The." *See Wizard of Earthsea*
Osiris, 5–9, 380

Othello (Shakespeare), 59–60
Ovid, 384–385

Parker, Bill, 220
"Paladin" (character), 322, 459–460, 462
Pan, 453
Pandora, 117
Paradise Lost (Milton), 454–462 *passim*
Parallèle des ancients et des modernes, Le (Perrault), 168
"Paul McCartney Death Rumor," 384
"Pearl Chavez" (character), 2
Peck, George W., 60, 97–98
Peckinpah, Sam, 86
"Peck's Bad Boy" (character), 60, 61, 97–101, 296
Peck's Bad Boy and His Pa (Peck), 60, 97–101
Pegasus, 266, 270–273
"Penrod" (character), 60
Pentamerone of Giambattista Basile, The, 168
Perrault, Charles, 168
Persephone, 162–166, 452
Perseus, 271n
Peter, Paul and Mary, 397
Petrarch, 385
"Phenomenology of the Spirit in Fairy Tales, The" (Jung), 211
"Philip Marlowe" (character), 322
Pierce Pennilesse, 459
Pierre (Melville), 162
"Pip" (character), 269–270
Playboy, 462
Poe, Edgar Allan, 3, 62
"Pogo" (character), 447, 450
"Polonius" (character), 214
"Polulu the Puma" (character), 267
"Poor Richard" (character), 258–262, 259
Poor Richard's Almanack (Franklin), 258–262
Popular Writing in America (McQuade and Atwan), 258
"Porky Pig" (character), 74–85
Portnoy's Complaint (Roth), 162
"Prankster, The" (character), 60
Presley, Elvis, 384
"Primitive Heroic Ideal, The" (Donaldson), 459
"Prince Arthur" (character), 464
"Prince Myshkin" (character), 269
Prince Valiant (Foster), 136–140
Procne, 388
Prometheus, 447
"Prospero" (character), 4

Puer Aeternus, 452
Puzo, Mario, 214

"Queen Bee, The" (Grimm), 265, 268, 273–275
Quest, the, 320–325, 382, 383

Radin, Paul, 58, 62–63
Raleigh, Sir Walter, 454, 456, 464
Ralph Roister Doister (Udall), 59
Rama, 434
Ramakrishna, 161
Ramayana, 434
Ranke, Kurt, 223
"Rappaccini's Daughter" (Hawthorne), 117
Reader's Digest, 462
Rebirth, 5, 9, 380–384
"Red Crosse Knight" (character), 321, 465
Redeemer Nation (Tuveson), 441
"Red Sonja" (character), 118
"Regan MacNeil" (character), 213, 238–245
Reinecke Fuchs (Goethe), 66
"Renard the Fox" (character), 66–69
"Rex the Wonder Dog" (character), 266, 267, 276–287, 323
Reynolds, Burt, 3
Rhea, 163–166 *passim*
Rilke, Rainer Maria, 445
"Rin Tin Tin" (character), 266, 267, 276
"Rip Van Winkle" (Irving), 162
Robertson, J. R., 337
"Robin" (character), 465
Robinson, W. R., 455
"Rocky Mountain High" (Denver and Taylor), 381–382, 383, 397–399
Roddenberry, Gene, 440
Rogers, Roy, 266
Rollin, Roger B., 454
Rolling Stones, The, 238
"Roman Castavet" (character), 214
Rose, William, 66
Rosemary's Baby (Levin), 214, 238
Roth, Philip, 162
Rusalka, 119, 126
Rush, Tom, 180

Sachs, Bernard, 276
"Sad-Eyed Lady of the Lowlands," 118
Salinger, J. D., 269
"Sam Gamgee" (character), 323, 355–364
Samson, 117, 451

Sandars, N. K., 325–326
"Sandman, The" (Hoffmann), 3
"Sarah Lee," 160
"Saruman the White" (character), 214
Satan, 214, 238, 461, 462
Saturday Night Fever, 235
"Scarecrow" (character), 266, 300–305
Schiller, J. C. F. von, 11, 273
"Secret of the Golden Crocodile, The"
    (Haney, Kane and Sachs), 276–287
"Secret Sharer, The" (Conrad), 3
"Sergeant Bilko" (character), 60
Sergeant Pepper's Lonely Hearts Club Band (Bea-
    tles), 179
"Sergeant Schulz" (character), 61
Set, 5–9, 381
Severin, Marie, 343
Severin, John, 343
Sewall, Richard B., 378
"Sexy Sadie," 118
Shadow, the, 1–4, 115, 161, 322, 324, 452
"Shadowfax" (character), 266
Shafer, Sanger D., 130
Shakespeare, William, 385
    Works: *Antony and Cleopatra,* 117; *As You
    Like It,* 319; *Hamlet,* 214; *King Lear,* 269;
    Othello, 59–60; *The Tempest,* 4
"Shang-chi" (character), 2, 12–24
Shangri-la, 324
Sharpe, Eric J., 159
Shazam!, 228
"Shazam" (character), 228–235
She (Haggard), 148–154
Shelley, Mary, 447, 448
Sherrill, Billy, 132
"Short Happy Life of Francis Macomber,
    The" (Hemingway), 117
Silmarillion, The (Tolkien), 355
"Silver" (character), 266, 268, 287–295
    passim
Silverstein, Shel, 236
Simon, Joe, 184
"Simpleton" (character), 265, 268, 273–275
Singer, Isaac Bashevis, 269, 308
"The Singing Bone" (Grimm), 9–11
Sirens, 119, 126
"Sir Gawain" (character), 321
"Sir Oliver Lindenbrook" (character), 211,
    267–268
Sisters, 115
Sita, 434
Slaughterhouse-Five (Vonnegut), 269
Smith, Cordwainer, 444

Smith, Courtland N., 173, 175
Soul Book, The (Anderson), 395
Soap operas, 118
"Sonny Sumo" (Kirby), 184–194
"Sophie Portnoy" (character), 162
Sophocles, 210, 215
Spenser, Edmund, 321, 385, 454–465 *passim*
Spider-Man, 60
"Spider-Woman" (character), 118
"Spirit, The" (character), 383, 400–408
"Spock" (character), 438–442 *passim*
"Squirrely the Squirrel" (Crumb), 59, 66,
    86–91
Starlin, Jim, 12
Starr, Ringo, 118, 179. *See also* Beatles
"Star Trek," 4, 437–442, 454
Star Trek Lives!, 440, 442
Star Wars (Lucas), 212, 253–258, 322
Steinbeck, John, 161
Steve Canyon (Caniff), 454, 455, 456
"Steve Canyon" (character), 454–456, 458,
    462, 463
Stevenson, Robert Louis, 4
Stoker, Bram, 116, 144, 213
"Story of Apollo and Hyacinthus, The"
    (Ovid), 384–388
Story of a Bad Boy, The (Aldrich), 60
"Stranger, The" (Joel), 43–45
Striker, Fran, 287–288
Succubus, 116
"Superman" (character), 4, 60, 228, 445,
    457, 463, 464, 465
Swinburne, Algernon Charles, 116
Sword of Shannara, The (Brooks), 213

"Take Me Home Country Roads," 397
Tales of Mother Goose (Perrault), 168
"Talus" (character), 464–465
Tammuz, 380
"Tar Baby (Water-Well Version), The,"
    69–74
Tarkington, Booth, 60
"Tarzan" (character), 136, 266, 267, 268,
    447
Taylor, Johnnie, 381, 395
*Teachings of Don Juan: A Yaqui Way of Knowl-
    edge, The* (Castaneda), 247–253
Teiresias, 210–211, 215–222
Tempest, The (Shakespeare), 4
Temptress, the, 115–119, 158, 323, 324, 452
Tereus, 388
Thomas, Roy, 343
Thompson, Stith, 266

Thoreau, Henry David, 324
"Three Feathers, The" (Grimm), 265
Three and the Moon (Dorey), 66
Thyestes, 388
"Tiger Man McCool" (character), 213,
    236–237
Time Machine, The (Wells), 447
"Times They are A'Changin', The," 340
Tin Pan Alley, 182
"Tin Woodman" (character), 266, 300
Tolkien, J. R. R., 213, 214, 266, 354–355,
    447
"Tonto" (character), 288–294 *passim,* 460
"Topper" (character), 266
"Toto" (character), 266, 300–305 *passim*
Traven, B., 213
Treasure of the Sierra Madre, The (Traven), 213
Trendle, George W., 288
Trickster, the, 58–62, 115, 161
Trickster, The (Radin), 58, 62–65
"Trigger" (character), 266
Tuveson, Ernest, 441
Twain, Mark, 60, 70, 108, 269
"Twentieth Century Fox," 118
2001: A Space Odyssey (Clarke), 412–421

Udall, Nicholas, 59
Ulysses. *See* Odysseus
"Ulysses and the Siren" (Daniel), 323
"Una" (character), 321, 465
Uncle Remus, His Songs and Sayings (Harris),
    70
Uses of Enchantment, The (Bettelheim), 168,
    273, 275, 337, 387, 433–437

Vallee, Rudy, 182
"Vamp," 117
Vampirella, 116, 118
Vegetation god, 5, 9, 380–381, 383
Venus of Wilendorf, 159
Verne, Jules, 211, 267
Virgin Mary, 158, 444
Voight, Jon, 3
Vonnegut, Kurt, 269

Wadjunkaga, 59, 60, 61, 62–65, 86
Walden (Thoreau), 324
"Waltons, The," 214
Ward, Artemus, 269
Wasteland, 9
Water Babies, The, 433
"Water of Life, The" (Grimm), 321, 333–
    337
Wayne, John, 321
*Way to Wealth, The. See Father Abraham's
    Speech*
Weaver, Ken, 235
"Weight, The" (Robertson), 337–339
"What Is an American" (de Crèvecoeur),
    382
"Whiteman" (Crumb), 3, 37–42
Whitman, Walt, 379
Whiz Comics, 228
Who, The, 118
"Who Mourns for Adonais?" ("Star
    Trek"), 438–441
Wild Bunch, The, 86
"William Wilson" (Poe), 3
"Winner, The" (Silverstein), 236–238
Wise Old Man, the, 210–214, 265, 267,
    323, 324, 333, 365
"Witchy Woman" (Henley and Leadon),
    118, 134–135
Wizard of Earthsea, A (Le Guin), 4, 29–37
Wizard of Oz, The (Baum), 161, 253, 266,
    300–305, 323
Woffinden, Bob, 340
"Woman to Woman" (Sherrill), 132–134
"Wonderful Tar Baby Story, The" (Har-
    ris), 70
"Woody Woodpecker" (character), 60
World of the Short Story, The (Evans and Fine-
    stone), 379
Wynette, Tammy, 132

Yeats, William Butler, 5

Zeus, 162–166 *passim,* 215–216, 271n, 444

79 80 81 82 83 9 8 7 6 5 4 3 2 1